Social Problems

Finding Solutions, Taking Action

Robert McNamara

New York Oxford
OXFORD UNIVERSITY PRESS

Oxford University Press is a department of the University of Oxford.

It furthers the University's objective of excellence in research, scholarship, and education by publishing worldwide. Oxford is a registered trade mark of Oxford University Press in the UK and certain other countries.

Published in the United States of America by Oxford University Press
198 Madison Avenue, New York, NY 10016, United States of America.

For titles covered by Section 112 of the US Higher Education Opportunity Act, please visit www.oup.com/us/he for the latest information about pricing and alternate formats.

Library of Congress Cataloging-in-Publication Data

Names: McNamara, Robert Hartmann, author.
Title: Social problems : finding solutions, taking action / Robert McNamara.
Description: New York, NY : Oxford University Press, [2022] | Includes bibliographical references and index.
Identifiers: LCCN 2021015472 (print) | LCCN 2021015473 (ebook) | ISBN 9780190056353 (paperback) | ISBN 9780190056360 (epub)
Subjects: LCSH: Social problems. | Social action. | Sociology.
Classification: LCC HN18.3 .M3996 2022 (print) | LCC HN18.3 (ebook) | DDC 301—dc23
LC record available at https://lccn.loc.gov/2021015472
LC ebook record available at https://lccn.loc.gov/2021015473

Printing number: 9 8 7 6 5 4 3 2 1

Printed by Quad/Mexico.
Mexico

To Doug: For all the lessons, the examples,
and the reminders of how difficult life can be for some people.
I know that on my worst day, people would do almost anything
for the opportunity to have my life, but I don't know how many
would have traded theirs for yours. RIP big brother.

Brief Contents

Contents

Preface

WHY DID I WRITE THIS BOOK?

For the past 30 years, I have been teaching, studying, and researching social problems in the United States. The topics have always been challenging and fascinating, while being frustrating and often disappointing. I always found examples of social programs that were effective at targeting a specific aspect of a complex problem, but too often these extraordinary ideas were applied beyond their capacity. Then, once the program failed to be a panacea, policymakers discounted the actual value of the program in its original design. I felt a similar frustration when enormous resources were dedicated to programs that, while politically popular, had little chance at succeeding because they were based on inaccurate assessments of the problem. It is easy to see why students might feel that a course on social *problems* offers little encouragement to find *solutions.*

When I had the opportunity to write a comprehensive social problems textbook for Oxford University Press, I was presented with a moment to frame the issues in an objective way: to explain clearly and effectively not only the nature and complexity of specific social problems, but also how sociological theory is a useful lens through which these problems can be understood. I also had the chance to point out that there are, in fact, solutions that work. As I tell my students, the question is not really what *caused* the problem—we know these are social problems and that means they have social causes. The interesting question is, what we are willing as a society to do about them?

TEACHING WITH *SOCIAL PROBLEMS: FINDING SOLUTIONS, TAKING ACTION*

I have designed this textbook to be accessible, flexible, objective, and solutions-oriented. A consistent chapter structure, compelling and timely photographs, robust presentation of quantitative data, and useful pedagogy provide the scaffolding for an effective introduction to the study of social problems. This scaffolding includes

- **An introduction to sociology as a discipline** Chapter 1, "What Is Sociology and Why Should I Care?" provides a useful overview to the basics of sociological theory and method for students who have not taken an introductory course as a prerequisite for the Social Problems course. The chapter is also a helpful review for students who did already take the introductory course.

- **An objective, balanced approach** *Social Problems: Finding Solutions, Taking Action* doesn't have a particular point of view; in fact, I have diligently tried to offer a balanced view of all the issues without any effort to sway readers toward any particular position or solution or another. My goal is for students to acknowledge their emotional responses to social problems that are indeed urgent, if not overwhelming—but then to move toward a perspective that is informed by the best available data and the facts as we know them (because all social science data is imperfect). It is not based on an agenda, a point of view, or a perspective that seeks to change your opinion. In an age of fake news and science denial, it is more important than ever that students develop the critical thinking skills to challenge ideology, dogma, and political affiliation as they make assessments of the challenges we face.

With the exception of Chapter 1, each chapter includes the following:

- **Engaging opening narratives** Each subsequent chapter begins with a brief, compelling narrative overview of the chapter's specific problem. This vignette is followed by "Sociological Story Time," a bulleted list of recent newsworthy events that reflect some aspect of the chapter's social problem.
- **Application of sociological theory** Each chapter includes a section that clearly explains how a social problem might be analyzed (and solutions sought), depending on the theoretical lens applied: functionalism, conflict theory, feminist theory, symbolic interactionism, and critical race theory, among others.
- **"You Make the Call"** A role-playing exercise concludes each chapter, asking students to apply what they've learned to a specific situation based on actual occurrences. These exercises could serve as discussion or role-playing prompts in a live or virtual classroom setting, as well as the basis for essays.
- **"Global Perspectives"** Most chapters include a boxed feature describing how another country approaches a particular social problem. For example, Chapter 4 ("Why Are There So Many Poor People? Poverty and Inequality") examines Finland's experiment with a universal basic income. Chapter 13 ("Are You Feeling Okay? Health and Health Care") considers why a Covid-19 tracking app developed by the Singapore government and required on all citizens' mobile devices works in a society accustomed to strict measures to ensure social cohesion.
- **"What Works?"** This section looks at programs that have successfully addressed some aspect of a social problem. Included is a discussion of how this

success was objectively measured, thus helping students better understand the social science context and methodology required to craft genuinely effective solutions.

- **"So What Can I Do?"** The sheer scope of the social problems described in these chapters can feel overwhelming to students. Our students in sociology courses tend to be idealistic, even hopeful; they are driven to better understand the challenges facing their families and communities in an effort to eventually participate in solutions for the common good. I have chosen to end each chapter with an appeal to that hope, suggesting ways in which students can take action on a micro scale to begin to alleviate some aspect of society that could function more effectively or compassionately.

CURRENCY IN THE FACE OF DRAMATIC CHANGE

The events of 2020 dramatically influenced each chapter of *Social Problems: Finding Solutions, Taking Action*. I began writing this book in 2018. When the Covid pandemic devastated the United States, I had to substantially modify all the chapters to reflect its impact. On top of that, the extraordinary momentum of the Black Lives Matter movement in the wake of the murder of George Floyd by police, the presidential election campaign of 2020, an attack on the US Capitol by citizens and domestic terrorists, a plot by domestic terrorists to kidnap and execute the governor of Michigan, and a second impeachment trial of the president, who allegedly incited an attack on the members of Congress, all sent me back into the manuscript to make additional revisions.

Of course, many of the issues discussed in this textbook were not unique to 2020. The structural inequities and systemic racism have been enduring features of US society. The events of 2020 not only exacerbated their intensity, but also brought them to the forefront of our students' awareness and concerns.

Ultimately, I hope I have done an adequate job of describing the problems and what is known about them, and provided students with the context and content they need as they contemplate possible remedies. It is easy to conclude that many of these issues are large-scale problems and one individual couldn't possibly have an impact on them. That's simply not true. The millions of people who participated in demonstrations for racial justice over the summer of 2020 are witness to the fact that if enough people come together to call for solutions, meaningful change can occur.

In the end, while I have written a number of books in my career and even other textbooks on other topics, this one has presented the greatest challenge for me, in part because of the range and impact of the topics discussed. As we move forward, I hope what I show you provides the impetus for meaningful changes.

RHM

Acknowledgments

Any project of this magnitude requires a real team effort. Fortunately for me, I have had the benefit of perhaps the best working experience with my friends at Oxford University Press. Sherith Pankratz, my editor, has been such a strong supporter of this project from our initial conversation. We had friends in common, and after our first phone call, I knew that I wanted to work with her and could see her as a lifelong friend. As I think about that time, which was nearly three years ago, I am more sure of that now than ever before. Thank you, Sherith, for all you have done.

Similarly, having worked with other major publishing houses in the past and benefitted from some exceptionally talented developmental editors, I hit a home run with Meg Botteon, my developmental editor. I was told by others in the industry that she is "the gold standard," "the best in the business," and "as good as it gets" in publishing. These comments were made by trusted friends and highly respected colleagues, and I am thrilled to join them in offering such ringing endorsements of Meg. She is just fantastic. Meg is thoughtful, inspiring, supportive, encouraging, and brilliant. I think of her as a partner on this project. Meg, you are extraordinary and I am so grateful for your wisdom, insight, and thoughtfulness. This book is so much better than anything I could have done on my own. Thank you so much!

Like Sherith, I have also benefitted from my relationship with Steve Helba, also an editor at Oxford University Press. I have worked with Steve on two other textbooks, and his friendship and level of professionalism is unparalleled. I can't imagine how difficult his job must be, particularly in the ever changing world of academic publishing, but Steve has a calming presence and never seems to get rattled. Thank you Steve, for your counsel, insight, and friendship. Like Sherith and Meg, I hope we get a chance to work together on something new in the future.

Finally, I need to thank all my students over the years who helped shape my understanding of various topics within sociology. I have taught at ten institutions over the course of my career, from four-year state universities to four-year private universities to religious-based colleges to community colleges to even ivy league institutions, with the two longest stretches occurring at Furman University and The Citadel. Thanks to all of you, even those students who seemed less interested or engaged in the discussions and the class, as you all have taught me what matters and how different learning styles require an elaborate teaching toolbox in order to be effective.

Lastly, as with all my endeavors I must thank my family for their support and encouragement. Writing can be an extremely lonely exercise, and while some people embrace that solitude, others look at it as a difficult but necessary experience. I am grateful for the time when I needed to be alone, as well as for the time Carey and Connor allowed me to escape my own thoughts and let me play games with them. You guys make team McNamara a success.

I am grateful to the many reviewers whose insights have shaped the development of this text:

John Teddy Ambenge, Middlesex Community College
David L. Briscoe, University of Arkansas at Little Rock
Carole Campbell, California State University Long Beach
Taylor Cannon, Mendocino College
Nicholas Dempsey, Eckerd College
Dianne Dentice, Stephen F. Austin State University
Nicole Farris, Texas A&M University-Commerce
Anna Marie Hammersmith, Grand Valley State University
Alissa Klein, University of South Florida
Ross Kleinstuber, University of Pittsburgh at Johnstown
Diane Lindley, The University of Mississippi
Beth Lyman, Radford University
John Malek-Ahmadi, Tarrant County College
Marguerite V. Marin, Gonzaga University
John R. Mitrano, Central Connecticut State University
David Pasick, SUNY Polytechnic Institute
Michael Polgar, Penn State University
Tiffanie Reed, Cuyahoga Community College
Amy Ruedisueli, Tidewater Community College
Roscoe Charles Scarborough, College of Coastal Georgia
Russell J. Willis

Teaching and Learning Support

Oxford University Press offers instructors and students a comprehensive teaching and learning package of support materials for adopters of *Social Problems: Finding Solutions, Taking Action*.

OXFORD LEARNING LINK

The Oxford Learning Link (OLL) at www.oup.com/he/mcnamara is a convenient destination for all teaching and learning resources that accompany this book. Accessed online through individual user accounts, the OLL provides instructors with up-to-date ancillaries while guaranteeing the security of grade-significant resources. In addition, it allows OUP to keep users informed when new content becomes available. The OLL for *Social Problems: Finding Solutions, Taking Action* contains a variety of materials to aid in teaching:

- **Instructor's Resource Manual**—A robust and innovative Instructor's Resource Manual that includes learning goals and objectives, lecture outlines/chapter overviews, essay questions, key terms and definitions, and review questions with discussion, essay, and critical response prompts.
- **Test Bank**—A robust test bank designed for both novice and advanced users. Instructors can create and edit questions, as well as upload the file into various Learning Management Systems.
- **PowerPoint-Based Lecture Slides**
- **Pop Culture Guide**—A valuable guide to media (movies, TV shows, podcasts) that can be used to demonstrate sociological ideas or concepts, organized by chapter. These come from multiple sources and include suggestions for clips, as well as full-length features. Each suggested clip includes the concept being represented, the time stamp (if relevant), as well as the streaming service where the media can be accessed.

DIGITAL LEARNING TOOLS

Social Problems: Finding Solutions, Taking Action comes with an extensive array of digital learning tools to ensure your students get the most out of your course:

- *In the News Weekly Quiz* is a resource for both instructors and students that provides current news articles on a weekly basis, along with low-stakes assessments that ensure student engagement and encourage students to connect the article to what they are learning in their course. These articles are selected specifically to relate to a particular sociological idea or concept and are designed to demonstrate to students the sociological relevance of everyday events.
- *Media+Data Literacy Exercises* are innovative, interactive exercises that help students build their data and media skills and assess their learning in a low-stakes environment. These exercises push students to critically analyze photos, charts, and graphs in an effort to highlight how easily information can be manipulated or misinterpreted. They can be assigned to students, or used as jumping-off points for class discussions or group activities.

Access to these tools is provided free to students with purchase of a new print or electronic textbook, through an access code or directly within the enhanced eBook. These and additional study tools are available at www.oup.com/he/mcnamara, through links embedded directly in the enhanced eBook, and within course cartridges. Additional tools are described as follows:

- **Enhanced eBook:** The enhanced eBook provides students with a versatile, accessible, online version of the textbook. Every new copy of the print text comes with an access code, which can be used to redeem premium OLL resources, or directly in your LMS, and the enhanced eBook will be available in all these locations. (Please note: Students should check with their instructor before redeeming their code to determine if their instructor is using an LMS integration. If neither is being used, students can redeem directly on OLL.)
- **Online Study Tools:** Additional online tools are available at www.oup.com/he/mcnamara for student use. For each chapter, these tools include interactive flashcards, a glossary, learning goals, and web links.
- **Learning Management System Integration**: OUP offers the ability to integrate OUP content directly into currently supported versions of Canvas, D2L, or Blackboard. Contact your local rep or visit oup-arc.com/integration for more information.

FORMAT CHOICES

Oxford University Press offers cost-saving alternatives to meet the needs of all students. This text is offered in a loose-leaf format at a 30% discount off the list price of the text; and in an eBook format, through RedShelf for a 50% discount. You can also customize our textbooks to create the course material you want for your class. For more information, please contact your Oxford University Press representative, call 800.280.0280, or visit us online at www.oup.com/he/mcnamara.

PACKAGING OPTIONS

Oxford University Press is pleased to offer the following packages at a discount to your students:

- *Social Problems: Finding Solutions, Taking Action* packaged with any one title from the *Very Short Introduction Series* for no additional cost. Each additional VSI beyond the first can be packaged with *Social Problems: Finding Solutions, Taking Action* for $5.00 per title (regular retail price $11.95.)
- *Social Problems: Finding Solutions, Taking Action* packaged with *Writing in Sociology: A Brief Guide* for an additional $9.95 (regular retail price $24.95.)
- *Social Problems: Finding Solutions, Taking Action* packaged with any title from the *What Everyone Needs to Know Series* for an additional $10.00 (regular retail price varies.)

For more information, please contact your Oxford University Press representative, or call 800.280.0280.

1

What Is Sociology and Why Should I Care?

LEARNING OBJECTIVES

- Define sociology and the sociological imagination.
- Understand the role of theory in the social sciences and in sociology.
- Identify the main theoretical perspectives or paradigms in the discipline.
- Describe the role of research in sociology and the various designs.
- Compare the differences between personal troubles and public issues.
- Discuss the process of how social problems are created.

Chapter Outline

Stories are important tools that teach people how to be a part of a social group.

If this is your first sociology course, you may be surprised to discover that you know more about sociology than you realize. If you have already taken an introductory course in sociology, the social problems course provides an opportunity to refresh your memory about sociological theories and concepts. Regardless of your classroom experiences with sociology, you have a great deal of insight and understanding about the culture and the society of which you are a part. Your experiences have shaped how you see the world around you.

This chapter provides a foundation for making sociological sense of your culture and your society, while avoiding conventional thinking about sociological issues in general and social problems in particular. Why is it important to recognize and avoid conventional thinking? When we think conventionally rather than critically, we often miss important information, or the conclusions we draw from those observations and perceptions are inaccurate or incorrect. My goal in this textbook is to share with you what we know about social problems based on compelling studies and the latest expert research. I hope both to expose the misguided notions about social problems that have contributed to conventional thinking and to offer examples of solutions based on critical thinking and careful observation that actually work. In a social problems course, it is very easy to come away with a sense of discouragement or pessimism about the possibility of solutions. And some of the problems we analyze can provoke fear and anxiety that the society we live in is falling apart. My intention here, which your instructor shares, is that you will complete this course with a sense of cautious optimism about social problems and how you can contribute to their solutions. While social problems are complicated and multi-faceted, some strategies to solve them are in fact effective. The outlook is far from pessimistic.

It is also important to remember that, while it is normal to think that a particular social problem is unique to the United States, this is far from true. Other countries wrestle with the same issues, although with key differences based on the culture, policies, and structural makeup of those countries. What is safe to say is that most of the time, the problems we will discuss extend beyond our borders.

The goal of this introductory chapter is for you to establish a sociological understanding of various problems. We will explore what sociology attempts to accomplish, and how sociologists use both empirical research and theory in offering explanations for social problems and working toward solutions. Theory is the primary method by which we can understand what's happening, and it also provides insight into possible solutions that might be developed to address problems. Think of it this way: if the problem was that simple, someone would have developed a solution a long time ago. The fact that we're still talking about these issues means the problems are complex and there remains a lot to learn about them.

SOCIOLOGICAL STORY TIME

- In response to the threat of Covid-19, which by November 2020 had killed more than 400,000 Americans, cities and states are taking dramatic steps to limit social interaction to curb spread of the virus. Included in these measures are the closing of bars, restaurants, sporting events, concerts, and places where large numbers of people can gather. In California, for example, the governor placed the entire state under a "shelter-in-place order," which is a lockdown measure designed to limit people from face-to-face interaction (Yan, Maxouris, and Almasy, 2020).
- Doug is a 61-year-old homeless veteran, who spent years living on the streets and in shelters. He was a substance abuser, a petty thief, and suffered from PTSD. He finally gets help through a program at the Veterans Administration and begins to turn his life around. Then he suddenly dies of a heart attack after getting his own apartment. Some see this as a tragic ending to a difficult life; others see it as a function of choices, and society is not responsible for Doug's decisions or his death.
- In response to numerous allegations that Harvey Weinstein engaged in sexual abuse of actresses while he was a Hollywood producer, the #MeToo movement was born. This started as the result of one particular actress, who decided to stand up to the industry that allowed such behavior to go unchecked for years. The #MeToo movement has encouraged many other women to report similar stories of abuse committed by Weinstein and

other influential men in Hollywood ("Harvey Weinstein Expected to Surrender," 2018).

- A recent ruling by the Trump administration to separate illegal immigrants from their children if they are caught sparked a backlash against a policy that had previously kept families together. Because of the overwhelmingly negative reaction by the general public and leading figures in society, President Trump signed an executive order in 2018 reversing this decision (Abramson, 2018).

WHAT IS SOCIOLOGY?

How does sociology explain the ways in which culture shapes our attitudes, values, beliefs, and behavior? A standard textbook definition of "sociology" might be: "Sociology is the scientific study of society, culture, group behavior, and social interaction." But such a definition seems very vague—if not downright boring.

Much of sociology can be summed up in the phrase "things are not always what they seem."

In fact, sociologists are interested in trying to figure out why people act the way they do. We want to be able to predict people's behavior, and we think that the groups they belong to significantly influence those actions. Think about it: Do you act differently when you are in church, with your friends at a club, or when you are spending time with your grandparents or small children? For example, are you mindful of language and the use of profanity when you are around children or the elderly? These observations are at the heart of sociology, the basic insight of which is that much of our behavior is influenced by the groups to which we belong and the interactions that take place in those groups.

Sociology is similar to other social sciences (such as psychology) in that sociologists attempt to find ways to predict people's behavior. The difference is that psychology attributes much of people's behavior to internal traits, such as personality and cognitive development. Sociology, in contrast, attempts to explain human behavior by the context of interactions—the groups that we belong to, the values, attitudes, and beliefs of those groups, and how the larger society impacts the person and their worldview. Sociology is an academic discipline, and sociologists are scientists who attempt to use the scientific method to empirically understand behavior, much in the same way that a chemist uses science to uncover the properties of and relationships between chemicals. The challenge, of course, is that because people don't always act consistently in a given situation, even one with the same circumstances, predicting what someone will do is an imprecise process. Have you ever done something and then wondered, "Why did I do that?" If individuals don't always know why they acted in a given way, think of how difficult it is for a scientist to predict what they are going to do in the future.

Stories as Tools

Stories have both educational and entertainment value. They are powerful tools for socializing people into their status and role in a culture or society. Stories can also shape and reshape our social relationships. In his book, *Healing the Mind Through the Power of Story,* Mehl-Madrona (2010) offers three primary benefits of storytelling. First, stories allow us to understand a person's world from their point of view and help us develop empathy. That is, stories tell us about the context and motivations of people, particularly if their lives are very different from our own. Second, stories can be instructive, because they frequently contain an element of morality. In fact, our social identities are formed through the stories we tell other people. Finally, stories offer a way to consider life beyond our own individual existence. In other words, stories can stimulate thought about the possibilities of life and people's places in it (Mehl-Madrona, 2010).

From a sociological point of view, Karen Sternheimer (2018) offers three important observations about the sociology of storytelling. First, a form of storytelling can actually be a part of a research design. Qualitative research methods (such as ethnography) involve researchers spending time living with and interacting with the people they study. In training students on how to employ ethnographic methods, professors often encourage them to "tell the larger story"—that is, to communicate to the audience how their subjects see and understand the world and how they experience the reality of life.

Second, Sternheimer notes that qualitative researchers tell a more comprehensive story when they are able to include personal accounts of their subjects and to place those experiences into some sort of larger context. For instance, while it can be instructive to read about a crime and its general circumstances, providing more detail about the offenders themselves or the contexts in which the crime occurred can provide much richer insight. For example, does the offender suffer from an emotional disorder, or do they come from a family of privilege? Does the neighborhood in which the offender lived have high rates of unemployment, excessive poverty, or a large number of transient residents who don't feel a sense of responsibility for the community? (Sternheimer, 2018). In other words, is there a back story about the offender that informs the reader of why they may have committed the crime? This is a common strategy in fiction writing, and qualitative researchers offer similar insight in "telling the tale" (Van Maanen, 2011).

Finally, Sternheimer observes that sociologists use stories to debunk conventional understanding of a topic or phenomenon (Sternheimer, 2018). For instance, many people might not understand how people become homeless, such as the story of Doug offered in "Sociological Story Time" at the beginning of this chapter. Or they may conclude that Doug made poor choices, and his life is simply the consequence of those decisions. The struggles of people in poverty, housed or not, may not be obvious to people who have never encountered others in this predicament. Telling Doug's story is not designed to excuse the behavior, but to better understand it and learn more about why people make decisions that impact their lives. In sum, stories are critically important tools in which to share information, form our social identities, pass along the culture, and understand more about the nature of social life and the people in it. So what is this thing called sociology and how does it relate to storytelling?

The Sociological Perspective

Stories are one way to help us make sense of the complex process of understanding behavior, culture, social interactions, and relationships to society. This is particularly true given the overlap between sociology and the other social sciences, including history, economics, political science, anthropology, geography, and psychology. Sociologists have developed what is known as the **sociological perspective** to provide a unique lens through which to study society. This perspective is an attempt to study society without the biases that cloud our understanding of the world around us (Berger, 1963). How does the sociological lens help us accomplish that?

Think about how difficult it is to study something with which you are very familiar. For example, let's say you've been a member of a soccer club for several years. You decide that you want to learn more about what it is like to be a part of your soccer team, and you plan to study why players act a certain way. In this example, you probably feel as though you know what is going to occur or why someone is acting a certain way in a given situation. But that kind of familiarity is exactly what leads us to make inaccurate assessments about people, events, and groups. We are all subject to the socialization we have received, and that socialization shapes our perspective. The sociological perspective, however, tells us that we will not really understand events or people if we approach those situations with built-in biases.

The sociological perspective requires us to approach the objects of our study as if we are seeing them for the first time. Imagine that you are from an entirely different planet, and you have landed in the middle of a neighborhood or campus on Earth. You are not familiar with the culture, society, or the behaviors of individuals—but your mission is to describe what you are seeing and to explain certain events and phenomenon. Ideally, this is how all sociologists would apply their sociological perspective. Of course, sanitizing their understanding of things, particularly if they are studying their own culture, is very difficult. You can never be certain that you are being completely objective. Given these difficulties, it may be better to think of the sociological perspective as a goal to aspire to rather than a technique or tactic.

Another way to think about the sociological perspective is to consider the level of analysis of a given topic. Imagine you have a camera and are taking photos of a sporting event. With a telephoto lens you can capture a picture of a player on the field in great detail, but you don't have the ability to capture where that player is on the field. On the other hand, a wide-angle lens gives you the ability to take a photo of that player in the context of everyone else around them. It gives you the ability to see the larger view so that the impact of the player is better understood. However, you lose the ability to obtain a lot of detail about that individual player.

Sociological perspectives are like those camera lenses, in that they provide us with different ways of looking at a common subject. In sociology, the terms **microsociology** and **macrosociology** describe this process. In microsociology, the level of analysis is focused on people's day-to-day interactions: how they go about their lives, the relationships they form, and how all that influences their perspectives and behaviors. In contrast, macrosociology is like a wide-angle lens. It considers the larger context of how society functions. While not focused as much on individual participants, a macrosociological approach examines society in general and how it contributes to social life.

The Sociological Imagination

Let's imagine that we have used our sociological perspective and tried to objectively and empirically (scientifically) study something about society, social relationships, social interaction, or individual behavior. What do we do with that information? How do we make some sense out of it sociologically? In other words, what is the unique contribution that sociology makes to understanding the world around us? The answer, which is really the heart of the discipline, is found in the **sociological imagination**. C. Wright Mills (1959) suggests that the "promise" of sociology is found in telling the story of a person or group by identifying the intersection between biography and history, or the interplay between the person and the world. What does that mean? It means we need to develop an understanding of phenomena and behaviors that offers more than an individual assessment.

For example, suppose you encounter Doug, that homeless person I mentioned at the beginning of the chapter. You meet him on the street and he asks you for money. You might think that Doug is lazy and does not want to be independent and self-sufficient. Alternatively, you might think he has made some poor individual choices that led him to his current situation. Either possibility could be true, but the sociological imagination asks you to further consider other alternative explanations that go beyond the choices that Doug may have made as an individual. Perhaps Doug once had a job but lost it through downsizing or corporate mergers and did not have the training to find another one. Perhaps Doug sustained an injury that prevents him from working, or maybe he is suffering from a severe form of mental illness that precludes him from living independently. Given the limited services available for the mentally ill in this country, Doug may have turned to the streets because he couldn't get the help he needed.

Such considerations are not making excuses for individual behavior. Rather, they acknowledge that there may be other explanations for people's actions that go beyond their individual decisions or our first impressions of why it happened. In other words, the sociological imagination looks for larger explanations of people's behavior. These larger explanations may involve the influence of race, social class, religion, economics, or politics in creating a context to understand a person's life and their behavior. This is what Mills means when he talks about the intersection between biography and history. That is, a person's behavior and worldview is shaped by the events that occur during their life that shape and influence the person's attitudes, values, beliefs and behaviors (Mills, 1959).

For example, Covid-19 has had a devastating effect on the economy, as many companies have closed, leaving workers who do not have sick leave or vacation time without a paycheck. Some experts are forecasting that the prolonged nature of the pandemic means the recovery process, both in the United States and abroad, will take many months (Figure 1.1). The pace of recovery is worse than the Great Recession of 2008–9 (Tooze, 2020).

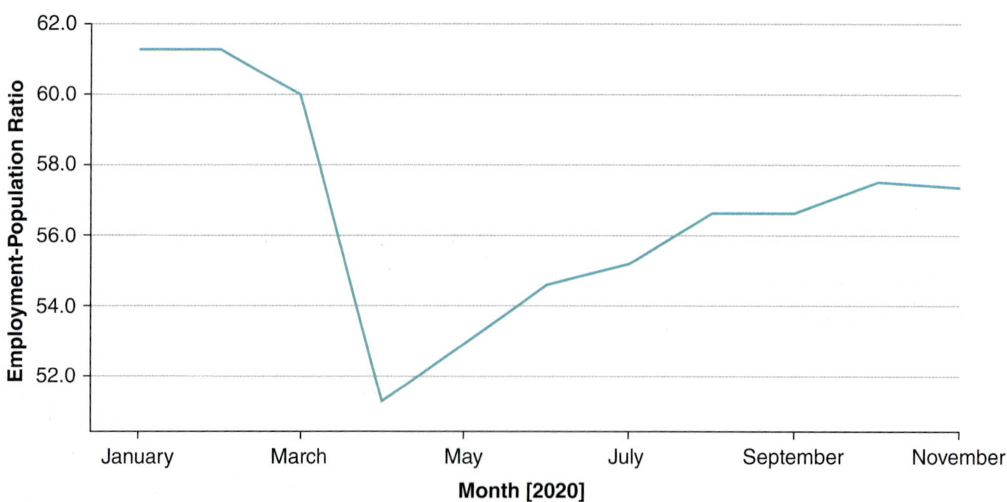

Figure 1.1 US job loss due to COVID-19 The Employment-to-Population ratio is the percentage of the US population that is gainfully employed. Beginning in March 2020, as COVID-19 led to quarantines and shutdowns across the country, the rate of gainful employment plunged. Due to the slow recovery so far, many Americans continue to struggle to find full-time work.

Add to this is the negative impact for the airline industry, where officials expect they will need more than $50 billion in assistance. While some experts are noting that the stimulus package proposed by Congress is an important first step, which includes sick time for those who are infected or caring for those who are, along with stimulus checks to most Americans, at a cost of an estimated $1 trillion, in the long run significant infrastructural improvements in health care and other industries are needed. This could be promising, but it is too early to tell the complete effects the virus will have on the economy (Tooze, 2020).

The airline industry was devastated by Covid-19.

In sum, one of the most important benefits of the sociological imagination is that it provides us with the ability to learn and appreciate explanations of events and behaviors that transcend our own limited experiences. In the process, we develop critical thinking skills, as well as a better understanding of how and why we believe the things we do and why we act a certain way (Mills, 1959).

WHAT'S THEORY GOT TO DO WITH IT?

For sociologists, theory provides clues to understanding the things we observe using the sociological perspective and our sociological imagination. Theory helps us ask good questions about what is occurring, what it means, and why it's relevant. Theory also gives us ideas about how we might create solutions to a problem. For sociologists, theory is one of the most important tools in our intellectual toolbox. Recall the distinction between macrosociology and microsociology: the former looks at social life from a broad perspective, while the latter examines the day-to-day experiences of people. This distinction is important, since it helps us understand the main focus of the different paradigms in sociology.

The three key sociological paradigms (or theories) we will review in this section were developed by European thinkers who tried to make sense of the extraordinary changes that resulted from the Industrial Revolution of the late 18th and early 19th centuries. This was one of the most significant events in the modern era, similar to what the Internet has done for contemporary society.

Industrial Revolution The Industrial Revolution forever changed economies, livelihoods, landscapes, and markets. This engraving shows workers in a German factory in 1840.

The transition from an agrarian to an industrial society, spurred on by the development of capitalism, led to new opportunities, as well as a host of social problems. A massive rise in poverty, overcrowding, disease, crime, suicide, depression, and other developments led these theorists to grapple with the causes of these problems, as well as propose solutions. There was a sense of urgency because the changes were so dramatic and significant. Political upheaval, including revolutions in France and America, restructured the social order of those countries and added to the sense of urgency. Often referred to as classical sociological theory, these explanations—structural functionalism, conflict theory, and symbolic interactionism—attempted to make sense of the current and future state of society as a whole (Hobsbawm, 1999).

Structural Functionalism

One of the earliest and most enduring explanations of how society operated is called **structural functionalism**. Here's a relatively easy way to understand this theory. Let's imagine you decide that you are going to lose weight and get in shape. Perhaps you have been inspired by the fitness models and their motivational quotes on Pinterest. You change your diet, start exercising, and drink more water. After a short time, you start to feel a lot better—you are getting more sleep, your energy levels are higher, and you can feel your clothes fitting differently. After a while, you're aware of your metabolism changing. You continue to lose weight even on those days when you miss a workout, or eat poorly. It may be that your body initially had trouble responding to the changes: you were really sore from those workouts and you craved carbs and sugar once you stopped eating them. Over time, however, your body adapted to the changes and actually grew stronger and healthier. What does this have to do with structural functionalism?

Imagine that society functions like your body. The individual parts (like your heart, lungs, muscles, and brain) are all technically independent of each other, but in order for your body to function properly, there needs to be some sort of interdependency. When you decided to introduce exercise and better nutrition, which can be seen as changes to the system, your entire body was affected. Now consider the individual parts of society: the family, the education system, religious institutions, the economy, and the political system. These are **social institutions**. While social institutions are independent and can operate on their own, in order for society to maintain balance or equilibrium, just like the human body, there needs to be an interdependency or synergy between the parts.

Structural functionalism argues that in order for society to be stable, this synergy is critical. For example, in socializing children about appropriate behavior and morality in society, all social institutions should send children the same or very similar messages. The parents instruct the child about what is appropriate; that message should be reinforced by teachers in school, priests and pastors at church, and by politicians and business leaders in the economy and in government. A consistent message allows the child to better learn and understand society's expectations. If all children are consistently socialized in this manner, then getting people to follow societal rules becomes easier and involves less conflict (Coser, 1999).

There is also an element of functionalism that borrows from Charles Darwin's theory of evolution. Functionalism argues that if some condition in society has existed for a long time, it must serve some useful or constructive purpose. If not, the condition would have withered away and died according to Darwin's theory. Conversely, if something does not contribute in a positive way, then that condition or phenomenon is considered **dysfunctional**. The three key points to remember about structural functionalism are

1. Synergy: how the parts of society fit together;
2. Balance: how the critically important equilibrium between the parts of society is maintained; and
3. Contributions to society: if a social institution exists, it must serve some useful purpose.

As it specifically relates to a social problem, the functionalist perspective would view even a problem such as crime as a good thing for society, in the sense that it identifies the boundary between acceptable and unacceptable behavior. Crime also serves as a unifying mechanism for society in that it creates a common bond for those who conform to society's rules (Lunden, 1958). Coming together against crime and criminals also enhances people's sense of social connectedness to one another. In the next chapter we will examine the impact of Neighborhood Watch programs and other forms of community crime prevention strategies. All of these efforts, including community policing, have a functionalist influence.

DURKHEIM AND FUNCTIONALISM

The basis of structural functionalism comes from the work of the French philosopher Auguste Comte (1798–1857), considered the father of sociology, and the French sociologist Émile Durkheim (1858–1917), whose work was central to the development of sociology as a whole and structural functionalism in particular. In fact, structural functionalism was the dominant theory in sociology in the mid-twentieth century. Durkheim saw what was occurring in France as a result of the Industrial Revolution and political upheaval, and he felt that what had been lost in the transition to the modern era was a connectedness of people to the larger society and to each other. In his first major work, *The Division of Labor in Society,* Durkheim offered insight into the nature of how people become and remain connected to one another (Durkheim, 1893:2013).

Because French society until the mid-19th century was largely agrarian, most people were held together in groups by the traditions and rituals they practiced and the commonality of their experiences. Durkheim called this **mechanical solidarity**. However, the Industrial Revolution brought about a division of labor or specialization. As a result, people were held together by the different tasks they performed. The banker needed the farmer to grow his food, and the farmer needed the butcher to ready his cows and sheep for market. Durkheim labeled this type of connectedness **organic solidarity**, arguing that it caused people to develop relationships and connectedness based on need (Durkheim, 1893:2013).

Another Durkheimian concept is the **collective conscience.** Imagine a situation when you made a poor decision and regretted it. Or perhaps you found yourself in a situation where you should have acted a certain way but did nothing instead. If the regret you felt continued to bother you, it is probably the result of your individual conscience nagging at you. Our individual conscience is developed by being a part of a society and its sense of morality. Without those attachments, we would not have any remorse or feelings of guilt over our actions (Durkheim, 1893:2013).

Instead of a person's individual conscience, Durkheim offered the collective conscience. To understand the collective conscience, think of it as the larger society's sense of morality. When the collective conscience is strong, people are in agreement about how to live their lives and what is considered appropriate and inappropriate behavior. Durkheim felt that in those societies characterized by mechanical solidarity the collective conscience would be strong, as people in such societies are on the same page with regard to social life. But as society changes and becomes more diverse, or **heterogeneous**, there is generally less agreement on how life should be organized. In those instances, the collective conscience would be weaker, leading to disagreements about what constitutes appropriate and inappropriate behavior.

Durkheim also discovered that people's level of connectedness to society influences their behavior. For instance, in his landmark study of suicide, Durkheim found that groups of people who took their own life might do so based on being overcommitted to society, which he called **altruistic suicide** (think of members of a cult and their willingness to sacrifice for the group), or because of a lack of connectedness to the larger society, which he referred to as **egoistic suicide.** Another reason people sometimes commit suicide is due to what Durkheim called **anomie,** or normlessness. In other words, when the norms that organize people's lives no longer have any value, are broken, or have yet to be replaced by a set of new ones, anomie creates tremendous anxiety and fear. As a result, some people take their own lives. Durkheim called this **anomic suicide**. Durkheim also had a term for people who committed suicide based on a sense of hopelessness. These were often found in enslaved societies, where people felt nothing in their lives was going to improve. Durkheim explained that people in such situations were more likely to engage in what he called **fatalistic suicide** (Durkheim, 1897:1965).

ADVANTAGES AND DISADVANTAGES OF FUNCTIONALISM

One of the greatest advantages of functionalism is that it attempts to provide a universal theory, a way of comprehensively explaining society and how it works. It also offers insight into what happens to society when things go astray or when disorder is generated. Since functionalism focuses on stability, this means it is a very conservative theory—and change, if it is to occur at all, must happen slowly. Why? To give the society an opportunity to regain its equilibrium or balance. Rapid social change disrupts the rhythm of society and time must be afforded to give society a chance to adapt. Of course, such a conservative approach means that something like the Internet might be seen as dysfunctional for society, as would protests or social movements that clamor for change (e.g., the Black Lives Matter movement or the #MeToo movement; Gans, 1964).

Second, the functionalist approach has received criticism based on its Darwinian roots. Remember, functionalists argue that if something exists for a long time, it must serve some useful societal purpose. One can easily use such logic to justify all manner of inequalities. Poverty has existed for a long time, so it must serve some useful purpose—like what? As some commentators have noted, one could argue that poverty provides a market for substandard goods and services, it provides an illustration or example of what not to aspire to be, and it provides jobs for people in the criminal justice system and social service agencies. This type of circular reasoning is the most looming criticism of functionalism—just because something has existed for a long time doesn't automatically make it useful (Gans, 1964).

Conflict Theory

Like structural functionalism, **conflict theory** is a comprehensive theory in that it attempts to explain how society in general operates. However, conflict theory explains society and its purpose quite differently from functionalism. For example, while functionalism tends to focus on a consensus model to explain the social order (where everyone is on the same page about social life), conflict theory argues that this does not reflect the way the world actually works. Conflict theory argues instead that life is about change, conflict, and competition. Because social consensus is rare, conflict occurs and results in winners and losers. Thus, conflict theory dedicates a considerable amount of attention to the inequalities that exist in society (Gans, 1964).

Conflict and competition are facts of life, and the source of conflict relates to who has access and control of scarce resources. Those with economic, social, and political power will use that power to keep what they have and to prevent others from acquiring it. It means that the wealthy and the powerful in society will use their influence to shape society's culture, education, law, and other social institutions aspects of life to reflect their interests. An interesting dimension to this perspective is that most people, even those who do not benefit from the existing system, tend to accept that system with all its inequalities as valid and appropriate. Few people attempt to change it.

Karl Marx (1818–1883) is the figure most closely associated with conflict theory. Like other theorists of his era, Marx believed that most of the problems of the Industrial Revolution were a result of capitalism, wherein some people were able to achieve enormous wealth while others struggled to survive. Marx felt that the capitalist system was unfair and unsustainable. At some point, he argued, dramatic social change would have to occur and a more equitable system be instituted. However, this would not occur organically or be achieved by a consensus; only a revolution would create a new system (Ritzer and Stepinsky, 2017).

Marx believed that capitalism contained essentially two classes of people: those who owned the **means of production**, or the **bourgeoisie**; and the **proletarians**, or workers. Marx identified two other classes of worker: artisans or craftsmen, who made up the middle class; and the **lumpenproletariat**, comprising vagrants, criminals, and others who did little to contribute to society. The means of production are all the things needed to create a commodity in order to sell it in the marketplace for a profit. This includes the land, the factory, the equipment, raw materials—everything except labor. The proletarians were former farmers, peasants, and laborers, who were forced to sell their labor once the Industrial Revolution occurred. Proletarians owned nothing else and were unable to directly benefit from their efforts. They frequently worked in an assembly line in a factory for hours each day and only received a small salary. Thus, workers never gained any level of satisfaction from their labor (Ritzer and Stepinsky, 2017).

As a result, the proletarians suffered from what Marx calls **alienation** from work. More importantly, given that the primary aim of capitalism is profit, the bourgeoisie attempted to pay workers as little as possible and to have them work long hours to maximize their level of productivity. Initially, the workers accepted this situation, as they felt that the owners of the factories had the right to pay them whatever they wanted. The workers also had few options in terms of job prospects, so they took what they could get without realizing the importance of their role in the process. Marx calls this acceptance a sense of **false consciousness** (Ritzer and Stepinsky, 2017).

Worker solidarity In 2019, many workers (including these McDonalds employees in Charleston, South Carolina) joined strike actions in support of the Fight for $15 minimum wage effort.

Marx argues that the situation for workers would only get worse, as any demands workers might make to improve their lives (such as higher salaries or better working conditions) would reduce the profits of the bourgeoisie, who would therefore be opposed. For Marx, the only way this situation would change is if the proletariat as a class recognize the role they play in the process and begin to demand more. This recognition is called **class consciousness**. Further, the tension between the workers and the capitalists will continue until the workers recognize that the only way they will be treated fairly is by overthrowing the capitalists in a revolution and taking over the means of production themselves. This idea of workers uniting and running the system would lead to more equitable solutions, where everyone would contribute but everyone would also share in the profits (Ritzer and Stepinsky, 2017).

WEBER'S THEORY OF RATIONALIZATION

The German philosopher Max Weber (1864–1920) was another central figure in the development of sociology. Like Durkheim and Marx, his work is critical to understanding society and its processes. Like Marx and Durkheim, Weber was concerned with the changes resulting from the Industrial Revolution. He was especially interested in how this shift from a more traditional society to a modern industrial one impacted social life. While some sociologists might argue that Weber's theory does not neatly fit into one of the three paradigms mentioned in this chapter, some of his work was a criticism of Marx. So in the interest of simplicity and ease of understanding the foundations of the discipline, we will include Weber in the category of conflict theory. One of the most important contributions Weber made was to understand the process of **rationalization** to social life (Ritzer and Stepinsky, 2017).

In *Economy and Society,* Weber argued that modern societies were characterized by the efficient, goal-oriented, logical processes that ensured the maximization of profit. However, not only was this process applied to industry and the way societies are governed; Weber argued that rationalization impacted social relationships as well. Individual behavior was said to be motivated not by tradition, values, or emotions, but by a more logical understanding of the utility of relationships. As people begin to understand the value of rational relationships and see the conveniences they represent, they embrace them and social life takes on an entirely new meaning and importance (Weber, 1921;2019). In his book *The Protestant Ethic and the Spirit of Capitalism,* Weber argued that people ultimately became trapped in an **iron cage of rationality** (Weber, 1905:2003). He meant that people don't realize how limited they have become in their relationships with others or how the use of technology dominates their lives; all people see are the conveniences technology presents. Think about how we communicate with each other: we text instead of call, or "like" each other's posts on social media. In fact, we seem to try to avoid face-to-face conversations. Why? For rational reasons: individual, in-person conversations take too long, and thanks to technology we can communicate with lots of people more efficiently.

Weber couldn't have imagined Facebook, texts, emojis, and the like during his own lifetime, but his observations about social life seem to be accurate. He would say that we don't realize how much of ourselves we are giving up when we resort to such superficial forms of communication; and we are even surprised when people communicate "the old fashioned way." However, Weber argues that direct communication is what makes us human. We are not simply machines that communicate with each other, and emotion and meaning is a critical part of how we develop meaningful social relationships.

This focus on the superficial and efficient in relationships, and ultimately the loss of significance of what makes us human, is what Weber calls *verstehen* (German, "understanding"), or a sympathetic understanding of the human condition. Thus, Weber argues that by using rationalization to reduce people and things to quantifiable variables, where we can tabulate, accumulate, and evaluate people on the basis of certain criteria, we think we are being fair minded and technologically savvy. In reality, however, we are giving up the very essence of what makes us human and never realize the costs (Weber, 1921:2019).

One way to understand the contemporary use of Weber's theory is to consider the ways in which society leverages technology (Chapter 5). As we embrace the luxury and convenience of online shopping, we lose the element of *verstehen* that Weber says is critical to social life. Similarly, as companies embark upon the use of automation, in part to reduce costs (which critics use to argue against an increase in the minimum wage in the United States), jobs disappear and workers in those industries will either need to be retrained or lose their place in the labor force altogether.

Similarly, Weber would be quite concerned about the rise of companies like Amazon or Walmart, which dominate the marketplace and squeeze out the small businesses, which cannot compete with those corporations in terms of price and availability. Thus, even problems related to jobs and the idea of entrepreneurship become challenged by rationalization.

ADVANTAGES AND DISADVANTAGES OF CONFLICT THEORY

One of the main advantages of Marx's theory is that it has shed light on the nature of conflict in society and on ways to challenge the status quo. In fact, one of Marx's most significant contributions to social theory is his notion of **praxis,** or practical action. In other words, people need to understand society, but they also need to act on that information in meaningful ways.

Conflict theory has a very different focus than structural functionalism, particularly in its emphasis on social life. For conflict theorists, the nature of relationships are not based on consensus or fit, but rather social relationships reflect the interests of those in power. However, such a focus can result in conflict theorists failing to identify or trivialize those aspects of society that are in fact orderly; where people are integrated based on agreed upon values or on relationships that are mutually beneficial. In other words, while society does have its share of disagreements and disputes, there are common values and beliefs that hold it together.

While conflict theory has sharpened our understanding of macro-level issues, such as women's rights, animal rights, and the systematic discrimination against other groups, it also contains elements of a micro-level analysis, such as understanding the relationship between employees and employers and the power distinctions between men and women and Whites and Blacks.

Symbolic Interactionism

Sociology's third main paradigm, **symbolic interactionism**, helps explain our individual personalities (and how they develop), along with how the social order and social change are developed. For symbolic interactionists, the focus is not necessarily on grand theories to explain society but on a more micro-level approach. Given that society is produced through the interactions of its members, those face-to-face interactions are the building blocks of society, particularly since much of our interactions involve the use of symbols, such as language. Interestingly, symbolic interactionism is the perspective that often has the most appeal to students, as they are able to apply its principles to their everyday lives more easily than the larger narratives of other theorists.

There are three basic ideas behind symbolic interactionism, according to Herbert Blumer (1900–1987), one of its founders. First, we act toward things on the basis of their meanings. Consider the letter A in the English language. That letter can be a musical note, an academic grade, or a part of a sentence; each of these meanings can result in people acting differently based on their understanding of its use (Blumer, 1986).

Second, meanings are negotiated through interaction with others. That is, people have to figure out what a particular symbol means when interacting with someone who uses it. In other words, nothing has intrinsic or inherent meaning—it is given meaning only as people create it. For example, I once had a college president tell me a story about a tree in front of the presidential house on campus. When he moved into the house, he saw that the tree was situated in front of a lake on the property. One day, he casually mentioned that fact to a member of his staff. To his surprise, early the next morning he saw workers out in his yard removing the tree. When he asked what was going on, thinking that perhaps the tree was diseased or dying, his staff member looked at him and said, "You said that tree was in the way of your view of the lake, so we had it removed." Heartbroken at the loss of such a beautiful tree due to a misunderstanding, this president learned a valuable lesson—one person saw the tree as a beautiful accompaniment to the landscape, another saw it as an obstacle. The perceived meaning of that tree determined the outcome of that interaction (Blumer, 1986).

Finally, meanings can change or be modified through the course of social interaction (Blumer, 1986). What does this mean? Sometimes our interactions can change the significance or meaning of an event. Let's imagine that you are an underachieving student in your classes and you suddenly start getting "A" grades in all of them—how do you feel about school and your place in it? The meaning has changed, right? Suddenly that professor isn't so incompetent; maybe this information isn't so boring or irrelevant; perhaps your confidence level goes up and you start thinking about the meaning of getting a degree in a different way.

As we will discuss in Chapter 7, the current US policy toward immigrants from Central America provides a telling illustration of how a group of people may be characterized and misunderstood. In the process of attempting to address an increase in the flow of undocumented immigrants from those countries, President Trump has characterized undocumented immigrants as "rapists," "criminals," "drug dealers," and "terrorists."

By repeating this narrative over the course of several years, the president attempted to symbolically and pragmatically change the status of immigrants from these countries as well as to redefine what it means to be an immigrant. Such an approach arguably suggests the Trump administration attempted to label this group as inferior and unworthy of assistance from the United States, as well as shape the public's understanding of this group of people and their relationships with them.

GOFFMAN AND SYMBOLIC INTERACTIONISM

One of the most noted symbolic interactionists is Erving Goffman (1922–1982). He enhanced our understanding of symbolic interactionism by suggesting that much of our social behavior is like a theatrical performance. Goffman calls this process **dramaturgy**. In other words, we are all acting when we interact with others, and through the process of **impression management** we attempt to present the most favorable impression possible (Goffman, 1969). Think of a first date or a job interview or any situation in which we attempt to control information about ourselves. We have both a **front stage** and a **back stage** to our performance. The front stage is where the actual interaction takes place; the back stage involves all the preparation—what to wear, questions to ask, and how we might answer certain questions about ourselves. Goffman argues that most of our interactions with others involve some form of impression management. We even have strategies developed in the event the interaction goes astray; Goffman calls these **face saving techniques** (Goffman 1969). While there are other sociologists who contributed to the development of symbolic interactionism, such as Herbert Blumer, Harold Garfinkel, and George Herbert Mead, Goffman's work is most familiar to non-sociologists because of its applicability to everyday life.

An illustration of dramaturgy and impression management can be seen in the way President Trump vilified and disparaged groups and individuals that disagree with him or with people that he sees as inferior. This approach has even raised concerns among his supporters, suggesting that he fails to act sufficiently "presidential." At the same time, however, Trump's extensive use of Twitter to proclaim his innocence on a wide assortment of matters, coupled with his insistence that he is being victimized by his political opponents or that his impeachment is a "witch hunt," are marvelous examples of Goffman's ideas about impression management.

ADVANTAGES AND DISADVANTAGES OF SYMBOLIC INTERACTIONISM

One of the primary advantages of the symbolic interactionist perspective is that it offers insight into how people understand the world around them. For instance, as people construct particular meanings for events and people's behavior, their understanding may shift even if the objective facts suggest otherwise. For example, as teenagers become more aware of the risks associated with smoking, the "coolness" associated with smoking (and more recently, vaping) may supersede any concern with the health risks. Symbolic interactionism helps us understand how powerful people's perceptions are in shaping their reality.

But critics of symbolic interactionism point out that such a micro-level approach to social life misses important factors such as large-scale structures and their influence on people's behavior. That is, some scholars point out that the heavy emphasis on the subjective construction of meaning can easily result in the loss of seeing the "larger picture" of how society is actually structured. Some experts also note that the symbolic interactionist approach, with its focus on qualitative analysis and methods, is of limited value compared to the more quantitative approach used by many sociologists.

OTHER IMPORTANT SOCIOLOGICAL THEORIES

There are many other theories beyond these three main paradigms that help sociologists study and explain social problems, as well as develop effective and sustainable solutions to those problems. Because gender and race, along with social class, play essential roles in the ways sociologists develop an understanding of society and people's behavior, it makes sense to touch on a few theories that go into more depth and detail about those variables.

Feminist Theory

Feminist theory emerged about the same time as the women's rights movement in the early part of the twentieth century. With its basis in Marx's works, feminist theory essentially examines how gender, and the inequalities based on it, may be understood and applied to various social institutions in society. Examples of the application of feminist theory include inquiries into conventional notions of how the family unit should be structured; how gender in the workplace results in wage differences; or how beauty and sexuality norms translate into perceptions of women and their behavior.

Claiming space During the summer of 2020, protests against police brutality and in support of civil rights erupted nationwide. Here, protestors with Claim Our Space Now, an intersectional movement "emboldening urgent action to dismantle white supremacy and save Black lives," rallied in Times Square, New York.

As we will see in Chapter 2, feminist theory is valuable in understanding how certain crimes significantly impact women. This would include domestic violence, human trafficking, and sexual harassment, which tend to impact women more profoundly than men. Similarly, one of the criticisms of criminological theory has been that many of the theories to explain crime use studies that have male subjects, who may have very different motivations for committing crime than women.

Feminist theory calls attention to gender-based inequalities, which sometimes result from unconscious biases formed about the role of women in society, while at other times are the result of intentional discrimination against women. Intertwined with gender are issues of power and control, and when other variables are factored into the discussion, such as race and ethnicity, social class, and sexual orientation (an **intersectional** approach), the realities of unfair treatment become even more pronounced. Why? Because there may be inherent biases built into those social factors as well. There are several different types of feminist theories, ranging along a continuum that starts with a more liberal interpretation of how gender impacts people's understanding of the role of women in society to more radical assessments of a paternalistic society that systematically discriminates against women (hooks, 2014).

Critical Theory

One of the most well-known applications of Marx's theory to contemporary society is called **critical theory** (sometimes referred to as the Frankfurt School or neo-Marxism). This theory was very popular among scholars in the United States from the 1930s to the 1960s. Critical theorists were among the first theorists to see the connection between popular culture and capitalism, and were also among the first to note the influence of the media in shaping people's understanding of social institutions and various classes of people. Critical theorists continue to call attention to the problems relating to consumerism, which could result in the loss of personal freedom and the decay of democracy. For example, the way in which Facebook has shared personal and private information of its users, even private messages, with other companies might be a source of particular concern for critical theorists. The original ideology of critical theory resulted in the development of many other radical thinkers, such as postmodernists and the cultural studies movement. In fact, some argue that critical theory was one of the most significant developments of theories during the 1980s and 1990s (Held, 1980).

Critical Race Theory

Critical race theory, which is an offshoot of critical theory, began with the Civil Rights movement of the 1960s and continued during the 1970s and 1980s. This theory argues that racism is deeply embedded in all American social institutions, and is easily seen in its laws and their application to certain groups. As institutional racism continues to marginalize people of color and perpetuates a form of white privilege, where people of color are disproportionately represented at all phases of the criminal justice system, many people do not even realize the extent of the prejudice and discrimination that occurs. In fact, some segments of American society remain skeptical of the idea that systemic discrimination and prejudice even exists in the United States (Delgado, 2017).

Queer Theory

Queer theory, which emerged from the gay and lesbian rights movement of the 1970s and 1980s, generated new thinking about how sexuality can be a tool to understand social, political, and economic inequalities. In the same way that feminist theories offer insight into the inherent biases against women, and critical race theory asserts that race is an essential variable in understanding how people of color are systematically discriminated against in society, queer theory offers the idea that no sexual category is inherently deviant or normal: each is socially constructed. What this means is that the traditional categories used by society (heterosexual is normal; non-heterosexual is deviant) are no longer relevant in today's world, and that more flexible broad-based definitions of categories should be used instead (Sullivan, 2003).

Postmodern Theory

In the late twentieth century, some social theorists began to wonder if we would ever be able to uncover the laws of the universe that regulate human behavior. In fact, some wondered if we can ever really grasp objective truth.

Modernism, which began with the 18th-century Enlightenment in Europe, placed great value on a scientific approach to the world and a belief in the universality of human nature. **Postmodernism**, on the other hand, argues that there are no absolutes, no claims to truth, logic, or order. From a postmodern perspective, everything is relative, fragmented, temporary, and variable; there are no universal human truths from which we can derive meaning about humanity (Hollinger, 1994).

Postmodernism sees the grand narratives with which society reinforces itself as stories that justify dominant beliefs and give people as false sense of coherence to the world. Instead, what we have are conflicting versions of what happened, based on particular accounts by different people, who may have agendas of their own. Postmodernists are interested in **deconstructionism**, or the taking apart and examination of existing narratives and explanations of life, rather than the pursuit of an objective truth. In place of those grand narratives are **mini-narratives**, which offer varying insights and explanations for the same event (Hollinger, 1994).

Some sociologists often criticize postmodernism for not embracing the scientific method and the knowledge it generates. Conservatives, whether they are political, religious, or otherwise,

The challenges of uncertainty A culture of conspiracy flourished during the COVID-19 pandemic and in the runup to the 2020 presidential election, as rumors and falsehoods spread rapidly online. Postmodern theory helps social scientists study how such conspiracies take root. Here, protesters in Colorado in 2020 who have been convinced that the media and scientists are lying rally against stay-at-home orders.

generally oppose postmodernism because it appears to ignore or dismiss existing moral standards. Others believe postmodernism has some merit, especially in areas which questions remain about the accuracy and validity of the current paradigm. Postmodernism allows us to explore the possibility that the scientific method is not the only means by which information, facts, and truth can be determined.

HOW SOCIOLOGISTS DO THEIR THING: RESEARCH METHODS

Sociology, as we defined it at the beginning of this chapter, is the scientific study of society, its people, culture, and social interaction. How does sociology use the scientific method? Recall that sociology is an academic discipline. That is, while many counselors or therapists who try to understand people's behavior have degrees in sociology, sociologists themselves are researchers who examine different dimensions of social life to learn more about how those events influence people's perceptions, attitudes, values, beliefs, and behaviors.

Given that studying human behavior is quite different from testing chemical properties in a laboratory, how do sociologists conduct research? Essentially, there are three main designs in social science research. Because we cannot really determine causality when studying human behavior (we haven't discovered those laws in the same way we have the laws of physics, for example), all of the conclusions are based on probabilities. This is not the same thing as saying one thing causes another. We can be 95 percent sure or even 99 percent sure a variable relates to another in a particular way, but we cannot know with certainty that this relationship will occur every single time. So how do we study social life in ways that contribute to our understanding of social problems?

People conducting a survey Surveys and interviews are essential tools for gathering information in social science research.

Surveys

One way to study society and social phenomena is to administer a survey, asking people questions about their experiences or feelings. Surveys are such a common factor in today's life (for example, think of all the times as a consumer that you're asked to complete a survey about your satisfaction with a purchase) that many people think that creating a survey is easy. It is not. There are many factors to consider. Even the way questions are worded or how they are ordered can make a big difference in how people might answer. More important, unless you are going to survey an entire population of people, which can often be impractical, you have to select a scientific sample that represents the population you are studying. In other words, the people you survey have to be a **representative sample** of the population you are studying, and that sample has to be **generalizable** so that the conclusions you draw from analyzing your data can be generalized to people other than the ones you survey (Babbie, 2015). These two concepts are linked: you can't generalize your findings from a survey unless you have a representative sample.

Experimental Methods

Many people are familiar with the elements of a scientific experiment. As you may recall from other courses in the sciences, there are two groups: an **experimental group** and a **control group**. You introduce the **independent variable** (that is, the variable we manipulate to see what kind of impact it has on the dependent variable) to the experimental group to see what effect it has on the **dependent variable** (this is the cause and effect variable—the one we want to see changed in some way). Figure 1.2 illustrates the general process of an experiment. The control group, then, serves as a safeguard against any outside factors that might influence your findings. Ideally, you will start with two comparable groups, and the only change during the experiment involves the independent variable, as seen in the posttest.

This model works great in laboratory settings where you can control all aspects of the environment, but how do you design an experiment for social science research that examines people in their daily lives? It is extremely difficult, which is why **quasi-experimental designs** are sometimes used by sociologists. This contains many of the same elements of a traditional experiment but acknowledges limitations of and inability to control all aspects of the environment (Babbie, 2015). In other words, there are experimental and control groups, along with independent and dependent variables, but the manner in which the population is determined is different from that used in a traditional experiment, and the ability to control all aspects of the environment is less precise.

Many years ago, my old friend and colleague Dennis Kenney conducted an experiment of subway riders in New York City. The experiment occurred at a time when politicians and the media argued that subway crime was out of control. This claim led to the rise in popularity of citizen patrol groups, such as the Guardian Angels, a New York-based group of volunteers who patrolled the subways

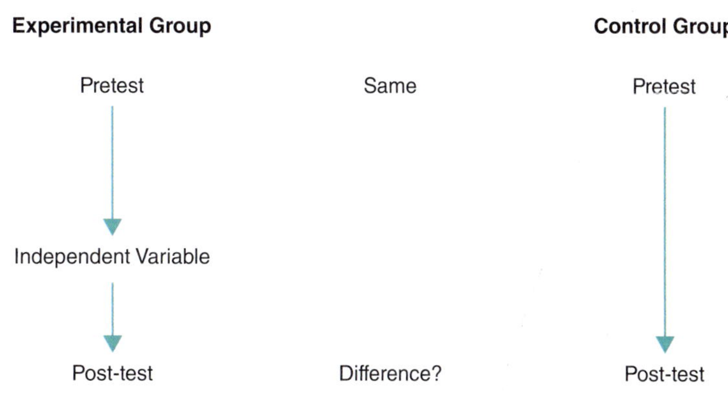

Figure 1.2 Interviews are a critically important part of the research process.

and intervened when they witnessed a crime. To test the effectiveness of this group, as well as attempting to determine whether subway riders were in fact afraid to ride the trains, Kenney (1985) used a quasi-experimental design. He used subway routes as experimental and control groups to measure crime. He also included the presence of Guardian Angels on the subway routes as an independent variable.

Kenney identified subway routes that were said by advocates and the police to have high rates of crime and compared them with routes that Guardian Angels patrolled. Thus, the elements of a traditional experiment were used, but no one knows exactly how many (or which particular) people use the New York City subways. Still, Kenney was able to measure passenger fear as well as the frequency with which Guardian Angels patrolled, along with changes in crime rates in those subway routes used in the study (Kenney, 1985). That said, in sociology, quasi-experimental designs are not used often. Instead, surveys and qualitative research designs are more common (Babbie, 2015).

Qualitative Research

Unlike other forms of research, which attempt to generalize to the larger population or use quantitative analysis to examine the data, qualitative research attempts to examine populations and phenomena in a more contextual manner. Instead of large representative samples and using mathematical calculations to describe the population under study, qualitative researchers study fewer cases in more depth and detail. The result is a context of understanding that is much deeper than what can be derived through a survey or an experiment. There are many variations of qualitative research designs, but two of the most common ones are Ethnography/Participant Observation and the use of interviews.

Ethnography/Participant Observation

Ethnography is one of the most commonly used research designs in the social sciences. A key element of this method involves spending a great deal of time studying the population in in the real world, observing and interacting with people in their neighborhoods, communities, and workplaces as they go about their lives. Also referred to as **participant observation research**, the researcher in these cases strives to become a member of that community or group under study, as well as being an observer of it. It can take months or even years in order for the researcher to gain a full understanding of the context of life among a group of people. Issues involved in this type of research, aside from the length of time it takes to complete such a project, include gaining access to the population, developing a rapport and trust among the members, and determining how to document all the observations in field notes (Daynes and Williams, 2018).

The ultimate goal of ethnographic research is **thick description**, which means writing about what was seen, heard, and understood in such a way that the reader gets a vivid image, as if they were standing next to the researcher as they made those observations (Geertz, 1973). My colleague Terry Williams, a sociologist and highly respected researcher, is a master storyteller in his ethnographic accounts and his books provide powerful thick description about the life of criminals and other deviant populations. As we discussed at the beginning of the chapter, stories are powerful tools which help us understand a great deal about social life, society, and our culture. Ethnographic research typically offers richly detailed stories about the life of a group of people, and in the process challenge our understanding of social interaction and group behavior (which can reshape our stereotypical thinking about people and groups). However, there is the problem of **replicability** and **representativeness** with ethnographic research. That is, researchers do not select a scientific sample of people to study; in fact, they become involved with only those people who are willing to talk to them. My professor Kai Erikson used to say the people we study ethnographically are more of a "chunk of humanity" than any meaningful sample. There is also the issue of bias that must be considered, or what some field researchers call 'going native.' This is the tendency of the researcher to become so involved in the study that they lose their objectivity as scientists, thereby biasing the findings.

Interviews

Interviews can be a part of the ethnographic process, either formally or informally, but for other projects, they become the primary tool to gather data. Interviews can also be used in conjunction with other research methods, such as an analysis of existing sources. In these types of studies, a focus group might be used to study a population, or perhaps a more scientific sampling method would be employed. Interviewing as a skill is similar to effective survey design, in that interviewing is so common in our media culture that some people believe they are more proficient than is probably the case. There is a real skill to designing the types of questions asked, how follow-up questions are offered, and whether the questions are open-ended or closed-ended. These skills are critical to the success of the interview process. Sometimes a **life history approach** is used, which involves the researcher interviewing subjects repeatedly over time so that the researcher gains a much more detailed insight into a respondent's behavior and attitudes. The advantage of using interviews is that the issues and problems can be identified and articulated in the respondent's own words, rather than simply checking a box on a questionnaire. Like ethnographic research, there are challenges related to sampling as well as the manner in which respondents answer interview questions. In some cases, for example, the respondent may recall an event incorrectly or in a different time sequence than is actually the case. These issues of validity, however, are challenges with virtually all forms of social science research (Daynes and Williams, 2018).

Using Research Methods in the Real World: Does This Program Really Work?

I was once asked to evaluate a diversion program for domestic violence offenders. This program was intended for first-time offenders who committed an act of domestic violence. Instead of going to jail, members in this particular program were given the opportunity to participate in group counseling sessions along with reviewing videos that provided additional understanding of domestic violence and its victims.

When I contacted the program director to learn more about the program and to design some type of overall assessment, the director quickly informed me that one was not needed. She claimed, "We have a 100 percent success rate in this program." I was curious about such a statement, so I asked her how such a remarkable track record was achieved. She said, "Well, we have never had any repeat offenders." I thought a moment and then asked, "What happens if an offender who completes your program commits a second offense?" She replied, "They go directly to jail." See the problem? The effectiveness of the program can't be determined by a lack of repeat clients because those individuals who commit a second offense never get to come back to the program.

If you are wondering why you need to know how to conduct research, such a story is not an uncommon one. Most people would probably come to a similar conclusion as that director unless they have been trained in how to conduct and evaluate social science research. In that instance, I suggested that one possible way to evaluate the program would be to identify individuals who were arrested on a domestic violence charge for a given time frame. After making sure the offenders were comparable (e.g., first offense, similar demographic characteristics, and other factors), the next step would be to randomly assign some offenders to the domestic violence prevention program (experimental group) while others received no treatment (control group). At the end of a given period of time, one could examine how many offenders in the experimental group were rearrested on a domestic violence charge compared to those who were in the control group. Also, when students discuss macro-level scale social problems, such as crime, poverty, education, or racism, I often hear them conclude that there are no viable answers or solutions. This is simply not the case. The "nothing works" approach taken by many policymakers, politicians, and even some academics is lazy thinking and is not reflective of what actually occurs. There are programs that are effective at addressing social problems, although no single program solves every problem or works with every population.

Like theory, research methods are tools that are used to gain further understanding into a phenomenon, condition, or population. Understanding how to use research to determine which programs work is critically important from a policy perspective. As we discuss various problems in this textbook, we will be examining programs that have been empirically shown to be effective.

WHAT IS A SOCIAL PROBLEM?

When I meet someone for the first time and they ask me what I do for a living, the next thing they ask me is what courses I teach. When I mention the social problems course, they often joke, "Well, you should study me because I have all sorts of social problems!"

I often smile at this, in part because they probably think they are the first person to ever say this to me, and in part because it shows they don't really understand what a social problem is from a sociological point of view. I believe those folks are telling me the truth about having problems, but what they are really referring to are individual struggles, such as psychological disorders.

C. Wright Mills, in his definition of a social problem, would refer to these as **personal troubles**. In contrast, Mills argues that the sociological focus of social problems should be on **public issues** (Mills, 1959)**.** Thus, a family with a teenage daughter who has an opioid abuse problem rightly feels that problem to be important and significant, but that the problem is really one for that particular family to address and resolve. A public issue, in contrast, involves a problem that affects a large number of people and is a topic worthy of societal intervention in the form of programs, laws, and/or policies. In this particular example, the social problem would be the increase in the number of teenage women who become addicted to prescription painkillers. See the difference? One encompasses a wider audience than the other.

When enough people in a society agree that a condition or situation exists that threatens the quality of their lives and their values, and they further agree that something should be done about that condition, this constitutes a **social problem**.

The Evolution of a Social Problem

There is rarely complete consensus on the severity, causes or the solutions of all social problems. What matters to many sociologists is how some issues become defined as social problems—much of the discussion of how social problems get defined is a political one. That is, what gets defined as a social problem, as well as what is to be done about it, is a product of debate, discussion, and often the use of economic, social, and political influence in that decision. This process is called **claims making.** Claims makers are people who identify a problem or condition in society as harmful to others and make the claim that the public should pay attention to the issue. The claims that are made are given greater credibility depending on the credentials and influence of those making them. In fact, sociologists have discovered that there is an evolution or sequence of steps to the development of a social problem (Specter and Kitsuse, 2001).

STAGE 1. IDENTIFICATION OF THE PROBLEM

Not every situation, condition, or behavior becomes a social problem, regardless of whether or not it is harmful to society. Rather, there is a political element to the process, because influential people in society (those who have social, economic, and/or political power) attempt to claim that the problem is a serious one and should be of concern to the general public. The people making the claims (be they concerned citizens, policymakers, or others) are identified as **moral entrepreneurs** because they not only have influence in society to convince people of their claim, they are also attempting to shape and reshape the society's moral stance on an issue—usually by changes in laws and/or social policy (Specter and Kitsuse, 2001). For instance, many years ago, a group of women who lost children in traffic accidents as a result of drunk drivers began to see a pattern. As a result of these tragedies, they began to act like moral entrepreneurs and founded the organization known today as Mothers Against Drunk Driving (MADD).

STAGE 2: ELEVATION OF THE PROBLEM

By engaging in claims making, moral entrepreneurs attempt to call attention to the seriousness of the problem by convincing the public the issue is one worthy of their attention. This is often accomplished through media campaigns, which frequently include the use of research or other data that suggests the scope of the problem is not simply a pet project of that individual or group. The goal here is to raise awareness and concern about the situation so that it warrants societal attention (Specter and Kitsuse, 2001). As it relates to MADD, in examining the data and making the claim that such a tragedy could happen to any family, the mothers and advocates of MADD elevated the problem of drunk driving from a personal trouble to a public issue.

STAGE 3 DEBATING THE CAUSES

Included in the efforts to raise awareness of the problem are explanations of why the problem is occurring. There are two general explanations for most social problems that cast the problem in different ways: personal and systemic. **Personal attribution** is when the cause of the problem is presented as a failure of certain individuals who contribute to the problem. The social problem is caused by *their* failure, *their* lack of effort or talent, or something attributed to the individual or person. For example, in the case of drunk driving, one might argue that the offender's inability to moderate their alcohol intake is the reason for its frequency. Deaths related to drunk drivers, then, are a result of the offender's lapses in judgment or carelessness in making the decision to drive while intoxicated.

In contrast, social problems can be attributed to factors beyond the individual's control. In such cases, there may be structural factors that explain the problem. This is sometimes referred to as **systemic attribution,** where the system or structure of society causes the problem. To use the example of drunk driving again, an explanation based on systemic attribution might argue that the reason so many deaths occurred at the hands of drunk drivers was a result of the legislatures' failure to pass laws specifically targeting drunk driving as a crime as well as law enforcement's failure to arrest offenders for DUI unless it was related to an accident.

This distinction between personal and systemic attribution illustrates the nature of social policy. More conservative approaches to a social problem tend to focus on personal attribution as an explanation, while more liberal interpretations of the problem are more likely to assert systemic attribution as a way to understand why the problem exists (Specter and Kitsuse, 2001).

STAGE 4: CHANGES IN SOCIAL POLICY

As debate about the nature, severity, and extent of the problem occurs, so too does the discussion about possible solutions to the problem. The role of sociologists in these debates is not always clear. On one hand, some sociologists argue that their role, as researchers, is to provide the most accurate information as possible about a problem. The argument here is that sociologists are not policymakers; they are researchers. Their job, then, is to provide policymakers with the insight they need to form accurate and comprehensive policy. On the other hand, some sociologists believe that, as experts on the topic, they should endeavor to influence social policy. Some researchers feel they are in the unique position to offer insight and guidance on how best to draft and implement policy on a given topic. The result can be the development of social programs to address the problem; changes in social policy; or even changes in legislation that mandate how the problem is to be prevented and addressed in the future (Specter and Kitsuse, 2001).

As a result of their efforts in convincing the public of the dangers of drunk driving, MADD and its members have had a significant impact on shaping social policy and drunk driving laws in this country. They tell a compelling story, one that is supported by data, on their website (MADD.org).

Further complicating the understanding of any particular social problem is that it is likely to have both objective and subjective features. Remember, what people consider to be negative and how extensive the problem might be varies quite a bit. In addition, well-meaning people can arrive at very different subjective conclusions about the same set of objective data.

This subjective component to all social problems is sometimes called **the social constructionist view** (Rubington and Weinberg, 2010). This view essentially argues that social problems are determined by people (such as policymakers, the general public, or other influential people in society) who determine whether a situation or condition should be elevated in status to a social problem. What this means is that the definition of social problems is a very political process. As people, policymakers, politicians, and the like attempt to shape our understanding and perception of a problem, they will attempt to influence the media about the problem, its causes, as well as the possible solutions. This is not to suggest these individuals are misrepresenting the problem or fraudulently creating a problem to further an agenda. Rather, the focus from a social constructionist viewpoint is not on the problem or condition itself, but on the process by which something becomes a social problem.

CONCLUSION

Sociology is a discipline that offers scientific explanations of events and people's behavior. I tell students that once they start thinking sociologically, they will see it wherever they go. Why? Because sociology occurs in real time in everyday life. I have had students email me, describing many such episodes when they were watching a movie and found sociological ideas and theories in it (several students have even lamented that I have ruined their ability to simply watch a movie without seeing the sociological implications—I wish I could tell them I was sorry, but I am actually thrilled to hear this). Others talk about understanding personal and systemic problems more intimately, because they have used their sociological imagination to grasp a phenomenon in a way they would have otherwise never considered. Still others often email me with ideas for research projects, including research design ideas that they learned in class.

After reading this chapter, you should have an understanding of the sociological imagination, a sense of the role of theory and why it's important, and a basic sense of how social problems are constructed and analyzed. You should also be able to explain how social problems emerge (and recognize new ones, which seem to crop up all the time) and what role sociology has in understanding and explaining them. Most important, you will begin to use the sociological imagination to consider different (and more systemic, or macro-level) explanations for things that occur in society. Once you recognize that people's behavior may be symptomatic of something larger rather than simply idiosyncratic or personal preferences, you can begin thinking about effective solutions for social problems.

SUMMARY

- Define sociology and the sociological imagination.
- Understand the role of theory in the social sciences and in sociology.
    - Theory is a tool to help you understand whatever it is you are studying or learning about. Theory can also help explain why certain events, phenomena, or behavior occur.
- Identify the main theoretical perspectives or paradigms in the discipline.
    - There are two main principles of functionalism. First, society is a stable, ordered system made up of interrelated parts or structures. Second, each structure has a purpose or function that contributes to the continued stability of the unified whole. Structures are seen in social institutions such as the family, schools, the economy, religion, and politics. They meet society's needs by performing different functions, and each one is needed to maintain that stability in society. Any disorganization or dysfunction leads to change and a new sense of balance.
    - According to conflict theory, the pursuit of profit in a capitalist system means there are winners and losers. People acquire economic power depending on their place in the system, whether they are part of the bourgeoisie or the proletariat, and the economic influence also gives them social power as well. However, the proletariat plays a critical in the process, but they are continually exploited in favor of profits. For Karl Marx, the only way the situation changes is if workers develop a sense of class consciousness and start a revolution to overthrow the existing system and institute a more

equitable distribution of resources. For Max Weber, rationalization has led to the loss of meaningful social relationships.
- Symbolic interactionism takes a micro-level approach by focusing on three basic ideas: the meanings of symbols; how those meanings are negotiated by people; and how meaning changes through the course of social interaction. Erving Goffman proposed that that social behavior is like a theatrical performance, or dramaturgy. We manage our social behavior like actors in a play.
- Gender, race, and sexual orientation factor into how people's places in society are determined and the influence of those factors. Feminist theory, critical theory, and queer theory might provide some insight. Some sociologists question the entire idea of truth, fact, and the use of science in explaining the world around you. In that instance, postmodernism might offer compelling explanations.

- Describe the role of research in sociology and the various designs.
  - Research methods are tools used by sociologists to gain further understanding into a phenomenon, condition, or population. Research methods can be quantitative, such as surveys and experiments, or qualitative, such as ethnography and interviews.
- Compare the differences between personal troubles and systemic issues.
  - Personal troubles are individual struggles at the micro level, such as a family dealing with a child's opioid abuse. Systemic issues impact society at the macro level, such as the easy availability of prescription painkillers.
- Discuss the process of how social problems are created.
  - There are four stages to the evolution of a social problem: identification; elevation; debate; and change. Each stage of this process is influenced by moral entrepreneurs.

KEY TERMS

Alienation 14
Altruistic suicide 12
Anomie 12
Bourgeoisie 14
Claims making 27
Class Consciousness 14
Collective conscience 12
Dramaturgy 18
Ethnography 24
False consciousness 14
Generalizability 23
Impression management 18
Iron Cage of Rationality 15
Macrosociology 7
Mechanical Solidarity 11
Microsociology 7
Moral entrepreneurs 27
Organic solidarity 12
Personal Attribution 28
Personal troubles 27
Postmodernism 21
Praxis 16
Proletariat 14
Public issues 27
Rationalization 15
Social constructionist view of social problems 29
Sociological imagination 7

Discussion Questions

1. How would you explain to a friend the difference between sociology and psychology?
2. Can you think of contemporary examples of Durkheim's idea of anomie? In what kinds of situations might individuals find themselves experiencing anomie?
3. Think about Weber's ideas on rationalization. When was the last time you wrote an email or a handwritten letter to someone instead of sending a text? Do you think people fully consider the costs associated with the use of technology and the conveniences it brings to their lives?
4. What are some of the difficulties of creating an effective survey? What are some of the challenges to conducting research using this method?
5. What do you make of the idea that social problems are sometimes created through influential people making claims about a problem? Can you think of conditions or problems in society that affect a large number of people but aren't really considered social problems by the general public? Which ones?

Learn more with this chapter's digital tools, including Data and Media Literacy Exercises, flashcards, and chapter self-assessments at **www.oup.com/he/mcnamara**.

2

Why Is Crime Always in the News? Crime and Interpersonal Violence

LEARNING OBJECTIVES:

- Describe the extent of crime in the United States.
- Discuss factors that contribute to the public's fear of crime.
- Summarize what makes crime bad for society.
- Analyze the public's role in the crime problem in the United States.
- Compare the different types of crime, including crimes of violence, property crime, juvenile crime, white-collar offenses, and cybercrime.
- Explain the role of sociological theory in understanding crime.
- Discuss the components of the criminal justice system and how it addresses crime in the United States.
- Identify several programs that work to reduce crime in the United States.

Chapter Outline

Scene of the crime The news media and popular culture are saturated with familiar images of crime scenes, including yellow caution tape and forensics experts.

Whether you get your news from a website, social media, or a podcast, it is difficult to not find stories about crime. There is a lot of information—and misinformation—offered about crime, and it is easy to see how those stories can generate fear. It may also be the case that prior to reading this chapter, you too are afraid of being a victim of crime. Indeed, public opinion polls show that more people are fearful of being victimized by crime than ever before.

In this chapter, we are going to stick with what sociologists and criminal justice experts know about crime—not news reports; not sensationalized accounts of single incidents; not dramatic recreations of events. Instead, we are going to examine the data as it relates to crime. This is critically important, because if you don't balance your own biases about the problem with the actual data that explains its causes, trends, and solutions, you won't be any better educated about the problem than the general public. As I tell my students, relying on research conducted by unbiased parties is more likely to provide a closer approximation of what's happening than someone who has an agenda, or seeks to exploit crime for entertainment or fear-mongering. That means you must use your sociological imagination and critical thinking skills to avoid falling victim to the biases that most people experience.

As you read this chapter, I will also suggest that while the public has heightened levels of fear of being victimized, some of our values, attitudes, beliefs, and behaviors actually contribute to the problem. This is not blaming the victim; no one is suggesting that people deserve to be victimized, yet it is fair to say that some of our actions may create opportunities for crimes to occur.

Finally, as you read this chapter, think about factors that might be important to minimize or eliminate this this problem. These factors will become clear to you as you read the section on solutions to crime. Remember, not every program or solution works with every population or for every crime. Some are specific to particular types of offenders or certain conditions in which crime occurs. This point is often where the general public and even policymakers make the mistake of looking for the panacea, or single solution, to crime. There isn't one.

SOCIOLOGICAL STORY TIME

- February 14, 2018. Nikolas Cruz, a 19-year-old male who had a history of disciplinary problems at Marory Stoneman Douglas High School in Parkland, Florida, entered the campus and killed 17 students and adults. Cruz was identified as a potential threat by a blogger who reported him to the FBI months before the attack (Hanna, Karimi, and Grinberg, 2018).
- A pastor at one of Newark, New Jersey's largest churches was arrested for stealing over $700,000 while acting as a plumbing company's bookkeeper in 2015. While not a CPA, the bookkeeper used his status as a pastor to engender the trust of his clients (Segal, 2017).
- Hollywood mogul Harvey Weinstein was charged in 2018 with three counts of rape and sexual assault involving three women. Weinstein has been accused by hundreds of women for sexual misconduct between 2013 and 2015, but has only been formally charged in this particular case. As of January 2020, Weinstein faced five criminal counts: one count of rape in the first degree, one count of rape in the third degree, one count of a criminal sexual act in the first degree, and two counts of predatory sexual assault. In late 2019, Weinstein's company offered to settle many of the assault and harassment suits against him for $25 million. In all of these instances Weinstein has denied any wrong doing and continues to argue that all the sexual acts were consensual (Bekiempis, 2020).
- In 2018, Wells Fargo Bank was charged with opening new accounts and credit cards in its customers' names without their permission. Estimates suggested that over three million fraudulent accounts were created and imposed improper fees on mortgages and auto loans. Regulators imposed a $1 billion fine on the company and required Wells Fargo to refund nearly $13 million to customers who were harmed by the bank's actions. In addition, the company recently agreed to pay $142 million to settle a class-action lawsuit by Wells Fargo shareholders for the misconduct (Cowley, 2018).

THE EXTENT OF CRIME IN THE UNITED STATES

How much crime occurs in the United States? This may seem to be a simple question, but the answer is extremely complicated. One reason the question is difficult to answer accurately is that a lot of crime goes unreported. For example, let's imagine you wake up one morning and as you leave the house, you realize that you left the window down in your car and someone stole minor items, including your coveted social problems textbook. As heartbroken as you might be about losing that important item, you really can't get your insurance company involved because your deductible is $500, and the cost of the items stolen is less than that amount. Given that you're already late for class and there's no way to get reimbursed for your loss, would you call the police and file a report? Probably not. But a crime has in fact occurred, right?

Unreported incidents create what is known as a **dark figure of crime**. However, based on the incidence of reported crime, we can use different measures to get an idea of how much actually occurs. This is accomplished by asking the police how many crimes have been reported to them; asking victims to describe their experiences with crime (and whether they reported those crimes to the police); and asking offenders about how often they commit crimes. The most common form of data collection is called the **Uniform Crime Reports** (UCR), which is compiled by the FBI and consists of all crimes known to the police across the country in a given year. This is what most media accounts and others use when they refer to the crime rate.

Crime Trends

The UCR program collects information on crimes reported by law enforcement agencies. There are two main categories of crime that it tracks: violent crimes (murder, non-negligent manslaughter, rape, robbery, and aggravated assault) and property crimes (burglary, larceny-theft, motor vehicle theft, and arson). According to the UCR for 2018, the estimated number of violent crimes in the nation decreased 3.3 percent from 2017, from 1,247,917 to 1,206,836. However, the violent crime rate has increased by nearly 5 percent since 2014 (Table 2.1). Similarly, in 2018, murder and non-negligent

Table 2.1 Violent Crime in the United States 2014–2018

2014	2015	2016	2017	2018
1,153,022	1,199,310	1,250,162	1,247,917	1,206,836

Source: Crime in the United States 2018. Available at https://ucr.fbi.gov/crime-in-the-u.s/2018/crime-in-the-u.s.-2018/topic-pages/violent-crime

Table 2.2 Homicides in the United States 2014–2018.

2014	2015	2016	2017	2018
14,164	15,883	17,413	17,294	16,214

Source: US Department of Justice, Federal Bureau of Investigation. (2018). *Crime in the United States 2018*. Available at: https://ucr.fbi.gov/crime-in-the-u.s/2018/crime-in-the-u.s.-2018/topic-pages/murder

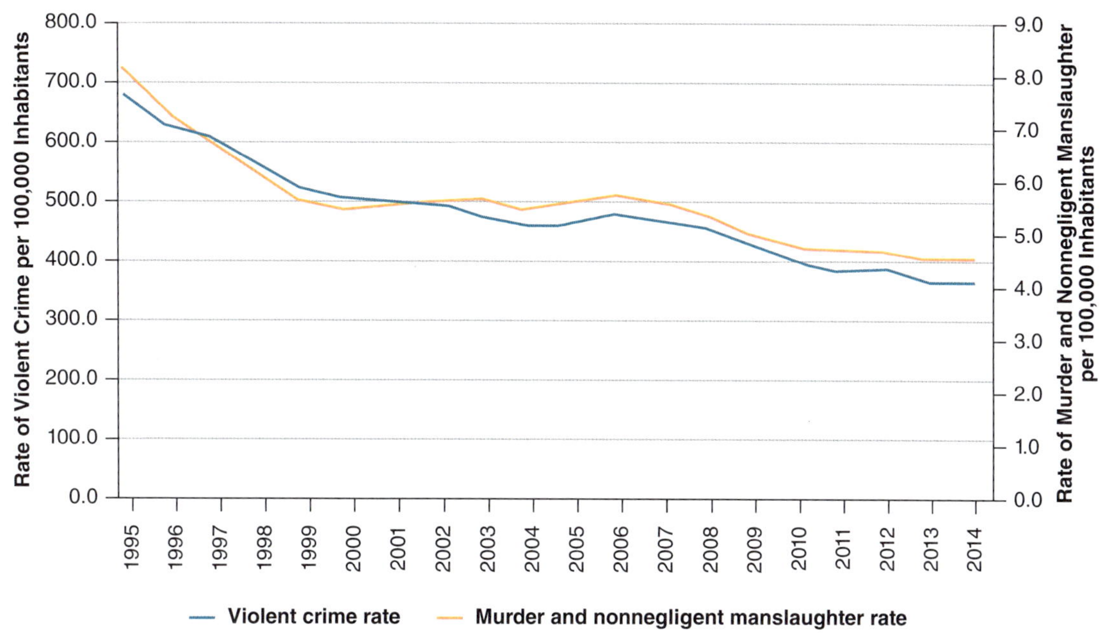

Figure 2.1 **Violent crime and murder and nonnegligent manslaughter rates in the United States, 1995–2014.**

manslaughter offenses decreased 6.2 percent compared to 2017. However, when compared to 2014 data, the rate has increased 14.5 percent (Table 2.2). Despite these recent increases, the violent crime rate and the homicide rate decreased steadily for over two decades until 2014 (Figure 2.1).

Nationwide, in 2018 there were an estimated 7,196,045 property crimes. Overall, property crimes decreased by 6.3 percent from 2017 and witnessed a ten year decline of approximately 23 percent (Table 2.3). Burglaries, larcenies, and motor vehicle thefts decreased in 2018 from the year before and had significant declines since 2014.

Overall, then, crime rates, as calculated by the UCR, have shown significant declines for years (Figure 2.1). However, fears and concerns about crime by the general public remain relatively high. Why would this be the case?

Table 2.3 Property Crime in the United States 2014–2018

2014	2015	2016	2017	2018
8,209,010	8,024,165	7,928,530	7,682,938	7,196,045

Source: Crime in the United States 2018. Available at: https://ucr.fbi.gov/crime-in-the-u.s/2018/crime-in-the-u.s.-2018/topic-pages/property-crime

GLOBAL PERSPECTIVES

Why is Crime in Japan So Low Compared to the United States?

For researchers studying the crime problem in the United States, Japan provides a fascinating comparison. Since Japan has low rates of crime (particularly violent crimes), few gun-related offenses, and a very different style of policing than the United States, it is held out as an example of what life could be like in the United States.

Japan, which has approximately 127 million people, has an extraordinarily low crime rate. According to official data, in 2017 there were a total of 915,111 crimes in Japan, a significant decrease from the 996,120 recorded in 2016, and about half of the 2.8 million crimes recorded in 2002. As in the United States, larceny and thefts present the largest share of all crime in Japan, with 655,541 thefts, a third of which consist of stolen bicycles. However, even with these crimes, in 2018 there was a ten percent decline in thefts from the previous year. Homicides and robberies are low in Japan with 9,037 homicides and 1,852 robberies recorded in 2018 (Kyodo, 2018).

Policing in Japan In Okinawa, Japan, police officers restrain a suspect. Crime rates in Japan are much lower than they are in the United States.

Japan's homicide rate is very low, hovering at about 0.3 per 100,000 people and is among the lowest in the world. In comparison, the homicide rate in the United States in 2018 was 5.0 (McNeil, 2018). Also, there are only about 10 gun-related deaths in Japan each year, compared to 10,265 in the United States in 2018. This is one of the reasons people sometimes point to Japan's model as a way to counter the gun-related violence in the United States (McNeil, 2018).

Also noteworthy are Japan's efforts to keep people from being sentenced to prison. Unlike the United States, which seems to use incarceration to punish offenders into compliance, in Japan reoffending rates are low. Japanese adults are incarcerated at a far lower rate, about 45 offenders per 100,000 people, than the United States, whose rate is about 666 per 100,000 people (Lopez, 2018).

To achieve such extraordinary success, however, Japan employs a very different system of justice. For instance, confessions result in nearly 90 percent of prosecutions in Japan, and these are often made under duress. Interrogations can be long and arduous. Japanese law allows suspects to be detained for up to 23 days, and access to attorneys is limited. Moreover, the constitutional protections afforded to suspects in the United States are virtually non-existent in Japan. Trials also usually result in convictions. Juries are rarely used and judges routinely defer to the wishes of the prosecuting attorney in most cases (Lopez, 2018).

Sexual assault is another crime that is relatively rare in Japan. However, it is unclear whether these figures are partly the result of enforcement efforts or actual criminal activity. The emancipation of women in Japanese society is not seen the same way as in the United States; as a result, offenses against women are said to be more widespread. Japanese police have been criticized for failing to take victims of sexual crimes seriously as a result of either chauvinist bias or an inability to investigate such crimes. Similar comments have been made against the police in the United States, but such a trend is noteworthy for Japan. Also similar to their US counterparts, critics point out that the police culture seems overly concerned with manipulating crime rates to demonstrate a higher level of effectiveness than might actually be the case (Bergo, 2014).

In sum, while Japan has achieved an extraordinary level of success in combatting crime, such a system requires from its citizens a sense of duty and compliance to the law (where the general sense is that people in Japan do not commit crimes so criminals must consist primarily of foreigners) as well as a criminal justice system that does not provide the same level of protections afforded to people in the United States.

ARE PEOPLE AFRAID OF CRIME?

Generally speaking, people are concerned about crime. Public opinion polls ask a sample of Americans about crime, such as whether they are afraid to walk alone at night, even in their own neighborhoods. Polls also ask people if they worry about crime and violence, and how serious the problem is in this country. Public opinion polls have also inquired about people's perceptions about the government's ability to address the crime problem. As Table 2.4 shows, a large percentage of Americans are fearful of being victimized by crime. For instance, when asked in 2017 how worried they are about being victimized, 84 percent said they were worried a great deal or a fair amount. This

Table 2.4 Gallup Poll: Americans Worried About Crime

Year	A Great Deal	Fairly Concerned
2017	57%	27%
2016	47%	29%
2015	53%	26%
2014	43%	37%
2013	47%	28%

Source: https://news.gallup.com/poll/190475/americans-concern-crime-climbs-year-high.aspx

Table 2.5 Gallup Poll: Perceptions about the Extent of Crime in Your Area

Year	More	Less	Same
2017	40%	38%	20%
2016	45%	37%	20%
2015	40%	33%	18%
2014	44%	32%	19%
2013	40%	33%	20%

Source: https://news.gallup.com/poll/190475/americans-concern-crime-climbs-year-high.aspx

is an increase from 2016, where 76 percent said they were similarly worried. In fact, over the past five years, about 70 percent of the people polled consistently stated that they were either fairly or a great deal worried about crime and violence (Davis, 2018).

Similarly, when asked about crime trends, the public does not seem to have a good understanding of the extent of the problem. As Table 2.5 shows, Americans are about evenly divided between thinking the problem is worse, better, or has remained the same, even in their own neighborhood. The table shows that about 40 percent of Americans think the problem has gotten worse, while a bit less think it has lessened in intensity and 20 percent consistently rate the problem about the same (Davis, 2018).

However, when it comes to assessing the problem on a national scale, people's perceptions become dramatically inaccurate. As Table 2.6 shows, between 2013 and 2017, most Americans think the crime problem has gotten worse across the country.

Table 2.6 Gallup Poll: American Perceptions about the Extent of Crime in United States

Year	More	Less	Same
2017	68%	19%	9%
2016	70%	20%	6%
2015	70%	18%	8%
2014	63%	21%	9%
2013	64%	16%	9%

Source: https://news.gallup.com/poll/190475/americans-concern-crime-climbs-year-high.aspx

Table 2.7 Gallup Poll: Public's Confidence in the US Criminal Justice System

Year	Great Deal	Quite a Lot	Some	Very Little	None	No Opinion
2018	9%	13%	41%	34%	2%	1%
2017	14%	13%	37%	32%	2%	1%
2016	9%	14%	40%	34%	2%	1%
2015	9%	14%	42%	31%	3%	1%
2014	10%	13%	40%	32%	4%	1%
2013	10%	18%	40%	30%	2%	1%

https://news.gallup.com/poll/190475/americans-concern-crime-climbs-year-high.aspx

Adding to these fears is a lack of confidence in the criminal justice system's ability to address crime. As Table 2.7 shows, only about a quarter have a lot of confidence in the system, while about a third of the population have very little or no confidence—findings that have been consistent over the past five years (Davis, 2018).

Significantly, this data suggests that Americans are generally afraid of being victimized and often take steps to address that fear. It also shows that a substantial portion of the population does not feel confident in the ability of the government to address the problem.

WHY IS CRIME BAD?

Americans have consistently rated crime as one of the most important social problems in society, and it is clear from public opinion polls that it causes them to be afraid. But what makes crime so bad for society?

Harm

When most people think of crime in the United States, particularly as a social problem, they most often think of street crime. While there are many types of crime, generally speaking, when the public talks about crime, it focuses attention on things like murder, rape, robbery, assault, burglary, larceny, and motor vehicle theft.

You might think crime is "bad" because of the harm it does to people. Victims of crime are physically hurt or killed by offenses such as murder, rape, robbery, and assault. Similarly, people who lose their possessions from property crimes, such as burglary, larceny, and motor vehicle theft, suffer harm too. However, if harm is the primary reason, consider other events that occur in society that are just as harmful (if not more so)

Harm and cost Car thieves often strip cars for parts that can be illegally re-sold for profit.

but not criminal. For example, more people are harmed in automobile accidents each year than by all of street crime; more workers are injured in work-related accidents, or die of heart attacks, than are murdered or raped each year. So what makes crime more problematic than these events?

Costs

If harm isn't the primary reason crime is bad for society, perhaps a related factor holds the answer: cost. That is, people lose money or the value of their possessions due to crimes such as burglary, auto theft, and larceny. There are costs associated with the apprehension, prosecution, and punishment of offenders. There are also costs related to the prevention of crime; costs to the insurance industry (which is passed along to the public in the form of higher premiums); medical costs; and other expenses related to crime.

Interestingly, when the general public considers the costs of crime, they tend to only consider street crimes. Yet it is the crimes that cost the most—white-collar crimes—that are often overlooked in the discussion. White-collar crime can exceed the costs of all those street crimes combined. For instance, consider the costs of the cleanup of the 2015 oil spill in the Gulf of Mexico, when a British Petroleum (BP) tanker ship ran aground and spilled millions of gallons of crude oil into the Gulf, causing damage to the environment and the area. Estimates of the cost of that single event act approached $65 billion (Bousso, 2018). Given that there are other things in society that are more harmful or costly than street crime, what makes crime so problematic for people?

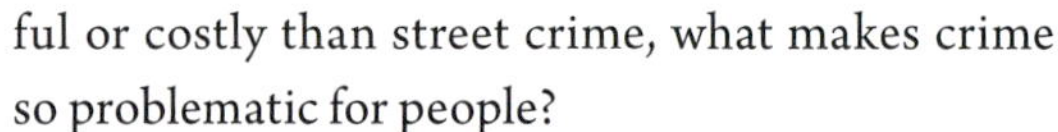

Crimes against the environment The harm done to the environment and the massive costs incurred for cleanup make oil spills due to negligence among the most devastating of industrial crimes.

PSYCHOLOGICAL IMPACT

What makes crime bad for society is not necessarily the harm or the cost, but the psychological impact it has on people. Street crime is sudden, it directly impacts the victim in meaningful ways, it is likely to be a surprise event, and it is usually confrontational. Street crime is in your face: there's a guy with a gun robbing you of your jewelry; there's a criminal breaking into your home to steal your possessions; someone attacks you or a loved one.

Not only is this a traumatic experience for the people involved in such incidents, but when people hear about incidents of street crime, the event serves as a reminder that something like it could happen to them. This creates a significant amount of anxiety and fear, which in turn changes people's behavior. People become less willing to interact with others, who might be seen as potential threats. As was saw earlier, public opinion polls indicate that about a third of the public is afraid to walk around their neighborhood at night (Davis, 2018).

THE PUBLIC'S ROLE IN THE CRIME PROBLEM

To understand crime as a social problem, it is important to study not just the activities of criminals but also the ways in which the community contributes to the problem. This line of inquiry is not victim-blaming (that is, the assumption that the victim caused the problem or brought it on themselves). Rather, whether intentionally or not, people sometimes create opportunities for crimes to occur.

For example, studies of auto theft examined the number of vehicles that were recovered after being stolen. The research found that about one in every eight vehicles had no damage to the steering column. Typically, car thieves break into the steering column in an effort to start the vehicle. One conclusion from such a finding is that the keys were left in the ignition. This is very common in colder climates, where drivers attempt to warm up their vehicles prior to leaving home. In fact, some states have laws preventing what they call "puffing" and issue fines for such actions (Tuttle, 2016).

Another example involves burglary, which is one of the most common crimes in the United States. Research points out that a significant proportion of burglaries occur through the front door with no signs of forced entry. This means it is very likely that the door was left unlocked. These and other examples point out that whether intentionally or unintentionally, the public creates opportunities for crime to occur (US Department of Justice, Bureau of Justice Statistics, 2016).

It is also important to acknowledge that, according to the data about violent crimes (which generate the most fear), it is likely that there is some sort of relationship between offender and victim. Again, to study this aspect of the problem is not to engage in victim-blaming, but rather to arrive at a better understanding of why and how crime occurs. That is, while we might be fearful of the unprovoked attack by a stranger, most of the time the offender is an acquaintance, a friend, or even a relative. This is true not only for interpersonal crime (such as homicide, rape, aggravated and simple assault, robbery, and stalking) but also for some property crimes, such as larceny and burglary. To be fair, property crimes tend to have fewer known relationships between the victims and the offenders, largely because the offender is not apprehended nor does the victim see the offender as the crime occurs. With regard to stalking, for example, according to one study, approximately three out of four stalking victims reported a relationship of some type with their offender, while only 1 out of 10 victims reported being stalked by a stranger (Baum, Catalano, Rand, and Rose, 2009).

This relationship between victims and offenders has implications for the criminal justice system. For instance, there is some evidence that the relationship could play a mitigating role in the decision to charge an offender (where a homicide might be reduced to manslaughter because of the circumstances and emotions surrounding the relationship). Similarly, crimes between intimates are more likely to generate images of victim provocation by juries and judges than are crimes involving strangers (Dawson, 2006).

Even the evidence about child abuse indicates that, despite fears and concerns about strangers attacking and harming children, more often than not the offender is usually a family member, a sibling, a relative, or a friend or acquaintance (Latzman, Vilijoen, Scalora, and Ullman, 2011). Similarly, the data on rape has consistently pointed to the fact that in a significant portion of cases, there is a relationship between the victim and the offender (Morgan and Kenna, 2017).

Finally, the community's inadvertent role in the problem of crime can result from a lack of understanding of the implications of certain social policies meant to address the problem. For example, while a "get tough" approach to crime was and remains a popular position for policymakers and some citizens, the research has shown that these policies, which began in the 1980s, have resulted in thousands of offenders receiving long prison sentences (Sentencing Project, n.d.).

One unintended consequence of this strategy has been the problem of addressing the health care needs of elderly inmates. This problem, in turn, results in significant funding and accommodation issues, as correctional facilities were never designed for wheelchair-bound inmates or dealing with chronic illnesses such as cancer and other ailments (McKollop and Boucher, 2018). This is not to say that inmates should be given light sentences or not held accountable for their actions, but a widespread policy change that required longer and mandatory sentences not only makes criminals worse when they are released, but there are other costs associated with such a strategy.

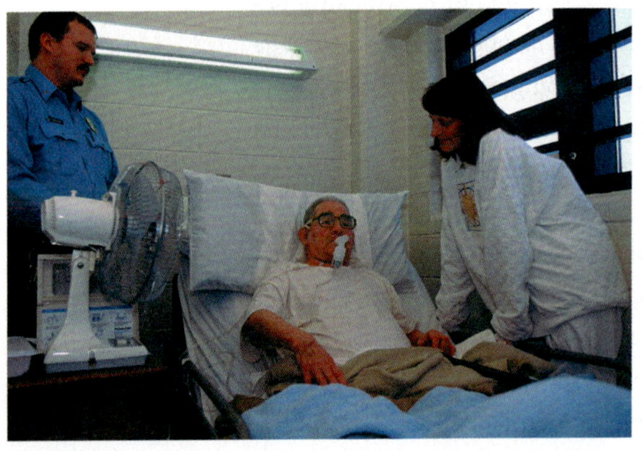

Sentenced for life An elderly prisoner receives care in the hospital at the Nebraska State Prison.

TYPES OF CRIME

While there are many types of crimes, and just as many ways to categorize them, for our purposes we will use the following categories: violent crime, property crime, juvenile crime, white-collar and corporate crime, and cybercrime.

Violent Crimes

As we have discussed, violent crime generates the greatest levels of fear, and public opinion polls indicate elevated concern regardless of the actual crime rates. As noted in the UCRs, violent crimes involve murder and non-negligent manslaughter, rape, robbery, and aggravated assault. The distinguishing characteristic in these crimes is the use or threat of force in the commission of the acts.

MURDER

The murder rate, like the overall violent crime rate, has been declining in recent years. According to the UCRs, the murder rate per 100,000 people in the United States is 5.0. Although other countries have noticeably lower rates than the United States, the trend in this country has been downward for the last decade. Criminal homicide takes two forms: murder, which is the unlawful killing of a human being with malice aforethought; and manslaughter, which is unlawful homicide without malice aforethought. (Malice aforethought means the offender thought about committing the crime, planned it, and carried out that plan.) In practice, it can be difficult to distinguish between the two because it requires knowing the offender's intent when they committed the crime.

While the public's perception of the problem suggests a more calculated and intentional type of offender, in reality, most homicides are not planned and are not committed by hardened criminals. In fact, most are a result of a dispute or argument between people who know each other (and are often intimately related), and the deadly outcome occurs when a conflict gets out of hand. Studies have shown a close relationship between homicide victims and their offenders. Often, the crime lacks premeditation. The dispute frequently occurs when both parties have been drinking and the dispute escalates. Add in the availability of guns, and it is relatively easy to see how the outcome can turn deadly (Fox, Levin, and Fridel, 2018; Katz, 1989).

Handguns were used in approximately 64 percent of all murders in 2018. The UCR data suggests that murders occur most often in large cities and in the southern portion of the United States. Some argue that this is the result of a culture in the South that suggests the use of violence is an acceptable solution to problems, as well as easy access to weapons. The percentage of handguns used in homicide has been consistent for many years (US Department of Justice, Federal Bureau of Investigation, 2019a). Race and gender also play a role in understanding homicide, as men are more likely to commit murder than women, perhaps because men are socialized to be more aggressive than women and are more familiar with guns.

With regard to race, more than half of all people who commit murder are members of a minority group, most often Blacks. Similarly, victims of homicide also tend to be minorities. This means that homicide tends to be an intra-racial crime, meaning people of the same race commit the crime against another member of that group. According to the UCR, about 81 percent of White murder victims were killed by White offenders, while about 89 percent of Black victims were killed by Black offenders (US Department of Justice, Federal Bureau of Investigation, 2019a).

MASS MURDER AND SERIAL KILLERS

Another form of homicide is **mass murder**—or the killing of multiple victims, either at one time, such as a school shooting, or over time, as in the case of a serial killer. Sometimes wars between criminal gangs lead to mass murders, while other times criminals commit multiple killings of witnesses or accomplices who might testify against them. For instance, the famous mobster John Gotti, was once known as the "Teflon Don" because he avoided prosecution in part because witnesses or victims either refused to testify against him or disappeared before the trial began (Dickson, 2018).

Still, the most frequent type of mass murder is not the gangland war—it is the family killing, where one member of a family kills several of his relatives. Often these killings are exaggerated responses to the emotions and pressures that can occur in families. Examples include the teenage child who feels wronged and takes revenge against his parents and perhaps everyone else in the house. Another example would be the rejected husband, angry with his wife over a divorce, who returns to kill her and her children (Ramsland, 2005).

Finally, there are the multiple murders of strangers. Unlike the crime-related killings or family slayings, these involve victims chosen almost at random. In some cases, the murders occur all at the same time. For example, on August 3, 2019, a 21-year-old male, Patrick Crusius, walked into a Walmart in El Paso, Texas armed with an assault rifle and killed 22 people. This was one of the deadliest mass shootings in US history (Murphy, 2019). Mass murderers in this category typically do not repeat their crimes. Either they kill themselves or are killed or captured by police (Ramsland, 2005).

Another type of murderer, the serial murderer, kills one or two victims at a time but repeats the crime several times over a period of months or years. Often there is an element of sexual sadism involved; that is, the killer derives sexual excitement and release by torturing and killing his victims (Fox, Levin and Fridel, 2019).

The research on serial killers suggests that their crimes are difficult for the police to solve because the murderer, the victim, or both live at the fringes of society. They often choose as victims people who have few stable relationships, such as the homeless, runaway children, or prostitutes (Fox, Levin, and Fridel, 2019). In their appearance and in their manner, serial killers appear friendly, intelligent, and approachable. Experts who study serial killers note that there is something deep in the psyche of the serial killer that motivates them to commit these crimes that we may never understand (Fox, Levin, and Fridel, 2019).

RAPE AND GENDER-BASED VIOLENCE

According to the UCR, there were 101,151 reported rapes in 2018, an increase of about 3 percent from the previous year and approximately an 18 percent increase since 2014 (US Department of Justice, Federal Bureau of Investigation, 2019b). In 2017, the UCR modified the definition of rape for reporting purposes. In the past, the definition included the term "forcible" and was confined only to females. In the revised definition, rape consists of any type of penetration against anyone without their consent. While this is a more accurate definition of the crime of rape, the statistics on rape continue to show that females are the primary victims, particularly younger ones (US Department of Justice, Federal Bureau of Investigation, 2019b).

For instance, according to the Rape and Incest National Network, girls and women between the ages of 16 and 19 are four times more likely than girls and women in other age groups to be assaulted or raped. Although much of the fear of victimization stems from being assaulted by strangers, when it comes to rape, in most cases the victim knows their assailant. According to the Rape and Incest National Network, an estimated 8 in 10 rapes are committed by someone known to the victim. Moreover, the costs of sexual assault are significant—an estimated $450 billion (Holler, 2019). Given the circumstances surrounding rape, including the harm it causes its victims and the way the justice system typically responds to these crimes, it is one of the least frequently reported crimes.

While rape is a crime that is tracked by the UCR data in the United States, rape is but one type of victimization of women. In fact, because violence against women and girls is such a prevalent theme around the world, the term **gender-based violence** is used. Gender-based violence is defined by the United Nations as "any act of violence that results in or is likely to result in physical, sexual, or psychological harm and suffering to women, including threats of such acts, coercion or arbitrary deprivations of liberty, whether occurring in public or private life."(United Nations Population Fund, n.d.) Examples of gender-based violence include rape, intimate partner violence, forced prostitution, female genital mutilation, infanticide of female children, and **human trafficking** (US Department of State, 2018).

In the United States, intimate partner violence is a growing problem, largely because of the way women are perceived in this country. The Harvey Weinstein incident, noted at the beginning of this chapter, is one such illustration of how actresses in Hollywood are seen and valued. So widespread was the problem that the #MeToo movement was created (Mahdavi, 2018). We will have more to say about the role of gender and crime in another chapter.

Property Crimes

Property crime includes larceny, burglary, motor vehicle theft, check forgery, shoplifting and vandalism. What distinguishes property crime from violent crime is that they do not usually involve the use or the threat of force. Property crimes are the types of crime that people are most likely to experience. You are more likely to have your wallet or a personal item stolen than you are to be murdered or raped. Because these crimes happen so frequently and because there is a lower chance that the crime will be solved, less information is known about offenders. As we noted earlier, property crimes are frequently crimes of opportunity (for example, keys left in the ignition of a car or a front door left unlocked).

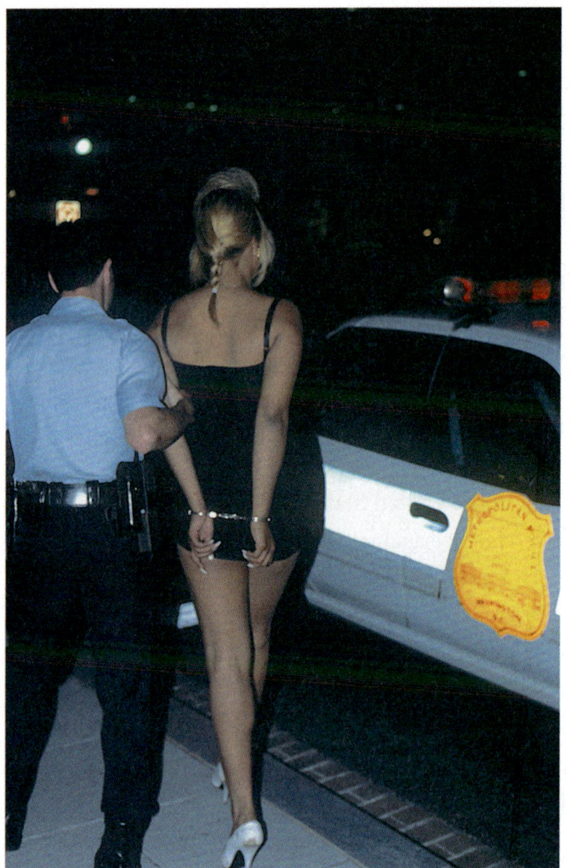

Victimless? Many activists contend that prostitution is not a victimless crime.

Public Order Crime

Another category of non-violent crime includes those that evoke public concern about morality. Public order crimes sometimes involve the use of violence, but what distinguishes them from other types of crime is the threat of the moral disintegration of society. In terms of sheer numbers, public order offenders are the largest category of criminals, with the incidence of such crimes exceeding those actually reported to the police. Public order offenses include prostitution, gambling, use of illegal substances, drunkenness, vagrancy, disorderly conduct, and traffic violations. These are sometimes called **victimless crimes** because some people believe they do not result in specific harms to anyone but the offenders. However, many activists and researchers argue that prostitution is in fact not a victimless crime. Still, society considers these acts to be crimes because they violate customs and society's sense of morality. We will explore this issue in greater depth in Chapter 8.

Juvenile Crime

Since the first juvenile court was created in Illinois in 1899, there has been an emphasis on treating juvenile offenders differently from their adult counterparts. The juvenile justice system recognizes that youth are still cognitively developing and can learn valuable lessons from a more rehabilitative approach to punishment. Thus, while juvenile crime can involve both violent and property crimes, the system is distinct from its adult counterpart and its goals are generally to provide individualized justice and rehabilitate young offenders instead of punishing them.

In a recent report by the UCRs, the overall number of arrests of juveniles has decreased by 60 percent since 2009. In fact, as Table 2.8 shows, the arrests of juveniles in 2018 decreased in every category from 2009. This is true of property crimes, violent crimes, and even status offenses showed significant declines.

One of the reasons offered by experts for the decline is that efforts are being made to divert youth who are experiencing trouble prior to their being processed through the system. In addition, there has been a greater recognition of the cost savings of diversion than of formally processing offenders. While there may be conflicting explanations for the decline in juvenile crime and arrests, disparities in the system exist. For example, Black and Hispanic youth are much more likely to be processed through the system

Table 2.8 Uniform Crime Reports Juvenile Arrests, 2018

Most Serious Offense	Number of Juvenile Arrests	Percent Change		
		2009–2018	2014–2018	2017–2018
All offenses	728,280	–60%	–29%	–10%
Murder and non-negligent manslaughter	920	–22%	21%	0%
Rape	NA	NA	NA	NA
Robbery	17,290	–45%	–11%	–11%
Aggravated assault	27,940	–44%	–8%	–1%
Burglary	22,250	–70%	–45%	–28%
Larceny-theft	92,630	–71%	–48%	–22%
Motor vehicle theft	14,780	–26%	16%	–9%
Arson	1,850	–65%	–41%	–18%
Simple assault	125,030	–43%	–11%	2%
Forgery and counterfeiting	1,040	–51%	–12%	–15%
Fraud	4,710	–23%	10%	–1%
Embezzlement	580	–4%	27%	–9%
Stolen property (buying, receiving, possessing)	9,320	–50%	–10%	–11%
Vandalism	30,600	–66%	–32%	–17%
Weapons (carrying, possessing, etc.)	17,170	–49%	–17%	–6%
Prostitution and commercialized vice	260	–81%	–65%	–6%
Sex offenses (except rape & prostitution)	NA	NA	NA	NA
Drug abuse violations	90,670	–47%	–20%	–4%
Gambling	180	–90%	–69%	–35%
Offenses against the family and children	3,340	–25%	–1%	–11%
Driving under the influence	5,450	–60%	–22%	–10%
Liquor laws	26,350	–76%	-49%	–21%
Drunkenness	3,270	–76%	–49%	–24%
Disorderly conduct	57,760	-66%	-28%	-8%
Vagrancy	680	–75%	–28%	–7%
All other offenses (except traffic)	140,500	–57%	–25%	–6%
Curfew and loitering	22,030	–80%	–59%	–27%
Violent Crime Index	NA	NA	NA	NA
Property Crime Index	131,500	–69%	–44%	–22%
Violent crimes*	46,140	–44%	–9%	–5%

(Source: US Department of Justice, Office of Juvenile Justice and Delinquency Prevention, 2018)

compared to White offenders (McNamara and Burns, 2020; Smith, 2015). Also troubling is the number of youthful offenders who transferred to adult courts and prisons increased in the early 1990s, when many states passed laws, making it easier for youth to be tried as adults. Finally, the number of female youth arrested has increased significantly, resulting in some experts asserting that females have become more violent than in the past. An alternative explanation for this trend is that school districts have passed zero tolerance policies that result in the arrest of females for behaviors that might otherwise be handled informally (Smith 2015).

Occupational (White Collar) and Corporate Crime

In the 1940s, Edwin Sutherland (1949) coined the term **white-collar crime** to describe the behavior of people who commit crimes as part of their normal business activity. An interesting aspect of occupational criminals is that such crimes are not seen as threatening to society compared to other types of crimes. White-collar crimes rarely come to the criminal courts, and even when they do, offenders are rarely judged as severely as other types of criminals. The likely reason for this is that the public does not perceive lawyers, accountants, or stockbrokers as "hardened" criminals. In fact, offenders rarely see themselves in this light either. Sutherland's theory of differential association suggests that occupational crime offenders do not intentionally go into a career with criminal activity in mind. Rather, they likely enter professions where their colleagues view such conduct as "business" or standard industry conduct rather than actual criminal behavior (Sutherland, 1949).

Corporate crime is committed by corporations or people working on behalf of a corporation, usually for some type of financial benefit for the organization. It can include a wide range of activities including environmental pollution, price-fixing, defrauding employee pension plans or illegal labor practices. The difficulty in prosecuting corporate crimes is that often the individual who is punished is a low-level employee who may or may not have gained as much in the process as those higher up in the corporate hierarchy. But who is responsible when a corporation commits a criminal act? Corporations cannot be sent to prison, and it is often the case that high-level executives escape any meaningful level of accountability. There are a host of examples in the media of such crimes, where no one is charged or the people who gained the most are not held accountable. Even when corporations are identified and fined millions of dollars for their actions, the fine usually pales in comparison to the amount of money the criminal acts garnered. Thus, corporations can see the fine as nothing more than a cost of doing business.

Cybercrime

One of the fastest growing crimes is **cybercrime,** a criminal behavior that includes fraud, theft, computer hacking, bullying, terrorism and other activities. The increasing numbers of e-services like online shopping, online banking, and social apps have given rise to the number of internet users who are easily targeted by cybercriminals. Because most people are limited in their understanding of protecting information online, they are easily exploited by cybercriminals (Singh and Kumar, 2018).

As with all types of crimes, there are many reasons why cybercriminals engage in this form of criminal activity. Common motives of offenders include:

- **Entertainment.** Some cybercriminals perform their activities of cyberattack to test their hacking abilities while seeking status among their criminal peers, especially for acts that other cybercriminals have failed to accomplish.
- **Hacktivism.** These cyberattackers are motivated by political, religious, and social objectives—either to promote their own particular agendas and/or to discourage others from doing the same things. A recent hacktivist behavior is to expose high profile individuals who are having secret affairs.
- **Financial gain.** Most of the cyberattackers perform cyberattacks to become rich. The target of cyberattackers may be the banking system, big companies, organizations, rich individuals, or wealthy countries.
- **Spying**. These types of cybercriminals, working on their own or as contracted by others, steal confidential information of specific countries, organizations, or individuals.
- **Revenge**. These types of cybercriminals conduct cyberattacks against a company as a form of revenge against it for various reasons, including disgruntled employees (Singh and Kumar, 2018).

Cybersecurity deals with the security of the cyberspace from cybercriminals.

The three basic fundamental principles of cybersecurity are confidentiality, integrity, and availability, known as the CIA triad. Cyberattacks on the information and data on the Internet can affect the confidentiality of information, the integrity of the network or security of the system to protect it, and availability of mechanisms to protect the network (Singh and Kumar, 2018).

WHAT ROLES DOES SOCIOLOGICAL THEORY PLAY IN UNDERSTANDING CRIME?

The key sociological theories and concepts we examined in Chapter 1 can help us to better understand and explain crime.

Anomie and Strain Theory

One theoretical explanation for crime comes from Durkheim's work on **anomie**. Anomie occurs when the norms that regulate people's conventional behavior no longer apply or are ineffective. For example, after a natural disaster such as a hurricane or earthquake, people often feel great fear, anxiety, and concerns about how they are supposed to act. After Hurricane Katrina destroyed the city of New Orleans in September of 2005, thousands were left without water, food, housing, or basic supplies. Frustrated by the slow response of emergency services and other officials, some people violated social norms by looting. [Some observers argued that the term "looting" was offensive, as people were simply trying to get access to basic needs like food and clean water.] Still, others took advantage of the situation and tried to profit from the devastation. In fact, because the situation was so desperate and local police were unable to control the problem, the National Guard had to be called in to patrol the streets and restore order (Wombel, 2009).

Anomie has been used to explain crime in other ways, such as **strain theory.** Strain theory was originally developed by Robert Merton to describe the tendency for some people to commit crimes due to an inability to achieve the American Dream (Merton, 1938). Merton argues that American culture promotes a certain idea of what success should look like; creates identity markers for people on the basis of what they own; and prescribes the means by which a person achieves that success. Hard work, sacrifice, perseverance, getting an education, saving and investing money, owning a home and a car, and taking vacations are all part of the American Dream. However, some people lack the opportunities to achieve that dream. They may never have the opportunity to obtain a well-paying job, graduate from a prestigious college, or own a home.

Merton says that the reason some people commit crime is because, while they believe in the American Dream, the conventional means to obtain that dream is blocked for them in some way. This blockage is the strain part of the theory. In response, people cope with this anomic condition through various adaptations. Merton determined that there are five types of adaptation to this situation: **conformity, innovation, ritualism, retreatism,** and **rebellionism** (Figure 2.2). Conformists are those who have the desire but not the opportunity to succeed. They will continue nevertheless conform to society's expectations and rules in hopes of eventual success. Others, however, may be innovative in that they accept the goals but reject the means. This group is more likely to

	Cultural Goals	Legitimate Means
Conformity	+	+
Innovation	+	–
Ritualism	–	+
Retreatism	–	–
Rebellionism	+/–	+/–

Figure 2.2 Strain Theory Modes of Adaptation

engage in criminal behavior. Think of a drug dealer as an example—when they achieve enormous wealth through crime, what types of things do they buy?

Ritualists respond to strain/anomie by focusing on the means of achieving the goal rather than the goal itself. Think of the last time you interacted with an employee who did not care about you or your problem, but only the rules that governed their job. They can cite company policy from memory, and their actions are always within the boundaries of that policy. Still other people respond to strain by retreating from society, rejecting both the conventional goals and the means to obtain them. Addicts, the homeless, and others who withdraw from mainstream society identify neither with societal goals nor the methods to achieve them. Instead, they focus on remaining on the fringes of society. Finally, there are rebellionists. These people selectively accept or reject the goals and means of success in society based on to the larger objective of overthrowing or replacing the existing system with something different. Examples include terrorists, who may work in jobs in society as they plan their next activity.

Conflict Theory and Crime

In the same way that strain theory extended Durkheim's ideas to explain criminal behavior, Marxist theory has been used to explain crime as well. Recall that Marx's ideas center around the exploitation of those who do not have access to economic, social, and political power. Those who do have it tend to use that power to further their own interests. One way to do that is to influence the process by which laws are created so that the elite's interests are protected. This means the type of people who threaten the elite's way of life are likely to engage in behaviors that are likely to be identified as criminal.

An example of applying Marx's theory to crime can be found in the work of Richard Quinney, whose **social reality of crime** offers important insight into how some people are more likely to end up as criminals. Quinney argues that not only do the powerful control the criminal justice system, but they are also able to influence what types of actions the general public considers appropriate or inappropriate. By controlling the media, the wealthy and powerful are able to convince the public that some acts should be considered criminal while others, which actually may be more harmful to society in the long-run, are not (Quinney, 1970).

For example, as a result of the fear of crack cocaine, offenders who were convicted for dealing in crack received longer sentences, on average, then traffickers in powder cocaine, who dealt in much larger quantities, and who represented an arguably larger threat to society (Alexander, 2012). Quinney might contend that such a disparity could be based not on the harm or costs of each activity, but that the threat of crack adversely affected those in power more dramatically, thereby justifying the promotion of crack as more dangerous than powder cocaine.

Quinney might also argue that some products are actually quite harmful but have not been deemed criminal because the sale and use of those products reflect the interests of the wealthy and powerful. For example, the popularity of caffeinated drinks such as Red Bull, Monster, and other brands, and even diet sodas have been heavily marketed to younger audiences, despite considerable research that shows the ingredients in these drinks has a host of negative consequences—including links to cancer and other illnesses—yet the companies that make and sell these products continue to market them as if they are safe and the companies are not seen as engaging in any criminal or inappropriate conduct.

Similarly, **feminist theory** argues that the unequal status of women in society is reflected in the justice system. A feminist theory of crime also criticizes the tendency of existing theories to assume that the motives behind criminality for women are the same as that for men. In other words, virtually all criminological theories use samples of only males and are based on assessments of the motives about why men commit crimes. Feminists argue that such logic is flawed; there may be many reasons why women commit crimes that are different from men, but none of the traditional criminological theories really offer insight into this fact (Simpson, 1989). For example, as it relates to homicide, the research generally shows that females who commit murder have different reasons for doing so than men. While men commit the vast majority of homicides, their motives and even their methods are often different from women.

As an illustration, a 2016 study in Sweden showed that men are more likely to use blunt instruments or firearms in committing homicide, while women are more likely to use sharp instruments. Similarly, men tend to commit homicide as a way to solve problems or achieve some sort of objective, while women tend to kill in response to some type of emotional connection to the victim, such as a history of physical or emotional abuse. This is not to say that all women only kill as a result of abuse, but the research does show that the reasons for committing such a dramatic act are different for men and women (Tragardh, Nilsson, Granth, and Sturup, 2016).

Symbolic Interactionism and Crime

From a symbolic interactionist perspective, such as Sutherland's **differential association theory** as well as **labeling theory**, there is much to be learned about how criminal behavior is a product of social interaction between the individual and the larger society.

Sutherland argues that people learn how to commit crimes in the same way they learn about most things in life: they are taught by people they respect who believe that criminal activity is a legitimate way to achieve societal success. A summary of Sutherland's theory suggests:

1. Criminal behavior is learned through the process of interacting with others.
2. When criminal behavior is learned, the learning includes not only the techniques of committing the crime, but also a set of motives, drives, rationalizations, and attitudes that justifies the action.

3. A person becomes delinquent because they associate with others who feel that criminal behavior is an acceptable course of action.
4. Differential associations may vary in frequency, duration, priority, and intensity.

A critical element of this theory argues that people become criminal when they are exposed to people who think criminal behavior is more acceptable than conformity. Also important to the theory is the nature of the relationship with those individuals: the more time the potential criminal spends with someone who thinks crime is acceptable, and the greater the intensity and importance the person places on that relationship, the more likely they are to learn from and emulate their actions. While not everyone who is exposed to people who think crime is acceptable necessarily becomes a criminal themselves, there is a great deal of research that supports social learning theory as a way to understand how people act (Sutherland, 1939).

A related perspective, labeling theory, argues that once a person commits a crime and gets caught, there is a process that reshapes their social identity and limits their opportunities to become full-fledged members of society again. Consequently, because of the way society shuns offenders, the person may be more likely to commit further criminal or deviant acts as a result of having a negative label or stigma attached to them (Becker, 1966).

The process of acquiring a label develops in five stages:

1. **The act (primary deviance):** In this stage the person has committed the act and been discovered. Most of the time a person's identity can tolerate a minor transgression without a change of social standing (Lemert, 1951).
2. **Status degradation ceremony:** However, depending on what the person has done, if he or she is discovered, society responds by calling attention to the act and making the offender take responsibility for it. As a result of this status degradation ceremony, the person's societal status is damaged and a negative label is affixed (Garfinkel, 1956).
3. **Label as master status:** A person so labeled by a status degradation ceremony takes on a new social status. While we all occupy many statuses in society, there is usually one that serves to primarily define us, which sociologists refer to as a master status. As a result of the act and the societal response, the person's new, negative label becomes their master status (Becker, 1966).
4. **Retrospective interpretation:** Because of the damage to the person's identity and reputation, the negative label causes others to withdraw from social interaction with the labeled person. It also results in people's recasting of that person's identity, or retrospective interpretation. That is, all of their past, present, and even future behavior will be understood in light of this new negative label (Schur, 1971).
5. **Internalization of the label:** The offender who has been negatively labeled begins to think about themselves in terms of how society has now defined them. That is, they internalize this negative label.

6. **Deviant subculture/career (secondary deviance):** Finally, in light of all of these factors, particularly society's exclusion of the negatively labeled person from full participation in society, the individual begins to interact with other similarly labeled individuals and embarks upon a criminal or deviant career (Becker, 1966).

To review, labeling theory is concerned with three inter-related ideas: the process by which laws are enacted and behaviors are condemned; the process by which a person acquires a label; and the negative consequences that the person experiences as a result of this new stigma. Because the creation of labels is a political process, labeling theory resembles conflict theories in that both recognize that people in power use their economic, social and political influence to create laws that further their interests. This means that some people are more likely than others to engage in behavior, and to be negatively labeled as a result, that is considered inappropriate, deviant, or illegal (Becker, 1966).

THE CRIMINAL JUSTICE SYSTEM AND ITS IMPACT ON CRIME

How does society address the problem of crime? The primary mechanism is the criminal justice system. This is a societal mechanism comprised of three related agencies: the police, the courts, and correctional institutions. This system provides for the administration of justice by apprehending criminals, while attempting to prevent crime, the prosecution of offenders, and the oversight of the punishment assigned to them as a result of their conviction. Each dimension of the system has its own set of challenges and a brief mention of some of them will be offered here.

The Police

The police represent perhaps the most visible representative of the criminal justice system and it is the agency that most people who come into contact with the system will experience. An important part of the role of the police is the identification and apprehension of criminals and to prevent crime from occurring. Traditionally this was accomplished by having police officers patrol geographic areas to act as a deterrent to those who might consider committing a crime as well as being available to discover crimes in progress. Research has shown that while patrol remains an important component

Encountering the criminal justice system Most people in the United States first encounter the criminal justice system through an interaction with the police.

of policing, other strategies, such as hot spots analysis, discussed in another section, can be more effective in addressing crime problems in certain areas.

In the past 20 years, an importing principle in policing has been what is known as the **broken windows theory**. This theory was first described in an article in *The Atlantic* by James Q. Wilson and George Kelling. The basic premise of the model is that disorder is a key element in understanding and preventing crime. Disorder, in the form of graffiti, trash, abandoned cars, furniture, poor lighting, and broken windows in abandoned buildings, creates a climate of fear that causes residents to avoid these areas (Wilson and Kelling, 1982).

Without a surveillance network of residents to report crimes when they occur, the area becomes ripe for all manner of criminal activity. The goal, then, is to prevent residents from becoming afraid of an area and the primary way to do that is to give the impression that the area is cared for, valued, and addressing minor forms of disorder (Wilson and Kelling, 1982).

The police play a critical role in preventing disorder by enforcing laws and countering the perception that an area is not safe. Despite its popularity with policymakers, police officials, and even the general public, the research on the effectiveness of the broken windows theory is mixed. For example, Braga, Welsh, and Schnell (2015) found that aggressive order maintenance efforts had no significant impact on reducing crime. However, other efforts can have modest reductions in crime, depending on the type of strategies used. Another problem related to the research on broken windows theory is that police departments often use strategies under the umbrella of broken windows theory, but these are not reflective of the actual definition of the theory, thereby creating problems in assessing the effectiveness of a given approach (Braga, Welsh, and Schnell, 2015). While there are other issues to discuss involving the police, such as the use of excessive force and racial profiling, these will be discussed in Chapter 6 on race and ethnic relations (Figure 2.3).

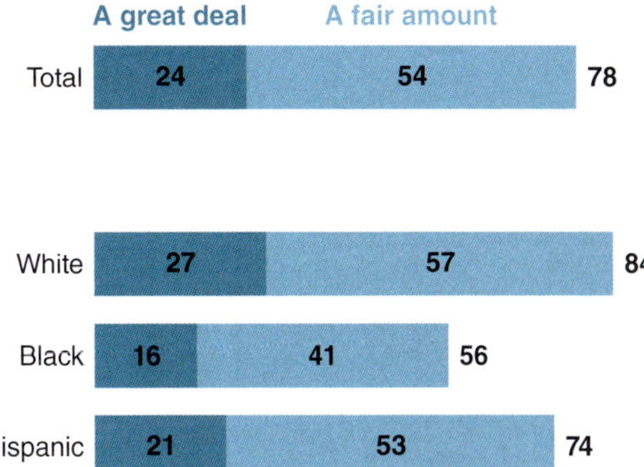

Figure 2.3 Public confidence in the police, April 2020
Note: Whites and Blacks include only those who are not Hispanic; Hispanics are of any race. Survey of US adults conducted April 20-26, 2020. Source: https://www.pewresearch.org/fact-tank/2020/06/05/a-month-before-george-floyds-death-black-and-white-americans-differed-sharply-in-confidence-in-the-police/ft_2020-06-05_viewsofpolice_01/

Courts

Another key element of the criminal justice process is the court system. While there are several different types of courts in the US that reflect the many local, state and federal laws, criminal courts are generally tasked with determining whether a suspect is guilty of committing a particular crime. After arrest, prosecutors generally bring formal charges against a suspect and the decision to move forward with a trial or plea bargaining the case occurs. A **plea bargain** is a negotiation between the prosecutor and the defense attorney that results in a guilty plea in exchange for a lighter sentence. This happens in more than 90 percent of all criminal cases and has become a primary method of processing cases (The Innocence Project, 2018).

If a case goes to trial, judges are responsible for sentencing offenders if they are found guilty. An important issue in the sentencing decision is the rationale or justification for punishing offenders. Generally there are four philosophies of punishment: deterrence, incapacitation, rehabilitation, and just desserts. Deterrence is generally the idea that the punishment is designed to send the message to others about the consequences of their actions—in other words, don't do what this person did or you will get the same punishment. Or deterrence can focus on the particular offender; trying to get that person to see that doing it again is a bad idea (Clear, Resig, Petrosino and Cole, 2018).

Incapacitation is a philosophy that suggests the person should be punished so that the rest of society is safer while they removed from society. In other words, society has incapacitated the offender's ability to harm society while they are in prison. Rehabilitation is a philosophy that argues people make mistakes and while they should be punished and held accountable for their actions, while incarcerated efforts should be made to correct their thinking and actions so that when released they will become productive members of society. Finally, just desserts suggests that the first three philosophies are future-oriented—they are based on what the offender might do in the future (Clear, Resig, Petrosino and Cole, 2018). But we can't really know what someone will do in the future; we can only assess what they have done in the past. This means the punishment should reflect the crime and the offender should be held accountable for his or her actions—not on what they might do in the future. These differing philosophies are guiding principles for issuing a sentence. For the past thirty years or so, we have held firm to a just desserts model of punishment. Our "get tough" on crime approach, where we have issued longer sentences, particularly for drug offenses, has led to significant increases in the number of offenders sentenced to prison (The Sentencing Project, 2018). It has also led to other strategies such as mandatory sentences for certain crimes and the famous "three strikes and you're out" approach, where a felon, upon his or her third conviction, would be sentenced to life in prison (The Sentencing Project, 2018; Clear, Resig, Petrosino and Cole, 2018).

Corrections

The third main component of the criminal justice system are the correctional agencies. This consists of jails and prisons, at the local, state, and federal levels. According to a 2018 report from the Bureau of Justice Statistics (BJS), nearly 2.2 million adults were held in America's prisons and jails at the end of 2016 and the prison population decreased in 2016 for the third straight year (Kann, 2019). While this may be an encouraging sign, it is important to recognize that while we may think of those in prison are there for drug crimes (and this is true primarily in federal prisons, but this makes up a small percentage of all inmates), the majority of incarcerated people are held in facilities controlled by state and local governments, according to the Prison Policy Initiative. According to the report, about 1.3 million people are held in state prisons, while more than 600,000 people behind bars are in one of the country's local jails. What is interesting about this is that jail is designed for people who have committed minor crimes, those with sentences of up to one year, as well as those who are awaiting trial and cannot afford bail (Kann, 2019).

As was mentioned earlier, the "get tough" approach to crime that sustained social policy has resulted in numerous offenders being sentenced to long and mandatory prison sentences. In fact, the United States is said to incarcerate more criminals than any other country in the world (The Sentencing Project, 2018). However, the data seems to suggest that many people who are incarcerated have not yet even been convicted of a crime. Even those who have been convicted of serious offenses, the problems of managing such a large inmate population has a host of unintended consequences. This includes an aging inmate population, where prisons and jails are ill-equipped to deal with disabled or chronically and terminally ill patients (McKillop and Boucher, 2018).

WHAT WORKS? EFFECTIVE SOLUTIONS TO CRIME

Students and the public tend to view social problems as unsolvable. Some of the more popular programs to address the problem have not been very effective. In fact, research has shown that the public clings to programs that have received a lot of media attention despite the evidence that they are not nearly as effective as initially portrayed. For example, in his 1981 study of the "Scared Straight" program, which brought juvenile offenders into contact with hardened criminals, who would graphically describe the youths' futures if they continued along their current behavioral pathway, James Finckenauer points to what he has described as the **panacea phenomenon** (Figure 2.4). This is the tendency for the public, policymakers, politicians, and others to seek a single cure-all solution to a problem such as crime. Because a cure-all solution is not likely to exist, virtually every program will be measured against such a benchmark and inevitably fail, thus leading to a cycle where an apparent solution leads to disappointing results and

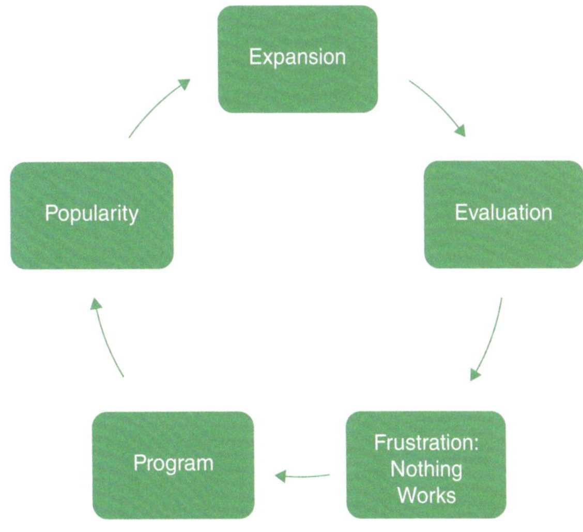

Figure 2.4 The panacea phenomenon

discouragement that "nothing works." This period lasts until the next solution emerges (Finckenauer, 1982).

In 1999, Finckenauer revisited the landmark findings of the Scared Straight through the lens of the panacea phenomenon. The goal was to examine the latest evidence of how Scared Straight programs are used in other countries. In characterizing the panacea phenomenon, Finckenauer used the concept of myths, or widely accepted beliefs that give meaning to events. Finckenauer concluded that panacea programs tend to remain popular because the public clings to the belief that people's behavior will change if the consequences are sufficiently severe, regardless of the data suggesting that such an approach lacks an empirical foundation (Gavin and Finckenauer, 1999).

Despite the panacea phenomenon, there are programs that have been shown to be effective. However, these programs may only target one dimension of the problem or a certain segment of the offender population. We also must be careful in how we determine success. Rarely does a program work all of the time with all offenders. Thus, it is important to set realistic benchmarks of what success looks like. Otherwise, the program will likely be seen as ineffective when in fact the opposite is occurring.

In assessing the effectiveness of a given program, it is important to set realistic criteria for what constitutes success. This can be reductions in certain types of crime, improvements in other areas, or some empirical-based assessment. The following programs have been evaluated and considered by scholars as effective in reducing certain types of challenges.

Big Brothers/Big Sisters Program

The Big Brothers Big Sisters of America (BBBS) Community-Based Mentoring (CBM) program is designed to help youth between the ages of 6 and 18, many of who come from single-parent households and neighborhoods where there is a high incidence of poverty, violence, and trauma. The program's philosophy is that if youth can develop strong, positive bonds to the community and to others, they will be less likely to engage in problematic behaviors. Also, with the help of encouraging adults, youth can develop positive self-images and make better choices in terms of their behavior. Volunteers work one-on-one with youth on a regular basis, attending sporting events, watching movies together, reading books, going on hikes, or engaging in other activities that encourages positive interaction (Tierney, Grossman, and Resch, 2000).

According to studies of outcome measures such as drug or alcohol use, anti-social behavior, or academic performance, participants in the BBS and CBM programs showed far more prosocial behavior than a control group of youths who did not receive mentoring. Tierney, Grossman, and Resch (2000) found that youths in the Big Brothers Big Sisters (BBBS) Community-Based Mentoring (CBM) program were 46 percent significantly less likely to initiate drug use and 27 percent less likely to initiate alcohol use, compared to control group participants. Youths in these programs were also 32 percent less likely to have hit another youth or adult in the previous 12 months. Mentored youth also felt more competent about doing their schoolwork, earned higher grades and were less likely to skip school than other youth. Finally, mentored youth also had better relationships with and trust of their parents, compared to a control group (Tierney, Grossman, and Resch, 2000).

Perry Preschool Project

The Perry Preschool Project, which originated in Michigan, is designed to target African American children ages three to four who are living in poverty and considered to be at high risk for school failure. The goal is to increase academic success, decrease teen pregnancy, reduce involvement in crime, and improve employment opportunities later in life. The underlying assumption is that family poverty and its associated hardships leads to poor academic performance, which in turn instills in children the belief that they are not intelligent and results in a dislike of school. Research has shown that children of poor families frequently do not perform at grade level and often end up in remedial classes. As a result, many youth drop out of school and are at greater risk to engage in delinquency and crime. Without a solid educational foundation, as adults, these children are often ineligible for well-paying jobs and are more likely to engage in crime (Schweinhart, Barnes, and Weikart, 1993).

During a school year, there is a daily 2½-hour classroom session and a weekly 1½-hour home visit for each child by a caseworker. The home visits are a way to involve the mother or primary caretaker, in the educational process and enable her to provide her child with support. Teachers also help mothers deal with any problems that arise during the home visits. Children are encouraged to engage in activities that involve making choices and solving problems that contribute to their intellectual, social, and physical development. These components of the program are heavily influenced by research in child, educational, and developmental psychology, which notes that children's innate curiosity and exploration should be incorporated into a formal learning environment (Schweinhart, Barnes, and Weikart, 1993).

To measure program effectiveness, researchers measured the academic performance of youth in the program along with rates of delinquency and crime and economic status at a later age. With regard to academic performance, the evaluation administered intellectual and language performance tests of Perry Preschool Project participants from preschool up to age 7, academic performance assessment at age 14 and a literacy test at age 19. The results showed that by age 17, participants, compared to a control group of students who did not participate in the program, had completed a significantly higher level of schooling than the no-program group (11.9 years versus 11.0). The group also had a significantly higher rate of regular high school graduation (66 percent versus 45 percent) and a nearly significant rate of regular high school graduation or the equivalent certification (71 percent versus 54 percent; Schweinhart, Barnes, and Weikart, 1993).

With regard to delinquency and crime, rates for the program group were significantly lower than for those in the no-program group. At the 27-year follow-up, the program group, compared with the no-program group, averaged a significantly lower number of lifetime (juvenile and adult) criminal arrests (2.3 arrests versus 4.6) and a significantly lower number of adult criminal arrests (1.8 arrests versus 4.0). There were significantly fewer program group members who were frequent offenders (arrested five or more times) by the time they were in the 27 to 32 years-old range, compared with the no-program group (7 percent versus 25 percent; Schweinhart, Barnes, and Weikart, 1993).

Economically, by the time participants reached age 27, they had significantly higher monthly earnings (mean of $1,219 versus $766, with 29 percent versus 7 percent earning $2,000 or more) compared to the control group. The program group's employment rate was noticeably higher and fewer participants received welfare compared to the control group in the previous ten years (Schweinhart, Barnes, and Weikart, 1993).

Hot Spots Policing

The **Hot Spots policing** strategy, a concentrated police effort to address the physical and social disorder in a community, was first implemented by the Lowell (Mass.) Police Department in 2005 (National Institute of Justice, 2011). The strategy is based on the broken windows theory of crime, which postulates that crime is likely to flourish in areas with high levels of physical and social disorder. The program used three primary approaches to reduce crime: an aggressive enforcement strategy designed to take high-risk individuals off the street; a crime prevention approach that creates a safer atmosphere by installing improved street lighting and cleaning up abandoned lots and buildings; and a social services approach, which provides assistance to residents in need, thereby improving the overall environment and feelings of safety for residents. It also includes mentoring programs for youth, mental health services for those who need them, and addressing the large number of homeless individuals in the area (Braga and Bond, 2008).

As a result of these efforts, outcome measures for the program, which included calls for service, observed disorder, and an overall improved physical landscape, indicated the program's success. For example, compared to a control group within the community, the total number of calls for service decreased by nearly 20 percent. Moreover, there was a 42 percent reduction in the number of calls relating to robberies and a 34 percent decrease in domestic violence calls to the police. There was also a decrease of about 35 percent in burglary calls for service in the program area. The types of calls also changed. Residents were less likely to call the police to address an issue related to disorder in the neighborhood. Not only were there substantial and statistically significant decreases in criminal activity in the program area, but there were also substantial reductions in loitering, public drinking, drug transactions, and homelessness, as well as statistically significant reductions seen in graffiti, visibility of trash in vacant lots, and abandoned vehicles (Braga and Bond, 2008).

POPULAR BUT LESS EFFECTIVE PROGRAMS

Some programs gain media attention, even though their actual impact is limited. This can happen for many reasons, such as policymakers attempting to capitalize on the popularity of a program without waiting for an empirical assessment, or the media searching for a sensational story. In both instances, the program's effectiveness can be inflated. Why? Sometimes the panacea phenomenon makes policymakers overestimate a program's ability to address problems relating to crime. This underscores the need for realistic and empirical assessments of the effectiveness of programs and their ability to impact crime.

D.A.R.E.

A school-based drug use prevention program called D.A.R.E., taught by police officers, was created in 1983 by Los Angeles police chief Darryl Gates in response to increases in drug arrests. The program quickly grew in scope and popularity. In fact, during the 1980s and 1990s, D.A.R.E. was implemented in nearly 75 percent of all schools in the United States. It received praise from policymakers, politicians, and anti-drug advocates and generated millions of dollars in funding and in revenue. However, from the outset, the empirical evaluations of D.A.R.E. not only showed that it had no effect on decreasing drug use, it had what was called a **boomerang effect**, meaning exposure to the effects of drugs actually caused some youth to experiment with drugs. The research on D.A.R.E. consistently showed that it had no statistically significant impact on drug use or attitude toward drug use compared with the control comparison group. While D.A.R.E. refused to accept the criticisms of its programs and even attempted to control the publication of studies that showed its limited effectiveness, the program eventually declined in popularity and funding (Cima, 2016).

Juvenile Boot Camps

Correctional boot camps (also called shock or intensive incarceration programs) are short-term residential programs that resemble military basic training and target convicted juvenile and sometimes adult offenders. The aim is to reduce recidivism by changing offenders' behaviors through positive reinforcement for positive acts and immediate punishment for negative acts. Most participants are young, first-time, nonviolent offenders. However, the eligibility criteria and selection process can vary substantially by program. Typically, boot camp participants are required to engage in military drills and ceremonies, including physical training. Correctional officers act as drill instructors, and punishment for misbehavior often involves pushups, extended drills, or other demanding physical activity.

There is no standard boot camp model, and individual programs can differ greatly. Some boot camps may also offer an after-care or reentry program designed to help program participants adjust to the community following their release. However, regardless of the model used, the research shows a limited level of effectiveness in changing the behavior of participants, particularly over time. A main reason for this is that there is no follow up to the boot camp intervention. Also contributing to the problem is the fact that participants often return to the environments that caused them to get into trouble in the first place. Thus, while there may be some evidence of short-term behavioral change while participating in the program, once offenders leave it, past behaviors and attitudes often return. Thus, the weight of the evidence suggests that although boot camps are a popular strategy with many policymakers and politicians, actual impacts of the programs to reduce crime and delinquency are not seen (Wilson, MacKenzie, and Mitchell, 2008).

Weed and Seed

Weed and Seed is a community-based approach that attempts to reduce and prevent crime, including violent crime, drug trafficking, and gang activity, while also attempting to revitalize the community by providing social services aimed at restoring the physical landscape and providing assistance to residents. The "weeding" portion of the program involves aggressive law enforcement activities designed to identify chronic and dangerous offenders, while the "seeding" portion of the program attempts to restore the elements of the community necessary for economic development and social cohesion among residents. A key role is played by the local US Attorney's Office to provide leadership in guiding multiagency efforts and mobilizing key stakeholders. Many sites develop joint task forces that help coordinate law enforcement agencies from all levels of government. Beginning in 1991 and consisting of hundreds of sites across the country, this program was funded until 2011 and had several advocates who continued to support the communitywide efforts that occurred under the umbrella of Weed and Seed (US Department of Justice, Executive Office of Weed and Seed, 2010).

Despite the popularity of Weed and Seed as an idea, and despite considerable funding from the federal government to implement these programs, the overall impact was quite limited in terms of its actual impact on reducing crime. Some research has found that despite aggressive law enforcement tactics and concentrated priorities in prosecuting offenders, the actual impact on crime and violence has not been systematically seen in comparison to a control group, nor have there been lasting reductions for drug offenses. While the seeding efforts to restore and revitalize the physical conditions of neighborhoods has occurred, it has not yielded the desired levels of economic development and resident cohesion (Roman, Cahill, Coggeshall, Lagerson, and Courtney, 2005).

SO WHAT CAN I DO?

You might be wondering at this point what you can do as an individual to impact crime. Like all social problems, the problem of crime is complex and not easily resolved. However, there are some things you can do to contribute to a solution. Reducing the opportunities for crime is perhaps the easiest and most immediate step you can take. It involves a greater level of awareness and mindfulness of the risks of being victimized. Simple measures such as not leaving your keys in the ignition and locking your doors and windows are important and meaningful steps to preventing crime. Most criminals are opportunistic, and if people can reduce those opportunities, the chances of victimization are greatly reduced.

This doesn't mean you have to become paranoid about your safety; it simply means taking a more intentional approach to reducing the risks of being victimized. Improving lighting around your home, cutting down shrubs and bushes so that burglars can't hide behind them while they break into your home, walking through parking lots with others, are all simple measures that can make a big difference. Now, will you know if they worked? This is a difficult question because one never knows how many crimes they would have prevented by their actions if they never occur. But given the high levels of fear people already possess, feeling as though you are doing something meaningful and tangible to reduce those risks could alleviate some of those fears. Your local police department probably has a crime prevention unit or a patrol officer who is assigned that responsibility. Contact them and get some tips on how to minimize your risks.

CONCLUSION

Crime is a complex problem that involves many variables. Research shows that people are generally afraid of being victimized and think that crime is getting worse. Those fears are real for some people, despite the fact that the data has shown that the crime rate has been decreasing for the past 30 years. We also must consider the public's role in the crime problem in this country, often through a lack of awareness of risks, as well as via involvement as offenders.

In explaining crime, there are a host of theories based on the three fundamental paradigms in sociology. Durkheim's notions of anomie, Marx's conflict theories, and the symbolic interactionist approach (including differential association theory as well as labeling theory) offer insight into the nature of social interaction and help explain crime. Finally, it is important to recognize that some programs that do in fact work to reduce crime and the involvement of offenders. And we must not fall victim to the panacea phenomenon, by desperately searching for a single solution to crime. Realistically, there is no single answer or solution to the crime problem; rather there are many reasons that people commit crimes, and a variety of programs are needed to address those motivations.

YOU MAKE THE CALL: SCHOOL SHOOTINGS

Imagine that you are a superintendent for a school district in your home town. As a result of the controversy surrounding recent school shootings, the local PTA has passed a resolution that supports the idea of arming teachers as a way of addressing the risks associated with an active shooter situation. Local politicians, many of whom are up for reelection and need the media attention, also support the strategy, which, coupled with the PTA stance and opinion polls that support the idea, puts enormous pressure on you to respond. Teachers are divided on the issue, so appealing to the local union does not seem to provide much help either. The pressure to do something is building and you worry that your job may be in jeopardy if you do not act in some meaningful way in the near future. So what do you do?

Questions to consider:

1. Do you implement a strategy that provides weapons and training for teachers? Is the plan mandatory or optional?
2. Do you come up with an alternative solution? One suggestion has been to elicit the help of former military veterans, who have had weapons training and some combat experience, who might be willing to volunteer to protect their local schools? What are the risks and benefits of such a strategy?
3. Is hiring additional school resource officers an option? Would additional officers really prevent such situations from occurring or result in less loss of life in the event one does happen? This approach can also be cost prohibitive and set a precedent for all other school districts, assuming there is money in the budget for such a plan.
4. Do you delay a decision by hiring a consultant to study the problem and make recommendations to the school board and to you about best practices? This is risky, since it means a delay of several months, and the research on the topic doesn't have many solutions to the problem.

SUMMARY

- Describe the extent of crime in the United States.
    - The Gallup poll data shows that people's perceptions of the crime problem contrast with the actual trends.
    - People think the crime problem is generally getting worse at a time when we have seen historic declines in overall crime.
- Discuss factors that contribute to the public's fear of crime.
    - While most people are afraid of stranger-on-stranger crimes, the vast majority of the time there is a relationship between the victim and the offender; sometimes an intimate one.
- Summarize what makes crime bad for society.
    - Part of what makes crime bad is the harm it causes to people as well as its costs to society.
    - Crime is problematic for society because of the psychological effects it has of increasing people's fears.
- Analyze the public's role in the crime problem in the United States.
    - Whether because of a lack of understanding of the risks of victimization,

a sense of carelessness, or even our own involvement in criminal activity, the public creates opportunities for crime to occur.

- Compare the different types of crime, including crimes of violence, property crime, juvenile crime, white-collar offenses, and cybercrime.
  - The two most prominent forms of crime are violent and property crimes.
  - Even within the category of homicide, there are different variations, including mass murder and serial killing.
  - Evidence shows significant declines in all of the major crime categories, including a dramatic decrease in juvenile crime in the last ten years.
- Explain the role of sociological theory in understanding crime.
  - Functionalism, conflict theory, and symbolic interactionism offer ways to understand the causes of crime.
  - Strain theory, Quinney's social realities of crime, along with differential association and labeling theory, provide valuable insight into why people choose criminal acts over conformity.
- Discuss the components of the criminal justice system and how it addresses crime in the United States.
  - The criminal justice system is made up of three interrelated agencies: the police, courts, and corrections.
  - Within each component, there are issues that impact our understanding of crime. These include the broken windows theory as it relates to policing, sentencing guidelines for courts, and philosophies of punishment for correctional agencies.
- Identify several programs that work to reduce crime in the United States.
  - Examples of effective programs include Big Brothers/Big Sisters.
  - Ineffective programs include D.A.R.E. and boot camps.

KEY TERMS

Anomie 51
Boomerang effect 63
Broken windows theory 57
Conformity 52
Cybercrime 50
Dark figure of crime 36
Differential association 54
Feminist theory 54
Gender-based violence 47
Human trafficking 47
Labeling theory 54
Hot Spots policing 62
Innovation 52
Internalization of label 55
Mass murder 46
Panacea phenomenon 59
Plea bargain 57
Primary deviance 55
Rebellionism 52
Retreatism 52
Retrospective interpretation 55
Ritualism 52
Secondary deviance 56
Social reality of crime 53
Status degradation ceremony 55
Strain theory 52
Uniform Crime Reports 36
Victimless crimes 48
White collar crime 50

Discussion Questions

1. Do you think that if people actually knew the extent of crime in their communities it would change their fear levels?
2. If a person is given a deviant or criminal label by society, can it ever be removed? What has to occur in order for the label to be removed? Or is it the case that the best the person can hope for is to minimize the impact of the label?
3. Why do you think D.A.R.E. was continually funded by the federal government despite evidence from the beginning of the program that it had little or no effect on drug use among youth?
4. How does a program like Perry Preschool Program change people's behavior later in life so that they do not get involved in crime?
5. Do you think people's unwillingness to take precautionary steps to avoid victimization is a result of a lack of awareness or some other factor? In other words, do people leave their keys in the ignition of their vehicles or leave the front doors of their homes unlocked because they are unaware of the risks of being victimized, or is there some other reason?

Learn more with this chapter's digital tools, including Data and Media Literacy Exercises, flashcards, and chapter self-assessments at **www.oup.com/he/mcnamara**.

3

Are More People Getting High? Drug and Alcohol Abuse

LEARNING OBJECTIVES

- Explain why alcohol and drug abuse is a social problem.
- Describe the extent of the tobacco use and abuse problem in the United States.
- Describe the extent of the alcohol use and abuse problem in the United States.
- Describe the extent of the drug use and abuse problem in the United States.
- Analyze sociological theories as they apply to alcohol and drug abuse.
- Summarize what works in terms of effective solutions to address alcoholism and drug abuse in the United States.

Chapter Outline

Underage drinkers The legal drinking age in the United States is 21, but many young people abuse alcohol.

In 2018, President Donald J. Trump declared the opioid crisis to be a public health hazard requiring the intervention of the federal government. In creating a committee to examine and address the problem, along with legislation that seeks solutions to the crisis, Trump's initiatives are the most recent of a long line of public health crises in the United States that relate to drug abuse.

The abuse of drugs in the United States is one of the most pervasive problems plaguing our society. This is true despite considerable efforts to increase awareness of the dangers of drug and alcohol abuse as well as the development of treatment programs to help people who have become addicted.

In fact, our historical fascination and fear of drug use in the United States could be seen as one of its defining features—we have routinely grappled with some type of drug that was seen as a public health hazard. The recent opioid crisis and its derivatives is part of a long-standing trend in American culture, where a drug has gained considerable public attention and resources to address its use.

As you read this chapter, consider the context in which certain drug and alcohol crises have been framed. Recall our discussions in Chapter 1 about claims making and the construction of social problems. As with crime, part of the challenge of understanding drug and alcohol abuse is that public perception of the problem does not always match what actual data reveals about the extent of the problem. And as we shall see in our discussion of alcohol abuse, sometimes the actual data itself offers conflicting conclusions. Therefore, it is important to understand the problem in its proper context.

Some drugs that are abused (such as tobacco and alcohol) are legal, and information about their effects are well-known. Other abused drugs, like heroin, are illegal. Heroin is just one example of why it is important to understand the larger context. Although it is an illegal drug, its abuse has exploded in recent years largely because of the problem of addiction to legal opioid prescription medicines. People who have become addicted to those legal drugs but can no longer obtain them are forced to seek illegal means to address their needs. The question that you as a student of social problems should ask is *why*: Why is it that people became addicted to prescription opioids in the first place? Why is it that they have to turn to illegal drugs, like heroin?

Another question you should consider as you read this chapter is how some drugs become illegal in the first place. Why is it that alcohol remains legal, despite all the negative consequences associated with its abuse, while the debate over the legalization of marijuana continues on a state-by-state basis?

Finally, you should consider how society has responded to the abuse of drugs and alcohol. The prevalent model is punitive; that is, offenders are punished for abusing, selling, or manufacturing drugs or alcohol. In what circumstances has a punitive approach been effective? In what ways has this approach failed to address the problem? And, finally, what might alternative strategies to solving drug and alcohol abuse (and their related problems) look like?

SOCIOLOGICAL STUDY TIME

- A police officer in Ohio pulled over a swerving Ford Explorer after it screeched to a stop near a school bus. The officer approached the Explorer and found two adults in the front and a four-year-old boy in the back. He immediately noticed the driver's erratic behavior and slurred speech. The passenger, who was the mother of the boy in the back seat, was unconscious and unresponsive. The officer realized the adults were suffering from a heroin overdose. Paramedics revived the two adults with the drug Narcan, which halts the effects of heroin, and took them first to the hospital and then to jail. The young boy was placed in county children's services (Project Know, 2018).
- College freshman Erica Buschick returned from a semester break and started to drink with friends. Buschick started drinking about 10 p.m. and consumed at least one bottle of champagne, while her roommate did the same. Then they filled a water bottle with vodka and drank that as well. The next morning Buschick's roommate found her unconscious in their dorm room, but she never recovered. This student's death has resulted in many colleges around the

country reexamining their policies on alcohol use on campus (Filby, 2017).

- In a decision that was heralded as precedent-setting by New York City's mayor, the New York City police department announced in 2018 that it would no longer arrest offenders for smoking marijuana in public. Instead, offenders would be issued a summons (unless other circumstances justified an arrest, such as outstanding warrants or the commission of other crimes). Critics of the long standing policy of arrest pointed out that African Americans are far more likely to be arrested for marijuana possession despite the fact that most groups use the drug at about the same rate. Such a decision is an effort to address this disparity as well as reflecting community sentiments about marijuana (Thompson, 2018).

WHY ALCOHOL AND DRUG ABUSE ARE SOCIAL PROBLEMS

American culture is defined by convenience. Americans generally want to meet their needs as easily as possible, even if that means paying a bit more for products and services. Entire industries serve this desire for convenience, with some paradoxical results: for example, weight loss programs that promise dramatic results in very little time, and food delivery services that bring anything from a pizza to a week's worth of groceries to your front door. Americans seem to be increasingly impatient when it comes to our appetites: we want to satisfy our needs when we have them—and we are not interested in delaying our satisfaction.

This cultural craving for immediate gratification has larger implications. For example, when we encounter a problem, such as a health issue like obesity, we don't want to address the root causes of the problem nor do we want to make the long-term changes that will result in a solution. Instead, we want to fix the problem quickly, easily, and painlessly. After all, we have a life to live and things to do.

This tendency creates an optimal climate for drug and alcohol abuse. Americans have been described as a pill-popping culture, where medications, both legal and illegal, are used to quickly address problems and issues that might more effectively involve a more concerted effort. Instead, the medical and pharmaceutical industries have responded by offering products so that people don't have to make those difficult choices. Instead of lifestyle changes, including better nutrition and regular exercise, there are medications to address excess body weight, cholesterol problems, or other obesity-related ailments. This is not to say that all medications are bad; in many cases they save lives. But in general, the problem such an approach creates is one of dependence—we rely on medications to fix many of the problems we encounter, even the ones we can resolve in other ways.

This need for immediate gratification also contributes to the problem of drug and alcohol use for recreational purposes. Tobacco, alcohol, and other substances create a sense of euphoria or positive feelings that we enjoy, but the replication of these feelings typically requires increased amounts of the drug to reach the same effect, leading to dependency and addiction. In this chapter, we will explore the use and abuse of alcohol and drugs as a social problem, since this reliance on drugs can not only creates physiological dependency but impacts people's social standing and society as a whole.

TOBACCO USE AND ABUSE

Some students might not immediately think of tobacco as a drug, especially since it has been legal in the United States for many years. However, tobacco use and abuse is a good illustration of the need to provide a context of understanding of addiction and abuse of substances as social problems. In examining the trends related to tobacco use, there is good news and bad news. The good news is that the rates of use by adults in the United States, particularly cigarettes, have declined in the last ten years, although this trend seems to have leveled out since 2015. This cannot be said of everyone around the world, however.

Unfortunately, about a billion people aged 15 and over smoke, with the vast majority (about 80 percent) living in what are known as low and middle income countries. According to Action on Smoking and Health, the evidence indicates that the number of smokers in these countries has been increasing, especially for adolescents—up to four times higher than the number of smokers in England. And by 2030, tens of millions of people in the developing world are predicted to die from tobacco consumption (Action on Smoking and Health Fact Sheet, 2019).

The bad news is that the US Surgeon General has asserted that tobacco-related deaths and illnesses in the United States are overwhelmingly caused by cigarettes. In fact, cigarettes are the most commonly used tobacco product among US adults, and about 480,000 US deaths per year are caused by cigarette smoking and **secondhand smoke exposure** (National Institute on Drug Abuse, 2018).

The use of cigarettes continues even though most people understand the risks associated with smoking as well as a strong anti-smoking societal response. Many states have laws that attempt to protect non-smokers from exposure to tobacco smoke in the form of bans on smoking in public places. Yet even with such a widespread effort, more than 1 in 7 US adults still smoke cigarettes, and one-quarter of the population in the United States (about 58 million people, including 15 million children aged 3 to 11 years old) is exposed to secondhand smoke. The problem does not only affect adults, however. About 3.9 million middle and high school students use at least one tobacco product, such as **e-cigarettes** (vaping) and conventional cigarettes (Center for Disease Control, 2018).

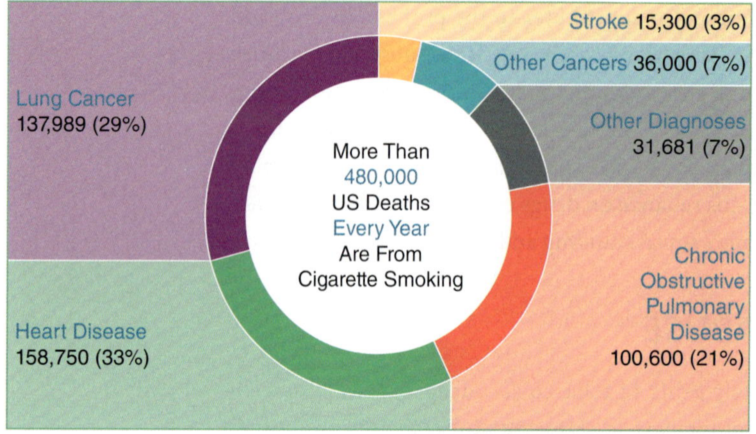

Figure 3.1 Annual deaths from smoking, United States. Note: Average annual number of deaths for adults aged 35 or older, 2005–2009. Source: Centers for Disease Control. (2018). Fast Facts and Fact Sheets." Available at: https://www.cdc.gov/tobacco/data_statistics/fact_sheets/index.htm?s_cid=osh-stu-home-spotlight-001

What are the consequences of the decision to smoke? Cigarette smokers miss more work, visit a doctor more often, are hospitalized more often, and die 10 to 12 years earlier than nonsmokers. In addition, the United States spends nearly $170 billion on medical care to treat diseases related to cigarette smoking in adults every year (see Figure 3.1). For those who are exposed to secondhand smoke, the problems are also considerable. Secondhand smoke exposure contributes to illnesses such as heart disease, stroke, and lung cancer in nonsmoking adults. In children, secondhand smoke can cause sudden infant death syndrome, acute respiratory infections, ear infections, and more frequent and severe asthma attacks (Center for Disease Control, 2018).

Who smokes? The answer varies according to race and ethnicity (Table 3.1).

Cigarette use was also higher among LGBTQ populations (21 percent) than among heterosexual adults (15.3 percent). It was also higher among those adults suffering from serious psychological distress (35.8 percent) than those without a serious psychological disorder (Centers for Disease Control, 2018).

Table 3.1 Percentage of Persons Aged 18 or Older Who Reported Cigarette Use "Every Day" or "Some Days" at Time of Survey

By Race/Ethnicity	Percentage
White, non-Hispanic	15.5%
Black, non-Hispanic	14.9%
Asian, non-Hispanic	7.2%
American Indian/Alaska Native, non-Hispanic	20.9%
Hispanic	8.8%
Other, non-Hispanic	19.7%

Source: https://www.cdc.gov/tobacco/campaign/tips/resources/data/cigarette-smoking-in-united-states.html#by_race

Lawsuits and the Tobacco Industry

The decline in tobacco use in many populations did not simply come about as a result of people's intuitive understanding of the dangers of smoking. Rather, information about the negative effects of using tobacco came as a result of lawsuits against the tobacco industry. That is, the legal system has often been used as a forum to address the challenges presented by various social problems. As it relates to tobacco use, in court proceedings, evidence was presented that showed how tobacco companies misrepresented the harmful effects of tobacco, used questionable marketing campaigns to target youth, and withheld evidence of the negative effects of using tobacco. However, this legal process took decades of litigation. In fact, initially, lawsuits against the tobacco industry typically resulted in rulings against plaintiffs.

For instance, when initial research linking cigarette use to cancer was published in the 1950s, plaintiffs that sued tobacco companies typically argued that companies failed to act with reasonable care in manufacturing cigarettes or engaged in fraudulent advertising. In response, tobacco companies argued that tobacco use was not harmful to users and that the cancer that occurred developed from sources other than cigarettes. Tobacco companies also argued that smokers assumed the risk of the possibility of getting cancer when they decided to start smoking in the first place. In all of these early cases, the tobacco companies refused to settle out of court and won their cases (Minchon, 2017). By the 1990s, as information about the addictive nature of tobacco became known, and that tobacco companies were aware of this finding, plaintiffs bringing lawsuits began to win cases.

Thus, the trend has been to hold tobacco companies accountable for their failure to adequately inform the public of the harmful effects of using tobacco products. What has also occurred has been a rebranding of tobacco products by tobacco companies as well as the marketing of its products in other countries. Examples of new products include e-cigarettes, which are heavily marketed to youth and young adults.

E-cigarettes/Vaping

According to the Office on Smoking and Health, a division of the Centers for Disease Control, e-cigarettes (also known as e-hookahs, mods, vapes, and vape pens), are sometimes made to look like regular cigarettes, pipes or cigars, while others resemble USB sticks or pens. Using an e-cigarette, sometimes called **vaping**, involves inhaling the aerosol that is created by a nicotine-based liquid in a container within the device. Bystanders can also breathe in the aerosol when the user exhales it into the air.

E-cigarettes Electronic devices for vaping deliver the addictive hit of nicotine without the stigma associated with cigarette smoking.

The aerosol contains not only nicotine, but also cancer-causing compounds and heavy metals such as nickel, tin, and lead. While researchers are still learning more about the long-term impact of e-cigarettes, the effects of nicotine are well-known. The research concludes that using e-cigarettes is detrimental to health, despite the fact that they appear to be (and are marketed as) less harmful than smoke from burned tobacco products (Center for Disease Control, 2018).

Interestingly, there is some evidence that vaping is also used with marijuana. While there are only a few studies about this trend, one national study found that about 6 percent of teens who had ever vaped had used marijuana that way, while other studies focusing on specific states estimate it as high as 18–20 percent (Miech, Megan, O'Malley, and Johnston, 2017).

While some people think using e-cigarettes is a way to quit smoking regular cigarettes, according to the US Preventive Services Task Force and the FDA, e-cigarettes are not considered an approved means to do so. In fact, some of the research suggests that most adults using e-cigarettes end up using both, known as **dual use**. According to the CDC, among adult e-cigarette users overall, 58.8 percent were also current regular cigarette smokers, 29.8 percent were former regular cigarette smokers, and 11.4 percent had never been regular cigarette smokers (Centers for Disease Control, 2018).

Whatever negative effects e-cigarettes may have on users, they are now the most commonly used tobacco product among youth. In 2016, more than 2 million US middle and high school students used e-cigarettes in the past 30 days, including 4.3 percent of middle school students and 11.3 percent of high school students, significantly higher than the 3.2 percent of US adults who were current e-cigarette users (Center for Disease Control, 2018).

In 2018, in an unprecedented decision, the FDA warned e-cigarette manufacturers to take meaningful steps to reduce teenage addiction to nicotine after retailers and online vendors were discovered to be illegally selling e-cigarettes to minors. The FDA also learned that there has been an increased use of nicotine by teens, primarily through the use of e-cigarettes. Citing the trends as a public health risk and approaching "epidemic" proportions, the FDA warned manufacturers they are willing to take aggressive action such as pulling flavored liquid tobacco off the market or requiring manufacturers to limit the amount of nicotine to make it less addictive, even if that means fewer products are available as a result (Ebbs, 2018). In 2020, they followed through on their concerns and banned companies from the manufacture and sale of flavored e-cigarettes to minors (US Food and Drug Administration, 2020). While the debate continues about the value of e-cigarettes as a strategy for adults to quit smoking conventional cigarettes, the health risks are still considerable and the threat to young people using them is a significant one (Ebbs, 2018).

Smokeless Tobacco

Smokeless tobacco Snuff, or snuf, is smokeless tobacco in the form of a pouch that a user places between the gum and the cheek.

Recently there has been an increase in the popularity of the various types of smokeless tobacco. Unlike the type that is burned, smokeless tobacco can be sucked or chewed. It is frequently flavored with cinnamon, berry, vanilla or apple, which makes the product appealing to youth. However, smokeless tobacco (like cigarettes) contains nicotine, and can be addictive. Smokeless tobacco is available in three forms: Chewing tobacco, which can be in loose leaf form, plugs or compressed packets wrapped in a tobacco leaf, or flavored twists, which are tobacco leaves intertwined like a rope; snuf/snuff, which is finely ground tobacco that can be inhaled into the nose or mouth (snuff) or packaged in pouches and placed between a user's cheek and gum (snuff); and dissolvables, which come in sticks, strips, orbs or even lozenges that slowly dissolve in the user's mouth. They are popular with youth because they look like candy and can easily be concealed (US Department of Health and Human Services, 2014).

What are the dangers of smokeless tobacco products? According to the Centers for Disease Control (CDC), many smokeless tobacco products contain cancer-causing chemicals including a radioactive element, Polonium-210, used in tobacco fertilizer as well as harmful metals including arsenic, cadmium, chromium, cobalt, lead, nickel, and mercury. The CDC warns that smokeless tobaccos causes cancer of the mouth, esophagus, and pancreas, along with gum disease, tooth decay and tooth loss. Other risks include heart disease, stroke, and nicotine poisoning in children (Centers for Disease Control, 2018).

ALCOHOL USE AND ABUSE

Like tobacco use, alcohol is a legal drug, if not highly regulated and both have been pervasively and persuasively marketed to be attractive to Americans. However, the acceptability of alcohol has not always been unanimous. During the 1920s, a constitutional amendment was passed that banned the manufacture, sale, and consumption of alcohol. Known as *Prohibition*, spurred on by a group of moral entrepreneurs, most notably the Women's Christian Temperance Movement, Prohibition was an unpopular law that was eventually repealed. Despite the long-standing acceptability of alcohol as a part of American culture, its abuse is significant (Ken Burns, n.d.).

While the issue of the opioid crisis is garnering a lot of attention, and rightfully so, alcohol abuse is another problem that deserves mention. According to the National

Institute on Alcohol and Alcohol Abuse, approximately 17 million people age 18 and older have an **alcohol use disorder** and 1 in 10 children live in a home with a parent who has a drinking problem (National Institute on Alcohol Abuse and Alcoholism, 2018). The Center for Disease Control and Prevention estimates that about 88,000 people a year die of alcohol-related causes, more than twice the number who die from opiate overdoses (Center for Disease Control, 2018).

Extent of Use

According to a 2017 study in *Journal of the American Medical Association, Psychiatry,* nearly 13 percent of the US population meets the criteria for abusing alcohol. Alarmingly, the rate of alcoholism has increased by nearly 50 percent since 2000 (Grant et al., 2017). Nearly 30 million Americans are struggling with alcohol abuse. According to the research, alcohol use disorders have almost doubled (92.8 percent) among the African American population since 2000 and increased nearly 84 percent among women. For those 45 to 64 years of age, alcohol use disorders increased by 82 percent. For the elderly, those individuals 65 and older, the data shows a 107 percent increase in alcohol use disorders. The study also found that rates of alcoholism were higher among men (16.7 percent), Native Americans (16.6 percent), people below the poverty threshold (14.3 percent), and people living in the Midwest (14.8 percent). Stunningly, nearly 1 in 4 adults under age 30 (23.4 percent) met the diagnostic criteria for alcoholism (Grant et al., 2017).

WHAT IS AN ALCOHOL USE DISORDER?

For the *JAMA Psychiatry* study, researchers used the definition of an alcohol use disorder found in the *Diagnostic Statistical Manual-IV* published by the American Psychiatric Association. This definition combines 11 factors of alcohol abuse and alcohol dependence, including:

- Drinking interfering with home, family, or job responsibilities.
- Drinking increasing chances of danger or injury.
- Withdrawal symptoms from intoxication.
- An inability to stop drinking.

Of the 11 criteria, the presence of two or more indicates an alcohol use disorder. Six or more indicates a severe alcohol use disorder (Grant et al., 2017).

While the study's findings are alarming, a different survey, the National Survey on Drug Use and Health (NSDUH), has shown that alcohol use disorder rates are lower and have in fact been falling, rather than rising, since 2002. A separate study looking at differences between the two surveys found that the disparities are probably caused by how each survey asks about alcohol disorders. As was mentioned, part of the challenge of conducting social science research relates to the imperfect nature of the data. It also underscores the differences between the perception of a social problem and what can be objectively determined through careful collection of information (Willingham, 2017). In the end, the findings from both studies call attention to the consequences of alcohol abuse, both in terms of health issues as well as social behaviors. One example of this is driving while under the influence of alcohol.

Driving Under the Influence

According to the National Transportation and Safety Board, nearly 30 people die every day in the United States in automobile accidents that involve alcohol. Drunk driving fatalities have decreased by nearly a third in the last 30 years, but the costs associated with these alcohol-related incidents are approximately $44 billion per year. Moreover, drunk drivers are typically repeat offenders: drivers with blood alcohol levels of.08 g/dl or higher involved in deadly accidents were 4.5 times more likely to have prior convictions for driving while intoxicated than were drivers with no prior record (9 vs. 2 percent; National Transportation and Safety Board, 2018).

Alcohol is absorbed into the body through the walls of the stomach and small intestine, where it passes into the bloodstream and remains until it is metabolized by the liver. Alcohol level is measured by the weight of the alcohol in a certain volume of blood. This is called the **blood alcohol concentration**, or BAC (Table 3.2). If the BAC is .08 grams of alcohol per deciliter of blood (g/dl), the risk of impairment is higher, which can lead to a fatal accident if the person decides to drive a vehicle. BAC is measured with a breathalyzer, which measures the amount of alcohol in a driver's breath. A better and more accurate measure of BAC is a blood test. Even a small amount of alcohol in one's system can impair you. In 2016, for example, there were over 2,000 people killed in vehicle accidents where the drivers had BACs of.01 to.07 g/dl, according to the NTSB (National Transportation and Safety Board, 2018).

According to the Uniform Crime Reports, there were 1,001,329 arrests for driving under the influence of alcohol or narcotics 2018, or about one arrest for every 215 licensed drivers in the United States. All 50 states, Washington DC, and Puerto Rico have enacted consistent laws regarding drunk driving, which is defined as a BAC at or above 0.08 for adults and 0.02 for drivers under the age of 21. The groups with the highest involvement in fatal vehicle crashes as a result of alcohol are those drivers under the age of 21 and those 21–34 years of age. As a result, prevention programs have specifically targeted these segments of the population. However, the data indicates that young drivers are those who are least responsive to awareness campaigns to reduce impaired driving (Insurance Information Institute, 2018).

Recall the discussion of Mothers Against Drunk Driving, where efforts were made to call attention to the problems of driving while intoxicated and to change laws regarding this practice. In an attempt to address the underage drinking problem in the United States, as well as to convince younger drivers of the risks associated with

Table 3.2 BAC and Its Effects

Blood Alcohol Concentration (BAC) in G/DL	Typical Effects	Predictable Effects on Driving
.02	Some loss of judgment; relaxation, slight body warmth, altered mood	Decline in visual functions (rapid tracking of a moving target), decline in ability to perform two tasks at the same time (divided attention)
.05	Exaggerated behavior, may have loss of small-muscle control (e.g., focusing your eyes), impaired judgment, usually good feeling, lowered alertness, release of inhibition	Reduced coordination, reduced ability to track moving objects, difficulty steering, reduced response to emergency driving situations
.08	Muscle coordination becomes poor (e.g., balance, speech, vision, reaction time, and hearing), harder to detect danger; judgment, self-control, reasoning, and memory are impaired	Concentration, short-term memory loss, speed control, reduced information processing capability (e.g., signal detection, visual search), impaired perception
.10	Clear deterioration of reaction time and control, slurred speech, poor coordination, and slowed thinking	Reduced ability to maintain lane position and brake appropriately
.15	Far less muscle control than normal, vomiting may occur (unless this level is reached slowly or a person has developed a tolerance for alcohol), major loss of balance	Substantial impairment in vehicle control, attention to driving task, and in necessary visual and auditory information processing

Source: National Transportation and Safety Board. (2018). *Alcohol Abuse and Cost*. Available at: https://www.nhtsa.gov/risky-driving/drunk-driving#alcohol-abuse-and-cost-5091

driving while intoxicated, 42 states and the District of Columbia have enacted laws holding sellers and servers of alcohol liable for the injuries and deaths caused by any alcohol-impaired driver. Further, 39 states have laws that individuals who serve liquor to people, such as at parties at their homes, to be held liable for any injury or death should a person become involved in a vehicle-related accident (Insurance Information Institute, 2018).

Treatment of Alcohol Abuse

The good news is that most people with an alcohol use disorder can benefit from some form of treatment. Research shows that about one-third of people who are treated for alcohol problems have no further symptoms one year later. Many others substantially reduce their drinking and report fewer alcohol-related problems. When asked how alcohol problems are treated, people commonly think of 12-step programs or 28-day inpatient rehab but may have difficulty naming other options. Generally speaking, there are three types of treatment available for alcohol abuse: medications, behavioral treatments or counseling, and mutual support groups, such as Alcoholics Anonymous (AA).

Alcoholics Anonymous A billboard encourages people who abuse alcohol to contact Alcoholics Anonymous for help.

MEDICATIONS

The US Food and Drug Administration (FDA) has approved three medications for treating alcohol dependence. Naltrexone can help people reduce heavy drinking, while acamprosate makes it easier for users to maintain their abstinence. Finally, disulfiram prevents the metabolism of alcohol in the body, which can result in nausea. These and other effects can help some people avoid using alcohol. Researchers at the National Institute for Alcohol and Alcohol Abuse have found that other drugs show promise for reducing alcohol dependence.

For example, the anti-smoking drug varenicline (marketed under the name Chantix) significantly reduced alcohol consumption and craving among people with alcoholism. Also, gabapentin, a medication used to treat pain conditions and epilepsy, was shown to increase abstinence and reduce heavy drinking. Those taking the medication also reported fewer alcohol cravings and improved mood and sleep. Finally, the anti-epileptic medication topiramate was shown to help people curb problem drinking, particularly among those with a certain genetic makeup that appears to be linked to the treatment's effectiveness (National Institute on Alcohol Abuse and Alcoholism, 2018).

Behavioral Treatments

Also known as **alcohol counseling**, behavioral treatments involve working with a health professional to identify and help change the behaviors that lead to heavy drinking. Behavioral treatments share certain features, which can include:

- Developing and enhancing the skills needed to stop or reduce drinking.
- Building a strong social support system.
- Addressing issues related to relapse.

Cognitive–behavioral therapy is focused on identifying the indicators that lead to heavy drinking and managing the stress that can lead to relapse. By developing the skills needed to cope with everyday situations that can result in drinking, cognitive therapy attempts to change the person's thought process on how to resolve problems. Motivational enhancement therapy is a short-term intervention to help users identify an optimal plan to build confidence while developing the skills and discipline to follow through on a treatment plan to limit one's drinking. Finally, marital and family counseling is based on research showing that a strong network of family members provides the type of support needed for recovery. Improving family relationships is a crucial step in maintaining abstinence for the user.

MUTUAL SUPPORT GROUPS

In terms of treating alcohol abuse, many rehabilitation facilities and communities rely on programs that can broadly be categorized as a **12-step model,** also known as **Alcoholics Anonymous (AA)**. Founded by Bill Wilson and Dr. Bob Smith (both recovering alcoholics) in 1935, Alcoholics Anonymous began as a means to encourage sobriety for other recovering alcoholics. Today, Alcoholics Anonymous boasts more than 2 million active members worldwide, with more than 50,000 groups nationwide. The original steps are still used and many people credit the group with helping them through recovery. The basic premise of the 12-step model is that the steps need to be completed sequentially, but members often use them as part of a circular process. Although the 12 Steps emphasize spirituality, many nonreligious people have found the program immensely helpful. In addition, the 12-step model has been adapted to treat a wide range of addiction disorders (Dodes, 2016).

The 12 Steps of Alcoholics Anonymous

1. We admitted we were powerless over alcohol–that our lives had become unmanageable.
2. Came to believe that a Power greater than ourselves could restore us to sanity.
3. Made a decision to turn our will and our lives over to the care of God as we understood Him.
4. Made a searching and fearless moral inventory of ourselves.
5. Admitted to God, to ourselves and to another human being the exact nature of our wrongs.
6. Were entirely ready to have God remove all these defects of character.
7. Humbly asked Him to remove our shortcomings.
8. Made a list of persons we had harmed, and became willing to make amends to them all.
9. Made direct amends to such people wherever possible, except when to do so would injure them or others.
10. Continued to take personal inventory and when we were wrong promptly admitted it.
11. Sought through prayer and meditation to improve our conscious contact with God as we understood Him, praying only for knowledge of His will for us and the power to carry that out.
12. Having had a spiritual awakening as the result of these steps, we tried to carry this message to alcoholics and to practice these principles in all our affairs.

Despite its popularity, not everyone agrees that the 12-step model approach to alcohol abuse is always effective. For instance, Gabrielle Glassner argues that there is a general acceptance of programs like AA despite the fact that there is no real data to support its overall success. In fact, not only AA, but virtually every 12-step based treatment center, either does not collect data or rarely publishes its success rate because they know the rates are quite low and the length of success varies considerably (Glassner, 2015).

One study that examined retention rates of Alcoholics Anonymous, along with studies on sobriety and rates of active involvement (attending meetings regularly and working the program) among AA members, placed AA's actual success rate somewhere between 5 and 8 percent (Dodes, 2016). This model also presumes that people uniformly suffer from alcohol abuse, which justifies the narrow approach to treatment. Alcoholics Anonymous offers a single path to recovery: lifelong abstinence from alcohol (Glassner, 2015).

This absence of empirical support regarding the success of 12-step programs is compounded by the lack of qualified personnel to treat alcohol abuse. As Glassner points out, most treatment providers carry the credentials of addiction counselors or substance-abuse counselors, for which many states require little more than a high-school diploma or a GED. Many counselors are in recovery themselves (Glassner, 2015).

Another problem with Alcoholics Anonymous is its one-size-fits-all approach. Alcoholics Anonymous was originally intended for chronic, severe drinkers—those who may, indeed, be powerless over alcohol—but its program has since been applied much more broadly. Today, for instance, judges routinely require people to attend meetings after a DUI arrest; about 12 percent of AA members are there by court order (Dodes, 2016).

Glassner also takes issue with the notion that alcoholism is a progressive disease. According to AA, alcoholism is progressive and follows an inevitable trajectory unless the person stops using it completely and forever. However, data from the National Epidemiological Survey on Alcohol and Related Conditions show that nearly one-fifth of those who have had alcohol dependence go on to drink at low-risk levels with no symptoms of abuse. This raises questions about the inevitability of abusing alcohol. Further, a recent survey of nearly 140,000 adults by the Centers for Disease Control and Prevention found that nine out of 10 heavy drinkers are not dependent on alcohol and, with the help of a medical professional's brief intervention, can change unhealthy habits. Thus, despite their popularity, extensive use, and perceptions of effectiveness in American culture, real questions remain about the actual effectiveness of 12-step programs and their lasting impact in the treatment of alcohol abuse (Glassner, 2015; Dodes, 2016).

DRUG USE AND ABUSE

The discussion thus far has focused on the use and abuse of legal drugs, such as tobacco and alcohol. As we begin to explore the abuse of other drugs, we start with prescription medications, such as the **opioid epidemic** facing the United States.

The Opioid Epidemic

The United States is experiencing a serious problem with the abuse of opioid-based drugs. Opioids are drugs formulated to replicate the pain-reducing properties of opium. They include both legal painkillers prescribed by doctors for acute or chronic pain (such as morphine, oxycodone, or hydrocodone) as well as illegal drugs like heroin or illicitly-made fentanyl. Experts point out that more than two million Americans have become dependent on or abused prescription pain pills and street drugs. The challenge opioids present is how they react in the human body. Opioids bind to receptors in the brain and spinal cord, disrupting pain signals. They also activate the reward areas of the brain by releasing the hormone dopamine, creating a feeling of euphoria or a "high" (CNN, 2018).

In 2018, President Trump declared the opioid problem in the United States a national emergency and promised to commit funds to address the issue. While heroin addiction has been a problem for years, and knowledge of its impact on people's lives is well-documented, the recent problem relating to opioids stems from the availability of synthetic drugs that are prescribed by physicians to treat legitimate illnesses such as back pain, the impact of surgical procedures, and other ailments. For instance, the number of opioid prescriptions dispensed by doctors steadily increased from 112 million prescriptions in 1992 to a peak of 282 million in 2012, according to the market research firm IMS Health. The number of prescriptions dispensed has since declined, falling to 236 million in 2016 (CNN, 2018).

The problem is that physicians overprescribed, people became addicted, and pharmaceutical companies misled the public and the medical community about the addictive properties of new opioid-based medications. And, to add further complexity, few people have answers on how to help addicts recover. While physicians are now being much more disciplined about prescribing opioid-based prescriptions, this does little for the millions of people who are already addicted.

EXTENT OF THE PROBLEM

In 2015, the National Survey on Drug Use and Mental Health estimated that two million people suffered from some form of **pain reliever use disorder**. Two of the most commonly-prescribed pain relievers, hydrocodone and oxycodone, are semi-synthetic opioids, manufactured in labs with natural and synthetic ingredients. Between 2007 and 2016, the most widely prescribed opioid was hydrocodone (Vicodin). In 2016, 6.2 billion hydrocodone pills were distributed nationwide. The second most prevalent opioid was oxycodone (Percocet). In 2016, 5 billion oxycodone tablets were distributed in the United States. Based on preliminary reports from *the New York Times*, more than 59,000 people died from drug overdoses in 2016 alone, making it the leading cause of death for people under the age of 50 (Figure 3.2; Deming, 2018).

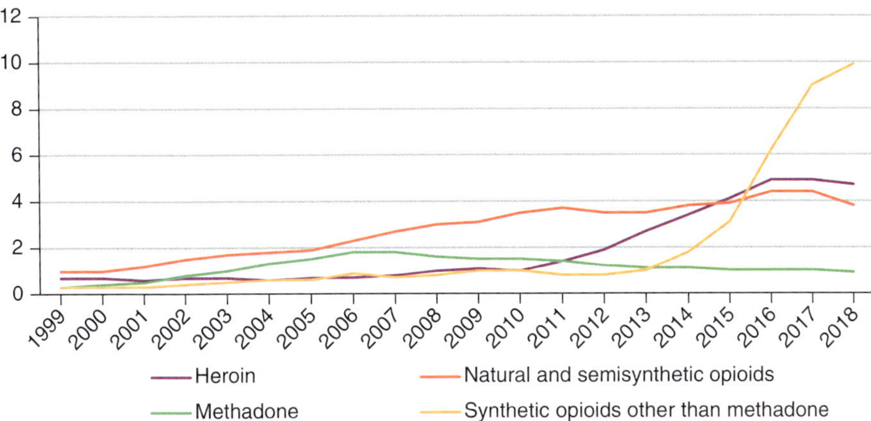

Figure 3.2 Drug overdoses by drug 2020 According to the CDC two of every three overdoses in the United States is some type of opioid. 1. Significant increasing trend from 1999 through 2006 and 2013 through 2018, with different rates of change over time, $p < 0.05$.2. Significant increasing trend from 1999 through 2018, with different rates of change over time, $p < 0.05$. 3. Significant increasing trend from 2005 through 2015, with different rates of change over time, $p < 0.05$. 4. Significant increasing trend from 1999 through 2006, then significant decreasing trend from 2006 through 2018, with different rates of change over time, $p < 0.05$. NOTES: Deaths are classified using the International Classification of Diseases, 10th Revision. Drug-poisoning (overdose) deaths are identified using underlying cause-of-death codes X40–X44, X60–X64, X85, and Y10–Y14. Drug overdose deaths involving selected drug categories are identified by specific multiple-cause-of-death codes: heroin, T40.1; natural and semisynthetic opioids, T40.2; methadone, T40.3; and synthetic opioids other than methadone, T40.4. Deaths involving more than one opioid category (e.g., a death involving both methadone and a natural or semisynthetic opioid) are counted in both categories. Deaths may involve multiple drugs. The percentage of drug overdose deaths that identified the specific drugs involved varied by year, with ranges of 75–79% from 1999 through 2013 and 81–92% from 2014 through 2018. Access data table for Figure 3.2 at: https://www.cdc.gov/nchs/data/databriefs/db356_tables-508.pdf#3. SOURCE: NCHS, National Vital Statistics System, Mortality.

According to the Centers for Disease Control and Prevention, the rate of heroin-related deaths quadrupled between 2002 and 2013, and people who are addicted to prescription opioids are 40 times more likely to become addicted to heroin. People who become dependent on pain pills may switch to heroin because it is less expensive than prescription drugs. Researchers at Washington University in St. Louis found that 94 percent of people surveyed indicated that they used heroin because prescription opioids were far more expensive and harder to obtain (Deming, 2018).

The National Institute on Drug Abuse estimates that half of young people who inject heroin turned to the street drug after abusing prescription painkillers, and that three in four new heroin users start out using prescription drugs. The number of overdose deaths related to heroin increased 533 percent between 2002 and 2016, from an estimated 2,089 in 2002 to 13,219 in 2016 (Deming, 2018). As a new population of users emerged whose addiction to prescription painkillers led them to dependency on stronger drugs like heroin, the discovery of fentanyl made addiction even more dangerous.

Fentanyl, which is 50 to 100 times more powerful than morphine, and carfentanil, which is 10,000 times stronger than morphine, are synthetic opioids known to cause overdoses with comparatively small amounts. As with any street drug transaction, users don't always know what they are buying as dealers typically dilute drugs with all sorts of additives. However, given the powerful nature of fentanyl and carfentanil, if they are added to any street drug (such as heroin) the results can be deadly. It is estimated that between 2013 and 2015 more than 9,000 deaths were caused by lethal doses of these synthetic opioids (Deming, 2018).

In 2013, the cost of medical care and substance abuse treatment for opioid addiction and overdose was an estimated $78 billion, according to a report in the journal *Medical Care*. The 21st Century Cures Act, passed in 2016, allocated $1 billion over two years in opioid crisis grants to states, providing funding for expanded treatment and prevention programs (US Department of Health and Human Services, 2017). In August 2017, Attorney General Jeff Sessions announced the launch of an **Opioid Fraud and Abuse Detection Unit** within the Department of Justice. The unit's mission is to prosecute individuals who commit opioid-related health care fraud. The Department of Justice is also appointing US attorneys who will specialize in opioid health care fraud cases as part of a three-year pilot program in 12 jurisdictions nationwide (US Department of Justice, 2017).

HOW DID WE GET HERE?

In the 1990s, a new prescription painkiller, **OxyContin**, hit the pharmaceutical market. With an estimated 100 million people suffering from chronic pain, patients were eager for a miracle drug to alleviate their aches. Opioid manufacturers were eager to educate both doctors and patients on this allegedly safe and effective way to help them find relief. A report by the *Los Angeles Times*, which examined internal documents and other evidence of effectiveness of OxyContin, along with the marketing tactics by Purdue Pharma, the company that created the drug, revealed that the company knew the drug was not as effective as it claimed and deliberately misled physicians and patients. Specifically, Purdue Pharma informed physicians that OxyContin could last for 12 hours instead of the typical eight hours pain killers lasted (Ryan, Girion, and Glover, 2016).

Such a claim turns out to be untrue, but the pressure for Purdue Pharma to produce a better product led to misleading physicians. The result of this effort was significant: in the same way that users did not know the full effect of street drugs they purchased, patients with legal prescriptions did not realize the impact of their painkilling medication. For much of the early years of the opioid epidemic, painkillers were the leading cause of drug overdose deaths, and most people who were addicted to opioids got started on painkillers. That has changed in recent years but painkillers were the initial cause of the current opioid crisis, fostering more misuse of and addiction to the drugs (Ryan, Girion, and Glover, 2016).

LAWSUITS AND OPIOID MANUFACTURERS

Similar to the tobacco industry's misleading claims about the effects of the use of its products, lawsuits have been filed against opioid manufacturers. These lawsuits were brought primarily on behalf of people who overdosed as a result of their addiction. The argument made in these cases was that manufacturers did not warn users about the addiction risks, while others argued companies deliberately withheld information about the dangers of their products; claiming they were safe to use when this was not in fact the case. These suits faced an uphill battle since the FDA approved the drugs and the companies that made them had a limited responsibility to warn users about the risks (Haffajee, and Mello, 2017).

One procedural strategy to overcome these obstacles was the **class action suit**, which is brought by a large group of individuals who experienced similar problems with the use of the drug. This was the strategy employed in lawsuits against tobacco companies based on smokers' behavior. While initially resisted by judges in granting class action suits for **opioid addiction**, in recent years such lawsuits have gained greater success against opioid manufacturers (Haffajee, and Mello, 2017).

Perhaps the most promising development in opioid litigation has been the advent of suits brought against drug makers and distributors by the federal government and dozens of states, counties, cities, and Native American tribes. Because the government itself is claiming injury and seeking restitution as a result of the increased costs they have incurred as a result of opioid addiction, there is greater likelihood of the success of these claims (Haffajee, and Mello, 2017).

Marijuana Use and Abuse

While the opioid crisis represents a good illustration of the costs and harms associated with the abuse of prescription drugs, along with the increased use of illegal drugs, another drug that appears to be making a transition from an illegal status to a more legal one is marijuana. This does not mean there are no harmful effects of marijuana, however, and the issue of decriminalization or legalization remains controversial in some states.

EXTENT OF THE PROBLEM

According to a 2015 survey by the National Survey on Drug Abuse and Health (NSDAH), about 36 million people reported currently using marijuana, defined as having used marijuana at least once or twice in the past year (National Survey on Drug Abuse and Health, 2015). In a 2017 poll conducted by Yahoo News and Marist College, that number increased to nearly 55 million, 35 million of whom are what the survey calls "regular users" who use marijuana at least once or twice a month. This latest figure puts usage on par with the number of cigarette smokers in the United States (59 million). According to a 2019 CBS News poll, the number of people who have ever tried marijuana has increased to fifty-five percent since 1987, up five percentage points from 2018 (Depinto, 2019). About half of this country's 55 million marijuana users are millennials (those born between 1981 and 1996). The majority of marijuana users are male, make under $50,000 a year and lack a college degree (Ingraham, 2017).

Public opinion polls show that support for legalization increased from just 12 percent in 1969 to 31 percent in 2000 to 64 percent in 2017, including 51 percent of Republicans (Ingraham, 2017). Prior marijuana use is one of the biggest predictors of support for recreational marijuana legalization. Fully 70 percent of Americans who have tried marijuana at least once support legalizing it for recreational use. Only 26 percent of those who have not tried it agree that legalization is a good idea. Part of the reason for the support of marijuana may be due to the perceptions of its harmfulness. In the NSDAH survey, 72 percent of respondents said that regular alcohol use is more of a health risk than regular marijuana use. Respondents felt that the harmful effects of marijuana were lower for use of tobacco (76 to 18 percent) as well as prescription painkillers (67 to 20 percent). This is not to say that people feel marijuana is harmless; rather it suggests that they think it is less harmful than other drugs they might use.

In a 2019 Gallup poll, about two-thirds of Americans support the legalization of marijuana, which is about the same as in 2018, but 30 points higher than in 2005. According to the poll, there were no meaningful differences by gender, education, income, or region of the country with regard to legalization. However, there were differences based on political ideology (82 percent of liberals versus 48 percent of conservatives supported legalization), religiosity (whether the person attended church services weekly, occasionally, or not at all, 42, 63, and 77 percent, respectively, favored legalization of marijuana), and age, with 81 percent of those under 30 in favor of legalization, while only 49 percent of those over the age of 65 supported legalization (Jones, 2019).

THE LEGALIZATION OF MARIJUANA: THE DEBATE AND REALITIES

In 2012, Colorado and Washington became the first two states to legalize marijuana for adult use. In some cases, approval started for medical use of marijuana, but since then much of the discussion has focused on recreational use. Two years later Alaska, Oregon, and Washington, D.C. followed suit. In 2016, California, Massachusetts, Maine, and Nevada also approved the legalization of marijuana in their states. In January 2018, Vermont was added to the list and more states are expected to follow this trend in the future. In addition, 13 states have chosen to decriminalize possession of small amounts of marijuana so that it no longer carries a jail or prison sentence. These laws vary from state to state, with some laws attaching a fine for possession, while others attach brief jail time (Figure 3.3). What is important is the amount the person has in

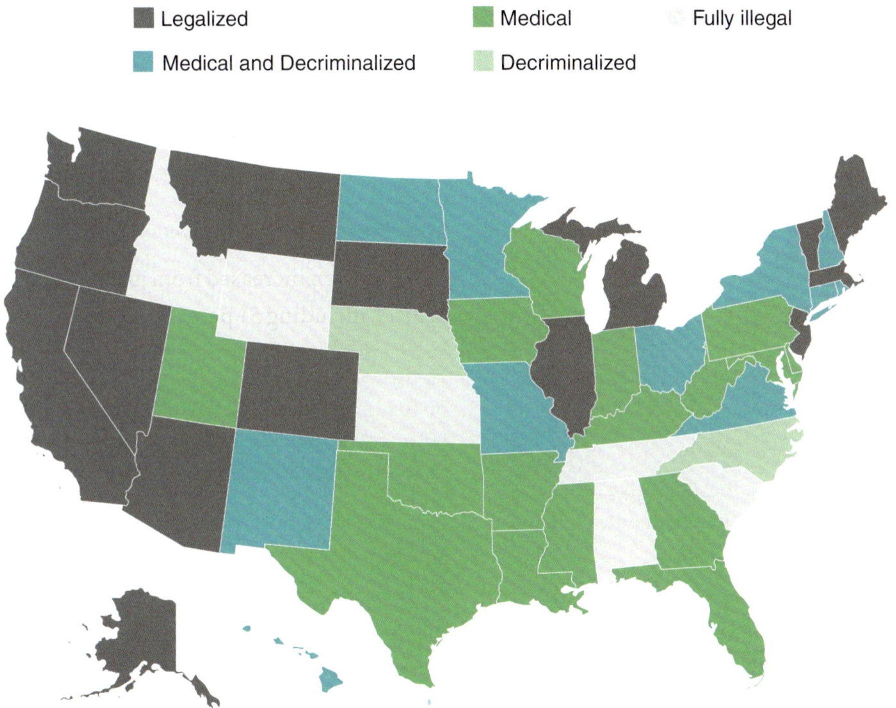

Figure 3.3 Marijuana legalization in the United States State status reflects current laws as of January 2021. Source: DISA Global Solutions https://disa.com/map-of-marijuana-legality-by-state

their possession, not its intended use. That is, some states define a small amount as between 10 or 100 grams, while possession of larger amounts for sale, distribution, or even recreational use remain illegal. Thirty states and Washington, D.C. allow marijuana for medical purposes, although some states allow for medical marijuana dispensaries while others only allow home cultivation of the drug (Hsaio, 2019, Lopez, 2018).

It is important to note that while several states have allowed marijuana, it is still considered illegal under federal law. That is, federal law classifies marijuana as a Schedule 1 drug, meaning it does not have any medical value and has a high potential for abuse (Table 3). This puts the drug in the same category as heroin and is more restrictive than Schedule 2 drugs such as cocaine and methamphetamine (Hsaio, 2019, Lopez, 2018).

Advocates in favor of legalizing marijuana argue that legalizing the drug would allow greater regulation as well as create revenue generated from taxes that could support treatment programs and other efforts to address substance abuse problems. Legalization would not only generate considerable revenue, it would also likely reduce the costs related to arresting, prosecuting and incarcerating offenders for relatively minor offenses. Proponents of legalization also argue that the war on marijuana has cost billions of dollars, has resulted in the creation of a black market for the drug, and has not

Table 3 Schedules of Controlled Substances

Schedule	Definitions	Examples
Schedule I	High abuse potential with no accepted medical use; medications within this schedule may not be prescribed, dispensed, or administered	Heroin, marijuana, ecstasy, gamma hydroxybutyric acid (GHB)
Schedule II	High-abuse potential with severe psychological or physical dependence; however, these medications have an accepted medical use and may be prescribed, dispensed, or administered	Morphine, codeine, hydrocodone, hydromorphone, methadone, oxycodone, fentanyl, methylphenidate, pentobarbital
Schedule III	Intermediate abuse potential (i.e., less than Schedule II but more than Schedule IV medications)	Hydrocodone/acetaminophen 5 mg/500 mg or 10 mg/650 mg; codeine in combination with acetaminophen, aspirin, or ibuprofen; anabolic steroids; ketamine
Schedule IV	Abuse potential less than Schedule II but more than Schedule V medications	Propoxyphene, butorphanol, pentazocine, alprazolam, clonazepam, diazepam, midazolam, phenobarbital, pemoline, sibutramine
Schedule V	Medications with the least potential for abuse among the controlled substances	*Robitussin AC*, *Phenergan* with codeine

Source: http://www.deadiversion.usdoj.gov/pubs/manuals/pharm2/pharm_manual.pdf

changed the use of the drug by millions of people. Thus, our drug policies are being viewed as a failure that requires a different approach, particularly since the public favors the use of marijuana (Hsaio, 2019).

Legalization would also address the problems of disproportionality since minorities, particularly African Americans, are more likely to be arrested for possession of marijuana. A 2013 report by the American Civil Liberties Union found that African Americans are nearly four times more likely to be arrested for marijuana use compared to Whites (American Civil Liberties Union, 2013). Advocates of legalization also contend that such a strategy would stimulate the economy by creating jobs, who would then become less dependent upon society and would be taxpaying citizens (Hsaio, 2019). Another benefit to legalization is that marijuana use can address the opioid epidemic. Given marijuana's properties to reduce pain, legalization would make it easier for people who are currently addicted to opioids to use a more stable and less harmful alternative (DiBenedetto, Weed, Wawrzynick, et. al, 2018).

In contrast, those who are against legalizing marijuana contend that legalizing the drug would make it more accessible and increase its abuse. A related argument against legalization is that it would allow businesses that sell marijuana to aggressively market to people who likely already have a drug problem, thereby increasing dependency and risks. There are also concerns that marijuana serves as a gateway drug to more dangerous substances, such as heroin and cocaine. This is particularly true of young users (Hsiao, 2019).

While the laws regulating the sale of marijuana may be restricted to adults, as is the case with current alcohol and tobacco laws, teenagers are able to acquire both illegally. The same argument could be made about marijuana; any form of regulation would create a type of black market that provides the product to those from whom it should be restricted. Arguments against legalization also contend that the number of traffic accidents and road fatalities would increase as more users would attempt to drive while under the influence of the drug (Hsiao, 2019).

An intermediate step between legalizing marijuana and keeping it illegal is decriminalization. This strategy does not punish offenders for possession of small amounts of marijuana for personal use. It is a "soft" policy of tolerance instead of a hardline approach that involves aggressive law enforcement and criminal prosecution. In fact, very few countries have legalized marijuana. Uruguay was the first country to legalize marijuana in 2014; Canada followed suit in 2018. Aside from these two examples, many other countries have opted to decriminalize the possession of marijuana, such as the policy of the Netherlands, which allows the sale of marijuana in various "coffee shops" around cities like Amsterdam (Johnson, 2018).

GLOBAL PERSPECTIVES

Marijuana Use in Other Countries

When Americans consider the drug abuse problem in this country, inevitably discussions turn to what other countries are doing to address the issue. One misconception is that the city of Amsterdam in the Netherlands has solved the marijuana abuse problem by legalizing its possession and use. Although the Dutch approach is an interesting contrast to the more punitive approach taken by the United States, its actual enforcement is more nuanced than popularly believed. While at one time the Dutch government took a harder line on all drugs, in the early 1970s a distinction was made between soft drugs (such as marijuana and sedatives) and hard

Amsterdam's marijuana culture A bounty of cannabis-based products on display in the window of an Amsterdam "coffee shop," where it is legal to purchase and consume marijuana.

drugs (such as cocaine, heroin and ecstasy). In the mid-1970s, marijuana was allowed to be sold in what are called "coffee shops" around the Netherlands—although no coffee is actually sold, just marijuana.

The rationale behind this decision was the realization that eliminating drug use was not possible and the public would be better served by trying to minimize the harm rather than fighting it. Thus, people who wish to use marijuana for non-medical purposes are allowed to do so in a safe place, like a regulated coffee shop. In addition, up to five plants can be grown at home for personal use, but large scale growth operations are considered a more serious crime. Such a position does not mean marijuana is legal in the Netherlands; rather, its use has been decriminalized. That is, possessing small amounts (5 grams) does not result in an arrest and jail sentence. Instead, it has relaxed the regulation of the use of marijuana, taken away the economic advantage of organized crime, and stimulated the economy by allowing coffee shops to sell it to customers. Police officers may still confiscate the drug from an individual if the person is under the influence, is in possession of greater quantities than is tolerated, or if the person is a minor (Johnson, 2018).

IMPACT OF LEGALIZATION AND DECRIMINALIZATION

Early evidence in some states suggests the advantages of legalization and decriminalization. For instance, data suggests that states are reducing the costs relating to the arrest and prosecution of offenders, while considerable revenue has been generated from legalizing marijuana. This revenue is being used to support many social programs. For instance, according to a recent report by Drug Policy Alliance, a pro-legalization advocacy group:

- Colorado distributed $230 million to the Colorado Department of Education between 2015 and 2017 to fund school construction, early literacy, bullying prevention, and behavioral health.
- Oregon allocates 40 percent of marijuana tax revenue to its state school fund, depositing $34 million into the fund so far. The state also distributes 20 percent to alcohol and drug treatment.
- Washington dedicates 25 percent to substance use disorder treatment, education and prevention. The state also distributes 55 percent of its marijuana tax revenues to fund basic health plans.
- Alaska will collect an estimated $12 million annually, which will fund drug treatment and community residential centers.
- California and Massachusetts will invest a share of their marijuana tax revenues in the communities most adversely impacted by drug arrests and incarceration, particularly low-income communities of color, to help repair the harms of unequal drug law enforcement (Drug Policy Alliance, 2018).

Despite concerns that legalization would result in higher rates of marijuana use by youth, the data seems to indicate that rates have remained stable, even in those states that have legalized marijuana. Again, according to Drug Policy Alliance:

- According to the 2015 Youth Risk Behavior Survey, 21.7 percent of American high school students used marijuana in the past month and this rate has been consistent over the past decade.
- In Washington, Colorado and Alaska, rates of marijuana use among high school students largely resemble national rates.
- In Oregon, Nevada, California, Maine, Massachusetts and Washington, D.C., rates of marijuana use mostly stabilized or declined over the years leading up to legalization (Drug Policy Alliance, 2018).

With regard to the potential for increased traffic fatalities and/or arrests while under the influence of marijuana, the data suggests that this concern has not been fulfilled in those states that have legalized the drug. The total number of arrests for driving under the influence (for alcohol and other drugs) has declined in Colorado and Washington, the first two states to regulate marijuana for adult use. The data suggests that crash rates in both states are statistically similar to comparable states without legal marijuana. The early data also suggests that the legal marijuana industry employs between 165,000 to 230,000 full- and part-time workers across the country. This is expected to grow as more states pass legislation regarding marijuana use (Drug Policy Alliance, 2018; Hsiao, 2019).

While the public use of marijuana remains illegal even in those states that have passed legislation regarding possession and consumption of the drug, one strategy used by several states that have legalized marijuana possession is to allow retail stores or other establishments that permit the consumption of marijuana on the premises. This is similar to the coffee shop strategy employed in the Netherlands. This could address some of the disproportionality issues relating to arrests of minorities, particularly African Americans (Drug Policy Alliance, 2018; Hsiao, 2019).

While there remain a host of issues yet to be resolved in the debate over the legalization of marijuana, it seems that the trend of public opinion is to lean toward a more permissive approach to recreational use of the drug. As many states begin to allow companies to market and sell the drug, and as other businesses are created to cater to user needs, the inevitable concerns about abusive business practices (similar to what was seen with tobacco and alcohol companies) as well as the long-term effects of increased accessibility and use of the drug have arisen.

Society's Response to Drug Abuse: The War on Drugs

In the 1970s, President Richard Nixon, in response to the increase drug use in the United States, declared a war on drugs. Nixon dedicated considerable effort to increasing the size of law enforcement agencies to address the problem as well as legislation that resulted in mandatory sentencing and allowing "no-knock" warrants. The latter allowed the police to serve warrants without warning to potential offenders. Interestingly, such measures came during a period when there was actually increasing evidence and support for decriminalizing the possession and distribution of marijuana for personal use. However, fear of widespread drug use by parents about teen drug use prompted a shift in public policy (Lopez, 2016).

The origins of Nixon's War on Drugs began in New York, when Governor Nelson Rockefeller took a dramatic stand against heroin users and dealers, which was creating a significant problem in his state. While he originally supported drug rehabilitation efforts, Rockefeller took perhaps the first zero tolerance approach to the drug epidemic. He proposed mandatory prison sentences of 15 years to life for drug dealers and addicts of any kind—even for offenders arrested for possession of small amounts of marijuana, cocaine or heroin. The initiative passed through the New York legislature and soon became popular in other states, where mandatory sentences and three-strikes laws (which sentenced offenders to life in prison upon their third conviction of a felony) were passed and impacted Nixon's efforts at the federal level (Mann, 2013).

This was not the first time that the United States wrestled with drug abuse, however Nixon's efforts, along with his successors' approaches, had numerous and lasting effects on social life in the United States and abroad. These effects have been felt primarily on those who use drugs, in particular minorities (Lopez, 2016).

While there is a great deal to unpack regarding the repercussions of the War on Drugs, including the violence that has occurred in other countries as result of the drug trade, along with an assortment of challenges with respect to the time, energy, and money dedicated to enforcing drug interdiction policies in the United States, one critical consequence has been the creation of disparities of punishment for those who have been arrested for drug offenses, particularly possession.

By one account, the number of people incarcerated for nonviolent drug law offenses increased from 50,000 in 1980 to over 400,000 by 1997 (Lopez, 2016). Perhaps even more importantly, because crack cocaine was seen as a serious threat to the country, in part because it was inexpensive and produced an intense high when smoked, much of the crack epidemic was linked to the poor in general, and to Black people in particular (Hendricks and Wilson, 2013).

As a result, efforts to address the drug problem overall and crack in particular focused on minorities. This is true despite consistent evidence that drug use patterns between whites and Blacks are remarkably similar. However, law enforcement efforts concentrated heavily on poor and minority neighborhoods. The result? More arrests and convictions for Black people for drug offenses (Alexander, 2012; Kurtzleben, 2010).

In addition, there is a clear disparity between the punishments for the possession of crack cocaine compared to powder cocaine, even though the two drugs are essentially the same. People who are charged with possession of just one gram of crack are given the same sentence as those found in possession of 18 grams of powder cocaine (US Sentencing Commission, 2015).

Ironically, this change is said to be an improvement over the original disparity—prior to the enactment of the Fair Sentencing Act of 2010, the disparity was not 18:1, but 100:1, meaning sentences for crack were far longer than those convicted of powder cocaine charges. For instance, according to the ACLU, in 2006, the distribution of just five grams of crack carried a minimum five-year federal prison sentence, while distribution of 500 grams of powder cocaine carried the same five-year mandatory minimum sentence (ACLU, 2006). Because crack users tended to be Black, low-income, and less educated, they were at higher risk than their white counterparts for those longer sentences (US Sentencing Commission, 2015; Alexander, 2012; Cullen, 2018).

This disproportionality applies not only to crack use, but also becomes a part of the narrative relating to the decriminalization and legalization of marijuana. The reason? As was mentioned, Blacks are much more likely to be arrested for marijuana possession than Whites, and the decriminalization of possession of that drug has important implications for what is known as the **mass incarceration of America** (Sawyer and Wagner, 2019; Cullen, 2018).

We will return to the disproportionality of Blacks in the criminal justice system and examine the mass incarceration of America in Chapter 6. However, it is important to frame the War on Drugs in light of what we know about moral panics and how policy changes driven by such fear can have serious consequences for those most affected by them.

SOCIOLOGICAL THEORY AND ALCOHOL AND DRUG ABUSE

As was mentioned in Chapter 1, sociological theory helps to understand the nature of social problems as well as serving to identify solutions to them. This applies to the challenges presented by drug and alcohol abuse as well.

Functionalism and Drug Abuse

In the discussion of functionalism in Chapter 1, we observed that the existence of a condition or phenomenon over time likely means that it serves some useful purpose for the growth and survival of society. While drugs and drug abuse might not seem to make a positive contribution to society, functionalists would point to the benefits of prescription drugs, such as preventing and curing disease and saving lives. Abuse of these drugs might seem to be dysfunctional, but drugs and their abuse, both legal and illegal, are functional for those who make money from growing, processing, distributing, and selling them. Further, the enormous profits made by pharmaceutical companies underwrite additional research to find cures for all sorts of diseases. The presence of drug abuse also enhances treatment modalities and the development of techniques to address addiction, not to mention the impact the rehabilitation industry has on the economy.

Conflict Theory and Drug Abuse

From a conflict approach, the manufacture, sale and distribution of legal drugs generates enormous profit for the medical and pharmaceutical industries. This results in significant economic, social and political power for these entities. The fact that many companies have misled the public and falsified the evidence about the harmful effects of the drugs is seen by conflict theorists as an example of how influential these companies can be in shaping not only the public's opinion about their power, but the narrative about their level of accountability. The tobacco industry and the drug manufacturers related to the opioid crisis are proof that the profits generated from these products results in virtual immunity from any meaningful level of accountability, despite the harm they inflict on the public. Conflict theorists would also point out that the use of existing drug laws are a means to control the poor and to keep them addicted to drugs, thereby ensuring the stability of the status quo that regulates their status in society.

Symbolic Interactionism and Drug Abuse

Symbolic interactionists would tend to look at how certain drugs evoke stronger or more negative reactions than others that might actually be more harmful. In the social construction of drugs and drug abuse, how people perceive drugs as well as the appropriateness of their effects become critical variables in the discussion. Examples such as Prohibition and the Temperance Movement against the evils of alcohol, mentioned earlier in this chapter, were replaced with a more casual attitude toward alcohol, one that continues to exist today, despite the harms involved. Similarly, the popularity of marijuana can be seen as simply a shifting of the emphasis and importance of the drug as a threat to society to one that is less harmful than existing legal drugs, such as alcohol.

Down the drain US law enforcement agents pour barrels of illegal liquor into the sewer during a raid on a producer of bootleg alcohol during the Prohibition era (1920–1933).

Thus, the stigma that certain drugs have, develop, and how they are perceived by society become the focus of attention for symbolic interactionists. In the past, cigarette smoking was seen as socially acceptable, but today it is seen far differently, in part because of the harms that were discovered about its use, but also because society has shifted its focus to other drugs that appear to be more dangerous, such as opioids.

Critical Race Theory and Drug Abuse

Recall that critical race theory offers insight into structural and institutional discrimination. This perspective is especially useful as it relates to the legal system, where minorities are disproportionately more likely to be arrested and involved in the criminal justice system. Data seems to indicate that minorities are more likely to be arrested for the possession of marijuana and more likely to be charged for this offense. Further, critical race theory could offer insight into the nature of the response by society regarding the opioid crisis, which seems to affect more Whites than any other group—thereby creating a public health crisis to which considerable resources and effort have been directed (Hansen and Netherland, 2016). Critical race theorists would point out that the crack cocaine epidemic that impacted more of the African American community in the 1980s did not garner nearly as much attention or resources. Finally, critical race theory offers insight into how the efforts to decriminalize marijuana use, or changes in how the police respond to people using it in public, likely stems from the fact that more Whites are using it than ever before (Hanson and Netherland, 2016).

WHAT WORKS? EFFECTIVE SOLUTIONS TO ADDRESS ALCOHOLISM AND DRUG ADDICTION

Efforts to address substance abuse vary according to the drugs involved and the reasons why people use and abuse them. Here, we examine three solutions that have proven effective.

Tobacco Use: Breaking The Habit

According to the Centers for Disease Control and Prevention, one promising strategy to reduce smoking is social media campaigns, which have a broad reach to young adult smokers with high engagement and retention rates. For example, a counseling intervention delivered via Twitter in combination with nicotine replacement therapy (NRT) yielded significantly higher short-term quit rates when compared to those receiving NRT alone. Another effective approach to reduce smoking is tobacco-free grounds policies (restricting use of any tobacco use on specific property). Research finds a significant decrease in client smoking behaviors after implementation of tobacco-free grounds in residential addiction treatment programs (Glandtz, 2018).

Finally, providing smoking cessation treatment to patients are already hospitalized may also be effective. Such smokers may be motivated to quit, especially if they are admitted for a smoking-related illness, and are forced to be temporarily abstinent because of hospital smoke-free policies. However, such strategies are only effective if counseling is continued after the patient is discharged. One way to do this is the interactive voice response system (IVR). The IVR is a telephone-based technology that allows a computer to detect voice and touch tones during a phone conversation and respond with prerecorded audio. The IVR system has been used successfully in several hospitals in the United States and Canada with improvement in cessation rates. In a 2017 randomized controlled trial of an IVR intervention for hospitalized smokers, the six-month abstinence rate of for participants was 26 percent compared to 15 percent in the control group (Glandtz, 2018).

Opioid Addiction: Combining Approaches

The challenges involving effective treatment for opioid addiction is not that there are no known cures. While the issues are significant for those who suffer from an addiction, there are medications that have been proven to work to reduce both the desire for the drug as well as the pain of withdrawal. Some argue that the use of such drugs is less than optimal; one is simply trading one drug for another. Others point out that patient compliance is a complicating factor: patients must continue to take the drug in order for treatment to be effective. It is not unusual for patients suffering from many different conditions to stop taking their medications, either because they feel better or because they convince themselves they don't need it. Drug addicts have the added challenge in that the cravings for the drug or the side effects from the opioid blocker often lead them to stop taking the medications all together.

However, studies have consistently shown that medication reduces the mortality rate among opioid addicted patients by more than half and is much more successful in keeping patients in treatment than non-medication modalities. For example, in a 2004 study of opioid addicts in France, when the government allowed doctors greater latitude in prescribing buprenorphine to address opioid addiction, overdose deaths from opioids was reduced by nearly 80 percent. At the same time, the number of people seeking treatment increased (Auriacombe et. al, 2004).

While the stigma connected to taking drugs is a real concern and while compliance is always an issue, the real problem with treating opioid addiction is lack of access to care. In a 2016 report by the Surgeon General's Office, only about 10 percent of people in the United States who have a drug use disorder can get specialty treatment. Even when treatment is available, fewer than half of treatment facilities offer opioid addiction medications. Why? Treatment providers face a significant challenge in reimbursement from insurance companies, making it less likely they offer this type of care. It also means there is a shortage of facilities in general and the ones that exist have waitlists, assuming the patient can afford the cost of the treatment (US Department of Health and Human Services, 2018).

In 2017, the state of Virginia acted to treat opioid addiction as a public health issue. Officials brought addiction treatment into the larger health care system by allowing patients to use Medicaid to pay for drugs like buprenorphine, methadone, and naltrexone, along with a comprehensive treatment plan that allows case workers to address issues such as housing and employment for patients. This boost to reimbursement rates created an incentive to addiction treatment providers, who were then not only guaranteed revenue, but at a rate that made it worthwhile to create programs for opioid addiction (Lopez, 2018).

To accomplish this goal, the state created the Addiction and Recovery Treatment Services (ARTS) in 2017. The ARTS program offers a full range of treatment options, from outpatient doctors' offices to intensive residential facilities. Patients are placed in treatment depending on their needs, based on guidelines by the American Society of Addiction Medicine. The state also established new Medicaid guidelines for painkiller prescriptions, setting rules and extra layers of approval for lengthier prescriptions. Such an approach is heralded as a best practice among experts on drug addiction since it addresses both medical and non-medical factors that contribute to addiction (Lopez, 2018).

Research by Virginia Commonwealth University demonstrates the promise of this combined approach. For instance, the percentage of Medicaid members with an opioid use disorder who received treatment went up by 29 percent from April to December 2017 compared to the same period the previous year. At the same time, emergency department visits related to opioid use disorders went down by 31 percent. That was more than double the 15 percent reduction in emergency department use among all state Medicaid members during the same time frame. The researchers also created computer models to determine what emergency room (ER) visits might be with and without the ARTS program. The conclusion? ARTS was really the reason for the majority of the decrease in ER use (Lopez, 2018).

Medicaid alone can't solve all the problems with addiction treatment in the United States, since it only targets low-income populations. However, the Virginia example points to the need for a greater understanding of the stigma of medications specifically designed to meet the needs of the opioid epidemic. As the opioid crisis will take years to address and cost the United States billions of dollars, integrating addiction treatment into the larger health care system is perhaps one of the most effective ways of finding a solution.

Alcohol Abuse: Limiting Access

One of the challenges relating to the abuse of alcohol relates to the rate of consumption, such as binge drinking, along with the availability of alcohol. While prevention efforts are noteworthy and valuable, a strategic challenge relates to access to alcohol. Researchers have discovered that there is a relationship between the availability of alcohol in certain location and crime, or what is known as **alcohol outlet density**. This refers to the number of locations where alcoholic beverages are available, including bars and restaurants, which serve alcohol on the premises, or convenience and grocery stores, which are defined as "off-premise."

Several studies have noted a statistically significant relationship between alcohol outlet density and alcohol-related harms, including crime. For example:

- In Los Angeles County, researchers estimated that in Los Angeles, each additional alcohol outlet was related to 3.4 additional violent incidents per year.
- In Cleveland, Ohio, when a tavern or bar was added to a given city block, the result was at least three more crimes occurring on that same block per year.
- In New Orleans, researchers found that a 10% increase in the number of convenience stores or other outlets that sell alcohol result in about a 2% increase in the homicide rate.
- In Newark, New Jersey, one study found that for every 1% decrease in the number of places that sold alcohol, there was a corresponding 1% decrease in violent crime (Jernigan, Sparks, Yang, and Schwartz, 2013).

But alcohol outlet density is not simply connected to criminal behavior. A review of 88 studies on alcohol outlet density concluded that it was also associated with increases in impaired driving, neighborhood disruption, hospitalizations, suicides and automobile accidents. Based on the wealth of data, a task force on community preventive services recommended the use of zoning and licensing laws to reduce excessive alcohol consumption. This was accomplished by limiting the number of outlets that sell alcohol in a given area; limiting the number of outlets based on population; limiting the hours of operation of these outlets and limiting the number of outlets based on total retail businesses in a given area (Jernigan, Sparks, Yang, and Schwartz, 2013). Although this approach demonstrates an effective way to limit the exposure to alcohol, it clearly does not address the issues that individual users might have with alcohol abuse. By starting at the source of the problem—availability—community efforts can target the supply side of the issue and has been shown to be an effective means of containing alcohol abuse.

SO WHAT CAN I DO?

We live in a medicine-oriented society. Medicines save lives, so they are not evil or bad in themselves. Short of not taking the drugs or strictly monitoring their use, one thing that individuals can do that might serve as a step in the right direction relates to the stigmatization of addiction. Very few people make a conscious choice to become an addict. This is not to say they didn't make a choice; individuals do have agency, and at some level they should be held accountable for their actions. But what about the context in which that decision occurred?

What if the person thought they were taking a drug that was non-addicting for a legitimate reason, such as a pain reliever as a result of a surgical procedure? What if they were misled or uninformed about the harms those drugs could cause? Does that change the nature of the choice involved? What if they were told by the manufacturers of those drugs that they were safe, such as e-cigarettes as a way to quit smoking? The point is, while people do in fact make choices about the decision to use drugs, there is more to understand about those choices and their consequences.

The stigma associated with medicines to treat substance abuse make it difficult to convince policymakers and other stakeholders to view these treatments as more than the simple substitution of one drug for another—yet that is exactly what is needed in order for the addict to recover. While models such as the 12-step approach can work for some people, they have not been proven to work empirically, and they remain the default category for treatment. What you can do individually is to recognize the flaws in the conventional wisdom about addiction and about treatment, and work to decrease the stigmatization that prevents effective measures from being taken.

CONCLUSION

Americans, who tend to use drugs for a variety of reasons, often find it difficult to effectively self-regulate their usage. This leads to the social problems of abuse and addiction. Part of the problem for users is the lack of information about the harmful effects of many drugs. We have seen evidence that the tobacco industry as well as opioid manufacturers conceal, mislead, and deny the harmful effects of their products. It is only after millions of people become harmed by and addicted to these substances that policymakers and legislators have been forced to act. We have also seen that alcohol abuse has far-reaching consequences, even for those who use it legally. The same can be said for tobacco products and prescription painkillers—the issue is what happens when they become addicted and cannot control the effects of the drugs. This leads to all manner of inappropriate behaviors, including the use of illegal drugs to compensate for the absence of legal ones.

We have also seen evidence that the United States has a poor track record when it comes to drug treatment. This comes in many forms, but primarily it is the stigma associated with using drugs to solve a drug-related problem. We have medications that are proven to work with those addicted to opioids for example, but the government's reluctance to make it easier for treatment providers to help abusers complicates the problem. The government has also continued to make it difficult for medical providers to become licensed and certified to dispense the drugs, which ultimately lead to a host of other problems relating to the black market of treatment drugs or sustaining addictions.

Finally, there are programs and treatments that we know work, but the availability and costs associated with these treatments prevent abusers from getting the help they need. In their place are programs like the 12-step model, which has a poor empirical foundation and success rate, yet has become the default approach to drug and alcohol addiction. Until we as a country make the decision to allow insurance coverage, such as Medicaid or Medicare to support the effective treatments, there will be very few treatment providers willing to absorb the costs of helping abusers to recover from their addictions.

YOU MAKE THE CALL: MARIJUANA AND ENFORCEMENT DISPARITY

You are a police chief in a major metropolitan city. As part of your commitment to addressing racial disparities in the criminal justice system, and in acknowledgement of changing public attitudes about marijuana use, you have changed your department's policy on enforcing laws against people for smoking marijuana in public. That is, people will no longer be arrested or issued a ticket for simply smoking weed outdoors. However, the sale and distribution of marijuana will be vigorously enforced, as that is, in your mind, a better use of police resources than processing offenders for simple possession of marijuana. This decision is praised by minority group advocates for your forward thinking and courage for attempting to address an obvious abuse of police authority, since minorities are disproportionately arrested for marijuana possession. Others praise your decision as one that will serve to improve police-community relations since it shows that you and the department recognize the public's preferences and are attempting to avoid what is seen as a form of harassment and interference with people's right to exercise individual choice.

However, not everyone is supportive of this policy change. Critics point out that such a stance essentially amounts to giving up on the enforcement of existing laws as well as creating a public health hazard. Some also argue that the decision flies in the face of other laws designed to prevent public health challenges.

Questions to consider:

1. How does such a strategy affect current policy about prohibiting people from smoking cigarettes in many public places?
2. What about contact highs that result from users smoking in public, similar to second hand smoke? Will there be restrictions on where someone can smoke in public, such as near a school?
3. Will such an approach really improve relations between the police and minority communities?

SUMMARY

- Explain why alcohol and drug abuse is a social problem.
    - The American culture of immediate gratification contributes to the problem of drug and alcohol use for recreational purposes.
    - Tobacco, alcohol, and other substances create a sense of euphoria, but the replication of that feelings requires increased amounts of the drug, leading to dependency and addiction.
- Describe the extent of the tobacco use and abuse problem in the United States
    - The rates of use by adults in the United States, particularly cigarettes, have declined in the last ten years, although this trend seems to have leveled out since 2015.
    - Globally, however, tobacco use continues to increase.
    - The US Surgeon General has asserted that tobacco-related deaths and

illnesses in the United States are overwhelmingly caused by cigarettes.

- Describe the extent of the alcohol use and abuse problem in the United States
    - According to the National Institute on Alcohol and Alcohol Abuse, approximately 17 million people age 18 and older have an alcohol use disorder and 1 in 10 children live in a home with a parent who has a drinking problem.
    - The Center for Disease Control and Prevention estimates that about 88,000 people a year die of alcohol-related causes, more than twice the number who die from opiate overdoses.
- Describe the extent of the drug use and abuse problem in the United States
    - According to the National Survey on Drug Use and Mental Health, an estimated two million people suffered from some form of pain reliever use disorder.
    - In 2016, drug overdose in 2016 was the leading cause of death for people under the age of 50.
    - Because of an inability to obtain prescription drugs, users often turn to illegal substances, such as heroin.
    - According to the Centers for Disease Control and Prevention, the rate of heroin-related deaths quadrupled between 2002 and 2013, and people who are addicted to prescription opioids are 40 times more likely to become addicted to heroin.
- Analyze sociological theories as they apply to alcohol and drug abuse.
    - Functionalists would point to the benefits of prescription drugs, such as preventing and curing disease and saving lives.
    - Functionalists would also argue that the abuse of drugs is functional for those who profit from growing, processing, distributing, and selling them.
    - From a conflict perspective, the fact that many drug companies have misled the public and falsified the evidence about the harmful effects of the drugs is an example of how influential these companies can be in shaping public perception as well the narrative about their level of accountability.
    - Symbolic interactionists might examine how certain drugs evoke stronger or more negative reactions than others that might actually be more harmful.
    - Symbolic interactionists would also point to the legalization of marijuana as reflecting a more casual attitude toward the drug.
    - Critical race theory would call attention to the disparities (especially racial) in the prosecution and punishment of offenders.
- Summarize what works in terms of effective solutions to address alcoholism and drug abuse in the United States.
    - Social media campaigns have proven to be effective at reducing tobacco abuse, particularly among young adult smokers.
    - For opioids, some medications have been proven to reduce both the desire for the drug as well as the pain of withdrawal.

- A key challenge to addressing opioid abuse is access to treatment.
- For alcohol abuse, one promising strategy is to limit access to alcohol. Researchers have discovered that there is a relationship between the availability of alcohol in certain location and crime (alcohol outlet density). Reducing the number of places to obtain alcohol in a community has been shown to reduce alcohol abuse as well as other problems, like criminal behavior.

KEY TERMS

12-step model 82
Alcohol counseling 81
Alcohol use disorder 78
Alcohol outlet density 99
Alcoholics Anonymous (AA) 82
Blood alcohol concentration 79
Class action suit 87
Dual use 76
E-cigarettes 73
Legalization of marijuana 88
Mass incarceration of America 95
Opioid addiction 87
Opioid epidemic 83
Opioid Fraud and Abuse Detection Unit 86
Oxycontin 86
Pain reliever use disorder 84
Secondhand smoke exposure 73
Vaping 75

Discussion Questions

1. What do you think is the basis of the debate about legalizing marijuana? How is the debate different from alcohol?
2. How should society respond to the opioid crisis? Should the company that created Oxycodone have been held responsible for misleading the public about its effects, similar to what has happened to the tobacco industry?
3. Do you think the efforts to increase awareness about tobacco use explains the declines in drug use or are there other explanations? If so, what are they?
4. What do you think about the controversy surrounding the 12-step method of treating alcohol addiction? We know this is one of the most popular modalities, but what are some of the challenges of using this model?
5. What level of responsibility should the medical community bear in creating the opioid crisis in this country? Do you think physicians are simply giving the public what they want, or are they creating a culture of addiction?

Learn more with this chapter's digital tools, including Data and Media Literacy Exercises, flashcards, and chapter self-assessments at **www.oup.com/he/mcnamara**.

4

Why Are There So Many Poor People? Poverty and Inequality

LEARNING OBJECTIVES

- Discuss the extent of poverty and social inequality in the United States.
- Discuss the concepts of social class and social inequality in the United States.
- Summarize how poverty is measured and profile the poor.
- Describe the extent of homelessness in the United States and how it relates to poverty.
- Compare and contrast sociological theories to explain poverty.
- Examine current welfare policies relating to the poor.
- Assess successful programs for the poor.

Chapter Outline

Skid Row In downtown Los Angeles, thousands of homeless people congregate in the district known as Skid Row, setting up encampments like this one for shelter.

When it comes to a problem as complex and universal as poverty, it is critical that you examine the claims that are being made and compare them to the empirical data. As you have likely observed in political debates and popular culture as well as your own community and personal experience, there are very different portraits of the problem presented. As we discussed in Chapter 1, there is a tendency to explain poverty from a few overly simplistic perspectives. From the perspective of **personal attribution**, people are believed to be poor because they are lazy, they lack a strong work ethic, or they have a sense of entitlement that prevents them from doing the things that would lead to their success. The other perspective, **systemic attribution**, tends to see the problems of poverty as symptomatic of a much larger set of factors that prevent people from getting the opportunities necessary for success regardless of how motivated they might be.

Regardless of which perspective you prefer, this chapter will challenge you to use critical thinking to consider other possible explanations, some of which you may have dismissed in the past because you were convinced they had little to offer. With a problem as pervasive and complex as poverty, it is important as a social scientist that you consider the entire spectrum of causes and solutions; while there are exceptions to every situation or circumstance, they do not constitute a trend or validation of a particular point of view. Your understanding of poverty also influences your views on social policy. You might not believe that, as an individual, you have much influence at the moment on social policy, but when it comes to poverty you are more powerful than you think. How you vote; how you participate in your community; and how you speak to friends and family about poverty are just as influential as any contributions you might make in the future as a professional working in a social science field.

I hope you will come away from this chapter with the realization that the causes of poverty are not as easily explained as some experts, politicians, or lay persons would make it seem. Finally, this chapter will challenge you to use your sociological imagination to go beyond individual cases and identify both causes of and solutions to the problem of poverty based on the data, not on what conventional wisdom or the media offers.

SOCIOLOGICAL STORY TIME

Fast Facts About Poverty

- According to UNICEF, an estimated 17,000 children under the age of five die every day, mostly from preventable or treatable causes. Nearly half of all deaths in children under age 5 are attributable to undernutrition. (United Nations Development Programme, 2016).
- In 2020, in response to the Covid-19 epidemic, many companies went out of business. The effect on low-wage workers has been devastating. Most workers, but particularly those in low-income jobs, do not get paid unless they are working and often they cannot work from home. In fact, 40 percent of Americans cannot cover an unexpected emergency that cost $400. Without the benefits of paid sick time or health insurance, many low income workers are at higher risk of contracting Covid-19 (Vesoulis, 2020).
- According to the US Department of Agriculture, nearly a quarter of children growing up in rural America were poor in 2016, compared to slightly more than 20 percent in urban areas. The report found the highest concentrations of child poverty, overall, in the Mississippi Delta, Appalachia and on Native American reservations (Booker, 2018).
- A recent report shows that a family of four earning $117,000 a year is considered low-income and qualifies for subsidized housing in San Francisco (Egan, 2018).
- In Los Angeles, where there are an estimated 53,000 homeless people, residents are critical of homeless encampments because it creates a climate of fear, but also oppose new housing for the homeless (Arango, 2018).

THE EXTENT OF POVERTY IN THE UNITED STATES

In 2020, the world was shocked by the devastating effects of the Covid-19 pandemic, which impacted millions of people all over the world and in the United States. As experts have noted, the pandemic has a particularly intense impact on the poor and the working poor (Vesoulis, 2020). The problems experienced by the poor had existed prior to the pandemic, of course, but the pandemic has exacerbated already existing challenges. In this chapter we'll explore the historical roots that created the vulnerabilities in the economic system.

Discussions of poverty in the United States are often hotly debated and emotionally laden. There does not seem to be much of a middle ground. Why? Perhaps because of how we see ourselves. In the United States, our culture promotes the idea that people are in charge of their own destinies. The "American Way" values self-sufficiency, independence, and the notion that if we work hard, we reap the rewards of our efforts (Herberg, 1955). To some extent, there is truth to that notion. However, the data suggests that much of our success goes beyond simply hard work, sacrifice, discipline and dedication. While those things are generally needed to achieve success, there are also systemic factors beyond the control of the individual that influence individual outcomes.

Sociological research has consistently shown that the best predictor of the quality of a person's life is based on the opportunities they receive, or their **life chances**: their education, their networks, their career possibilities, all of which are based on their parents and their social class standing (Griswold, 2014). In other words, individual success almost always has to do with the single greatest factor over which an individual has no control: where, and to whom, one is born.

Such a finding would not sit well with most Americans, who believe in the idea that their success is based on what *they* do, not on what others have done for them. But in order for someone to succeed, they must have access to opportunities: to get into a good college, to make friends and develop networks that will help them later in life; or to obtain resources, such as loans from family members to start a business or buy a house. Americans without certain advantages from birth are denied opportunities like these that many others might take for granted.

Why is this important? If we acknowledge that there are factors beyond the control of the individual that leads to their success, the devastating economic collapse brought about by the 2020 pandemic makes it clear that there are obstacles beyond the control of any individual that prevents them from getting ahead. While you may have heard some successful individuals claim that they "make their own chances," the reality is that opportunity doesn't happen in a vacuum.

The American Way and the American Dream: Middle Class Perceptions of Poverty and the Poor

What, exactly, is the American Dream? If you asked people to define the American Dream, they might say it involves owning your own home; having a good marriage and great kids; a career that you enjoy and pays well; having the leisure time for vacations and the income to buy not just what you need, but what you want. For most Americans, the American Dream also means that no matter what social class you were born into and no matter what your circumstances, there is a chance that—with enough hard work—you can succeed. Historian James Truslow Adams, in his book *The Epic of America*, once described the American dream as a land in which life should be better, and richer and fuller for everyone, with opportunities for people according to their ability. He goes on to describe America as a place where people can prosper regardless of where they started or the obstacles they faced (Adams, 2001).

A problem with this belief is that it reinforces the idea that everyone has the same chance to get ahead and that success depends on the person. That is, if the person succeeds the rewards are justified and if they do not, the person is to blame for their failure. (Hochschild, 1996). What reinforces this belief system are the examples that exist in the United States, where people start off with very little and end up enormously wealthy. However, we generally endorse the sentiment that people can accomplish anything if they try hard enough. These rags-to-riches tales are appealing, and found their most popular form with the writer Horatio Alger.

The American Dream? In the years after World War II, the "American Dream" suggested that every American could, with enough hard work, own a house and a car and raise a family.

HORATIO ALGER MYTHS

Horatio Alger was an author at the turn of the twentieth century who wrote fictional stories about the life and times of youth in New York. The theme for these stories was one in which the main character, a young man who was destitute and orphaned, was nevertheless resourceful and was of good character. As the stories unfold, there was usually some sort of sensational event that put the boy in a situation where, after having done the right thing, he is rewarded for his efforts and uses that opportunity as a springboard to a better life.

These stories were very popular during the twentieth century and continue to be a part of our cultural understanding of life's struggles. We love rags-to-riches stories, where the person begins at a disadvantage, but through hard work, sacrifice, dedication and perseverance, ends up achieving the American Dream. Such stories are inspiring and remind us of the possibilities of what life could bring, if we remained focused on the goal. And because we can often point to real-life Horatio Alger stories, they are not simply a part of cultural lore; they really do occur.

The problem with Horatio Alger stories, and why we refer to them as **Horatio Alger myths,** is not that they are fictional, but that is how our culture chooses to interpret their meaning. Instead of using these dramatic and iconic stories as an inspirational source of motivation or a reminder that anything is possible, we use them as a benchmark: If the main character in the story can achieve success, why can't anyone do the same thing? The problem with such an approach, of course, is that these are rather unique and dramatic examples—the odds of anyone achieving this level of success, particularly given their lack of initial opportunities, are nothing short of remarkable. We should celebrate these moments, of course, and we should note that there is a chance that it could happen, but that is far different from saying everyone should be able to achieve that level of success.

That's like saying because there are students on campus who have earned a perfect 4.0 grade point average, those who do not have one are not as talented, not as willing to work hard, or are not sufficiently disciplined to get those same grades. There are many factors that go into such an extraordinary level of success, as evidenced by the fact that very few students can accomplish this goal. But it doesn't mean that those students who fell short of a perfect score are somehow less worthy, gifted, or dedicated.

Sociological research raises questions about whether the American Dream is a realistic goal for most people in the United States. For instance, Rank, Hirschl, and Foster (2014), in their book *Chasing the American Dream: Understanding What Shapes our Fortunes,* argue that the data suggests the American Dream isn't realistic for most people. They point out that while rag-to-riches stories do occur, it is a rare event—they estimate such situations occur about 8 percent of the time-regardless of how hard someone works or how dedicated they are to their own success. Instead, the vast majority of people who are born poor often remain so as adults—and more than half are going to experience some type of poverty-related event over the course of their lives (Rank, Hirschl, and Foster, 2014).

Another sociological study examined trends in social mobility since 1940. Chetty et al. (2016) found that while the idea of a person doing better economically than their parents is expected, in reality, these trends have not occurred and it is getting increasingly more difficult for people to surpass their parents in terms of wealth and achieving some version of the American Dream. In fact, there are a host of sociological studies and articles that support these findings (see for instance Hoschild, 1996; Semerets, 2016; Tankersley, 2016; Yglesias, 2016; Hauhart, 2015; Halikias and Reeves, 2016).

Let's look at the notion of poverty, social inequality and social class in more depth.

SOCIAL CLASS/SOCIAL INEQUALITY IN THE UNITED STATES

In order to understand the issues surrounding poverty, we have to begin with a discussion of social class. After all, if we are talking about people at the bottom of the social hierarchy, it is reasonable to ask how they were given that designation in the first place. We begin with a brief discussion of what is known as **social stratification**—or the segmenting of people into different groups based on some set of criteria. In our society, we base it on their access to society's valuable resources (Grusky, 2014).

One type of stratification system classifies individuals based on their occupations, incomes and skills. This stratification based on social class is a system that ranks groups of people based on such factors as wealth and power. However, there is a great deal of disagreement among sociologists on how to distinguish groups as well as the boundaries between one group and another. As you recall from Chapter 1, Marx argued that the distinction between people in a social hierarchy was based on whether or not they owned the means of production. In his view, social class was based on economic wealth. This was part of Marx's concept of **economic determinism**; that is, the idea that a person's place in society is based on their standing in the economy. The proletariats and the *lumpenproletariats;* the vagrants, homeless and criminal populations, will always be destined for the lowest ranks of the system because workers never see any of the profits of their efforts (Doob, 2012).

Weber, as you will recall, disagreed with such a narrowly defined view of stratification. He felt that while Marx was correct in that economic wealth plays an important role in a person's place in the stratification system, it is not the only factor. In addition to wealth, access to power and prestige are critical components of stratification as well. That is, one could be seen as highly valued in society even though one does not have great wealth or make a lot of money. For example, scholars, priests, and others with social influence are also given status in society in the absence of money or wealth (Weber, 1922).

Thus, as Bill Kornblum asserts, social class has essentially two dimensions: an objective quality, which can be easily documented and identified (income, wealth, etc.), and a subjective component, which includes assessments of people's contributions and value to society that are not as easily measured, but are still highly valued (Kornblum, Seccombe, and Joseph, 2017).

The result is that when sociologists discuss social class, most sociologists use **socioeconomic status (SES)** as the marker of distinction. Because income is only one indicator of social class, SES is an index comprised of income, education level, and occupational prestige. The unequal distribution of wealth, power and prestige results in what is known as **social inequality.**

Another concept related to social class and inequality is **social mobility**. This involves the movement of people from one social class to another. In the United States, we theoretically have an open class system, which means it is possible for people to move up or down in the social class structure. This is in contrast to closed systems, such as the caste system in India. In a caste system, people are born into a certain social class and remain there regardless of their effort or desire to change it. In fact, the opportunity to move up or down in social classes is what makes America so attractive to people—after all, America is the land of opportunity. But is it? Some data suggests that perhaps there isn't as much social mobility in this country as one might think.

For example, consider a 2017 United Nations report that points out that the United States has the lowest rate of social mobility of any industrialized country. That means that despite the promise that anyone can become rich and successful, the realities are that they typically do not. As the report points out, in 1982 the top 1 percent of adults earned about 27 times more than the bottom 50 percent of adults. Today, the top 1 percent earns 81 times more than the bottom 50 percent (The United Nations, Office of Human Rights 2017).

An understanding of the actual data about social mobility clarifies the ways in which two perspectives about poverty in the United States have shaped both popular opinion and public policy. The first perspective attributes poverty (and the overcoming of poverty) to the individual; the second perspective urges consideration of structures, or systems, over which individuals have little (if any) control.

Personal Attribution

As we have seen, many Americans believe—contrary to evidence—that anyone can be whatever they want to be if they are willing to work hard. Conversely, individuals who don't succeed are often seen as lazy or lacking sufficient motivation for success. These are often called individualistic explanations of poverty; that is, a belief that the poor have only themselves to blame for their situation.

Sociologists describe American society as a **meritocracy**, a system in which you reap the rewards of your efforts. This fits with the general public's ideas of how they achieve the American dream and also what makes those Horatio Alger stories so compelling—they remind us of the possibilities regardless of where we start in life (Pew Research Center, 2014). While the promise of social mobility is a part of American culture, the realities of it are often quite different. There have been periods in American history when a greater proportion of people did enjoy the opportunity to be more successful than their parents.

However, while wealthy people can almost always give advantages to their children that increase their chances of being successful as adults, most Americans tend not to increase their mobility. That is, most people reproduce the social class they are born into, largely because of the limits on the opportunities that exist for people in those classes. If you grow up poor, the odds are that you will likely be poor as an adult (Rank, Hirschil, and Foster, 2014). Nevertheless, people's general understanding of why people are poor are based on the idea that the person fails to succeed due to their lack of discipline, initiative, talent, or willingness to sacrifice to get ahead.

Personal attribution Many Americans believe that personal success is entirely due to character. This may make it easy for people who have steady jobs and reliable incomes to ignore the plight of people in need of both.

Systemic Attribution

Systemic attribution seeks an explanation for poverty in the elements of a system that either keep people from rising out of their situations or by limiting their chances to succeed. For example, the fact that most people who are poor are employed suggests that poverty is not simply a matter of laziness; it is difficult to argue that people are lazy if they are working one or more jobs. Rather, the problem relates to the wages those jobs pay, and the availability of good jobs. These are systemic factors that individuals and families cannot control.

Outsourced and out of work Auto workers in Detroit picket the North American International Auto Show in 2014 to protest the loss of jobs in Detroit's once-flourishing automobile manufacturing economy.

Similarly, if more companies export jobs to other countries to reduce production costs, workers in the United States are impacted. Escalating costs of goods and services also affect the ability of people to stay out of poverty. For example, as the costs of health care in this country continue to rise, and as insurance coverage continues to expect patients to pay more of their care in out-of-pocket expenses, those costs hurt the poor since they have less money for these expenses. Also, child care is a necessity for working parents. As those costs continue to increase, it affects the amount of money available for other necessities and may require the parent(s) to take additional jobs to make ends meet. These are **structural factors** that contribute to poverty and over which individuals have no control.

DEFINING POVERTY

For those at the bottom of the social class structure, the poor, we must begin with a qualification about the intensity of the experience. Poverty in its most extreme form, where people do not have enough food to eat, clothes to wear, or access to the most basic health and education services, is called **absolute poverty**. When people in the United States talk about poverty, they don't usually refer to its absolute forms. In this country, most people do not experience the level of poverty that comprises the lack of basic necessities. Instead, we often use what is known as **a relative definition of poverty.** That is, poverty is understood in reference or relation to some standard that is used to compare everyone. While we may have millions of people who are living in poverty in this country, the poorest ones have a far higher standard of living than anyone in developing countries.

The idea of programs like Finland's basic universal income scheme is a different approach than what is typical in the United States, where having a job is not only an identity marker, it is a requirement for full participation in society. At the same time, however, the notion of universal income in the United States is being tried in places like Stockton, California. The outcome of this approach, offered on a much smaller scale than what was attempted in Finland, is unclear. Universal Basic Income gained some national attention during the 2020 Democratic presidential campaign, as candidate Andrew Yang's "Freedom Dividend" drove the idea into mainstream conversations

GLOBAL PERSPECTIVES

Finland's Universal Basic Income

The population of Finland is about 5 million. Despite being small, Finland is well-known for its impressive education and national social welfare system. In fact, the poverty rate in Finland is among the lowest in the world, behind only Denmark, the Czech Republic and Iceland. Finland's economy is open and transparent. It has well-maintained laws and a very low tolerance for corruption. While the economy struggled in the early part of the 2000s, by 2015 it was growing again. Given its emphasis on social programs to benefit its citizens and economic growth, particularly as its population ages and the country is witnessing a decline in productivity in certain industries, Finland began an experiment in 2018. Known as **Universal Basic Income,** Finland's pilot program, which was supposed to last for two years, was designed to pay 2,000 randomly-selected citizens unemployment benefits of €560 every month. The experiment aimed to limit bureaucracy, reduce poverty, and increase employment. Critics argued that the program would encourage laziness, since people will be receiving a paycheck without working (Braunstein, 2017).

An assessment of the program in 2020 generally showed that the experiment was a failure. However, there were several factors that need to be considered before dismissing the idea of universal income as a strategy. First, in the case of Finland, the amount of money allocated for the program was far less than originally promised, thereby limiting the number of people who could participate in it, as well as how much money each subject actually received. The prime minister of Finland also accelerated the timeline for implementation of the experiment, leading researchers to alter the original protocols. An added challenge was the fact that the subjects in the experimental group had the stipend tied to the benefits they were already receiving, such as unemployment compensation and housing subsidies. The end result was that the monthly stipend for those subjects only amounted to about an increase of $50. Complicating the results further, the response rate for the survey of subjects was very low, thereby reducing the recorded number of people who actually found jobs during the study, not because fewer people looked for work, but because fewer of them completed the survey. In the end, it isn't clear whether universal income as a tool to address poverty and unemployment in Finland would be effective, largely because of methodological challenges found in the study (Bendix, 2020).

(Jagannathan, 2020). However, changes to current welfare policies—whereby an increasing number of programs, including Medicaid, Food Stamps, Section 8 housing, and other "entitlements," are requiring participants to work as a condition of their benefits—suggests the issue is far from settled.

In the United States, there is a strong belief that if one is able-bodied and over the age of 18, the government owes the person nothing in terms of benefits; that person needs to go out and get a job and make a life for themselves. However, at the same time, we have programs that align with the notion of a basic income program. Think of Social

Security; where people sign up and they get a check for the rest of their lives. Or consider the existing idea of Medicare for everyone, already a reality with a large percentage of Americans getting free health care in this country. In higher education, many states are experimenting with free tuition for residents who wish to attend college. All of these ideas are based on the same idea of a Universal Basic Income.

An idea like a Universal Basic Income is also more holistic and simpler to implement. Unlike the United States, which has particular programs for different needs (e.g., Medicare and Medicaid for health care; food stamps for the hungry; and Section 8 housing for the unhoused), the notion of a basic income for everyone resolves many of those issues in one step. This is what is giving the idea traction in other countries, even those who have a manageable poverty problem like Finland (Lowery, 2017).

The Poverty Line

Official definitions of poverty in the United States are based on a formula which uses the cost of a minimum family food budget, assuming that an average low-income family spends about one-third of its total income on food. If we multiply that cost by three, we obtain an income threshold to determine eligibility for government assistance. The formula also takes into account the number of people in the household and for changes in the cost of food (Fisher, 1997).

This measure was developed in 1965 by Mollie Orshansky, an economist who worked for the Social Security Administration, who argued that food consumption was a good measure of a person's overall standard of living. There is considerable debate today as to whether this is a good indicator of poverty. For example, critics of the current model argue that if benefits (such as Medicaid and subsidized housing) provided to poor people are included in the calculation of income, then the extent of poverty is much lower than its current levels. This means some people might be classified above the poverty line (Fisher, 1997).

The current model also has multiple poverty thresholds. While most media accounts talk about the income threshold for a family of four, it is important to recognize that poverty thresholds vary according to the number of people in a household. Thus, there are many poverty thresholds, but they are all calculated the same way (Table 4.1). In Table 4.1, thc first column on the left provides the size of the family, based on whether or not the person is under the age of 65 as a single person. There are two income thresholds based on this factor. The next column consists of a family of two people, and whether there is someone in the household under the age of 65. Like the first example, there are income thresholds based on age of the householder, as well as if they have a child under the age of 18 in the home. Moving down the column, you can see the size of the family and how it corresponds to the number of children under the age of 18 living in the household. For four people in a family of two children, the income threshold is $24,339, which was the poverty threshold in 2016 for a family of four.

Table 4.1 2016 Poverty Thresholds by Size of Family Unit Poverty Thresholds for 2016

Size of Family Unit	Weighted Average Thresholds	Related Children under 18 Years								
		None	One	Two	Three	Four	Five	Six	Seven	Eight or More
One person (unrelated individual):	12,228									
Under age 65	12,486	12,486								
Aged 65 and older	11,511	11,511								
Two people:	15,569									
Householder under age 65	16,151	16,072	16,543							
Householder aged 65 and older	14,522	14,507	16,480							
Three people	19,105	18,774	19,318	19,337						
Four people	24,563	24,755	25,160	24,339	24,424					
Five people	29,111	29,854	30,288	29,360	28,643	28,205				
Six people	32,928	34,337	34,473	33,763	33,082	32,070	31,470			
Seven people	37,458	39,509	39,756	38,905	38,313	37,208	35,920	34,507		
Eight people	41,781	44,188	44,578	43,776	43,072	42,075	40,809	39,491	39,156	
Nine people or more	49,721	53,155	53,413	52,702	52,106	51,127	49,779	48,561	48,259	46,400

Source: (Source: University of California, Davis, Center for Poverty Research, 2016).

Some argue that the existing formula used to calculate the poverty threshold underestimates the number of poor people. For instance, when the poverty line was initially created, the calculation resulted in an income threshold that was about half of the median income of Americans. However, since then, with the increased costs of food, child care, and housing, not only are there more poor people than officially counted, but these families experience considerably more poverty than those who were counted in the 1960s.

In addition, critics argue that taxes, work-related expenses and out-of-pocket health-care costs should not be included in the income calculation because this money can't be used to purchase necessities. Nor does the calculation take into account the cost of living in different parts of the country. In places like New York City or San Francisco, where the cost of living is extraordinarily high, the income threshold does not reflect the actual costs to live there—only what a person makes in terms of income.

Finally, the poverty threshold does not address the **working poor**, who are above the income level but are still poor. These individuals and families earn more than what would trigger assistance, but not enough to significantly improve their quality of life. In fact, their earnings are just enough to disqualify them from government assistance.

As of 2019, according to the Brookings Institution, about 40 percent of those living in poverty who were of working age were labor force participants. In general, the working poor constitute about 13 percent of the population. Members of this group are generally not well-educated; most do not have a high school diploma and have low literacy rates. They also tend to lack work skills that would likely result in a well-paying job. The types of jobs the working poor occupy are usually minimum wage jobs, housekeeping, day labor, and agricultural or landscape work. Because some of the work is seasonal or sporadic, this group tends to have higher rates of unemployment than other workers (Bauer, Moss, and Shambaugh, 2019).

PROFILING THE POOR

The federal poverty line is an income threshold below which a family would be eligible for government assistance, or **welfare.** In 2019, the poverty threshold was $25,750 for a family of four (U.S. Department of Health and Human Services, 2019). How many people fall below the poverty line? In 2019, 12.7 percent of the population, or 38.1 million people, were considered to be living in poverty (Bauer, Moss, and Shambaugh, 2019). During the past forty years, the percentage of people living in poverty has never dropped below 10 percent.

Contrary to some political and cultural narratives, most poor people are employed. In fact, if an individual works full-time at a minimum wage job (assuming the federal minimum wage is $7.25 per hour), those earnings still result in an income threshold below

Just Get a Job, But Can You Really Live on Minimum Wage?

The federal minimum wage has never really been a mechanism that pulls people out of poverty. So if the minimum wage puts people above the poverty line, can people realistically expect to make it, even at a basic level? The data tells us that a full-time minimum wage job is not enough for a person to support themselves and a family. This means that either both parents must work (which triggers child-care costs and medical expenses) or the primary provider must work more than one job to make ends meet. But let's do the math and look at this reality in practical terms (Table 4.2).

Table 4.2 Life On Minimum Wage

Monthly Wages:[1]	Monthly Expenses:
$1,160	$950 Housing[2] $114 Utilities[3] $844 Child care[4] $756 Transportation[5] $731 Food[6]
Total Monthly Income: $1,160/$2,320	Total Monthly Expenses: $3,395
	Difference: -$2,235/–$1,075

[1] Based on the current minimum wage of $7.25 per hour and working 40 hours per week.

[2] Based on national average for a two bedroom apartment. https://smartasset.com/mortgage/what-is-the-cost-of-living-in-south-carolina

[3] National Average of utilities for a family of four. https://smartasset.com/mortgage/what-is-the-cost-of-living-in-south-carolina

[4] According to Care.com, the average child-care cost is about $10,468 per year. This is for center-based child care and costs approximately are $211 per week per child. https://mic.com/articles/182482/cost-of-kids-how-much-child-care-costs-on-average-in-2017-and-the-most-affordable-us-states#.o3Ku6hSME Let's also remember that this amount is per child. In a family of four, the costs of child care in this example double since there are two children in the family that require care.

[5] This includes the costs of a vehicle or public transportation. See https://bettermoneyhabits.bankofamerica.com/en/saving-budgeting/average-household-monthly-expenses

[6] According to the USDA's Center for Nutrition Policy and Promotion, the average cost for a low-cost meal plan for a family of four was $731.20 in 2017. A liberal food plan, which has more elaborate meals, was $1,093 for a family of four for a month.

Bear in mind, these are only the basic costs; there are usually other expenses involved, including health insurance, which can easily add another $300 or more to the monthly budget. It also means the family takes no vacations, does not purchase any birthday or Christmas presents, or any of a host of other expenses that are part of having a family. It also does not take into account taking a sick day (since most of the minimum wage jobs do not have sick time or vacation days), nor does it provide anything for improving one's situation, such as tuition for college or retirement contributions. These costs are national averages; while expenses in some parts of the country may be lower, they are also much higher in major metropolitan areas. This budget provides housing, food, child care and transportation to and from work; that's it.

Let's imagine that both spouses worked full-time in minimum wage jobs. Assuming both spouses work full-time, that figure increases to $2,320 per month, which is still almost $1,100 short of making ends meet, again, before taxes. While the family might get most of that back at the end of the year, taxes are still taken out of each paycheck, leaving less available to pay bills. And remember, if both parents work, their combined yearly income is $30,160, which puts them above the poverty line of $24,620 for a family of four.

the poverty line if that individual is trying to support a family. To be clear, many states and municipalities have set much higher minimum wages for workers, but generally speaking, many employers use the federal minimum to pay workers. Because of the extensive use of the federal minimum wage, more than 80 percent of low-income minimum wage workers, even if they are working full-time, are not earning enough to afford basic necessities. In response, some people take additional jobs just to make ends meet, but even then the wages aren't always enough to keep up with rising costs of living (Bauer, Moss, and Shambaugh, 2019; Gould and Cooke, 2015).

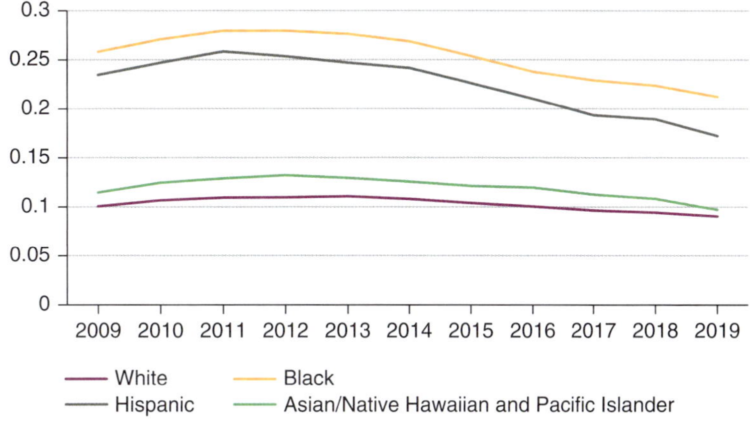

Figure 4.1 Poverty rate by race/ethnicity, 2009–2019 Data are for the total population and may not sum to totals due to rounding. Estimates based on the 2008–2019 American Community Survey, 1-Year Estimates. Source: Kaiser Family Foundation

Poverty is not equally distributed in the population. Poverty is higher among the elderly, the disabled, and for children as well as single-parent families. In fact, about one-third of female-headed families are below the poverty line (Kaiser Family Foundation, 2019). One reason for this is because of the decreases in government assistance to low-income mothers and their children. For example, benefits from the Supplemental Nutrition Assistance Program (SNAP) helps more than 47 million low-income Americans afford nutritious food each month. Nearly three-quarters of SNAP recipients are in families, most often single mothers (Dickinson, 2019). Poverty is also unequally distributed by race (Figure 4.1).

In 2018, Congress significantly cut the funding for the SNAP program, which would have resulted in reducing or eliminating benefits for more than 2 million people. It would make significant overall cuts to SNAP and put in place additional work requirements as a condition of receiving the benefits. While those funding cuts were rejected, President Trump issued an order to change the eligibility requirements for the program that resulted in fewer people receiving the benefits (Dickinson, 2019).

Studies have shown that children raised in households without enough nutritious food are more likely to suffer poor health, face deficits in cognitive development, and exhibit behavioral and emotional problems. SNAP already requires working-age adults (with limited exceptions) to register for work and accept a job if offered. There are a host of concerns about these new regulations, particularly as they relate to the expanded work requirements and the consequences to children if parents fail to comply with them (Center for Budget Analysis and Policy Priorities, 2018).

Challenges of child care Although most industrial nations subsidize child care for most families (or even provide it for free), in the United States families are on their own when it comes to arranging and paying for safe, high-quality child care like that provided by this Detroit day care center.

Children and the Poor

In the United States, approximately 21 percent of children live in poverty. An important element to understanding child poverty relates to single-parent families (National Center for Children in Poverty, 2018). In fact, the United States leads all affluent nations in the number of children allowed to live in poverty. Most other industrial nations provide assistance to low-income families and their children, including quality child care. In the United States, in contrast, child care is a major obstacle for many low-income mothers who want to work and could be successfully employed. For example, many of the available jobs for single mothers sometimes have split shifts or evening hours, which make finding and affording child care quite difficult. There are a host of consequences for children who experience poverty, such as poor physical health, mental health issues, poor academic performance, greater risk of dropping out of school, and a greater likelihood of criminal activity (National Center for Children in Poverty, 2018).

HOMELESSNESS: THE OTHER SIDE OF POVERTY

The challenges faced by the poor often involve structural factors, regardless of work ethic or desire to succeed. At an extreme, the problems for the poor can lead them to bouts of homelessness. According to The National Alliance to End Homelessness, on average there were 553,742 people who experienced homelessness on any given night in the United States in 2017 (National Alliance to End Homelessness, 2018). While there are many different ways to define homelessness, the most common one used is a person who is not "sheltered," meaning having a temporary bed to sleep in.

Like the poor, the homeless population is not a homogeneous group. There are many different subsets of the homeless population, from individuals to families with children as well as veterans, the mentally ill, and the chronically homeless. Similarly, there are many reasons people end up becoming homeless. Unfortunately, like the discussions of poverty, the general public knows and understands very little about the homeless population or the reasons for their plight.

A Profile of the Homeless

In a 2018 study by the National Alliance to End Homelessness, of the 553,742 people who were homeless on any given night in 2017, about 67 percent, or 369,081, were single adults and about half of those were considered *sheltered*. The remaining

48 percent were considered unsheltered. Of the single adults, about 61 percent were men and 39 percent were women. For this group, the primary reason for their experiences with homelessness is the lack of affordable and available housing (National Alliance to End Homelessness, 2018).

Figure 4.2 Changes in housing and wages Source: Harvard Joint Center for Housing Studies

The affordable housing crisis is especially serious in major urban areas. As the cost of housing continues to increase beyond people's capacity to pay for it (because wages, as we have seen, have not kept up with the cost of living), people and families are often faced with some extraordinary choices (Figure 4.2).

This is not a recent phenomenon either; The Economic Policy Institute estimates that since 1973, wages have only grown about 10 percent, from $16.74 per hour, to $17.86 in 2016. In comparison, the average cost of a new home in 1970 was $23,400 while the costs in 2016 were $289,500, a twelve-fold increase. Even adjusting for inflation, it is easy to see that wages have not kept up with housing costs (Figure 4.3). The problem then, is that housing costs continue to rise while wages have not, and this makes it difficult for virtually everyone to make ends meet (Hamm, 2014; Siddiqui, 2018).

Other circumstances can precipitate homelessness. Life events, such as losing a job, the death of a partner, or a health emergency, can result in the person being displaced. Contrary to popular belief, most adults who experience homeless do so for a short period of time and it does not occur on a regular basis. Another misconception about homelessness is that the reason for the problem stems from substance abuse or mental illness. While this is more likely to be true of the chronically homeless, discussed below, most homeless people do not attribute their circumstances to these factors.

Another segment of the homeless population is the chronically homeless. While most people's experiences with homelessness are brief and can sometimes occur more than once, there is a segment of the homeless population, perhaps 25 percent, whose experiences with homelessness last longer and occur more frequently. These individuals have serious emotional and physical disabilities and once they become homeless, it is difficult for them to secure permanent housing. According to a 2018 report by the National Alliance to End Homelessness, about 70 percent of chronically homeless people live on the street, in parks or in cars or other structures not designed for long-term living, such as tents. That said, the number of chronically homeless individuals has decreased by about 25 percent since 2007 (National Alliance to End Homelessness, 2018).

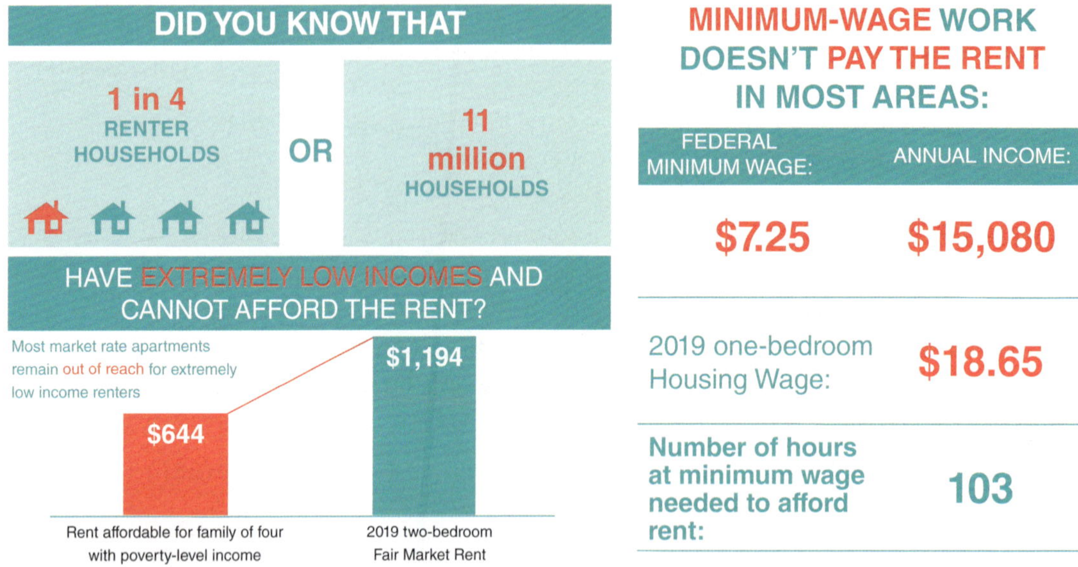

Figure 4.3. Out of reach Source: National Low Income Housing Coalition

Families with children make up another segment of the homeless population. According to one estimate, this group made up about 35 percent of the homeless population in 2017, which included about 185,000 people in families or approximately 58,000 family households. Nearly 17,000 were families living in a car, on the street, or another place not intended as housing. During the previous year, about 500,000 people in families made use of shelters and transitional housing programs; of that number, almost two-thirds were children, many of whom are under the age of six (National Alliance to End Homelessness, 2018).

Homeless families Hundreds of thousands of people in families are without permanent housing in the United States. Even if they stay overnight in shelters, many have no choice but to spend the day on the street.

The reasons for this group's experiences with homelessness are similar to those of single adults: the loss of a job, an unexpected expense, or a medical emergency. In addition, conflict with a family member or domestic partner can also trigger an experience with homelessness and result in the mother and children seeking assistance from social service agencies as they are displaced from the home.

The impact of homelessness is particularly taxing on children. The research suggests that children who experience homelessness have higher levels of emotional and behavioral problems, are more likely to encounter academic difficulties, including repeating a grade, lower academic performance, and more likely to be expelled or drop out of school. Homeless children are also at greater risk of serious health problems and more likely to be separated from their families (National Alliance to End Homelessness, 2018).

Veterans make up about 9 percent of the homeless population, according to the National Alliance to End Homelessness. The largest percentage of this group appear to be veterans of the Vietnam War, but there are also veterans from recent conflicts, such as in Iraq or Afghanistan, are also seen as members of the population. Some experts argue the experiences of combat are likely the main reasons for this trend, where soldiers suffer from injuries such as traumatic brain injuries, PTSD, or other emotional disorders (National Alliance to End Homelessness, 2018; McNamara, 2008).

Another explanation may involve the role of the military in a positive way. To explore this in more detail one must look at the person's life prior to their military service. If they were chronically poor and without job prospects, it may be that they would have become homeless had they not joined the military. Thus, while they were not homeless while serving their country, when they returned from military service, they may have ended up in the same set of circumstances and difficulties. In this way, the military experience did not necessarily cause them to be homeless; rather it may have actually prevented the person from being homeless while they were in the military (McNamara, 2008).

SOCIOLOGICAL THEORY AND POVERTY

With a basic understanding of the distinctions between individual and structural explanations of poverty, inequality, and barriers to social mobility, we turn now to the application of theoretical paradigms further investigate the nature of poverty. Specifically, we will look at how structural functionalism, conflict theory, symbolic interactionism, and postmodernism help us to understand the challenges of poverty in society.

Functionalism and Poverty

Recall that structural functionalism focuses on the social order where, as a result of consensus, the elements of society work synergistically to contribute to its overall growth and survival. One way to apply a functionalist perspective to the problem of poverty is to consider the ways in which different kinds of work are compensated in our society. The assumption is that some roles require more training and a time commitment than others, and therefore the incentives offered (such as a high salary) for performing more difficult jobs should be higher. This assumes, of course, that there is consensus about which types of work are most in need of incentivizing, either in terms of the scarcity of people wanting to perform that job or in the qualifications needed to do so.

However, while functionalism helps explain the existing system of stratification, it does not really explain the structural inequality that persists as a result. Is it really functional, for example, that wealth is so unequally divided among members of society? While we might agree that physicians are important to society, and their salaries reflect the years of training and dedication to their profession, how do we explain Hollywood entertainers or athletes, who make millions of dollars a year? This is particularly true when compared to trash collectors, store clerks, food service workers, or others who earn minimum wage, but whose roles in society are important and easily identified. So while functionalism explains the differences in the labor market, and that some people are poor, it does not offer an explanation of how such a system developed or continues. It also offers a weak argument to explain the value and purpose of the poor. That is, functionalism argues that the purpose of the poor helps society by having a ready supply of people to perform low-paying jobs and to serve as consumers of cheap and inferior products.

Conflict Theory and Poverty

Explanations of poverty from the conflict perspective draw heavily from Marx's ideas about the exploitation of workers because of the pursuit of profit in capitalism. That is, those who own the means of production will reap the profit from the selling of commodities on the market place, while at the same time trying to reduce the costs of production by paying workers as little as possible. Such a situation means that there will inevitably be a large divide between the haves and the have-nots, and that those individuals who have access to resources are the ones who are given many more life chances than those who do not.

For conflict theorists like Marx, the problems of the poor are embedded in the control of the economy. The reasons for poverty stem from the fact that workers are underpaid, undervalued, and do not share equally in the profits that come from selling commodities on the market. Also consistent with Marx's ideas of control of scarce resources, those who benefit from the status quo will use their economic, social, and political power to prevent others from acquiring any similar influence. The elite will also control the legal system to uphold promotion of their interests while suppressing change or revolt. Thus, the exploitation that occurs because of a capitalist society means some people are winners and some are losers: the proletariat are the losers since they make an equal contribution to the success of a commodity but do not share in the profits.

A place at the table Many people lost their jobs during the Covid-19 pandemic of 2020 and had to rely on private charity for groceries. Here, volunteers with the Central Texas Food Bank distribute food parcels to people in need.

Cultural Explanations

A variation on the personal attribution perspective of poverty involves cultural explanations. These are often framed as **a culture of poverty** attribution. Some people argue that what keeps people poor is not public policy or some other systemic attribution, but a set of attitudes, values, and beliefs that do not promote mainstream societal values about self-sufficiency and independence. Anthropologist Oscar Lewis studied poor Hispanics in the United States and concluded that the working poor, because they were excluded from mainstream opportunities for success, developed a way of life that allowed them to cope in world designed for the middle-class. An important feature of this adaptation was the notion of **fatalism**, which means people accept their fate rather than trying to improve their situations. The culture of poverty also promotes the notion of **present orientation**—living for the moment rather than the future or spending money now rather than saving it. This is in contrast to middle-class values, which promote **deferred gratification**. Lewis argued that once this culture is formed, it is passed from one generation to the next, resulting a reluctance of people to change their perceptions and orientations (Lewis, 1966).

The culture of poverty therefore attributes the problem not directly to individuals, but to a type of collective approach to living that accepts one's situation. One of the implications of this position, of course, is that society should do little to address the poverty problem since nothing will work as long as the culture of poverty operates in some communities. Another problem with the culture of poverty perspective is that it does not take into account the structural factors that existed before people developed an approach to cope with it.

William J. Wilson rejected the idea of the culture of poverty, claiming that it is a label that does not fit in many instances. There are long periods of poverty for individuals and families that have long-term consequences for children and grandchildren, but poor people share the same values and have the same aspirations as more affluent Americans. The difference is that their ability to achieve these goals is diminished by their life experiences. For Wilson, the issue isn't a culture that promotes complacency, or even necessarily that race is the most important factor in explaining poverty. Rather the issue is more about social class and how the structure of the economy and labor market perpetuates a chronic underclass of people (Wilson, 1987). Sociologist Herbert Gans also disagrees with the culture of poverty assertion, primarily because it assumes that poor people are a homogeneous group. Gans (1995) points out that some families have been poor for generations and others are only periodically poor, so it is unrealistic to make sweeping assessments of the impact of cultural values on an entire group of people. Gans also argues that the influence of the value system of a group of people is only one factor in explaining their behavior (Gans, 1995).

Postmodernism and Poverty

While not an explanation of poverty per se, postmodernism has something to offer in terms of explaining social class. Grusky (2018) explored Pierre Bourdieu's notion of **social reproduction**, which is the process and consequences of passing social class from one generation to the next. Bourdieu argues that children learn to acquire habits, ideas, and expectations from their parents, what he calls **cultural capital** (Grusky, 2018). In other words, cultural capital provides guidance on how institutions function and how best to navigate the world to one's advantage. Cultural capital can be seen in how children approach learning and studying in school, particularly their work habits. Cultural capital also shapes how others see a person.

For example, most employers place significant importance on "fit" when hiring an employee. Because a job candidate needs to be able to work well with others, the more the candidate has in common with other employees, the greater the likelihood that they will be successful. Candidates who understand how to present themselves and display a certain level of sophistication, along with an ability to adapt to different environments and people, will likely be preferred compared to someone who is equally talented but lacking the same cultural background and social cues.

People who lack cultural capital are at a distinct disadvantage in many social contexts, even if they try to develop or acquire more of it. People who grow up in low-income neighborhoods, for example, may not be able to circumvent some of the markers of their social class; this can be taken as a lack of sophistication or adaptability. Accents, the use of certain words or phrases, a familiarity with certain types of art or music, even the kinds of sports one follows can mark one as either possessing or lacking certain types of cultural capital.

HOW WE HELP THE POOR: WELFARE AND SOCIAL POLICY

While the reasons for the existence of poverty are complex and can be controversial, the issues become even more challenging when the discussion turns to what we should do about the problem. What is society's obligation to help the poor? One school of thought suggests that government assistance gives people a chance to become self-sufficient and productive members of society. Another school of thought contends that welfare and government assistance create a sense of dependency, ruins the incentive to become self-sufficient, and creates other problems for society.

How Did We Get Here?

The economic success seen in the United States during the late 19th and 20th centuries led to increasing class disparity and economic challenges for the poor. So acute was this problem that experts argue the uncontrolled capitalistic model actually contributed to the Great Depression. This nearly catastrophic event in American history resulted in the creation of a modern welfare state.

To address the growing gap between the rich and the poor, many politicians and business leaders felt that capitalism could expand if people in this country could be promised a basic standard of living. The resulting welfare state primarily benefitted the White middle-class with housing assistance and educational opportunities. The system also helped the poor through Social Security, stipends for single parents and the disabled, and a minimum wage for workers. Later programs like food stamps, public housing and health care in the form of Medicare and Medicaid provided even more comprehensive assistance for the poor (Axim and Stern, 2005).

In the aftermath of the Great Depression, between 1933 and 1939 President Franklin D. Roosevelt created a series of programs called the **New Deal**. This included programs such as Social Security, unemployment compensation, and Aid to Families with Dependent Children (AFDC), which is now called **Temporary Assistance to Needy Families** (TANF). These programs were intended as a safety net for those who found themselves facing adversity: the loss of a job, little in the way of savings, or some other problem. The safety net was designed to give them a chance to get back on their feet (Axim and Stern, 2005).

In the 1960s, President Johnson declared a "**War on Poverty.**" This led to programs including Medicaid, Medicare, Head Start (which promotes health and education for poor children), food-purchasing assistance (food stamps, now known as the Supplemental Nutrition Assistance Program), and job training. The "war on poverty" metaphor was significant since it attempted to attack poverty on many different fronts: hunger, health care, income, and job training. In fact, one could argue that this was one of the most comprehensive efforts ever to address the poverty problem in this country. The evidence seemed to indicate that it worked: between 1960 and 1970, the poverty rated had declined from 22 percent to about 12 percent, the sharpest decline ever recorded (Axim and Stern, 2005).

By the 1980s, with a more conservative White House and Congress, many politicians began to question the effectiveness of welfare programs. The argument was that despite years of efforts to eliminate poverty, the problems remained. Conservatives further held that welfare programs created a permanent class of people who were dependent upon the government for support. These critics of welfare also argued it undermined d individual incentive to find a job and become self-sufficient (Trattner, 1999).

The general public supported this idea, perhaps because of a mistaken if widely-held belief that welfare constitutes a large part of the federal government budget. In reality, then and now, safety net programs generally consist of only about 9 percent of the federal budget, or about $357 billion. This compares to about 15 percent for defense spending and the War on Terror, along with 24 percent for Social Security, 26 percent on Medicare and related programs, and 7 percent for interest on the federal debt (Figure 4.4; Center on Budget Analysis and Policy Priorities, 2019).

Nevertheless, the argument by conservatives was that the funds used to support these programs could be dedicated elsewhere to stimulate the economy and get

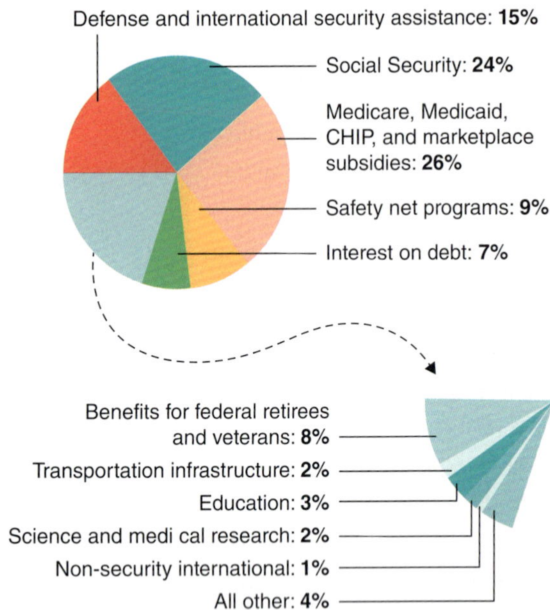

Figure 4.4 US Budget Priorities Most of the US budget goes toward defense, Social Security, and major health programs. Source: 2017 figures from the Office of Management and Budget, FY 2019 Historical Tables

people back to work. Massive cuts to welfare programs were seen in the 1980s under the administration of Republican president Ronald Reagan (Trattner, 1999).

By the 1990s, Democratic president Bill Clinton was able to achieve a reform of the welfare system. With unusual bipartisan support, Congress passed the Personal Responsibility and Work Reconciliation Act in 1996, also known as the Welfare Reform Act. **Welfare reform** ended the notion of entitlements for welfare recipients. As the name of the legislation implies, it required recipients of government assistance to take personal responsibility for themselves by getting a job and becoming self-sufficient. (Axim and Stern, 2005).

Under welfare reform, the federal government allowed states to design their own welfare programs according to the needs of their own populations and situations. To fund these initiatives, block grants were used. A block grant is an allocation of money given to states for a specific purpose. In this particular instance, the grants contained several caveats: welfare recipients were given a lifetime eligibility of benefits of five years, with consecutive benefits for no more than 24 months at a time. This means that people on welfare had five years to reach independence, after which point their benefits would be terminated, and could only be on welfare for two years at a time. The idea was to encourage people to find jobs and work their way out of poverty. By 2003, Congress added further restrictions to the law, requiring a larger percentage of recipients to take jobs and work longer hours. While states can exempt some individuals from these parameters, the emphasis has been on pushing people off welfare and into jobs (Axim and Stern, 2005).

What has been the result of such a change in policy? Some supporters of welfare reform point to the decreased numbers of people on welfare as evidence that welfare reform has worked. To be fair, if the goal was to reduce the number of welfare recipients, then perhaps the program has been successful. By one estimate at least 5 million people are no longer receiving welfare benefits as of 2015 (Administration for Children and Families, 2015).

However, evidence suggests that moving people from welfare to work does not increase their income levels, particularly if the jobs people obtain are low-paying minimum wage jobs. In other words, poverty levels have not changed, even though fewer people are receiving welfare benefits. Why? The main reasons are structural: increased costs of child care, health insurance, and transportation make it impractical for people to be able to sustain the expenses while living on a minimum wage job.

In the book *$2 a day: Living on Almost Nothing in America,* Edin and Shaefer (2016) report that while there has been a 75 percent decline in welfare recipients since 1996, the number of Americans living in absolute poverty has increased to 1.5 million families. The problem became most acute during the Great Recession (2007–2009), when well-paying full-time jobs were difficult for most people to obtain, along with the fallout in the mortgage and banking industries. The upshot of the latter event was that many people were forced into bankruptcy and/or homelessness. So how have people been able to support their families? People have resorted to a wide range of strategies, including making greater use of food pantries and soup kitchens, donating plasma, living in cars or with friends and family—in short, they are not getting by—despite a robust economy and low unemployment (Edin and Shaefer, 2016).

What have been the consequences of welfare reform? Now that there is no single welfare program, each state has their own set of policies. This diversity makes a thorough analysis of which particular set of work support, financial incentives, waivers and work responsibilities is the most effective difficult to achieve. As you can see, the number of people removed from welfare rolls does not tell the entire story.

As Edin and Shaefer point out, about 40 million Americans live in poverty, nearly half of those in **deep poverty** (those whose income is half of the poverty line). The United States has the highest child poverty rates (25 percent) in the developed world. Then there are the extremely poor who live on less than $2 per day per person and don't have access to basic human services such as sanitation, shelter, education and health care—often referred to as **extreme poverty.** These are people who cannot find work, who have used up their five-year lifetime limit on assistance, and do not qualify for any other programs (Edin and Shaefer, 2016).

Welfare is not simply a cash subsidy offered to people who are poor. In the United States, welfare consists of a series of programs designed to meet particular needs that poor people encounter. For example, the SNAP (food stamp) program addresses hunger; Section 8 provides housing subsidies; Medicaid addresses the costs related to health care; and Temporary Assistance to Needy Families (TANF) provides cash for expenses not covered by these other programs. However, those benefits are offset by other expenses incurred by working families, such as child care. The ways in which some benefits are used can actually be detrimental to families trying to climb out of poverty. For example, if a family uses TANF money to pay for housing costs, the reductions in benefits coupled with rising housing prices puts them at risk. To illustrate, according to the Department of Housing and Urban Development' Fair Market Rents, the average monthly TANF disbursement for a family of three is less than half the average rent in 30 states. Because affordable housing is out of reach for so many people, particularly the poor, a family that doesn't qualify for subsidized housing is likely to find that the TANF benefit inadequate for housing. Instead, they must resort to living in substandard conditions, live with friends and relatives, or become homeless (U.S. Department of Housing and Urban Development, 2020).

WHAT WORKS? EFFECTIVE SOLUTIONS TO POVERTY

The topic of poverty is controversial in the United States, largely because of the persistence of the personal attribution perspective (that is, people are poor because they are lazy or lack a work ethic). Unfortunately, such beliefs continue to translate into social policies to that prove ineffective against poverty. Often, these policies follow political lines, where conservatives often believe that public assistance programs enable the poor and create an atmosphere of entitlement that keeps people from getting out of poverty. While these schools of thought continue to exist, the 2020 Covid-19 pandemic is having an enormous effect on our understanding of poverty and the issues that are related to it, and these are forcing politicians and the public to reshape policy solutions.

The pandemic has also resulted in the need for dramatic changes that require an unprecedented level of flexibility and understanding about poverty. It may also cause many in Congress to reconsider long-standing positions about the structural factors that create vulnerabilities millions of people are experiencing because of the virus. This includes considerations such as national paid sick leave, healthcare, entitlement programs, and other issues.

Some programs have been proven effective at keeping people out of poverty. This is true for the poor in general as well as those in deep poverty. The question of whether or not these programs are effective is not disputed; the data is fairly self-evident. The challenge is found in convincing policymakers and the general public that such programs should be continued, expanded, or curtailed.

For instance, according to the Center for Budget Analysis and Policy Priorities, more so than any other program, Social Security is and has remained one of the most effective programs to prevent poverty. This single program kept nearly 26 million American above the poverty line in 2016 (Center for Budget Analysis and Policy Priorities, 2019). While Social Security is critical to the nearly 17 million senior citizens who rely on it, there are also nearly 2 million children who are directly or indirectly benefitting from the program. Children can be eligible for Social Security benefits through survivor payments if a working parent has died or if a family member retires or goes on disability (Center for Budget Analysis and Policy Priorities, 2019). Moreover, Social Security is a program that workers contribute to, making it quite different from other entitlement programs (see Figure 4.5).

Another effective program to address poverty is the Supplemental Nutrition Assistance Program, (SNAP). In 2015, using corrected data for underreporting from the Census Bureau, this program kept 8.4 million people above the poverty line, about half of whom were children. SNAP also helped keep 2 million children out of deep poverty and extreme poverty, more than any other assistance program (Figure 4.6; Center for Budget Analysis and Policy Priorities, 2019).

However, in recent years, funding to the SNAP program has been reduced and other requirements are being added as a condition of receiving benefits. This puts pressure on families, especially single mothers, who then have to find affordable child care while they are working in order to receive funding for food for their children.

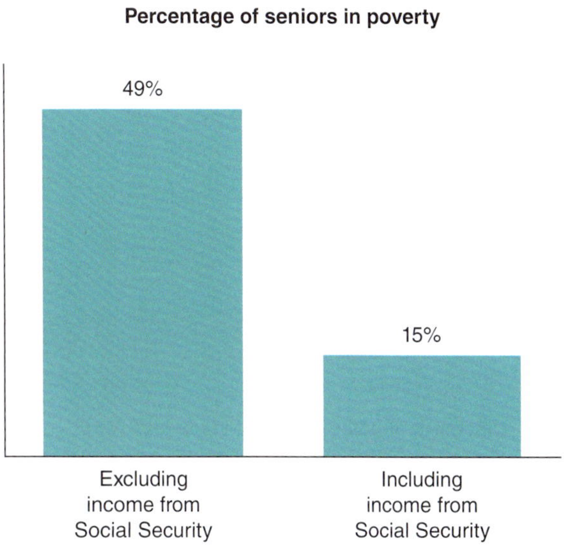

Percentage of seniors in poverty

49%

15%

Excluding income from Social Security

Including income from Social Security

Figure 4.5 Social Security and poverty among seniors
Note: Figures are for 2016 and use the federal government's Supplemental Poverty Measure (SPM). Source: U.S. Census Bureau

Finally, tax credit programs such as the Earned Income Tax Credit (EITC) and the Child Tax Credit (CTC) support low-income working families. These combined programs keep about 11 million people, about half of whom are children, above the poverty line. The Earned Income Tax Credit provides an incentive for workers by giving them a credit or refund of the taxes that would be taken out of their wages. In 2016, almost 6 million workers received the EITC and reduced the severity of poverty for another 19 million people in those workers' households. The amount received, which averaged $3,176, depends on marital status and the number of children in the household. If the amount of credit is more than what the worker would pay in taxes, they receive a "refund" from the IRS (Figure 4.7). The EITC encourages workers, especially single

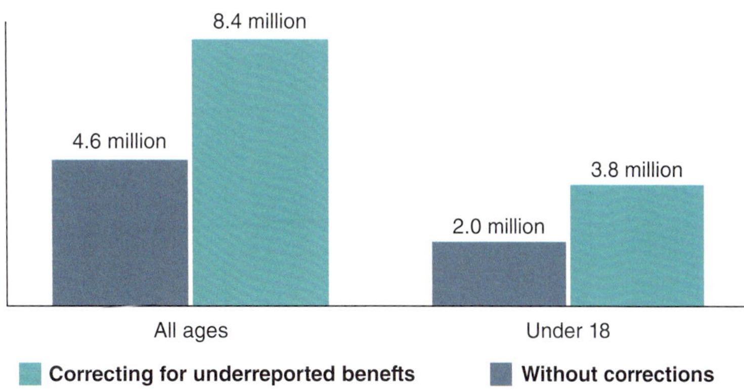

Figure 4.6 Supplemental Nutrition Assistance Program (SNAP) and poverty
Note: Figures are for 2015 and use the federal government's Supplemental Poverty Measure (SPM)> Source: CBPP analysis of Census Bureau data from the Current Population Survey and SPM public use files; corrections for underreported government assistance from Department of Health and Human Services/Urban Institute Transfer Income Model (TRMI)

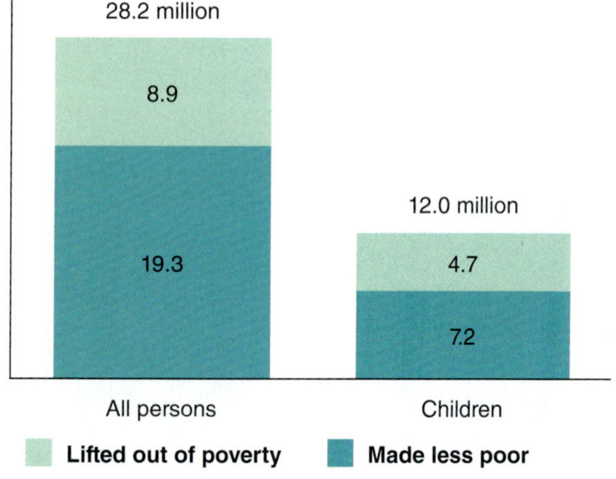

Figure 4.7 Antipoverty impact of Earned Income Tax Credit and Child Tax Credit Millions of persons lifted out of poverty or made less poor (using Supplemental Poverty Measure) by EITC and CTC, 2016. Note: Unlike the Census Bureau's official poverty measure, the SPM counts the effect of government benefit programs and tax credits. Source: CBPP analysis of Census Bureau's March 2017 Current Population Survey and 2016 SPM public use file

mothers, to transition off welfare and to work more hours because they get to keep more of what they earn. In fact, some research indicates that the EITC was more significant in getting single mothers back to work than welfare reform or a strong economy (Center for Budget Analysis and Policy Priorities, 2019). These and other programs are getting greater attention and consideration as larger scale issues, particularly from presidential candidates in the 2020 election, largely because so many people will need support to overcome the economic and social effects of the Covid-19 pandemic.

The Child Tax Credit (CTC) helps families by providing up to $2,000 in tax credit per child. This means families reduce the amount of taxes they owe and, like the EITC, if the credit exceeds the amount of federal income tax owed, the family receives a refund. The CTC lifted approximately 2.7 million people out of poverty in 2016, including about 1.5 million children, and lessened poverty for another 12.3 million people, including 6.1 million children (Figure 4.8; Center for Budget Analysis and Policy Priorities, 2019).

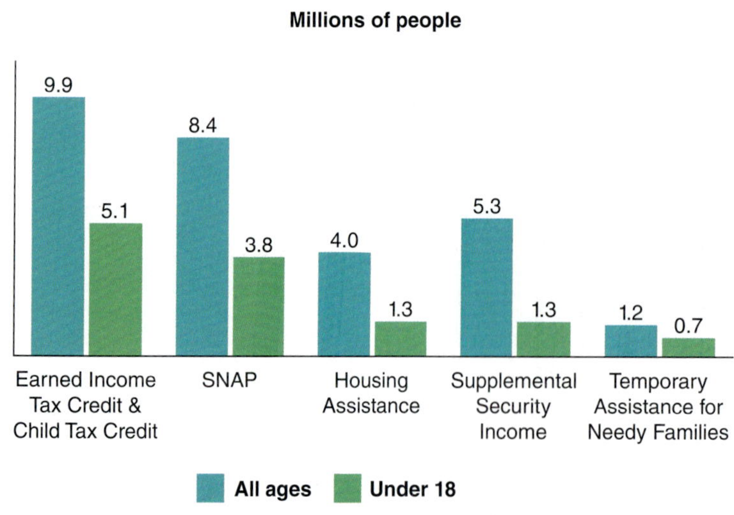

Figure 4.8 Impact of major tax credits and need-based programs on poverty Note: Figures are for 2015 and use the federal government's Supplemental Poverty Measure (SPM). Source: CBPP analysis of Census Bureau data from the Current Population Survey and SPM public use files; corrections for underreported government assistance from Department of Health and Human Services/Urban Institute Transfer Income Model (TRIM)

It should be mentioned that housing programs such as Section 8 are considered less effective as a poverty prevention tool than other programs like SNAP. This is due to the limited funding available for the program. However, for those who can take advantage of it, the impact of subsidized housing is considerable. For example, in 2018, a third of those people receiving housing assistance, over 5 million households, would be considered poor but above the poverty line if they did not receive it. While this number is smaller than those people who received SNAP or the ETIC, the impact on keeping people out of poverty is significant (Center for Budget Analysis and Policy Priorities, 2019).

SO WHAT CAN I DO?

Poverty and its related problems are complex. It may seem impossible for a single individual to do anything to solve it. However, think of the ways in which the 2020 Covid-19 pandemic impacted your life. How did you participated in or benefit from a solution to poverty that was a result of the pandemic? Even if you think the reasons people are poor are a result of their own choices, consider those individuals who were negatively impacted by the pandemic and experience poverty as a result.

In your community, look for opportunities to contribute time and resources. You might begin by volunteering at an agency or organization that assists the poor. This may be a food pantry, a soup kitchen, or a homeless shelter. If you would like to help children, contact your local Department of Social Services about mentoring opportunities. The research on this topic strongly indicates that positive role models are critically important to a child's or youth's overall development. You might even want to look around your neighborhood and see if there are single mothers struggling to raise their children. Offer to babysit so the mom can get a break or save a little on child care; prepare a home-cooked meal so they can stretch their food budget, or simply make friends with them and let them know you are there to support them in some way. While they may not take you up on your offer, knowing you are there and willing to help can go a long way in helping that family. Your professor and your campus career center may have additional ideas for volunteering opportunities.

You will also benefit by deepening your own understanding of this very complex social problems. At the very least, you can offer insight into the nature of poverty and the poor by reshaping people's perceptions—where they cling to the idea that laziness is the primary cause of poverty. You can serve as an ambassador of accuracy about social problems like poverty and share with others what you have learned. They may not agree or they may not change their opinion, but in this day and age of access to information, you can point them to the evidence about the problem. In sum, while it may seem that you can't do much to address the issue of poverty at an individual level, there are actually many ways you can make a contribution to improving the lives of others.

CONCLUSION

Perhaps the most important message of this chapter is similar to what many sociologists would say is the fundamental lesson of sociology: things are not always what they seem. In other words, much of what you may know or have heard about poverty is misleading and inaccurate. The majority of people who are struggling with poverty are, in fact, employed. Many of them hold down several jobs at once while supporting a family. The obstacles they face are structural and systemic: for example, they are stuck in low-paying jobs with few if any benefits. Social safety nets have stringent eligibility requirements and are time-limited. As society changes dramatically in the wake of the 2020 pandemic, we clearly see the need for robust subsidizing of things like housing, child care, and health insurance.

Another myth is that one can survive on minimum wage jobs. Given the high costs of housing, child care, health insurance, and transportation, a person (much less a family) simply cannot survive on minimum wage. Third, and more hopefully, there are programs that address poverty that do in fact work; the problem is that the public and policymakers believe that these programs create a form of unhealthy dependency and keep people from being self-sufficient. The reality is that most of the poor are already self-sufficient and are doing what is expected of them to be productive—they just can't meet all the costs given the job market and other factors beyond their control.

YOU MAKE THE CALL: LAW ENFORCEMENT AND THE HOMELESS

You are a police officer in a neighborhood that contains a growing number of homeless individuals. As a part of a community policing initiative, you have been spending time getting to know the members of the homeless population. One person in particular, Doug, has a similar story as one of your siblings; he is a veteran who suffers from PTSD, he has a substance abuse problem, and has not been able to hold a job. You find a program to help him become more self-sufficient and Doug makes good progress: he has entered a 12-step program and has applied for a disability pension through the Social Security Administration. Doug has been staying in the shelter but now is eligible for transitional housing, which is the next step toward independent living. Doug has also been seeing a therapist regularly and appears to be on track to get his life in order.

One day you find Doug in an alley and he appears disoriented, perhaps under the influence of some kind of drug. He doesn't recognize you, and becomes aggressive and hostile. You attempt to talk to him, but it is clear he is not in a logical state of mind. You decide to place him in handcuffs for his protection and yours while you figure out what to do next. You know that if he is arrested he will lose his place in the shelter, in the program, and is likely to lose the opportunity for his own apartment and disability benefits. Technically, he just tried to assault you, so you are justified in making the arrest. What do you do?

Questions to consider:

1. Does Doug's previous behavior cause you to pause and consider handling the matter informally?
2. Do you think Doug's current behavior is a result of illegal drugs or perhaps a reaction to something his therapist gave him?
3. Do you simply arrest Doug because he made a bad choice and you can't determine all of the circumstances that led him to his current state?
4. Are there other options besides letting him go or arresting him? If so, what are they?

SUMMARY

- Discuss the extent of poverty and social inequality in the United States.
    - Public perception of issues surrounding poverty differs considerably from what the data says about poverty and the poor.
    - Americans often have difficulty in understanding the structural barriers many poor people experience and how they prevent them from being successful.
- Discuss the concepts of social class and social inequality in the United States.
    - Social class is a concept that distinguishes people in terms of their social standing in society.
    - Social class a complex topic that is better described by an index, called socioeconomic status, which is comprised of a person's income, ed ucation, and occupational prestige.
- Summarize how poverty is measured and profile the poor.
    - Poverty is often measured by using income thresholds, where if a person or family earns a certain amount, they are identified as poor and eligible to receive government assistance.
    - Poverty falls disproportionately on single parent families, Blacks, Hispanics, and American Indian/ Alaska Natives.
- Describe the extent of homelessness in the United States and how it relates to poverty.
    - Homelessness, an extreme form of poverty, is largely the result of the lack of affordable housing in the United States.
    - Not all homeless people remain in their current circumstances, but there is a smaller segment of the population that are referred to as the chronically homeless.
- Compare and contrast sociological theories to explain poverty.
    - Conflict theory, functionalism, symbolic interactionism and postmodernism offer insight into why people become and remain poor.
- Examine current welfare policies relating to the poor.
    - Welfare programs address, housing, food, health care and other needs.
    - TANF provides a small cash stipend for incidental expenses.
    - Block grants from the federal government fund each state's individual plans.
- Assess successful programs for the poor.
    - Social Security is the most important strategy that keeps the elderly and children out of poverty.

KEY TERMS

Absolute poverty 113
Cultural capital 126
Culture of poverty 124
Deep poverty 129
Deferred gratification 125
Economic determinism 111
Extreme poverty 129
Fatalism 125
Horatio Alger myths 109
Life chances 108
Meritocracy 112
New Deal 127
Personal attribution 106
Present orientation 125

Relative definition of poverty 113

Social inequality 111

Social mobility 111

Social reproduction 125

Social stratification 110

Socioeconomic status (SES) 111

Structural factors 113

Systemic attribution 106

Temporary Assistance for Needy Families (TANF) 127

Universal Basic Income 114

War on Poverty 127

Welfare 117

Welfare reform 128

Working poor 117

Discussion Questions

1. Given the available information about poverty and the working poor, why do you think the general public still believes poverty is caused by laziness or a lack of work ethic?
2. Should welfare recipients be required to submit to drug testing and have work requirements even if they are single parents with young children?
3. Is the widening gap between the wealthy and the poor a problem for all of society? What strategies can be used to slow the growth or close the gap?
4. What structural factors inhibit people's ability to become and remain self-sufficient? How do we remedy the problem so that everyone has a chance to become independent?

Learn more with this chapter's digital tools, including Data and Media Literacy Exercises, flashcards, and chapter self-assessments at **www.oup.com/he/mcnamara**.

5

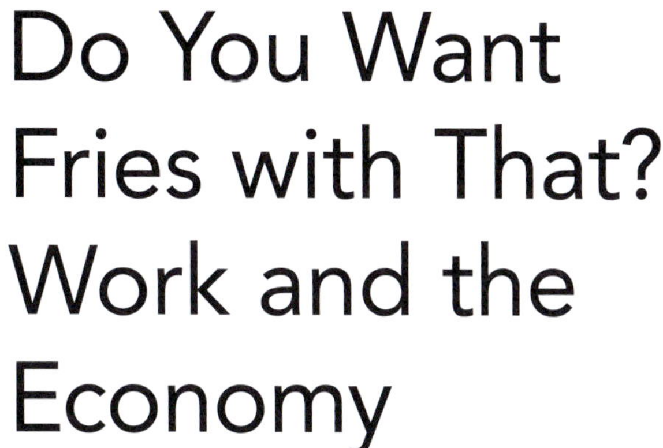

Do You Want Fries with That? Work and the Economy

LEARNING OBJECTIVES

- Describe the different types of economic systems.
- Summarize examples of government intervention in the US economy.
- Analyze the nature of work and employment in the United States.
- Describe the impact of broader economic changes on workers.
- Compare sociological paradigms as they relate to work and the economy.

Chapter Outline

The changing face of labor As the American economy faces extraordinary challenges, the need for a more diverse and creative workforce becomes increasingly urgent.

As we discussed in Chapter 4, poverty is one of the most persistent social problems we face. Many reasons that people remain poor have to do with the way our economy is structured. However, as we will see in this chapter, changes in the US economy and the development of technology have resulted in the elimination of many industries and the jobs they supplied. Semi-skilled and low-skilled workers have found it especially difficult to adjust to this new economic reality. Adding to these trends, the 2020 Covid-19 pandemic has challenged everything we took for granted about our economy, changing the workplace as we know it and even erasing entire industries. In this chapter we'll explore the systems and structures that created that fragility—as well as how resilience and creativity might help us to reimagine a more just economy and sustainable workforce.

As we examine the subject of labor, we will also reflect on the cultural dimension of work in the United States. Americans generally believe that people who are able-bodied should actively seek and find employment. We feel that work serves as a way to contribute to society as a taxpayer and set an example to others. We also believe that people who work are less dependent upon the government. While there are some exceptions to this rule (for the elderly or disabled, among others), in American culture a job serves as an identity marker as well as a fulfillment of one's responsibility to society.

Finally, as it is very likely you have experienced some of the adversity as a result of the 2020 Covid-19 pandemic, including significant events relating to your job or economic well-being, this chapter will help you apply theory and data to understanding what happened. Hopefully, you will be able to use your sociological imagination to think creatively about possible solutions to the challenges highlighted in this chapter.

SOCIOLOGICAL STORY TIME

- In 2020, the spread of Covid-19 virus into the United States resulted in the massive closing of factories, shops, restaurants, and other industries. By March, the Labor Department estimated that more than a million workers are expected to lose their jobs by the end of the month, and a total of nearly three million could lose their jobs in 2020, a stark contrast to the near record unemployment seen just a month earlier. As workers are attempting to access unemployment benefits, they are discovering the system is incapable of handling so much volume so quickly (Long and Bhattarai, 2020).
- President Trump has argued that America's $500 billion trade deficit—a measure of how much more we buy from other countries than they buy from us—is a national disgrace. He promised to eliminate the deficit by creating agreements that are more advantageous to the United States (Grunwald, 2017).
- In 2015, Seattle, WA became the first state to implement a $15 per hour minimum wage. Senator Bernie Sanders (along with other members of the US Senate) introduced a bill for a national $15 minimum wage. Advocates say the increase helps low-skilled workers earn a livable wage, while critics point out that it will lead to layoffs or reduction in the number of hours for those same workers (Chen, 2018).
- In 2018, President Trump announced a $12 billion bailout of US farmers who were negatively impacted by trade tariffs imposed on other countries, such as China. Critics pointed out that this short-term strategy would not sustain farmers indefinitely, as the tariffs' impact are felt worldwide (Johnson, 2018).

THE NATURE OF ECONOMIC SYSTEMS

As part of his 2016 presidential campaign, Donald Trump convinced many Americans that we needed to "make America great again." What this suggested, of course, is that the United States was no longer "great." He may have been referring to our position economically in the world; as well how much we spend on certain federal programs, or perhaps our business dealings with other countries. Those business dealings, along with the excessive spending habits of many American consumers, had resulted in a **trade deficit**. That is, America imports more products than we export. Said another way, we owe others more than we earn. This will have far-reaching consequences unless the United States finds a way to lower spending and increase revenues.

In this chapter, we will explore the consequences of capitalism as well as consider alternative economic systems. During the 2020 US presidential election campaign, along with the Covid-19 pandemic, made the urgency and need for changes to our health care system strikingly clear. While many people felt that "socialism" (or another alternative economic system, communism) implies a lack of choice and runs counter to the notion of a meritocracy, in reality, the economic system in the United States already contains many elements of what might be called socialism. But capitalism also includes many negative features, some of which (such as poverty) Americans blame on the individuals who experience them, rather than the larger structural problem. In reality, capitalism is structured in a way that ensures big winners as well as big losers, regardless of how hard the losers might work. Some of the social problems we will explore in this chapter include issues such as unemployment, wage inequality, deindustrialization, and the perils of a global marketplace. We will also examine how other countries address some of these problems to gain further insight into possible solutions to those issues.

There are several ways to describe various economic systems. Traditional social problems textbooks compare capitalism with communism. This approach is valuable because it offers insight into a system with which we are very familiar, while offering a view of a system that is quite different from our own. Historically, however, many Americans have seen communism with something negative—likely the lack of choice, excessive governmental control, or the loss of autonomy as citizens.

While we will compare the two types of economies, we will also describe other primary economic systems that are used around the world. An economic structure, by definition, is the manner in which scarce resources are distributed. To that end, we can identify four main types of economies: traditional, command, market, and mixed.

Traditional Economy

A **traditional economy** is perhaps the oldest form of economy. Today, it is used in countries that tend to be less developed and where farming is a primary industry. Durkheim might refer to such societies as examples of mechanical solidarity, in which members have close-knit relationships with each other and specific roles to play. While a surplus of resources is considered rare, and access to technology and advanced medicine tend to be lacking, the people in traditional economies are said to be socially satisfied with life in general (Intelligent Economy, n.d.). A country like Bhutan might be the best example of a traditional economy (Lipse, 2020). Many experts now contend that a truly traditional economy is a thing of the past, largely due to the fact that virtually all countries are no longer considered pre-industrial or pre-modern. While there are still many countries that have a large proportion of people living in subsistence conditions

Traditional economy Women harvest rice in Bhutan, a country that most closely represents a traditional economy in today's world.

or lag behind in their economic development, a more accurate term would be a "Least Developed Country," a term used by the United Nations to describe those places that have the lowest indicators of socioeconomic development (Lipse, 2020).

Command Economy

As the name suggests, in a **command economy** most of the system is controlled by the government or a central power. The government is involved in all aspects of economic development, including the distribution of resources and ownership of railroads, utilities, and airlines. Ideally, such power allows the government to create an ample supply of needed items at affordable prices. It also means, theoretically, that the government could create enough jobs to prevent high levels of unemployment. In a command economy, the government can focus on efficient use of resources and act in the best interests of society. At the same time, one of the disadvantages of a command economy is that the government can't determine the demand for resources, since it is the one that sets the prices. This can lead to rationing of goods and services. In addition, because the government is in control, there is more of an emphasis on compliance and obedience than innovation; and in a command economy, workers do not have many options in their career paths because they must do what the government asks of them. Examples of command economies today include China, Iran, North Korea, and Russia (World Population Review, 2020).

Socialism

Socialism is an example of a command economy. In a socialist system, the **means of production** (all those things that are needed to produce wealth: land, equipment, factories, raw materials, etc.) are owned by all citizens—that is, by the government. The goal of such a system is not the pursuit of profit, as it is in capitalism, but rather the needs of society are considered more important than those of the individual. Because of the lack of competition for scarce resources, people don't compete with one another, but instead work cooperatively for the good of society. In Marx's view, the best outcome of socialism would be a classless society—instead of the clearly defined stratification that exists between the wealthy and the poor in capitalism. Thus, for Marx, a single class system would reflect a **communist society** (Krupa, 2018).

Command economy North Korea is an example of a command economy. In May 2020, North Korean leader Kim Jong Un (second from right) attended the opening of a new fertilizer factory.

Market Economy

In a **market economy** (also known as a **free market economy**), people act in their own self-interests. The allocation of resources, the types of goods

Market economy The Causeway Bay area of Hong Kong, with is bustling department stores and shopping arcades. Hong Kong is an example of a market economy, which drives innovation and aligns with consumer needs.

that are produced, and who gets to buy them (and in what quantity) are determined by the market, not the government (as in the case of a command economy). In a free market system, the actor (an individual or a company) who takes risks and is successful gets to keep the profits. This relative freedom leads to significant innovation in the economy. In this type of economic system, there is a separation of the government and the market. This keeps the government from becoming too powerful and keeps the market in alignment with what consumers actually want and need. The advantage of a free market economy is that the price of products is determined by the consumers of that product, not artificially set by the government. Moreover, businesses only involve themselves in profitable ventures, producing goods and services that consumers want, and competition between businesses keeps prices in check. According to the 2019 Index of Economic Freedom, countries such as Hong Kong, New Zealand, Switzerland, and Australia are examples of a market economy (Depersio, 2019).

At the same time, however, the competition seen in a free market has no place for compassion for the less fortunate. The phrase "it's nothing personal, it's just business" is a defining feature of a free market system. There is an interest in profit and there is no interest in the poor, the disadvantaged or the elderly, except as they have resources to buy the goods in the market. Things like health care for the poor or other "entitlement" programs like Social Security or welfare are seen as a drain on profits and not part of the self-interest of capitalists (Krupa, 2018).

CAPITALISM

Capitalism is a form of market economy. Capitalism involves the private ownership of the means of production. The goal of capitalism is the pursuit of profit: as people try to maximize their own self-interests, they will (ideally) act in ways that benefit society. This means products are manufactured, services are provided that people need and want, and people are willing to pay for both. As a result, the economy and society in general improve. How does that work?

Well, people are competing with others who also want to maximize their self-interest and try to get people to buy their products and services instead of those offered by a competitor. This can be accomplished by lowering prices, added value beyond a product's price point, or some other way to attract and improve demand for goods and services. Competition is key to capitalism, since it keeps prices reasonable and prevents anyone from getting greedy and either overcharging or underperforming. Economist

Adam Smith argued that competition acts as an **invisible hand** to make sure the system works organically, without any need for involvement by the government to control or regulate the economy. This is what people sometimes refer to when they talk about a "free" market system or a "free enterprise" system. When you hear a government described as **laissez-faire**, it reflects the idea that there should be minimal involvement by the government (hands-off) and that the economy is self-regulating. As long as there is competition and similarly motivated people are involved in the pursuit of profit, with supply and demand regulating the amount, cost, and volume of goods and services, the capitalist system works (*Economic Times*, 2018).

Social Security The Social Security system is the primary economic safety net for older Americans.

Mixed Economy

A **mixed economy** is a combination of different types of economic systems. More often in these types of systems, the government generally stays out of market involvement, but it does control critical areas such as defense, transportation, or some other industry. The government is also involved to some extent in the oversight of private business, so they can correct market failures and prevent monopolies from being created. The government can also create programs such as Medicaid and Social Security to help the poor and needy. In doing so, as well as through their power to tax businesses and individuals, the government can address or attempt to reduce extreme inequality that exists. The main problem with mixed economies is achieving the balance of allowing the market to solve its problems while also finding a place to regulate and oversee it so that there is enough intervention when needed. Another problem is that at times if industries are subsidized by the government, there is a lack of competition which can lead to complacency and inefficiencies (*Economic Times*, 2018). Examples of mixed economies include Sweden, Iceland, France, and the United States (Moser, 2018).

Comparing Capitalism and Socialism

In Chapter 1, we observed that people tend to take many aspects of society for granted, just as a fish does not notice the water in which it swims. For sociologists, understanding the role of perception is critical. Whether their perceptions are objectively true or not, for most people their perceptions *are* reality. When it comes to thinking critically about the economic system in which we live, one's perceptions (and experiences) determine one's ability to understand how the system perpetuates inequality.

For most Americans, especially those who have never lived in another country, there is a general acceptance that capitalism is the best type of economic system. After all,

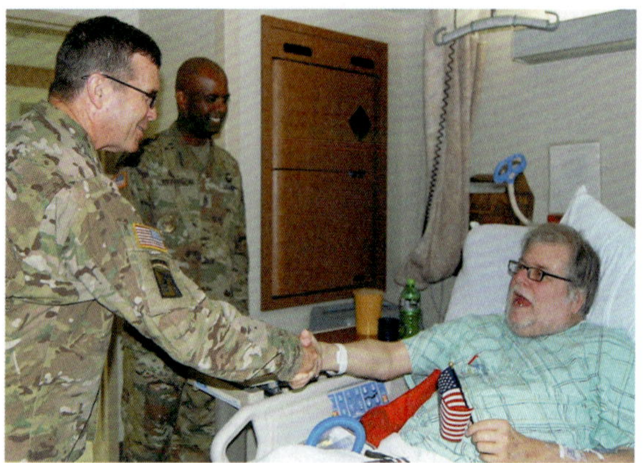

Government safety nets The Veterans Administration (VA) is a government agency that provides many types of medical and financial support and benefits to those who have served in the US military. Here, VA officials visit with a patient at the Louisville Veterans Administration Hospital. Despite their efforts, however, many US veterans go without adequate care and shelter.

our society and our media tell us that America is the land of opportunity. We believe that what makes this country so attractive to immigrants is the possibility of achieving success, regardless of where one starts in the social structure. It is natural, then, for people to believe that capitalism is a better paradigm than what is offered in other countries. As for socialism, the Covid-19 pandemic of 2020 changed how many Americans understood the perils of capitalism as well as the possibilities of socialism.

You might be surprised to learn that the United States is not a truly capitalistic country. In fact, we have several government programs that can be categorized as socialistic, such as the Veterans Administration. They are popular programs that provide services and a safety net for millions of people. So what's with all the negativity? Examining this issue in more detail, I think you'll see that some of what we are witnessing is stigma-created fear.

In fact, capitalism and socialism are two major economic systems that characterize modern society. Because no society is purely capitalistic or socialistic, it makes sense instead to consider them on a spectrum with a host of variations in between. For example, the US government is heavily involved in the regulation of many industries.

In 2020, as a result of the Covid-19 pandemic, Congress quickly passed legislation to address the economic impact felt across the country. This package, estimated to cost taxpayers $1 trillion, included more than $50 billion for the airline industry and another $150 billion other industries to prevent them from bankruptcy. It also includes a cash award to families along with up to two weeks of paid sick leave if workers are being tested or treated for Covid-19 or have been diagnosed with it. Also eligible would be those who have been told by a doctor or government official to stay home because of exposure or symptoms. It is likely that this will not be the only effort by Congress to address the fallout from the pandemic (Foran and Barrett, 2020).

So, between socialism and capitalism, can we say which system is "better"?

This is a difficult question to answer. Most Americans would say that capitalism is the better system, largely because it is all they have ever known. To be fair, the merits of capitalism versus socialism have been debated for decades. On one hand, capitalism results in greater economic growth, in part because it provides an incentive for innovation and creativity. Capitalism also allows for greater freedoms and liberties, in part because its main component involves private ownership of property and the pursuit of self-interest/profit. That is, the needs and desires of the individual are stressed in this model, and there is less emphasis on government involvement in economic, political and social life. That's not to say, however, that capitalism, even in its purest form, is perfect.

Importantly, by definition, capitalism contains and even promotes more economic inequality than socialism. Why? Because not all economic growth is equal, and there is a significant divide between the rich and the poor. A capitalist model also means there is less concern for those at the bottom of the market. Social programs like welfare, health care, and care for the elderly and disabled are not highly valued, because they take away from profits.

Culturally, people are socialized in a capitalist model to focus on their individual needs rather than the needs of the larger society. In this way, capitalism can encourage selfish, greedy, and even unethical behavior, all in the name of profit. And such actions are encouraged by business schools and experience in the business world. After all, what makes for a shrewd business person?

In contrast, in a socialist society people tend to collaborate and cooperate rather than compete (after all, with competition, someone has to lose). Further, whereas capitalism focuses on what's good for the individual, socialism focuses on what benefits the group. Such a system requires less emphasis on individuality and freedom; in order for the model to function efficiently and effectively, there can't be a great deal of variation in how tasks are accomplished. Also, under socialism there tends to be less incentive to work hard and innovate. Workers are paid regardless of their efforts, and there is no meritocracy. There is also a lack of "skin in the game" so to speak, whereby workers would benefit from making improvements, as is possible in the case of capitalism. At the same time, however, there is stability and assurance that everyone is provided for and there is less distance between the rich and the poor. Moreover, there is an emphasis on ensuring that those in need are cared for in a socialist model.

Democratic socialism At this 2016 Asheville, North Carolina rally in support of presidential candidate Bernie Sanders, supporters held signs and wore t-shirts with messages promoting democratic socialism.

The Best of Both Worlds? Democratic Socialism

The challenges presented by each model, with their corresponding limitations and impacts on society, have led some countries to develop a modified version of the two systems, what some call **democratic socialism**. This term has gotten a great deal of media attention, since 2020 presidential candidate Bernie Sanders described himself and his agenda with this term. This model combines elements of capitalism and socialism. Examples include many of the Scandinavian countries, such as Denmark, Sweden, Norway, and Finland. In such a model, the government owns and manages key industries, but most property remains in the hands of private citizens. Political freedom occurs under this model and there is a concerted effort to help the poor and needy (Democratic Socialists of America, n.d.).

In Chapter 4, we examined Finland's pilot of the **Universal Basic Income**, which provides a standard amount of money each year to everyone, including those who cannot work. The idea is that there will be more money saved by not having to support social programs and other efforts if people were simply given a certain amount of money each year. While the experiment in Finland was considered a failure, there were many factors that obscured the overall effect of the idea in shaping the contours of public assistance. Critics of universal income continue to argue that such a model breeds complacency and dependence, but a counter argument is that chronic dependency on welfare results in a similar type of dependence, not to mention the enormous burden the government bears to manage these massive programs. Countries that practice democratic socialism have high tax rates to pay for such programs, but culturally the people living there feel it is a better model since it contributes to the greater good and provides a better alternative to other models such as capitalism or socialism alone (Democratic Socialists of America, n.d.).

GLOBAL PERSPECTIVES

Social Democracy in Action

The Nordic nations of Denmark, Finland, Iceland, Norway, and Sweden are all social democracies. Their governments own important industries, such as mass transit and utilities, while their citizens enjoy a great deal of political freedom. Each nation has three branches of government—executive, judicial, and legislative—and each nation has a national parliament to which people are elected.

Social democracy In Sweden, child care is heavily subsidized by the government. Here, children enjoy lunch with two teachers in a day care center.

Social democracies are often called controlled capitalist market economies. A key feature of these social democracies' economies is that inequality in wealth and income is not generally tolerated. Employers, employees, and political officials work closely to ensure that poverty and its related problems are addressed, and because such a perspective is part of the value system and culture, there is a cooperative effort to solve the problem of inequality rather than the tension about inequality seen in the United States.

In this type of economy, the concept of **universalism** means that all members of society receive free or heavily subsidized services such as child care and health care. Paying for these services is expensive, so taxes paid by citizens of these countries are very high. However, most people accept this tax burden as a necessary feature of life there.

This attempt has not been entirely free of difficulties but overall has been very successful, as the Scandinavian nations rank at or near the top in international comparisons of health, education, economic well-being, and other measures of quality of life. The Scandinavian experience of social democracy teaches us that it is very possible to have a political and economic model that combines the best features of capitalism and socialism while retaining the political freedom that citizens expect in a democracy (Berman, 2006).

WORK AND EMPLOYMENT IN THE UNITED STATES

While many people may understand intellectually how economic constraints and larger scale problems affect society, they may not grasp how these problems affect them in their everyday lives. However, it is important to place these micro-level problems in their proper context because the challenges on a personal level are often connected to larger structural issues. One example of a macro-level problem that affected millions of people's lives is the Covid-19 pandemic, which began to cripple the global economy in 2020. This event was arguably the largest and most severe financial event since the Great Depression, reshaping the global economy and erasing entire industries.

In addition to the government influencing a country's economy, the pandemic of 2020 illustrated how sudden large-scale shocks can affect workers in a variety of ways, including whether they have jobs in the future. In this next section we examine the nature of globalization and deindustrialization because they significantly impact millions of workers and their opportunities to achieve the American Dream.

The Impact of Globalization

In a globalized world, economic markets are interconnected. What happens in developing countries impacts and is impacted by what happens in the United States. According to the Peterson Institute for International Economics, globalization is the economic, cultural and social interconnectedness between countries by trading goods, services, technology, people, and information (Peterson Institute for International Economics, n.d.). Although **globalization** was originally presented as a positive step for the world, it has in fact contributed to a rise in overall inequality as well as geopolitical tensions. Examples of those countries who are not in favor of globalization include Britain's decision to leave the European Union, known as Brexit, or President Trump's policy decisions that reflect an America-first position internationally. The rapid spread of the Covid-19 virus around the world, as well as the fallout of what happened in those countries affected by it, also serves as a reminder of the fragility of a globally interconnected economy, particularly when key players are forced offline.

Many experts agree that globalization has been a good thing for many developing countries, which were given the opportunity to export inexpensive goods and offer services previously unavailable to the rest of the world. This means there are employment opportunities which can stimulate economic growth in those countries. Globalization and free trade has made it possible for consumers in less developed countries to purchase goods and services as well.

However, there remain many barriers to **free trade**, which is an international policy where a country does not apply fees (tariffs) for its imported goods or financially subsidize its exported ones to other countries (Collins, 2015).

As of 2019, the United States has a trade deficit $616.8 billion, according to the Bureau of Economic Analysis (Figure 5.1). In 2019, the United States imported $3.12 trillion in goods and services from other countries and exported $2.5 trillion (US Bureau of Economic Analysis, 2020).

This means we import more goods than we export. In addition, the outsourcing of jobs from the US to countries where labor is less expensive creates a problem for the US economy, particularly since a large segment of the job market involves low-skill jobs which pay minimum wages. When those jobs are outsourced, where do unskilled and semiskilled employees find work? Trade agreements such as the **North American Free Trade Agreement** (NAFTA), are designed to allow companies the option of reducing their cost

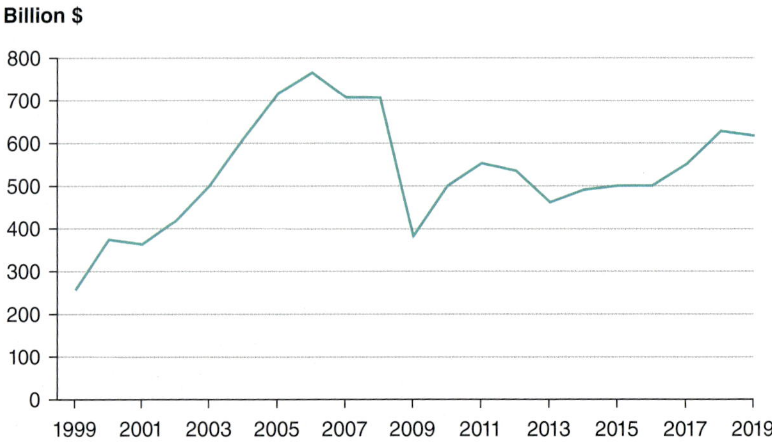

Figure 5.1 Annual goods and services trade gap/deficit 1999–2019 Source: U.S. Bureau of Economic Analysis, 2020.

of production of goods by outsourcing jobs (in the case of NAFTA, to Mexico or Canada) to maximize profits. Theoretically, such a model also stimulates all three countries' economies since consumers are able to purchase goods and services without additional costs. Critics of NAFTA argue that the agreement has simply eliminated jobs in the United States and expanded our trade deficit (Collins, 2015).

Deindustrialization

What is deindustrialization and how does it relate to jobs and unemployment? If industrialization means the growth of industry, jobs, and the overall economy, **deindustrialization** is the opposite. At one time, the United States was heavily involved in the production of goods. In fact, while our products cost more than those manufactured in other countries, they were generally of higher quality than what other countries produced. The goods cost more because of the higher standard of living in the United States, where workers were paid more than in other countries. However, particularly in the 1970s, policymakers and business leaders in the United States began to realize that other countries, such as Japan, had developed technological advances that enabled them to manufacture products of equal or better quality, and then sell those products on the global marketplace at a lower price. Those countries were able to undercut the prices of US products because the standard of living in those countries was lower. Such companies paid workers less than American workers earned and passed the cost savings on to consumers (Crossman, 2018).

This realization started the process of deindustrialization. Many US companies realized they could not compete on the global market since the cost of producing those items would remain high. Given that these companies could no longer argue the quality of the product was better than what other countries produced, many US companies were faced with the decision to get out of the manufacturing of products altogether. The United States began to shift its focus away from a product-oriented economy to a **service economy** (Crossman, 2018).

The toll of deindustrialization At its peak, Bethlehem Steel employed 180,000 people at its massive steel mill in Bethlehem, Pennsylvania. The plant closed in 1995 after years of decline brought about by deindustrialization. Ironically, a casino now operates on part of the site of the former factory.

As the name suggests, in a service economy, in contrast to an agricultural or product-based economy, a service economy focuses its efforts on providing various types of services, including things like information technology, legal and medical services, along with things like transportation, investments, and jobs such as those found in the restaurant and housekeeping industries.

In fact, a service economy is often divided into a category of worker that has a certain level of expertise or competency (e.g., attorneys, accountants, computer programmers) as well as relatively unskilled workers to support or participate in tourism and food industries (e.g. restaurant servers, cooks, checkout staff at grocery or department stores). In the case of the former group, the level of training and skills needed are higher than an employee who worked in a factory that produced items to be sold in the marketplace.

THE IMPACT OF ECONOMIC CHANGES ON WORKERS

As was mentioned, it is important to understand how large scale changes in the economy, such as globalization, deindustrialization, natural disasters, and other factors cause a ripple effect through society. At a micro-level, such changes dramatically impact workers and the nature of work. This not only includes the loss of jobs, but also the changing nature of the jobs that are left for workers. These challenges are particularly acute for the semi-skilled and unskilled segments of the labor market. Thus, one concern about deindustrialization is the elimination of millions of jobs as the economy shifted its focus. It also meant that not every worker would be suitable for the new jobs in a service sector economy, which tends to focus on either technology or in low-paying minimum wage jobs (Figure 5.2; Crossman, 2018).

However, not everyone agrees that deindustrialization has been a bad thing. While it is true that many manufacturing jobs have been lost due to outsourcing, some economists point to the increased production in manufacturing. The reason? Many

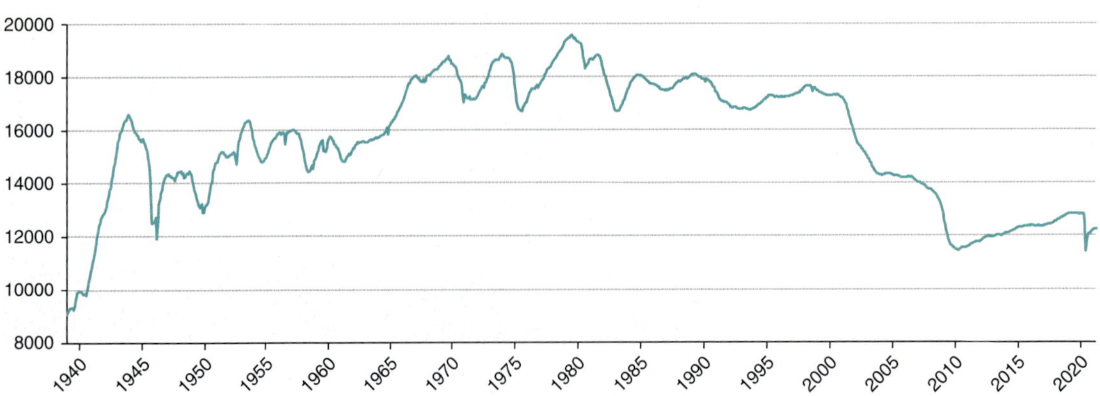

Figure 5.2 Employment decline in the manufacturing sector Shaded areas represent US recessions. Source: US Department of Labor: Bureau of Labor Statistics.

manufacturers have turned to automation and technology to increase production instead of outsourcing the tasks to other countries.

From the earliest days of the Industrial Revolution, capitalism has been fueled by the use of machinery to both improve productivity and to reduce the dependence on human labor to create products. While machinery also has costs, in the long run, there is more profit to be made through the use of automation than in relying on human labor. This explains what might seem like a paradox: that even though there are 8 million fewer manufacturing jobs in the US, the absolute output of manufacturing in this country is at its highest levels, over $2 trillion. In fact, the National Association of Manufacturers recently pointed out that if this sector of the US economy were its own country, it would have the eighth largest economy in the world (Movahead, 2016).

Whether one considers the decline in manufacturing jobs or deindustrialization in general as a bad thing for the economy, the reality is that once-reliable manufacturing jobs are no longer available to unskilled and semi-skilled workers. In their place are low-paying minimum wage jobs that do not provide retirement plans, vacation or sick time, or health insurance. It also means that workers who have been displaced from well-paying manufacturing jobs might have to take on multiple jobs to make ends meet. In addition, the burden of re-training for jobs in an economy based on service and technology falls disproportionately on displaced workers themselves. As we saw in Chapter Four, minimum wage jobs actually put people below the poverty line for a family of four. Thus, the minimum wage is not a solution to the problem of the loss of well-paying jobs.

Automation and Artificial Intelligence in the Workplace

In addition to globalization and deindustrialization that results in the loss of jobs, a significant development in the workplace involves the use of artificial intelligence and automation. While technology is, by definition, a labor-saving device, the changing nature of jobs as a result of artificial intelligence has created concerns about the future of work and what it means for employees. In 2019 Amazon announced it was spending over $700 million to retrain 100,000 of its employees by 2025 so that they will be ready to assume new jobs. The implication is that many jobs currently performed by humans will be replaced with robots (Press, 2019).

Robots never strike Many manufacturing and retail workplaces are replacing jobs that used to be performed by human workers (like welding car body panels, as shown on this factory production line) with robots.

Such a development obviously creates concerns for all employees, but especially those who are most likely to be affected by this change. According to a 2018 Pew Research Center survey, between 65–90 percent of respondents in advanced countries believe that robots and computers will either probably or definitely replace many jobs currently performed by humans (Wike and Stokes, 2018). Similarly, according to a 2018 online opinion poll by Gallup and Northeastern University in the United States, Canada, and the United Kingdom, about seven in ten respondents felt that technology will eliminate more jobs than it creates, and many fear that their particular jobs will be eliminated in the near future (Gallup and Northeastern University, 2018).

Thus, while many experts note that the less skilled segment of the workforce will likely be negatively impacted by automation and artificial intelligence, these same experts also note a sense of optimism about the creation of new opportunities for workers, as well as the rethinking of how education and training can be offered in a changing economy. The challenge, of course, is how to retrain these employees for the new tasks that will be needed in the job market of the future. This is particularly problematic given that about 40 percent of the US workforce has less than a high school education (Miller, 2019).

A Living Wage

As we have noted, the minimum wage in the United States is inadequate for sustaining a family of four above the poverty line. In addition, the minimum wage has not kept up with the pace of inflation.

In response, a new type of labor activism focused on a **living wage** (often set at $15 per hour) has emerged. This higher amount accurately reflects the actual costs of living instead of artificially increasing the minimum wage, which at $7.25 per hour has long been insufficient.. However, in what is described by some observers as an **alt-labor movement**, efforts such as the **Fight for $15** are designed to bring the discussion to the public domain and even meaningful protests. One such example occurred in November 2012 when nearly 200 non-union workers at fast-food chain restaurants in New York City marched through the streets to protest the need for a $15 per hour minimum wage as well as to dispel the notion that minimum wage workers are not teenagers looking for spending money—many adults rely on minimum wage jobs to support their families (Movahed, 2016; Levitz, 2018).

Fight for $15 Workers representing many different unions, along with their supporters, rally in New York City to advocate for a $15 minimum wage.

The Gig Economy and Part-time Workers

As a result of the financial crisis of 2008, many workers displaced from full-time jobs found themselves scrambling to piece together enough work to replace the lost income. Using a term from the music industry, the resulting **gig economy** is made up of part-time workers who are technically independent contractors. Among musicians, having a gig meant a job that involved playing music. For millions of workers today, it means a form of part-time labor that has changed the job landscape (Frazier, 2019).

Gigs involve a wide range of activities, from senior executives who work from home and serve as consultants to workers who attempt to work for companies like Uber or GrubHub and deliver food and other products and services (Kim, 2020).

A number of factors have contributed to the development of the gig economy. One important factor has been the effort by companies to reduce the number of full-time employees, whose benefits (such as health insurance and contributions to retirement accounts) are an additional expense on top of their base salary. As a cost-cutting measure, hiring contingent workers or independent contractors means that companies can pay people for the work they do, but have no obligation or responsibility to them in terms of health care, retirement plans, vacation or sick days. As more companies begin to see the cost savings to such an approach, most experts agree that the gig economy is likely to become the new norm in the future. Such a situation does not bode well for workers in general who wish to have the benefits, stability, and protections of working full time for a company (Frazier, 2019).

Demographics have also played a role in the rise of the gig economy. As Millennials have reshaped the culture and the nature of work, where they strive to find a work/life balance, such a position has redefined what a job and a career can look like. Instead of working a 9 to 5 job in corporate America, many Millennials prefer the autonomy and freedom that part-time work in the gig economy provides. While this comes at some costs in terms of stability and income, some experts argue that many Millennials see greater benefits of working from anywhere and maximizing their skills to enhance their flexibility of when, where, and how they work. Such an approach has had a ripple effect through the job market (Frazier, 2019).

Still, not everyone is enamored with the gig economy nor are all workers benefitting from its development. According to Kim (2020), the rise of the gig economy and the way technology is being leveraged by corporations is squeezing employees out of the labor market altogether. Kim points out that some industries, such as hotels and transportation, are increasingly finding that consumers can obtain the services they need more readily and less expensively than traditional avenues. Citing the hotel industry's decline in the use of room service in favor of food delivery apps or the rise in popularity of apps like Uber and its negative impact on doormen and bellhops in the hotel industry (who rely heavily on tips to supplement their low salaries), Kim laments that many of the jobs for the semi-skilled and unskilled are being replaced by part-time workers who have few options but to participate in the gig economy (Kim, 2020; Figure 5.3).

Interestingly, the report calls attention to the advantages and disadvantages to working in the gig economy, where some people have "side hustles" that simply allow them to earn extra money in addition to a full-time job. Others, however, and an increasing

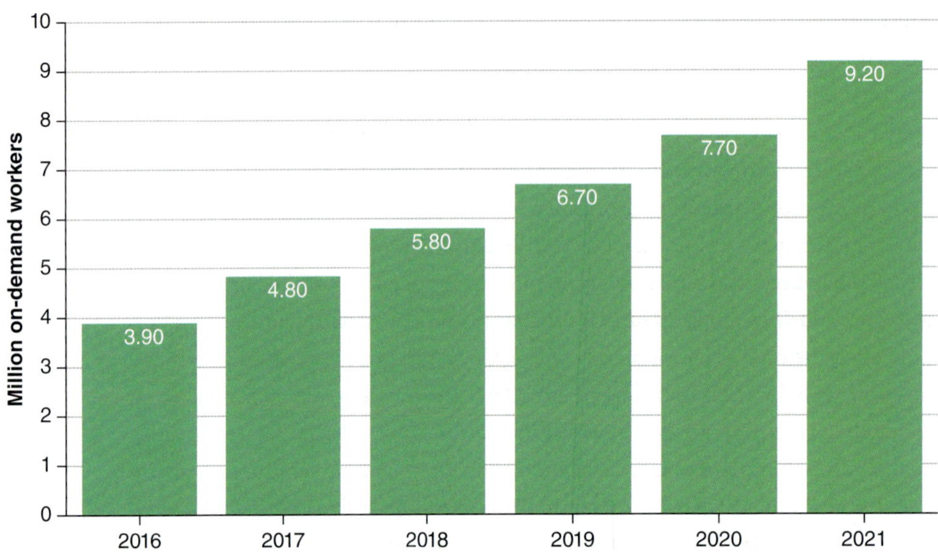

Figure 5.3 Numbers of Americans working in the gig economy

number of people fall into this category, are working in the gig economy out of necessity and struggle to find consistent employment (Torpey and Hogan, 2016).

For example, contingent workers are more likely to not have health insurance, a retirement plan, are more likely to be employed part-time and on average earn much less than full-time workers. They are also more likely to express a desire to have a full-time job; meaning most do not choose contingency labor, as some observers have suggested (Torpey and Hogan, 2016).

Unemployment and Underemployment

Is unemployment really a problem? By many accounts in the media the unemployment rate has been decreasing as the economy has thrived and is near historic lows (Cox, 2020). This suggests that people are working and that the economy is booming. But what do we know about the unemployment rate, and how does it reflect the health of the economy? And what about those people who are in minimum wage jobs: are they really that much better off than being unemployed? Let's take a look at the data.

We should begin with an understanding of what the unemployment rate actually describes and how it is calculated. The unemployment rate, expressed as a percentage, is a ratio that compares the number of unemployed people to the total workforce (Sherman, 2018). But we have to be careful to examine the rate because the way it is calculated can give a distorted perception of what is actually going on.

For example, in April 2018, the number of jobs increased by 164,000, but the number of unemployed dropped by 239,000. How can that be explained? When the number of unemployed workers are no longer counted, unemployment appears to drop. But it's not because these folks found jobs; they simply were no longer counted as unemployed. This means that changes in definitions of what constitutes an employed worker or a modification of the criteria in a given category can change the unemployment numbers without necessarily getting those people jobs (Sherman, 2018).

As Figure 5.4 shows, the employment to population ratio, which is the percentage of all people of working age (and including those who have stopped looking for work) that are employed decreased slightly (60.4 percent to 60.3 percent) in 2015 because more people were no longer counted in the labor rolls. Looking at the substantial drop in 2010 after the financial crisis and recession shows some improvement but it is still a long way away from the percentages in 1999, where it was close to 65 percent (Sherman, 2018).

Why would some people drop out of the labor force and not look for work? Women might leave the workforce to have children, and retirees might be able to leave the workforce altogether. College students might not be counted in the workforce. For whatever the reason, the United States is just below 63 percent in terms of labor participation, after reaching a high of over 67 percent in the mid-2000s (Sherman, 2018).

Thus, the data indicates that the reason that the unemployment rate keeps dropping is not that more people are back to work. Rather, it keeps dropping because more people have given up on finding work and are no longer counted as either working or unemployed. It's not the case that the economy is getting better and life has improved for more people. In fact, the fact that so many have given up on finding work means less long-term economic stability and more pressure on social programs designed to help the poor.

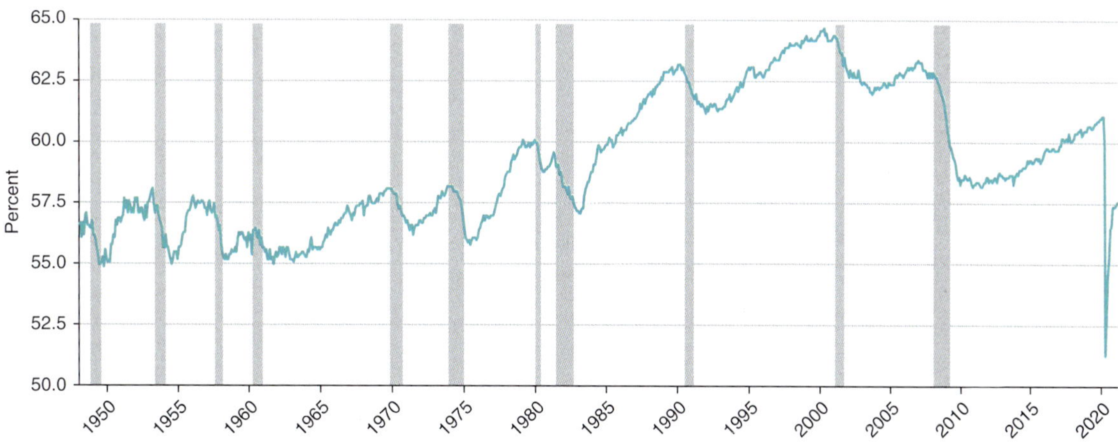

Figure 5.4 Civilian Employment-Population Ratio Shaded areas represent US recessions. Source: US Bureau of Labor Statistics; Federal Reserve Bank of St. Louis.

This trend also explains why wages have not improved for most workers. If more people were working, wages would increase because employers would have to respond to the market and the selectivity of workers. However, the Federal Reserve has noted that while people may be earning more than in the past, inflation detracts from the extra money earned. With so many people dropping out of the labor force, there is little need for employers to increase wages to keep and obtain workers (Sherman, 2018).

Unions and the Protection of Workers

Historically, unions have served as a countermeasure to the exploitation of workers. Unions were instrumental in providing workers with a collective voice to employers about working conditions, salary, and other considerations that resulted in a number of protections for workers. In fact, at one time, unions were a mainstay to the US economy. In the 1940s and 1950s, for example, union membership consisted of about a third of all US workers. In 2018, according to the US Bureau of Labor Statistics, only about 11 percent of American workers are members of unions (Figure 5.5).

Part of the decline of union membership relates to the changing nature of jobs in the United States, where health care, restaurant, and hospitality jobs, which have not had high unionization membership, are some of the fastest growing segments of the labor market. These types of jobs are also a considerable part of the gig economy and the rise of contract-based jobs and contingency work. As was mentioned, manufacturing jobs, which is generally characterized by organized labor, has been declining over the past thirty years (Kopf, 2019). The decline of unions is also said to explain the increase in income inequality in the United States. In a 2018 study, over the past eighty years union workers have earned approximately 20 percent more than non-union workers,

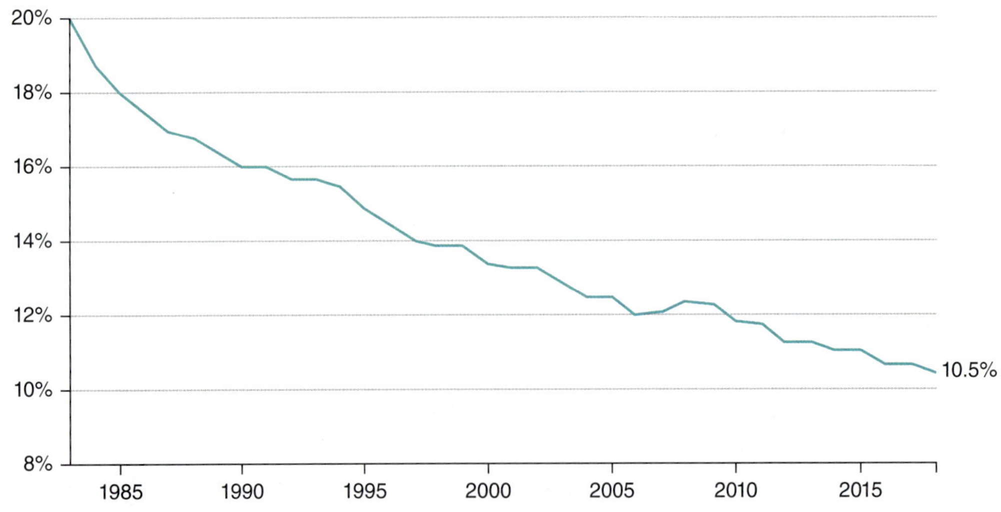

Figure 5.5 Decline in US workers in unions Source: Irina Ivanova. (2019). "Union Membership Hit Record Low in 2018." CBS News, January 21.

in part because of their ability to collectively bargain with companies. As unions have declined, so have wages and worker protections (Kopf, 2019).

In his book *Beaten Down and Worked Up*, Steven Greenhouse (2019) argues that the declining influence of unions, once a paragon of championing worker needs and concerns, have left workers on their own to fight those battles. Greenhouse characterizes the vulnerability of American workers to various types of exploitation and abuses by employers, including unfair labor practices, harassment and discrimination, and unreasonable demands on worker productivity that benefits the company's bottom line. So limited have unions become in the market that many have even refrained from going on strike because they fear that workers will simply be replaced and the strike as a strategy no longer holds the same bargaining power with employers (Greenhouse, 2019).

The Underground Economy

By many accounts, many of the problems discussed thus far have resulted in the growth of what is known as **the underground economy**, a term used to describe any economic activity that generates unreported income (Johnston, 2019). This term typically evokes images of criminal behavior, such as drug deals, buying and selling stolen merchandise or various forms of sex work, but in reality, the underground economy encompasses a wide range of illegal activities within traditional industries such as construction, auto repair, landscaping, or food service (Johnston, 2019).

Participants in the underground economy work for an employer "off the books" or without paying taxes or being counted as an employee. Such a situation can easily become exploitative in that workers are paid less than what other employees receive and there is little in the way of recourse if the employee is cheated out of earnings or injured on the job. In addition, employers don't have to contribute to Social Security or payroll tax for these workers. Given that the vast majority of people working in the underground economy are semi-skilled and unskilled, coupled with the limited opportunities for obtaining a steady job, many employees in this economy are vulnerable to a host of job-related risks.

Individuals may also work for themselves in the underground economy so that they do not have to pay taxes on the money or obtain the necessary licenses or permits to operate. This places a strain on legitimate businesses since these costs are normally absorbed by employers, but people working in the underground economy can charge less for those same goods and services. While data on the size and scope of the underground economy is difficult to obtain, primarily because concealment is part of the nature of these activities, some experts estimate that the underground economy is about 11–12 percent of US gross domestic product (GDP). In 2018, GDP was $20.5 trillion, so the underground economy was estimated to be approximately $2.25 trillion to $2.46 trillion. This is significant, along with the loss of tax revenue for the US, which is estimated to be about $500 billion (Johnston, 2019; Goldstene, 2014).

SOCIOLOGICAL THEORY, WORK, AND THE ECONOMY

The preceding discussion shows that large scale changes in the economy have a host of intended and unintended consequences for workers. This includes challenges to the declining influence of unions, the loss of millions of jobs for semi-skilled and unskilled workers, and the tendency for companies and corporations to redefine how and in what way it provides for its employees. How can we make sociological sense of these and other trends? There are many ways to apply sociological theory to this discussion, but given our emphasis on applying sociology to the real world, we will take a specific topic discussed in the chapter, globalization, and use the three main sociological perspectives to understand it.

Recall that globalization is the economic, cultural and social interconnectedness between countries by trading goods, services, technology, people, and information (Peterson Institute for International Economics, n.d.). Many experts agree that globalization has been a good thing for many developing countries, which were given the opportunity to export inexpensive goods and offer services previously unavailable to the rest of the world and it also presented opportunities for jobs in those countries.

Functionalism and Work

Recall that the functionalist perspective emphasizes, among other things, the maintenance of social equilibrium, the interconnectedness between groups and people, and the social cohesion that emerges when there is consensus on the way people live their lives. In this sense, functionalists would argue that globalization is an important feature of social life because it brings people together both economically as well as socially. As discussed by Durkheim in *the Division of Labor in Society,* this type of social connectedness is known as organic solidarity.

In addition, globalization can also contribute to a stronger collective conscience—where the people begin to see the commonality across groups of people in different countries, which further enhances their understanding of the economic, social and cultural connectedness. As people begin to grasp how similar we are to one another, and learn to appreciate the differences, our overall sense of concern and compassion toward one another increases the social cohesion among different groups.

As it relates to the 2020 pandemic, functionalists would likely see this event as a form of anomie, where there has been a breakdown in the normative structures in society. This is particularly true as it relates to the economy and job situations for many people. Anomie also offers insight into how people are coping with this sudden change and societal breakdown of the norms. As people consider the severity of events and as many attempt to form some sort of response, panic-driven behavior in the form of stockpiling food and other essentials has occurred.

Conflict Theory and Work

While the promise of globalization was to elevate and expand opportunities for other countries to prosper economically, along with more opportunities for jobs, it has instead resulted in greater economic and social inequality and few real job opportunities. In fact, from a conflict perspective, globalization has in fact perpetuated existing economic inequalities, increased worker exploitation, and contributed to what Marx describes as an alienation from work. Recall the discussion of alienation in Chapter 1, where we said this idea is what occurs as workers are exploited by capitalists who are attempting to maximize profits over worker safety or better wages (Ritzer and Stepinsky, 2017).

Alienation from work is most readily seen in the rise of the problems relating to contingency work, the gig economy and the challenges of people obtaining jobs with benefits such as sick time, vacation time, and retirement benefits—all of which have been linked to globalization. It also emerges as worker exploitation increases as well as unfair labor practices as vulnerable workers have few options but to accept the conditions employers provide workers and perpetuates the dramatic social, economic, and political differences between workers and capitalists.

Symbolic Interactionism and Work

At first glance, a concept like globalization might not seem to lend itself to symbolic interactionist analysis, given the latter's emphasis on micro-level interactions. In one sense, that's correct, but remember in chapter 1 we said that one of the primary advantages of the symbolic interactionist perspective is that it offers insight into how people understand the world around them.

One way to apply the symbolic interactionist approach to globalization would be to analyze how people's understanding of the value of diversity and multiculturalism is enhanced by their exposure to and experiences with people from other cultures and countries. In other words, as workers begin to realize that the experiences they have in the workplace transcend their particular job or country, a greater understanding of social inequality is achieved.

Another illustration of the symbolic interactionist approach as it relates to globalization refers to how workers, particularly Millennials, attempt to achieve some work/life balance—where a job is not necessarily seen as a primary identity marker. This idea was explored earlier in the chapter regarding why some Millennials, after seeing the effects of globalization and a changing job market, reconceptualize the meaning of work and its value in achieving a happy life (Frazier, 2019).

Symbolic interactionists would examine the 2020 pandemic in terms of how it is reshaping the nature of social interaction. The practice of social distancing, where people are being told to limit the size of groups and the actual physical distance they remain from one another when they do gather, changes the nature of interaction. As the fear of the virus spreads, it also leads people to refrain from interacting in person all together.

WHAT WORKS? EFFECTIVE SOLUTIONS TO WORKPLACE PROBLEMS

What can be done about problems relating to unemployment, the minimum wage, globalization, and the disappearance of low-skilled jobs in the manufacturing sector? These are clearly macro-level problems that require a great deal of consideration and a commitment of resources beyond the simplistic solution of "create more well-paying jobs" or "get people better training and education so they are more marketable." While these sound like good ideas, exactly how to implement such strategies is much more complex. Moreover, in a free market system, constraining employers by shouldering them with additional costs related to increasing wages or re-training workers ultimately hurts their ability to remain competitive, eventually crippling the economy. We can't find fault with employers who turn to automation to reduce their labor costs, since that is the largest expense they encounter in running their business. Nor can we find fault in their decision to continue to pay low wages if there is an ample supply of workers willing to work for that amount. This is the nature of a free market economy.

As we have seen, however, the existing system burdens everyone. Low wages cost taxpayers more in assistance programs, diminish tax revenue, and fuel the creation of an underground economy, where workers pay no taxes at all. While employers don't generally mind this as a system, since the costs are spread out across everyone and doesn't impact their bottom lines in a direct way, these costs are larger than what it would take to simply provide adequate salary increases to workers. What can be done and what might work? While there are no easy or simple solutions to this problem, and while there are no guarantees that any strategy will work, one idea relates to how we approach the nature of jobs and where work is performed.

Flextime and Telecommuting

One promising strategy relates to the use of flextime and telecommuting to allow workers the opportunity to create a better work/life balance. According to Taylor (2019), the idea behind flex time allows workers to leverage technology and remain productive, but without the burden of a traditional 9 to 5 job. This is important since many traditional opportunities appear to be diminishing, so companies and employees are searching for ways to build in flexibility in an ever-changing world. In fact, in 2018 there were over four million employees who worked from home at least part-time, an increase of 140 percent since 2005. Many companies have realized that as business occurs on a global scale, it requires employees to be available beyond the traditional business hours (Taylor, 2019).

Not only do strategies like telecommuting result in greater flexibility for businesses, it also appeals to the latest generation of workers. This is important since Millennials make up the largest population of workers and it is expected that 75 percent of the US workforce will consist of Millennials by 2025. Given that this group is technologically savvy and wants greater freedom when it comes to work, there is every reason to think that strategies like flextime and telecommuting will be a common feature of many businesses in the future (Figure 5.6). Such strategies also benefit businesses who will continue to use outside contractors and part-time employees (Taylor, 2019). The popularity of these strategies was leveraged in the early stages of the 2020 pandemic in the United States, as many employers encouraged and even required employees to work from home (Hadden, Casado, and Sonnemaker, 2020).

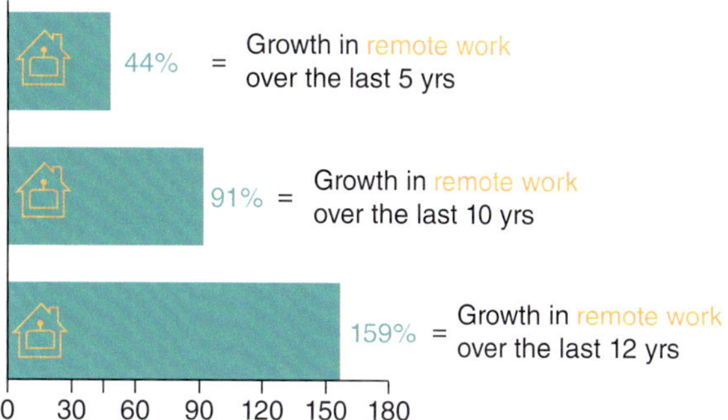

Figure 5.6 Trends in remote work growth Source: Beth B. Hering (2020). "Remote Works Statistics: Shifting Norms and Expectations." Flexjobs.com, February 13.

SO WHAT CAN I DO?

When it comes to a macro level issue as complex as the global economy, structural issues influence the steps any individual might make to remedy them. You cannot, for example, change the trends in globalization, deindustrialization, or the creation of a gig economy, but you may be able to influence how you spend your money—which can affect how companies treat its employees.

As an illustration, Nike Corporation subcontracts with employers in sweatshops in countries like South Korea to manufacture Nike apparel. In some cases, children working in the factory earn about two dollars a day making sneakers that generally cost around five dollars to make. These sneakers are then sold in the United States for upward of $100. The use of sweatshop labor became a battle cry by many labor advocates and forced Nike and other companies to make changes to such a strategy (Segran, 2017).

However, under capitalism, the actions by Nike and other corporations is understandable: after all, they are simply doing whatever they can to lower their costs of production and the use of sweatshop labor is one way to do that and maximize their profit. It was only after public outcry resulted in consumer distaste and the potential loss of revenue that Nike was forced the company to find a more reasonable and equitable alternative.

CONCLUSION

The nature of capitalism requires a need to maximize corporate profit at the expense of the individual worker. Over the last several decades, this has resulted in unskilled workers finding it increasingly difficult to find steady employment at fair wages, due to outsourcing or automation. This crisis has been especially obvious in the manufacturing sector, which shows greater output despite the loss of millions of jobs in those industries.

Such a movement is a natural consequence of an evolving economy and it also means that discussions about things like the gig economy, where part-time work may be what's left as companies begin to reduce the number of full-time employees or use technology to eliminate many jobs performed by humans. It also plays a role in the development of the underground economy, as unemployed workers attempt to find some means to earn a living if legitimate jobs are not available.

In addition to the emerging trends about the nature of work and the economy in the United States, the 2020 pandemic has forced us to reconsider everything we understand about the economy and the workplace. One question to consider is how we use the past successes in overcoming the enormous obstacles to meet this new challenge? Another question to consider is how sociological theory helps us to frame our understanding of these challenges.

YOU MAKE THE CALL: FAIR PAY

You decide to start your own business. One of the things you quickly realize is that your biggest expense is labor. As any small business owner will tell you, every expense matters and you will constantly be pressured to make decisions, often difficult ones, if you want your business to turn a profit. Because you majored in sociology as an undergraduate, you are very sensitive to the issues and challenges many minorities and people of color face in the United States. You make a decision that you are going to pay your employees above the minimum wage so that they have a chance to make ends meet. Instead of the normal $7.25 per hour you decide to pay your employees $10.00 per hour.

You are feeling pretty good about your decision and your employees are grateful, especially when they know the going rate for the work they do is normally worth $7.25 per hour. They are loyal to you because they know this is a sacrifice for you to make, as it means less profit, particularly as the number of employees hired increases.

However, the state recently mandated that the new minimum wage, effective next month, will be $15 per hour. This means that the minimum wage has more than doubled in a short period of time. As news of this development spreads, your employees come to you, asking if they will be paid the new minimum wage or one that is prorated to reflect the difference in what they currently make and the old minimum wage. Already facing a 50 percent increase in labor costs (from $10 to $15 per hour), you are faced with an even larger expense if you make it proportional (you were paying $2.75 more per hour prior to the change). You may also need to consider laying off workers or turning to automation to address the long-term expenses of having employees. Even though technology has costs associated with it, you begin to weigh out the benefits of using artificial intelligence and technology to do the things currently performed by people. Suddenly you find yourself with much more complicated dilemmas about your compassion for people and what you thought was responsible and ethical business practices. You began with the decision to treat your employees fairly and now, because of a new law designed to help low wage workers, you are actually weighing the decision to eliminate much if not all of your staff.

Questions for you to consider:

1. Do you simply pay the workers the new minimum wage, which is a significant increase over what they were making before?
2. How do you respond to their complaints that they were worth almost 40 percent above the minimum wage prior to the change but now are only worth the minimum?
3. Are you worried about employee resentment and a lack of commitment to you and your business? Will your employees, whom you have spent money training and have gained experience in your operations, simply leave to find a better job?
4. Do you pay the employees nearly $18 per hour, which would make it challenging to turn a profit?
5. What about employees who are experienced—they will be paid the same as a new employee—are you concerned that this might create problems among the staff and affect their productivity?
6. Do you use the new minimum wage but create a profit-sharing plan for experienced employees, so that their efforts are tied to the profitability of the company?
7. What types of things do you consider as you contemplate using automation instead of paying workers a higher salary?
8. Do you inform your employees that one possible outcome of the increases may be that you will be laying them off or cutting their hours back to part-time?

SUMMARY

- Describe the different types of economic systems.
  - The various economic systems include traditional, command, free market, and mixed economies.
- Summarize examples of government intervention in the US economy.
  - Globalization means that changes in one country's economy inevitably impact others across the world.
  - During the US financial crisis in 2008, banks were bailed out by the government because the impact could have been catastrophic not only in the United States, but in every other country.
- Analyze the nature of work and employment in the United States.
  - Changes in the economy such as globalization, deindustrialization, and the role of technology have reshaped the nature of work in the US.
- Describe the impact of broader economic changes on workers.
  - Micro-level implications of economic changes on workers include changes to the minimum wage; the movement for a living wage; the rise of a gig economy; the growth of the underground economy; and an overall increase in the extent of employment in the US.
- Compare sociological paradigms as they relate to work and the economy.
  - Using the three main paradigms in sociology, several of the topics discussed, such as the gig economy and the challenges workers face in a shifting marketplace, were examined.

KEY TERMS

Alt-labor movement 152
Capitalism 143
Command economy 141
Communist society 141
Deindustrialization 149
Democratic socialism 146
Fight for $15 152
Free market economy 141
Free trade 148
Gig economy 152
Globalization 147
Invisible hand 143
Laissez-faire 143
Living wage 152
Means of production 141
Mixed economy 141
Mortgage-backed securities 000
North American Free Trade Agreement (NAFTA) 148
Service economy 149
Socialism 141
Trade deficit 139
Traditional economy 140
Underground economy 157
Universal Basic Income 146
Universalism 147

Discussion Questions

1. How would you explain the reasons behind the economic recession in 2008? What factors were critical to the reason banks failed and the government had to bail them out?
2. Why would the federal government decide to bail out the auto industry? Should the government have let GM and Chrysler fail because they did not respond to changes in the market, as did other companies, like Honda and Toyota?
3. Do you think President Trump's decision to increase tariffs on goods from other countries is consistent with free trade or is this a business ploy to get a better trade agreement with those countries?
4. Should people who have declared bankruptcy be required to submit to financial oversight by the government? After all, bankruptcy tends to show they cannot adequately handle their finances so shouldn't the government be allowed to restrict some of their decision making when it comes to spending? Why or why not?
5. Should we follow the pathway of other countries, such as Finland, which has begun to experiment with the idea of a universal income for everyone? What might be some of the problems with this approach?

Learn more with this chapter's digital tools, including Data and Media Literacy Exercises, flashcards, and chapter self-assessments at **www.oup.com/he/mcnamara**.

6

Can't We All Just Get Along? Racial and Ethnic Inequalities

LEARNING OBJECTIVES

- Define the concepts such as race, ethnicity, minority groups, racism, prejudice and discrimination.
- Define the social construction of race and its significance to minority groups, the relationship between prejudice and discrimination, and White privilege.
- Identify institutional discrimination and systemic racism and its impact on housing, education, criminal justice and employment.
- Analyze sociological theories as they relate to race, ethnicity, racism, and discrimination.
- Assess examples of issues and problems relating to race, along with assessments of programs to improve diversity and address discrimination.

Chapter Outline

Solidarity against violence Protestors raised their fists in a gesture of solidarity and defiance outside of the Fifth Police Precinct headquarters in Minneapolis, Minnesota, following the murder of unarmed Black man George Floyd by police officers.

As with poverty, the topic of race is highly emotional. There are numerous examples of controversial incidents that have a racial undertone to them including police officers' use of force against minority suspects, policy decisions that separate immigrant children from their families, anti-Asian policies in college admissions, or fears and concerns about the innocuous behavior of Black men in public.

In 2020, many of these issues were brought to the forefront of people's thinking and behavior, with the death of George Floyd, yet another Black man who was killed by White police officers. This event prompted protests across the country, some of which became violent, and elevated the issues to a new level of urgency. Demonstrations calling for the removal of statutes of Confederate leaders, as well as changing the names of military bases or university buildings, have also become part of the narrative. In addition to the protests, the Black Lives Matter movement gained a higher profile in the discussion and has raised important questions about various forms of systemic racism and discrimination. All these events have shaped the political, economic, and social landscape.

An important part of the challenge in discussing issues related to race, prejudice and discrimination is countering the misinformation about what is known compared to what is offered to the public from the media. It is fair to say that the media has contributed to these problems, and their credibility has been called into question when some outlets fail to provide accurate information in an attempt to control or contain the narrative about race. The result is that the public is often only provided partial information or distorted versions of the events. It also leads some people to wonder which news agencies are trustworthy sources from which to learn about current events.

As with our explorations of poverty, it is critical that you as a social scientist both acknowledge your strong feelings about and experiences with racism and make every effort to ground your observations and thoughts in the data. If we are going to work together to constructively solve the social problems relating to prejudice, discrimination, and racism, it is imperative that our discussion remain focused on the data, not on emotion.

While individual acts of discrimination and prejudice can be problematic for those who experience them, of greater concern are the challenges related to what can be described as **institutional discrimination** or **systemic racism**. While there is some debate about how these terms differ, what they have in common is that the negative attitude or behavior against certain groups is embedded into the structure of society. That is, systemic racism goes beyond individuals acting inappropriately. In some cases, this type of unconscious bias can actually lead people to conclude everyone is treated equally. For instance, many police advocates argue that they treat all suspects equally, and those that do not are isolated cases, reflecting a "bad apples" theory of policing. Such a position ignores the structural factors that contribute to perceptions and understanding of certain groups, both within policing as well as society in general, what is sometimes referred to as systemic racism.

In the bad apples theory of why Black men are so often targeted by police officers, the argument is that those particular officers who hold negative attitudes against Black people should be treated as isolated cases. Others who point to systemic racism or institutional discrimination as the problem assert that what makes the problem of racial profiling or excessive use of force by police officers against Black men so dangerous is that the discriminatory behavior becomes so common that people are unaware that they are contributing to and/or are participating in it.

The uprisings that have occurred in 2020 called attention to, in part, what seems to be individual acts of racism. There are many such examples. In New York City, a White woman, Amy Cooper, called 911 about a Black man who asked her to leash her dog in an area of Central Park where leashing is required. The woman told the dispatcher to send the police immediately because the man was threatening her. The allegations were untrue and Cooper was charged with making a false statement. She was also fired from her job as a result (Martinez, 2020). While these events may not seem to be part of a systemic problem and this particular incident may seem trivial, they not only reflect a pattern of perception of Black men that systematically stigmatizes them, the consequences for Black males can have fatal consequences.

SOCIOLOGICAL STORY TIME

- On May 25, 2020, in Minneapolis, Minnesota, George Floyd, a Black man, was arrested outside a convenience store for allegedly using a counterfeit $20 bill to purchase cigarettes. Officer Derek Chauvin, the White responding officer, handcuffed Floyd and placed him face down on the ground. He also placed his knee on Floyd's neck for over eight minutes while waiting to transport Floyd to the station house for processing. Floyd repeatedly pleaded with Chauvin, claiming "I can't breathe." Chauvin and two other responding officers restrained Floyd. After a short time, Floyd became unresponsive and ultimately died. The four officers involved in this case were fired and Chauvin was charged with murder (Graves, 2020).
- On March 13, 2020, in Louisville, Kentucky, police officers attempted to serve a search warrant at the apartment of Breonna Taylor and Kenneth Walker, Taylor's boyfriend. The police had reason to believe that residents of the home were selling drugs. A "no-knock" warrant, authorized by a judge, allowed the police to use a battering ram to force open the door. Upon entering the apartment, Walker, who had a license to carry a gun, fired at the officers, thinking they were intruders. The other officers returned fire, accidentally hitting Taylor at least eight times. Taylor was pronounced dead at the scene. Questions remain about whether the police announced themselves while entering the home and whether one of the three officers serving the warrant blindly fired into the apartment from the exterior of the residence. Protests against the actions of the police occurred throughout Louisville, calling for the arrest of the officers involved (Carrega and Ghebremedhim, 2020).
- Harvard University has adopted a stance in its admissions policies that focuses on factors other than academic achievement. In 2018, the university claimed that the reason for its failure to admit more Asian Americans was due to the fact that they rated lower on social variables relating to their ability to fit in with other students, despite having extraordinarily high SAT scores. As a result, a group, Student for Fair Admissions, has filed a lawsuit claiming such a strategy is without merit and is a form of micro-aggression against Asian American students. Data indicates that if academic achievement alone were used for admission, nearly half of the students admitted would be Asian Americans (Lowry 2018).

DEFINITIONAL MATTERS

A foundational myth of American society is the idea that people from different backgrounds can peacefully coexist in a society that embraces cultural diversity. As a nation of immigrants, many different groups have defined the character and identity of America. The data suggests that with each generation, the United States becomes more diverse (Table 6.1). In 2019 Whites made up about 76 percent of the population;

Table 6.1 Racial and Ethnic Populations in the United States

Group	Percentage
White	76.3%
Black	13.4%
Hispanic	18.5%
Asian	5.9%
American Indian/Alaska Native	1.3%
Native Hawaiian/Other Pacific Islander	< 1%

Source: US Census Bureau, 2019.

Hispanics/Latinos represented about 18 percent, Blacks comprised about 13 percent; Asians about 6 percent; and Native Americans 1 percent of the population (US Census Bureau, 2019).

However, not everyone sees themselves as belonging to only one category. And, of course, neither Native Americans nor many Blacks whose ancestors were brought here as enslaved people would consider themselves "immigrants." In 2000, the US Census Bureau gave people the opportunity to identify with more than one race, creating a possible 57 racial categories. In 2019, about three percent of the population self-identified as multiracial; a figure that is expected to double by 2060 (US Census Bureau, 2019). Given the increased likelihood of people to see themselves as belonging to more than one race or ethnic group, it raises questions about whether race and ethnicity will be as important as a defining feature of individuals in the future.

Race and Ethnicity

For our purposes, it is important that we clearly define what we mean by terms like "race" and "ethnicity." In our society—and especially in media coverage of related issues—these terms are used interchangeably even though the distinctions are meaningful and important.

RACE

The idea of distinguishable groups based on race is something that has existed for many years. In the nineteenth century biologists attempted to develop a typology that grouped humans into three categories: Negroid, Mongoloid, and Caucasoid, which essentially translates into Black, Asian, and White. The notion was that there were distinguishing features of these groups that made separating them possible. From a sociological point of view, according to the American Sociological Association, **race**

Irish pride Spectators at the St. Patrick's Day Parade in New York City celebrate Irish ethnicity, whether or not they are actually of Irish descent.

refers to "physical differences that groups and cultures consider socially significant" (American Sociological Association, n.d.).

ETHNICITY

Ethnicity is another social category we use to distinguish groups of people. Instead of physical characteristics however, what distinguishes one ethnic group from another relates to their cultural ancestry and heritage. Things like language, religion and history are the markers of distinction. Think of Italian Americans, Irish Americans, and Hispanics as an ethnic group. By way of a definition, according to the American Sociological Association, ethnicity "refers to shared culture, such as language, ancestry, practices, and beliefs"(American Sociological Association, n.d.).

THE SOCIAL CONSTRUCTION OF RACE

Sociologically, while it is fascinating to learn how societies use certain physical characteristics to separate racial groups (even though they are rather imperfect and not scientifically valid), the important point is that people think of race as more of a social category, whether or not these biological differences actually exist. Modern research has shown, however, that there are no scientifically valid races; further, the lines between races, a result of intermarriage over generations, means there is no pure racial group.

There is also no such thing as a "superior" race as the characteristics one group might have little or nothing to do with the physical characteristics used to identify one racial group from another. Moreover, even within one racial group, such as Asian, there is wide variation in talents, abilities, and other features, making any meaningful distinction impossible. But if, by definition, physical characteristics are the mark of distinction between one racial group and another, can one really tell if someone is black just by their skin color? Not necessarily.

This use of race and ethnicity as social categories rather than biological ones is sometimes referred to as the **social construction of race.** This concept suggests that the particular physical characteristics a society uses to distinguish one racial group from another are relatively meaningless. There is no scientific proof that skin color, hair texture, earlobe size, or any similar designations proves that there is a distinction between one group and another. Rather, two ideas about race are critical for sociologists: first, that each society determines for itself which particular features matter; and second, how the response to those characteristics shapes and influences people's perceptions of that group. In other words, sociologists are concerned with the identities people construct based on arbitrary distinctions to determine the difference between racial groups. In reality, there are more similarities than differences between people (Haney Lopez, 1995).

The brutality of apartheid The entrance to the Apartheid Museum in Cape Town, South Africa, reminds all visitors of the brutal oppression of non-White people in that country during the years of apartheid.

Minority Groups

Sociologists define a **minority group** not in terms of its numerical size but rather as a group that suffers from unequal treatment. A minority group is denied access to social, economic and political power and resources that are given to the dominant groups in society. Membership in a minority group may become an identity marker for individuals, transcending gender, age, or other affiliation. Because of the mistreatment they receive at the hands of the dominant group, members of minority groups tend to develop a strong sense of solidarity and common identity.

Thus, it is possible to be numerically superior in a given society and still be considered a minority. Under the **apartheid** system in South Africa, for example, Blacks constituted the numerical majority, but all the social, economic and political power remained with the much smaller White population. Historically, in the United States Whites have been considered the majority both in terms of population as well as in access to resources. While Whites currently make up about 76 percent of the US population, in the 1960s that percentage was close to 85 percent. While the proportion of African Americans has remained stable over the past few decades, the number of Hispanics/Latinos and Asian has grown considerably. If predictions hold true, by 2044 Whites will make up about 48 percent of the US population (Colby and Ortman, 2015).

Prejudice, Discrimination, and Racism

It is important as a social scientist to understand the distinction between prejudice and discrimination. **Prejudice** consists of a negative attitude toward a group of people. Prejudice involves a strong emotional component that is unlikely to change. In fact, prejudiced people are often so strong in their beliefs about a group of people that they will continue to maintain their prejudice despite evidence to the contrary. This inflexibility and connection to emotion instead of evidence and logic is what makes prejudice so dangerous.

Discrimination can be defined as the behavioral component of mistreating those who are members of a particular group. To treat a subordinate group member as inferior is to discriminate against them. While discrimination is normally overt behavior, at times it can be difficult to identify. In other words, while prejudice is the abstract idea related to mistreating a group of people, discrimination is the acting out of that

Table 6.2 Merton's Typology on Prejudice and Discrimination

Unprejudiced Non-Discriminator	Holds no negative attitudes against other groups, and does not discriminate against them.
Prejudiced Discriminator	Has negative attitudes against groups and these translate into negative forms of discrimination.
Prejudiced Non-Discriminator	Has negative attitudes but does not discriminate; closet bigot.
Unprejudiced Discriminator	May discriminate against certain groups but the reasons for doing so may not relate to negative attitudes against them. Motives for discrimination may be due to profit or because others hold negative attitudes against the group.

idea (Table 6.2). In a now classic article, sociologist Robert K. Merton offered further explanation of the relationship between the two concepts (Merton, 1949).

The value in Merton's analysis is that it shows how prejudice and discrimination are related as well as offering insight into some of the different ways they can function to result in negative behaviors (Merton 1949).

Racism is behavior based on the belief that humans have distinctive characteristics that determine their abilities. Racists tend to believe that their own race is superior to all other races. Racism can be a way to describe an individual or it can be used to describe the organization and operation of an entire society. Examples of the latter include South Africa under apartheid or Nazi Germany during the early part of the twentieth century, as well as groups in the United States such as the Ku Klux Klan or the Proud Boys.

Many Whites may claim that race no longer matters and that we live in a color-blind society. This notion of **color-blind racism** essentially dismisses race in the discussion of social inequality. As some sociologists argue, color-blind racism is just a new form of racism; one that is even more difficult to eradicate since people think racism is no longer a problem.

Racism on parade At a 2017 "Unite the Right" rally in Charlottesville, Virginia, White nationalists and other racist groups flaunted racist symbols such as the Confederate flag. The rally turned violent, resulting in the death of a counter-protester.

White Privilege and White Fragility

Another important concept that relates to the discussions of race and racism is **White privilege**. This is a set of benefits granted to those who resemble the people—almost always White—who dominate powerful positions in our institutions. Color-blind racism is one result of White privilege, because privilege is often invisible to those who have that advantage. One of the primary privileges of being White in our society is greater access to power and resources than people of color. For example, given the same financial history, White people in the United States are two to ten times more likely to get a housing loan than people of color. All White people have White privileges, although the extent to which they have them varies depending on gender, sexual orientation, socioeconomic status, age, physical ability, size and weight, and so on.

While those who call out White privilege assert that White people have been socialized and convinced that they should come to expect certain benefits simply because they are White, those who deny the existence of White privilege offer two key arguments. They claim either that White privilege does not exist at all, or that it applies only to certain segments of the White population; primarily the wealthy and powerful. The concept of **White fragility** refers to that state of denial which for some White people leads to outrage when their privilege is called out (DiAngelo, 2018). In response to the first argument, sociologist Joe Feagin argues that American culture has socialized Whites to think they should view their dominant status as natural. Further, Feagin argues that racial inequalities should be viewed not as a product of Whites' privileged position, but as something over which they have no responsibility for or obligation to remedy (Feagin, 2006).

With regard to the second point, sociologist Arlie Hochschild interviewed working-class White people in Louisiana and discovered a level of discouragement by many residents who feel that the government caters to other groups such as minorities, immigrants, and Blacks. The implication is that these working-class Whites should be designated as a protected class (Hochschild, 2016).

Some critics of White privilege argue that working-class Whites should not be expected to acknowledge their favored position in society. After all, Whites who experience poverty and hardship, especially in a severe economic downturn such as that occasioned by the Covid-19 pandemic, will indeed have difficulty appreciating their enhanced societal position. Whites in such circumstances do not see nor do they accept the argument that they are benefitting from any enhanced position based on their race. Instead, the narrative becomes one in which minorities blame all Whites for their circumstances and do not take responsibility for their own behavior (Starkey, 2017). In fact, some evidence indicates the development of "Black

Acknowledging White privilege A participant at a 2020 Black Lives Matter protest in Portland, Oregon, holds a sign reading, "I am White, I am privileged, use your privilege to fight!"

privilege," where Whites complain of being accused of racism for the same celebration and identification of their race (Starkey, 2017).

This weaponization of White despair has been a common assertion by certain politicians who falsely claim that the problem is really about poor choices by Blacks who commit crimes, resist commands by the police, and face the consequences of their actions. This explains the high number of deaths by Black Americans. In July 2020, when asked in an interview with *CBS News* about why so many Blacks had been killed by the police, President Donald Trump's response was, "So are white people! What a terrible question to ask." He added that "more White people by the way, are killed by police than Black people." Consistent with an unwillingness to recognize the problem, what President Trump failed to acknowledge is that Blacks are killed by the police at a far higher rate than Whites (Montanero, 2020).

One of the greatest challenges to White privilege is convincing Whites that there are systemic obstacles and strategies that inhibit Blacks in ways that Whites have never experienced, considered, or encountered. For example, social policies of the past, such as the G.I. Bill for soldiers after World War II provided funds for education and home purchases were not made available for Blacks. Such strategies created and perpetuated a form of privilege for Whites that have been denied blacks (Starkey, 2017).

Is the Problem about Race or Social Class?

Some experts suggest that the challenges minorities have experienced may have to do with social class as well as race. William Julius Wilson, a noted expert on race issues, has long argued that the discriminatory treatment of minorities can be seen not so much as a result of their racial identities, but as a function of social class. Wilson argued that the US labor market created a Black underclass, largely because the jobs for which they were qualified were in the lowest paying sectors of the market.

His controversial findings generated a great deal of research by scholars. In subsequent work Wilson has continued to argue that economic class has become more important than race in explaining the status of African Americans in the United States. In fact, Wilson has argued that income inequality has increased across all racial and ethnic populations, and that social class has become more significant a factor in determining one's life chances than ever before (Steinhauser, 2015).

INSTITUTIONAL DISCRIMINATION AND SYSTEMIC RACISM

The significance of Robert Merton's description of the relationship between prejudice and discrimination shows the many ways in which the two are connected. One can have negative attitudes toward a group of people, but it does not always translate into discriminatory behavior. However, what Merton's typology does not explain is the

GLOBAL PERSPECTIVES

Racial Tolerance

The Black Lives Matter movement has brought attention to racism in the United States and around the globe. According to the World Value Survey, the United States is fairly tolerant of others than other places in the world. The survey asks participants in more than 80 countries what kind of person they would want as a neighbor. Those who said they would not want someone of a different race were identified as racially intolerant (Figure 6.1).

The findings from the survey indicate that

- Countries in the Middle East and Asia were found to be the least racially tolerant.
- Latin and Anglo countries were the most racially tolerant.
- Jordan and India were the least racially tolerant.
- France was the least racially tolerant country in Europe (Perry, 2017).

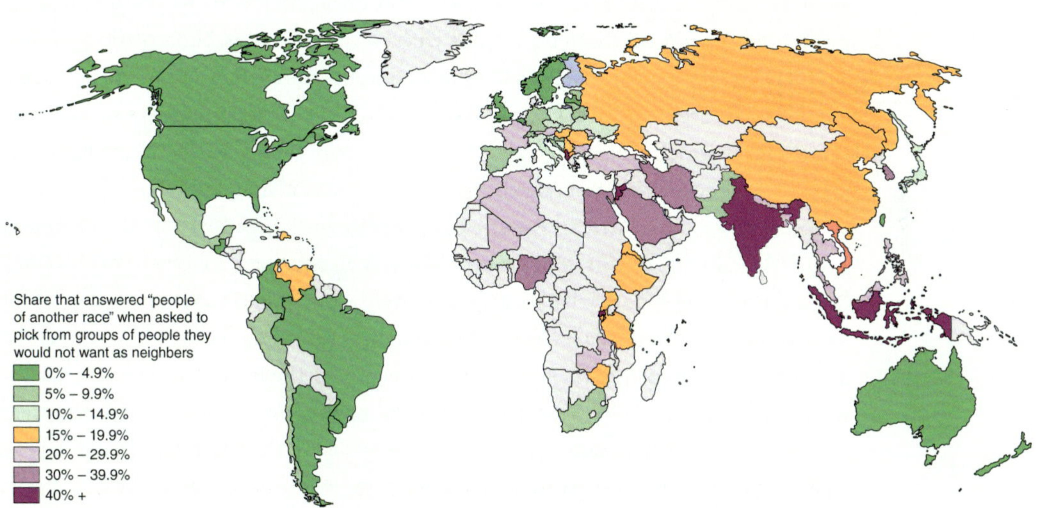

Figure 6.1 Racial tolerance around the world Data source: World Values Survey. Map source: Max Fisher/The Washington Post.

notion of institutional discrimination; which is the type of discrimination built into the structure of society. The process by which African Americans have been excluded from equal participation in society is systemic racism, or institutional racism. It is important to acknowledge the structural (societal) impediments that have kept African Americans from being successful (Clair and Denis, 2015; Stokely and Hamilton, 1967).

While institutional discrimination focuses on particular aspects of the problem, systemic racism involves a more holistic devaluing of African Americans in society.

Whether one focuses on the actual discriminatory behavior or a more general assessment of structural or systemic racism, what makes this phenomenon so dangerous is that people working within the system may not even notice that any mistreatment is occurring. In some extreme cases, people may believe that everyone involved is being treated fairly. Evidence of institutional discrimination, or systemic racism, pervades social life for Black and Hispanic people in the US. These inequalities are especially evident in issues related to housing, access to education, employment and income, the criminal justice system, and health care.

Housing

While housing segregation has diminished in recent years, it remains a serious problem. While some data indicates that Blacks have become less isolated from Hispanics and Asians, their exposure to Whites has remained relatively stable. In other words, regardless of income affluent Blacks have only slightly more frequent contact with Whites than do poor Blacks. One study showed that minorities at every income level live in poorer neighborhoods than do Whites with similar incomes. In fact, the average affluent Black or Hispanic household lives in a poorer neighborhood than the average lower income White resident. How can this be? Part of the problem relates to **racial steering**, a practice by which real estate agents attempt to convince minority home buyers to live in neighborhoods with more minorities (Massey and Fisher, 2004).

Another issue for African Americans is **redlining.** This practice, which essentially justified racial discrimination, prevented many Blacks from being eligible to purchase homes. President Roosevelt's New Deal to help Americans recover from the Great Depression during the 1930s included opportunities for residents to purchase their homes as part of a federal program. As a way of determining those neighborhoods that had the most promising recovery, The Home Owners' Loan Corporation, the agency given the responsibility to offer loans to residents, created a color-coded map to identify which neighborhoods were suitable. Green colored areas were considered the best, and those that were undesirable were colored red. Urban areas with a large share of Black families were most likely to be redlined, meaning their neighborhoods were coded red on the map, while neighborhoods made up mostly of White families were most likely to be deemed "best" and colored green (Figure 6.2). In redlined neighborhoods, it was virtually impossible to get a loan (Richardson, 2020).

Education

There is a strong relationship between income and education in our society. The more education a person achieves, the higher their income is likely to be. Our culture also believes that everyone has equal access to getting an education, which is critical to getting a well-paying job. There is little question that earning an education is vitally important in American society. Educational achievement is correlated with money, career

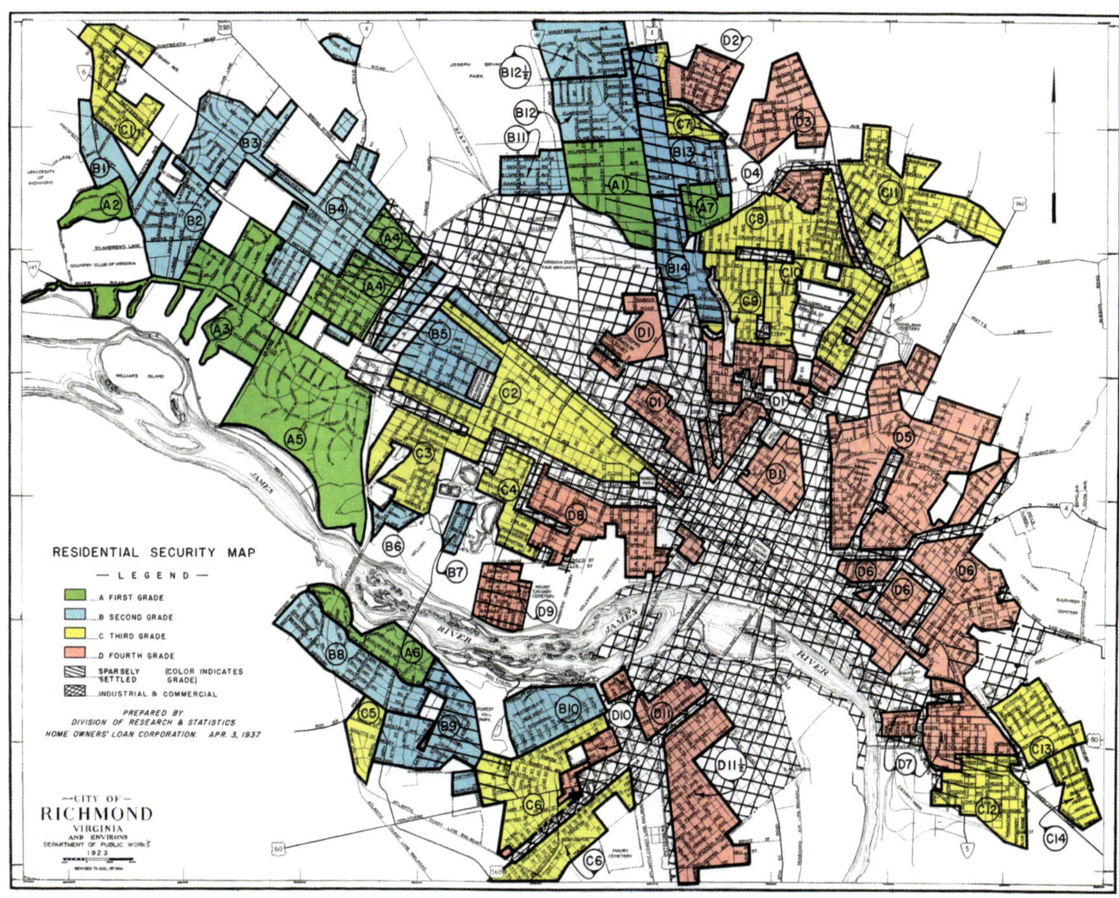

Figure 6.2 Redlining and housing discrimination This 1935 map of Richmond, Virginia, is labeled a "Residential Security Map." Issued by the Home Owners' Loan Corporation, the map key identifies districts in red as "fourth grade"—majority-Black districts for which homeowners would be highly unlikely to quality for a mortgage.

opportunities, social status, and the acquisition of cultural capital that can play an important role in other areas of social life.

The problem is that the promise of educational opportunity is different from the reality of access to those opportunities, especially for minority groups. High school graduation rates, a marker of early educational success, show that Hispanics and African Americans lag behind their White and Asian counterparts (Figure 6.3).

According to the US Department of Education, in 2018, 90 percent of Asians and 88 percent of Whites graduated high school, and 78 percent of Hispanics and 75 percent of African Americans graduated. Despite an increase in the number of years of school completed by all students, minority students remain less likely to finish high school or attend college than Whites (US Department of Education, National Center for Education Statistics, 2017). The disruption to the education system caused by the Covid-19

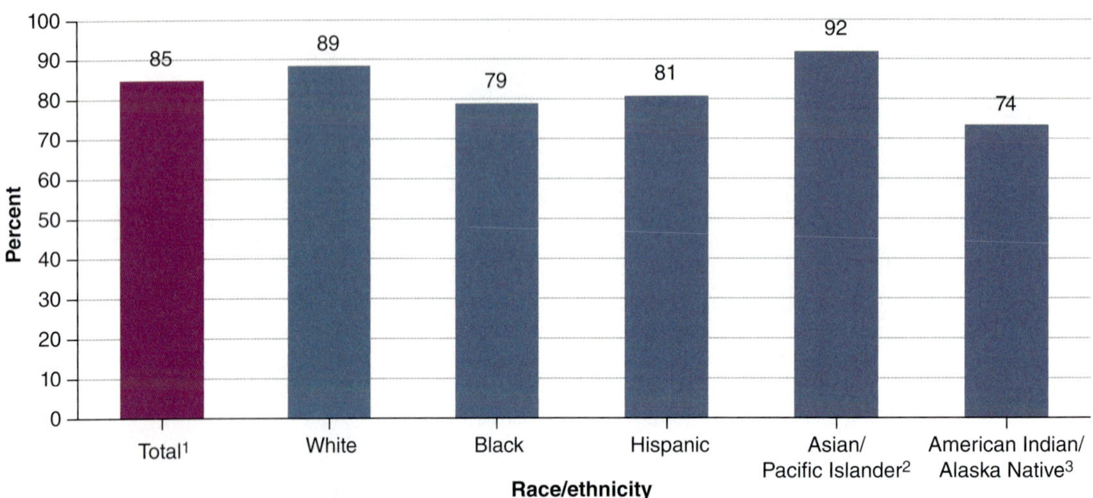

[1]Indudes other race/ethnicity categories not separately shown.
[2]Reporting practices for data on Asian and Pacific Islander statdents vary by state. Asian/Pacific Islander data in this ndicator represent either the value reported by the state for the "Asian/Pacific Islander" group or an aggregation of separate values reported by the state for "Asian" and "Pacific Islander." "Asian/Pacific Islander" includes the "Filipino" group, which only California and Hawaii report separately.
[3]Estimated assuming a count of zero American Indian/Alaska Native students for Hawaii.

Figure 6.3 Graduation Rates by Race/Ethnicity 2018 Adjusted cohort graduation rate (ACGR) for public high school students.

pandemic (which disproportionately impacts African American families) is likely to exacerbate this inequality.

At the college level, there is further evidence of this disparity. In 2018 far more Asians and Whites earned a college degree than Blacks or Hispanics (Figure 6.4; Duffin, 2020).

Economic disadvantage is a key factor in educational achievement. Some of the problems relating to education intersect with housing issues. Because educational spending is related to property values and taxes, schools in poor urban neighborhoods do not benefit from adequate tax revenues for their funding. Wealthy communities can pay higher salaries to teachers, attract more experienced faculty, and properly equip schools with the resources they need. White families who can afford to do so move to the suburbs, leaving minority students in poorer districts. Thus, schools often became and remain segregated based on race.

One study examined how minority achievement in education related to parents' wealth. The study found that the level of education of one's parents and their net worth (not only income but also the total of all owned assets or wealth) are the two best predictors of the quality of higher education their children will receive. Since Black students tend to come from less affluent homes than White students, their ability to attend the most prestigious universities and colleges that lead to the best jobs are more limited (Conley, 1999).

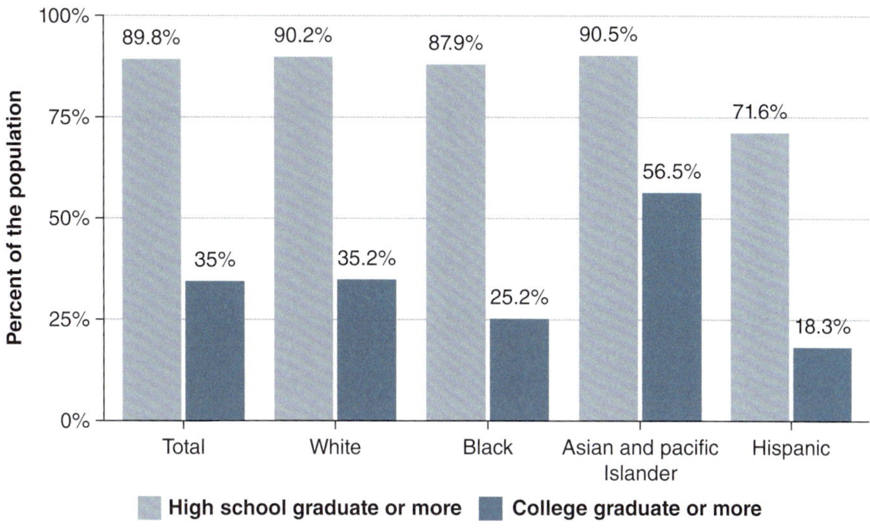

Figure 6.4 College degree by race and ethnicity

Although we have seen more minorities increase their educational achievement, and despite many colleges dedicating scholarship money for low-income students in an effort to increase the diversity of their campuses, the cost of attending one of these colleges often puts it out of reach for many minority students. This, too, limits their ability to gain an equal footing in the best paying jobs (Conley, 1999).

Employment and Income

If fairness dictated how someone found a job, we would probably see an equal representation of all races across all levels of the labor market. In 2018, Whites made up about 78 percent of the total workforce, African Americans made up 13 percent, while Hispanics represented about 17 percent. Asian Americans representing about 6 percent. Jobs occupied by African Americans and Hispanics tend to be in the lower paying sectors of the market. African Americans and Hispanics made up about 9 percent each of all management, professional and related occupations. Many of these positions require advanced degrees, which, as we saw in the discussion of education, Blacks and Hispanics are behind Whites (Bureau of Labor Statistics, 2019).

People of color find primarily find themselves in semi-skilled or unskilled jobs. In 2018, 38 percent of all nursing, psychiatric, and home health aides were Black. Similarly, 24 percent of all postal clerks were Black. Nearly half of all Hispanics (45 percent) were employed in the agricultural industry and as house cleaners and maids (47 percent). Except for nursing, these jobs do not require advanced training or education. It follows then, that those who are less likely to earn a degree will be confined to the lowest paying

Table 6.3 Median Family Income by Race and Ethnicity 2018

Race/Ethnicity of Household Head	2017 Median Household Income (2018 dollars)	2018 Median Household Income
All races/ethnicities	$62,626	$63,179
Asian	83,376	87,194
White, not Hispanic	69,851	70,642
Hispanic (any race)	51,389	51,450
Black	40,324	41,361

Source: United States Census Bureau. Current Population Survey. 2018 and 2019 Annual Social and Economic Supplements.

Note: The differences between the values shown are not all statistically significant at the confidence level used by the US Census Bureau.

jobs in the workforce (Table 6.3). This trend can be seen if one examines household incomes of families of color (Bureau of Labor Statistics, 2019).

During the Covid-19 pandemic, many Black and people of color workers in various industries were deemed "essential" and made it possible for people to purchase groceries, obtain medical assistance, and order items online. These workers, heralded as heroes by the public, took significant risks to allow the rest of the country to meet their essential needs. For the most part, however, their salaries were not increased nor were their working conditions improved or effectively safeguarded from the risks of infection.

For instance, Table 6.3 shows the median family income by race and ethnicity in 2018. However, caution must be used in assessing these numbers because it does not always take into account the number of family members working in that household (Peterson Foundation, 2019). Clearly job opportunities as well as income influence people's life chances differently in the United States (Bureau of Labor Statistics, 2019).

Criminal Justice

There is little disagreement that some minority groups, particularly African Americans, are overrepresented in crime statistics. This disproportionality is seen at every stage of the system and raises questions about whether racism is at work.

RACIAL PROFILING AND POLICE STOPS

According to a 2013 Justice Department report, an estimated 63 million people in the United States (about 26 percent of the population) have some form of contact with the police every year. The majority of persons with contact with the police thought the police behaved properly during the contact (Langton and Durose, 2013).

As it relates to **racial profiling**, Black drivers were more likely than White and Hispanic to be pulled over by police in a traffic stop; however Blacks, Whites, and Hispanics, even though they may have been subject to a search, generally believed the police were respectful and behaved properly (Table 6.4).

Table 6.4 Stopped Drivers Who Were Searched by Police
Stopped drivers age 16 or older who were searched by police, by driver's demographic characteristics and perception that police behaved properly, 2011

Demographic characteristics	Percentage of all stopped drivers searched by police	Percentage of stopped drivers[a]		
			Police behaved properly	
		Searched	Searched drivers	Drivers not searched
Total	3.5%	100%	61.3%	89.1%
Sex				
Male	4.5%	75.7%	61.0%	88.1%
Female	2.1	24.3	62.2	90.5
Race/Hispanic origin				
White[b]	2.3%	46.6%	62.4%	90.0%
Black/African American[b]	6.3	22.8	61.6	84.1
Hispanic/Latino	6.6	23.1	64.8	88.1
Other[b,c]	4.4!	7.4!	42.5!	91.3
Age				
16–17	1.4%!	0.7%!	–%!	93.5%
18–34	4.8	58.0	58.7	88.1
35–54	3.1	33.8	69.8	88.9
55 or older	1.4!	7.5!	49.0!	91.3

Note: Includes respondents for whom the most recent contact with police was as a driver in a traffic stop.

– Less than 0.05%.

!Interpret with caution. Estimate based on 10 or fewer sample cases or the coefficient of variation is greater than 50%.

[a] Denominator includes about 6% of searched drivers and 2% of other stopped drivers who did not know or did not report whether the police behaved properly.

[b] Excludes persons of Hispanic or Latino origin.

[c] Includes persons identifying as Native American, Alaska Native, Asian, Native Hawaiian, or other Pacific Islander, and persons of two or more races.

Source: Davis, Harrell, and Kena.(2018). Bureau of Justice Statistics, *National Crime Victimization Survey*, Police-Public Contact Survey. 2018.

About 63 percent of White, 62 percent of African American, and 65 percent of Hispanic drivers in traffic stops believed officers behaved properly (Langton and Durose, 2013), a finding that has been reported since 2005 (Langton and Durose, 2013). In general, a significant proportion of the population thinks the police are doing a good job; however, minorities generally feel less confident in the police and are generally less satisfied with police services.

ARRESTS

Is race a factor in the arrest of a suspect? What is clear is that minorities are arrested out of proportion to their representation in the population. According to the *Uniform Crime Reports*, in 2018, African Americans represented about 13 percent of the population but approximately 27 percent of all arrests while Hispanics, who represented about 18 percent of the population, accounted for 18.8 percent of all arrests. In 2018 approximately 69 percent of all individuals arrested were White, with the remaining 3.5 percent from Asian Americans and American Indian/Pacific Islander (Table 6.5).

The death of George Floyd and other high-profile cases have generated many questions regarding what happens to suspects while they are in custody. However, the answer to this question is anything but clear. Congress passed the Death in Custody Reporting Act of 2013, which went into effect in December 2014. The law requires the Attorney General to collect data from each state and each federal law enforcement agency on the deaths of suspects while in custody and produce a public report on trends and issues. However, a recent report from the US Inspector General's Office indicates that the Department of Justice (DOJ) has had problems implementing the law—in fact in 2020, the DOJ revealed that they have not completed the data collection nor be able to generate a report for the foreseeable future (Orway, Wihby, and Kille, 2020).

What data that does exists consists of a 2011 report, based on data from 2003–2009. That report showed that about 40 percent of custody deaths were related to suicide, death by intoxication, accidental injury, or other causes. In 2016, another report by the

Table 6.5 Arrests by Race/Ethnicity 2018

All Arrests	White	Black	American Indian/ Alaska Native	Asian	Native Hawaiian or Pacific Islander	Hispanic
7,710,900	69% 5,319,654	27.4% 2,115,381	2.1% 164,430	1.2% 92,737	0.2% 18,698	
6,343,684						18.8% 1,191,334

(Source: US Department of Justice, 2018).

Bureau of Justice Statistics indicated that there is an uneven collection of data, but what is known is consistent with previous studies on this topic (Table 6.6; Banks, Ruddle, and Kennedy, 2016).

In the absence of recent information about this topic, many organizations have started to collect their own information about the number of deaths in police custody. However, this is an uneven process and does not produce a complete picture of the scope of the problem (Orway, Wihby, and Kille, 2020).

THE COURTS AND MINORITIES

Several studies demonstrate racial bias in sentencing. More recently, a meta-analysis of 85 research studies revealed that, after considering the defendant's criminal history and the seriousness of the offense, Blacks and Latinos were generally sentenced more harshly than Whites. In general, there appears to be some evidence to suggest that

Table 6.6 Arrest-Related Deaths 2015 Manner of death by identification source, June-August, 2015

	All Deaths		Media-Identified Deaths		Agency-Reported Deaths	
Manner of Death	**Number**	**Percent**	**Number**	**Percent**	**Number**	**Percent**
All manners of death	425	100%	377	100%	48	100%
Homicide[a]	270	64	268	71	2	4
Suicide	76	18	62	16	14	29
Accident	48	11	26	7	22	46
Natural	7	2	1	0	6	13
Undetermined	8	2	8	2	0	0
Unknown/investigation incomplete	16	4	12	3	4	8
Data source		100%		100%		100%
Indicated on incident form	300	71	257	68	43	90
Imputed from open source information[b]	125	29	120	32	5	10

[a] *Homicide is the willful killing of one person by another. It includes justifiable homicide by a law enforcement officer.*

[b] *Manner of death was imputed from open source information when it was not completed on the incident form from the state reporting coordinator (SRC) or medical examiner/coroners' (ME/C) office or because no SRC or ME/C form was completed. Manner of death was not measured on the law enforcement agency incident form.*

Source: Bureau of Justice Statistics, Arrest Related Deaths Program Redesign Study, June–August 2015.

disparities in sentencing still occur, even with the use of sentencing guidelines (Mitchell and MacKenzie, 2014).

The conclusions from such findings explain varying racial perceptions of crime and criminals and foster understanding why Blacks and Latinos, while accounting for 30 percent of the general population, represent nearly 60 percent of the prison population. These perceptions also drive the belief by some groups that the criminal justice system is biased against Blacks. Such a belief is underscored by the results of the survey, which showed that over two-thirds of African Americans saw the system as biased compared to only 25 percent of Whites (Mitchell and MacKenzie, 2014).

CORRECTIONS AND MINORITIES

There is a long history of disproportionality in the criminal justice system regarding race and this is clearly reflected in statistics regarding incarceration. In 2018, according to the US Department of Justice, there were an estimated 1.4 million prisoners in state and federal correctional facilities, a decrease of nearly two percent from 2017. It seems that by any measure, African Americans are disproportionately incarcerated (Table 6.7). While they represented approximately 13 percent of the overall population in this country in 2018, African Americans represented 33 percent of those incarcerated in state and federal prisons (Carson, 2020).

In 2018, Black males age 18–19 were nearly 13 times more likely to be imprisoned as White males, while Hispanic males age 18–19 were about 3.3 times more likely to be imprisoned as White males at the end of 2018 (Figure 6.5). Black females age 18–19 were nearly four times as likely and Hispanic females nearly twice as likely to be imprisoned as White females in 2018 (Carson, 2020).

Health Care and Illness

Another important dimension that is influenced by race is health. One broad and imprecise way to measure health is to look at life expectancy. When we do this, we see racial disparities. For instance, a White child born in 2015 has a life expectancy of 76 years while White females can generally expect to live 81 years, according to the

Table 6.7 Incarceration in State and Federal Prison by Race/Ethnicity, 2018

Total Prisoners	**White**	**African American**	**Hispanic**
1,414,162	430,500 30.4%	465,200 32.8%	330,200 23.3%
Change from 2017	–1.4%	–2.2%	–1.9%

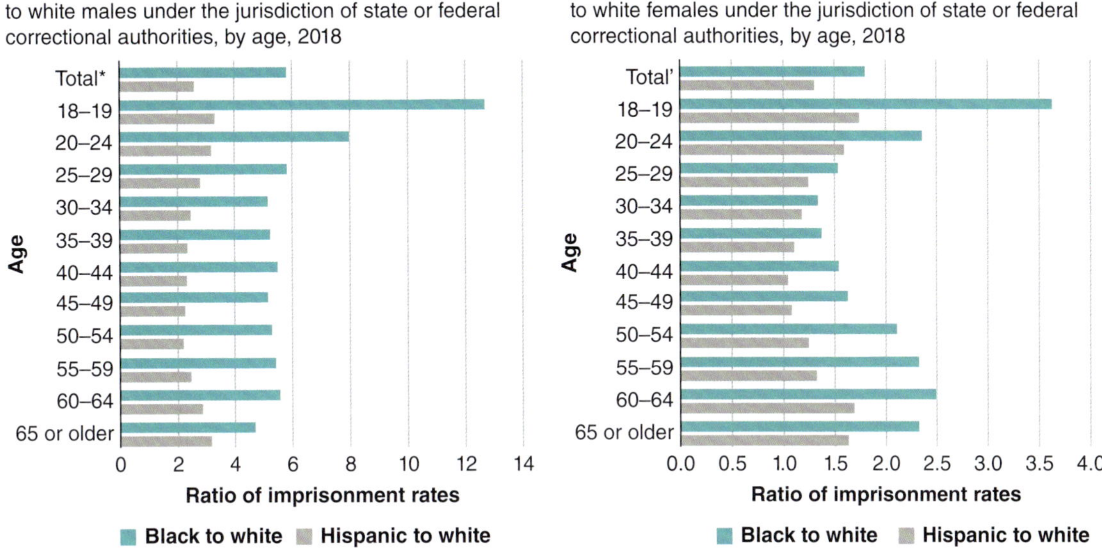

Figure 6.5 Ratio of Imprisonment of Black and Hispanic Males and Females to White Males and Females by Age, 2018

Center for Disease Control. In comparison, an African American male's life expectancy is 71 years and African American females can expect to live to about 78 years old. Generally, Whites live longer than Blacks, although there is some evidence that the gap between the two has narrowed. Interestingly, Hispanics have the highest life expectancy rates for both men and women of all groups; males can expect to live 79 years while Hispanic women have a life expectancy of 84 years (Centers for Disease Control, 2017).

The Covid-19 pandemic impacted the lives of millions of people, but the data also shows that there was a disproportionate impact on people of color (The Covid Tracking Project, 2021). The reasons for this are still not completely understood, but the fact that people of color are also more likely to suffer from a variety of illnesses that make them particularly susceptible to Covid-19 is an important consideration (Figure 6.6).

Part of the explanation in general for the disparities in health relate to access to health care in the form of health insurance. The lack of access to quality health care along with environmental factors, such as dangers in the type of work minorities perform, violence, stress, and toxins in the environment, all contribute to shorter life expectancies for minorities. David Williams, a well-known expert in medical sociology, argues that the combined effect of segregation has had an impact on minorities, but particularly African Americans, in terms of employment opportunities, housing, educational achievement and access and utilization of health care. It also creates stressors that contribute to the poor health of many African Americans (Williams and Mohommed, 2018).

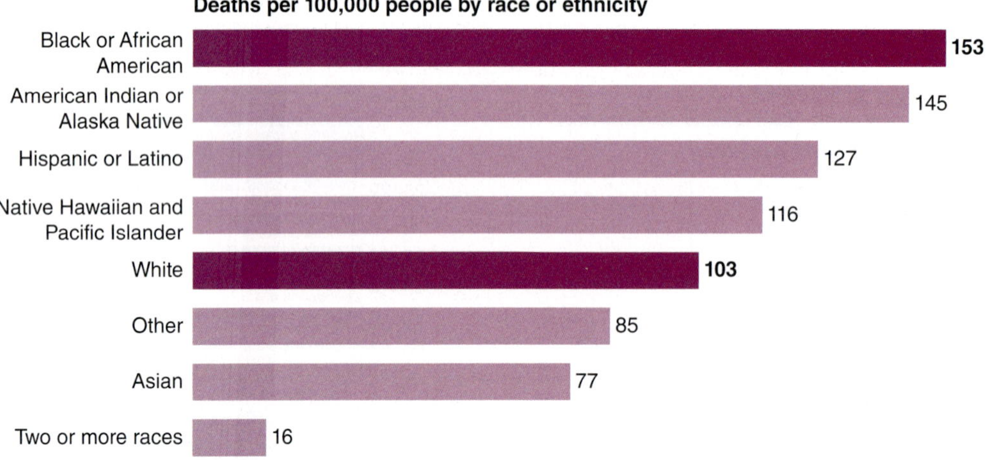

Figure 6.6 Nationwide, Black people have died at 1.5 times the rate of white people These calculations are based on data from the Covid Racial Data Tracker and the US Census Bureau. Race categories may overlap with Hispanic/Latinx ethnicity. Rates are not age-adjusted and some rates are underestimated due to lack of reporting of race and ethnicity categories for Covid-19 deaths. Source: The Covid Tracking Project at *The Atlantic*, covidtracking.com/race. Accessed February 21, 2021.

SOCIOLOGICAL THEORY AND RACE

Sociologists generally disagree with the idea that there is a scientific basis to racial categories. Instead, sociologists focus on the social construction of race, and the ways in which a society decides how those distinctions are understood. The meaning attached to those distinctions guides social interaction as well as determining the group's place in the social hierarchy.

Functionalism and Race

Functionalism has offered insight into the nature of social solidarity and group cohesion. Functionalists assert that the positive feelings of being a part of a group, even a subordinate one that has less access to social, economic and political power, tends to promote and maintain strong ties among group members. However, such strong feelings can also lead to divisions within groups, particularly other races and ethnic groups, where Whites may feel that their concerns are not being addressed. This is the basis of the White Power movement and other White Supremacy groups in the United States. At the same time, functionalists also argue that the disconnectedness felt by many minority groups can lead to a sense of isolationism as well as perceptions of fear and hostility toward majority groups. This can explain why some groups tend to have strained relationships with others as well as tensions between dominant and subordinate classes.

Conflict Theory and Race

Conflict approaches, particularly those that use a classic Marxist approach, explain how some minority groups in the labor force perpetually receive lower wages. This wage discrimination compounds the problems of racism and poverty. As we have noted, this discrimination is what William Julius Wilson argues has led to the creation of an underclass that personifies the Black experience in the United States. However, unlike other racial theorists, Wilson argues that the problem of the underclass is more economic than race-based. While conflict theory offers an interesting explanation of the problems facing this group, it does not explain all forms of racial stratification. Some of the more recent attempts to use conflict theory to explain racial inequalities address settler-colonialism, or the impact of the appropriation of Indigenous lands by Whites on the Native American community today (Robertson, 2015). Other sociologists focus on the issues relating to the class system, which impacts both the economic and political realms of social life. Still others, using an intersectional lens, have offered insight into the ways in which race, class, and gender inequalities are related.

Critical Race Theory

As we learned in Chapter 1, **critical race theory** argues that racism has become institutionalized in American society, especially in the legal system. This explains the disproportionate involvement of Blacks in the criminal justice system and the unfair treatment minorities generally receive when they become involved with the system. Critical race theory (which has links to conflict theory) suggests that to understand racism, one must recognize the intersectionality of race with gender, class, sexuality and other social statuses. Of great importance to critical race theory is the advocacy and activism that attempts to identify and challenge racist laws and policies that target minorities and to breed a type of color-blind social justice (Delgado and Stefanic, 2012). More recently, critical race theory has provided a framework for analyzing and advancing the Black Lives Matter movement (Dixon, 2017). This is important since it shows how theory can actually have a significant impact on practices and policies in addition to making sense of the world.

Symbolic Interactionism and Race

A symbolic interactionist approach to race examines how people perceive and respond to race in everyday life, in social relationships, and in larger social institutions. This approach reflects the sociological argument that people construct identities for themselves and others based on physical characteristics. From those immediate assessments, we put people into certain categories. Some of the labeling that occurs when we categorize others can help us to identify and understand members of those groups. It can also help us to reframe our relationships and interactions with them. This is urgently

Monuments to hate Many monuments to the Confederacy, such as this statue of Robert E. Lee in Richmond, Virginia, were vandalized and eventually taken down in response to calls from Black Lives Matter and other advocates for racial justice.

important, especially if the public's perception of a certain group—such as Black people tend to be violent or engage in oppositional behavior—is inaccurate. Such perceptions have an impact on the policing of majority-Black communities as well as media coverage of the Black Lives Matter protests of 2020.

While events in 2020 surrounding race and how racism is expressed in our society are dramatic, controversial, and even contested, one example of how a symbolic interactionist might understand how race influences relationships and interactions among people can be seen in the protests to remove statues of famous Confederate leaders in cities and on campuses around the country. These protests, sparked in part by the murder of George Floyd and others who were killed by the police, point out that these memorials are reminders of the very type of White supremacy that creates systemic racism and the lack of equality for Blacks in the United States.

For example, the cities of Birmingham and Mobile in Alabama took down memorials to Confederate soldiers, recognizing the offensive symbols they represent. Similarly, in Richmond, Virginia, efforts are under way to remove a statute of Confederate General Robert E. Lee, with four more statues being considered for removal as well (Elliott, 2020). These symbolic representations are a key element to understanding people's perceptions of those individuals, their historic significance, and the accepted treatment of enslaved people in this country. They also shape our understanding of the role and place for African Americans today.

WHAT WORKS? EFFECTIVE SOLUTIONS TO PREJUDICE, DISCRIMINATION, AND RACISM

It is difficult to find answers to complex problems such as racism, prejudice, and discrimination. Unlike other social problems, which can be more easily defined and documented, the problems that stem from issues related to race can be subtler in nature. This is not to say that outright discrimination does not occur and should not be addressed; programs such as affirmative action (which we will examine more closely) attempt to remedy the unequal treatment of minorities. Because the nature of prejudice can be found beneath the surface of social interaction, we will also look at ways in which people can be made aware of their unconscious biases and encouraged to address and remediate their impact.

Affirmative Action

Until the mid-1960s, some universities would not admit minorities, some employers would not hire them, and minorities were generally excluded from many other opportunities that were rightfully theirs as citizens. The Civil Rights Act of 1964 attempted to change discrimination in the workplace by making it illegal under federal law. A year later Congress passed the Voting Rights Act, which empowered the Justice Department to take steps to eliminate discrimination. President Lyndon Johnson assigned the responsibility of enforcing affirmative action to the US Department of Labor, which began a mandate that government contractors examine the demographic makeup of their workforce and develop strategies to diversify their staff (Kelly, 2010).

The original idea behind **affirmative action** was to increase the representation of minorities in the workplace at all levels. In doing so, it was felt that minorities would then take steps to further the diversification initiative when they were in a position to hire employees. Thus, affirmative action, from the beginning, was intended to be a short-term measure. During this time, the US Supreme Court defined the scope of affirmative action, particularly as it relates to quotas. In 1965 the federal government-mandated colleges and universities to establish minority goals for enrollment and to set quotas that outlined the number of minorities that had to be admitted each year.

Most people can understand the idea and logic of preferential treatment. That is, particularly as it relates to African Americans, the legacy of slavery has created an environment and structure that could potentially limit the opportunities for Blacks that requires some type of remedy. The problem is not in the idea or the sentiment behind it; the challenges and controversies emerge in the execution of that concept. Most people have a difficult time understanding the issues surrounding affirmative action, so it makes sense to offer both sides of the debate (Jencks, 1999).

There are two key arguments made by advocates of affirmative action. The first, which is sometimes called the shackled runner's argument or the argument from compensatory justice, contends that preferential treatment is justified based on the history of mistreatment of minority groups, particularly African Americans. The argument is that Blacks were denied opportunities over the sweep of history, starting with slavery, to which they should have been entitled. As a result, they were not given the same chances to succeed as Whites. Conversely, many Whites were given certain advantages, or privileges, over time that they were not entitled to. As a result, generations later, Whites were indirect beneficiaries of slavery and Blacks are indirect victims of that discrimination.

While today's Whites did not own slaves, some family members may have, and they were able to pass this privilege to their grandchildren and great grandchildren in the form of life chances. In the same way, Blacks who did not get the same opportunities could not pass the advantages of privilege to their grandchildren and great grandchildren. Thus, the idea of preferential treatment today is based on this legacy of slavery, where one group gained a considerable advantage over another. To remedy that historical mistake, preferential treatment is justified (Jencks, 1999).

A second argument is that of social justice. In this instance, proponents argue that given a fair representation of all people in society, minorities should see their level of participation in all walks of life. If Blacks comprise 13 percent of the population, then that proportion should be seen in school enrollment, among physicians, CEOs, police officers, secretaries, teachers, and so on. Similarly, if Hispanics represent about 18 percent of the population, their involvement in occupations and other endeavors should be seen proportionally as well. The basis of preferential treatment should be seen in those instances where equally qualified candidates are involved. That is, affirmative action would be seen in those cases where there are two equally qualified candidates; in such a circumstance, the minority should be given the preference for a job, an application to a college or in some other capacity (Jencks, 1999).

Opponents of affirmative action argue that it constitutes **reverse discrimination**. They suggest that Whites who are equally or even more qualified are disadvantaged by giving minorities preferential treatment constitutes the same type of discrimination that minorities argue is unfair. The problem, as they see it, is that the pool of equally qualified African Americans is much smaller than the one for Whites. As a result, even if preferential treatment was a good idea, finding equally qualified candidates from each category will be difficult. The result? Preferential treatment is increasingly given to less qualified blacks over more qualified Whites. This is what inflames the issue and creates resentment and lawsuits about reverse discrimination (Jencks, 1999).

In his book *Rethinking Social Policy*, Christopher Jencks investigates the impact of affirmative action, and who has benefited from the policies. While the goal of affirmative action was to provide opportunities for working class and poor minorities, Jencks observes that many middle-class and wealthy African Americans also benefit from affirmative action programs, even though they were not the intended beneficiaries of the program. Jencks further points out that preferential treatment appears to negatively impact working class or poor Whites. These individuals, according to this position, did not gain any particular privilege as a result of slavery or anti-Black discrimination. Thus, while wealthy and privileged Whites, who have the cultural capital, social networks, and resources to do so, will find other opportunities to succeed if preferential treatment is afforded to minorities, working class or poor Whites are asked to give up the few opportunities they have earned to remedy a historical tragedy from which they gained no tangible benefit.

Finally, Jencks addresses the personal and systemic doubts that accompany—however unfairly—recipients (or perceived recipients) of the benefits of affirmative action. While some White people might wonder if minority colleagues were hired because of their race rather than their qualifications, Whites do not themselves have to deal with that skepticism. As a result, some minority people in workplace and other contexts might always feel unfairly pressured to have to prove their worth beyond what a White person would have to do in a similar situation. This lament by Jencks is an important one that should not be overlooked.

Jencks further observes that this issue can also unjustly affect the minority member's sense of internal competency or credibility. Again, Whites have the advantage of not having to concern themselves with such questions. In conclusion, Jencks argues that while we need some type of program to address the issues of diversity and inequalities in many dimensions of social life, but the current affirmative action programs appear to increase the level of hostility rather than harmony among and between different groups of people (Jencks, 1999).

Education

To effectively address prejudice, discrimination, and racism, it is important to educate people on the actual and perceived differences between groups of people. This is particularly true in those instances where people may not be aware of their tendency to hold negative views about, or bias against, members of other racial groups.

Education-based solutions proceed from the understanding that a lack of contact with others creates barriers of understanding and interaction. Effective anti-racism education strategies include cooperative learning, peer-based learning, and creative ways to enhance positive contact and break down barriers. Of course, simply increasing contact between groups does not, by itself, improve race relations or reduce prejudice. Indeed, the wrong type of contact can promote further insensitivity and confirm stereotypical thinking. The most sustainable approaches find threads of commonality as well as showing how different groups can celebrate their differences in a non-threatening manner.

One education-based strategy to reduce prejudice involves recognizing the dominant White ideology and the many ways it reveals itself, particularly among White teachers, in diverse classrooms. As Brookfield (2019) points out, there is a natural tendency for White teachers, who have grown up in a White society, to have an unconscious tendency to engage in what are known as *micro-aggressions* against minority students. Brookfield argues this happens in a variety of subtle ways, but the result is that minorities are excluded from classroom discussions and are generally not given the same opportunities as their White counterparts.

Micro-aggressions are the small acts of exclusion and marginalization committed by a dominant group toward a minority. The danger with micro-aggressions is that they maintain the White dominated status quo by diminishing the contributions of others. Micro-aggressions are not overt or explicitly racist, but recipients are often left to wonder if the sender was being consciously or subconsciously insulting. Also, when people who engage in micro-aggressions are confronted with this behavior, they often do not or cannot see its injurious nature—often they claim that the receiver is being too sensitive, they are imagining the slight, or that no exclusion was intended. In addition, when such moments occur, offenders will argue they were simply being forgetful, misspoke, or did not articulate their position clearly enough (Brookfield, 2019). Brookfield's approach is to enhance teachers' tendency to fall victim to these perceptions, which are just one type of marginalization of minority students (Brookfield, 2019).

Workplace Diversity Training

Diversity training comes in many forms, including role plays, discussions, and instructional videos. The goal is the same: recognizing biases and hidden assumptions and developing empathy and understanding for others. Much of what constitutes diversity training is done in the workplace and the research on its effectiveness varies widely (Dobbins and Kalev, 2016; see also Bezrukova, Spell, Perry, and Jehn, 2016). However, the most effective diversity training programs are those that promote social accountability and engage managers and coworker contact with minority workers and colleagues. It is especially important that such efforts are not simply initiatives driven from the top of the organization. Rather, the best programs are those that are grown organically with staff input and support.

Still, the effects of a short-term seminar or workshop tend not to last. Some companies actually experience resistance from workers, particularly if these training programs are mandatory. Companies that make such workshops voluntary tend to see positive results, including the hiring of minorities into management and leadership positions. Of course, such an approach can lead to a form of self-selection, where only those who are interested in diversity will attend such workshops, but overall the data suggests that this is a far better approach to sensitizing the workforce than compulsory programs (Dobbins and Kaley, 2016).

Media Campaigns

Given the pivotal role the media plays in promoting and shaping people's perception of and behavior toward others it is central to the discussion of prejudice and discrimination. The messages conveyed in the media are part of the socialization of society's members and often serves to reinforce popular perceptions and stereotypes. Used as a tool to reduce prejudice and discrimination, media campaigns tend to be a popular approach to raise awareness, encourage the reporting of discrimination, and to highlight the positive contributions of certain minority groups.

Unfortunately, social media can also be part of a negative campaign; one that spreads racism and seeds hostility between groups. The use of hate speech and misinformation has been the subject of considerable debate and has become a global phenomenon as more people are online. To spread information about a group's ideology, many organizations have used fake news, misinformation, and hate speech, which can incite violence against certain groups. The use of social media to foment unrest and violence in the wake of the 2020 presidential election, culminating in the January 6, 2021, attack on the US Capitol building, is a subject of ongoing investigation and concern.

The problem of using social media to spread hate has become a subject of considerable debate in the United States. Companies such as Facebook and Twitter struggle to find ways to control hate speech and inflammatory comments by some individuals and groups while at the same time not engaging in censorship. The sheer volume of information coupled with limited technology to screen and control information has resulted in an uneven and poorly controlled process of information. Even with the use of algorithms and human oversight, the spread of misinformation and hate speech has become a widespread problem (Laub, 2019).

While the issue of misinformation and hate speech will continue to be a challenge, media campaigns can be used to improve people's understandings of different groups. For example, evidence indicates that media campaigns that target children under the age of eight improve attitudes about different groups of people. A review of 32 studies that used a variety of interventions across different countries to reduce prejudice in early childhood found that using media as part of an educational curriculum which used stories of intergroup contact among peers were quite successful in improving students' negative attitudes about other groups (Plaut et. al, 2011).

Despite the problems related to social media and regulating inaccurate or hurtful information, the goal of generating empathy and compassion are generally considered the most effective ways of challenging existing attitudes, so there is value in offering media campaigns clustered around a message (Plaut et. al, 2011).

SO WHAT CAN I DO?

A challenge in the discussion of race is recognizing the extent to which it permeates all aspects of our lives. For those who think we live in a color-blind society, the facts are overwhelmingly against such a position. Significant progress could be made if we were all honest about the role of race in American society. At least then we could have meaningful conversations and try to understand where other people are coming from in their description of the issues.

More concretely, there are many things you can do to begin sensitizing yourself to the issues surrounding race and ethnicity. If part of the challenge relating to prejudice and discrimination relates to a lack of understanding and sensitivity to issues, a first step toward an increased understanding might be to expose yourself to more diversity. Have you ever attended an ethnic festival in your city? Have you ever explored the significance of displaying your own identity—are you comfortable doing so and if so, why? If you are not comfortable, have you examined or asked others about that? Is it due to stereotypes about people of your race/ethnicity?

Some of you may have participated in one of the many demonstrations being held around the country to call attention to racial injustice and inequality. You may be a proponent of the Black Lives Matter movement. But do you really understand what the movement is about or how it is different from the organization with the same name?

At its core, the Black Lives Matter movement is about recognizing the disparities that have existed for many years. The organization itself, however, was created in 2013 in specific response to the acquittal of George Zimmerman, a self-styled vigilante who shot and killed an unarmed Black teenager named Trayvon Martin. While the movement promotes a philosophy similar to the original organization, there are subtle differences between the two that has created confusion and controversy. For example, some people responded to the original call of "Black Lives Matter" with phrases like "Blue Lives Matter" (which promotes the work of the police), and "All Lives Matter" (which argues that no one group should get special treatment). Both of those alternate phrasings obscure, co-opt, or distort the purpose and message of the Black Lives Matter movement.

An important part of what you can do as an individual is educate yourself about the Black Lives Matter movement and its goals. It is about more than parity of rights, and it certainly is not about promoting violence against the police (Lucero, 2020; Schumer, 2020). If you really want to be a part of addressing the problems of race and racism, it begins with understanding what the issues are and the specific missions of different organizations and movements in which you can participate. That can only happen if you educate yourself. As an individual, you aren't going to end prejudice and discrimination; but if you refuse to acknowledge it, passively tolerate it, or stop learning about it, you become part of the problem. So why not keep your sociological hat on and go into the field and ask questions?

CONCLUSION

The problems of racism, prejudice, and discrimination are engrained in American society but have become especially urgent since emergence of the Black Lives Matter movement and the uprisings of 2020. Part of the problem relates to a lack of understanding of other groups, perhaps due to the isolationism that the culture appears to be promoting. As long as groups remain apart and do not interact, explanations of motives, behaviors, and attitudes will be based on stereotypes, conjecture and inaccurate appraisals of others. Moreover, these perceptions can generate hostility toward others as groups become sensitive to slights and accusations. Evidence of this is seen in the way people (particularly White middle-class women, sometimes referred to as "Karens") have interpreted innocent behavior of others, for instance, asking a person to leash their dog in a public park, when it is required by law or ordinance, is seen as behavior that warrants calling the police.

The effects of Covid-19 has laid bare many of the race-based deficiencies that may have been ignored or neglected in the past. Whether it is the economic vulnerability of African Americans, many of whom had been working in low-paying jobs that were eliminated during the country's shutdown, or the health disparities for many African Americans who are disproportionately being affected by Covid-19, or the offensive ways society has celebrated events and actions of the past, life for African Americans, historically and currently, has been anything but easy. Add to the fact that there continues to be limits on the opportunities for Blacks to achieve a meaningful level of success in the United States (as evidenced by the disparities in the quality of education they receive or the tendency to treat them differently by the justice system), and one begins to see a disturbing pattern.

The challenges related to race, discussed in this chapter, are only magnified by the reluctance of the dominant group to understand and remedy these obstacles—an unwillingness to acknowledge White privilege and White fragility means traditional avenues or solutions are not available to most Blacks. In its place, the Black Lives Matter movement has been a main agent of social change. As one commentator pointed out, very little progress will be made toward racial and ethnic sensitivity if one group is labeled racist for saying and doing the things that others are given the freedom to express. An understanding of the problems and the social movements created to address them is a critical starting point for any meaningful conversation about how to resolve the role of race in American society.

YOU MAKE THE CALL: POLICING WHILE WHITE

You are a White police chief in a medium-sized city with a department made up of approximately 100 sworn officers. There is a sizeable minority population, many of whom are African American and Hispanic, and who are active in their community. Because of several instances in which White officers have been involved in altercations with suspects and residents when called to those locations, arrests have increased as have the number of injuries sustained by officers.

In an effort to find a solution to the tensions within the community, a committee made up of residents has argued that what is needed is a more customized type of service from the police department. To that end, the community is demanding that when a resident calls the police and an officer is required to visit that address, he or she should be of the race of the family that needs assistance. In other words, Black officers should respond to calls from Black families, Hispanic officers should handle calls from members of the Hispanic community and White officers should answer calls for service from White residents.

A local politician has been exceptionally vocal about such a plan, which has only further increased the media attention and public outcry for a more racially sensitive police department. After all, the politician argues, the police are there to serve the public and if the public wants someone to whom they can better relate on the basis of race or ethnicity, shouldn't the police department give the public what they need?

Questions to consider:

1. How would you respond to both the community activists in the neighborhoods in terms of the conflicts officers have had with suspects and residents? Do you respond with the details of celebrated cases which offers a context of understanding or do you not respond at all for fear of a public and likely emotional debate?
2. What would you say to the media and the residents about the idea of customized service? Can you provide this service, given the demographic makeup of your department? Even if you could respond with a plan of action, should you implement it? What are the potential consequences of such a decision—will this ease the tensions with the public or will it create other problems for the department and the community?
3. How do you think minority officers will respond to such a plan? Given that the majority of calls for service are in the most dangerous sections of the city, and given that these neighborhoods generally are comprised mostly of minorities, how would the rank and file respond? What does such a policy, if implemented, do to enhance officers' understanding of the issues in these neighborhoods? What happens if minority officers act the same way White officers have in these situations? Will that inflame the tensions further? What if they respond differently—what are the implications of that course of action?

SUMMARY

- Define the concepts such as race, ethnicity, minority groups, racism, prejudice and discrimination.
  - Race is generally defined as the separation of groups based on physical characteristics.
  - Ethnicity is a distinction based on cultural heritage.
  - Racism is when some groups feel they are superior to subordinate groups and feel justified in the mistreatment of those members as a result.
  - Prejudice is a negative attitude against a group of people.
  - Discrimination is the unequal or mistreatment of others based on their membership in a particular group.
- Define the social construction of race and its significance to minority groups, the relationship between prejudice and discrimination, and White privilege.
  - The social construction of race suggests that each society determines for itself which particular physical features

distinguish one group from another and how the response to those characteristics shapes and influences people's perceptions of that group.
    - Minority groups are those who do not have equal access to social, economic, and political power.
    - There is an interplay between prejudice and discrimination, where people may hold negative attitudes against certain groups, but that does not always mean it translates into negative behavior.
    - White privilege describes the benefits granted to those who resemble the people—almost always White—who dominate powerful positions in our institutions.
- Identify institutional or systemic discrimination and racism and its impact on housing, education, criminal justice and employment.
    - Institutional or systemic discrimination and racism is the type of mistreatment that is built into the structure and operation of society.
    - There are clearly identified obstacles that adversely impact Black people in terms of access to housing, a quality education, and well-paying jobs, as well as a higher than normal probability of involvement in the adult and juvenile justice systems.
- Analyze sociological theories as they relate to race, ethnicity, racism, and discrimination.
    - Functionalists assert that the positive feelings of being a part of a group, even a subordinate one that has less access to social, economic and political power, has a tendency to promote and maintain strong ties among group members.
    - Conflict theorists generally explain how wage discrimination against minority groups compounds the problems of racism and poverty.
    - Critical race theory suggests that to understand racism, one has to recognize the intersectionality of race with gender, class, sexuality and other social statuses.
    - A symbolic interactionist approach argues that the ways in which people construct identities based on physical characteristics, such as skin color, drives much of the interaction that occurs within and across groups.
- Assess examples of issues and problems relating to race, along with assessments of programs to improve diversity and address discrimination.
    - Examples include the debate about affirmative action, and the challenges of integrating race into students' educational opportunities. This includes the unconscious biases related to the dominant White ideology that can result in micro-aggressions against minority students.
    - Efforts to address prejudice and discrimination in the United States fall into three categories: educational and curriculum programs, short-term diversity training programs and media campaigns.
    - The weight of the evidence suggests that educational programs can be valuable in raising people's understanding of the differences between groups, while diversity training tends to be more successful when it is not mandated from employers.

KEY TERMS

Affirmative action 189
Apartheid 171
Color-blind racism 172
Critical race theory 187
Discrimination 171
Ethnicity 170
Institutional discrimination 167
Micro-aggressions 191
Minority groups 171
Race 169
Racial profiling 181
Racial steering 176
Racism 172
Reverse discrimination 190
Prejudice 171
Prejudiced discriminator 172
Prejudiced non-discriminator 172
Redlining 176
Social construction of race 170
Systemic racism 167
Unprejudiced non-discriminator 172
Unprejudiced discriminator 172
White fragility 173
White privilege 172

Discussion Questions

1. Think about the events mentioned at the beginning of the chapter, where people are calling the police when African Americans are engaging in routine behavior such as eating lunch in a public place. What is the source of these concerns?
2. Do you think the reason for the disproportionate number of African Americans in the criminal justice system is due to the fact that the system is racist or is it the case that many African Americans are committing more crimes?
3. What do you make of the controversy surrounding white privilege? Is it a real thing or is it a crutch used by minorities to justify their lack of initiative and effort?
4. What is the significance of symbolic racism and micro aggressions? Why is it considered even more dangerous and debilitating than overt forms of racism?

Learn more with this chapter's digital tools, including Data and Media Literacy Exercises, flashcards, and chapter self-assessments at **www.oup.com/he/mcnamara**.

7

Can I Stay A Little Longer? Immigration and Refugees

LEARNING OBJECTIVES

- Describe an overview of immigration in the United States.
- Summarize the extent of immigration in the United States.
- Analyze the issues and challenges of refugees, both in the United States and in other countries.
- Discuss issues surrounding immigrants in the criminal justice system.
- Compare and contrast various sociological theories that help explain immigration in the United States.
- Examine effective solutions to address the problems of immigration.

Chapter Outline

The border wall Former US president Donald Trump sought to build a wall along the US/Mexico border that would prevent immigrants and refugees from crossing into the United States. A symbol of intolerance as well as a failed immigration policy, President Joseph Biden halted construction of the wall immediately after taking office.

Social problems become social issues with the involvement of moral entrepreneurs, who argue that an issue that is important to them should be made known to the general public (Chapter 1). Such claims making elevates the discussion to a national level, fostering debate as to the causes of the problem, as well as possible solutions. This process is clearly seen in the social discourse about immigration. As a social problem, immigration is an example of what happens when claims making clashes with the general public's willingness to engage in constructive debate and collaborative problem-solving. In such instances, it becomes imperative for moral entrepreneurs to raise awareness about the problem to such a degree that its threat to most people becomes evident. This escalation of a problem to a threat has happened in the narrative about immigration. While it is reasonable for any country to limit immigration based on capacity and resources, questions remain in the United States about whether immigrants, particularly undocumented/illegal ones, are a threat to national security and have links to terrorism, the spread of disease, drug trafficking, and violent crime.

As you read this chapter, consider what a reasonable response to the problem of immigration would be. You should also consider the possible explanations for the problem. It is far too easy to simply attempt to treat the symptom by limiting the number of people allowed into the country. Instead, evaluate the evidence for what makes immigration a problem and why so many people are fleeing their native countries. Perhaps that exploration will lead to ideas and opportunities for solutions that do not require people to make such enormous sacrifices to achieve what they hope will be a better life.

While much of the rhetoric on the threat of immigration to the United States focuses on an "America first" approach, in a globalized world, everyone is interconnected and the differences between people are small compared to their commonalities. Thus, the problems of immigration are not approached in an "us" versus "them" approach or in a sense of self-protection against another group. Instead, the idea is that diversity is not a bad thing and it does not mean that one group loses if another one wins some concessions.

SOCIOLOGICAL STORY TIME

- On October 12, 2018, a group of about 160 Hondurans left the town of San Pedro Sula—often referred to as the "murder capital of the world"—in hopes of asylum in Mexico or the United States. After only a few days the group of people had swelled to nearly 3,000 refugees, many of whom were women attempting to escape violence in Guatemala as well as Honduras (Lind, 2018).
- As part of his 2016 presidential campaign, Donald Trump promised to build a border wall along the Mexican border that would stem the flow of illegal immigration. Trump also promised that the Mexican government would pay to build the wall, something that the country has consistently refused to do. By 2020, the Mexican government had not dedicated any funds toward the wall and questions remain about how much of the wall had been built compared to the replacement of existing border fencing. According to one account, about 245 miles of the wall has been built, but nearly all of it has been to replace older and shorter barriers of the existing wall. Trump has used about $5 billion in funds that were appropriated by Congress and another $10 billion in Defense Department funding that had been shifted from other priorities (Associated Press, 2020).
- In October 2018, more than 200,000 separate signed petitions were delivered to the Greyhound bus company headquarters in Dallas, Texas, protesting the company's decision to allow Customs and Border Patrol agents to question passengers about their immigration status. These petitions were signed by local Greyhound bus driver's union, the American Civil Liberties Union, and other immigrant advocates who argue that Greyhound has the legal right to refuse border patrol agents onto their buses when they have neither legal warrants or probable cause. By demanding passengers produce evidence of US citizenship, agents are accused of violating their constitutional rights and engaging in racial profiling (Immigration Direct, 2018).
- A major US-Mexico border crossing in San Diego was closed for hours on November 25,' 2018, after a group of migrants on the Mexican side rushed the border area, leading US Border Patrol agents to fire tear gas at the group. About 500 migrants on the Mexican side of the border overwhelmed police blockades near the San Ysidro Port of Entry. US Customs and Border Protection said the migrants threw projectiles that struck several agents, thus warranting the response to disperse the crowd (Emmanuela and Castillo, 2018).

AN OVERVIEW OF IMMIGRATION IN THE UNITED STATES

Why is immigration such a controversial topic in the United States? The subject generates considerable emotion for some people, who seem especially anxious to stop a perceived threat to the American way of life. During the Trump administration, the President's exhortations about building an enormous border wall near the Mexican border and his executive orders to separate families of illegal immigrants make it difficult to imagine how anyone could not be affected by the subject. This is particularly true given the narrative about how immigrants drain US resources or place a burden on the system. In fact, some experts argue that immigration is the rallying point around the rise of **separatism**, where proponents of an "America first" narrative assume an anti-immigration stance to protect the United States and its way of life (Zeitz, 2017).

To understand the origins of this controversy, a brief overview of the history and politics of immigration is in order.

History of Immigration in the United States

With the exception of the hundreds of thousands of enslaved Africans brought to this country against their will, America has a long history of immigrants searching for a better life. Some of the first settlers in the 17th century were fleeing religious persecution in Europe. These 100 or so Puritans established a colony in Plymouth, Massachusetts, and were followed by many others. Experts estimate that nearly 20,000 Puritans came to Plymouth in the decade between 1630 and 1640 (History.com, n.d.).

Another major wave of immigration occurred from around 1815 to 1865. The majority of these newcomers came from Europe. Devastating famine in the mid-19th century led many Irish people to migrate to the United States. In addition, during the 19th century, nearly five million German immigrants came to America, many of whom settled in cities such as Milwaukee, St. Louis, and Cincinnati. Also, by 1920 nearly four million Italians and over two million Jews from Eastern Europe migrated to America. In total, in the 40 years of enormous growth in the United States, more than 20 million immigrants came to America (History.com, n.d.).

A new home Italian immigrants arriving at Ellis Island, an immigration station in New York Harbor, in the early 20th century. Laden with their belongings, some of the immigrants are holding their immigration papers in their teeth.

In response to the massive influx of immigrants from several countries, many Americans began to resent their presence, seeing them as a threat in the job market. Congress passed the Chinese Exclusion Act of 1882, which banned Chinese laborers from coming to America. In 1917, Congress enacted legislation requiring immigrants over 16 years of age to pass a literacy test. The Immigration Act of 1924 created a quota system that restricted entry to 2 percent of the total number of people of each nationality in America (History.com, n.d.).

By the early 1960s, calls to reform US immigration policy had increased, largely due to the momentum generated by the Civil Rights Movement (Chapter 6). At the time, immigration was based on the quota system established by the Immigration Act of 1924. In 1965, Congress passed the Immigration and Nationality Act, which did away with quotas and allowed Americans to sponsor relatives from their countries of origin. The Act allowed preferences to be made according to categories, such as relatives of US citizens or permanent residents; those with skills deemed useful to the United States; and refugees from violence or unrest (McNamara, 2020).

Though it abolished quotas per se, the system did place caps on per-country and total immigration, as well as caps on each category. This new immigration policy would increasingly allow entire families to establish their lives in the United States. This change in policy also reconfigured the face of immigration in that while more than half of all immigrants in the 1950s came from Europe, today the majority of US immigrants come from Asia and Latin America compared to the European influence of decades before (McNamara, 2020).

Throughout the 1980s and 1990s, illegal immigration was an increasingly volatile topic of political debate. The Immigration Reform Act in 1986 attempted to provide better enforcement of immigration policies and creating more avenues toward legal immigration for undocumented people. For example, the Act included amnesty programs for nearly 3 million unauthorized immigrants (McNamara, 2020).

The economic recession that hit the country in the early 1990s was accompanied by a resurgence of anti-immigrant feeling, including among lower-income Americans competing for jobs with immigrants willing to work for lower wages. In 1996, Congress passed the Illegal Immigration Reform and Immigrant Responsibility Act, which addressed border enforcement and the use of social programs by immigrants (McNamara, 2020).

In response to the terrorist attacks on 9/11, in 2002 the Homeland Security Act of 2002 created the Department of Homeland Security, which has taken over the enforcement of immigration policy. Today, immigrants can enter the United States either by receiving a temporary or a permanent admission. A member of the latter category is classified as a lawful permanent resident, and receives a green card granting them eligibility to work in the United States and to eventually apply for citizenship (McNamara, 2020).

THE EXTENT OF IMMIGRATION IN THE UNITED STATES TODAY

In 2018, the United States had approximately 44.8 million people living in the US who were born in another country, more than any other country in the world. Since 1965, the number of immigrants living in the US has more than quadrupled. Immigrants today

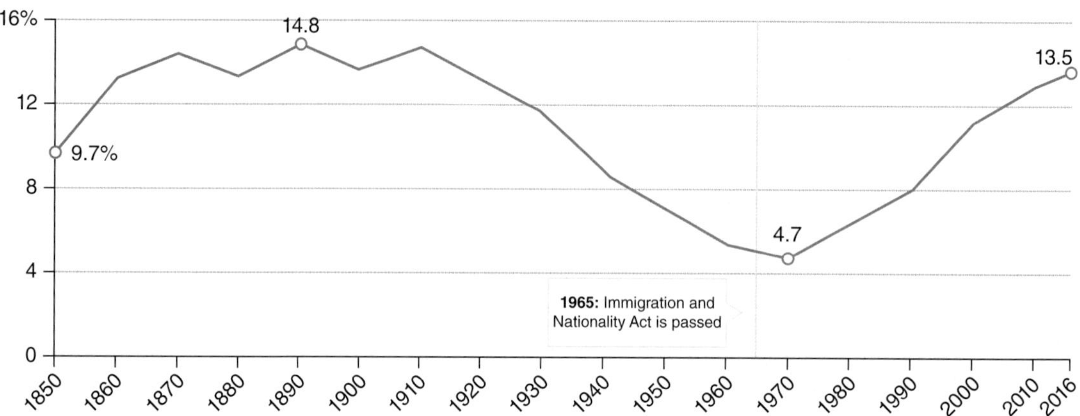

Figure 7.1 Immigrant share of US population Source: US Census Bureau, "Historical Census Statistics on the Foreign-Born Population of the United States: 1850–2000"; and Pew Research Center tabulations of 2010 and 2016 American Community Survey (IPUMS).

account for 13.7 percent of the US population, nearly triple the share (4.8 percent) in 1970 (Figure 7.1; Budiman, 2020).

According to the Pew Research Center, in 2017, 77 percent of immigrants (about 35.2 million) into the United States were in the country legally, while about 23 percent (10.5 million) were considered unauthorized (Figure 7.2; Budiman, 2020).

The process by which an immigrant living in the United States becomes a US citizen is called **naturalization**. Prior to Covid-19, the normal processing time for a typical application for naturalization was between five and seven months.

In 2019, there were 2.2 million immigrants who applied for naturalization. Until 2019, the number of naturalization applications showed a steady increase in recent years. However, the USCIS reports that the number of applications for green cards and naturalizations decreased by 14 percent and 12 percent in 2019. Mexican immigrants have the lowest naturalization rate. According to Mexican-born green card holders, the reasons for this stem in part from language challenges as well as a general lack of interest and financial obstacles (US Immigration and Customs Enforcement, 2020).

That said, in 2018 Mexico accounted for approximately 25 percent of all US immigrants, while immigrants from South and East Asia comprised another 28 percent of all immigrants into the United States. In fact, Asians are projected to become the largest immigrant group in the United States by 2055, surpassing Hispanics. Researchers at the Pew Research Center estimate that in 2065, Asians will make up some 38 percent of all immigrants; Hispanics, 31 percent; Whites, 20 percent; and Blacks, 9 percent (Budiman, 2020).

Assuming current immigration trends, immigrants and their descendants are expected to account for nearly 90 percent of population growth in the United States through 2065, according to the Pew Research Center. This is particularly true given that the percentage of immigrant women who gave birth in 2017 was higher (7.4 percent) than among US-born women (5.9 percent; Lopez, Bialik and Radford, 2018).

Immigrants: A Profile

According to the US Census Bureau, immigrants comprise about 14 percent of the US population. If we include US-born children of immigrants, they constitute about 27 percent of the US population. The United States granted nearly 2.2 million individuals temporary legal residency in 2017, either due to family reunification, employment opportunities, meaning they are needed in various industries, or other reasons. Hundreds of thousands of individuals work legally in the United States under various types of nonimmigrant visas. In 2017, the United States granted close to 180,000 visas for high-skilled workers and nearly 250,000 visas for temporary workers in agriculture and other industries (Budiman, et al., 2020).

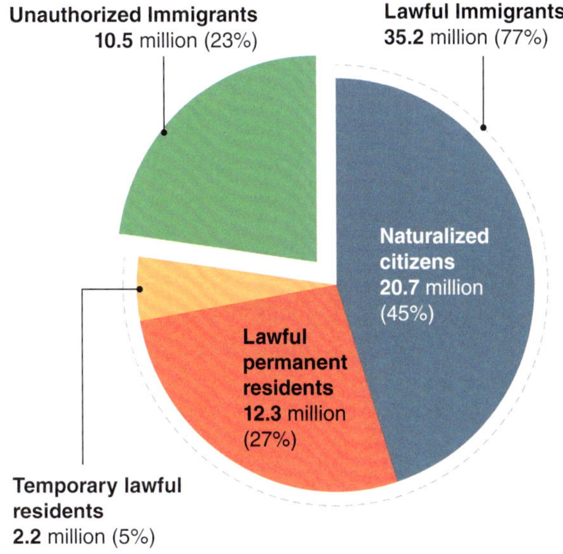

Figure 7.2 Percentage of unauthorized immigrants among US foreign-born population. Note: Figures for the total and subgroups differ from published US Census Bureau totals because census data have been augmented and adjusted to account for undercount of the population. All numbers are rounded. Unauthorized immigrants include some with temporary protection from deportation under Deferred Action for Childhood Arrivals (DACA) and Temporary Protected Status (TPS), as well as pending asylum cases. Source: Pew Research Center estimates based on augmented US Census Bureau data.

In fact, immigrants made up roughly 17 percent of the US workforce in 2017, according to the Pew Research Center; of those, around two-thirds were in the country legally. Collectively, immigrants represent almost half of all domestic employees and a third of workers in the manufacturing and agricultural industries. Thus, the US economy needs immigrants and many of the jobs performed by immigrants are those that many US workers are unwilling to do. According to another study, if the United States policy against immigration continues, the US workforce is expected to decline considerably in the future (Budiman, 2020).

Where some of the controversy exists about immigration relates to those who enter the country illegally. According to the Pew Research Center, unauthorized immigrants comprise about 11 million people. While it is obviously difficult to accurately count this population, the available data suggests that the rates of illegal immigration have declined, particularly since 2009 when the economic crisis eliminated many jobs for all workers in the United States. Many returned to their home countries in search of job opportunities, and since that time, rates of illegal immigration have remained low. For instance, in 2017 the Customs and Border Protection reported a 26 percent drop in the number of people apprehended or stopped at the southern border while arrests of suspected undocumented immigrants jumped by 40 percent (Lopez, Bialik, and Radford, 2018).

Another interesting pattern regarding illegal immigration is that once people cross the border into the United States, they tend to find jobs and build a life for themselves. According to research by the Pew Research Center, more than half of the undocumented have lived in the country for more than a decade and nearly one-third are the parents of US-born children (Lopez, Bialik and Radford, 2018).

What is also noteworthy is that while the controversy surrounding border security continues, most of the undocumented population in this country are what are known as **overstayers,** or people who obtained visas legally and simply remained in the United States once it expired. Thus, much of the debate about unauthorized immigration tends to focus on a relatively small portion of the immigration problem (Lopez, Bialik, and Radford, 2018).

Immigration and Politics

In 2018, largely due to the media attention given to a "caravan" of immigrants from Central America headed toward the US border, along with President Trump's response by sending over 5,000 National Guardsman to protect the border, immigration has risen to near the top of the list of the public's most pressing concerns for the United States. Concern about health care has also risen, probably a result of media attention about Obamacare and its impact as Democrats took control of the House of Representatives in January 2019. Republicans have always maintained a strong stance against immigration, many favoring the construction of a massive border wall, increased arrests and deportation of immigrants, and a reduction in the number of legal immigrants who can enter the United States (Stableford, 2018).

Has it always been the case that Republicans and Democrats are at such odds on the issue of immigration? During the 1990s, Democrats and Republicans were comparatively close in their stances on the issue of immigration. However, since that time twice as many Democrats as Republicans believe that immigrants provide a positive contribution to the nation. There are several reasons for this shift, one of which is the growth of the Hispanic population in the 2000s, which became the fastest growing ethnicity within the Democratic party. More Hispanic leaders became involved in politics, and they lobbied successfully for policies that favored immigrant workers. Organized labor has also changed its position on illegal immigration. In the past, labor unions felt that illegal immigrants took jobs away from US workers. However, now that immigrants represent a sizable proportion of the workforce, performing jobs that many US-born

Migrant "caravan," 2019 Migrants fleeing violence and economic despair in Central America gathered in thousands to move in "caravans" through Mexico and on to the United States. Most were detained in Mexico and forced to return home. This group gathered in Escuintla, Mexico, in April 2019.

workers do not want, unions see them as allies in the efforts to further worker benefits (Thompson, 2018).

The difference between Democrats and Republicans on the subject of immigration became a rallying point during the 2016 presidential campaign. Focusing on a narrative that blamed illegal immigration on employment problems and the lack of economic growth, President Trump has used the resentment felt by many less educated Whites to present an anti-immigration platform. In addition to the narrative that illegal immigrants take jobs away from US-born Americans, Trump has also bundled the illegal immigration issue with threats of terrorism, crime, and illegal drug trafficking to portray all illegal immigrants as a threat to national security. Such a narrative defies the overwhelming evidence to the contrary, but such a platform has gained some measure of appeal to some segments of the American people (Thompson, 2018). Despite such a strong and vocal anti-immigration stance, during the 2020 Republican National Convention, President Trump presided over a naturalization ceremony for several immigrants, a clear departure from his consistent rhetoric against immigration. The move, heralded by some as a political ploy to encourage suburbanites, people of color, and women to vote for him in the 2020 presidential election, is in stark contrast to Trump's consistently derogatory messages about immigrants, particularly those from Mexico and Central America (Shear, 2020).

Public Opinion and Immigration

Given the media attention to topics such as the "border wall" and "migrant caravans," as well as the plight of immigrant families separated at the US-Mexico border, it might seem that most Americans consider immigration in general (and unauthorized immigration in particular) to be a topic of utmost importance. It may even seem, as some politicians have portrayed it, that the general public is worried about the negative impact immigration could have on the economy and American culture. However, the data suggests a different picture.

For example, a 2020 Gallup poll found that 77 percent of Americans considered immigration a "good thing" for the United States (Figure 7.3). In 2020, 34 percent of Americans prefer to see immigration to the United States increase, a 7 percent increase from 2019, while the number of Americans who said they wanted to see immigration decrease dropped in 2020 to 28 percent. This poll marks the first Gallup poll in which the percentage of people wanting to see increased immigration was higher than those who wanted it decreased (Younis, 2020).

Between 2018 and 2020, surveys by various agencies consistently found that a substantial majority of Americans have positive views about immigrants. Polls conducted by CBS News, Quinnipiac University and the Public Religion Research Institute found that between 70–86 percent of Americans say immigrants strengthen the country "because of their hard work and talents," as well as their strong family values (National Immigration Forum, 2020). While some variation occurs based on political affiliation,

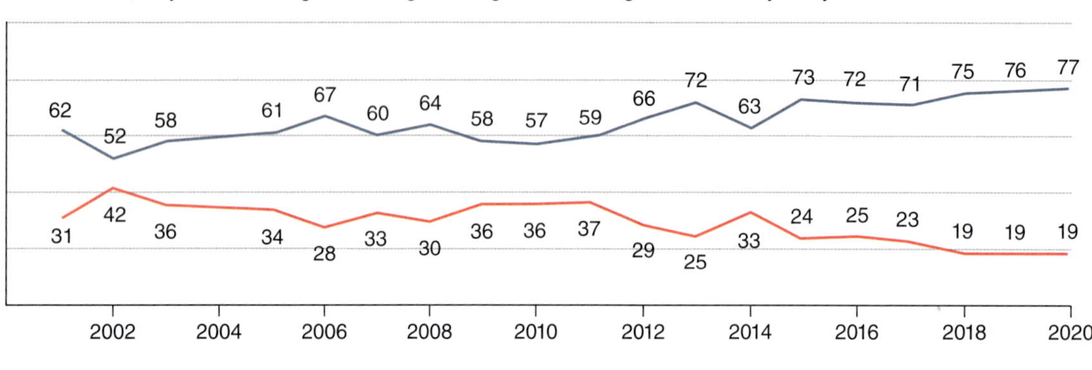

Figure 7.3 Percentage of Americans who believe immigration is "good for the country." Source: Gallup.

even many Conservatives think immigrants are good for the country. Moreover, the data also indicates that most Americans feel that immigrants should have some type of pathways toward citizenship, even undocumented immigrants in some circumstances. This trend has been consistent since 2013, according to a poll by the Public Religion Research Institute (Figure 7.4).

The fact that most people think immigrants make an important contribution to the country and its culture, coupled with opinion polls that look favorably upon immigration, questions arise about whether immigration is on the minds of the American people as much as it is for some politicians and pockets of dissatisfied people.

BENCHMARKS: IMMIGRANTS AND EDUCATION

Critics of immigration argue that immigrants are a drain on the system because they have low education levels, high unemployment, and are unable or unwilling to become fluent in English. Such disturbing statements are inconsistent with the available data on these trends. Overall, the data suggests that immigrants in the United States have lower levels of education than the US-born population (Table 7.1). In 2016, immigrants were three times as likely as the US born to have not completed high school (29 percent vs. 9 percent). However, when examining immigrants from other countries such as those from South America and Southeast Asia, Europe, and

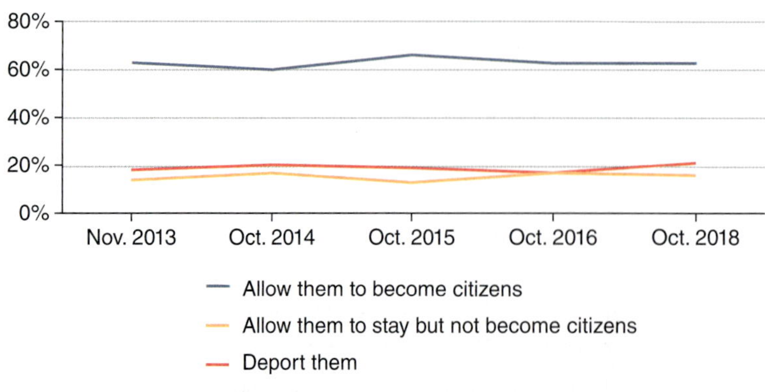

Figure 7.4 Support for paths to citizenship remained stable from 2013 to 2018 Source: National Immigration Forum, 2020.

Table 7.1 Education Levels: US born versus Foreign Born

	Less than high school	High School graduate	Some college	Bachelor's or higher
All US Born	9%	28%	31%	32%
All Foreign Born	29%	22%	19%	30%
Central America	49%	26%	16%	9%
Mexico	57%	25%	13%	6%

Source: Gustavo Lopez, Kristen Bialik, and Jynnah Radford. (2018). "Key Facts About U.S. Immigration." *Pew Research Center.* November 30th. Available at: http://www.pewresearch.org/fact-tank/2018/11/30/key-findings-about-u-s-immigrants/

Canada, immigrants were just as likely as the US born to have a college degree or more, 32 percent and 30 percent, respectively.

Among all immigrants, those from South and East Asia (52 percent) and the Middle East (47 percent) were the most likely to have hold a bachelor's or higher degree (Lopez, Bialik, and Radford, 2018).

BENCHMARKS: IMMIGRANTS AND EMPLOYMENT

In 2018, about 28 million immigrants were working or looking for work in the United States, making up some 17 percent of the total civilian labor force. Approximately 20 million workers were lawful immigrants, who made up the majority of the immigrant workforce, with unauthorized immigrants making up an additional 7.8 million immigrant workers (Lopez, Bialik and Radford, 2018; Table 7.2).

The Covid-19 pandemic had a significant impact on immigrant workers, many of whom were considered "essential" workers during the quarantine. According to a 2020 report

Table 7.2 Immigrant Workers and Labor Force

Total US labor force grows since 2007, but number of unauthorized immigrant workers declines

Labor Force Estimates, in Millions

	2007	2016	Change
US total	153.3	162.8	+9.6
US born	127.9	134.4	+6.5
Lawful immigrant	17.2	20.6	+3.5
Unauthorized immigrant	8.2	7.8	-0.4

Note: All numbers are rounded; changes calculated from unrounded numbers. Based on civilian labor force.

Source: Pew Research Center estimates based on augmented US Census Bureau data.

"US Unauthorized Immigrant Total Dips to Lowest Level in a Decade"

PEW RESEARCH CENTER

by the Center for Migration Studies, 69 percent of immigrants in the labor force and 74 percent of undocumented immigrants were considered essential infrastructure workers, meaning they worked in industries such as health care, agriculture, and others that helped Americans through the quarantine period, a figure higher than native-born workers who were considered essential. Despite these risks, it was during the pandemic that President Trump issued a proclamation banning immigrant workers, arguing that they would take "American" jobs during the Covid-induced recession (White House.gov).

Consistent with President Trump's proclamation, critics of immigration often argue that immigrants are taking jobs from American workers, while others claim that immigrants are a drain on federal resources when they come to the United States. There is, by any measure, a significant need for immigrant labor in the near future. By most accounts, the retirement of many Baby Boomers in the near future, immigrants are projected to become critical to the labor force. That is, immigrants are expected to add about 18 million people of working age between 2015 and 2035. It is important to note that immigrants pay taxes and contribute to the Social Security system even though they are ineligible to use it (Lopez, Bialik, and Radford, 2018).

With regard to the concern that immigrants are a drain on federal resources, according to a 2016 report from the National Academy of Sciences, first generation low-skilled immigrant adults often do receive more in health care, income support, and retirement benefits than they pay in taxes. However, beyond the first generation, most immigrant families end up contributing more, particularly as they spend decades working in the United States (Thompson, 2018).

BENCHMARKS: IMMIGRANTS AND INTEGRATION TO AMERICAN SOCIETY

Opponents to immigration often point out that members of some groups create tension within American culture by their inability or unwillingness to learn English. The **English-first movement** is a product of a backlash against bilingual education and the dilution of English as the official language of the United States. This remains controversial since the United States has not formally declared English as the official language, but critics are quick to point out that the ability to communicate is a critical component of assimilation—and if immigrants want to become citizens, they should learn the language of their new country.

It should not be surprising that the longer a person stays in a country where they are not native speakers, the greater the likelihood that they become proficient or fluent in their new country's language. According to data from the Pew Research Center, about 44 percent of immigrants living in the United States for five years or less are English proficient, and those who have lived in the United States for more than 20 years have a proficiency rate of 55 percent (Lopez, Bialik and Radford, 2018).

Many immigrants who come to the United States are already proficient English speakers. According to recent data, a bit more than half of immigrants ages 5 and older are **proficient English speakers** (defined as either speaking English very well or only speaking English at home). While immigrants from Europe or Canada and the sub-Saharan Africa and the Middle East have the highest rates of English proficiency, with some above 75 percent, immigrants from Mexico and Central America have the lowest levels of English proficiency, hovering around the 33 percent mark for each group (Lopez, Bialik and Radford, 2018).

Thus, in three critical areas (educational achievement, employment, and fluency in English), immigrants have clearly distinguished themselves as being productive members of society, in some cases at a higher rate than US-born residents. Given that immigrants are taxpayers and contribute to programs such as Social Security, and because they often take jobs that most American workers refuse, real questions remain about the value, purpose, contribution, and potential threat they face to the American people and its economy.

REFUGEES

More than 60 million people across the globe are fleeing conflict, poverty and persecution within their home countries. According to data from the United Nations, **85 percent** of arrivals to Europe came from the world's top 10 refugee-producing countries. Most people pass through Greece via Turkey and go on through the Balkans; others travel by way of the central Mediterranean, starting in Libya and ending in Italy. These people are generally trying to move north to Austria, Germany and Sweden—places with high standards of living and welcoming asylum policies. With the number of displaced people across the world tripling in the last decade, the number of people attempting to reach Europe is not expected to slow down any time soon (Office of United Nations High Commissioner on Human Rights, 2018).

Since 1980, about 3 million refugees have been resettled in the United States—more than any other country. In 2017, a total of 53,716 refugees were resettled in the United States. The largest origin group of refugees was the Democratic Republic of the Congo, followed by Iraq, Syria, Somalia, and Burma (Myanmar). Among all refugees admitted in 2017, 22,861 are Muslims (43 percent) and 25,194 are Christians (47 percent). California, Texas and New York resettled nearly a quarter of all refugees admitted in 2016 (Figure 7.5; Connor, 2018).

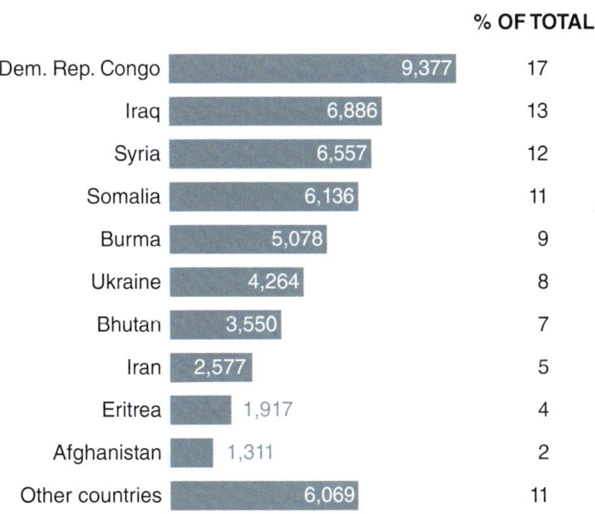

Figure 7.5 Distribution of US refugees by country (2017) Number of refugees entering the United States in fiscal 2017, by origin country. Note: Data do not include special immigrant visas and certain humanitarian parole entrants. Source: US State Department's Refugee Processing Center accessed August 30, 2018.

GLOBAL PERSPECTIVES

The Refugee Crisis in Yemen

Internal conflicts often wreak havoc on the civilian population and its infrastructure. For already less developed nations, the problems magnify and can easily reach epidemic proportions. Such is the case with Yemen. As a breeding ground for terrorist activity, US-backed forces are at war against Iranian-backed troops. The unrest began in 2014 after an Arab uprising forced the Yemen president to resign. However, a failed political transition resulted in rebels taking over the capital city of Sanaa (BBC.com, 2020; Keleman, 2019). While thousands of troops and civilians have been casualties of this conflict, the economic and social fallout has been extraordinary. Currently there are more than 3 million people that have been displaced by the war, and the United Nations says the risk of famine is high for nearly 75 percent of the Yemen population.

What's more, at least 1 million civilians have contracted cholera, which poses a threat to spread internationally. The reason for this outbreak stems from the fuel shortages that disrupted the operation of wastewater treatment plants, along with shortages of medical supplies, food, water, and other essential items. Already one of the poorest countries in the Arab world, international and humanitarian aid has come from several sources, including many from Egypt and Saudi Arabia, who are attempting to improve conditions in that country as it suffers the effects of war (Sipress, Karklis, and Meko, 2018).

The toll of civil war A Yemeni woman does laundry in a plastic tub surrounded by four of her five children. The family had been displaced from their village by the civil war and live crowded into a single room in Sanaa, Yemen.

Adding to the struggle is the Covid-19 pandemic, which has had an enormous impact on Yemen. While the problems in this country before the pandemic caused the United Nations to label Yemen as the world's worst humanitarian crisis in the world, the pandemic has exacerbated many of these problems and added to the burdens, including the loss of education for the nearly 7 million children who are out of school (Karasapan, 2020).

In addition, there is a severe shortage of equipment and medical staff. According to a report by the Brookings Institute in 2020, about 20 percent of the districts in Yemen have no medical doctors—a number that continues to shrink. Some hospitals have halted health services and the country has a total of 500 ventilators (Karasapan, 2020).

IMMIGRANTS AND THE CRIMINAL JUSTICE SYSTEM

During the Trump administration, increased enforcement of immigration policies led to an increase in the number of immigrant apprehensions, deportations, and prosecutions of illegal immigrants who have committed crimes. For example, the number of apprehensions at the US-Mexico border sharply decreased between 2006 and 2017, from over a million to about 300,000 in 2017. However, in 2019, there was a spike in apprehensions—851,000, which was nearly triple what occurred in 2017 and more than double that number in 2018. The reasons for this stem from an increase number of migrants seeking asylum to the United States (Gramlich, 2020).

In response, the Trump administration changed the protocols for applying for asylum and instituted obstacles that made it more difficult for people to apply. One of these strategies is known as the "Remain in Mexico" approach, where people seeking asylum have to remain in that country while their case was adjudicated. In the past, immigrants were allowed to remain in the United States until the case was resolved, which could take years. A recent court case struck down the use of this program (Gramlich, 2020).

Deportations

In 2019, according to the US Immigration and Customs Enforcement data, there were approximately 486,000 immigrants deported from the United States. Immigrants convicted of a crime made up about half of deportations in 2019, the most recent year for which statistics by criminal status are available. Of the 486,000 immigrants deported in 2019, about 50 percent had criminal convictions, a trend that had been consistent since 2001.The largest category of offenses for which immigrants were deported were traffic offenses; others included minor offenses such as liquor law violations, health and safety violations, or obstructing the police or Congress (US Immigration and Customs Enforcement, 2020).

While President Trump's immigration policies included the separation of children from immigrant families when they cross the border illegally, the Obama administration was also involved in large scale deportations of immigrants. In fact, President Obama deported more people than any other president in US history.

In 2015, Obama declared three priorities for deporting immigrants. The main thrust of this approach, which Obama framed as "felons, not families; criminals not children" focused on individuals who were threats to national security, border security, or public safety. This included gang members, convicted felons and those who were caught trying to cross the border illegally. Of all the people deported during the Obama administration, 91 percent fell into this category (Marshall, 2016).

Another priority was those who committed misdemeanor offenses or new immigration violations. These included people who were convicted of three or more misdemeanor offenses other than traffic violations. A third priority were those individuals who were unaccompanied minors sent across the border by their parents and relatives. In sum, the Obama administration made an attempt to move away from deporting immigrants who were working in the United States and who did not have a criminal record (Marshall, 2016). This was decidedly not the approach taken by the Trump administration, which did not distinguish between different types of offenders and clearly targets immigrants from Mexico and Central America. The incoming administration of President Joseph Biden is making immigration reform central to its agenda.

Detentions

The United States first imposed **immigration detention** in the late 19th century. By the early 1950s, detaining migrants no longer seemed necessary. European and Asian migration had fallen drastically as a result of the Immigration Act of 1924 and the Great Depression. In 1954, government officials felt that many migrants could be released while their cases were being reviewed. Detention was reserved for migrants who were deemed likely to flee or who posed some sort of threat to the country. This position changes in the 1980s with the migration of Cubans and Haitians into the United States.

During the 1980s, Americans came to see Cuban exiles as a dangerous threat and led to the use of detention as a primary strategy to deal with immigration. However, the exiles who fled Castro's revolution were wealthy, politically conservative, and very integrated into Miami's society. The group that was part of the Mariel boatlift, which included approximately 125,000 Cubans fled for the United States, included many poor Cubans as well as some of whom President Castro had released from hospitals and prison. Regrettably, many of these people were not criminals, but were labeled "antisocial" by Cuban officials. Thousands of immigrants were interned on US military bases while they waited to be sponsored by someone until they could become self-sufficient (Clemens, 2017). Without sponsorship, the only way they could leave the internment camps was by leaving the United States. But government officials could not deport them because the Castro government refused to take them back (Clemens, 2017).

Mariel boatlife A small boat crowded with "Marielitos," or refugees from Cuba, off the Florida coast in May 1980.

By 1982, about 400 Mariel Cubans who still had not been sponsored were sent to prison, including to a maximum-security penitentiary in Atlanta.

This trend, coupled with a fear of another large migrant group coming into the United States, led to the development of a policy that focused more on detention as a default strategy than the previous policy of allowing immigrants to remain free while their applications for citizenship were being considered. As we saw in Chapter 2, this was an era of "getting tough" on criminals in general, where there was an unprecedented level of incarceration of all types of offenders in the United States. This trend has continued, and US policy reflects the growth of detention as a strategy and the development of privately-run prisons. In 2016, this led to the detention of 360,000 people in over 200 detention facilities, at a cost of $2.6 billion per year (McNamara, 2020).

In early 2018, the Trump administration implemented a zero-tolerance policy, wherein all unauthorized immigrants were arrested and criminally prosecuted. As a result, thousands of children were detained separately from their parents or guardians. In response to widespread protests and criticisms, Trump ended the family separation policy (McNamara, 2020).

FEDERAL, STATE, AND LOCAL POLICIES AND IMMIGRATION

During his administration, President Obama attempted to provide temporary legal relief to many undocumented immigrants. In 2012, the **Deferred Action for Childhood Arrivals (DACA)** offered renewable, two-year deportation deferrals and work permits to undocumented immigrants who had arrived in the United States as children and had no criminal records.

Obama argued that this effort was an intervening step but attempted to influence Congress to pass the Dream Act, which first began in 2001, that would have benefited many of the same people. The first version of the **Development, Relief, and Education for Alien Minors (DREAM) Act** was introduced in 2001. As a result, young undocumented immigrants have since been called Dreamers. Since its creation, there have been multiple versions which outline a pathway for undocumented youth who came into the United States. Despite support in Congress from various Senators and Congressmen, none of the versions of the legislation has become law (American Immigration Council, 2017).

The Senate version of the Dream Act, introduced in July 2017, allows current, former, and future undocumented high-school graduates and GED recipients a three-step pathway to US citizenship through college, work, or the armed services. For instance, an individual may be able to obtain **Conditional Permanent Resident status (CPR)** if they entered the United States under the age of 18, have been living in the United States for four years, have not been convicted of a felony, and the individual has graduated high school, obtained a GED or is currently enrolled or admitted to an institution of higher education (American Immigration Council, 2017).

Anyone who maintains their CPR status can apply for **Legal Permanent Resident status** (**LPR**, also known as obtaining a "green card") by completing at least two years of military service with an honorable discharge or show that they have been employed over a total of three years. After maintaining their LPR status for five years, a person can apply to become a US citizen (American Immigration Council, 2017).

In 2014, Obama attempted to extend similar benefits to undocumented parents of US citizens and permanent residents. However, nearly half of US states sued his administration, alleging that the program, known as **Deferred Action for Parents of Americans (DAPA),** violated federal immigration law and the US Constitution. The US Supreme Court ruled in 2016 that the program was unconstitutional (American Immigration Council, 2017).

During his administration, President Trump signed several **executive orders** that increased enforcement and expansion of detention as part of his immigration strategy. These are controversial because questions remain about the legality and constitutionality of the use of executive orders in such cases without Congressional approval. For example, Trump signed an executive order that expanded the deportation of any unauthorized immigrant who could not prove they have been in the United States for two years, without a court hearing (American Immigration Council, 2017; Felter and Renwick, 2018).

Another executive order focused on preventing terrorists from entering the United States by banning nationals from Iran, Iraq, Libya, Somalia, Sudan, and Yemen from entering the United States and suspended the US refugee program for 120 days. These actions, particularly the ban on travelers from seven Muslim-majority countries, drew widespread protests and legal challenges (Felter and Renwick, 2018). The so-called **travel ban** was reversed by President Joseph Biden as one of his first acts in office.

While the federal government is generally responsible for enforcing immigration laws, it may delegate some immigration-control duties to state and local law enforcement. However, the degree to which local officials are obliged to cooperate with federal authorities is a subject of intense debate. Proponents of tougher immigration enforcement have labeled state and local jurisdictions that limit their cooperation with federal authorities as **sanctuary cities.** There is no official definition or count of sanctuary cities, but the Immigrant Legal Resource Center identifies more than six hundred counties where with such policies are located.

President Trump issued an executive order to block federal funding to sanctuary cities and attempted to reinstate the **Secure Communities program**, in which state and local police provide fingerprints of suspects to federal immigration authorities and transfer individuals to federal authorities who were assumed to be illegal immigrants.

In 2020, an analysis of the effects of the Secure Communities program indicates that there are a number of important consequences from its use. For instance, East (2020) points out that once President Trump implemented the use of the program, the result was about 80,000 immigrants being deported, 83 percent of which were related to the Secure Communities program. Although the goal of the program was to deport serious criminals, some data suggests that nearly 80 percent of those deported under the program were convicted of traffic offenses and immigration violations, such as illegal entry. In fact, East (2020) points out that research fails to show any evidence that the implementation of Secure Communities had the effect of reducing crime (East, 2020).

The use of the Secure Communities program also reduced the number of men who were available for low-skilled jobs, and it had a corresponding effect on the number of immigrant women, who make up the majority of housekeepers in the United States but became afraid to leave their homes out of a fear of being deported. The program also had the effect of reduced reporting rates of crime, as many immigrants did not report crimes to the police because they feared being deported (East, 2020).

SOCIOLOGICAL THEORY AND IMMIGRATION

How does sociological theory inform us about the issues surrounding immigration? How can sociology offer insight into the nature of the problem and possible solutions? In the following section, we offer several perspectives in an effort to provide a comprehensive understanding of the issues.

Functionalism and Immigration

Recall that functionalism focuses on the recognition of how elements of society contribute to its overall growth and stability. Immigration is a mechanism for providing the labor required for that growth to be achieved. Immigrants, as we have seen, are often willing to (or have no choice but to) take jobs and perform tasks that most US.-born workers will not, and often at wages that are considered below acceptable levels. As Herbert Gans noted about poverty, immigrants offer a way for society to perform its "dirty work" at a wage it is willing to pay. By providing this labor, immigrants meet an important societal need.

Doing the work no one else wants to do Migrant labor is essential in many US sectors, especially agriculture. These Mexican migrants are harvesting strawberries near Ventura, California.

A functionalist perspective would also observe that immigrants and immigration offer ways for society to enhance diversity. By bringing differences in culture, language, and ways of life that allow society to improve its level of sophistication and understanding of groups and of human nature.

Functionalists would also argue that the controversy surrounding illegal immigration fosters a sense of social solidarity as people come together against a common threat, whether or not that threat is supported by objective evidence. As Durkheim observed of crime and criminals, when people rally around a common threat they develop stronger ties with each other than might otherwise be the case.

Conflict Theory and Immigration

Conflict theorists consider the economic, social, and political aspects of power. They also study how power is used to further a particular group's interests. The experience of immigrants to the United States is determined by the absence of these types of power. Immigrants, who are denied the rights, privileges, and entitlements enjoyed by citizens, are at a significant disadvantage when they attempt to enter the United States. Unauthorized immigrants face especially challenging problems, as they attempt to evade scrutiny in the shadows of society.

At a macro level, policies that limit immigration are exercises of social, economic and political power by those who have it. Immigration policies that emphasize arrest, detention, and deportation are seen as efforts to limit the opportunities for immigrants because they represent a threat to the status quo. Indeed, as most projections indicate, immigrant groups (particularly Hispanics and Asians) are increasing in size and will eventually supersede Whites as the numerical majority group in the United States. Thus, immigration provides a good example of how groups with power attempt to preserve the status quo.

Symbolic Interactionism and Immigration

A symbolic interactionists perspective would view immigration in terms of the process by which a group of people learn to become a part of society. The process used by immigrants to assimilate into the United States, particularly as they learn to navigate the culture and its language, is of particular interest since it reshapes the immigrant's attitudes, values, beliefs, and behaviors. This is true even if the person has no intention of ever becoming a US citizen.

Another feature of immigration that would be of interest to symbolic interactionists is the response of US-born citizens to immigrant presence in the United States. While a small segment of the population usually views new members with suspicion or condemnation, likely out of fear that immigrants might take jobs away from citizens or dilute US culture, the current anti-immigrant climate in the United States relates to the labeling perspective (Chapter 2). As immigrants continue to come into the country under a cloud of suspicion and fear, questions arise about the place for immigrants and their status as residents, even temporary ones, in this country.

Symbolic interactionists would also be interested in the process by which an immigrant becomes a citizen. Given the many steps involved and the requirements outlined for each one, a symbolic interactionist might question whether the standards used to justify citizenship could be achieved by US-born residents. Thus, there may be questions about the criteria and protocols used that make it more difficult for immigrants to achieve citizen status that are not reflected in the actual knowledge or understanding of US culture that cannot be met by most current citizens.

Welcome to America New US citizens taking the Oath of Allegiance during a 2019 naturalization ceremony in Oakland Park, Florida. More than 150 people from 42 countries participated in this ceremony.

Critical Race Theory and Immigration

Critical race theory argues that racism is deeply embedded in all American social institutions and is easily seen in its laws and their application to certain groups. As institutional or systemic racism continues to marginalize people of color and perpetuates a form of white privilege, where people of color are disproportionately represented at all phases of the criminal justice system, many people do not even realize the extent of the prejudice and discrimination that occurs. In fact, some segments of American society remain skeptical of the idea that systemic discrimination and prejudice even exists in the United States (Delgado, 2017).

As it relates to immigration, critical race theorists argue that the federal government's policies and rhetoric that portrays them as criminals, drug traffickers, terrorists and animals that prey upon middle class whites is a telling example of the way they are perceived as a group of people. Such a distinction, coupled with an extreme set of enforcement policies that attempt to deport virtually all immigrants from certain countries, including the excessive use of detention and the separation of immigrant children from their families when they cross the border, serves to devalue the contributions and status of all Hispanic/Latinos, even those who are US citizens (Sanchez and Romero, 2010).

WHAT WORKS? EFFECTIVE SOLUTIONS TO ADDRESS PROBLEMS OF IMMIGRATION

The debate about immigration is a long standing one, particularly as it relates to immigrants from countries like Mexico and those in Central America. What is not debatable is the need for immigrant labor—the US economy cannot function without it and the country's failure to admit and recognize this fact is part of the problem—immigrants are needed, particularly in certain industries where it is difficult to find US-born workers to perform those jobs. In truth, the inability or unwillingness to create citizenship pathways for these immigrants to remain in the United States has actually created a system that demands unauthorized workers.

In trying to find reasonable solutions to a very complex problem, Tom Jawetz, vice president for the Center for American Progress, an organization that takes an admittedly liberal approach to economic and social issues, outlines a set of strategies to improve the immigration system in the United States. This plan attempts to take a more comprehensive approach to immigration that balances the needs of immigrants, the economic realities of immigrant labor, as well as retaining features of the rule of law that build in a fair and just mechanism that creates reasonableness and accountability for those who violate the boundaries related to immigration.

The plan consists of four parts: 1) a flexible immigration system; 2) an asylum and refugee system that recognizes the need for a compassionate approach to the problem; 3) an enforcement arm of a system that resembles our existing criminal justice system; 4) and a series of pathways toward citizenship for those immigrants who desire to remain in the United States (Jawetz, 2019).

SO WHAT CAN I DO?

Unless you are a Native American, just about everyone in the United States is a descendant of immigrants. This means the issues we wrestle with today are similar to the ones many immigrant families struggled with in the past. Regardless of your background or ancestry, immigration is an important issue and the decisions we make about the country's immigration policies should matter to everyone.

As with many of the social problems discussed in this textbook, it is critical for you to understand the issues accurately. It is also important as a sociologist for you to analyze the narratives being presented, along with the rhetoric offered to support them, that are inconsistent with the empirical evidence about what is occurring. In other words, while you cannot change social policy alone, you can separate fact from fiction and call attention to misrepresentations and false narratives about a problem like immigration.

You can influence the process by not allowing politicians to pass laws based on incorrect information or on their perceptions of a small but vocal support base, when the rest of the country feels differently. You can do a lot by being informed so that when those inaccurate portrayals of immigrants occur, you can counter them with facts and objective data, rather than emotion, divisive commentary, or claims of "fake news." You can remind those who have taken a particular stance on immigration that there are many layers to this problem regardless of one's political views. You can educate others in terms of what we know rather than what we think we believe. That is an ambitious goal, but the only way meaningful change occurs, or the correct decisions are made is with people who are armed with the knowledge of what is occurring not the editorializing in an attempt to secure votes.

CONCLUSION

There is considerable controversy surrounding the subject of immigration. Legal and unauthorized immigrants alike face problems related to their status, even as they may differ in terms of their reasons for coming to the United States. In addition, the contributions made by immigrants to American society are frequently overlooked. Increasingly, however, many American citizens are beginning to appreciate the value of immigrants, both in terms of their social and cultural contributions to a more diverse society as well as the positive economic and political contributions immigrants make. By taking jobs most US-born residents do not want and by paying taxes and contributing to programs such as Social Security, (even though they are ineligible to benefit from such programs themselves), immigrants continue to strengthen our society.

Politically, Democrats and labor unions have become more receptive to the value immigrants make to the United States, as they have come to appreciate that the US economy would suffer greatly without the contributions of immigrant workers. In contrast, conservative Republican groups often espouse views that favor greater restriction of access into the United States. While most presidents have attempted to stem the flow of immigrants at one time or another, President Trump's approach is much more aggressive and controversial, in that he has maintained that illegal immigration is tied to terrorism, drug trafficking, and violent crime.

The United States, like the rest of the world, must also address its refugee problem. More than 60 million people across the globe are fleeing conflict, poverty and persecution within their home countries. According to data from the United Nations, the problem is growing worse and refugees are increasingly finding it more difficult to find a country to host them. As countries that have welcomed refugees begin to reach their capacity to do so, some of which end up living in refugee camps, some leaders are enacting asylum policies that are more restrictive and complicated.

YOU MAKE THE CALL: FAMILIES AT THE BORDER

You are a border patrol agent who has discovered a family of immigrants from Central America attempting to sneak over the border into the United States. The family, which consists of a husband and wife, along with two children, ages seven and 15, are likely to be separated once you begin to file the paperwork about their arrest and detention. Then you discover that the two children are actually US-born. Under the current policy, this likely means that the children will be placed in foster care while the parents are assigned to a detention facility while they await a deportation hearing. The parents nor the children have no criminal history and traveled back to Central America upon learning of the death of the maternal grandmother. They attempted to reenter the United States, where they have been living for more than 15 years. The husband and wife obtained a work visa to legally enter the country but neglected to renew it after it had expired. The husband works in the agricultural industry, while the wife cleans people's homes and is self-employed. Both have been paying taxes, contributing to Social Security, and rent a home in the El Paso, Texas area. The children are doing well in school, where they have no history of behavior problems and are even in leadership roles in sports and student government.

You realize that to detain this family, you are likely ruining any chance for them to return to the life they have built. You also realize that the children will likely become a burden to the state as they will be part of the foster care system. The family will no longer pay taxes or contribute to the community in any meaningful way if the parents are deported. You are faced with an ethical dilemma of whether or not to release them or follow the protocol outlined by the Department of Homeland Security. What do you do?

Questions to consider:

1. While you have a duty to act by the oath you took to enforce the law, is this a black and white case that does not allow you any discretion?
2. What is gained or lost by processing them into the system? It is true that they have violated the law by staying beyond the time allotted to them in their visa, but are there other mitigating factors to consider?
3. Have you ever released someone who has committed a crime in the past or would you ever consider doing so if the situation warranted it? If so, what factors would you consider?
4. Is there some other alternative you can think of that allows the family to remain intact but still hold them accountable? If so, what is it?

Separated families Detained immigrant children lined up at the Homestead Temporary Shelter for Unaccompanied Children in Florida.

SUMMARY

- Describe an overview of immigration in the United States.
    - Immigration into the United States is an historically important feature in the development and growth of US culture and its economy.
    - While media accounts often portray immigration as a threat to national security and public safety, such a position typically comes from a small and politically conservative segment of the population.
    - Most public opinion polls show that Americans think immigrants make important social, economic, and political contributions and provide many benefits to society.
    - On the issue of immigration as a problem, most polls show that Americans

generally do not think of it as an issue of any significant priority.

- Explore the extent of immigration in the United States.
    - Immigrants represent a significant portion of the workforce, a fact that is important as an increased number of Baby Boomers retire, and the United States experiences lower birthrates.
    - The need for immigrant labor will become more important in the future.
    - In 2018 there were about 44.8 million immigrants in the United States, about 25 percent from Mexico and 28 percent from Asia, 13 percent from Europe and about 8 percent from Central America.
    - Most immigrants are authorized to live and work in the United States, with about 10.5 million considered undocumented or unauthorized.
- Analyze the issues and challenges of refugees, both in the United States and in other countries.
    - Civil unrest, violence, and corruption drive many people from their homes and to the borders of other countries.
    - Problems in countries like Yemen demonstrate that many people experience severe deprivation and questions remain about the ability and responsibility of other countries to accept refugees as these conflicts endure.
    - The United States has made it difficult to gain asylum for many refugees, in part by changing the criteria under which someone can apply for asylum as well as where they must remain while their application is being considered.
- Discuss issues surrounding immigrants in the criminal justice system.
    - While President Obama both deported many immigrants who presented a threat to national security, he also attempted to find ways to assist immigrants in the transition to American society, most notably the Dreamers Act and DACA.
    - President Trump's administration took an opposing view, stepping up enforcement at the border, with increased arrests, detention as a strategy, and deportation proceedings for those apprehended.
    - By casting the issue of immigration in the same light as terrorism and the war on drugs as well as violent crime, Trump apparently hoped to convince the American people that immigration is a much greater threat to national security than most Americans believe it to be.
- Compare and contrast various sociological theories that help explain immigration in the United States.
    - Functionalism focuses on the recognition of how elements of society contribute to its overall growth and stability. Immigration is a mechanism for providing the labor required for that growth to be achieved. Functionalists would also argue that the controversy surrounding illegal immigration fosters a sense of social solidarity as people come together against a common threat, whether or not that threat is supported by objective evidence.
    - Conflict theorists would argue that policies limiting immigration are exercises

of social, economic and political power by those who have it. Immigration policies that emphasize arrest, detention, and deportation are seen as efforts to limit the opportunities for immigrants because they represent a threat to the status quo.

- A symbolic interactionist perspective would view immigration in terms of the process by which a group of people learn to become a part of society. The process used by immigrants to assimilate into the United States is of particular interest since it reshapes the immigrant's attitudes, values, beliefs, and behaviors. This is true even if the person has no intention of ever becoming a US citizen.
- Critical race theory explores the ways that laws and policies perpetuate racial subordination. Critical race theorists argue that repeated assertions by politicians that anti-immigration measures are efforts to enhance public safety and enforce the rule of law in society are prime examples of systemic racism. They further observe that the stigmatization of immigrants demonstrate a type of structural prejudice identified by the theory.

- Examine effective solutions to address the problems of immigration.
  - Jawetz (2019) offers a proposal that creates a more humane immigration and asylum system. It contains many of the due process protections and proportionality of punishment that reflects the current adult and juvenile justice systems. This model also creates a reasonable and fair pathway toward citizenship for those immigrants who wish to pursue it.

KEY TERMS

Conditional Permanent Resident status (CPR) 215

Deferred Action for Childhood Arrivals (DACA) 215

Deferred Action for Parents of Americans (DAPA) 216

Deportation 213

Development, Relief, and Education for Alien Minors (DREAM) Act 215

English-first movement 210

Executive orders 216

Immigrant apprehension 213

Immigration detention 214

Legal Permanent Resident status (LPR) 216

Mariel Boatlift 214

Naturalization 204

Overstayers 206

Proficient English Speakers 211

Refugees 211

Sanctuary cities 216

Separatism 202

Secure Communities Program 216

Discussion Questions

1. What do you think about the proposed security wall along the Mexican border? Do you think the construction of a wall will stop the flow of illegal immigrants into the United States? Why or why not?
2. Why is the refugee problem such a difficult one to resolve? Is it a problem of capacity for countries that are refusing to admit refugees or are there other issues that prevent more countries from becoming asylum-friendly?
3. How would you propose to improve English proficiency for many immigrants? Is the continuation of bilingual education a reasonable solution? Should immigrants be required to pass a proficiency test at some point during their time in the United States?
4. How do you feel about the elimination of the DACA program? Is it reasonable to separate immigrant families or should the United States be more accommodating to children since they had no choice in the decision to migrate here?
5. What do you make of the differences between the facts about immigration, as offered in the available data, and the fiction offered by politicians and policymakers about this group? How do you make sense of the differences? What does the evidence say about critics of immigration who argue that immigrants take jobs away from US-born citizens?

Learn more with this chapter's digital tools, including Data and Media Literacy Exercises, flashcards, and chapter self-assessments at **www.oup.com/he/mcnamara**.

8

Does Education Really Lead to a Better Life? Educational Inequalities

Chapter Outline

LEARNING OBJECTIVES

- Summarize an overview of public education in the United States.
- Analyze the impact of educational inequalities in the United States.
- Discuss challenges to public education.
- Compare schools in the United States and international schools.
- Analyze the reasons that some schools fail in the United States.
- Describe the response to the challenges in public schools.
- Assess the problems in higher education in light of race and class influences.
- Analyze how sociological theory can explain some of the challenges in education.
- Evaluate effective solutions to some of the problems in education in the United States.

The outbreak of Covid-19 in early 2020 has had especially far-reaching consequences for the already fragile US public education system. As school districts went under quarantine, parents and caretakers of school-age children suddenly found themselves responsible for supervising their children's education. Teachers and administrators scrambled to create online delivery of lessons, activities, and resources. The crisis laid bare the stark inequalities of education in the United States, as students and districts alike grappled with disparities in everything from health and safety to hardware and bandwidth. For an as-yet-unknown percentage of American students, the last half of the 2019–2020 school year and at least the first semester of the 2020 school year might be a total loss.

Learning during a pandemic Fifth graders at a private school in California began the 2020–2021 school year in classrooms equipped with socially distanced learning stations and individual tablet computers. For most US students in struggling public school systems, however, the academic year began with even fewer resources than usual.

In response to the crisis, many parents in privileged communities pooled their resources to form learning "pods" for their children and a few select classmates. These families benefited from high-speed internet connections; parents and caretakers who either did not need to work, or could easily work from home without financial penalty; the resources to hire additional tutors, coaches, or babysitters; and the incalculable advantages of safe and quiet environments with nutritious food and opportunities for outdoor recreation. Still other parents took their children out of the public school system altogether, opting for other forms of homeschooling or "road schooling." The common denominator for these families is that their resources provided them with options.

Poor families, immigrant families, and others who lacked such resources had to either do their best with the confusing messages from their public school systems (in New York City, for example, the mayor rescinded plans to re-open schools within days of the planned re-opening date, throwing the plans of mostly working-class and poor families into chaos) or go without any educational structure altogether. For many children in such situations, public schools provided not just education but also hot meals, safe supervision, counseling, and recreation.

Inequality in educational opportunities, some experts argue, prevents some members of society from having the life chances to achieve a higher standard of living. As you read this chapter, think about the issues stemming from what we have learned about poverty, discrimination, prejudice and racism. Is the education system suffering from some of these same structural challenges?

SOCIOLOGICAL STORY TIME

- On February 14, 2018, in Parkland, FL, a troubled teen, Nikolas Cruz, walked into Marjory Stoneman Douglas high school and shot 24 people, killing 17. He then dropped his rifle and backpack and escaped by blending in with panicked students who were leaving campus. He then walked to a Walmart, bought a drink at a Subway restaurant and then went to a McDonald's. About 40 minutes later he was arrested on the street without incident (CBS News, 2018).
- A 2017 documentary, *Teach Us All*, chronicles the issues and challenges facing poor and minority students in inner-city environments. The film calls attention to the intersection between race, class, and education. Critics are calling it one of the most significant films on education in decades (CBS News.com, 2018).
- In 2018, New York attorney Aaron Schlossberg was caught on camera complaining that workers in a restaurant were speaking Spanish with customers. His argument was that they should be speaking English because, "this is America." Schlossberg went on to say: "My guess is they're not documented, so my next call is to ICE to have each one of them kicked out of my country." The irony is that unlike other multilingual countries, the United States has not declared English as its official language. However, comments like these are reflective of the English-first approach to education. Some states have passed laws eliminating bilingual education programs and replacing them with English-only immersion programs (Kaur, 2018).

AN OVERVIEW OF EDUCATION IN THE UNITED STATES

Education has been a path out of poverty to achievement of the American Dream. The problem is that the promise of an education conflicts with the realities of actually getting one. In fact, one could argue that the inequalities discussed in previous chapters, as they relate to poverty, race and crime, affect the ability of poor people and racial minorities to obtain the kind of education that leads to a well-paying job.

Sociologist C. Wright Mills offered important insight into the nature of social life by observing the intersection between biography and history (Chapter 1; Mills, 1959). Perhaps there is no better example of what Mills describes than the interconnectedness between poverty and education, poverty and race, and race and education. The inequalities that minorities experience are often reinforced by the educational experiences they receive. Let's look at this interplay in more depth.

History of Public Education in the United States

Although the (male) children of elite families have long had access to education in the West, systems of public education for most children began to emerge in the Enlightenment era 18th century. Social thinkers of the time, such as John Locke, in his book *Some Thoughts Concerning Education* (1728), believed that modern society would be enhanced if the population was better educated and could use reason and logic to solve problems (Locke, 1728). In the United States, schooling became compulsory for students up to a certain age. In the 1850s, Massachusetts became the first state to mandate schooling for children under the age of 16 (Pulliam, 2002).

By the early 20th century, public education became a mechanism for the assimilation of immigrants as well as preparing workers with the knowledge and skills to be successful in the job market. Schools eventually developed curricula that offered potential pathways for students, depending on whether they were destined for an academic-based or trade-based career. By the 1930s, public schooling had been organized into elementary, junior high, and high schools in virtually every state. Land-grant colleges were created in the United States to provide further training to youth once their primary education was completed (Pulliam, 2002). Whereas before 1900 less than 2 percent of Americans finished high school and even fewer went on to college, by 2018 the high school graduation rate was approximately 85 percent (National Center for Educational Statistics, 2020).

THE IMPACT OF EDUCATIONAL INEQUALITIES IN THE UNITED STATES

Educational inequalities are both entrenched and persistent in the United States (Table 8.1). There are significant differences in educational achievement among states as well as between different racial and ethnic groups (National Center for Education Statistics, 2020).

The success in **graduation rates** corresponds with decreases in the number of students who drop out. High school **dropout rates** in the United States were about 11 percent in 2000, 6 percent in 2016, and 5.4 percent in 2017, the latest data available. While the dropout rate is still higher for Blacks and Hispanics compared to Whites, decreases

Table 8.1 2018 US Public High School Graduation Rates

Category	Percentage
Overall Average	85%
White	89%
Black	79%
Hispanic	81%
Asian	92%
American Indian/Alaskan Native	74%

Source: Ke Wang, Amy Rathbun, and Lauren Musu. (2019). *School Choice in the United States: 2019.* National Center for Education Statistics. Available at: https://nces.ed.gov/pubs2019/2019106.pdf

in dropout rates for Blacks and Hispanics are partially due to a greater number of African American and Hispanic students who have completed high school (McFarland et al., 2020).

Why is this important? As we noted, education is related to life chances. That is, the more education a person receives, the better their income levels. For instance, according to the Pew Research Center, workers with a doctoral degree will earn $3.3 million in average lifetime wages, compared to $2.3 million for workers with only a bachelor's degree. Those with an associate's degree will earn over their lifetime $1.3 million, and those with only a high school diploma, about $975,000 (Pew Research Center, 2014).

This connection between education level and jobs also impacts the unemployment rate. The unemployment rate for those without a high school diploma was about 5.1 in 2017; for those with a bachelor's degree or higher it was just 2.2. Race plays a role in unemployment in addition to education: African Americans had the highest unemployment rate at 6.6, while Hispanics were at 4.5. In comparison, the unemployment rate for Whites was about 3.4 as of July 2018 (US Department of Labor, 2018). Of course, the Covid-19 pandemic severely impacted the number of layoffs, but some of the differences in the types of people who became unemployed had a great deal to do with their education levels. While millions of workers across the labor market were impacted, those near the bottom were most affected by the pandemic and subsequent job losses.

Research about the inability of public schools in the United States to lift all students out of poverty points to a connection between poverty and academic performance. According to a report by the National Center for Education Statistics, about half of all public school students in the United States live in poverty (National Center for Education Statistics, 2020). Further, only about half the students from high-poverty schools *attend* college, which is different from graduating with a diploma, making poverty one of the most important predictors of academic achievement and **educational attainment** (the number of years of schooling completed.) Also, all colleges are not the same. Some colleges provide a far less valuable education, despite their costs; this is especially true of some for-profit colleges. This will be discussed later in the chapter, but it is important to note that because race and poverty are also correlated, the issue of underachievement in education significantly impacts minority students, who also tend to be poor (Sparks, 2013).

Race and Educational Inequality

The challenges facing all public schools in the United States are considerable: from funding to high stakes testing to an increasing number of regulations regarding the education of students. While a greater number of US students are finishing high school and going on to college, the picture is not an even one; minority students are consistently behind their White and Asian counterparts on most measures of academic success. While the gap between most minority groups and Whites has narrowed since the turn of the century, largely due to everyone receiving more education in this country, much of the problem involving educational attainment rests with structural issues that impede some students more than others.

Academic success in high school also translated into attendance and graduation from college. For instance, in 1980, about 25 percent of Whites between the ages of 25 and 29 had completed a bachelor's degree or higher, compared with only 12 percent of Blacks and 8 percent of Hispanics. Today, 58 percent of Asian/Pacific Islanders have at least a bachelor's degree, while 40 percent of Whites, 21 percent of Blacks, and about 17 percent of American Indian/Alaska native and about 16 percent of Hispanics have achieved that mark (Musu-Gillete et al., 2018).

BLACK STUDENTS AND EDUCATIONAL INEQUALITY

How do Black students compare to their White peers in terms of educational achievement? What are the factors that contribute to this difference? This is a complicated question, but one factor that contributes to the challenges faced by Black students relates to the unemployment rate. Research consistently shows that the employment status of parents or caregivers is a critical factor in educational attainment. Children of low-income households are more likely to drop out of school.

Segregation is a persistent factor that contributes to lower educational achievement. Low-income neighborhoods, which are predominantly minority, have much lower rates of home ownership. Because public school funding relies on property tax revenue, schools in these neighborhoods have far fewer resources than those in higher-income (and majority White) districts. This inequality of resources means that poor districts find it much more challenging to recruit and retain experienced teachers, provide advanced courses, offer abundant extracurricular activities, or guarantee a safe school environment. According to a recent report by the National Center on Educational Statistics, Black students are more likely to receive in-school suspension and are less likely to read at grade level. They are also more likely than any other group except Native American students to report being threatened or injured with a weapon on school property during the previous 12 months (Musu-Gillete, et al., 2018).

Cultural constraints also inhibit poor children who want to succeed academically. In many communities, there is a sentiment that efforts to succeed through conventional means is akin to "selling out" one's culture or race. Thus, some Black students, who are already underperformers because they have not been given an adequate educational foundation to succeed in school, adapt to this stigma by shunning academic success. As a result, some Black students who are academically talented often have to hide their ambition out of fear of retribution from underperforming peers. Thus, even those few students who have the academic talent to succeed are often prevented from doing so because the community standards reject mainstream societal values about how one achieves success (Musu-Gillete et al., 2018).

Bilingual classrooms and student engagement Dodge City, KS, invested in public bilingual education for Hispanic children like this first-grade girl. Her classroom promotes literacy (reading, writing, and speaking) in both English and Spanish.

HISPANIC STUDENTS AND EDUCATIONAL INEQUALITY

The educational achievement of Hispanic students is similarly hampered by segregation and poorly-funded (and underperforming) schools. That some Hispanic students do not speak English well enough to succeed in an English-speaking education system (especially a system that does not accommodate second-language learners) poses another obstacle to success. Another factor to consider is immigration enforcement. Undocumented children or those who live with undocumented guardians might leave school because of fear of deportation (Chapter 7).

Since the late 1960s, efforts have been underway to improve the ability of Hispanic students to speak English, including **bilingual/bicultural education**, where students are taught in their native language until they are proficient in English. Research has shown that bilingual education is effective and can improve all students' understanding of multiculturalism and their knowledge of other cultures. However, in recent years, a backlash against immigrants has led to the reduction in funding for bilingual programs and a focus on English-first initiatives (Musu-Gillete et al., 2018).

AMERICAN INDIANS, ALASKA NATIVES, AND EDUCATIONAL INEQUALITY

As with Blacks and Hispanics, American Indian/Alaska Native students are less likely to finish high school and are less likely to attend college than White or Asian students. This means these students are less likely to obtain a well-paying job. American Indian/Alaska Native students have the option of either attending public school or **tribal schools**, which are funded by the Bureau of Indian Education (BIE). The BIE school system, which includes **tribal colleges**, were created to preserve the culture, heritage, and learning styles of native students. However, outcomes for American Indian/Alaska Native students at both public and schools, remain much lower than any other racial category of students. That is, due to poverty, segregation, and/or language issues, there continue to be challenges for Native students that prevent them from completing their education (Clarron, 2017; Northwest Evaluation Association, 2014).

ASIAN STUDENTS AND EDUCATIONAL INEQUALITY

Asian American students (including East Asian, Pacific Islander, and South Asian students) represent a rather different problem for public education. Instead of the experiences of their Black and Hispanic counterparts, many Asian students outperform even White students academically. The reasons for this are many, but one factor is the emphasis many Asian American families place on education and the amount of time many Asian American students dedicate to their studies (Northwest Evaluation Association, 2014).

While Asian Americans represent only about 4 percent of the population in the United States, they comprise about 20 percent of students attending Ivy League colleges and universities. In fact, many Asian students feel they are being discriminated against for their academic success. A group of Asian students at Harvard University filed suit against the school, claiming that Harvard was limiting the number of Asian students admitted to their campus despite the fact that they have higher test scores and better credentials than other students. In 2019 a federal judge ruled that while there was statistical evidence to show that Asian American students were negatively impacted in admissions, the students in this case failed to show that Harvard, in using the criteria to deny them admission, was intentionally discriminatory toward them (Gertsmann, 2019).

CHALLENGES TO PUBLIC EDUCATION

Racial and economic inequality, as we have seen, pose significant challenges to public education in the United States. Let's take a closer look at other issues that have a significant impact on the learning environment, academic achievement, and the manner in which schools are organized.

No Child Left Behind Act

One of the most significant challenges in public education relates to its quality. Because each state has its own standards regarding curricula and the content of material, this can create issues in ensuring all students receive the same quality of education. This disparity led to the creation of the **No Child Left Behind Act of 2001** (NCLB). Policymakers, concerned not only with inequality among students within the United States but also with the failure of US students on many indicators of academic success compared to international students, sought four goals:

1) Accountability**:** the law was designed to create accountability for schools in terms of actual results.
2) Research-based decision making: implementing strategies and curricula that were based on research that showed effectiveness.
3) School choice: expanding school choice options for parents, particularly if their child was in an underperforming school.
4) Flexibility: given the diversity of populations across the country, the law increased local control and flexibility at the state level (Klein, 2015).

Under NCLB, states had to describe how they would close achievement disparities and make sure those students who were underperforming were able to achieve academic proficiency. Schools that failed to meet these objectives would be required to provide services that enhanced learning. If after five years of poor progress, individual schools were required to make substantial changes, such as state oversight of schools, reassigning teachers and administrators, and converting some campuses into **charter schools**. The main method of determining academic success was through standardized testing, which demonstrated school performance across all states.

Most teachers quickly realized that the problems relating to academic proficiency were larger than any individual school's ability to solve them. This meant they would likely continue to see low performance scores by students even if they altered the curriculum and expanded services to students. As a result, many schools started to "game" the system by teaching the students how to improve their test scores. In some exceptional cases, cheating or even the fabrication of data was the result (Wong and Ross, 2015) . Teaching to the test was a desperate attempt to address the symptoms of the problems, but it did not help students to learn.

Test-based policies remain a prominent feature of US education policy. Federal grants through a program called **Race to the Top**, as well as flexibility waivers that give some struggling schools a chance to opt out of the NCLB requirements, were designed to incentivize states and local school districts to improve student test scores as well as provide comprehensive assessments of teachers and principals. Further regulations passed in 2016 attempted to expand the testing model. Questions remain, however, around the number of tests, who should be tested, and the expanding role of state and federal governments in local school districts. Missing from the discussion, however, is whether high stakes testing actually improves academic achievement. Also missing from the conversation are the outside factors that impact student performance in the classroom, such as poverty (Strauss, 2018).

These outside factors, such as the Covid-19 pandemic and subsequent economic recession, impacted the funding for underperforming schools, as did spiraling housing costs and unemployment. However, even these dramatic circumstances are not the reason some schools continue to underperform. Poverty, the lack of funding, and structural racism remain major impediments to academic success. Perhaps most importantly, the challenges presented by uneven educational opportunities for students will not be remedied by testing. Moreover, if educational improvement is the goal, then it is underperforming schools (as measured by the tests) that should actually receive more funding than the successful ones to make up ground (Strauss, 2015).

GLOBAL PERSPECTIVES

How US Students Are Falling Behind

The inability to address the linkages between poverty, race, and education is one reason that US students continue to lag behind their international counterparts. A 2016 report by the National Conference of State Legislators noted that not only was the United States being outperformed by a majority of advanced industrialized nations, but a growing number of less-developed countries were ranked higher than US students on critical benchmarks. In fact, compared to students in 33 countries on literacy and problem-solving ability, US students scored at or near the bottom in every category (Carpentier, 2016).

The report also pointed out that academic success is not simply about funding. In other countries, schools spent far less than the United States and still managed to improve students' level of academic success, even among low performing or disadvantaged students. In many Asian countries, for example, students are expected to meet high standards, but the commitment to their success included hiring the best teachers, offering competitive salaries and professional development, and giving them the autonomy needed to gain results (Carpentier, 2016).

School Violence and School Shootings

Safety is a critical issue in public schools. School shootings, as dramatic and tragic as they may be, occur far less frequently than such everyday violence as bullying, intimidation, and assaults that occur on campus. Moreover, the problems of school shootings (as well as all on campus forms of crime and violence) changed once students were not able to attend school due to Covid-19.

School shootings are perhaps the most dramatic example of how crime and violence can influence the school environment. Some of the causes that have been offered as explanation include the emotional distress of the offenders; easy access to guns; the effects of bullying and intimidation on some students; and the failure of parents and guardians to effectively supervise their children. Whatever the causes, such events evoke fear in students and their parents and have a significant impact on faculty and staff in those schools as well. According to a study conducted by CNN, between 2009 and 2019, there were 180 school shootings, with 356 victims in schools around the United States (CNN, 2019).

While school shootings get much more media coverage, **bullying and intimidation** can also influence the ability of students to learn and succeed in school. In fact, these are the types of events that generate the most fear because students are more likely to experience them. The good news is that it appears that these problems are decreasing in schools across the country. Between 2005 and 2017, the percentage of students ages 12–18 who reported being bullied at school during the school year decreased from 29 to 20 percent. In fact, decreases were seen in virtually every type of student and school: males, females, Blacks, Whites, Hispanics, Asians, urban schools, public or private schools—they all saw significant declines in instances of bullying. The only exception to this trend is an increase in bullying in rural schools (Figure 8.1; Wang, et al., 2020).

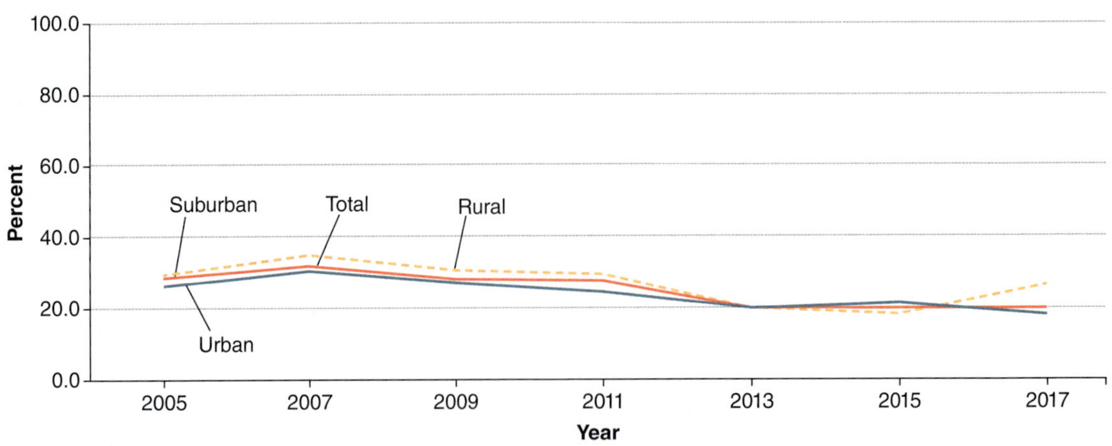

Figure 8.1 Percentage of students aged 12–18 who reported being bullied at school during the school year, by urbanicity: Selected years, 2005 through 2017 Source: U.S. Department of Justice, Bureau of Justice Statistics, School Crime Supplement (SCS) to the National Crime Victimization Survey, 2005 through 2017.

While the figures show a decline in the extent of the problem in recent years, in part a result of target-hardening measures by school officials, which make criminal activity more difficult, including installing metal detectors and hiring school resource officers, the fear such events generate among students who are not direct victims can be considerable and can even cause them to miss school out of a fear of being victimized.

Protesting zero-tolerance discipline Students in Detroit, MI, lead a protest against zero-tolerance disciplinary school policies that they argue disproportionately punish youth of color.

Zero-Tolerance Policies and Academic Achievement

Zero-tolerance policies were created in part due to the passage of the 1993 federal Gun-Free Schools Act (HR 987). Such policies are in alignment with the "broken windows" theory of crime (Chapter 2), which asserts that if minor crimes and disorderly conduct are not addressed quickly and decisively, they will lead to more serious problems in the future (HR 987).

The challenge of a zero-tolerance policy is that it removes discretionary authority from the teachers and administrators to resolve issues that occur on school grounds. Such policies also disproportionately target minority students, who are more likely than White students to be disciplined or expelled, thereby limiting their opportunities to receive a quality education.

In 2008, a task force from the American Psychological Association examined the evidence regarding the overall effectiveness of zero tolerance policies and found them to be lacking. Moreover, the task force found that minority students appear to be disproportionately targeted for discipline in schools with zero tolerance policies, and that the weight of the evidence points out that the punishments for minority students was greater compared to Whites who committed similar offenses. Later research continues to support the task force's report, indicating that zero tolerance policies are unnecessary, negatively influence the overall educational environment for all students, and more severely impacts minority students (American Psychological Association, 2008).

HOW DO US AND INTERNATIONAL SCHOOLS COMPARE?

Discussion of educational reform in the United States often centers on a comparison of the performance of American students with their peers worldwide on standardized tests. However, as some experts have pointed out, the ranking of US students may not be the most accurate way of presenting the data. While some politicians and media accounts protest loudly about how far behind US students are academically compared to other countries, with some critics pointing out that even Third World countries are doing better to educate their children than the United States, the reality is far less dramatic. Most education experts, particularly those with a research background argue that while there is indeed room for improvement, US students aren't doing that badly (Tures, 2018; Loveless, 2017).

A common mistake occurs when policymakers use international test score rankings to determine which country is better than another—one expert observed that the rankings aren't like football rankings, where the goal is to get into the playoffs. Rather, while rankings are simple to understand, they can be rather misleading and provide little in the way of context or consider the many factors involved in the creation of rankings (Tures, 2018; Loveless, 2017).

A 2017 report from the Brookings Institute showed that using a more sophisticated form of analysis of trends, the PISA (Program for International Student Assessment) scores for US students have remained relatively flat from 2000 to 2014. In addition, the data from the latest TIMSS (Trends in International Mathematics and Science Assessment) test in 2015 show Americans scored their highest marks in the 20-year history of US tests (Loveless, 2017).

Using this form of statistical analysis, the United States was above average in comparison to the top 69 countries tested in the PISA in reading, math and science. A good way to frame the comparison is with another sports analogy—the United States are in the playoffs but we aren't the top rated team. This is a very different picture than the one created by the ranking system and such information is important in terms of what changes need to be made to improve our standing compared to our international counterparts. So the United States does not need to go into a "rebuild" mode, like some teams do when they are consistently losing; instead, incremental changes are needed to show consistent increases and improvements (Tures, 2018; Loveless, 2017).

WHY DO SOME PUBLIC SCHOOLS FAIL?

It is true that not all public schools operate equally in this country. Students in low-income communities contend with challenges that prevent them from obtaining a quality education. In some cases, the problems are structural in nature, while in other instances, cultural adaptations to these conditions generate behaviors that add to the problem.

Structural Factors

Earlier in this chapter, we considered the impact of social problems such as racism and economic inequality on access to public education. Let's look more closely at these issues.

PROPERTY TAXES AND INADEQUATE FUNDING

An important part of bringing accountability, competency, and equality to public schools relates to how schools are funded. As Jonathan Kozol (1999) points out in his now classic book, *Savage Inequalities,* most school districts receive funding from property taxes. This means that inequalities are built into the education system, since some communities generate more tax revenue than others. Why? Property taxes are based on the value of the property. The more the property is worth, the higher the taxes that are levied on it. Wealthy neighborhoods pay substantially more in property taxes than poor ones. This influences the type and quality of education for children living in those communities. With more resources available, wealthy school districts can offer a wide range of options to students, invest in nicer facilities, and purchase upgraded equipment and technology compared to low-income schools (Kozol, 1999).

SEGREGATION

The landmark decision reached in *Brown v. the Board of Education of Topeka, Kansas* (1954) called attention to the segregation between Blacks and Whites in public schools. The case made clear that segregation had a negative effect on Black students even when their school facilities were equal, which rarely occurred. In response to the decision, many White parents withdrew their children from public schools and enrolled them in private institutions. In the 2007 case of *Meredith vs. Jefferson County Board of Education,* the US Supreme Court reversed its decision in *Brown* and found that policies based on race to achieve a more integrated classroom were unconstitutional.

The consequences of this decision are considerable: currently, a typical minority student finds him or herself surrounded by other minority groups, but very few White students. Moreover, these minority-dominated schools are also more likely to have higher dropout rates and lower academic achievement than predominantly White schools. They are also likely to receive less funding.

The *Meredith* decision stemmed from a case involving schools in Seattle, WA and Louisville, KY, because they used race when assigning some students to schools in an effort to end racial isolation and prevent segregation. In Louisville, the school system combines school choice, neighborhood school assignment, and assignment based on race in order to maintain schools that are between 15 and 50 percent minority. Seattle had a system that allowed all high school students to rank the school of their choice. If too many students listed a particular high school, the race of the student was used in an effort to keep the schools in some sort of balance between White and non-White students. Some parents sued because they were not allowed to exercise their choice of schools because they were White. While the Supreme Court, acknowledged that it had previously held that racial diversity can be a compelling government interest in university admissions, race cannot be the sole factor in deciding assigning high school students to public schools. The upshot of the decision forced schools and parents to accept the notion of racially segregated schools (Totenberg, 2007).

INEXPERIENCED TEACHERS AND TEACHER BURNOUT

Related to disparities in funding is the quality of teachers a particular school district can attract. Like professionals in any career path, teachers seek out the best-paying jobs with schools that offer opportunities for innovative ideas and forms of instruction. Because of the funding issue, low-income schools cannot readily compete with their wealthy counterparts, thereby ensuring that teachers who work in low-income schools are likely to be less experienced and/or likely from the same neighborhoods as their students. This means they likely lack the social networks and experiences of suburban teachers, which limits the opportunities for students. In addition, because they are less experienced and perhaps less well-credentialed, these teachers are likely to remain in poorer schools (Isenberg et al., 2016). For those teachers who remain in these schools over time, burnout becomes a problem. Even the most experienced, effective and caring teachers can be overwhelmed not so much by the challenges of a poor school as by the sheer lack of support from administration, large class sizes, the lack of professional development opportunities and other challenges. In response, many of these teachers leave education altogether instead of moving on to more privileged school districts.

THE DIGITAL DIVIDE

As many children begin the 2020 academic year online or in some form of hybrid delivery system, the challenges presented by the **digital divide,** or the gap in access to technology and the utilization of sources like the Internet, become especially troubling for low-income families. In a recent study by the Pew Research Center, 59 percent of US parents with lower incomes say their child may face digital obstacles in school work (Vogel, 2020).

Driving across the "digital divide" In El Cenizo, TX, school buses equipped with wi-fi provide internet access to the mostly low-income residents whose children participated in remote learning during the COVID-19 pandemic. Nationwide, a lack of high-speed internet access in communities of color and low-income communities made remote learning especially difficult for students.

Educators have known that inequalities in internet and technology access long preexisted the pandemic, disproportionately impacting Black, Hispanic, Native American, and low-income families. In April 2020, a Pew Research study found that 36 percent of low-income parents reported that their children were unable to complete their schoolwork at home because they did not have access to a computer. This contrasts sharply with 14 percent of middle-income parents and 4 percent of upper-income parents (Vogel et al., 2020). Among the more than 50 million students in the United States, an estimated 15 percent live in homes with no access to high-speed internet. This means either students are required to complete homework assignments on a cell phone or find a location with public wi-fi access, or simply not turn in the assignments at all (Vogel, et al., 2020).

Cultural and Individual Factors

The structural factors that inhibit many minority and low-income students significantly impact their ability to receive a quality education. Given that these are structural factors, there is little that the student or the parents can do to remedy the problem. At the individual level, however, what may appear to be choices that suggest minorities are not as interested or committed to a quality education may reveal that structural factors are at work as well.

LIFE CHALLENGES

Many students in low-income schools bring with them a host of life challenges to the classroom. Whether it is because they are caring for younger siblings while parents work, have to take a job themselves to help support the family, or care for sick and elderly relatives as part of their family dynamic, the challenges presented to these students are considerable and often show up in lower academic performance. Many students are also left unsupervised and do not receive the academic support they need to be successful in the classroom. In addition, some students also experience physical and mental health challenges as a result of being poor, which only further complicate their ability to succeed academically.

LACK OF INVOLVEMENT BY PARENTS OR GUARDIANS

At first glance it may appear that low-income and minority parents are not as involved in their child's education as their wealthy and suburban counterparts. This tendency could easily be mistaken for a lack of interest in education by minority parents. However, it is important to recall that many poor families must take more than one job to make ends meet. Thus, what may appear to be apathy is simply parents addressing the realities of low-paying jobs and a rising cost of living. For single parents and guardians, or in households where adults work multiple jobs, there is less time to dedicate to the education needs of children or find it challenging to participate in school-related activities, such as student-teacher conferences, afterschool activities, or parent-teacher association meetings (Beckhusen, 2019). The challenges presented by Covid-19 have impacted all parents, as many have had children at home during the pandemic and have significant challenges in managing not only their children's school-related responsibilities, but their own work demands as well (Harris, 2020).

PEER PRESSURE

The problems students encounter in school are considerable, particularly if students have gaps in their understanding of foundational topics that have not been adequately addressed. In those situations, academic failure becomes cumulative. Such circumstances can result in students becoming convinced that they cannot be successful in school, and they choose to drop out. As it relates to race, one way of rationalizing their poor performances or the decision to quit school all together, many youths begin to perceive that academic success is akin to selling out one's race. In such situations, students are pressured not to become a race traitor and show considerable disdain for "book learning" and school in general.

Gender and social class also factor into peer pressure. Girls, for example, can also feel pressured to seem more interested in their social status than their studies. And if girls get pregnant they are certainly at risk of dropping out. Similarly, lower-income white students might feel that they should leave school to help support their families. So, the issues surrounding peer pressure are complex and it is important to recognize how and in what ways this can contribute academic problems.

Students who demonstrate some level of academic success often find themselves in a dilemma: if they show their talent for school, they will likely be socially outcast, and perhaps even physically harmed, but if they embrace the anti-school/education movement, they will not likely graduate or create other opportunities for themselves (Edyson, 2018).

RESPONSES TO CHALLENGES IN PUBLIC EDUCATION

As we noted at the beginning of this chapter, the ways in which parents coped with the impact of Covid-19 on their children's education made the inequalities of the US public education system dramatically clear. While many privileged parents sought alternative solutions to cope with education in the age of Covid-19, the fact is that for years many parents have responded to problems in the education system by removing their children from public schools. Among the strategies that have been used include charter schools, home schooling, and school vouchers; this last option allows parents to take the tax dollars they would normally contribute to their local public school and apply it toward tuition at a private or charter school. The problem with these individual choices is that they erode the funding available to taxpayer-funded school systems that serve the greater community.

Charter Schools

Dissatisfaction with the public school system is the main reason that parents who can afford to do so enroll their children in private school. However, this can be costly and there are no tax benefits for doing so; parents still have to pay the taxes that fund local schools. **Charter schools** are funded like public schools but are organized locally and centered around a particular theme such as STEM or the arts and humanities. Because they are operated locally and on a smaller scale (most have 300 or fewer students), these schools can customize the educational experience for students and are not bound by bureaucracy. These schools can also address deficiencies that minority students have faced in the public schools, thereby giving them an opportunity not only to catch up academically, but also to customize the learning experience. In 2017, the latest data available, there were 7,200 charter schools in the United States, serving approximately 3.1 million students, an increase of 2.7 million since 2000 (National Center on Education Statistics, 2020).

Parents for school choice A 2019 rally in support of charter schools in Los Angeles, CA.

Approximately two-thirds of charter school students are racial or ethnic minorities and more than half of students qualify for free or reduced lunch. The latter is significant because this eligibility is often used as a primary indicator of poverty or membership of the working poor (National Center on Education Statistics, 2020). While the idea of charter schools appears reasonable, particularly as it relates to addressing minority students' academic needs, research suggests that charter school students fare no better on reading and math tests than students in non-charter schools with similar student populations. Also significant is whether the charter school is a for-profit or non-profit: the data shows that for-profit charter schools tend to show lower academic achievement levels of its students than non-profit ones (National Center on Education Statistics, 2020).

School Vouchers

School vouchers allow parents to behave more like consumers. If they find their child to be enrolled in a low-performing school, vouchers allow them the option of transferring to a more successful school (public or private), and the funding should follow the student. Theoretically, this creates competition among schools, builds in accountability, and promotes efficiencies and cost effectiveness while not sacrificing quality. School vouchers are perhaps the ultimate example of school choice and are consistent with American values about independence and autonomy. Currently there are nearly 180,000 voucher students in the United States (Balonon-Rosen, 2017).

Critics of school vouchers point out that such a strategy is more likely to be used by well-educated and wealthy parents, who have more familiarity with education and who would likely use the voucher to supplement their child's private education. Moreover, taking funding out of existing schools not only decreases their ability to make positive changes, but also leads what some educational experts refer to as a "brain drain," where academically talented students leave the schools in search of better opportunities.

Research indicates that the success of students using vouchers to attend private schools have been mixed, with students not showing significant overall academic improvement.

Most of the early research indicated mixed results, mostly indicating modest improvements in some subjects and among some student groups but rarely had studies shown vouchers causing such dramatic decreases in test scores. However, the trend seems to be shifting, where students using vouchers seem to be regressing academically (Balonon-Rosen, 2017).

Home Schooling

Another strategy used by families to address issues in the public schools is to **home school** them. While some parents home school their children so that they can better integrate a faith-based curriculum into their children's education, others believe they can do a better job of educating their children than the schools. According to the National Center for Education Statistics, in 2016, the latest data available, there are 1.7 million children home schooled in the United States, which makes up about 3.4 percent of all students in the United States (Wang, Rathbun, and Musu, 2019). As a result of the Covid-19 pandemic, however, many children are likely to consider home schooling, particularly as schools reopen and parents express concerns about their safety. While the data on this is yet to be revealed, it is reasonable to conclude that many parents may opt to keep their children home instead of sending them back to school.

In a 2017 report on home schooling, White children were overwhelmingly represented among those who were homeschooled, at 60 percent, while Hispanic students represented 26 percent. Only about 8 percent of Black students are home schooled and about 3 percent of Asian students as well. (Cavanagh, 2017).

In terms of the impact of home schooling, according to some research, homeschooled children perform as well, if not better on average, then those graduating from public schools. At one time, critics of home schooling argued that the social component of educating children was lost by not giving students an opportunity to interact and develop leadership skills (Redford, Battle, and Bielick, 2016). However, with the development of co-ops and other strategies, including sports teams, extracurricular activities, and even proms, many of the problems associated with home schooling in the past may have been addressed.

English First Movement

Bilingual education has also emerged as a strategy. In 1968, Congress passed Title VII of the Elementary and Secondary Education Act, also known as the Bilingual Education Act, which mandated bilingual education to give immigrants an opportunity for an education in this country in their native language (National Center for Education Statistics, 2017).

This approach is controversial. Some argue that preserving the language and culture of minority groups is important, while others argue that in order for minorities to be successful, they must learn English in to better assimilate and become productive citizens.

According to the National Center on Education Statistics, in fall 2017 there were about 3.8 million Hispanic ELL students (Figure 8.2). Asian students were the next largest racial/ethnic group among ELLs, with 530,900 students and 327,300 White ELL students. Blacks represented 211,000 Black ELL students (National Center for Education Statistics, 2020).

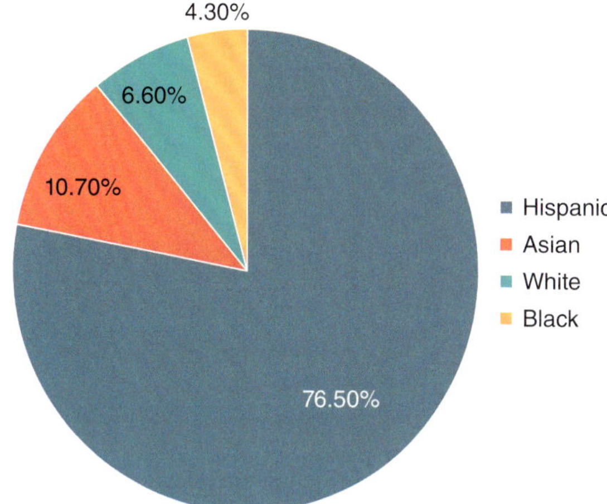

Figure 8.2 English Learners in US Public Schools by Race/Ethnicity Source: National Center for Education Statistics, 2020.

In each of the other racial/ethnic groups for which data were collected (Pacific Islanders, American Indians/Alaska Natives, and individuals of two or more races), fewer than 40,000 students were identified as ELLs. While advocates of bilingual education argue that there is evidence that teaching students initially in their native language ultimately improves their academic performance in other areas, even after they transition to English, others, as part of an **English-First Movement**, contend that bilingual education is expensive and interferes with English development and stigmatizes children who participate in them (Lu, 1998).

More recently, as part of an isolationist approach to multiculturalism, several states have passed laws curtailing the use of bilingual education, citing threats to America's "national identity" and that it divides people along ethnic lines. Proponents of the English-only movement also contend that widespread use of bilingual education implies to immigrants that they need not assimilate by being required to learn the language.

THE PROBLEM DOES NOT END IN HIGH SCHOOL: HIGHER EDUCATION ISSUES

Problems in higher education, especially those related to public funding, further perpetuate racial and economic inequalities. Minority students and poor students are at a considerable disadvantage in the higher education landscape. The lack of a college diploma, or the persistent economic difficulty that comes with a student loan burden, also has a negative impact in terms of lifetime earnings.

Is a College Education Really Worth It?

The idea that one's education translates into job opportunities is not disputed. The more education one receives translates into additional income over one's lifetime (Figure 8.3).

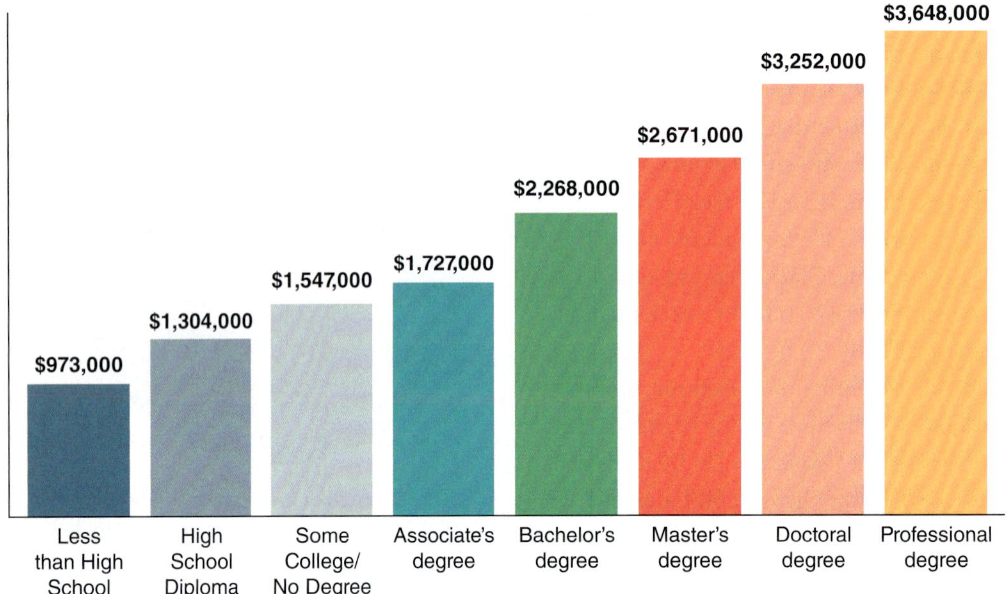

Figure 8.3 Lifetime earnings by education attainment Source: Pew Charitable Trust

A college degree seems like a good investment, as it confers a lifetime advantage in earnings. But the cost of earning that college degree is complicated to determine. Variables include the type of college one chooses; whether or not one works while attending school; family obligations; the field of study; and the length of time to degree completion. How tuition is financed also makes a difference, as student loans can create an insurmountable debt in the post-graduate years. According to the Peter G. Peterson Foundation, in 2017, the total amount of student loan debt is about $1.4 trillion (Figure 8.4).

For students who graduate from an affordable four-year college, it takes about nine years before the costs of attending is covered by the higher income earned than had they gone to work right out of high school. For those who graduate from a private college, the point at which the cost of attendance is covered by higher income may be as long as 17 years (Carnevale, Cheah, and Hanson, 2015). And for some students who graduated from prestigious and expensive institutions but found themselves post-graduation trapped in a tight labor market and forced into jobs for which they are overqualified, the cost of getting a degree may not feel justified at all—especially if they are carrying significant student loan debt (Capelli, 2015).

The High Cost of Dropping Out of College

Whether a degree is worth the money is only relevant if the student actually finishes college. According to the National Center on Education Statistics (2019), there is a good deal of variation on graduation rates from college. About 60 percent of students

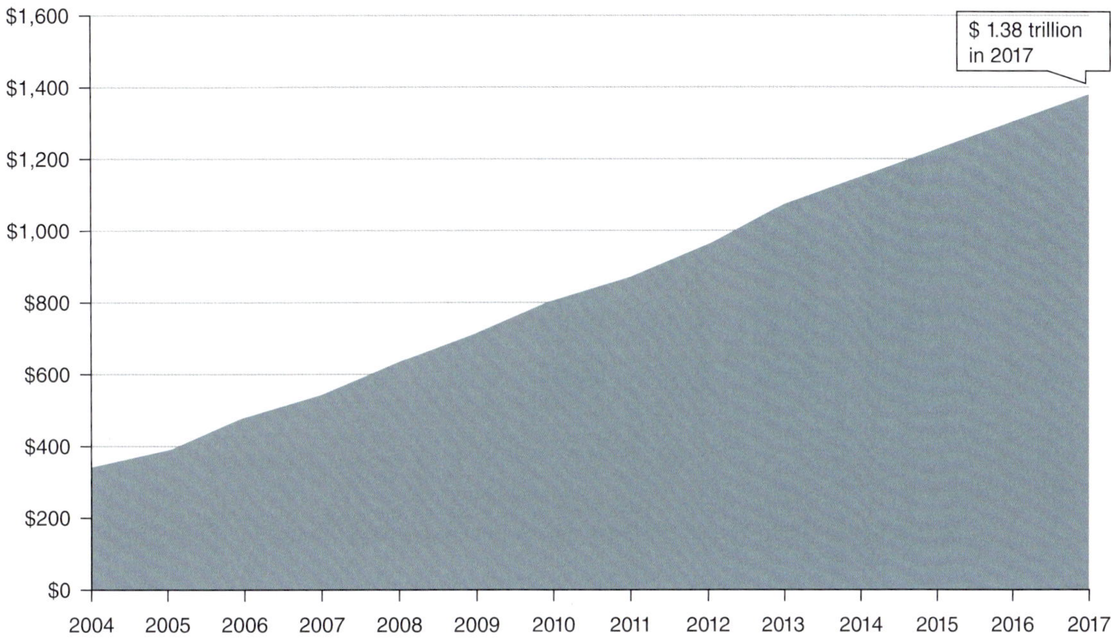

Figure 8.4 Student loan debt burden Source: Federal Reserve Bank of New York, 2018 Student Loan Update, July 2018. Compiled by PGPF.

graduate within six years of beginning their program of study, but that figure ranges from a high of 74 percent for Asians to a low of 39 percent for American Indian/Alaska Natives (Figure 8.5).

Traditional students, those who began college right after high school, had the highest graduation rates, about 59 percent within six years, but completion rates were much lower for those who started at age 20 to 24, which is approximately 33 percent. Like traditional students, this figure is about 5 percent lower than the previous year. For those who enrolled after age 24, the completion rate is about 39 percent, a decrease of about 3 percent from the previous year. Private colleges have higher completion rates, generally about 80 percent after six years (Chuck, 2015).

While critics of higher education point to the spiraling costs of attendance, what is often missing from the discussion are the additional costs colleges must absorb as accrediting bodies and state regulatory agencies require compliance with increasingly complex state and federal laws, regulations, and policies.

Because federal and state funding for higher education has continued to shrink, the only option for colleges and universities is to increase tuition and fees to offset these costs. Added to the enormous operating costs for most colleges is deferred maintenance. These costs, which include construction, insurance, and updating, continue to rise as well.

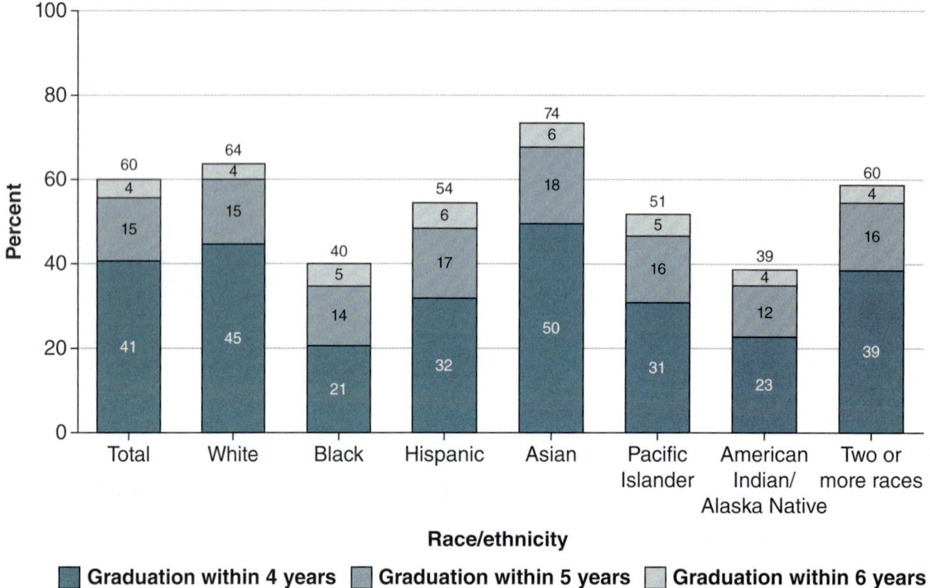

Figure 8.5 Graduation rates from first institution attended for first-time, full-time bachelor's degree-seeking students at 4-year postsecondary institutions, by race/ethnicity and time to completion: Cohort entry year 2010.

For-Profit Colleges and Online Education

The growing popularity of for-profit colleges has made them a significant factor in the higher education landscape. By definition, a for-profit college is one that is owned by shareholders and governed by a board of directors. The main difference between a for-profit college and a traditional one is that the decisions about its operation are driven by profits, like most businesses (BestSchoolGuides.org). There are a host of issues related to for-profit colleges compared to a traditional college, including cost and academic success.

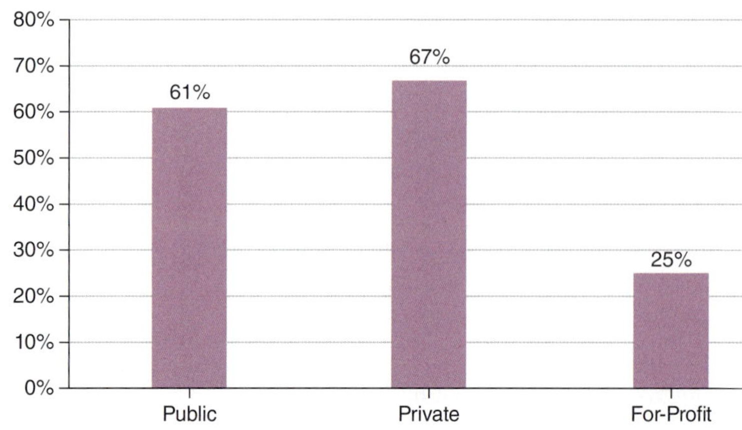

Figure 8.6 Graduation rates by type of institution (2018). Source: National Center for Education Statistics, 2020.

For instance, in 2017, students graduate at a much lower rate from private for-profit colleges than other students (Figure 8.6).

For-profit schools are also far more costly than most public and private colleges and universities (College Board, 2018). According to the College Board, the

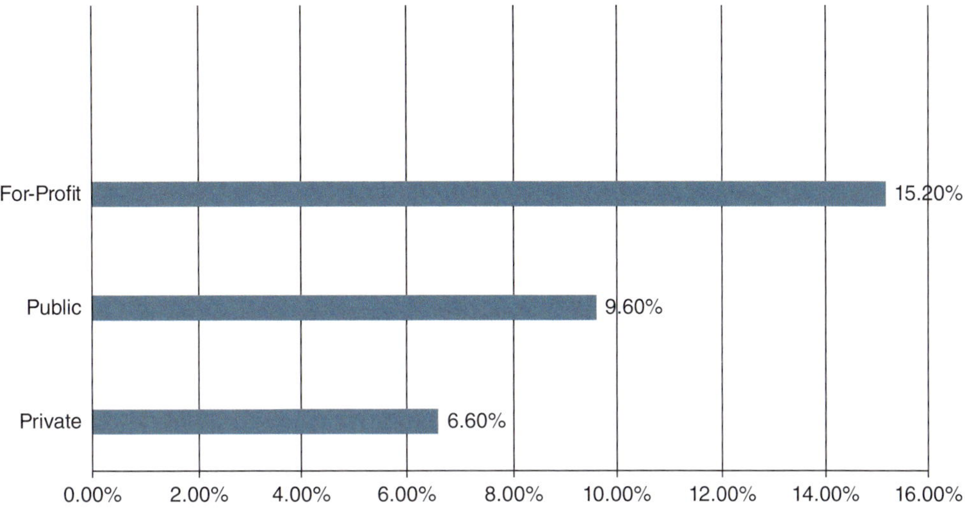

Figure 8.7 Default rates on student loans by type of institution Source: National Center for Education Statistics.

average cost of tuition and fees in 2017–18 was about $16,000 per year. This compares to the $3,570 at two-year public non-profit schools and just under $10,000 at the four-year public institutions ($9,970 per year). Only private nonprofit colleges cost more, at $34,740 per year (College Board, 2018).

How do students afford these expenses? The majority of students take out loans to pay for college. The problem is that not only are these students taking out more in loans, they are also more likely to default on them (Powell, 2018; Figure 8.7).

Why do so many students enroll in for-profit programs, given their relative expense and their lack of both effectiveness and accountability? To a certain extent, predatory recruitment practices are to blame. A number of for-profits were found to exploit veterans eligible to apply their 9/11 GI Bill benefits to education. Some investigations of for-profits also noted intimidation tactics and false promises used by admissions counselors to get students, particularly minorities and those from low-income families, to enroll in costly programs and to incur enormous debt, on the promise of well-paying jobs (Cottom, 2017).

Since 2010, when the Obama administration began holding for-profit colleges accountable for questionable marketing and admissions practices, more than 2,000 for-profit have closed. Some for-profit colleges were also the subject of a federal investigation into questionable business practices and abuse of predatory lending laws. One example was Corinthian College, which violated several state and federal laws and was ultimately shut down. Similarly, ITT Technical Institute generated tens of thousands of complaints from students who said they were left with worthless degrees. In response to this and other allegations of misconduct by for-profit colleges, the Obama administration responded by forgiving nearly $450 million in taxpayer funded student debt to for-profit graduates who could not find decent jobs with the degrees or certificates that they earned (Taylor and Appal, 2014).

SOCIOLOGICAL THEORY AND EDUCATION

The intersection between poverty, race, and education appears to present significant challenges for some students, parents and schools. How would a sociologist frame the issues and offer insight into the state of affairs in the public schools, particularly the inequalities that exist?

Functionalism and Education

An important distinction of the functionalist perspective is the difference between **manifest functions** (the intended effects of a particular condition and **latent functions** (the unintended consequences or effects of something). As it relates to education, manifest functions include the idea that schools provide students with the basic skills of reading, writing, and critical thinking, as well as reinforce cultural values such as the respect given to authority figures, adapting and accommodating to a structured environment, doing one's duty, or following through on commitments, and perseverance.

Another manifest function of education is the organization of students based on their talents and abilities so that they are best prepared to benefit society as a whole. For example, schools will direct some students toward academic subjects, while others are encouraged to pursue more vocational pathways.

Examples of latent functions of public education include providing a place for teenagers to go during the day so that they do not compete with adults in the job market, as well as for similarly aged youth to meet, socialize, and potentially select life partners.

Because the schools are organized bureaucratically, with rigid structures and a host of policies and procedures that, in theory, allow for some level of standardization in the product provided to all students, it also means that it is not easily modified. From a functionalist perspective, it means that students must accommodate to the system, not the other way around.

Conflict Theory and Education

Conflict theorists point out that education in general, and public schools in particular, perpetuate existing social inequalities. In his book *The Great School Legend*, Colin Greer identifies three objectives behind the original development of public education: to foster an understanding of the elements of a democratic society; to train and develop workers who would sustain US economic growth; and to improve social mobility (Greer, 1972).

Greer argues that such a romantic view of public education does not reflect the realities of what occurred. Instead of teaching students the value and purpose of a democracy, for example, Greer argues that the real reason behind compulsory public education in this country was the need to indoctrinate immigrants into the dominant culture. By teaching democracy, newly arrived immigrants would be trained to accept the status quo, avoid problems of political dissent, and ensured a smooth transition into American culture (Greer, 1972).

Greer's comments lie at the heart of the conflict approach to education. While it is true that schools offer important information to students so they can navigate the social landscape, they also act as a gatekeeper and perpetuate the status quo. Similarly, the curriculum is designed to encourage acceptance of existing inequalities. Greer also points out that education in this country is only theoretically a path out of poverty. Given the dramatic and systemic inequalities of the US education system, students in poor school districts are less likely to graduate. Even if they do, they are ill-prepared to succeed in college compared to White students. The result is that minorities, even those who have received an education, have fewer opportunities for a well-paying job (Greer, 1972).

Symbolic Interactionism and Education

Symbolic interactionists examine the process of education from a micro-level perspective. An example of how they would study educational inequality is through the application of the labeling theory (Chapter 2). For example, **tracking** is a common strategy by public schools to organize students based on their abilities as well as their post-graduation path. This sounds like a reasonable approach to managing schools with a diverse population. However, the process is a form of labeling students. In fact, these tracks are inflexible, and students who wish to change tracks find it very difficult to do so—not because of a lack of intelligence or ability, but because it means changing a student's label.

Symbolic interactionists also point out that teachers often label students in terms of their perceived ability based on stereotypes, such as race, social class, or other factors. If biased teachers label students as failures based on stereotypes, and shape how they teach those students as a result of those low expectations, any subsequent failure on the part of the student is due in large part to their unequal treatment by those teachers.

In some cases, students internalize those labels and doubt their own potential. At an extreme, this is what causes many students to give up on their educational goals and drop out. Research on the effects of tracking and labeling has consistently found that this self-fulfilling prophecy and its impact on student perceptions of their own abilities, along with the effects of teacher expectations, has the greatest impact on poor and minority students (Avelar, Johnson, and Johnson, 2018; Loveless, 2016).

According to Pierre Bourdieu's **theory of social reproduction**, children learn to acquire habits, ideas, and expectations from their parents. Bourdieu calls this process the development of **cultural capital** (Chapter 4). Cultural capital can be seen in how children approach school, particularly their work habits and their perception of the importance of getting a good education. Cultural capital, importantly, also shapes how others see a person.

One of the problems with cultural capital is that without it, people are at a distinct disadvantage, even if they try to develop or acquire more of it. People who grow up in low-income neighborhoods, for example, may not be able to circumvent some of the markers of their social class, and this can be taken as a lack of sophistication or adaptability. An example of how cultural capital is relevant to education relates to the use of slang terms and the way a person presents information to others. Such distinctions are essentially meaningless but are powerful predictors of a person's life chances and their educational opportunities. In fact, there is some evidence of minority students from low-income families who attended private schools, who express considerable difficulty navigating how their teachers and colleagues saw them (American Speech, Language, and Heritage Association, 2018).

WHAT WORKS? EFFECTIVE SOLUTIONS TO ADDRESS PROBLEMS OF EDUCATION

Given all the challenges facing public schools and higher education, are there programs that effectively address some of these issues? Can minority students actually receive a high quality education compared to White students? Can the gaps created by the history of segregation, discrimination and prejudice be closed to give minority students a fair chance at success? Can the intersection of race, poverty and education be addressed in a meaningful way? While no single approach can solve all of these interconnected problems, some programs have demonstrated success in enhancing the educational experience of disadvantaged students by increasing student academic achievement and/or preventing students from dropping out.

Head Start A Head Start classroom in Texas.

K-12 Programs

HEAD START

This program, which began in the 1960s, has consistently shown that children make gains that continue throughout their later school years. **Head Start** offers poor families a comprehensive program that provides health and nutritional services to preschool children while also developing their skills. Measuring the success of Head Start, as with all programs, is difficult. Advocates argue that it saves taxpayers money because participants are more likely to graduate from high school and get a job compared to those who don't participate in the program. Head Start graduates tend to be healthier and receive preventive medical and dental checkups, which is also a cost savings. But the program isn't cheap: in 2019, the costs of the Head Start program was $11.6 billion (Federal Safetynet.com, 2019).

THE FIRST GRADE CLASSROOM PREVENTION PROGRAM

The First Grade Classroom Prevention Program combines a classroom management strategy designed to curtail disruptive behavior while at the same time improving overall academic performance. Teachers receive approximately 60 hours of training in the program prior to implementation, as well as supervision and feedback from program experts monthly during the year. The behavioral component is addressed using the Good Behavior Game, which reward positive group behavior instead of punishing individual outbursts. The teacher divides the class into three diverse teams and each team receives a tally on a posted chart when one member of a particular team acts inappropriately. Any team with four or fewer checks at the end of a period of time (a portion of the day, the entire day, etc.) earns a reward (usually something like stickers or activity books).

Over the course of the year, rewards are eliminated altogether. In addition, teachers lead weekly class meetings to build students' problem solving skills. For those students who remain disruptive, individual teams are created, and other incentives are offered to encourage compliance. On the academic side, the curriculum incorporates exercises such as interactive read-aloud periods, journal writing, dramatic presentation of written work, critical analysis of issues from students' daily life.

A randomized controlled trial with a sample of 18 first grade classrooms in nine high-poverty Baltimore schools found that disruptive behaviors such as smoking, and the experimental use of hard drugs decreased by 26 percent and 50 percent respectively. Academically, by age 19, participants, compared to those in a control group who did not participate in the program, increased high school graduation by 21 percent and by college attendance by nearly two-thirds (Evidence Based Programs.com).

CAREER ACADEMIES

Sometimes called Small Learning Communities, these are cohorts of students, typically less than 200, that operate within larger high schools in low-income urban areas. These programs combine academic and technical curricula focused on a particular theme or career field (e.g. health care, hotel management). Career academies partner with local employers and universities to provide work-based opportunities for students as well as insight into their chosen field (College and Career Academy Support Network, 2018).

Higher Education Programs

EARLY COLLEGE HIGH SCHOOLS AND DUAL ENROLLMENT PROGRAMS

One innovative solution to control college costs as well as benefit high-achieving public high school students is the emergence of **early college high schools**. These programs are designed for students who might have difficulty transitioning into college, as well as the financial costs of attending college. The evidence of the success of these programs indicates that participating students were significantly more likely to graduate from college, with minority students witnessing the largest increase in success (Berger et al., 2014; Heacox, 2018). **Dual enrollment programs** provide an opportunity for high school students to attend and receive credit for college courses at a local campus, and better understand what's needed to be successful (Heacox, 2018). Dual enrollment programs can significantly decrease the amount of time and expense related to obtaining a degree while the student is still in high school.

COMMUNITY COLLEGES AND TRANSFER PROGRAMS

Students in two-year community can take courses that transfer to a four-year institution, ultimately completing their degree at a significant savings (National Student Clearinghouse Center, 2018). However, the advantages of using a community college as a springboard to a four-year degree are not without challenges. For example, the current graduation rate for those who attend a community college is about 13 percent in 2019 (Figure 8.8).

While this may seem a disappointing figure, we must recognize that there are several problems with calculating graduation rates from community colleges. Many community college students transfer to a four year institution before they complete their associate's degree. In fact, as Chen (2020) points out, about 25 percent of all college students who began at a community college transfer to a four year institution. And we have seen that about 60 percent of students complete a bachelor's degree within six years.

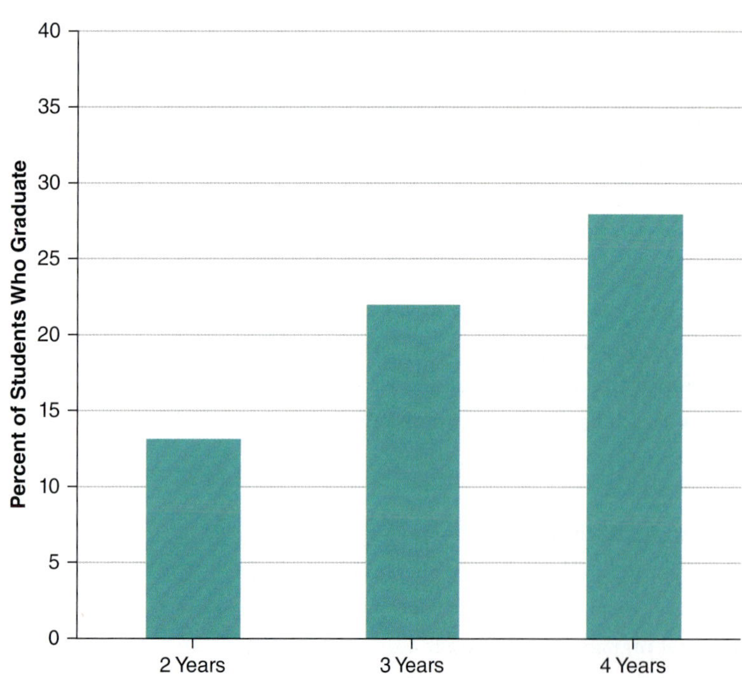

Figure 8.8 Graduation Rates for Community College Students Percent of US students enrolled in public two-year institutions who graduate in two, three and four years. Source: National Student Clearinghouse Research Center.

Thus, while the community college experience may have improved the chances of some students in completing their bachelor's degree, these decisions adversely affect the outcome measures for community colleges (Chen, 2020).

Another key challenge for the community college system is its dependence on state and federal funding. In addition, many students in community colleges require remedial classes, as they were not adequately prepared for the rigors of college level work by their public school. Even with remedial courses, many students fail and choose to drop out (National Student Clearinghouse Center, 2018).

SO WHAT CAN I DO?

If you are a parent or guardian of a child, you know all too well from your experience with remote learning during Covid-19 the extraordinary challenges faced by students and educators. At the micro level, you may be struggling along with your child to keep motivated and focused without the social reassurance of friends and the academic benchmarks that indicate progress. At a meso level, your school district might be struggling to ensure that students and teachers have adequate technology and training to conduct remote learning efficiently and effectively. And at a macro level, as we have explored in this chapter, the gulf between the abundant educational opportunities available to wealthy families and the limited possibilities for those who rely on public schools may never have seemed so wide. Given that you may already be doing all that you can to support school-age children in your own household or family, is it fair to ask you to consider doing even more?

Think about the ways—however small they may seem—in which you are already taking action for and advocating on behalf of students and teachers. You are gaining expertise in how your local school board makes decisions: do they communicate clearly and effectively with the community, or have decisions been made without adequate input from teachers and parents? What would an effective communication plan look like?

Are you assisting other parents and guardians with setting up and troubleshooting the technology required for remote learning? If so, what recommendations might you make to the district to better support the acquisition and use of technology in the future?

Do you live in a multilingual household? If so, what resources are available to assist families who need a translator's help to understand communications from individual teachers as well as the district? Are there opportunities for you to volunteer as a translator, or work with other parents to create a network of translators that reflects your district's diverse needs?

Even if you do not have a school-age child in your immediate household or family, you are likely a product of the US school system and your taxes go toward supporting public education. We all have a stake in the success of our schools and the potential of every student.

CONCLUSION

Problems of poverty, race, and education are all connected. While we would like to believe that education is the path out of poverty, in reality the educational experiences of poor and minority students reinforce the challenges they already face. This is a key reason that people tend to reproduce the social class they were born into: their life chances are shaped by the opportunities presented by the schools they attend. Moreover, many of the problems in schools are structural in nature.

Thus, those who claim that minority students simply don't want an education, and that there are cultural factors explaining the poor progress of minority students, fail to recognize that poor performance is likely a consequence of systemic inequality. Further compounding the problem is that some of the programs that have attempted to remedy educational inequalities are political in nature. As such, they become subject to distortions and inaccurate portrayals by politicians and the media. Programs that are known to work typically get less attention and funding.

In the end, one has to wonder if parents and the general public really want a fair and equitable education system. Given that many minorities are already so far behind, assuming some students want to succeed, the funding and support that would be needed for these school districts would have to be far greater than current levels. This might mean a redistribution of resources from academically successful schools in privileged communities As the response to Covid-19 related quarantine suggests, however, the reaction would be that parents who could afford to do so would enroll their children in private school or provide advantages in other ways. While some of the data suggests that progress has been made and improvements are seen in academic performance for minority students, the problem is that all groups have made advances; some more so than others. Thus, the educational gap that has existed for some time remains a visible feature of social life for low-income families.

YOU MAKE THE CALL: PRINCIPAL OR POLICE?

You are a principal of a junior high school located in a low-income community, where many of the children come from minority families. The school district in which you work has recently passed a zero tolerance policy to address the crime and gang problems in your schools. This policy, supported by the federal legislation designed to keep campuses and students safe, calls for the police to be involved in any criminal matter and expulsion for students who violate school policy on matters related to safety, including possession of dangerous instruments or bringing weapons to school. The school district has also installed metal detectors at the entrances to the facility and have hired school resource officers to patrol the campus.

One day during the school year a student brings a razor blade to the main office she found on the ground during recess. She claims that she picked it up because she didn't want anyone to get hurt and brought it directly to the office after it was discovered.

Under the zero tolerance policy, this constitutes possession of a dangerous instrument and the police should be called and an arrest made. Such a circumstance would also trigger expulsion for the student. What do you do?

Questions to Consider

1. Do you think it matters that the student found the razor blade and was trying to protect the students and the school?
2. Should the student's reputation factor into whether or not you believe the student?
3. Do you think you have the ability to ignore the facts and circumstances in this case: it is, after all, a zero tolerance policy?
4. What implications does the arrest of this student have among the student body as well as with everyone on campus? Are there more important lessons at stake here, and if so, what are they?

SUMMARY

- Summarize an overview of public education in the United States.
  - While there appears to be some improvement in terms of educational attainment for all students, inequalities still exist in terms of in academic success among minority students.
- Analyze the impact of educational inequalities in the United States.
  - A consistent problem in education is that minorities generally lag behind Whites in terms of graduation from high school as well as college.
  - While all graduation rates have improved in recent years, Blacks, Hispanics, and American Indian/ Native Alaskan students have lower graduation rates than Whites or Asian Americans.
  - Not graduating from high school translates into higher unemployment rates as well as lower paying jobs.
- Discuss challenges to public education.
  - The linkage of educational funding to property taxes results in unequal sources. Poor communities do not have the same resources to spend on public schools as wealthier communities.
  - The bureaucratic nature of schools can prevent innovation.
  - The No Child Left Behind laws have been shown to be ineffective and complicate educational success for most students since they only focus on testing benchmarks and do not consider the context in which those tests are offered.
- Compare schools in the United States and international schools.
  - The United States continues to lag behind other nations in part because US schools are decentralized.
  - The philosophy guiding the education of students in the United States does

not center on student learning as much as in other countries.

- Analyze the reasons that some schools fail in the United States.
    - The intersection between education, poverty, and race has a significant impact on the overall success of students.
    - Despite court rulings that segregation is illegal, many schools continue to be segregated, primarily on the basis of race.
    - Underfunded schools can lead to teachers who are inexperienced or suffer burnout, magnifying problems related to academic achievement.
    - Low-income families tend to have less involved parents in their child's education, along with a host of cultural and individual factors that contribute to low academic achievement.
- Describe the response to the challenges in public schools.
    - Head Start programs as well as certain types of charter schools, along with efforts to combine academic and vocational training in the form of career academies, have shown success compared to traditional schools.
- Assess the problems in higher education in light of race and class influences.
    - The inequality seen in public schools is evident among college students and graduates, with minority students being the least likely to attend, graduate, and earn well-paying jobs.
    - For-profit colleges have offered a different model of education, although serious questions remain about the value of an education from these institutions.
- Analyze how sociological theory can explain some of the challenges in education.
    - From a functionalist perspective, one needs to distinguish between the manifest or intended functions of education, from its latent or unintended consequences.
    - A conflict approach to education would point to the structural inequalities that exist in schools and act as a gatekeeper to perpetuate the status quo..
    - Symbolic interactionists examine the process of education from a micro-level perspective. An example of how they would study educational inequality is through the application of the labeling theory (Chapter 2).
- Evaluate effective solutions to some of the problems in education in the United States.
    - Programs that have demonstrated success in increasing student academic achievement and/or preventing students from dropping out include Head Start, K-12 program, Career Academies, and the First Grade Classroom Prevention Programs.
    - In higher education, programs like Early College, Dual Enrollment, and College Transfer programs are designed to give students an opportunity to get a head start on completing a college degree.

KEY TERMS

Bilingual/bicultural education 232

Bullying and intimidation 236

Charter schools 234

Cultural capital 252

Dual enrollment programs 254

Early college high schools 254

Educational attainment 231

English First movement 245

Head Start 252

Home school 244

Latent functions 250.

Manifest functions 250

No Child Left Behind Act of 2001 234

Race to the Top 235

School vouchers 243

Theory of social reproduction 252

Tribal schools/tribal colleges 233

Discussion Questions

1. Why do you think for-profit colleges are able to charge such high tuition? What is their added value compared to traditional colleges? Do you think they provide the same quality education as traditional colleges? Why or why not?
2. Given some of the recent policies by universities that limit the number of Asian American students, does this constitute a form of discrimination? Should we admit students who have the best scores and grades, or should there be some attention given to minorities, including those who score higher than average?
3. Consider the backlash against public education, where more parents believe they can do a better job than teachers and schools by home schooling their children. Do you think home schooling results in higher academic achievement on average than public school? What lessons can we learn from such a model?
4. What do you think explains the problems in the United States, where we spend so much more per pupil on education but the outcomes, compared to other countries, is lower than what one might expect?

Learn more with this chapter's digital tools, including Data and Media Literacy Exercises, flashcards, and chapter self-assessments at **www.oup.com/he/mcnamara**.

9

Why Can't a Woman Do That? Gender Inequalities

Chapter Outline

LEARNING OBJECTIVES

- Define gender and contrast the differences between gender and sex.
- Summarize the history and current state of the Women's Movement in the United States.
- Describe gender socialization and the social institutions that contribute to it.
- Analyze gender inequalities and life chances.
- Compare sociological theories of gender and how they explain the inequalities that exist.
- Summarize effective solutions to gender inequality.

A historical first Kamala Harris is the first woman and first person of color to be elected Vice President of the United States.

In our discussions of poverty, race, and ethnicity, we saw that certain groups can be targets of discrimination and mistreatment based on their membership or characteristics. Recall that in Chapter 1 we pointed out that people tend to categorize others on the basis of physical and social cues. When enough cues emerge, we tend to put that person into a social category that attributes their attitudes, values, beliefs in addition to their behavior based on those cues. This becomes the basis of stereotypes and a misunderstanding of groups of people—in part because we overgeneralize what they think and feel in addition to how they act. In addition to skin color, one of the more easily identifiable characteristics or cues is a person's gender.

In sociology, a minority group is defined not by its size but by their access to social, economic, and political power. Women, who make up 51 percent of the US population, are sometimes seen as a minority group. Women are often not treated equally to men in terms of prestige, wealth, or power. Prejudice and discrimination based on sex or gender that gives rise to and perpetuates this inequality is known as sexism.

In this chapter, we will discuss the role of women in American society as well as challenges they face. We will investigate the unequal and unfair treatment of women based on membership in a minority group. As in our considerations of race and ethnicity, it is important to note that we are often not aware of the biases we have toward certain minority groups. We also tend to overlook the significance of unequal treatment unless we are a member of that particular group. To the extent that recent movements for social justice have revealed pervasive unequal treatment of minority groups, it is important to understand how mainstream society—including other women—perceives the role of gender in social interaction and relationships.

SOCIOLOGICAL STORY TIME

- Alexandria Ocasio-Cortez, first elected to Congress in 2018, ran on a shoe string campaign and a message about humility. She was criticized in the media for a magazine shoot in which she wore an outfit that cost upward of $3,500. How, critics argued, could someone who claimed to grow up poor, wear designer clothing that only a wealthy person could afford? In response, Ocasio-Cortez explained that the magazine paid for the outfit, which she returned after the photo shoot (Watson, 2018).
- Since 2017, an estimated 425 men, including many Hollywood actors, politicians, and CEOs of large corporations, have resigned, been fired, or have left their positions as a result of allegations of sexual misconduct against women. Others have denied any wrongdoing after accusations were filed and often questioned the motives of their accusers. The #MeToo movement has been instrumental in shaping the narrative about how men have seen and acted toward women (Griffin, Recht, and Green, 2018).
- In 2015, Kristen Greist and Shaye Haver became the first two women to ever complete the US Army Rangers course and were commissioned as officers after completing their education at West Point. However, the Army had not yet changed its policy on prohibiting women from serving in combat areas and it was a year later before both officers were allowed to serve. The women faced online death threats as well as having to prove their competence to their male counterparts on a regular basis (Myers, 2018).
- In 2018, President Trump mocked the account of a woman who accused Supreme Court nominee Brett M. Kavanaugh of assault and told a Mississippi crowd that the #MeToo movement was unfairly hurting men. Trump also said that men were going to be fired after being unfairly accused of sexual harassment (Dawsey and Sonmez, 2018).

DEFINING GENDER

It is important to be precise in the language we use to describe gender and sexuality, especially if we are to investigate inequalities based on these characteristics. In Chapter 10, we will specifically address issues of inequality based on sexual identity and orientation as well as explore how members of the LGBTQ community experience their place in American society. For the purposes of this chapter, however, we must first distinguish between gender and sex.

For the purposes of this chapter, **sex** is defined as the biological difference between males and females. At or before birth, we are each identified with our first label or status on the basis of our sex organs and genes. **Gender** is a social category that constructs roles and defines behaviors for men and women. Through socialization, men and women learn to identify these roles and uphold the behaviors expected of them when they occupy these statuses. Men are supposed to be masculine (Lippa, 2005). Some qualities of masculinity include aggression, independence, toughness, and strength. In contrast, women are expected to uphold feminine behaviors. This includes being more emotional, gentle, and nurturing. The social category of gender also reinforces for men and women how they perceive themselves and their roles in society (Lippa, 2005). That is, not only does society have expectations for men and women based on socially constructed identities, but individuals internalize these ideas and define themselves in that way as well.

It would be a mistake, however, to think of gender roles as only being socially constructed. There is an interplay between biological and sociological differences between men and women. Biological differences between men and women are underscored, highlighted and reinforced beginning in childhood.

Differences Between Boys and Girls

Socialization about gender influences our perceptions of the world and of ourselves from very early in our lives. Long before children begin making decisions about their lives and who they will become, research shows that parents send gender messages to their sons and daughters (Lippa, 2005). For example, several studies have shown that female children are held more tenderly and with greater affection, while male children are often treated more playfully and aggressively (Coon and Mitterer, 2008). In general, our culture, our parents, and our peers send the message that women should be passive and emotional while men should be independent and action-oriented (Coon and Mitterer, 2008).

Influences begin early Children are socialized about gender from a very early age. Boys are typically expected to be more interested in trucks, while girls are given dolls and dollhouses to play with.

One implication of this standard is that men are supposed to have jobs that embrace masculinity. Consider the stigma associated with being a male nurse, an occupation that has traditionally been associated with women and femininity. Men who deviate from the standards set by their culture are not considered "real men," and can be mocked for their choices (Savran, 1998). Many people think that there is something inherent about the differences between men and women, and to some extent this is true. However, we must be careful not to attribute too much of this difference to biology.

PHYSICAL DIFFERENCES

Whatever one believes about the differences between men and women, it is true that men and women have different physical abilities. On average, males are 10 percent taller, 20 percent heavier, and 30 percent stronger, especially in their upper bodies, than women. Women tend to live longer than men; on average, women live 79.8 years, compared to 74.4 years for men (US Department of Health and Human Services, 2018). Research shows that there are no overall differences in intelligence between the sexes. Together, these findings suggest that while there are biological differences between men and women, there is no evidence to suggest that one sex is naturally superior to the other (Tavaris and Wade, 2001).

Boys and girls also differ in their developmental progress. Girls learn to speak earlier and are more adept overall in their verbal skills than boys. Boys tend to develop their mechanical and dexterity skills faster than girls. Furthermore, cognitive differences increase in scope as boys and girls are socialized, making these natural inclinations some of the most significant markers of the differences between the two sexes (Halpern and LaMay, 2000).

SPECIALIZED DIFFERENCES

Children are taught from an early age about the differences between men and women. They also learn which behaviors are appropriate in masculine or feminine terms. Gender, therefore, also shapes our thoughts, feelings, and behaviors.

For example, girls between the ages of eight and eleven years generally view themselves as strong and confident, and are not afraid to say what they think. But as they enter adolescence, girls feel pressure to adopt the more traditional roles associated with women. They become concerned with upholding expected feminine behaviors, and with their physical and sexual attractiveness. These social pressures often impose negative self-images onto young girls, which can lead to eating disorders, depression, and low self-esteem (Jackson and Hong, 2007; Greenfield and Brunberg, 2002).

Beauty standards and expectations The media, including women's magazines, promote standards of female beauty and expectations for proper female behavior that are unrealistic for most women and serve to perpetuate stereotypes.

In her book *The Beauty Myth*, Naomi Wolf argues that American culture serves to damage women's self-esteem by teaching them to measure themselves in terms of physical appearancestandards for beauty are largely unrealistic and the inability to meet those standards results in lowered self-esteem for many women (Wolf, 1990). Wolf argues that the same myth that designates standards for women's physical appearance also defines their

Table 9.1 Moral Decision Making Between Males and Females
According to Gilligan's argument, boys and girls will react differently to situations because of different viewpoints.

	Males	Females
Perspective	Justice	Care and responsibility
Description	Reliance on formal rules to develop sense of morality	Reliance on compassion and sense of responsibility for others
Example	Objection to stealing because it breaks the law	Sympathy for the offender by asking why someone would steal in the first place

roles in relationships with men. In short, women are evaluated based on physical appearance, and they gain status by using their physical traits to attract men. In social terms, such standards effectively reduce women to the status of objects (Wolf, 1990).

Psychologist Carol Gilligan has examined gender in terms of behavior. In trying to answer the question of whether girls are more naturally nurturing than boys, Gilligan argues that much of the difference can be explained through the process of socialization. For example, Gilligan argues that boys and girls use different strategies for making moral decisions (Table 9.1).

Like Wolf, Gilligan also found that self-esteem issues can be discussed in relation to gender. She found that young girls are often much more self-confident than girls reaching, or going through, adolescence. Gilligan attributes this difference to the ways in which young women are socialized in American culture, as well as to the culture's lack of strong female role models (Gilligan, 1990).

Another important dimension of female identity involves maintaining relationships. Girls experience a great deal of pressure to be popular among their peers, and this pressure can manifest in negative behaviors, including delinquency (Greenfield and Blumberg, 2002; Anderson, 2018). Thus, while relationships are essential to the overall well-being of young girls, and they are important to the development of their identities, relationships are also one of the more stressful experiences of growing up. Some experts refer to the manifestations of this stress as "relational aggression," characterized by negative behaviors like spreading rumors, threatening or withdrawing from friendships, and reacting to power issues within a group (Craig et al., 2020). Sometimes girls inflict forms of hazing and social isolation on their female peers, which can result in emotional trauma. It can also lead to delinquent acts as girls attempt to fit in and be part of the group (Craig, et al., 2020).

Social media also plays a role in contributing to negative behaviors. According to a 2018 report by the Pew Research Center, 59 percent of teens have personally experienced at least one of six types of abusive online behavior—harassment, threats, name calling, rumor spreading, etc. While boys and girls are about equally likely to experience what we might call cyberbullying, girls are more likely to be targets of online rumor spreading and non-consensual explicit messages. In fact, girls are more likely to experience several different forms of online bullying: 15 percent of teenage girls were the target of at least four negative online behaviors compared to 6 percent for boys (Anderson, 2018). Other studies point to the idea that the more teens are using social media, the greater the likelihood they will be victimized by cyberbullying (Craig et al., 2020).

THE WOMEN'S MOVEMENT IN THE UNITED STATES

Women's struggle for equal rights has spanned much of our nation's history and has laid the groundwork for the advancement of women to their present-day social status. Today, the continuous efforts and campaigns promoting the belief that males and females should be politically, socially, and economically equal are referred to as **feminist movements. Feminism** is a belief or doctrine that advocates equality in the social, economic, and political treatment of women in society. Feminist scholars discuss these movements as having occurred in three/four waves (See for example Case and Craig, 2019; Paglia, 2018; Cavanaugh, 2018).

The first wave of feminism occurred in the nineteenth and early twentieth centuries and focused on women's legal rights. This wave occurred in response to the rise of the modern industrial society, which saw an increase in economic and political opportunities for women and inspired many to question their traditional status in society. This wave culminated in women winning the right to vote in 1920.

During the period following World War II, the US economy experienced a boom. Both world wars had brought women into the workforce in large numbers, and as a result, inequities between the sexes in terms of pay, job security, benefits, and the overall treatment of employees became more apparent. In general, women began demanding that society allow them to take on more important roles (Cavanaugh, 2018).

Women's suffrage movement These Connecticut women rallied in 1914 for the right to vote. The nationwide women's suffrage movement finally triumphed on August 19, 1920, with the ratification of the 19th Amendment to the Constitution.

The second wave of the feminist movement peaked in the 1960s and 1970s, and focused on the emergence of a formal identity for women. This wave coincided with other movements, such as the Civil Rights Movement and anti–Vietnam War protests in the United States. The 1964 Civil Rights Act had recognized and guaranteed equal protection under the law for minorities. Feminist groups observed these movements and found inspiration in the experiences of minorities (Case and Craig, 2019; Cavanaugh, 2018).

In the 1970s, women's groups like the National Organization for Women (NOW) sought to overturn laws that enforced discrimination in matters such as contracts, property rights, employment, and wages. Perhaps the greatest effort of this period was the attempt to pass the Equal Rights Amendment (ERA), a constitutional amendment that would have granted women equal protection under the law, and which had been denied in Congress since its proposal in 1923. While the ERA is yet to be made into law, feminists continue to use it to pressure legislators to address women's issues (Cavanaugh, 2018; Case and Craig, 2019).

Taking action A January 2018 combined #MeToo and #TimesUp protest in San Francisco.

The third wave of feminism began in the 1980s and though it bears much resemblance to earlier feminist movements, third-wave feminism chooses to address issues of equal rights from *within* the political and legal establishments, rather than criticizing them from the outside. A related effort, sometimes referred to as the fourth wave of feminism, stresses the need to broaden the scope of feminism, emphasizing global networking, human rights, and a more holistic understanding of the role of all women in society (Cavanagh, 2018).

According to a 2018 report by Progressive Women's Leadership, the fourth wave of feminism is highlighted by events such as the **#MeToo movement** and the #Time'sUp movement, which together bring assault cases against influential men (including celebrities such as Matt Lauer, Bill Cosby, and Mario Batali) and amplify demands by high-profile women to make significant changes in those industries. The fourth wave also includes a greater number of women seeking political office and leadership roles (Progressive Women's Leadership, 2019).

GENDER SOCIALIZATION AND SOCIAL INSTITUTIONS

Part of the discussion of the differences in the way women and men understand their roles and meet societal expectations relates to how they are socialized as well as how society constructs people's perceptions of what is acceptable and expected of men and women.

Parents and Caretakers

Parents and caretakers contribute to gender stereotypes by the ways in which they raise their children. The purchase of particular toys, for example, can signal and reinforce gender-specific roles and behaviors. Thus, if parents buy guns, tanks, footballs and soccer balls for boys, this will tend to encourage the type of aggressive play typically associated with "boy" behavior. Similarly, if parents buy their daughters dolls, cosmetics, and miniature ovens and doll houses, that too shapes the types of activities in which girls are likely to engage. These items and activities also develop various skills that reinforce notions of what boys and girls are supposed to do (Klass, 2018).

Another way parents contribute to gender socialization is in the chores they assign their children. Think about the tasks you were given as a child—if you are a female, were your chores things like taking out the trash, mowing the lawn, carrying the recycling bin to the street? Or were they more likely to be household chores, such as cooking, cleaning, wiping off the counters, emptying the dishwasher, and minding younger siblings? Boys get the chores that require a willingness to get one's hands dirty while girls are given activities that perpetuate a traditional woman's role in the household.

Peers

Peers are extraordinarily important agents of socialization, particularly at certain ages. Sociological research points out that children tend to be accepted by their peer group when they conform to that group's gender-based behavior. This is particularly true for boys, who put pressure on other boys to engage in masculine activities and to refrain from and show disdain for feminine activities. The penalty for failing to live up to gender-appropriate expectations? Banishment from the male peer group. Such punishment has a coercive effect on boys' behavior, even if they do not wish to participate in many activities, but it is better than being ridiculed, ostracized, or excluded. For girls, the expectations may be related to what they wear, how they style their hair, whether they engage in typically male dominated activities (e.g. playing football or hunting) or whether or not their circle of friends consists of mostly boys or girls.

Media stereotypes of gender relations Long-running reality TV shows like The Bachelor reinforce rigid gender expectations of roles and behavior. In Season 20, Lauren Bushnell competed with several other women and endured many "rose" ceremonies to "win" a marriage proposal from bachelor Ben Higgins. Their relationship broke up within two years.

Media

The media children begin to consume at an early age both shapes and reinforces cultural values about appropriate behavior for boys and girls, and men and women. From video games to news broadcasts to popular television shows and movies, the media is a powerful influence on how our society perceives gender. The news media and social media especially shape how our society understands and addresses gender-based inequality.

A 2017 report by Common Sense media confirms that gender stereotyping begins early in a child's life and persist throughout adulthood. These stereotypes are effective at teaching children and young adults what American culture expects from boys and girls. For preschoolers, for example, the characters they see on television and in the movies are often associated with certain traits that are seen as valuable and important, such as being strong or brave (Ward and Aubrey, 2017).

These traits morph into something different when the child begins watching shows as a teenager, where relationships become important. Bravery and strength translate into aggression and hostility. Such oversimplifications, particularly those that characterize women as meek, fearful, submissive, and weak, are reinforced again and again by the story lines in a wide array of shows and movies. It is challenging for parents and caretakers to dispel some of these stereotypes. This is an important development since many of our ideas about men and women have been reinforced since childhood, making awareness of inconsistencies or inaccuracies difficult to identify (Ward and Aubrey, 2017).

Schools

The bureaucratic nature of public education in this country brings with it a host of policies and procedures, not to mention informal practices, that are designed to provide a quality education to a wide range of students (Chapter 8). However, what if gender stereotypes influence the way teachers act toward male or female students? What if these subtle and not so subtle tendencies perpetuate ideas about the value and role of women in society among students?

Recent studies have indicated that while girls tended to excel in elementary school, they began to lag behind boys when they reached middle and high school. Other research pointed out that girls tended to test more poorly than boys and lacked confidence in their abilities. The research suggested that one explanation for this trend was that teachers tended to call on boys more often than girls and were given more praise by the teachers for their answers (Ahern, 2019).

In response, some educational experts argue that the gender bias traditionally found in schools was the focus of educational reforms of the 1990s. Those efforts helped girls to succeed but did so at the expense of boys' learning. This argument suggests a form of reverse sexism has occurred (Whitmire, 2011). Evidence of the trend is seen in the success of girls in education, where more girls apply to, attend, and graduate from college more than boys (Chapter 8).

Different learning styles Research suggests that boys do not respond as well as girls do to literacy-based learning.

In his book *Why Boys Fail*, Richard Whitmire conducted a meta-analysis of research on the learning style of boys compared to girls. Whitmire found that while there are only minor differences in intelligence between male and female students, the socialization and experiences in schools for boys lead them to greater likelihood of failure in an academic setting. This is not because boys are lacking in intelligence, but rather that the school environment is not geared toward the ways in which boys' brains process information. Boys tend to take longer to process information and they absorb it differently than girls. However, most public schools rely on literacy-based learning, which favors the way most girls process information. As a result, boys, who tend to be slower readers, get behind, earn a poor grade, and then dislike reading. However, of all the skills learned in school, reading is perhaps the most important, since it relates to students' ability to write, reason, and problem solve. Thus, boys tend not to do as well in school compared to girls, not because they lack the aptitude, but because of the ways in which they are socialized into the school environment (Whitmire, 2011).

GENDER, LIFE CHANCES, AND INEQUALITIES

What are the implications of the stereotypical images that characterize socialization about gender? In what ways do gender stereotypes shape social interaction between men and women? How do men and women experience inequality differently? Let's take a look at the data and see if there are any noteworthy trends.

Work and Income

Among the more tangible limitations women experience as a result of gender are in the workplace. As more women have embarked upon careers, and as more have achieved high levels of education (Chapter 8), it would seem that women should be treated equally to men when it comes to hiring for, performing, and being compensated for the same job. After all, if they are equally qualified, wouldn't fairness dictate that the best qualified person obtains the job or promotion? However, the data suggests different story.

In fact, however we analyze the data on employment, most experts contend that gender inequality is extraordinarily visible. This inequality is evident in rates of participation in the work force, the kinds of jobs, levels of pay, and the additional responsibilities men and women assume outside of the workplace, among other areas.

The **wage gap** is the difference between what women and men earn. Despite changes in the number of women entering the workforce, some experts note that women still earn approximately 81 percent, on average, of what men earn. This wage gap results in significant differences in median incomes between men and women in many occupations. Interestingly, the wage gap varies by race and ethnicity as well as by gender (Figure 9.1). If the earnings ratio continues at its current rate, and, assuming a host of other factors, it will take more than 40 years for wage parity to be reached between men and women (Hagewisch, 2018).

Whether male or female, Black and Hispanic workers earn considerably less than Whites and Asians. One conclusion from this trend is that the gender earnings ratio is narrower within races or ethnicities, but wider when compared to White workers. Asian workers as a group have the highest median annual earnings, primarily because of historically higher rates of educational attainment for both genders (Hagewisch, 2018).

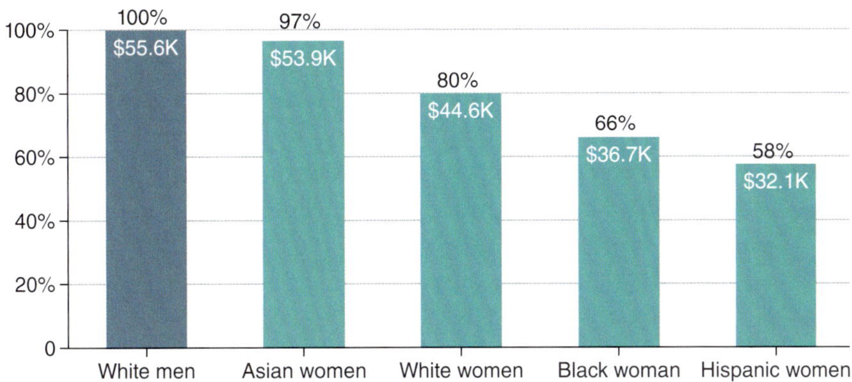

Figure 9.1 Women's annual earnings compared to white men's Note: Data shows media earnings for full-time, year-round civilian employees 16 and over in 2018. Source: US Census Bureau, "2018 Community Survey".

Part of the problem with the wage gap is the inaccurate assumption that gains for women in terms of salary comes at the expense of men's salaries. Another issue that needs to be considered is how to close the wage gap; logically women's real wages would have to rise faster than men's, a tall order even in the best of economies. In a booming economy, all workers' wages would increase, not just those for women. Thus, closing the wage gap requires giving more attention to one group over the other and this likely results in a significant backlash against the idea (Hagewisch, 2018).

Critics of the wage gap contend that the difference between what women and men make relate to the types of jobs people are performing. That is, if women traditionally take jobs such as teachers, nurses, and other professions that are low-paying, while men take jobs in other industries that pay better, such as banking, insurance, or finance, then the differences in wages simply reflects the value society places on those jobs by the salary they pay. But what about the same types of jobs? Sociologists who analyze the wage gap consider **comparable worth**, meaning the jobs are similar and the wages paid for that job should reflect the value placed on those tasks rather than the gender or race of the worker performing it.

To measure comparable worth, researchers calculate the amount of training and education needed to perform a certain job, how much responsibility a person is assigned when taking a particular job, and the working conditions. A point system is allocated for these variables to determine if men and women are being paid equally for comparable jobs. For pay equity to exist, men and women in occupations that receive the same score should be paid the same. The data tends to show that pay equity only exists for a few jobs—and that those people who choose certain professions are often penalized and unfairly compensated (Hagewisch, 2018; Sonam, Gal, Hoffman, and Ward, 2020).

Family and Career

In recent decades, more women have entered the workforce in addition to having a family (Chapter 12). At the same time, men have increased their level of participation in housework and child care. In addition, an increased number of men are choosing to stay home while their wives embark upon careers. That said, the data continues to show that women still assume the majority of the responsibilities for maintaining the household (Brenan, 2020). As Hochschild and Machung (2012) pointed out in their book, women must not only deal with the demands of a career, but then continue to manage a household and family responsibilities, something she refers to as the **second shift** (Hochschild and Machung, 2012).

Moreover, the household tasks that are performed by women tend to be the ones that are needed regularly, while research tends to reveal that the tasks often performed by men are those that are not needed every day. These everyday tasks, such as laundry, preparing meals, and caring for the children, add to the stressors and workload of working women. In response, many women, in their attempt to manage the many tasks at home that require their regular attention, give up leisure activities and sleep (Brenan, 2020). As was mentioned in Chapter 8, the impact of the Covid-19 pandemic placed greater burdens on women, who were primarily responsible for supervising the remote learning of their children when schools closed while balancing their own careers while working from home (Graves, 2020).

Military

Women have always been involved in some capacity in the US military. During World War I and World War II, when there were shortages of personnel to carry out non-combat tasks, women stepped up and contributed to supporting combat troops. Until recently, however, women were prohibited from serving in combat units. Changing technology as well as a greater appreciation for the contributions of women's roles in the military have led to modifications of the Department of Defense policy on women in combat. In 2013, the first two women were integrated into the US Army Rangers. Both women are now serving in leadership roles in combat units.

A proud first 1st Lt. Shaye Haver, one of the first female graduates of the Army Ranger School.

In that same year, the Secretary of Defense ended the Ground Combat Exclusion Policy and gave the military until 2016 to integrate women in direct combat units. While women could still be excluded from certain jobs, this should be the exception and based on the approval of the Secretary of Defense. The policy change was criticized by many in the military, particularly because of concerns that women would not be able to meet the physical demands of members of direct combat units (Constitutional Rights Foundation, 2014).

While the number of women who can meet the physical fitness requirements to join specialized combat units will likely remain small, the fact that the policy changed to allow women to participate is an important moment in the journey toward equality for women. While there still remain individuals who do not think women should be allowed to serve in the military, an increasing number of women are members of the various branches of the armed forces in both rank and file as well as in leadership positions (Task and Purpose, 2017). However, problems still remain.

According to a 2020 report from the Department of Defense, there were 7,825 reported sexual assaults in 2019, a 3 percent increase from 2018. The increase consisted primarily of enlisted female service members between the ages of 17-24 and junior officers. Related to sexual assault is sexual harassment (Department of Defense, 2020).

In 2019 there were 1,021 official sexual harassment complaints filed by military personnel, an increase of more than 10 percent since 2018. Active duty women who experience sexual harassment are three times greater risk of sexual assault than those who were not sexually harassed. Part of the challenge is that male and female service members have difficulty defining sexual harassment and victims often feel a complaint is not addressed adequately or at all. Most women's advocates argue that the military has generally done far less than necessary to address the problems of sexual assault and sexual harassment (Kenney, 2020).

In 2019, in an attempt to address the problems of sexual assault as well as sexual harassment, acting Defense Secretary Patrick Shanahan issued a memo making sexual harassment a separate military charge. In addition, a Catch a Serial Offender program was created to allow victims to anonymously submit information about their complaint in an effort to identify individuals who are frequent offenders of both types of crimes (Department of Defense, 2020).

Crime and Victimization

While females are victimized by all types of crime, perhaps the most alarming trend as it relates to gender involves victimization as a result of violent crime. This includes acts such as sexual assault, stalking, and domestic violence. Interestingly, according to the Bureau of Justice Statistics, between 2018 and 2019 the rates of sexual violence decreased slightly. That is, the rates of sexual violence for both women and men experienced no significant change, nor did reporting practices to the police (Morgan and Truman, 2020).

RAPE

According to the Center for Disease Control and Prevention, nearly 20 percent of women in the United States (nearly 22 million women) have been raped in their lifetime. Less than 2 percent of men in the United States reported having been raped at some point in their lives, nearly 1.6 million men (Smith et al., 2018).

Nearly half of all women (44 percent) and nearly a quarter of all men (22 percent) experienced sexual violence victimization other than rape at some point in their lives. This equates to more than 53 million women and more than 25 million men in the United States. About 13 percent of women reported experiencing sexual coercion in her lifetime, which translates to more than 15 million women in the United States. Six percent of men reported sexual coercion in their lifetimes (almost 7 million men; Smith et al., 2018).

Victims of rape vary by race and ethnicity. Approximately 22 percent of Black and 19 percent of White non-Hispanic women were raped at some point in their lives, while about 15 percent of Hispanic women reported that experience. More than one-quarter of women (26.9 percent) who identified as American Indian or as Alaska Native reported rape victimization in their lifetime.

STALKING

While many people don't automatically think of stalking as a violent crime, the issue is worthy of inclusion in the discussion because of the psychological effect it has on its victims. For example, about 16 percent, or about 19 million women, in the United States has experienced stalking at some point in their lifetime. In the United States, approximately 20 percent of Black non-Hispanic women experienced stalking in their lifetime (Stalking Prevention Awareness and Resource Center, 2019).

A variety of tactics are used to stalk victims. More than three-quarters of female stalking victims reported receiving unwanted phone calls, voice or text messages, or hang ups. More than half of female victims reported being approached by the stalker. Two-thirds of female victims of stalking were stalked by intimate partners. For both female and male victims, stalking was often committed by people they knew or with whom they had a relationship. Two-thirds of the female victims of stalking reported stalking by a current or former intimate partner and nearly one-quarter reported stalking by an acquaintance (Stalking Prevention Awareness and Resource Center, 2019).

INTIMATE PARTNER VIOLENCE

Intimate partner violence includes physical violence, sexual violence, threats of physical or sexual violence, stalking and psychological aggression by a current or former intimate partner. Intimate partner violence may occur among cohabitating or non-cohabitating romantic or sexual partners and among opposite or same sex couples. Previous large-scale surveys of intimate partner violence have primarily examined only certain aspects of intimate partner violence (e.g., physical or sexual violence) or have examined these forms of intimate partner violence within the context of crime or public safety (Centers for Disease Control, 2020).

More than one-third of women in the United States, or 42.4 million, have experienced rape, physical violence, and/or stalking by an intimate partner at some point in their lifetime About a third of women (32.9 percent) has experienced physical violence by an intimate partner. About ten percent of women in the United States has been raped by an intimate partner in her lifetime, while nearly 17 percent has experienced sexual violence other than rape by an intimate partner which includes sexual coercion or unwanted sexual contact. Nearly a third of all women in the United States has been slapped, pushed or shoved by an intimate partner at some point in her lifetime. This translates to approximately 36.2 million women in the United States (Centers for Disease Control, 2020). Approximately one quarter of women in the United States has experienced *severe* physical violence by an intimate partner in her lifetime, translating to nearly 29 million women. An estimated 17 percent of women have been slammed against something by a partner, 14 percent have been hit with a fist or something hard, and 11 percent reported that they have been beaten by an intimate partner in their lifetime (Centers for Disease Control, 2020).

The Covid-19 pandemic had a significant impact on intimate partner violence. As stay-at-home orders were put in place, schools closed, and workers laid off, many intimate partner violence victims were more vulnerable and at greater risk of victimization. While some evidence indicated that calls for services decreased in some areas, most practitioners realized this was not due to actual decreased cases but by the inability of victims to access services. The problems continue as some restrictions are lifted, but many experts express concerns about an increase in cases if a second round of restrictions are implemented (Evans, Lindauer, and Farrell, 2020).

Female criminality

While most people think of women primarily as victims of crime, there is increasing evidence that women are also becoming involved in the criminal justice system as offenders. In fact, according to the Sentencing Project (2019), women are a fast-growing criminal justice population according to trends over the past 30 years.

What types of crime are women more likely to commit? The available data suggests that women are more likely than men to commit property crimes such as larceny-theft and fraud, and are also more likely to commit drug offenses, including drug possession and trafficking (Figure 9.2). Women are less likely than men to have been convicted of a violent crime, but when they do commit a violent act, the

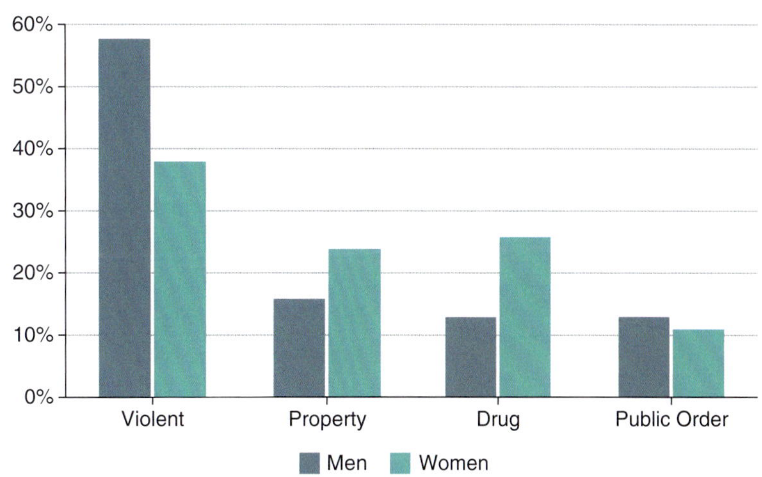

Figure 9.2 Offense type by gender in state prisons, 2018 Source: Carson, E. A. (2020). Prisoners in 2019. Washington, DC: Bureau of Justice Statistics.

reasons for this often stem from efforts to protect themselves or their children from attackers. That is, women who engage in violence do not typically do so in a premeditated manner, but instead are engaging in a form of self-defense. Because the motives for engaging in violence are different from men, it should not be surprising to learn that violent female offenders are not as likely to engage in further violence once incarcerated or reoffend once they are returned to the community. Arrest rates for women, like those for men, reflect a disproportionality. Black women are more than twice as likely to be imprisoned compared to White women, and Hispanic women being only slightly more likely to be incarcerated as Whites (The Sentencing Project, 2019).

By contrast, women who commit non-violent acts are more likely to reoffend, particularly if their actions are drug-related. Overall, about one-quarter of women released from prison fail within six months (i.e., have an arrest for a new crime), one-third fail within a year, and two-thirds fail (68 percent) five years out from release (The Sentencing Project, 2019).

Female offenders are still likely to experience victimization, either before or after their incarceration. For those who are in jail or prison, studies point out that victimization can occur either by other inmates or correctional staff. In general, most research shows that about half of incarcerated women interviewed report experiencing physical or sexual abuse in their lifetime. Given their extensive histories of trauma, it is not surprising then that women in jails and prisons report high rates of mental health problems such as depression, post-traumatic stress disorder (PTSD), and substance abuse. About a third of incarcerated women meet the criteria for current PTSD, with about half meeting criteria for lifetime PTSD. A national survey found that 55 percent of male adults in state prisons exhibited mental health problems as compared to 73 percent of women prisoners (The Sentencing Project, 2019).

Sexual Harassment

Sexual harassment is a form of gender discrimination that violates Title VII of the Civil Rights Act of 1964. It involves all unwelcome sexual attention that affects an employee's job and work environment. Sexual harassment can occur in all types of work dynamics involving all sorts of organizations. According to the US Equal Employment Opportunity Commission, most reported cases of sexual harassment involve the harassment of women by men, although there are cases where men have filed sexual harassment complaints against female supervisors and colleagues (Pflum, 2018).

While many observers note that people accused of sexual harassment claim that their actions are harmless fun, most experts contend that sexual harassment, like rape, is not really about sex at all. Instead, it is about power and its abuse. Those who are harassing victims are usually in a position of authority, and the subordinate does not feel she is in a position to resist, report, or fight back.

The research on sexual harassment shows that individuals at particular risk include low-income women or recent immigrants, illegal aliens, nannies and hotel housekeepers and others who feel vulnerable about reporting an attack against an offender for risk of losing their jobs or being deported. Other victims contend that they do not feel their accusations will be believed, particularly if the offender is especially influential or well-known (Pflum, 2018). In fact, the primary significance of the #MeToo movement is that powerful Hollywood executives, such as Harvey Weinstein, and celebrated personalities such as Matt Lauer, were finally held accountable for their actions after allegedly getting away with such behavior for years. In 2017, actress Alyssa Milano tweeted her opinion about Weinstein: "If you've been sexually harassed or assaulted write 'me too' as a reply to this tweet." Within 24 hours, thousands of people replied. Many women offered candid accounts of being harassed, raped, and losing jobs because of sexually aggressive coworkers like Weinstein (Pflum, 2018).

Civil rights activist and #MeToo founder Tarana Burke

While Milano amplified #MeToo, the movement itself originated a decade earlier through the work of Tarana Burke, an activist who wanted to raise awareness about the problem of sexual harassment. The #MeToo movement has led many well-known male figures to be charged with sexual harassment and sexual assault who may have gotten away with it had the movement not become so widespread (Pflum, 2018).

In addition to workplace harassment, women experience public forms of sexual harassment such as groping, sexual comments, and public statements that objectify them while commuting to and from work, traveling in airports, subways, or while walking on the street. Tolerance of such behavior creates an invasive environment where women are often made to feel victimized or even afraid for their safety. The long-term consequences of such behaviors is that it reinforces gender stereotypes about the value of women and could impact public perceptions of their competence in their chosen profession (Pflum, 2018).

SOCIOLOGICAL THEORY AND GENDER

As with each of the chapters in this book, sociological theory offers important insight into the nature of inequalities and the mistreatment of minority groups. The following analysis examines how sociological theory applies to gender.

Functionalism and Gender

It should be noted from the outset that critics of the functionalist approach, including many feminists, argue that this perspective serves to perpetuate and uphold social structures that work to oppress women in society. How? Functionalists tend to examine gender inequalities through the lens of biology. Sociologist Talcott Parsons described the division of labor in the household as being comprised of **instrumental tasks** and **expressive tasks**. Instrumental tasks, which often require greater physical strength and are focused on accomplishment, traditionally were taken on by men in their role as breadwinners. Expressive tasks are focused on nurturing, well-being, and group cohesion. Women, Parsons observed, in their primary role of mother take on the expressive tasks of the household. Such clearly defined roles allowed the nuclear family institution to remain stable and viable.

Moving from the household to society as a whole, functionalists argue that differences in wages and salaries are based on the particular talents of certain individuals who are willing to undergo extraordinary training to enhance these skills (Chapter 5). Functionalists would further point out that women and men differ in their particular skill sets, with women being more nurturing and compassionate; they might bring different but equally valuable capabilities to a task. Thus, the different treatment of women, particularly in the area of work, justifies the differences in wages. Even in those instances where men and women have the same credentials or perform the same job, functionalists might argue that those who are more gifted and talented in performing those tasks should earn higher wages.

With more women entering the workforce, a functionalist perspective would likely argue that certain occupations are more conducive to women's natural inclinations. For example, women, given their greater abilities at relationship building and nurturing, would be better suited for public relations positions or family law if she were to work as an attorney, whereas men would be better suited for leadership roles and those found in finance and operations.

Conflict Theory and Gender

Conflict theorists examine social inequalities based on gender and attribute them to power differentials. They might argue that life is more about access to economic, social, and political power. An important element of this dynamic is preserving the acquired power so that others do not obtain it. This may explain why members of dominant groups (in this case, men) try to maintain control over society and its scarce resources by limiting women's access to those opportunities. It is important to note, however, that conflict theorists do not see this struggle as simply between men and women. While it is true that many women have been and continue to be excluded from opportunities that men receive, not all males are treated equally either. The issue is power and its utilization, more so than gender—even though women are at a particular disadvantage in the pursuit of power.

A Marxist perspective analyzes gender inequality by considering those who have control of the means of production and the ownership of private property. From this perspective, men gain a particular advantage because women stay at home providing unpaid labor in raising children, caretaking, and housekeeping. This frees men to concentrate on building businesses and enhancing profits. Further, inequalities in the workplace are explained not by a particular discrimination or dislike of women, but because paying women less means greater profits. Since women, like the proletariat in Marx's discussion of capitalism, have little choice but to accept the conditions of the job market, they are forced to accept unequal wages. What is missing, of course, in this discussion, is the unequal treatment of men in the labor force. If business owners are purely about the pursuit of profit, then all workers, not just women, should be mistreated and paid less.

Symbolic Interactionism and Gender

From a symbolic interactionist perspective, the study of gender and inequality focuses on micro-level interactions and relationships. These interactions between men and women include spoken language as well as body language and gesture, all of which can indicate perceived and actual power differentials. In speaking and writing, many still refer to women in a traditionally male profession with an added descriptor: female doctor, female firefighter. This seems to suggest that women are the exception, not the default, in these career fields, and might even serve to devalue the contributions of women to these professions. In terms of body language, men typically control more physical space than women, whether they are sitting or standing. The term "manspreading" was recently coined to describe how men arrogantly take up more space when seated in public places as a symbolic expression of male dominance ("There's a Reason Men Take Up So Much Space When They Sit." 2017). Men also tend to invade women's personal space by standing close to them, staring at them, or even touching them. While not necessarily sexual in nature, such actions symbolically reflect male dominance.

While some sociologists are critical of the symbolic interactionist approach to gender, arguing that its concerns are relatively trivial, in fact language and communication patterns are critical to relationship development and typically persist for generations. In short, they shape our understanding of and response to perceived and real impressions of women.

Manspreading Men are more likely than women to physically take up and dominate more space. Here, a man assumes a wide stance while a woman folds her limbs to make herself smaller.

Feminist Theory and Gender

Feminist theory offers multiple perspectives useful to an understanding of gender-based inequality. Among these are liberal feminism, phenomenological feminism, socialist feminism,

Marxist feminism, and radical feminism. While each feminist perspective described below differs on a number of important elements, there are five general principles on which most agree:

1. **Equality.** Feminist ideology is critical of the status quo and tries to change the perception and treatment of women.
2. **Human choice.** Feminists maintain that cultural notions of gender limit individual choice. For instance, it is traditionally presumed that certain traits belong to the female domain (such as nurturing and cooperation) while traits like rationality and competition belong to the male domain. These preconceptions, reinforced by culture, influence the personal and professional decisions of men and women alike. Feminists, on the other hand, believe that all people, regardless of their gender, should feel free to make choices based on the things that matter most to them.
3. **Elimination of gender-based stratification.** Feminists are opposed to laws that limit economic, political, and social opportunities for women. While the Equal Rights Amendment was defeated in the 1970s in Congress, this legislation has given momentum to other women's rights efforts.
4. **Elimination of sexual violence.** Many feminists argue that in our male-dominated society women are generally seen as sexual objects. They would further argue that violence against women, such as domestic violence, rape, sexual harassment, and pornography, are symptoms of this perception of women.
5. **Sexual freedom**. Feminists support the idea of women having control over their own bodies, particularly as this control relates to reproduction. The decision whether to bear children or to terminate a pregnancy, for instance, is referred to by many feminists as "a woman's right to choose." One aspect of sexual freedom on which some feminists disagree, however, is prostitution. While feminists defend a woman's right to choose what to do with her body, many argue that prostitution is not a choice. Instead, these feminists believe that women turn to prostitution in response to economic hardship and as a means of survival in a society that otherwise limits opportunities for women (Case and Craig, 2019). The topic of sexual freedom as it relates to prostitution and pornography is a contentious one in feminist circles, and one that has gathered more nuanced opinions in feminism's third/fourth wave.

Liberal feminism focuses on equal opportunities for women and the freedoms that allow women to make decisions about their lives. Liberal feminists do not believe that the political system is inherently biased or that discrimination against women is institutionalized or systematic. They instead believe in the idea of equality and in the promise that men and women can work together cooperatively. By their standards, policies such as affirmative action and fair labor laws, as they apply to women, demonstrate that it is possible for men and women to find common ground when it comes to equal treatment and protection under the law. The ideas that Freda Adler articulated in *Sisters in*

Crime, when she argued that adolescent females are imitating males in order to achieve similar economic and social goals, could be described as adhering to a liberal feminist agenda (Adler, 1975; Case and Craig, 2019; Paglia, 2018; Cavanaugh 2018).

When it comes to female delinquency, **phenomenological feminism** focuses on how women and girls are treated by the system. Phenomenological feminists examine the discriminatory treatment of female delinquents by the juvenile justice system. For instance, females are much more likely to run away than males, but they are also much more likely to be arrested and adjudicated for that offense. The reasons for this may stem from a chivalrous approach to treating female offenders. That is, officials may be attempting to protect females either by dealing with criminal offenses informally, thus keeping them out of the system, or by punishing them more severely, so that they recognize the error of their ways and begin to engage in more appropriate conduct (Berger, 1996).

Given how class and gender are interrelated, **socialist feminists** argue that it makes no sense to think of only one of these variables at a time. Looking at the larger picture, socialist feminists suggest that crime results from the lack of access to political power for women. Female delinquency occurs because women are more likely to be poor, and so lack the same professional and educational opportunities as men. Lacking social opportunities often means lacking political influence as well. As a result, socialist feminists believe that women's needs and concerns are often ignored by policymakers and government officials (Case and Craig, 2019).

Marxist feminism contends that the control of private property in the early days of capitalism set in motion a series of events whereby men controlled the social institutions of society. Because most of the economic, political, and social power belonged to men, women were left without sufficient opportunities to achieve societal success. As with the *lumpenproletariat* in Marx's theory—the segment of society that consisted of vagrants, criminals, and other people without resources—crime for women became one of the only means by which economic survival was possible, largely because men controlled the means of production and excluded women from benefitting from a capitalistic system. Thus, Marxist feminists explain female involvement in economic crimes, such as shoplifting and prostitution, as the symptom of a society that systematically discriminates against women (Case and Craig, 2019).

Finally, **radical feminists** view the control of society by males to be the source of all social inequality. According to this perspective, a **patriarchal society,** or one in which males dominate every aspect of economic, social, and political life, has resulted in women's oppression throughout history. Masculine control of society has also resulted in the objectification of women, with women's sexuality valued above all. As a result, the oppression of women is more widespread and has become internalized in the attitudes, values, and beliefs of American culture. Radical feminists are especially sensitive to women's oppression and the domination of men over women. They also contend that eradicating this type of discrimination is exceptionally difficult and requires women to maintain a heightened sensitivity to abuse (Case and Craig, 2019).

WHAT WORKS? EFFECTIVE SOLUTIONS TO GENDER INEQUALITY

While gender inequality is a persistent issue, there have been some efforts to address dimensions of the problem. Domestic violence is one such dimension. The Community Advocacy Project (CAP) is one promising program. This evidence-based program is designed to help survivors of intimate partner abuse regain control of their lives. The project has been shown to decrease survivors' risk of re-victimization and to increase their quality of life, level of social support, and ability to obtain the community resources they need. During the 10-week-long program, advocates offer insight to survivors about setting goals and identifying what makes them happy. This self-empowerment program has been evaluated through longitudinal data and has been shown to result in statistically significant improvements in the lives of domestic violence victims. This program has been used with a variety of populations, including at-risk adolescent females, as well as in other countries. The CAP program is also included in the National Registry of Evidence-Based Programs and Practices and the Domestic Violence Evidence Project (Research Consortium on Gender-Based Violence, n.d.).

SO WHAT CAN I DO?

While issues relating to gender may seem to be confined only to women, males and females are equally invested in seeing an elimination of the inequalities based on gender. If you are a male, you likely have a female relative who is impacted by gender inequalities. Thus, gender inequality is not something only for women to address; men have a responsibility to recognize how they have contributed to the problem, much in the same way that race and ethnicity has a long and uncomfortable history with the way these groups have been treated.

Part of the solution, of course, is to not tolerate inequalities when you see them. Especially if you are a male, one of the things you can do is to speak up against the catcalling that occurs against women in public places and to hold your friends accountable for telling sexist jokes or making lewd comments about women in public. In the workplace, make space to amplify the voices and contributions of female colleagues. It is only when men see the real value of women as equal partners and not as some sort of threat, that women will be afforded the type treatment to which they are entitled.

If you are a woman, there are also steps that you can take to address the problem. It is indeed tempting to lash out at any perceived or real threat against women, particularly those instances where women are objectified and seen as sex objects. However, rarely does a forceful and angry approach convince people to change their behavior. It is understandable, though, that changing people's understanding of the role of women can be time-consuming, exhausting, and more than a little frustrating. In a perfect world it shouldn't be up to women to expend the emotional energy to educate everyone else about oppression in general and women's oppression in particular. As it is the case for men who must step up and take exception to the mistreatment of women, one way to consider this effort is to think of it as part of society's resocialization process, which often takes time and effort to achieve positive results.

CONCLUSION

Inequalities based on gender play a critical role in the definition and treatment of women in society. While there is some reason to be optimistic about positive changes, there is still much to do before women can feel as though they are on equal footing to men. Thus, the issue is not so much about whether you think men and women are the same, but rather that one group is discriminated against and mistreated based on physical characteristics or other factors that have little to do with whether they should be given opportunities to achieve equality.

Some things are in fact improving. According to the Center for American Women and Politics, in 2019 there were 126 women who held seats in the United States Congress: 25 in the Senate and 101 in the House of Representatives (Center for American Women and Politics, 2020). The number of women graduating from medical and law schools continue to outpace men, and the number of women in leadership positions in higher education and in corporate America also continue to increase. This is not to say that the tasks are complete and we need not do any more to further the issue of equality between men and women, but it also indicates that progress is in fact occurring.

Finally, it is important to note what we might call intersectionality with regard to gender. That means we should pay attention to the interplay between gender and things like race and ethnicity; gender and social class issues, such as poverty, and gender and sexual orientation. These are important issues alone but they do not occur in isolation. In fact, some experts argue that being Black and a woman is a form of double marginality, since discrimination comes as a result of both of those categories.

YOU MAKE THE CALL: GENDER STEREOTYPES AND CHILDREN

You are a fourth-grade teacher in a private K–12 and your class is made up of about 15 students, with eight girls and seven boys. One boy, Alex, is new to the school, having just transferred in the fall. Alex is a shy but thoughtful ten-year-old, who is smaller than most of the children in his class and does not really seem interested in playing with the other boys. Those boys like to roughhouse, and their imaginative play usually involves some sort of wrestling, competition, or physical activity. Because of his small stature and quiet personality, Alex has not really fit in well with this group, despite repeated requests from the other boys to play with them. Alex is content to sit in a corner with a book or to sit with the girls as they talk about various topics that might traditionally be seen as "feminine."

As the teacher, you worry that Alex may encounter difficulty fitting in over time, particularly as the classes are small and the students are likely to progress together through subsequent grades and into middle school. You want Alex to fit in, but the stereotypical behavior the boys are engaging in doesn't seem to fit with Alex's personality. The girls are friendly and welcome, but you wonder if they will always allow him to be a part of their group either, particularly as they grow older.

As someone invested in the well-being of your students, you wonder if it is your place to help Alex better integrate into the class, particularly with the boys. You already see evidence of gender-appropriate behavior and how this can shape students' perceptions of themselves and others, as they interact. At the same time, one of the benefits of a small school experience is that it provides the freedom for children to figure out who they are and what they want to be—Alex may simply be one of those children who is uncomfortable around aggressive people and might even be a bit of an introvert—is it really your job to push him out of his comfort zone and try to change his personality?

At some point you realize that the boys in the class will begin to exclude Alex and may even engage in a bit of taunting, as is often the case with people who violate gender-specific activities. You want to be proactive and know that Alex could be friends with many of the boys; all of whom are kind, considerate, and polite—but still remain a bit of a wild bunch. You also have to be mindful of the role you play in Alex's development in terms of your own gender, so what do you do?

Questions for you to consider:

1. Do you take a hands-off approach and allow Alex to figure out how he wants to interact with the boys, knowing that this could potentially be a problem if he continues to refrain from participating in the activities with the other boys?
2. Do you encourage Alex to find his own pathway and if that means interacting with the girls in the classroom, that's perfectly acceptable and he should not be made to feel inadequate for his choices?
3. Do you try to create activities where Alex's talents and abilities can be seen and experienced by the other boys, so they realize he has something to offer them and even excels beyond their abilities?
4. Do you pull Alex aside and try to encourage him to engage with the boys and "toughen up" a little so that he can make friends and feel a part of the class—which will be particularly important given that these are the children he will grow up with if he remains at the school?

SUMMARY

- Define gender and contrast the differences between gender and sex.
    - Sex is defined as the biological difference between males and females.
    - Gender is a social category that constructs roles and defines behaviors for men and women.
    - Children are socialized into acceptable societal roles for their gender.
- Summarize the history and current state of the Women's Movement in the United States.
    - Women's struggle for equal rights has spanned much of our nation's history and has laid the groundwork for the

advancement of women to their present-day social status.
- The first wave of feminism occurred in the nineteenth and early twentieth centuries and focused on women's legal rights.
- The second wave of the feminist movement peaked in the 1960s and 1970s and focused on the emergence of a formal identity for women.
- The third wave of feminism began in the 1980s and addresses issues of equal rights from *within* the political and legal establishments.
- The fourth wave of feminism is highlighted by events such as the #MeTooMovement and The Time's Up movement, and greater involvement of women in politics.

- Describe gender socialization and the social institutions that contribute to it.
    - The differences in the ways women and men understand their roles and meet societal expectations relates to how they are socialized.
    - Society constructs people's perceptions of what is acceptable and expected of men and women.
    - Parents and typically create gender stereotypes for children by treating babies of each sex differently.
    - Schools, the media, and peers contribute to perpetuating inflexible ideas about what it means to be a male or female in society.
- Analyze gender inequalities and life chances.
    - Stereotypical ideas and expectations about men and women and the roles they can play in society translate into particular life chances for women.
    - Inequalities faced by women in American society include the wage gap, the role of women in the military, the extent and type of victimization they experience, and sexual harassment.
    - The way society and US culture perceive and respond to women and their needs is reflected in all manner of interactions and relationships, something that occurs both in the United States as well as in other countries.
- Compare sociological theories of gender and how they explain the inequalities that exist.
    - Though heavily criticized as perpetuating the oppression of women, functionalists argue that differences in wages and salaries are based on the particular talents of certain individuals who are willing to undergo extraordinary training to enhance these skills. Functionalists would further point out that women and men differ in their particular skill sets, with women being more nurturing and compassionate; they might bring different but equally valuable capabilities to a task.
    - Conflict theorists examine social inequalities based on gender and attribute them to power differentials.
    - From a symbolic interactionist perspective, the study of gender and inequality focuses on micro-level interactions and relationships.
    - Feminist theory offers multiple perspectives useful to an understanding of gender-based inequality. Among these are liberal feminism, phenomenological feminism, socialist feminism, Marxist feminism, and radical feminism. There are five general principles on

which feminists agree: equality, human choice, elimination of sexual violence; elimination of social stratification based on gender; and sexual freedom.

- Summarize effective solutions to gender inequality.
    - The Community Advocacy Project (CAP) is an evidence-based program is designed to help survivors of intimate partner abuse regain control of their lives. The project has been shown to decrease survivors' risk of re-victimization and to increase their quality of life, level of social support, and ability to obtain the community resources they need.

KEY TERMS

#MeToo movement 267
Comparable worth 271
Expressive tasks 278
Feminism 266
Feminist movements 266
Gender 262
Instrumental tasks 278
Liberal feminism 280
Marxist feminism 281
Patriarchal society 281
Phenomenological feminism 281
Radical feminism 281
Second shift 272
Sex 262
Sexism 262
Sexual harassment 276
Socialist feminism 281
Wage gap 270

Discussion Questions

1. While one does not have to adopt the label "feminist" to support the notion of equality for women, which of the feminist theories makes the most sense to you? What do you think is the main differences between them?
2. Has the #Me Too movement raised awareness about sexual assault against women or has it created a backlash by men, where prominent figures, such as President Trump and Jeopardy host Alex Tribek have argued that it is a "dangerous time to be a man" in the United States?
3. Debate the merits of women in the military. What roles, if any, should women be allowed to play in the armed services and what are the potential challenges for such a policy?
4. Is there really a wage gap between men and women? If so, why do you think it persists? If not, what are the arguments used to minimize the differences in salaries between men and women?

Learn more with this chapter's digital tools, including Data and Media Literacy Exercises, flashcards, and chapter self-assessments at **www.oup.com/he/mcnamara**.

10

Love Is Love: Sexuality and Sexual Behavior

LEARNING OBJECTIVES

- Define sexual orientation and describe various types of sexual identity.
- Summarize the history of the experiences of LGBTQs in the United States.
- Analyze some of the issues and challenges for LGBTQ people in the United States.
- Analyze the challenges for LGBTQ people in the criminal justice system.
- Summarize sociological explanations of the inequalities LGBTQ groups encounter.
- Describe effective programs to address issues surrounding sexuality in the United States.
- Summarize what individuals can do in addressing the challenges many LGBTQ persons face.

Chapter Outline

Rally for equal justice LGBTQ activists gather at the Supreme Court on October 8, 2019 as the Justices consider three cases dealing with workplace discrimination based on sexual orientation.

In recent years, movements to address inequalities and oppressions faced by LGBTQ people have gained social momentum as well as legislative accomplishment. Yet even as the topic of sexual orientation has become part of our civic discourse, on an interpersonal level it can still evoke strong feelings. Many people (including many people with social capital, such as politicians and religious leaders) still feel strongly that heterosexuality is the "normal" lifestyle, and that any alternatives pose a threat to the status quo.

Our primary objective in this chapter is not to get you to change your personal opinion on the social acceptability of one's sexual orientation or identity. Rather, our objective is to offer insight into how sexual identities are formed, along with the challenges faced by people whose identities are not part of the mainstream. As we observed in Chapter 1, our social interaction with others often depends on very little information about the identities, beliefs, and behaviors of individuals. We tend to label and stereotype each other based on broad social categories rather than objective assessment. Such labels have enormous influence over the way we interact with people, as well as their standing in society.

A secondary objective for this chapter is to understand the ways in which certain minority groups (in this case, LGBTQ people) are treated. As a society, we are only recently beginning to understand ways in which discrimination and prejudice experienced by LGBTQ people are similar to and different from the obstacles faced by members of other minority groups.

Finally, we will compare the issue of sexuality and sexual identity in the United States to how other countries around the world have responded to and resolved the inequalities faced by LGBTQ people. Many countries accept people of diverse sexual orientation and provide mechanisms to prevent oppression and discrimination in the same way they would any other group of people targeted for unfair treatment. There may be lessons here for the United States that could result in changes to social policy.

SOCIOLOGICAL STORY TIME

- In a move that is seen as an attempt to scale back the rights of LGBTQ people, President Trump announced in October 2018 that he was considering revoking civil rights protections for transgender people and further requiring that all US citizens identify themselves by the gender listed on their birth certificates. The proposed policy stated gender would be determined by a "biological basis that is clear, grounded in science, objective, and administrable." (Sampathkumar, 2018).
- A recent report by Human Rights Watch indicate trends in discrimination against LGBTQ populations. In a nationally representative survey conducted by the Center for American Progress in 2017, 8 percent of lesbian, gay, and bisexual respondents and 29% of transgender respondents reported that a health care provider had refused to see them because of their sexual orientation or gender identity in the past year. Interviewees described being denied counseling and therapy, refused fertility treatments, denied a checkup or other primary care services, and in one instance, told that a pediatrician's religious beliefs precluded her from evaluating a same-sex couple's 6-day-old child (Human Rights Watch, 2018).
- In July 2017, then-President Trump reversed an Obama-era commitment to allow transgender people to serve in the military. In March 2019, the Department of Defense issued a new policy, which allows transgender people to serve only in their biological sex, and only if they have not had a recent diagnosis of gender dysphoria—a feeling of distress that can occur when a person's gender identity differs from their sex assigned at birth (Naylor, 2020). As one of his first acts in office, President Joseph Biden reversed Trump's ban.
- A ruling by the 7th Circuit Court of Appeals found that the US Civil Rights Act prohibits workplace discrimination against LGBTQ employees. The ruling came from a case of an employee who sued Ivy Tech Community College that the school violated Title VII of the Civil Rights Act of 1964 when it denied her employment (DeVogue, 2017).

DEFINING SEXUAL ORIENTATION

Sexuality is a broad term that is used to describe sexual behavior and desires. Sociologists use the term to describe sexual orientation or identity. In the same way that "Asian American" does do not constitute a single homogeneous category, sexual orientation also comprises a tremendously diverse range of individual experiences, relationships, and behaviors. It is overly simplistic to think of sexual orientation as binary; that is, either "gay" or "straight." Further, it is important to remember that sexuality is just one part of how an individual perceives their identity and status; the intersection of sexuality with gender, race, and class means that no two LGBTQ people experience either opportunity or oppression in the same way.

People who identify heterosexual (straight) feel desire primarily for people of the opposite sex. People who identify as homosexual (gay or lesbian) feel desire primarily for people of the same sex. According to the National Survey of Sexual Health and Behavior, about five percent of adults in the United States identify themselves as gay or lesbian. About 3 percent of males and 4 percent of women consider themselves to be bisexual, or attracted to both sexes. A much smaller percentage of US adults identify as asexual, or not sexually attracted to any group.

The word "homosexual" was first used in Germany in 1869. It appeared in a political pamphlet intended to protest the criminalization of sodomy in the German constitution. The term coincided with increased public awareness of gay male life in urban Europe and North America, as well as increased policing and punishment of gay men. Interestingly, despite a long history of males and females engaging in same sex relationships, the inclusion of lesbian relationships as it relates to public opinion or societal laws, has been largely ignored (Morris, 2017).

Sexual orientation is a sexual attraction toward people either of the same gender, the opposite sex, or both. Sexual identity is now understood to be fluid, and while individuals may self-identify as heterosexual or homosexual, it is important to acknowledge that identification does not necessarily correspond to behavior. For example, many heterosexuals have had homosexual encounters, and vice versa. Simply because a person engages in homosexual activity does not mean that he or she must be a homosexual (Mustanski et al., 2014).

The biologist and sexologist Alfred Kinsey's studies in the 1940s and 1950s American males and females found that 37 percent of males and 13 percent of females in his sample had at least one homosexual encounter (Kinsey, 1948; Kinsey, et al., 1953). In the 20th century, psychiatry attempted to explain homosexuality by attempting to link homosexual behavior to childhood trauma or abusive adult sexual relationships. More recent research has contributed to an understanding that sexual orientation is complex and not simply a matter of "choice" (Ganna et al., 2019; Ghose, 2015).

This has led to considerable cultural controversy, as both science and popular culture argue that individuals are "born this way" while other political and religious figures insist that homosexuality is a learned or chosen behavior that is disordered and should be changed. Some biologists argue that homosexuality might be related to hormonal imbalances in the mother during pregnancy. Others argue that homosexuality might be related to brain functioning. Some studies have shown that homosexual men react differently to human pheromones than heterosexual men (Zhou, et al., 2014). Whatever the explanation, most theorists agree that homosexual orientation tends to arise at an early age (Ganna et al., 2019; Ghose, 2015).

For most of the twentieth century, the term **queer** was used (often disparagingly) to describe homosexual men. By the 1990s, the term was reclaimed by gay, lesbian, and bisexual people. **Queer theory**, a branch of academic critical theory that attempts to understand social and cultural issues through a queer lens, emerged at about the same time. Queer theory rejects the notion of a binary heterosexual/homosexual identity categorization as oppressive. Instead, queer theory suggests that queerness reflects the nuances and gaps between artificially constructed categories based on sexuality. In fact, the term "queer" is broader in scope than either "gay" or "trans," and has led to a more comprehensive discussion about society's ideas about gender and sexual identities (McCann and Monaghan, 2019; Sullivan, 2003).

As discussions of how to define sexual orientation and identity continue to evolve, many activists argue that other groups who have been oppressed for their sexuality should be acknowledged. Thus, the acronym **LGBTQIA,** which includes intersex and asexual people, is considered more appropriate by activists and may be more familiar to you on your campus or in your community. For the purposes of this chapter's study of social problems as they relate to sexuality, we will continue to use the acronym **LGBTQ** to include all the groups that define themselves on the basis of their sexual orientation and who experience some level of discrimination and mistreatment. This is not to negate the value or importance of intersex and asexual people, but to recognize some mechanism is needed for the purposes of discussion. There are instances, however, where the term homosexual or gay is used, primarily as part of the historical chronology of the development of the larger sexual identity discussion.

THE HISTORY OF LGBTQ PEOPLE IN THE UNITED STATES

The perception of homosexuality in American culture has evolved over the course of history from sinful conduct to a disease model to the development of gay identities (Bronski, 2012). Religious institutions have been largely responsible for the overall cultural condemnation of homosexuality. In colonial America, ministers cited Scripture to justify the harsh punishment inflicted on homosexuals. In every colony, sodomy was a capital offense while other homosexual acts, such as lewdness between women, were punished with whippings and fines (Bronski, 2012).

Sodomy and "crimes against nature" continued to be criminalized through the 19th century, and sexual activity between women was also increasingly criminalized. By the late 19th century, the medical profession diagnosed homosexuality as a form of mental illness. The development of Freudian psychoanalysis led many physicians and psychiatrists to conclude that homosexuality was an acquired affliction that required medical treatment. Some of that "treatment" was barbaric; electroshock therapy, lobotomy, hysterectomy, and even castration was used in an attempt to "cure" people of homosexuality (Brooks, 2015).

The development of psychiatry during this period also reinforced the medical model used to understand and treat homosexuality. Reflecting the attitudes, values, and beliefs about homosexuality at the time, many states enacted sexual psychopath laws to regulate consensual sex among same-sex partners. This medical model translated into behavior deemed criminal for some adults. Not only were homosexuals determined to be in need of treatment, and more likely to spend time in mental institutions, district attorneys often used the sexual psychopath laws to criminally prosecute them (Rupp and Freeman, 2017).

Despite these risks, in the late 19th century, a homosexual urban subculture began to emerge. At first certain parks, streets, and bath houses became meeting places for gay men. Bars and clubs also appeared in or near **red-light districts** (centers for prostitution) of major cities. By the 1920s and 1930s, this subculture was flourishing (Bronski, 2012; Brooks, 2015; Rupp and Freeman, 2017).

After World War II ended, as many soldiers returned to cities rather than going home to small towns, the number of gay bars in urban areas began to increase (Marcus, 2002; Bronski, 2012; Rupp and Freeman, 2017). In the 1950s, during the time of the Cold War, not only communists perceived as a threat to the American way of life, but Senate investigations portrayed homosexuals as a threat as well. In fact, this perception was so pervasive that President Dwight D. Eisenhower issued an executive order barring gay men and lesbians from all federal jobs. In response, state and local governments followed suit as did many companies in the private sector. The FBI created a surveillance program against homosexuals, and local police departments conducted undercover operations in gay bars, making mass arrests on a regular basis. Wichita, Dallas, Memphis, and Seattle were among the cities that most intensely persecuted the gay community, averaging 100 misdemeanor charges against gay men and lesbians per month (Bronski, 2012; Brooks, 2015).

In the 1960s, as the Civil Rights Movement and protests against the Vietnam War convulsed society and brought demands for social justice to the forefront of the cultural agenda,, the gay community began to organize politically. By 1969, nearly 50 gay rights organizations existed in the United States, with membership running in the thousands. When police in New York City raided the Stonewall Inn, a gay bar in New York City's Greenwich Village, on June 27, 1969, the gay community fought back. The angry response from patrons resulted in three nights of rioting and violence in the City. The **Stonewall uprising** also spawned the "Gay Power" movement. A massive grassroots gay liberation movement began, similar to that of Blacks, women, and college students of that era (Marcus, 2002; Faderman, 2016).

Like their militant counterparts, gay people challenged both how they were perceived by society at large as well as how they were treated by social institutions. They sought to change the narrative, proclaiming that their lifestyle was "alternative" rather than "deviant." The phrase "coming out of the closet" was born during this time to solidify their identity and their presence in (as well as value to) the larger society. By 1973, there were almost 800 gay and lesbian organizations in the United States. By 1990, the number was several thousand (Faderman, 2016; Brooks, 2015).

The Stonewall Inn This New York City gay bar is the site of the historic June 27, 1969, Stonewall Uprising that sparked a civil rights movement for LGBTQ people.

This politicization of the gay community resulted in changes in legislation, public policy, and the way gays were perceived by American society. Not only did half the states decriminalize homosexual behavior over the next 20 years, but public and political pressure reduced the number of police raids, harassment, and arrests as well. Many cities included sexual orientation in their civil rights statutes, and the American Psychiatric Association removed homosexuality from its list of mental illnesses in 1974. In 1975, the Civil Service Commission eliminated the ban on the employment of gays for federal jobs. In short, the gay and lesbian world was no longer hidden from public view. Gay people were increasingly visible: there were gay businesses, political clubs, and community centers. Gay candidates ran for public office (Faderman, 2016).

However, the "coming out" experience and homosexual identity was not universally welcomed. Mainstream society still had difficulty adjusting to the visible and militant presence of gays. The late 1970s and 1980s were a turbulent time for this community. Singer Anita Bryant, best known for her commercials promoting orange juice, began an anti-gay campaign in Dade County, Florida. Building on her momentum, by the 1980s, a conservative, Christian based anti-gay movement had begun. Fundamentalist ministers such as Jerry Falwell, who formed the Moral Majority, Inc., worked with other groups to oppose gay rights (Marcus, 2002; Rupp and Freeman, 2017).

The AIDS epidemic in the early 1980s intensified anti-gay groups' efforts against homosexuals, this time from a public health perspective. However, the threat of AIDS also galvanized the homosexual community. As a result, many gay organizations were created to address the practical consequences of infection with the disease as well as its

ACT UP The activist group ACT UP (AIDS Coalition to Unleash Power) was formed in 1987 to fight for a much stronger and more cohesive political, medical, and social response to AIDS.

treatment. While a catastrophic event in the lives of many gay men, their collective response to the social, medical, and political challenge of AIDS was instrumental in shaping and changing the gay rights movement (Faderman, 2016).

Despite great advances in recent years, such as the widespread acceptance of same-sex marriage, LGBTQ activists remain steadfast in their attempts to secure equal rights at a time when the public seems to be moving toward the legitimacy of a gay identity. However, the backlash against LGBTQ people can be seen in the ways that they are victimized and discriminated against in the criminal justice system.

CHALLENGES FACING LGTBQ PEOPLE

Like many minority groups, LGBTQ people face a wide range of challenges. As it is with others, much of the problem stems from the unfair treatment and access to societal resources. The issues facing LGBTQ people include various forms of prejudice and discrimination, problems surrounding same-sex marriage, workplace and housing discrimination, as well as their standing in the military.

Prejudice and Discrimination

While public opinion polls indicate there is growing acceptance of same-sex marriages and alternative lifestyles, people generally fear what they do not understand. In the case of the LGBTQ community, society continues to treat this group as abnormal and the target of mistreatment. Evidence of this trend is seen in the discriminatory behavior against LGBTQ people in parenting, at work, for those who wish to serve their country in the military, and in violent hate crimes.

Same-Sex Marriages and Parenting

While the topic of **same-sex marriage** remains a controversial subject (Chapter 9), in the United States there is increasing support for these types of marriages. In 2019, a survey conducted by the Pew Research Center show that almost two-thirds of Americans support the idea of same-sex marriage (Pew Research Center, 2019; Masci, Brown, and Kiley, 2019).

That said, while there has been a dramatic overall increase in support for same-sex marriage, there remain pockets of opposition to it. For instance, among white evangelical Protestants, only about 29 percent favor same-sex marriage, with 63 percent

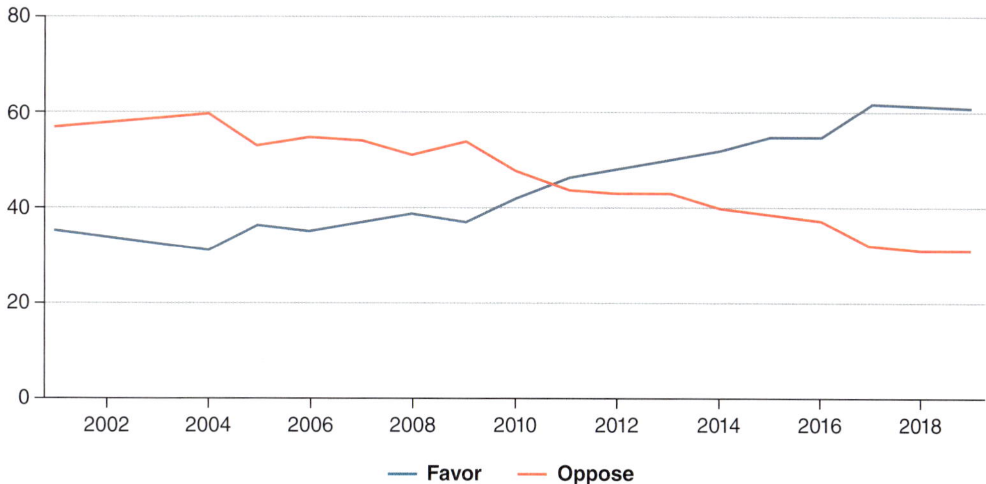

Figure 10.1 Trends in public opinion about same-sex marriage Percent of US adults who favor/oppose same-sex marriage, 2001–2019.

opposed (Pew Research Center, 2019). These figures are in contrast to public opinion about same-sex marriage ten years earlier (Figure 10.1).

A 5–4 decision in 2015 by the US Supreme Court in *Obergefell v. Hodges* declared that same-sex marriages are constitutional, making it easier for same-sex couples to marry. The ruling legalized same-sex marriage, including in the 14 states that did not previously allow gays and lesbians to wed. The justices ruled that limiting marriage only to heterosexual couples violates the amendment's guarantee of equal protection under the law (Masci, Brown, and Kiley, 2019). While one might think that this settles the issue, the controversy is far from over. One of the most significant issues relating to same-sex marriage (as well as **domestic partnerships**, in which same-sex couples have chosen not to marry but still want the rights and privileges of a married couple), involves parental rights.

Parental rights refer to all of the legal rights and obligations that are associated with being a parent of a child. This includes physical custody, the right to visitation with the child, the right to inherit property from the child and to have parents leave things for their child to inherit, the right to consent for medical treatment, and the ability to contract on behalf of the child, among other rights.

According to the Williams Institute at the UCLA School of Law, by 2017 there were about 114,000 same-sex couples in the United States who were raising children. According to the study, most same-sex couples who are raising children have biological children (68 percent), but same-sex couples are significantly more likely than different-sex couples to be raising adopted or foster children. One in five same-sex couples (21.4 percent) are raising adopted children compared to just 3 percent of different-sex couples,

Family pride Children representing COLAGE (Children of Lesbians and Gays Everywhere) march in the 2009 Northampton, MA Gay Pride Parade.

and 2.9 percent of same-sex couples have foster children compared to 0.4 percent of different-sex couples (Williams Institute, 2018).

Children enter LGBTQ families in ways similar to many heterosexual families. For instance, in some cases one LGBTQ partner may have been in a heterosexual relationship and is the biological and legal parent of the child. This can create challenges for the non-biological parent in that they have no legal standing with the child. About two-thirds of all children under the age of 18 living with a same-sex couple have one who is their biological parent (Williams Institute, 2018).

Other children arrive through adoption, surrogacy, or foster care. Estimates vary, but about 20 percent of same-sex couples who have children in the household have acquired them through adoption. Part of the burden for LGBTQ couples, as it is with all adoptions, is that they must show that they will be fit parents and the child's development will not be affected by the parents' sexual orientation (Williams Institute, 2018).

With regard to same-sex couples serving as foster parents (Chapter 11), many LGBTQ couples have experienced discrimination when attempting to become foster parents. While most states do not prohibit LGBTQ couples from becoming foster parents, some couples have experienced challenges because of the misguided notion that foster children raised by same-sex foster parents will witness immoral conduct or be "recruited" into homosexuality as a result. Many advocacy groups that successfully countered such arguments and gay rights advocates are more optimistic about social norms regarding adoption and fostering children. The issue is properly whether the couple can act in the best interests of the child and be successful parents, not their sexual orientation.

Moreover, according to the Williams Institute, there is ample research to suggest that same-sex couples can be just as effective at parenting as heterosexual couples.

Workplace Discrimination

In recent years, LGBTQ people have had to resort to legal action against companies that have discriminated against them on the basis of sexual orientation. In a 2018 survey by the Human Rights Campaign, almost half of LGBTQ employees do not feel they can reveal their sexual orientation in the workplace. The report, found that 46 percent of LGBTQ employees are not open about their sexuality at work for fear of being stereotyped, making people feel uncomfortable or losing connections with coworkers. This figure has not changed in more than ten years, despite the fact that many companies have created anti-discrimination policies. Although many companies have invested in creating non-discrimination policies and inclusive benefit packages, 31 states still don't have fully inclusive nondiscrimination protections for LGBTQ people. The responses to the survey present a conflicting picture:

- 80 percent of non-LGBTQ employees believe no one should have to hide who they are at work.
- 59 percent of non-LGBTQ employees said they think it's unprofessional to talk about sexual orientation and gender identity in the workplace.
- 36 percent of non-LGBTQ employees said they would feel uncomfortable hearing an LGBTQ colleague talk about dating.
- 20 percent of LGBTQ workers report having been told that they should dress in a more feminine or masculine manner (compared to 1 in 24 non-LGBTQ workers).
- 53 percent of LGBTQ workers report hearing jokes about lesbian or gay people at least once in a while.

Because of the stigma that is still associated with being a member of the LGBTQ community, workers who might otherwise share personal information about themselves and their families with their colleagues, cannot do so. This can result in social isolation from peers and even outright discrimination by supervisors (Yancey-Bragg, 2018).

From a legal standpoint, until 2020, the courts were divided on the issue of granting LGBTQ people the same protections afforded other groups. For instance, The US Court of Appeals for the Eleventh Circuit declined to hear a case involving a child welfare worker who claims he was fired because of his sexual orientation. The question before the court was whether protections ensured by Title VII of the Civil Rights Act of 1964 extend to sexual orientation, in addition to race, national origin, religion and sex. The issue has divided federal appeals courts, as well as government agencies. The other case from the Second Circuit, *Zarda v. Altitude Express*, was heard before a full panel, which found that Title VII protections should extend to gay workers. That ruling followed the same result in the Seventh Circuit, *Hively v. Ivy Tech Community College*, mentioned in the Sociological Story Time segment at the beginning of this chapter.

The US Supreme Court clarified several of the issues in *Bostock v. Clayton County, Georgia*, No. 17-1618 (S. Ct. June 15, 2020). In that case, the Supreme Court held that firing individuals because of their sexual orientation or transgender status violates Title VII's prohibition on discrimination because of sex. As the Court explained, "discrimination based on homosexuality or transgender status necessarily entails discrimination based on sex; the first cannot happen without the second" (US Equal Employment Opportunity Commission, 2020).

Until the Bostock case, sexual orientation was not considered a protected category by the courts. The **US Equal Employment Opportunity Commission** and gay rights advocates have instead argued that sexual orientation should be considered a protected category under sex discrimination under Title VII. In some of these cases, the US

Justice Department has argued against such protections, furthering the position of the Trump administration that LGBTQ people should not be protected (Mulvaney, 2018).

Housing Discrimination

The **Federal Fair Housing Act of 1968**, which focuses on discrimination on the basis of race, color, religion, sex or national origin, was further amended in 1988 to provide protections against discrimination against families with children and people with physical or mental disabilities. However, the Fair Housing Act does not provide protection for LGBTQ people against discrimination.

In July 2017, a study by the Urban Institute found a pattern of discrimination against gay men and transgender people in three major cities in the United States. Researchers attempted to compare the housing experiences of gay men to heterosexual men and lesbians to heterosexual women. In this study, researchers posed as qualified renters who differed only in their sexual orientation. Another variation of this study was conducted in Washington, DC comparing the experiences of transgender and non-transgender people seeking a rental home (Levy et. al, 2017).

The study found that gay men and transgender people were treated differently by landlords and management companies. Gay men were told there were fewer units available, were quoted higher prices, and were less likely to schedule appointments to show gay men the available units. Transgender people had similar experiences compared to non-transgender people as well (Levy et al., 2017).

While federal law does not protect LGBTQ people from discrimination on the basis of sexual orientation, more than 20 states have laws prohibiting such discrimination. Much of the justification for addressing discrimination against LGBTQ people comes from the Fair Housing Act of 1968, and this research points to some of the nuances of how discrimination unfolds in the early stages of LGBTQ renters and the impact of that discrimination (Levy et al., 2017). Such studies increasingly show the need for protection of LGBTQ people beyond what is offered by the Fair Housing Act of 1968 (Levy et al., 2017).

Discrimination in The Military

In 1993, President Bill Clinton attempted to overturn the existing ban on gays and lesbians serving in the military. The prevailing policy at that time was that while many gay and lesbians had indeed served in the military, such individuals were assumed to present a security risk because of their vulnerability to blackmail if their sexual orientation was discovered. President Clinton attempted to dispel such a notion, but military and religious leaders strongly opposed an elimination of the ban. In 1993, Clinton issued a policy where military officers could no longer ask about a person's sexual orientation. Under such a rule, which became known as **don't ask, don't tell,** as long as service members did not reveal their sexual identities and as long as their sexual behaviors were not discovered, they could remain in good standing in the military.

President George W. Bush continued to support this policy during his administration. When President Obama was elected, he vowed to end the "don't ask, don't tell" policy, which Congress ultimately did in 2010. Obama felt that the law's constitutionality would eventually be challenged and likely overturned by the courts, so he took a more proactive approach to repealing the law conventionally.

The issue of gays in the military took different turn under President Trump, particularly as it relates to transgender people. As noted in Sociological Story Time, Trump's original plan was to deny recruits' applications or to not move forward on their processing until the official policy on transgender people in the military could be changed. This came at a time when personnel shortages have been reported in the military and when many members of the LGBTQ community have applied to various military branches. The current policy allows transgender people to serve only in their biological sex, and only if they have not had a recent diagnosis of gender dysphoria. When he took office in January 2021, one of the first acts of President Joseph Biden was to reverse Trump's decision, and transgender people can now serve in the military.

Criminal Victimization and Hate Crime

On April 23, 1990, Congress passed the Hate Crime Statistics Act, which mandated that data be collected "about crimes that manifest evidence of prejudice based on race, religion, sexual orientation, or ethnicity." Management of this data was given to the FBI and the Uniform Crime Reporting program.

In 1994, Congress augmented the Hate Crime Statistics Act by passing the Violent Crime and Law Enforcement Act of 1994. This act expanded the scope of the Hate Crime Statistics Act by including bias against persons with disabilities. In 1996, Congress mandated that hate crime data become a permanent part of the Uniform Crime Reporting program. (US Department of Justice, 2020).

In 2018, there were over 16,000 law enforcement agencies participating in the Hate Crime Statistics program. Of approximately 7,120 hate crimes reported, about 58 percent were motivated by race/ethnicity/ancestry bias, about 20 percent based on religious bias, and about 17 percent related to sexual orientation bias (Figure 10.2).

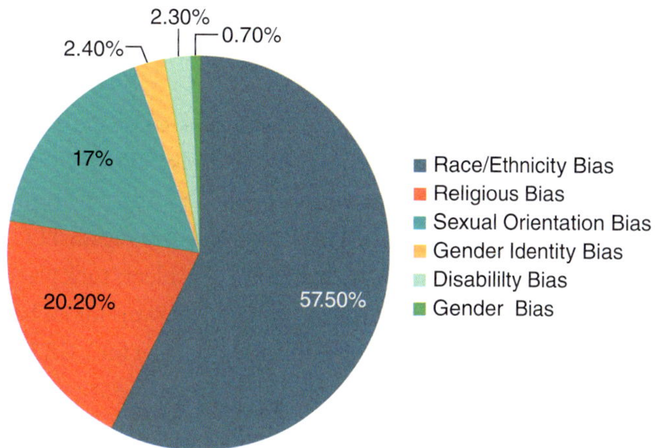

Figure 10.2 Hate crime statistics by motivation bias Source: U.S. Department of Justice, 2020

Focusing specifically on sexual orientation and gender identity bias (Table 10.1), there were 1,196 incidents of hate crimes with 1,404 offenses, with 1,445 victims and 1,268 offenders in 2018. In most instances, the motivation behind the acts involved an anti-gay (male) bias, although more

Table 10.1 Incidents, Offenses, Victims, and Known Offenders by Bias Motivation, 2018

Bias Motivation	Incidents	Offenses	Victims[1]	Known offenders[2]
Total	**7,120**	**8,496**	**8,819**	**6,266**
Single-Bias Incidents	**7,036**	**8,327**	**8,646**	**6,188**
Sexual Orientation:	**1,196**	**1,404**	**1,445**	**1,268**
Anti-Gay (Male)	726	839	863	841
Anti-Lesbian	129	171	177	105
Anti-Lesbian, Gay, Bisexual, or Transgender (Mixed Group)	303	353	360	294
Anti-Heterosexual	17	20	24	13
Anti-Bisexual	21	21	21	15
Gender:	**47**	**58**	**61**	**38**
Anti-Male	22	26	28	21
Anti-Female	25	32	33	17
Gender Identity:	**168**	**184**	**189**	**180**
Anti-Transgender	142	157	160	156
Anti-Gender Non-Conforming	26	27	29	24
Multiple-Bias Incidents3	**84**	**169**	**173**	**78**

[1]*The term* victim *may refer to an individual, business/financial institution, government entity, religious organization, or society/public as a whole.*

[2]*The term* known offender *does not imply the suspect's identity is known; rather, the term indicates some aspect of the suspect was identified, thus distinguishing the suspect from an unknown offender.*

[3]*A* multiple-bias incident *is an incident in which one or more offense types are motivated by two or more biases.*

Source: FBI/UCR https://ucr.fbi.gov/hate-crime/2018/tables/table-1.xls

than 25 percent consisted of a mixture of bias against lesbians, bisexuals or transgender people. The data also indicated that gender identity related hate crimes, about 184 cases, consist primarily of an anti-transgender bias (US Department of Justice, 2020).

Most hate crime incidents against LGBTQ people reflected similar trends against other groups. That is, most incidents took place in or near residences (between 25 and 29 percent for LGBTQ and 25.7 percent for all hate crimes) and on or near some type of roadway (between 19 and 22 percent for LGBTQ people and 18.7 percent for all hate crimes). The remaining incidents occurred at a variety of other locations, including schools and houses of worship, commercial and government buildings, restaurants and nightclubs, parking lots and garages, playgrounds and parks, and even medical facilities.

Hate crime victims can be individuals, businesses, government entities, religious organizations, or society as a whole, and they can be committed against persons, property, or society. In 2018, law enforcement reported overall that 65.5 percent of hate crimes were against individuals, with approximately 31 percent as crimes against property. As it is similar with most of the hate crime data, victimization trends of LGBTQ people are similar to what all hate crime victims experience. For instance, overall most hate crimes against persons consist of intimidation (30.1 percent) or simple assault (22.3 percent), addition, about 22 percent of hate crimes involve destruction of property or vandalism. The data on LGBTQ victimization reflects similar percentages on all these variables (US Department of Justice, 2019).

CHALLENGES FOR LGBTQ PEOPLE IN THE CRIMINAL JUSTICE SYSTEM

Gender and sexuality impact law enforcement practices, interactions with court personnel and its operation, and the correctional system. Each of these branches of the criminal justice system has a host of challenges related to gender and sexuality. Each agent of the criminal justice system will be considered next, along with how sexuality impacts practitioners within the system as well.

LGBTQ People and the Police

One area of interaction between LGBTQ people and the police in which research has shown evidence of bias is in the standards used by police to stop and search suspects. For example, it is common for LGBTQ people (especially women, transgender people, and youth) to be perceived as involved in sex work. As such, police in some jurisdictions use possession of condoms by suspects as evidence supporting arrests for prostitution-related offenses (Hanssenset al., 2014). Another study pointed out that LGBTQ people are often targets of harassment by the police. Transgender people of color in particular are three times more likely to be victims of harassment and assault than non-transgender people. However, according to the National Coalition of Anti-Violence Programs, about half of the survivors who reported the violence to the police also reported incidents of police misconduct (National Coalition of Anti-Violence Programs, 2012).

In a 2015 national survey of LGBTQ people, a quarter of respondents who had recently had contact with the police reported at least one type of misconduct or harassment, including false arrests, verbal or physical assault by officers. Moreover, LGBTQ people of color were five times more likely to be asked about their immigration status by police officers than White survey respondents (James et al., 2017).

It should therefore not be surprising that many LGBTQ respondents in the study were uncomfortable seeking the help of the police should they need it (James et al., 2017). Yet given the fact that homelessness, poverty, and other social challenges further marginalize this group, the likelihood of victimization is much higher than the rest of the population. In fact, one 2012 study found that, over the previous decade, the police had been among the top three categories of offenders against LGBTQ people (National Coalition of Anti-Violence Programs, 2012).

Because many LGBTQ youth are homeless or housing challenged (by one estimate LGBTQ youth make up 40 percent of all homeless youth in the United States), LGBTQ people are impacted by police sweeps as well as by laws that restrict the use of public spaces (James et al., 2017; Greenblatt, 2013; Human Rights Campaign, 2012). According to one report, about half to two-thirds of homeless LGBTQ youth in New York reported that they had been stopped, searched, threatened with arrest or falsely arrested by police, compared to only 25 percent of LGBTQ youth who live in their own apartments (James et al., 2017; Welfare Warriors Research Collaboration, 2010). Further, LGBTQ people face further challenges when they are arrested. According to the National Prison Rape Elimination Commission, as well as reports by human rights organizations, women and LGBTQ people in police custody often experience unlawful searches and sexual assaults while in detention. Some of these searches and assaults, either on the street or in lock up, are ostensibly for the purpose of assigning a gender to detainees, but it is a short step from that to abuse (James et al., 2017; National Prison Rape Elimination Commission, 2011; Harrell, 2013).

The Courts and LGBTQ People

The LGBTQ community has also faced challenges in the courts. Some scholars argue that the status of homosexuals in society is reflected in the kind of treatment they get by the courts. This is particularly true regarding **jury bias.** Trial by jury is a cornerstone of the US legal system in this country. A jury is required to be composed of a fair cross-section of the population. If a jury is biased against LGBTQ people, a defendant might be convicted for being a homosexual rather than for the crime they have committed. Further, jury bias against LGBTQ people can raise questions about the credibility of a gay witness even though this should have no bearing on whether they are telling the truth. Bias against LGBTQ people can also result in reduced sentences against an offender who victimizes a member of the LGBTQ community since the jury might perceive the victim as deserving of what happened to him or her (Brunelli, 2004). Thus, the composition of juries, their perceptions of LGBTQ people, and how sexuality factors into jury decisions all play a role in understanding the relationship between LGBTQ people and the justice system.

One example of jury bias is how defendants who victimize gay people are treated. According to the **homosexual advance theory,** courts may allow a non-violent homosexual advance to constitute sufficient provocation to incite a reasonable man to "lose his self-control and kill in the heat of passion, thus mitigating murder to manslaughter." The homosexual advance theory is different from self-defense in that it does not attempt to justify the behavior of the offender. Rather, the theory states that it is a mitigating factor that should reduce the severity of the crime. While not all courts allow this theory to be introduced in homicide cases, the fact that some do raise concerns that perhaps some juries and judges allow their individual biases against LGBTQ people to interfere with equality of justice (Minson, 1992).

For example, in *Schick v. State (570N. E. 2d 918 (Ind. Ct. App. 1991),* the defendant, Timothy Schick, claimed that after being propositioned by a man for sex, Schick attacked him, knocking him to the ground. When Schick stopped hitting and kicking the man, he heard "gurgling noises" coming from the main's chest. Schick took the man's wallet and left the scene. The man later died. At trial, Schick argued that he was so repulsed by being propositioned by another man that he lost control. The jury found Schick not guilty of murder while attempting to commit robbery, but he was convicted of voluntary manslaughter.

In other cases, however, the homosexual advance played no part in the decision at trial. For example, in *State v. Volk,* (421 N.W. 2d 360 Minn. Ct. App. 1988) the defendant, Jerry Volk, was convicted of second-degree murder after the trial court refused to give a manslaughter instruction to the jury. Volk allegedly was hitchhiking with his friend, who testified that they planned to pose as prostitutes, pick up a gay man, and rob him. They found the victim at a store and he invited Volk and his friend to his apartment.

Volk allegedly hit the victim over the head with a liquor bottle and tied him up. When Volk's friend left to search the victim's car for money, the victim freed himself and attacked Volk. During the fight, Volk shot him twice. At trial Volk argued that, in part, he was revolted by the victim's homosexual advances and that this should serve, like intoxication or exhaustion, as a mitigating factor in the crime. The court found that there "was no provocation sufficient to elicit a heat of passion response." The court further found that a reasonable person finding themselves in such circumstances would have simply walked away (Brunelli, 2004).

While the homosexual advance theory remains controversial, there is greater agreement about the introduction of jury bias against LGBTQ people in the voir dire, or jury selection process. At issues is whether or not jurors should be questioned about their own sexual orientation, and how such information should be used.

Sexual orientation is frequently one of the main issues presented to the jury in cases involving hate crimes or sexual discrimination. In such cases, potential jurors' attitudes toward homosexuality may affect whether attorneys can select an impartial jury. What is less clear is whether or not jurors in other sorts of cases should be questioned about sexual orientation when the defendant or the victim is gay. Considering that jury bias against LGBTQ people plays a crucial role in the outcome of such cases, is it fair for a court to ask individual jurors about their sexual orientation? Or is it an invasion of privacy?

Some experts believe that an unbiased jury will not allow evidence of sexuality of the victim or the defendant to affect the outcome of the case. They will not care if the defendant in a rape case is gay or if the murder victim made a homosexual advance (Brunelli, 2004). Jury bias and homophobia by court personnel may also affect decision making. While the courts have never provided a constitutional protection of a jury of one's peers (meaning that a gay person cannot ask for a jury made up of only other gay people), they have provided that a jury will come from a cross-section of the population. Steps can be taken to minimize the bias many people feel toward gay defendants and victims.

LGBTQ People and Prison Life

For LGBTQ people, prison life presents additional challenges. For instance, a 2009 study found that transgender prisoners experience **sexual victimization** at a rate 13 times higher than non-transgender prisoners (National Coalition of Anti-Violence Programs, 2012). In response, the National Prison Rape Elimination Commission mandated that correctional facilities take more pronounced steps to protect this segment of the inmate population from harm. While the violence and victimization that occurs in prison has been well documented, the issues related to protecting and providing adequate care for LGBTQs are significant, and many correctional institutions are limited in their ability to provide adequate care (Langness, 2020).

The solution by many correctional facilities has been to place LGBTQ people in solitary confinement for their protection. However, such a practice results in a lack of access to mail, job opportunities, and programs while incarcerated. Some reports indicate that LGBTQ people remain in protective custody for years, meaning that they are likely to serve much of their sentence in isolation. They are also more likely to serve the maximum time since they are not eligible for good time credit and early release (Langness, 2020; National Coalition of Anti-Violence Programs, 2012).

Immigration issues further complicate the incarceration of some LGBTQ people. According to one estimate, there are at least 267,000 undocumented LGBTQ immigrants in the United States. While an exact figure cannot be determined, it is estimated that a significant percentage of those detained in immigration detention and holding facilities are LGBTQ people (Immigration Equality, n.d.).

Further, because of changes in immigration policy in the United States, the number of persons detained by immigration officials has dramatically increased in recent years. Advocates estimate that almost 70 percent of the 420,000 persons detained by Immigration and Customs Enforcement (ICE) were held in state and local facilities. While LGBTQ immigrants experience the same challenges as US-born LGBTQ people, there is the added burden of filing a claim for asylum during the one-year window, which impacts nearly 20 percent of those people fleeing persecution (National Coalition of Anti-Violence Programs, 2012).

SOCIOLOGICAL THEORY AND SEXUALITY

Similar to the way it helps to understand the issues surrounding other minority groups, sociological theory offers important insight into the ways in which sexuality and sexual identity shapes people's interactions, relationships, and standing within society.

Functionalism and Sexuality

The functionalist approach to sexual orientation examines how social norms ensure stability to social institutions and society overall. In explaining why non-heterosexual behavior is considered deviant and unacceptable, functionalists would argue that their existence disrupts the equilibrium of society and interferes with its ability to maintain the social institution of the family.

Homosexuality, for example, would from a functionalist perspective undermine the function of the institution of marriage and procreation for society. The notion of traditional family values (Chapter 11) along with religious beliefs proscribing homosexuality may explain why some groups do not believe LGBTQ people should not be afforded equal rights and should remain a deviant category. Approaches critical of functionalism, most notably queer theory, argue that such conventions and belief systems reflect an outdated and unrealistic definition of the institutions of marriage and the notion of what families should look like.

Conflict Theory and Sexuality

From a conflict theory perspective, the reason LGBTQ people continue to be discriminated against and not afforded equal rights in society is the same as it would be for any minority group: lack of access to social, economic and political power. The modern conflict approach argues that all groups compete for this power, and that those with the most power get to decide the social norms regarding all aspects of social life, including the acceptability of one's sexual orientation or identity. In addition to the exercise of power and control over policy, those who have power and influence also drive the narrative of the status quo and what the public understands the issues to be. In the case of LGBTQ people, many conflict theorists argue that those in power continue to promote the idea that heterosexuality is the default category and the public's perceptions of the problems are shaped by the elite-controlled media (Quinney, 1970).

Bigotry on display Before the 2015 Supreme Court decision legalizing same-sex marriage nationwide, protesters in different states fought to keep LGBTQ people from marrying. These protesters are attending an anti-same-sex marriage in Austin, TX.

In explaining the lack of complete equality for LGBTQ people, the conflict approach might argue that the process is yielding some success. Members of the LGBTQ population are gaining access to economic, social and political power, which is why there has been progress on the social acceptability of LGBTQ people. As more gay, lesbian and transgender people are elected to public office or are given high-profile positions in society, they can shape and influence the public's perceptions of non-heterosexuals and gain societal acceptability. While this group continues to experience discrimination and mistreatment, building on the work of generations of LGBTQ people before them, advocates are increasingly finding support among the general public.

Symbolic Interactionism and Sexuality

Symbolic interactionists might examine how a person defines and accepts their sexual identity. The process for many LGBTQ people (especially young people) can be quite unsettling, particularly given the historically strong condemnation by heterosexual groups. Thus, the decision for someone who might have an attraction to individuals of the same sex to express their identity is not easy, nor does it come without negative consequences. In fact, as Erving Goffman points out, there can be a stigma associated with "coming out," one that can have lifelong negative consequences (Goffman, 1963).

In recent years, fortunately, it is increasingly likely that LGBTQ people who are defining and expressing their identity can connect with others who went through the same process for affirmation and advice. This exposure to the LGBTQ subculture is an important step in the process, as members can offer insight into what the person may be experiencing themselves.

Developing a sexual identity involves the integration and acceptance of the label by adopting the attitudes, values, beliefs, and behaviors of the members of that particular group. While an LGBTQ identity is not necessarily a deviant label, as it was in the past, the process of claiming that identity is similar to what labeling theorists offer in managing a deviant identity.

Trevor Project Volunteers representing the Trevor Project participate in a 2019 Gay Pride Parade in New York City. The Trevor Project is a nationwide organization providing free crisis intervention and suicide prevention services to (LGBTQ) young people under 25 (thetrevorproject.org).

Feminist and Queer Theory and Sexuality

Feminist theory offers a robust and nuanced lens through which to understand sexuality and sexual orientation. It examines how gender influences the construction of identities, with a particular focus on how the idea of being female influences a woman's place in the power structure of society. Feminist theory addresses the pursuit of equality between men and women, and feminist theorists have exposed the ways in which a patriarchal society disadvantages women economically, politically, and socially.

Queer theory, like feminist theory, also addresses the formation of a social and sexual identity. Queer theory rejects the idea that one's sexual identity must fit into the neatly defined binaries of heterosexual and homosexual. In fact, queer theory argues that the conventional social construction of identity is unnecessarily limiting and oppressive. It provides an alternative identifier ("queer") which embraces all alternatives that can't be defined in the existing paradigm (Piantato, 2016).

WHAT WORKS? EFFECTIVE SOLUTIONS TO LGBTQ INEQUALITY

Although their social position has greatly improved in recent decades, LGBTQ individuals still experience discrimination, violence, and victimization. As a result, many LGBTQ people suffer from psychiatric disorders, substance abuse, and suicide. Isolation due to the lack of social acceptance by family and friends also has a negative impact on the health and well-being of members of the LGBTQ community. Programs that address the specific physical and mental health challenges faced by the LGBTQ community became a more urgent priority during the AIDS crisis, with many such programs emerging from within the LGBTQ activist community itself. Research into the effectiveness of these programs offers guidance for determining solutions.

LGBTQ youth are at a higher risk of suicide. Data from the 2019 Youth Risk Behavior Survey (YRBS), found that while about 19 percent of students overall had given serious consideration to suicide, 46 percent of LGBTQ youth had considered suicide attempts (Ivey-Stephenson et al., 2020). Other research found that LGBTQ youth are nearly three times more likely to report suicidality and were more likely to exhibit depressive symptoms than non-LGBTQ youth. Although research on effective suicide prevention for LGBTQ youth is limited, evidence-based programs that are designed for all youth who express some level of suicidality suggest possible solutions (Center for Disease Control, 2020).

For example, Sources of Strength is a suicide prevention program designed to help students who are experiencing suicidal thoughts and behaviors. The program trains youth as peer leaders who work with adult advisors to other youth about coping strategies and to minimize problem behaviors. The activities employed by peer leaders are designed to reduce the frequency of suicidal thoughts, attempts and related behavior by promoting the acceptability of seeking help and developing healthy coping mechanisms. The messages offered by peer leaders also reduce the stigma of asking for help from other youth and adults. An outcome evaluation of the Sources of Strength program indicated that training was highly effective in increasing peer leaders' adaptive norms about suicide as well as positive coping, connectedness to adults, and supportive behaviors with their friends, with most changes being highly significant (Wyman et al., 2011).

Programs like Sources of Strength build social support and self-efficacy among youth by changing the way youth perceive suicide as a means of coping with stressors. This is critically important for LGBTQ youth, since they experience the world differently from non-LGBTQ youth in that they encounter greater levels of discrimination and victimization. Having peer leaders provide a source of support, encouragement and offering opportunities for LGBTQ youth to work out and talk through their experiences is said to be a critical feature of the program (Topper, 2015).

SO WHAT CAN I DO?

You might be thinking that you are limited in what you can do to help LGBTQ people cope with the problems they encounter. After all, what can you realistically do to change the societal stigma or the discrimination LGBTQ people encounter? You might also think you are ill-equipped to help those who might be facing this type of discrimination or their consequences. You are not likely trained as a therapist or a counselor and you may not have any experience in dealing with members of this segment of the population. You would be correct in all of those conclusions, but it doesn't mean you have no role to play in the process.

As has been mentioned in many of the chapters in this book about various macro-level social problems, the role you play cannot be to fix the problem; that is beyond your capabilities. But it does mean that you can offer your support, assistance, encouragement, and input at a micro-level. This is especially true in this post-MeToo moment as well as the many instances in which trans rights and queer visibility is such a prominent issue on many campuses and communities across the country.

One thing you might consider is becoming an "ally" to LGBTQ people. Go to engage youth.gov at https://engage.youth.gov/resources/being-ally-lgbt-people. Everyone needs allies or supporters and this website shows you how you can become one by staying informed about LGBTQ issues, speaking up against inequality or issues related to LGBTQ people, and showing compassion for this group, even when you don't understand all of the problems they face.

Another thing you might consider is learning more about and being supportive of those who are transgender. The National Center for Transgender Equality has a list of 52 things you can do in support of transgender equality. Go to their website at: https://transequality.org/issues/resources/52-things-you-can-do-transgender-equality and find something that interests you. Some of these suggestions are as simple as inviting a transgender person to lunch to holding a job fair for transgender employees looking for work.

Another suggestion is to get involved with an organization called the Trevor Project. This non-profit organization provides crisis intervention and suicide prevention services to LGBTQ people under the age of 25. There are many ways to get involved—visit their website at: https://www.thetrevorproject.org/get-involved/

In the end, much of what you can do is to be present and willing to help someone in need. Even if you don't agree with LGBTQ people on their sexual orientation, their sexual identity, their lifestyle choices, or encourage their behaviors, you can be supportive of the problems they experience and offer some level of encouragement, particularly if they are expressing suicidal thoughts. Most people simply want to be heard and understood. Think about those times in your life when you were struggling and wished someone would just be there and listen—not solve any problems, not to judge, or even offer advice; but just to be present, to listen, and to show compassion to another human being who is struggling.

CONCLUSION

Although the problems faced by the LGBTQ community are similar to those faced by other disadvantaged groups in the United States, there are some important distinctions. The prejudice against LGBTQ people is very deeply rooted in both religious as well as social and political systems that uphold the heterosexual family unit as the norm, and label anything outside of that unit as deviant. Until recently, many also believed that people chose to be anything other than heterosexual, or had suffered some sort of psychological trauma that caused them to be homosexual (and that they could therefore be "cured"). As a result, many in the LGBTQ community felt compelled for reasons of personal safety as well as the need to maintain a position in society to conceal their sexual identity—to be "in the closet."

LGBTQ people, like other marginalized groups in the United States, have encountered discrimination in the workplace, in obtaining health care, in attempts to secure housing, and in starting families. However, while the law in many states prohibits such behavior on the part of people and organizations, there is as yet no equivalent federal protection of LGBTQ rights as there is for other marginalized groups.

YOU MAKE THE CALL: ADOPTION AND THE LGBTQ COMMUNITY

You are the director of a Christian-based international adoption agency. An LGBTQ couple has applied to adopt a child from your agency and meets all the necessary criteria to be eligible to adopt. They are financially stable, with good jobs, and were legally married in a state that recognizes same-sex marriages. They own a home in a neighborhood with lots of young children and are active volunteers in their community.

Your agency has a policy against same-sex couples adopting; the state in which your agency is based does not recognize same-sex marriages; and your Christian beliefs oppose two people of the same sex adopting a child. Under other circumstances, their application would be fast tracked, and the adoption process would move forward. Thus, from a professional and personal standpoint, you must deny their application on the basis of sexual orientation.

Questions for you to consider:

1. Do you recommend an alternative adoption agency that would allow this couple to adopt a child, or does your personal beliefs prohibit you from doing that?
2. What would happen if you simply approved the application?
3. Could there be a lawsuit filed, which might bring unwanted negative attention to your agency?
4. What is the rationale behind the agency's policy and/or your personal beliefs?
5. How does the denial of this application impact the child?

SUMMARY

- Define sexual orientation and describe various types of sexual identity.
    - Sexuality is a broad term that is used to describe sexual behavior and desires. Sociologists use the term to describe sexual orientation or identity.
    - Sexual orientation also comprises a tremendously diverse range of individual experiences, relationships, and behaviors. It is overly simplistic to think of sexual orientation as binary; that is, either "gay" or "straight."
- Summarize the history of the experiences of LGBTQ people in the United States.
  This chapter offered insight into the history of how LGBTQ populations have been perceived as well as the various types of discrimination members of the LGBTQ community experience as a result of their sexual orientation and sexual identity. This includes events such as perceiving homosexuality as a form of mental illness or deviance, as well as the Stonewall uprising in the 1960s.
- Analyze some of the issues and challenges for LGBTQ people in the United States.
    - LGBTQ people face prejudice and discrimination in a variety of circumstances, including housing and work discrimination, challenges surrounding same-sex marriage and parenting, and their standing in the military.
- Analyze the challenges for LGBTQ people in the criminal justice system.
    - LGBTQ people face considerable challenges within the criminal justice system, including harassment from police officers, many of whom believe LGBTQ people are involved in sex work.
    - LGBTQ people face challenges from the courts, in that there are sometimes credibility issues when they serve as witnesses.
    - Hate crime statistics offer further evidence of the victimization of LGBTQ people
    - Incarcerated members of the LGBTQ community are vulnerable and must be segregated from the general population of offenders.

- Summarize sociological explanations of the inequalities LGBTQ groups encounter.
    - A functionalist perspective to sexual orientation examines how social norms ensure stability to social institutions and society overall. In explaining why non-heterosexual behavior is considered deviant and unacceptable, functionalists would argue that their existence disrupts the equilibrium of society and interferes with its ability to maintain the social institution of the family.
    - Conflict theorists would argue the reason LGBTQ people continue to be discriminated against is the same as it would be for any minority group: lack of access to social, economic and political power.
    - Symbolic interactionists might examine how the development of sexual identity involves the integration and acceptance of the label by adopting the attitudes, values, beliefs, and behaviors of the members of that particular group. While an LGBTQ identity is not necessarily a deviant label, as it was in the past, the process of claiming that identity is similar to what labeling theorists offer in managing a deviant identity.
    - Feminist theory focuses on how gender influences the construction of identities. Queer theory argues that the conventional social construction of identity is unnecessarily limiting and oppressive.
- Describe effective programs to address issues surrounding sexuality in the United States.
    - The data suggests that LGBTQ people are at higher risk of suicide than other populations. Programs like Sources of Strength build social support and self-efficacy among youth by changing the way youth perceive suicide as a means of coping with stressors.
    - Having peer leaders provide a source of support, encouragement and offering opportunities for LGBTQ youth to work out and talk through their experiences is particularly helpful.
- Summarize what individuals can do in addressing the challenges many LGBTQ persons face.
    - While the problems LGBTQ people experience are serious and perhaps beyond the scope of a single individual's effort, there are things that can be done—including becoming and staying informed about LGBTQ issues. There are a host of resources available to offer support and ideas about how individuals can assist member of the LGBTQ community.

KEY TERMS

Discussion Questions

1. Why do you think other marginalized groups received equal protection and recognition decades ago in the United States, while the LGBTQ community still struggles with similar recognition from the federal government?
2. As more people consider these partnerships as acceptable, do you think this is the result of greater exposure to LGBTQ people?
3. Compared to similar civil rights movements in the United States, how does the perception of homosexuality as a choice pose challenges for the LGBTQ community in their pursuit of equal rights?
4. What are your thoughts about the use of public restrooms by transgender people—should they be allowed to use whichever restroom they choose or should they be restricted to the one that is associated with their assigned gender at birth? Why or why not?
5. While transgender people are now generally allowed to serve in the military, albeit under carefully crafted criteria, how might military service by transgender people help change the negative perception some people have with this group?

Learn more with this chapter's digital tools, including Data and Media Literacy Exercises, flashcards, and chapter self-assessments at **www.oup.com/he/mcnamara**.

11

Is Our Understanding of Family Changing?

LEARNING OBJECTIVES

- Operationalize and define concepts such as the family and some of the recent trends in the literature about family structure in the United States.
- Summarize the research on changes that have occurred to the family institution, such as cohabitation, women in the workforce, same-sex families, grandparent-led families, or blended families.
- Analyze a variety of problems families experience, such as family and domestic violence.
- Compare the differences and similarities between child abuse, neglect, and the foster care system.
- Identify how child abuse can be detected and prevented.
- Illustrate how sociological theory helps us understand and diagnose problems and challenges families experience.
- Assess the effectiveness of empirically supported programs to help families.

Chapter Outline

What does family look like? A traditional family structure might include members of several generations under the same roof.

There are many forms of family in American society today. This diversity reflects the complexity of social life. Family formation is shaped not only by emotional ties but also by economic, social, and political constraints. The commonality of divorce has led to many **blended families**, and the recent legalization of same-sex marriages and increasing ability of same-sex couples to adopt or have their own children provide options for forming a family unimaginable just a decade ago. Economic constraints, drug and alcohol abuse, and other social problems have contributed to a rise in grandparent-led families. In addition, more families are having fewer children than in the past, while some couples are opting to remain childless. This last trend in particular has long-term implications for society.

SOCIOLOGICAL STORY TIME

- Research has shown that loneliness is related to a shorter life span, with an impact comparable to smoking nearly a pack of cigarettes a day. Loneliness is also associated with greater risk of heart disease, depression, anxiety, and dementia. Nearly a third of people older than 65 (and half of people age 85 and over) live alone (Baker, 2017).
- In 2012, David Mullins and Charlie Craig asked Masterpiece Bake Shop, a bakery in Colorado, to bake a cake to celebrate their planned wedding. Mullins and Craig planned to marry in Massachusetts, where same-sex marriage was legal; it was not legal in Colorado. The owner of Masterpiece Bake Shop, Jack Phillips, said he couldn't create the product they were looking for without violating his faith. Mullins and Craig filed a complaint with the Colorado Civil Rights Commission, which ruled in their favor, citing a state anti-discrimination law. Phillips appealed, arguing that requiring him to provide a wedding cake for the couple violated his constitutional right to freedom of speech and

free exercise of religion. The court held that the state anti-discrimination law did not compel Phillips to "support or endorse any particular religious view." It simply prohibited Phillips from discriminating against potential customers on account of their sexual orientation. Upon appeal the US Supreme Court ruled in favor of Phillips, in a 7 to 2 vote (DeVogue, 2018).

- As the opioid epidemic intensified, there has been an increase in children entering the foster care system. State budgets are stretched, social workers are overloaded, and not enough families are willing to provide children with temporary homes. American foster care, experts say, is in crisis. "It's pretty much every state — except maybe four or five — that have seen an increase in the number of children in foster care," said John Sciamanna, vice president of public policy at the Child Welfare League of America. "What you are seeing now is just a straining of the system." (Stein and Bever, 2017).
- Recent data indicates that teen pregnancies are at an all-time low in the United States. According to the National Center on Health Statistics, the teen birth rate has declined 67 percent since 1991. The reasons? The economy, greater access to and use of contraceptives by teenagers, as well as a decrease in the percentage of teenage girls having sex (Livingston and Thomas, 2019). The birth rate for older women, however, has seen historic increases. For women between the ages of 30 and 34, the birth rate increased to the highest rate for this age group since 1964. Similarly, the birth rate for women who are between 35 and 39 increased in 2015 to the highest rate since 1962. Even older women, those between the ages of 40 and 44, showed a substantial increase, to its highest rate since 1966 (Scutti, 2018).

DEFINING FAMILY

The definition of "family" has evolved over time and varies between cultures. According to the U. S. Census Bureau, a family consists of "two or more people, one of whom is the householder, related by birth, marriage, or adoption and residing in the same housing unit." A family differs from a household, which "consists of all people who occupy a housing unit regardless of relationship. A household may consist of a person living alone or multiple unrelated individuals or families living together." (US Census Bureau, 2018). The function of a family is to meet its members' needs for food, shelter, and intimacy as well as to provide socialization, or the transmission of culture from one generation to the next. Most discussions of assume a **nuclear family**, which is a family unit composed of parents and their children. This smaller unit contrasts with the extended family, which often includes grandparents, uncles, aunts, and others living in the household with the nuclear family. The nuclear family has been the standard structure in the United States for many years (Khimm, 2015).

Many of our perceptions of the family are rooted in this traditional thinking about family structure that was reflective of the 1950s. When you hear the word "family," do you think of a father who is the sole breadwinner, a stay-at-home mother who raises the children, and one or more children in the household? Many people still think of the "typical" family in this way (Livingston, 2018).

However, this is not the norm. Most families have both parents working at least part-time and the **stay-at-home parent** is a relatively small percentage of all families. Recent data indicates that about 18 percent of families have one stay-at-home parent. Interestingly, there has been a dramatic increase in the number of stay-at-home fathers. While some of this may be due to unemployment and an inability to find work, the data indicates that many fathers are intentionally making the decision to stay home and raise the children (Livingston, 2018).

CHANGES TO FAMILIES

In Chapter 4, we saw that poverty, deindustrialization, and high housing costs are social structural factors that impact individuals in significant ways. These factors all place a strain on families as they reduce the amount of time parents can spend supervising their children and limit family resources.

The Decline of Marriage and the Birthrate

As social stigmas about sexual activity outside of marriage and childbearing outside of wedlock have softened, people's ideas about the actual value of marriage have changed. It is now socially acceptable as well as much easier to obtain a divorce, and it is also socially acceptable for people to live together in a committed relationship without marrying. Since the 1960s, the development of effective contraception as well as the availability of safe and legal abortion reduced the risk of sexual activity and the likelihood of unwanted parenting. This trend, combined with the rising independence of women, encouraged the delay of marriage and childbearing, particularly for women who are highly educated and have well-paying jobs. As a result, traditional notions about families and marriage are changing.

According to the US Census Bureau, in 1970, median age at first marriage was 21 for women and 23 for men. In 2018, it was 29.8 for men and 27.8 for women (Figure 11.1; US Census Bureau, n.d.) Clearly, people are waiting longer to get married.

Households have also grown smaller. According to the US Census Bureau, the average number of people living in a household has decreased. In 1960, the average number was 3.3, in 2019 it was 2.52. This reflects two primary trends: people having fewer or no children, and the increase in people living alone. In fact, about 36.4 million people were living in a single person household in 2019, an increase from the 30.4 million in 2006 (Figure 11.2; Duffin, 2019).

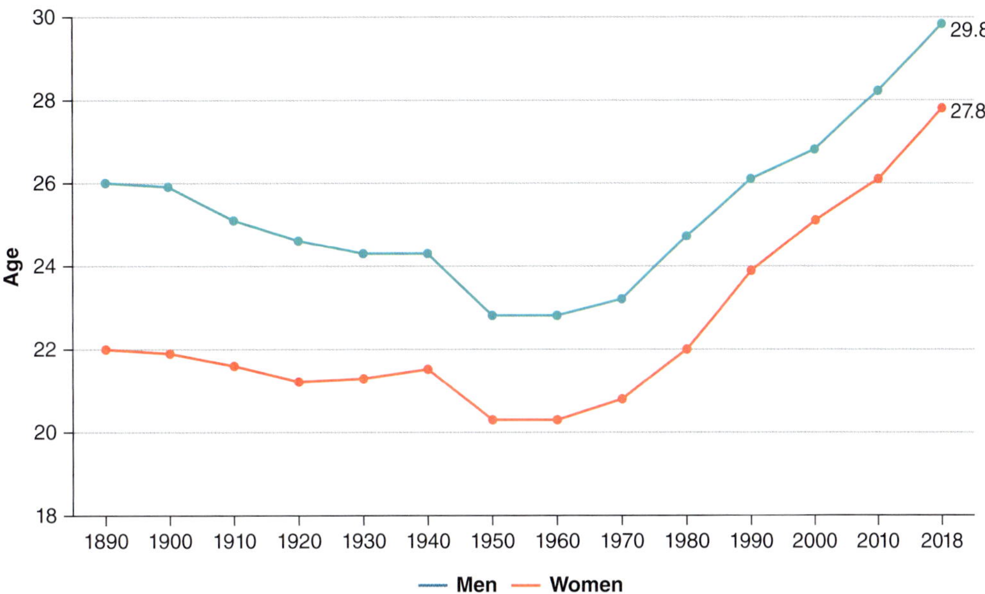

Figure 11.1 Median Age at First Marriage: 1890 to Present Source: 1890 to 1940 Decennial Censuses and 1950 to 2018 Current Population Survey, Annual Social and Economic Supplements.

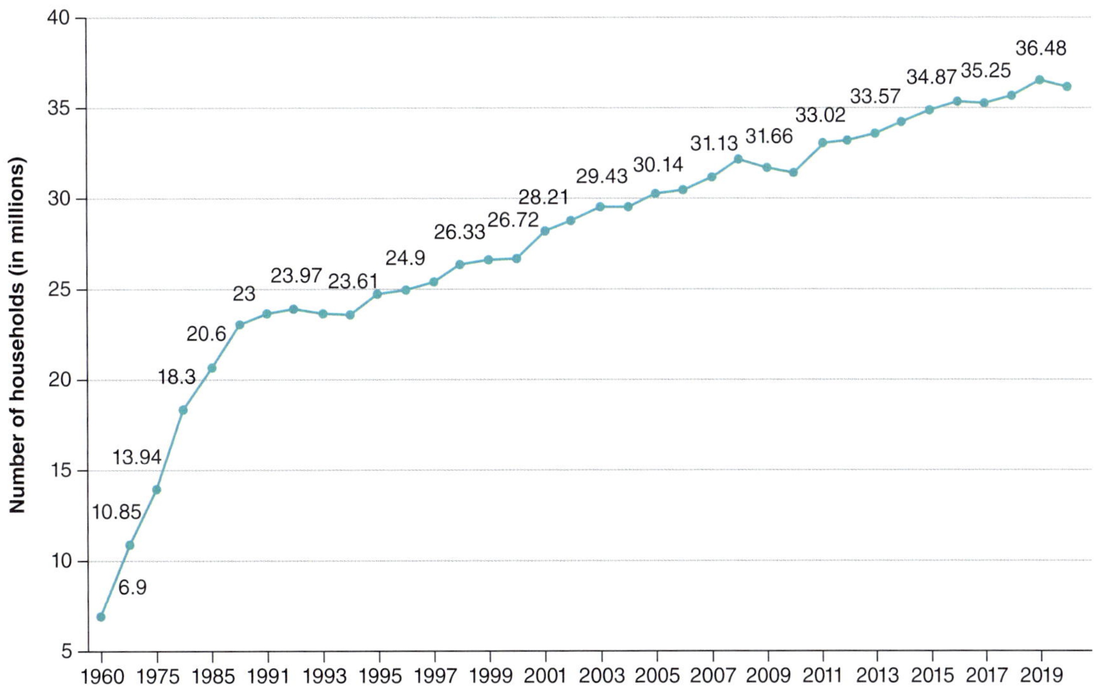

Figure 11.2 Number of single-person households in the US, 1960-2019. Source: (Duffin, 2019).

Cohabitation and Childbearing

While marriage rates have witnessed steady declines in the United States, cohabitation has increased. According to a 2019 report by the Pew Research Center, marriage rates have seen a steady decline since 1995 (Horowitz, Graf, and Livingston, 2019). The decline in marriage is particularly noteworthy among those under the age of 30 (Table 11.1). However, cohabitation appears to be increasing across all age groups (Figure 11.3).

While the trend of living together is increasing, it still makes up a small segment of the US population. This is particularly true of older adults (Horowitz, Graf, and Livingston, 2019). Some cohabiting couples have children from previous relationships while others decide to start a family without being formally married. Although some cohabiting couples may have decided to live together as a prelude to marriage, there is no data to support the contention that living together beforehand helps prevent divorce. What is known is that **cohabitation**, particularly if children are a product of such a situation, makes it more difficult to break up. For example, some experts observe, the predictability and familiarity of living together may mean that people often marry someone they would have otherwise left. The consequences of such a decision, however, can impact

Table 11.1 Percentage of Population Married 1995–2019

	Year	
	1995	**2019**
Age Group		
Under 30	31%	18%
30-49	68%	62%
50 +	65%	62%

Source: Juliana Horowitz, Nikki Graf, and Gretchen Livingston. (2019). "The Landscape of Marriage and Cohabitation in the U.S." Pew Research Center, November 6. Available at: https://www.pewsocialtrends.org/2019/11/06/the-landscape-of-marriage-and-cohabitation-in-the-u-s/

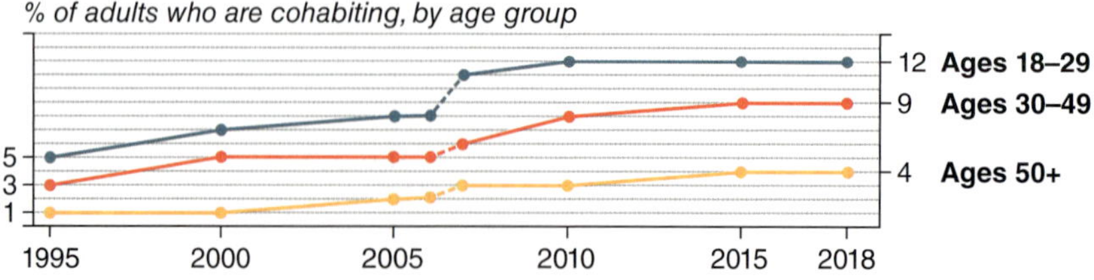

Figure 11.3 Cohabitation rates in the US. Note: In 2007, the Current Population Survey added a new cohabitation question. Estimates from 2007 to 2018 are based on this measure. Source: Pew Research Center analysis of 1995-2018 Current Population Survey, Annual Social and Economic Supplement (IPUMS). "Marriage and Cohabitation in the U.S." Pew Research Center.

the quality of the marriage. A consistent trend in the research shows that those who start living together before deciding to marry say their marriage is of lower quality (compared to couples who did not live together prior to marriage) and are more likely to divorce (Horowitz, Graf, and Livingston, 2019).

Prior research has shown that serial cohabitation is strongly associated with economic disadvantage among unmarried couples, lower odds of marriage, and increased odds of poor marital outcomes (Horowitz, Graf, and Livingston, 2019). More recent data from the Pew Research Center in 2019 suggests that a significant number of people (either those currently cohabiting, or those who are neither cohabiting nor married) already lived with two or more partners (Horowitz, Graf, and Livingston, 2019).

Another trend associated with cohabitation is the tendency for mothers to have children by different fathers. This tendency is often referred to as **multiple partner fertility (MPF)**. According to a Census Bureau report, more than a quarter of families with minor children have MPF and about 17 percent of children live with a half sibling, while roughly a third of parents who have been married two or more times have MPF. Parents who have MPF tend to both begin childbearing earlier and to have more children, compared to all parents. MPF parents are also less likely to be married and to have ever been married, compared to all parents (Monte, 2017).

MPF parents are also more likely to live in poverty for several reasons. They are less likely to be White or Asian, and more likely to be Black, Hispanic, or to identify as multiracial. MPF parents as a group also tend to have lower education levels than all parents. Given demonstrated differences by age, education, and race, it is perhaps unsurprising that nearly 20 percent of MPF parents (18.4 percent) live below the poverty line, compared to 12.4 percent of all adults, and 11.5 percent of all parents (Monte, 2017).

Divorce

The availability and convenience of **divorce** has changed the face of American families. According to the Census Bureau, about 40 percent of first marriages end in divorce. **Remarriage** also occurs regularly, as shown in divorce rates for subsequent marriages. Divorce rates for second and third marriages are even higher than first marriages: 60 percent of second marriages and 65 percent of third marriages end in divorce (Table 11.2).

Table 11.2 Divorce Rates for First and Subsequent Marriages

Number of Marriages	Rate of Divorce
First Marriage	43%
Second Marriage	60%
Third Marriage	65%

Source: US Census Bureau.

Factors that diminish the chance of divorce include religion (Catholics are substantially less likely than Protestants to get divorced), older age, higher income, more education, absence of divorce in family history, and a child after marriage (Popenoe and Whitehead, 2006). For many years the prevailing view has been that divorce is very traumatic for children. However, studies of divorced couples have found that about 75 percent of children of divorce do not have serious psychological, social, or academic problems. That said, the other 25 percent, which in absolute terms represents a large number of children, have significant problems (Brand, et al., 2019; Anderson, 2014).

The first two years after a divorce are often physically, emotionally, and psychologically draining for everyone in the family. Erratic behavior, depression, and physical ailments are common. Divorce is especially traumatic for children whose parents have kept their problems hidden, as these children experience a greater sense of loss (Al-Ubaidi, 2017). On the other hand, children whose parents' marriage created a chaotic environment often find things more peaceful after divorce in a stable single-parent home. Interestingly, children from non-divorce, high-conflict homes have similar problems as children from divorced homes, which suggests that "staying together for the children" is not beneficial if the home is not a peaceful one (Al-Ubaidi, 2017).

Preschool children can find coping with divorce especially difficult. Young children often regress in their behavior through action such as baby talk, clinging, or thumb sucking. Young boys, who typically have greater difficulty coping and adjusting to divorce than young girls, often act out, even becoming aggressive with peers and others. Girls tend to internalize their feelings about the divorce experience, and they can develop depression, headaches, or experience changes in their eating or sleeping habits (Al-Ubaidi, 2017).

The good news is that for most children and teenagers these problems do not cause long-term harm. Teens that do well in such situations tend to have a strong connection to at least one adult, not necessarily a biological family member. Schools also provide ways for teens to feel a sense of belonging and to experience success (Popenoe and Whitehead, 2006).

The impact of divorce Some studies have shown that girls tend to internalize their feelings about divorce and are at greater risk of depression.

Women in the Workforce

Women in the labor market and who have professional careers may rethink the value of marriage and childbearing as a form of identity and self-fulfillment. Women who expect to have fewer children and who see less value in marriage will dedicate more time to their educations and careers and less to finding a husband and starting a family. Women now attend college at higher rates than men, particularly women from disadvantaged families. Moreover, women attend professional school in equal or greater or equal numbers than men—approximately 51 percent of law students and medical students are women (Association of American Medical Colleges, 2017; Jaschik, 2016).

According to a report by the Pew Research Center, overall, about 72 percent of US mothers are working either full-time or part-time, a significant increase since 1968, when that figure was about 50 percent. More mothers are also working full-time: 55 percent of all US mothers are employed full-time in 2019, compared to 34 percent in 1968 (Figure 11.4; Horowitz, 2019).

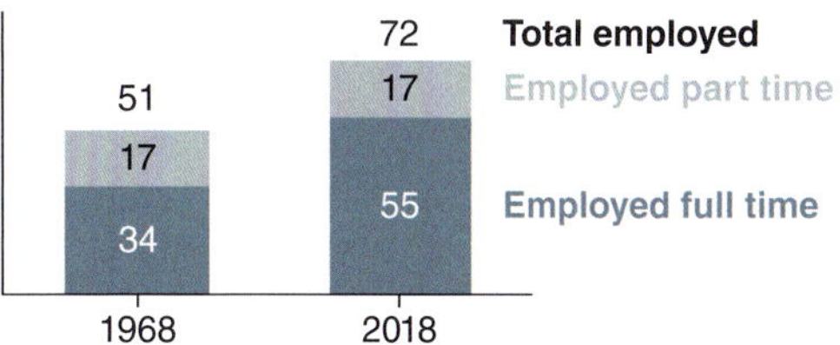

Figure 11.4 A majority of US mothers are employed full time Note: Based on employment status in the prior year among women with children younger than 18 in the household. "Full time" includes those who reported working at least 35 hours a week in the previous year. Source: Pew Research Center analysis of 1968 and 2018 March Current Population Survey Annual and Social Economic Supplement (IPUMS).

Census Bureau data also show that most women are working. Women with younger children work less than those with older ones (Figure 11.5). About 75 percent of mothers with children ages 6–17 (school age) were employed full-time compared with 62 percent of mothers with preschool and school age children. Mothers with only school age children are more likely to be able to work full-time and for more weeks during the year than mothers with either preschool and/or school age children (Christnacht and Sullivan, 2020).

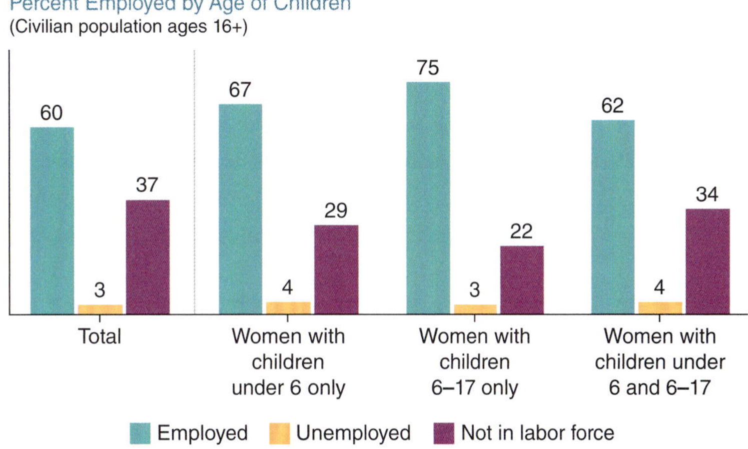

Figure 11.5 Percent of working mothers with children Source: U.S. Census Bureau, 2018 American Community Survey 1-year estimates.

For married women with children, having a career changes the structure of the family and affects the family's parenting styles, financial situation, and choices about how to use their time. While college-educated women who are active in their professional lives have more stable marriages than those without college educations, they also tend to have fewer children, and the dynamics of decision making in their families tend to be more egalitarian. Because they contribute financially, women want more say in how finances are handled and more input in all decisions within the household (Bianchi, Robinson and Milkie, 2006).

Women who work outside the home have less time to spend with their children. Some mothers try to compensate for their absence, for example by getting less sleep or

Pandemic parenting For many women, the strains of trying to maintain a career from home while also supervising children's remote learning and shouldering the burden of housework is driving them from the labor market altogether.

participating in fewer leisure activities. Mothers of adolescents find spending quality time with their children to be exceptionally challenging: research has shown a consistent decline in the amount of time mothers spend with their teens in recent decades (Bianchi, Robinson, and Milkie, 2006). The Covid-19 pandemic and the associated quarantines meant that many working women had to juggle their career obligations while also supervising their children's remote learning and maintaining the household. While there is evidence that women tend to have difficulty re-entering the labor force the longer they are out of it, the challenges presented by the pandemic may exacerbate this trend, meaning potentially greater obstacles to mothers who wish to return to work. There is some preliminary evidence that the pressure of these multiple roles might force some women out of the workplace altogether (Cohen and Hsu, 2020).

Some critics claim that problems with the American family could be resolved if we simply went back to traditional family structures. This type of thinking blames women and calls for a return to **traditional family values**, which means women should be in the home raising children. It is unreasonable to blame women for the massive changes in society over the past 50 or 60 years. Social changes have many causes, not all of them are harmful, and most children emerge unscathed even from the most difficult home situations.

Same-Sex Marriages

As was mentioned in Chapter 10, there has been an increase in the number of **same-sex marriages** in the US. In addition, public support for same-sex marriage has steadily increased, with the latest figures showing most Americans in support of this type of union. While having children biologically in a same-sex marriage creates some challenges, the rise in adoption and surrogate births can serve as solutions to the creation of families in these types of marriages. While some debate still exists regarding whether attraction to the same gender is a choice or has a biological explanation, the fact is more people are able and willing to publicly proclaim themselves as part of the LGBTQ population and legally marry.

Single-Parent Families

The traditional composition of a family with children in the United States involves a child or children under the age of 18 living with two married parents. According to the US Census Bureau, this trend still holds true. Between 1970 and 2018, the percentage

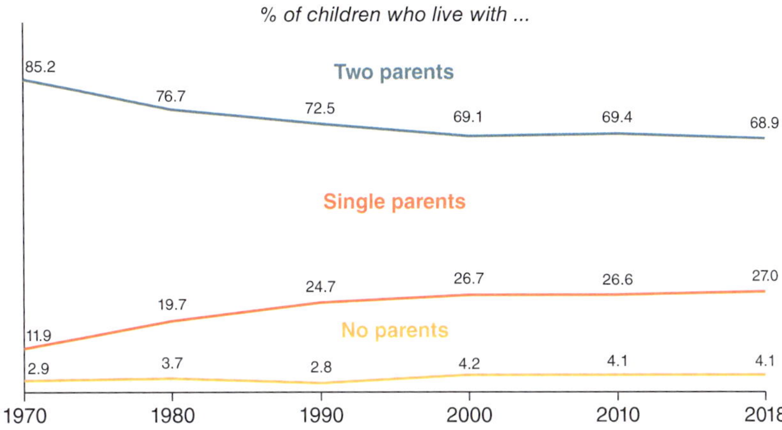

Figure 11.6 Children's living arrangement by presence of parents in the home, 1970-2018. Source: Current Population Survey Annual Social and Economic Supplement (CPS-ASEC) 1970-2010 and CPS March 2018. (IPUMS)

of children living in families with two parents decreased from 85 percent to just under 70 percent (Figure 11.6). An increasingly common family arrangement is a child living with a single mother. Between 1970-2018, the percentage of children living with only their mother increased by more than 125 percent. Thus, while the two-parent family remains in the majority in the United States, the data is clear that other configurations like single-parent families are becoming more common (Wang, 2018).

While many people think of single-parent families as only those that live in poverty or a result of divorce, this is only one explanation of a **single-parent family**. The death of a spouse can create one, as can the situation in which one of the parents is unknown, absent from the family, or has abandoned the spouse and children. In addition, social class plays an important role in the success of a single-parent family. That is, those parents who have sufficient wealth or extended family members who can offer assistance in raising the children tend to be better able to adapt to such a circumstance. As the research also shows, there are an increasing number of single people who are opting for a family without a spouse (Schondelmyer, 2017).

Grandparent-led Families

Another trend in the changing structure of families involve **grandparent-led families**, where the grandparents are assuming the primary caregiver role. Approximately eight million children, about 10 percent of US children aged five through 18, are raised by their grandparents. About 20 percent of these children live at or below the poverty line. Grandparents often step into the role of parents due to abuse and neglect, substance abuse, HIV/AIDS, homicide, mental illness, incarceration, military deployment, teenage pregnancy, and death. Grandparents also become involved through child welfare

Grandparents and grandchildren In the US, about ten percent of children are raised by their grandparents.

policies that attempt to keep families intact by encouraging family members to intervene.

Research shows that children who live with one or both grandparents do well in terms of academic achievement and physical health, and report fewer behavioral problems than children living with one biological parent. However, even if children thrive, there are social costs to the grandparents. About half of grandparents who take care of their grandchildren are 55 years old or older and about 15 percent are 65 years or older. More than half of all grandparents providing care are single parents. About 25 percent of grandparents struggle with physical or mental health problems, which complicates their ability to care for young children. Finally, the financial strains of raising children take their toll on grandparents, many of whom are poor or have fixed incomes (Sham'ah, 2017).

FAMILY PROBLEMS

Many of the changes to the structure of families has also revealed a number of problems families encounter. While not all families experience these problems, they are serious enough to warrant discussion and understanding.

Family Violence

Family violence includes physical and sexual abuse of children, child neglect and maltreatment, intimate partner violence, and elder abuse. Children do not have to be direct victims of abuse to be harmed by it: witnessing violence in their homes make them indirect victims. Children who witness abuse often have the same types of problems as those who experience it directly: low self-esteem, depression, stress disorders, poor impulse control, and feelings of powerlessness. They are also at high risk for alcohol and drug use, sexual acting out, running away, isolation, fear, and suicide (Morgan and Kena, 2017). Sadly, children exposed to violence at an early age are likely to become either perpetrators of abuse or victims of violence in adulthood (Morgan and Kena, 2017). In fact, boys who have witnessed abuse of their mothers are 10 times more likely to batter their female partners as adults (Redden, 2008).

Consider some other facts about the impact of family violence:

- Children of battered women are fifteen times more likely to be battered themselves than children whose mothers are not abused.

- Because the abuser often uses the children's behavior as an excuse for battering the woman, children come to blame themselves for their mother's abuse.
- Divorced and separated women, who compose only 10 percent of all women, account for 75 percent of all battered women and report being battered 14 times as often as women still living with their partners (Redden, 2008).

In trying to make sense of family violence, particularly as it relates to children and teens, many experts agree that it involves a **cycle of violence.** That is, parents and caretakers discipline their children using violence because that is the way they were raised. The consequence is that victims of such abuse can become violent offenders themselves as they get older (Office of Juvenile Justice and Delinquency Prevention, 2001; O'Hara, 2018). In addition, children who do not become offenders or victims are still likely to suffer from attention deficit disorders, educational difficulties, substance abuse, mental health problems, symptoms of post-traumatic stress disorder, and lack of appropriate social skills (Office of Juvenile Justice and Delinquency Prevention, 2001; O'Hara, 2018).

Not only are children directly or indirectly affected by domestic violence, but the extent and seriousness of domestic violence clearly impacts women far more than men. Some experts contend that intimate partner violence, which includes domestic violence, is the most common violent crime in the United States (O'Hara, 2018; Redden, 2008). Data indicates that one in every four women will experience **domestic violence** in her lifetime. Also, it is estimated that about 4.8 million incidents of physical assault by an intimate partner occur each year, and 75 percent of those victims are females (O'Hara, 2018).

According to the Violence Policy Center, which uses Bureau of Justice statistics in its annual reports on female homicide victims, early three women are murdered every day in the US by current or former romantic partners. While domestic violence occurs across boundaries of race, class, and gender, the National Center on Victims of Crime estimates that American Indian and Alaska native women have the highest rates of intimate partner violence (Figure 11.7).

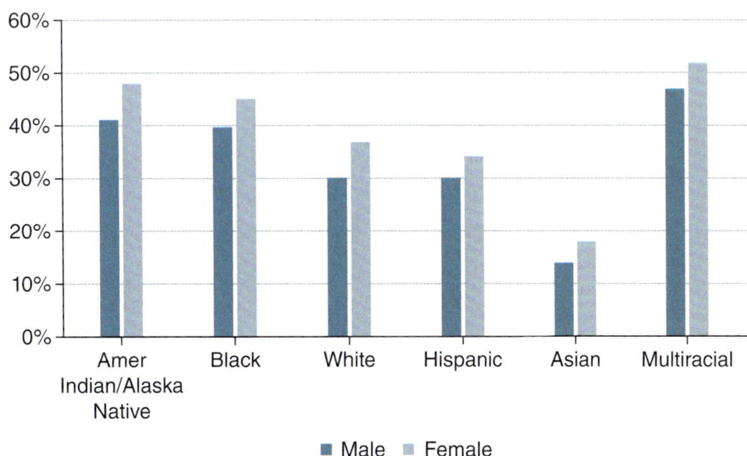

Figure 11.7 Percent of victims of intimate partner violence by race Source: National Center on Victims of Crime, 2018.

CHILD NEGLECT AND ABUSE

What is the difference between a bad parent and a neglectful one? This is a difficult question faced by case workers, police officers, and child welfare advocates. The structure and fabric of all American families are challenged by economic and social stresses as well as issues of mental and physical health and safety. What happens when these challenges overwhelm parents' ability to adequately socialize their children? For some families, failure to meet these challenges results in inadequate care (or neglect), while for others it leads to abuse.

Child neglect is the most prevalent form of child maltreatment in the United States. The National Child Abuse and Neglect Data System (NCANDS) defines **neglect** as "a type of maltreatment that refers to the failure by the caregiver to provide needed, age-appropriate care although financially able to do so or offered financial or other means to do so." (O'Hara, 2018). Neglect occurs when parents or guardians do not provide the kind of care needed, even though they can do so. Neglected children suffer from poor hygiene, weight loss, frequent absence from school, and extreme neglect is usually easily recognized. Physicians, nurses, day care personnel, relatives, and neighbors often suspect and report neglect in infants, toddlers, and younger children. Once children are in school, teachers and administrators usually notice the characteristics of child neglect (O'Hara, 2018).

Types of Neglect

While neglect can be a difficult concept to define, and while there are a wide range of activities that can be considered neglectful behavior by parents, experts and treatment professionals typically characterize neglect under four types: physical, educational, emotional, and medical.

PHYSICAL NEGLECT

When the parent or caregiver does not provide the child with basic necessities (adequate food, clothing, and shelter), **physical neglect** is the result. Physical neglect also includes child abandonment, inadequate supervision, and failure to provide for the child's safety and physical and emotional needs. Physical neglect can severely impede a child's development by causing **failure to thrive**; malnutrition; serious illness; physical harm in the form of cuts, bruises, burns or other injuries due to the lack of supervision; and a lifetime of low self-esteem. This accounts for the majority of neglect cases (O'Hara, 2018; Redden, 2008).

Abandonment is also a category of physical neglect. An abandoned child has been deserted by a parent without arranging for reasonable care and supervision. This category includes cases in which children were left by parents or substitutes, the children were not claimed within two days, and their caregivers have no information about the parent's whereabouts (O'Hara, 2018).

EDUCATIONAL NEGLECT

The failure to enroll a child in school or to provide appropriate home schooling or needed special educational training is called **educational neglect**. Parents may be punished for educational neglect when their children are chronically truant (Chapter 3). Educational neglect has links to disruptive behavior, chronic delinquency, as well as adult unemployment and poverty.

EMOTIONAL/PSYCHOLOGICAL NEGLECT

Not all neglect is physical. Engaging in spousal abuse in the child's presence, allowing a child to use drugs or alcohol, refusing or failing to provide needed psychological care, constantly belittling the child, allowing or even encouraging the child to engage in antisocial behavior, and withholding affection are all forms of emotional and psychological neglect. This type of neglect is the most difficult to identify and prosecute because the trauma is not as evident as other types of neglect.

MEDICAL NEGLECT

The failure to provide appropriate health care for a child even though the parents are able to do so, is referred to as medical neglect. Medical neglect is most evident when a parent refuses emergency treatment for a child, but it also occurs when a parent ignores recommendations for treatment of a chronic illness or disease. Child protective services agencies can intervene in an emergency, if a child is suffering from a life-threatening disease and is not receiving medical treatment, or if a child has a chronic disease that can cause disability or disfigurement if left untreated. In these situations, a court order is required to provide medical treatment (US Department of Health and Human Services, Adminstration of Children and Families, Children's Bureau, 2016).

The behaviors of the mother during pregnancy can also lead to medical neglect, as in the case of **fetal alcohol syndrome (FAS)**. Drinking during pregnancy can cause FAS, one of the leading known preventable causes of mental disability and birth defects. Children with FAS are at risk for psychiatric problems, criminal behavior, unemployment, difficulty getting along with others, and incomplete education (US Department of Health and Human Services, Center for Disease Control, 2019).

Reasons for Neglect

Why do some parents neglect their children? Some experts argue that neglectful parents have a **present orientation**, or an inability to plan for the future. This mindset prevents parents from thinking about buying clothes for their children, groceries, cleaning the house, or planning for emergencies (McNamee and Miller, 2004).

Other parents are neglectful through lack of knowledge. Women who have children at an early age may not know how to manage a household or meet their children's needs. This knowledge was not passed along to them from their parents because it is likely they themselves had children at an early age and failed to develop adequate life skills or to understand the psychological and emotional needs of children.

A third explanation for neglectful behavior is poor judgment. Some parents assume their children can handle responsibility before they are ready. They may not impose a curfew for their teens or overlook experimental drug use because they believe their children "can handle it." While some parents may have good intentions and want to teach their children to be responsible adults, excessive or non-existent boundaries can easily lead to neglect.

Finally, some parents simply give up providing adequate care for their children. For some, it may be due to a feeling of being overwhelmed with the responsibilities of being a parent while others may simply ignore their children (Wallace, 2005; Zimbardo and Boyd, 2008; Orford, 2008; Banfield, 1970).

Types of Child Abuse

While neglect is perhaps the most common form of family disruption, the incidence of reporting child abuse is on the rise. According to the US Department of Health and Human Services, in 2018, there were about 3.5 million children who were the subject of an investigation of child maltreatment (which includes abuse and neglect), which resulted in about 678,000 actual cases of abuse and neglect (US Department of Health and Human Services, Administration of Children and Families, 2020). **Child abuse** and neglect are defined by Federal and State laws. The federal Child Abuse Prevention and Treatment Act (CAPTA), which provides minimum standards that states must incorporate in their statutory definitions of child abuse and neglect, defines "child abuse and neglect" as "Any recent act or failure to act on the part of a parent or caretaker, which results in death, serious physical or emotional harm, sexual abuse, or exploitation, or an act or failure to act which presents an imminent risk of serious harm" (US Department of Health and Human Services, 2020). According to the latest data available, most cases of child maltreatment involve neglect, but it is also common for a child to have multiple incidents of maltreatment (Figure 11.8).

Obviously, there are problems with reporting rates of child abuse, so it is likely that the number of actual cases is underestimated (US Department of Health and Human Services, Administration of Children and Families, Children's Bureau, 2017). Parents are the most frequent offenders when it comes to physically abusing their children. Nearly 80 percent of the time, a parent is responsible for abusing their children.

Infants are most likely to be the victims of physical abuse. The incidence of abuse decreases as children get older, likely due to the ability of the children to flee their parents or victimizers by running away or leaving home. Unlike neglect, which may be more difficult to detect, physical abuse results in obvious signs and symptoms. Still, there are often questions about whether a child's injuries were a result of normal childhood activity or if parents caused them through abuse.

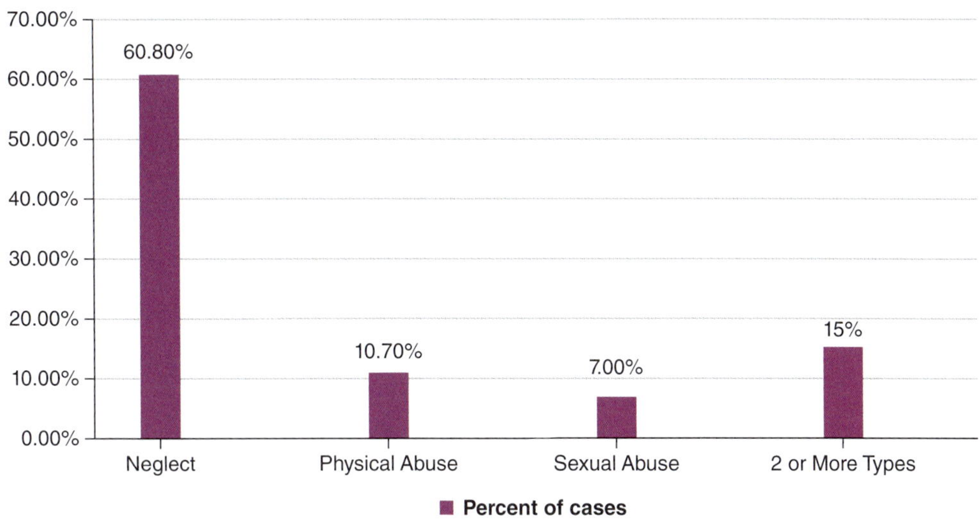

Figure 11.8 Percent of abuse and neglect cases, 2018 Source: US Department of Health and Human Services, 2020.

Sexual Abuse

Notorious cases of the sexual abuse of children generate media outrage, especially those involving members of the clergy, cases of incest, or care providers. However, sexual abuse happens to children in both rural and urban areas, in all socioeconomic and educational levels, and across all racial and cultural groups. The Child Abuse Prevention and Treatment Act (CAPTA) defines **sexual abuse** as "The employment, use, persuasion, inducement, enticement, or coercion of any child to engage in, or assist any other person to engage in, any sexually explicit conduct or simulation of such conduct for the purpose of producing a visual depiction of such conduct; or the rape, and in cases of caretaker or interfamilial relationships, statutory rape, molestation, prostitution, or other form of sexual exploitation of children, or incest with children" (US Department of Health and Human Services, 2019).

Statistics indicate that girls are more frequently the victims of sexual abuse, but that the number of boys is also significant. Estimates suggest that boys account for 25 to 35 percent of child sexual abuse victims. Boys tend not to report sexual abuse as often as girls and may fail to report sexual abuse for fear of appearing weak (US Department of Health and Human Services, 2020).

Most sexual abuse of children is perpetrated by someone the child knows. Sexual abuse can occur within the family (by a parent, stepparent, guardian, older sibling, or relative) or outside the family (often by a person the child and family know well; Table 11.3).

In 90 percent of child sexual abuse cases, the offenders are male. Other common offender characteristics include a history of abuse (either physical or sexual), alcohol or drug abuse, little satisfaction with sexual relationships with adults, a lack of emotional

Table 11.3

Sexual Abuse Offender Relationship to Victim	
Relationship	Percentage
Relatives	30%
Day-care Staff	25%
Parents	3%

Source: US Department of Health and Human Services, Administration for Children and Families. (2020). "Child Abuse, Neglect Data Released" Available at: https://www.acf.hhs.gov/media/press/2020/child-abuse-neglect-data-released

control, or severe mental illness. Females can also be perpetrators of sexual abuse against children. Unlike male offenders, who tend to use threats or actual force, females tend to use persuasion. Boys are more likely than girls to be abused by a female (US Department of Health and Human Services, 2020).

INTERVENTION IN ABUSE CASES

Child abuse cases present a host of challenges—they are often emotionally charged, often go unreported, often occur over time, and impact arguably the most vulnerable victim: children. Children are not fully developed physically or emotionally, they often do not wish to talk about their abuse/neglect experiences and may only tell part of the story when they are forthcoming with information. Adding to the difficulty is the mixed feelings children often have toward their offenders—most know the person who abused them and sometimes there is a strong emotional connection between the two. This creates internal conflict for the child; while they may want the abuse to stop, at the same time they may not want the offender to be punished. In addition, abuse, particularly sexual abuse, usually have no witnesses and occur in private locations. This makes identifying, prosecuting, and preventing such cases extremely difficult. Often, the discovery of abuse occurs when caregivers, such as teachers or physicians, who may have more regular contact with the child, observes symptoms consistent with abuse or neglect. In the end, law enforcement becomes involved when evidence exists that a crime has occurred.

Teachers

Depending on the age of the child, teachers have perhaps the most contact with children outside of their parents. This gives teachers opportunities to observe a child's typical demeanor, behavior, and changes that make the teacher suspect some form of child maltreatment is occurring. Some of the signs are physical: bruises, burns, lacerations, or other injuries, are potential signs that a problem is occurring at home. However, particularly with boys, many such injuries are also a normal part of childhood. However, when a teacher suspects something is occurring that goes beyond normal minor injuries that occur on the playground, they are required to report their concerns to school authorities.

Medical Personnel

Medical personnel, such as school nurses or pediatricians, who have regular contact and interaction with a child, can also be a source of intervention if neglect or abuse is occurring. These providers may also come into contact with a child as a result of a referral by a teacher or other concerned adult, who make them aware of the possibility of potential abuse or neglect. Like teachers, medical personnel have a legal duty to report any findings to the police for further investigation.

Law Enforcement

In most child abuse or neglect cases, the police become involved in one of two ways—either by a referral from a teacher/school; by a physician/medical provider; by a social worker who has been made aware of an allegation by a parent, neighbor, or a child; or through a direct report to the police department by a concerned citizen. The primary role of law enforcement in child abuse cases is to determine if a violation of the criminal law has occurred, and to identify and apprehend the offender. At that point the case is turned over to the district attorney for prosecution or resolution.

Foster Care

Children are placed in **foster care** when a child protective services worker and a court have determined that it is not safe for the child to remain at home because of the risk of maltreatment, including neglect and physical or sexual abuse.

Youths in the foster care system must cope with two sources of trauma: the experience that brought them into the system in the first place as well as their experiences while in the system. Compared to non-foster children, they are more likely to suffer from mental disorders, health-related illnesses, low academic achievement, substance abuse, and delinquency (US Department of Health and Human Services, 2020).

The number of children in foster care rose steadily in the 1990s; decreased a bit in the early 2000s and has since risen again (Figure 11.9). One possible explanation for this increase is the opioid epidemic, as many parents have lost custody of their children due to addiction (Chapter 3; US Department of Health and Human Services, 2020).

As is the case with many social problems, minority children are overrepresented in the foster case statistics, where Black children account for about a quarter of the children in foster care, even though they only represent about 14 percent of all children in the United States.

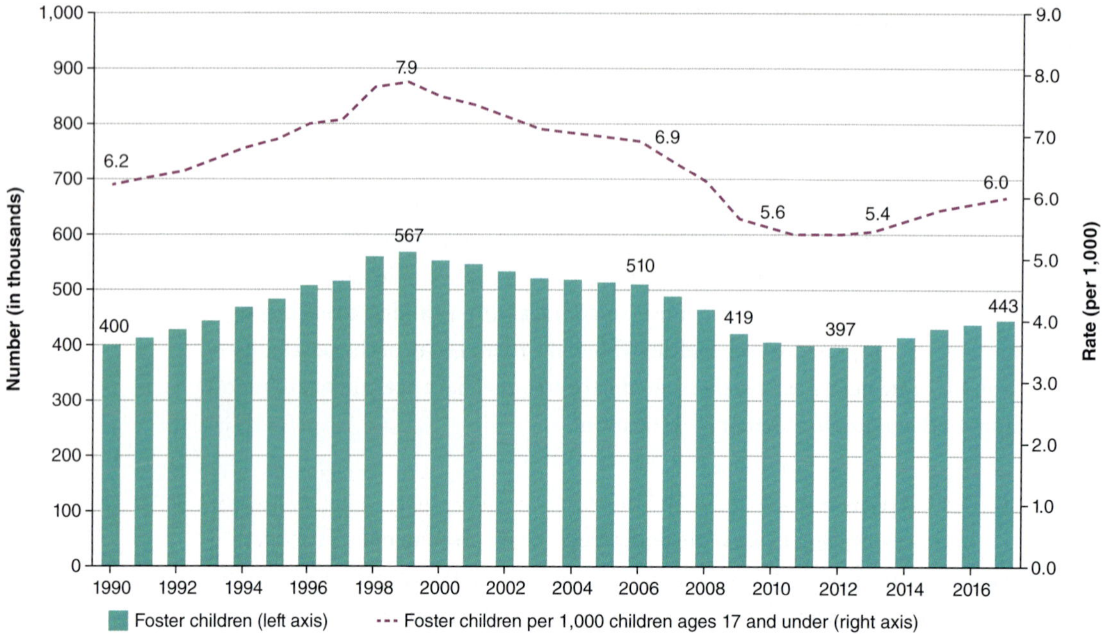

Figure 11.9 Number and rate of children in foster care, ages 17 and younger: 1990-2017 *Data for 2004-2017 are preliminary estimates as of August 10, 2018. Revised estimates may be forthcoming. Sources: US Department of Health and Human Services, U.S. Census Bureau.

Similarly, Hispanic children (of any race) were 18 percent of US children, and accounted for 21 percent of foster children in 2018 (Figure 11.10; US Department of Health and Human Services, 2020). One encouraging sign in recent years is the reduction in the length of stay in foster care for children (US Department of Health and

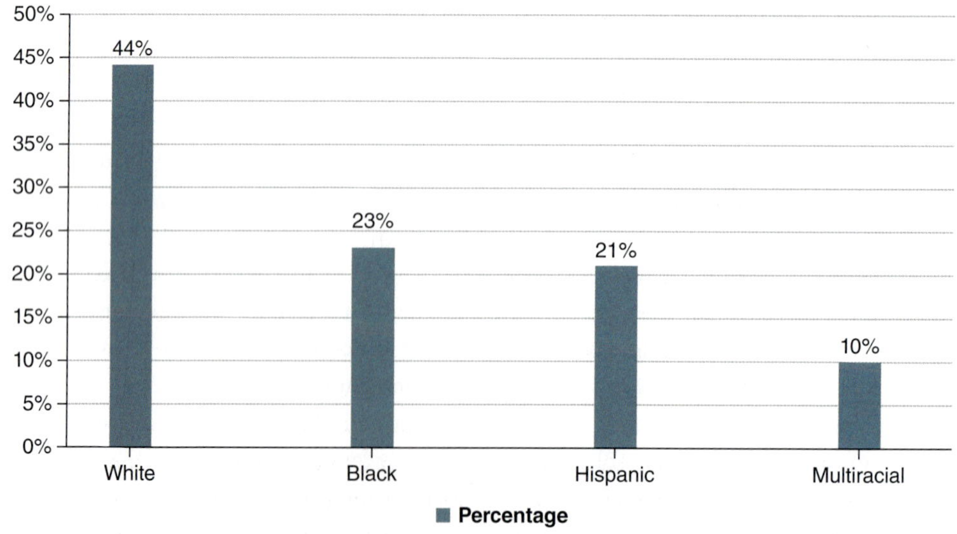

Figure 11.10 Children in foster care by race/ethnicity 2018 Source: US Department of Health and Human Services.

Human Services, Administration of Children and Families, Children's Bureau2017; US Department of Health and Human Services, 2020).

SOCIOLOGICAL THEORY AND THE FAMILY

How sociologists describe the role of the family in society is important to understanding the nature of social life. At a macro level, changing configuration of families may be symptomatic of structural changes occurring in society. At a micro level, families play a critical role in the socialization of children. Families are also the child's first reference group, making it a critical component of developing a child's understanding of societal morality and expectations for its members.

Functionalism and the Family

A functionalist perspective emphasizes the importance of the family to maintaining the stability of society. Durkheim observed that marriage as an institution is symbolic of the larger society, as it involves the blending of diverse people into a more cohesive unit. Parsons saw the family as a synergistic component of society that met people's economic needs and provided for the care and raising of children in an efficient and effective manner.

For contemporary functionalists, the family provides a mechanism to address critical needs for people in society, such as caring for the elderly, properly socializing children to understand and accept society's sense of morality and providing an acceptable outlet to regulate sexual behavior of individuals. Disruptions to the family unit threaten those functions. Deindustrialization and globalization result in the loss of economic well-being for many Americans, threatening the ability of the family to sustain itself. Similarly, no-fault divorce has made the disintegration of families more commonplace. Finally, the increase in the number of single-parent families threatens the ability of the family to fulfill its function of raising well-balanced children with both parents contributing to their development (Parsons and Bales, 1955).

Conflict and Feminist Theories and the Family

While functionalists emphasize the need to restore families in order to ensure stability and cohesion, conflict and feminist theories observe that family structure has always contained an element of exploitation. They argue that rather than operating as a synergistic and harmonious unit, families have always been a source of inequality and conflict.

Conflict theorists argue that, like workers in a factory setting, some family members are dominated by others and exploited for their efforts. Women are dominated by men in the home like the way the elite exploit factory workers. The labor wives contribute to the family, such as cooking, cleaning, and raising the children, is not usually recognized and compensated in the same way as the man's income and professional success.

Feminists argue that this subordination and exploitation of women is not necessarily a function of capitalism, however. Rather, they see it as a product of **patriarchy**, or a male-dominated society that tends to devalue the contributions of women, thereby justifying their exploitation.

For conflict and feminist theorists, problems seen in the family are a product of social inequality. The problem of domestic violence, they argue, is not just about the use of violence by men, but a reflection of the subordinated role of women in general, and laws regulating this behavior tend to reinforce the fact that women have long been oppressed.

Symbolic Interactionism and the Family

While conflict and feminist approaches might argue that the issues in families is about access and utilization of power, and functionalists might contend that the family is the basis for social stability and organization, symbolic interactionists would argue that there is no such thing as "family." They would observe instead that people conceptualize many different types of families based on social interaction and the development of relationships.

That is, while traditional definitions of "family" refer to kinship ties, or the legal status of marriage or adoption, many families include close relationships with people who do not have a kinship or legal obligation. Thus, while there are certain rights and expectations afforded to those who are related by kinship, marriage, or adoption, the configuration of those relationships differs greatly. For many people, "family" includes individuals who are more present in a meaningful way than those who might be a product of biology or a legal treatise (LaRossa and Neitzes, 2009).

Queer Theory and the Family

While feminist theory, like conflict theory, focuses on social inequalities perpetuated by male dominance, queer theory calls attention to similar challenges faced by same-sex couples. For example, queer theorists point to the concept of the **head of household**. This concept typically implies that the male occupies this status and reflects the power to manage the home and make decisions for its members. Queer theorists question this concept: if males are considered the heads of households in heterosexual families, which person occupies this position in a non-heterosexual relationship? For queer theorists, traditional ideas about heterosexuality being the norm are outdated and unrealistic. In such an example, an egalitarian model of the family does not need such requirements to function effectively (Allen and Mendez, 2018).

WHAT WORKS? EFFECTIVE SOLUTIONS TO FAMILY PROBLEMS

While it may seem that the problems families experience are unique to their particular configuration, there are strategies, programs, and changes in social policy and legislation that can help families resolve some of the more serious and enduring issues they encounter. While not every program or tactic will work with every family, there are a number that can be used successfully.

Family Skills Education

One way to help parents improve their ability to raise children is to provide them with an effective program that has a demonstrated track record. An excellent example is the Strengthening Families Program (SFP), created through the US Department of Health and Human Services.

The SFP involves elementary school-aged children and their families in family skills training sessions. SFP increases resiliency and reduces the risks of behavioral, emotional, academic, and social problems by strengthening family relationships, improving parenting skills, and increasing youths' social and life skills. Parents learn how to increase desired behaviors in children by increasing attention to and rewards for positive behaviors. They also learn about clear communication, effective discipline, substance use, problem solving, and limit setting. Children learn how to understand their feelings, control anger, resist peer pressure, comply with parental rules, solve problems, and communicate effectively. Children also develop their social skills and learn about the consequences of substance abuse. Families also practice therapeutic child play, learn communication skills, and reinforce positive behaviors in each other.

Studies of SFP consistently demonstrate that appropriate behaviors in children were increased, fewer instances of aggression and depression symptoms occurred in children, and substance abuse by parents and children decreased. Perhaps most promising is a five-year follow-up study that showed 92 percent of families continued to use parenting skills learned in the program and over two-thirds still used family meetings as a tool in collective decision making (US Department of Health and Human Services, Strengthening Families Program, n.d.).

Aging Out of Foster Care

The challenges facing older youth in foster are considerable, particularly since many of these youth do not have a stable family to rely on. Data indicates that there can be significant impacts on these youth into adulthood, such as unintended pregnancy, homelessness, involvement in crime, unemployment, and other challenges (Rosenberg and Abbott, 2019).

The data indicates that allowing foster children to extend their participation in the foster care system beyond age 18 has a significant impact on their ability to navigate through many of the challenges of adulthood and their experiences. A 2019 study of children who were allowed to remain in extended foster care at age 19 or to age 21, were more likely to be enrolled in school and receiving educational aid and were more likely to be employed or attend training programs than those who aged out of foster care at that same age (Table 11.3). In addition, youth who were allowed to remain in extended

Table 11.3 Comparison of Youth in Extended Foster Care and Youth Who Aged Out, 2019

	NYTD cohort 1 for age 19	NYTD cohort 1 for age 21
Outcome Domain	**Odds**	**Odds**
Having a diploma/GED	1.2x higher	No significant difference
Employment	1.2x higher	1.3x higher
School enrollment	2.8x higher	3x higher
Disconnectedness	2.8x lower	3x lower
Receiving educational aid	1.9x higher	1.4x higher
Homelessness	3.1x lower	2.7x lower
Young parenthood	1.7x lower	2x lower

Results significant at the $p < .05$

foster care had lower odds of being homeless, unemployed, not enrolled in school or being disconnected, compared to youth in foster care who aged out at age 19 or age 21 (Rosenberg and Abbott, 2019).

The Fostering Connections to Success and Increasing Adoptions Act of 2008 is one such effort to improve the chances of foster children to extend care. This federal law gives states the opportunity to continue providing compensation to families for fostering or adoption for children up to the age of 21. There are criteria that foster children have to meet to be eligible, of course, such as enrolling in full-time secondary education programs or working toward preparing for participation in such a program, the foster child is working at least part-time or has a medical condition that prevents them from working (National Conference of State Legislators, 2017).

SO WHAT CAN I DO?

The changing configuration of families presents many challenges to American society, most urgently how children navigate their way through life. In some instances, children simply need the support and encouragement of a responsible adult. This is particularly true of children who have experienced abuse or neglect, but it can also be important for children who are witnessing the divorce of their parents or trying to find their place in a newly constructed blended family.

One thing you can do is offer your time and energy to support one such child. There are many opportunities for you to participate in child advocacy, and reputable organizations provide volunteers with the support and training required to participate in improving a child's life. Perhaps you are interested in the legal dimensions of family dynamics. In such cases, you can volunteer to serve as a Guardian ad Litem in your community. Guardians serve as advocates for the child in cases of neglect and abuse, and work with social workers, attorneys, and judges to find a solution that reflects the best interests of the child.

Or perhaps you enjoy spending time with younger children. Big Brothers Big Sisters of America and similar mentoring programs are a good way to volunteer your time and provide a constructive role model to a child.

Another way for you to offer help is to identify a single parent family and provide some dimension of help there. This could be in the form of respite care for the children or running errands and grocery shopping for a working mother. There are a host of ways you can help; you simply need to be present and extend the offer.

CONCLUSION

Nearly every social problem we have examined so far in this textbook has an impact on families. For example, the opioid epidemic has led to an increase in the number of children in the foster care system (Chapter 3). Challenges relating to poverty and a changing job market have contributed to the rise in the single parent family structure (Chapter 5). And remote learning during the Covid-19 epidemic places additional burdens on household schedules (Chapter 8).

As we have seen, much of what constituted a family unit in the past is evolving into new definitions of "family." With the greater acceptance of same-sex couples and the legitimacy of same-sex marriages, it makes sense that there would be an increase in the number of same-sex families as well as adoptions. Similarly, as people begin to question the value and purpose of traditional marriage, and opt for other alternatives, it is likely that children will increasingly be raised in non-traditional family structures.

Sociologists who study the family provide important insight into the consequences of social problems at the macro level and the micro levels of social life. These changes also influence the nature of social interaction and our understanding of diversity issues.

YOU MAKE THE CALL: FOSTERING A TROUBLED CHILD

You are an educated, married, and successful middle class parent of two daughters, ages six and four. Because you want to help others in the community, you decide to take in a foster child. After contacting the local Department of Social Services and receiving the necessary licensure to be certified as a foster parent, you and your spouse decide to help the group of foster children in greatest need: teenagers.

After meeting with a 14-year-old boy who has been in the foster care system for years due to an absent father and heroin-addicted mother, you decide he is a good fit for your family. The boy seems polite, kind, and friendly. While you are told by his caseworker that he has some minor behavioral issues typical of a teenager, you feel that you can handle whatever problems come with love, compassion, gentleness and setting reasonable boundaries. Surely, this young man will see what you are doing for him and he most certainly will be open to following rules that are established with his input, right?

About two weeks after he arrives, the young man begins pushing those boundaries and becomes a different person than the one you met during the interview. In fact, so dramatic is the behavioral change you wonder if you had been misled in his assessment. He refuses to follow even basic rules of the household and when held accountable, he flies into a destructive rage. You quickly realize that the strategies used when you were growing up are completely ineffective and the ones you considered before he moved in are also not working. You are not a trained therapist and are beginning to see that you are not at all equipped to handle the young man's behavior.

Soon, you become fearful of leaving the boy alone in the house with your spouse and the children. Your social worker refers you to a family therapist, who tells you that if you feel your safety is threatened you must have the social worker remove the boy from your home or, in extreme cases, call the police.

Questions to Consider

1. Do you contact the social worker and demand some type of immediate intervention by a therapist?
2. Do you tell the social worker that the boy's behavior is beyond your ability to manage? What are the implications of such a decision? Will this only add another layer of rejection to the boy's self-esteem and make him an even greater challenge for the next family?
3. Do you address the issue in unconventional ways, such as recognizing that perhaps he doesn't respect compassion and kindness, seeing them as weaknesses to exploit? What are some of the consequences of that approach?
4. What impact is the boy's behavior having on your family, particularly your two young daughters?

SUMMARY

- Operationalize and define concepts such as the family and some of the recent trends in the literature about family structure in the United States.
    - According to the US Census Bureau, a family consists of "two or more people, one of whom is the householder, related by birth, marriage, or adoption and residing in the same housing unit."
    - A family differs from a household, which may consist of a person living alone or multiple unrelated individuals or families living together.
    - The function of a family is to meet its members' needs for food, shelter, and intimacy as well as to provide socialization, or the transmission of culture from one generation to the next.
    - Most discussions of family assume a nuclear family. This contrasts with the extended family, which often includes grandparents, uncles, aunts, and others living in the household with the nuclear family. The nuclear family has been the standard structure in the United States for many years (Khimm, 2015).

- Summarize the research on changes that have occurred to the family institution, such as cohabitation, women in the workforce, same-sex families, grandparent-led families, or blended families.
    - Social changes have resulted in new conceptualizations of families.
    - Single-parent families, blended families, same-sex families and other variations are increasingly common and accepted.
    - Changes to concepts of family may be structural, as modifications to the economy, the changing role of women, and other issues may cause people to reconsider the value of marriage and how families are created.
- Analyze a variety of problems families experience, such as family and domestic violence.
    - Challenges to families in the United States include divorce, family violence, child neglect and abuse.
    - The foster care system also has many challenges.
    - While the trends on child abuse appear to be decreasing slightly, most cases are not reported to authorities.
- Compare the differences and similarities between child abuse, neglect, and the foster care system.
    - The overall term used to describe child abuse, neglect and other offenses against children is called child maltreatment.
    - Neglect, by definition, occurs when parents or guardians do not provide the kind of care needed, even though they have the ability to do so.
    - Child abuse consists of actions or behaviors that cause physical harm to a child.
    - Many children who experience abuse and neglect end up in the foster care system, which consists of state monitored families who provide guardianship for a child. In some cases, children in foster care are placed in facilities or group homes, which house many foster children.
- Identify how child abuse can be detected and prevented.
    - Child abuse can be detected by teachers, parents, police officers, social workers and others. Each has a legal obligation to report any evidence that abuse or neglect has occurred.
    - In some cases, evidence of abuse is seen in physical injuries to children or in the way a child is dressed, but in other instances, abuse and neglect can be difficult to detect.
- Illustrate how sociological theory helps us understand and diagnose problems and challenges families experience.
    - Functionalists view changes to the American family as a potential threat to society since functionalism tends to see the family as a critical variable in the stability and survival of society.
    - Conflict, feminist, and queer theories tend to see families as a reflection of the larger instances of social, political and economic inequalities in society, whereby the work and role of women tends to be devalued, minimized, trivialized when abuses occur.
    - Symbolic interactionists tend to look at the dynamics of what constitutes a family and the social construction of reality for people as they interact with each other and develop relationships. Thus, there are many versions of families, and biological connections do not

necessarily ensure stable, successful, or involved relationships with its members.

- Assess the effectiveness of empirically supported programs to help families.
    - There are programs that have been shown to be successful in addressing some of the problems that emerge as a result of changes to the family system.
    - While the trauma and issues created by children who are abused and neglected are serious, and while foster children tend to encounter unique and life-long issues, extending care and providing support can offer some opportunities to recover from these events and give those children a chance at a normal life.

KEY TERMS

Blended families 314
Child abuse 328
Cohabitation 318
Cycle of violence 325
Divorce 319
Domestic violence 325
Failure to Thrive (FTT) 326
Family violence 324
Fetal Alcohol Syndrome (FAS) 327
Foster care 331
Grandparent-led families 323
Head of household 334
Multiple partner fertility (MPF) 319
Neglect 326
Nuclear family 315
Patriarchy 333
Present orientation 327
Remarriage 319
Same-sex marriages 322
Sexual abuse 329
Single-parent family 323
Stay-at-home parent 316
The Fostering Communities to Success and Increasing Adoptions Act of 2008 336
Traditional family values 322

Discussion Questions

1. Why do you think fewer people are getting married? Is it due to a decline in religious beliefs, the lack of a financial incentive, the simplicity of divorce, or a larger disconnectedness among people?
2. What factors contribute to the large percentage of single-parent families in the United States?
3. What factors do you think are most important in explaining the rise in birthrates among older single women?
4. In Sociological Story Time, there was an article that discussed loneliness as a public health crisis in the United States, particularly for men. How would Durkheim explain this sense of loneliness, even for those who have spouses, children, and families?
5. Given the apparent success that grandparent-led families seem to have on children's overall well-being, what types of incentives might society offer to encourage this option over placing children in the foster care system?

Learn more with this chapter's digital tools, including Data and Media Literacy Exercises, flashcards, and chapter self-assessments at **www.oup.com/he/mcnamara**.

12

Is 70 the New 40? Population and Aging

LEARNING OBJECTIVES

- Discuss the changing configuration of the elderly population in the United States.
- Describe the economics of aging, including income, retirement issues, and job discrimination among the elderly.
- Analyze crime and the elderly, including victimization patterns among the elderly and crime as offenders.
- Characterize the health care challenges facing the elderly in the United States.
- Describe family relations and aging, including widowhood and social isolation. familial and health-related issues for the elderly.
- Compare various sociological theories as it relates to aging and the elderly population.
- Assess effective programs that assist the elderly and their empirical support, such as Meals on Wheels.
- Discuss what individuals can do to address the challenges of an aging population.

Chapter Outline

Attitude is everything In the US, although the social safety net for senior citizens is increasingly frayed, some older people find health and strength in community. In Brooklyn, NY, these seniors gathered in 2012 for a free outdoor exercise class.

In many Western societies today, people take extraordinary steps to prevent or delay the aging process. Although aging—and, ultimately, dying—are fundamental human experiences, these natural processes for many people lead to a fear of a loss of status, loss of social identity, and marginalization by a society that values youth, beauty, and health.

While other societies celebrate the aged and revere the wisdom that comes from the experience of time, in the United States many people have discomfort with aging and an anxiety about becoming a burden to their family and community. While other countries show deference and respect to older family members, often seeing their care as a form of honorable role reversal as a parent gets older, sometimes referred to as **filial piety**, in the United States there seems to be greater willingness to require providers to offer that care. The rise of assisted living facilities and other industries that cater to delaying the dependence of older people is a reflection of the American value of autonomy.

The inequalities we have examined in previous chapters can be especially severe for older populations. That is, the problems people experience as a result of their race and social class become magnified as they get older and have fewer resources to sustain themselves when their working lives have ended. The disproportionate toll the Covid-19 virus took on the elderly made these inequalities all the starker.

For younger people—especially people who do not live with, or very close to, older family members—it can be difficult to imagine or plan for life after the age of 65. Unfortunately, the persistent social problems associated with aging (such as health care, poverty, and isolation) are not likely to be resolved within the next few decades. Moreover, the decisions of current policymakers, such as how the Social Security system and Medicare will be managed, will significantly impact your future when you reach that age. Thus, it is important to analyze the consequences of these decisions and to understand the experiences of those in the past as a precursor to what could happen in the future.

SOCIOLOGICAL STORY TIME:

- In the wake of the devastation of Covid-19 and its impact on the elderly, particularly those in nursing homes, and despite the nearly $7.5 billion in relief from the federal government to nursing homes around the country, many experts and nursing home officials predict that nearly two-thirds of nursing homes in the United States may permanently close. In 2020, nearly 100,000 Covid-19 related deaths occurred to the elderly in nursing homes, which comprised approximately 40 percent of all Covid-related deaths in the United States (Snelling, 2020; Fulmer et al., 2020).
- On January 20, 2021, Joseph Biden was given the distinction of being the oldest person in US history to ever be sworn in as President of the United States. Prior to his inauguration, Biden offered important insight into the benefits of being an older adult. He said, "Hopefully, I can demonstrate not only with age has come wisdom and experience that can make things a lot better." Biden also said in an interview, "I am an adult and I will bring back normalcy and I will bring back a sense of decency and demonstrate maturity" (Diaz, 2021).
- Despite a 1.3 percent cost of living increase in Social Security payments for 2021, which generally results in a $20 per month increase in benefits (Konish, 2020), a Kaiser Family Foundation report noted that people 65 and older pay an average $5,460 per year in out of pocket expenses for health care. In addition, people without supplemental health insurance beyond Medicare, about 20 percent of the elderly, pay an average of $7,473 per year in out of pocket expenses. Given the rising costs of other items, such as prescription drugs and dental care (which are generally not covered by Medicare), people who rely primarily on Social Security as their source of income are increasingly finding it difficult to make ends meet (Cubanski et al., 2019).

THE AGING AMERICAN POPULATION

At what point do you categorize someone as "elderly" or "old"? You may be surprised to know that there is no official consensus in determining when someone is considered "elderly." Most people use 65 years old as marking the point when someone is considered elderly. This is the usual retirement age, the point at which one is eligible for Social Security benefits, pensions, retirement income, and Medicare. But the number is rather arbitrarily designated. While there are problems in determining what constitutes "elderly," the generally accepted age category is 65 and older.

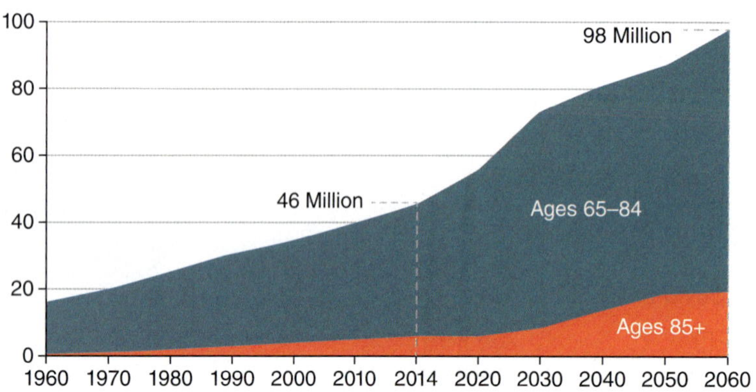

Figure 12.1 US population ages 65 and older will more than double by 2060
Source: PRB analysis of data from the U.S. Census Bureau.

According to the Administration on Aging, a division of the US Department of Health and Human Services, in 2019 there were 52.4 million people over the age of 65 in the United States, or about 16 percent of the US population. This number is an increase of more than 35 percent from 2008 (Administration on Aging, 2020). The projection for the size of this segment of the population is expected to grow considerably in the coming years (Figure 12.1).

As a result of improvements in health and medicine, people are living longer in this country. According to the Center for Disease Control, the life expectancy of an American in 1960 was 69.7 years, in 1990 it was 75.4 years, and in 2016, it was 78.9 years (US Department of Health and Human Services, Center for Disease Control, 2004). All of the age categories one might use to describe the elderly—55 and over, 65 and over, and 75 and over—witnessed dramatic increases in size since 1980 (Figure 12.2; Medina, Sabo, and Vespa, 2020).

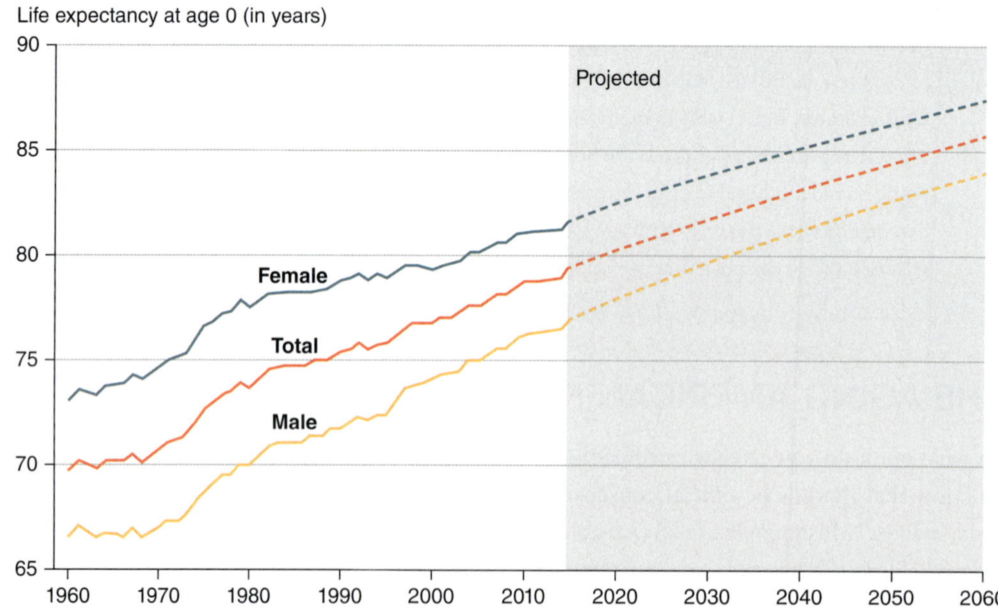

Figure 12.2 Historical and projected life expectancy for the total US population at birth: 1960–2060.
Source: Medina, Lauren; Sabo, Shannon; and Vespas, Jonathan. (2020). "Giving Longer, Historical and Projected Life Expectancy in the United States, 1960-2060." US Census Bureau, February.

As the population of the United States ages, the implications of the changes for our society are striking. For instance, the elderly population will become more racially and ethnically diverse (Figure 12.3). About 23 percent of the elderly in the United States is a member of a racial or ethnic minority group. Of this group of people 65 years and older, a small number (0.7 percent) identified themselves as being of two or more races.

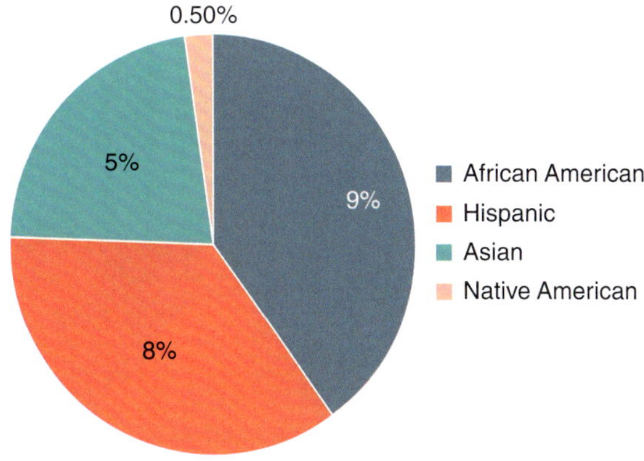

Figure 12.3 US Elderly Population by Race/Ethnicity 2019 Source: Administration for Community Living, 2020

In addition, nearly 70 percent of the elderly are married (Figure 12.4). However, an increasing number are living alone. This is especially true for women. Among women age 75 and older, nearly 44 percent lived alone in 2019.

In general, then, the population as a whole is getting older, the number of people considered elderly is growing, and they are living longer. Increases in lifespan are driven by improvements in health care as well as general changes in health behavior, such as reductions in the number of people suffering from obesity and smoking (US Department of Health and Human Services, Center for Disease Control, 2004). There can be little doubt that as the elderly population continues to grow, the social and economic issues they represent are considerable. One of those costs relates to health care, another relates to crime. It is important to recognize the diversity of elder Americans as individuals as well as generational cohorts, as each of these cohorts experiences (or will experience) these problems differently.

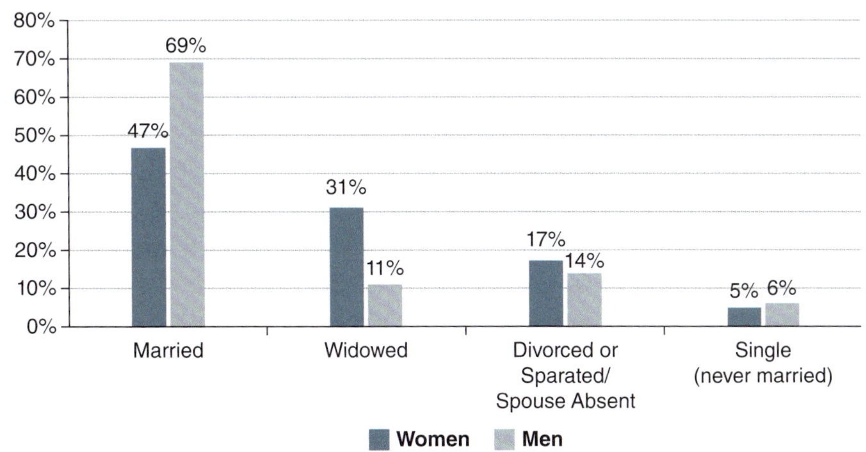

Figure 12.4 Marital status of persons age 65 and older, 2019 Source: U.S. Census Bureau, Current Population Survey, Annual Social and Economic Supplement

Golden years The baby boom generation, which enjoyed unparalleled prosperity during their lifetimes, has for the most part enjoyed both health and wealth as they retire.

The Elderly as Baby Boomers and Generation X

The main population of people aged 65 and over in the United States, the **baby boomers**, were born between 1946 and 1964, representing about 28 percent of the overall US population. Baby boomers are responsible for some of the most dramatic changes in American history. From the Vietnam War protests to the Civil Rights Movement to the rise of feminism and the hippie movement, boomers have been at the center of the debate, discussion, and social change (Zemke, Raines, and Filipczik, 2000). Boomers have also been referred to as the "Me" generation for their emphasis on narcissism and individual pleasure. In fact, this group has fundamentally altered the way in which the elderly are understood in American society. Not content to simply age gracefully like their parents, this group has remained (with important exceptions) healthy, wealthy, and active into their retirement years. As a result, boomers have changed the way most Americans conceive of normal aging (Zemke, Raines, and Filipczik, 2000).

The baby boom generation focused on their careers and leisure activities rather than marrying young and starting families. As a result, many boomers delayed having children or remained childless. The subsequent generation, far fewer in number, were born between 1968 and 1979 (Zemke, Raines and Filipczik, 2000). This generation, numbering about 41 million, are referred to as **Generation X (Gen Xers).** Although the oldest members of this generation are still many years away from retirement, they are likely to experience both the aging process and the quality of life in retirement in a significantly less comfortable fashion than their boomer parents. Many experts argue that this group has been ignored, misunderstood, and disheartened (Kraus, 2017).

Gen Xers are generally marked by their lack of optimism for the future and an absence of trust in traditional values. They grew up during the end of the Cold War and witnessed the economic depression of the 1990s. They watched as their parents coped with job loss due to outsourcing, deindustrialization, and corporate mergers. This had a profound impact on many Gen Xers, who realized that company loyalty and sacrifices to get ahead did not always pay off. This lack of stability in the job market left many Gen Xers cynical about their lives, future, and the country as a whole. This group is also generally critical of the boomer generation, whom many Gen Xers look upon as self-centered and impractical (Kraus, 2017).

ECONOMICS OF AGING

In previous generations, older Americans might have relied on a comfortable cushion of savings, a modest pension, and the care and support of extended family to provide for them after their working years. Since the boomer generation, however, Americans are increasingly on their own when it comes to a safe and stable retirement.

Income

According to the US Census Bureau, the median income of older persons in the United States in 2018 was $25,601 (Figure 12.5). The median income for men was $34,267 and $20,431 for women.

The median household income of a person age 65 or older in the United States in 2018 was $64.023. However, this figure varies considerably by race and ethnicity (Figure 12.6).

While the source of that income can be from pensions, investments, or savings, the largest source for most people comes from Social Security. Although many workers in the baby boomer generation enjoyed a traditional pension plan from their employers, which provided a modest income

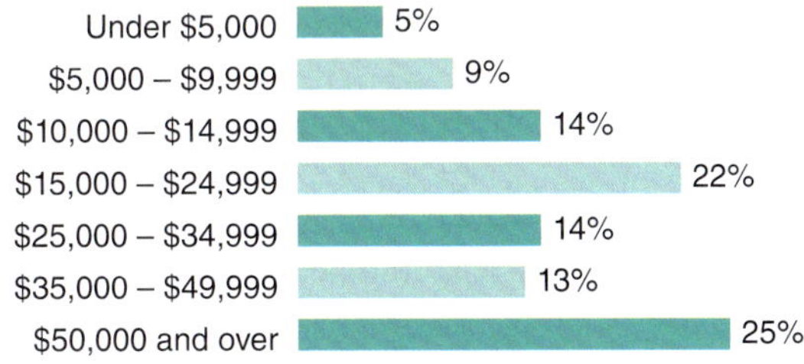

Figure 12.5 Median income of older persons in US, 2018. Note: Percentages may not add to 100 due to rounding. Source: U.S. Census Bureau, Current Population Survey, Annual Social and Economic Supplement.

Figure 12.6 Median family income of US elderly by race/ethnicity, 2018. Note: Percentages may not add to 100 due to rounding. Source: U.S. Census Bureau, Current Population Survey, Annual Social and Economic Supplement.

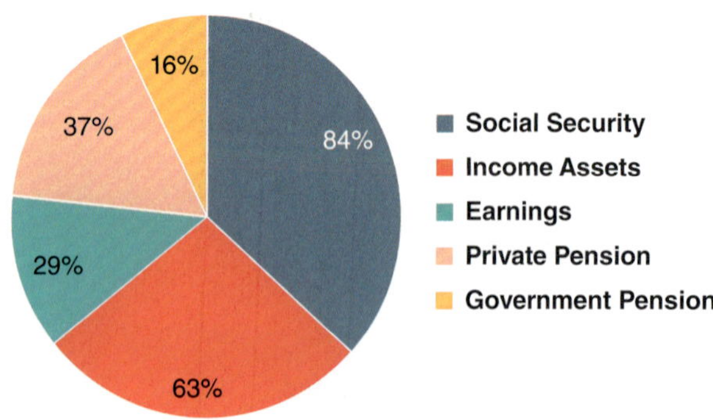

Figure 12.7 Median family income of US elderly by race/ethnicity, 2018

after their retirement, most employees today (if an employer offers any sort of retirement plan at all), will have a 401k or similar plan. In such instances, the employer makes a contribution to the fund based on matching from the employee's own contributions (which are deducted from her paycheck). The individual employee is then is responsible for managing the plan herself.

According to the US Census Bureau, Social Security constituted 84 percent of the income for people 65 and older in 2019 (Figure 12.7). The Center for Budget and Policy Priorities (2020) suggests that Social Security was generally designed to supplement about 40 percent of a person's working income, so it is not designed to be the primary source of income in retirement (Center for Budget and Policy Priorities, 2020).

Older Americans in the Workforce

One of the consequences of an aging population is that there will be more older people in the workplace. Also, the lack of a pension, retirement plan, or adequate savings means that many older workers must either keep their current job or find another one as they age. While some workers are able to retire and live comfortably without having to find a job, for others a part-time or even a full-time job is a necessity.

According to a 2017 Congressional report on America's aging workforce, there is considerable evidence to indicate a growing elderly workforce in the labor market (Figure 12.8). For instance, the number of Americans over age 55 is expected to represent nearly 25 percent of the overall labor force by 2026 (US Senate, Special Committee on Aging, 2017). The report also notes that the growth of the overall labor force between 2016 and 2026 is only about 0.6 percent per year, but workers in the 65–74 age group will grow 4.2 percent per year while those in the 75 and above category will grow by 6.7 percent per year. While the participation rates for workers 25–54 and even those in the 55-64 categories will remain about the same, the projections for workers who are 65 and older and 75 and older are expected to grow considerably by 2026 (US Senate, Special Committee on Aging, 2017).

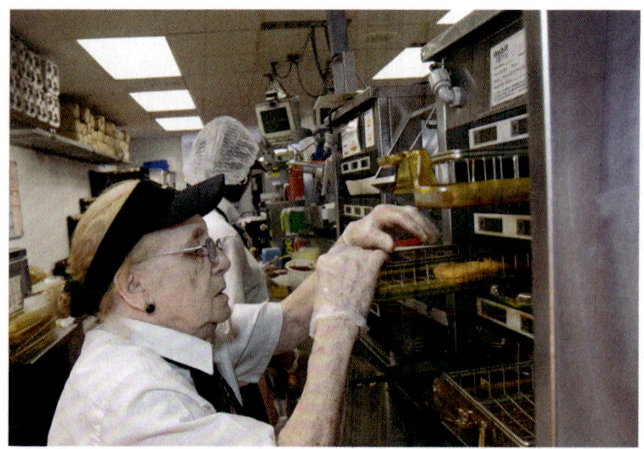

Retirement out of reach Many older Americans find they have to continue working to support themselves long after the traditional retirement age. Here, 80-year-old Angela DiNoto prepares a sandwich at a McDonald's in Michigan.

Another finding of the Senate Committee's report is that there are actually many advantages

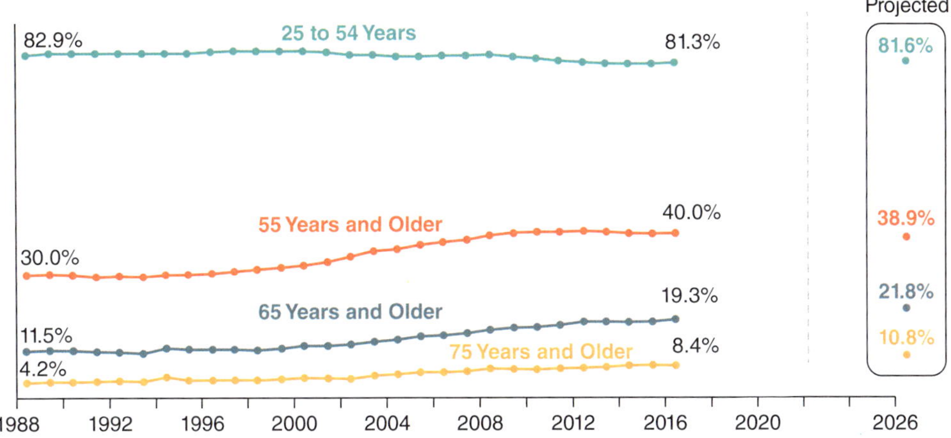

Figure 12.8 Sources of income in retirement, 2019 Source: Administration for Community Living, 2020

for elderly workers remaining in the labor force. For instance, there is considerable research that suggests work improves one's physical, psychological and cognitive health, improves their quality of life as well as providing some level of financial stability and security (US Senate, Special Committee on Aging, 2017).

Elderly workers are also valuable resources for organizations, given their experience, wisdom, insight, and dedication to their jobs. Older workers are also valuable in terms of their ability to mentor younger workers. In many ways, employers are learning that not only will elderly workers become a reality in the labor force in the future, they bring substantial and added value to the organization (US Senate, Special Committee on Aging, 2017).

At the same time, however, older workers face obstacles that many of their younger counterparts do not. For some, there are health-related issues that impede older workers and require some flexibility and accommodations by employers. Other elderly workers are facing caregiver responsibilities, such as caring for an ailing spouse. For still others, retraining is needed to reach a level of competence, but not all older workers are able to quickly transition into new roles. Furthermore, some elderly workers need full-time employment in their later years but can only find part-time work to make ends meet (US Senate, Special Committee on Aging, 2017).

Finally, there is **ageism** that operates in the labor force—where older workers are discriminated by employers. This can occur in many ways, such as older workers being denied promotion opportunities, hiring and layoff decisions based on age, or limiting training opportunities to younger workers based on the belief that older workers are not sufficiently savvy or competent in a given area or task. In 1967, Congress passed the **Age Discrimination in Employment Act (ADEA),** which made it illegal for employers to discriminate against employees who were 40 years of age or older. This law included prohibiting policies that required older workers to retire at specific ages and other forms of discrimination that prohibited older workers from applying for jobs. Despite this legislation, age discrimination continues to exist and employers have found ways to circumvent the laws in a variety of ways (US Senate, Special Committee on Aging, 2017).

Retirement Savings

Retirement is romanticized as a stage in the life course where the person is relieved of their occupational and parental responsibilities and are able to pursue their interests in a carefree manner. However, the realities of retirement for most people are far different from the imagined depictions people use during their working lives. This is especially true for poor White Americans as well as Blacks and Hispanics/Latinos.

Low-wage jobs, discrimination in the workplace, and changes in the economy have affected the earning power of these groups over their working lives. They may not have been offered a pension or retirement savings plan, and may have depended on their employers for health insurance. As a result, many are either unable to retire since there is no pension or retirement plan, or they are forced to continue working until the mental and physical challenges of aging make it no longer possible.

In some cases, employers can provide private sector plans such as 401k plans, where they contribute a certain percentage of the employees' contribution. Such programs, however, usually require some understanding and knowledge of how stocks, bonds, mutual funds, and other investments work. Those who are sufficiently savvy in this area can create a portfolio that provides income into retirement, but many Americans are ignorant of financial planning, which is what made pension plans of the past so attractive: workers knew that if they achieved a certain number of years with a company, they would be given a pension (usually a percentage of their salary) for the rest of their lives. The increased life spans of Americans also means that any money saved for retirement has to last longer.

Financial experts suggest that people should expect to live at least 18 years after they retire, and plan accordingly. They also argue that, by age 55, American workers planning for retirement should have saved about seven times their current working salary. If the typical worker in the United States earns approximately $50,000 per year, that means the amount saved by age 55 should be approximately $350,000. However, according to the Economic Policy Institute, the median retirement account balance for households of those in the 50-55 age group is $8,000. For those in the next older category, 56-61 years of age, the median retirement account is only $17,000 (Backman, 2017). Factors such as credit card debt and student loan debt both make it difficult to save at the pace recommended by experts.

Instead, many retired Americans rely on Social Security to support themselves. Social Security was never intended to be the primary source of income for retirees.

From the beginning of the program, the expectation was that retirees would have other sources of income, either in the form of pensions, investments or other resources (Backman, 2017).

Retirement also presents challenges for the elderly that go beyond its financial dimensions. Chief among these challenges is the increased cost of health care. As of 2020, the typical recipient of Social Security collects just $18,170 a year in benefits, but most experts project that a healthy person is likely to spend up to $10,000 per year in health care costs (Bloom, 2017; Leonhardt, 2019; Center on Budget and Policy Priorities, 2020). Either way, this means additional expenses for those who are not earning incomes during retirement.

Making ends meet Social Security was never intended to be a long-term primary source of income for retirees. Many seniors rely on private charity, such as this food bank in New York City, to help stretch their limited incomes.

CRIME AND THE ELDERLY

Since the early 1970s some attention has been paid to the relationship between crime and the elderly (Seigel, 2005; Sykes and Cullen, 2005). The majority of this focus has been on fear of crime as well as elderly victimization. While conventional wisdom has been that the elderly are at the greatest risk of becoming the victims of crime, research has consistently shown that they have the lowest rates of actual victimization (Livingston, 1992; Adler, Mueller and Laufer, 1995). However, fear itself can be seen as a form of victimization, and the elderly, along with women, express the highest levels of fear. Moreover, the consequences of actual victimization can be more severe for the elderly than other age groups because of their physical limitations and their limited economic ability to recover from the financial losses sustained by crime.

Elderly Victims

As a person ages, rates of victimization tends to decline. According to the National Crime Victimization Survey (NCVS), elderly persons, those over the age of 65, experienced less violence and fewer property crimes than younger persons between. Property crime (such as identity theft, elder fraud, and larceny) provided the greatest threat to those age 65 or older. Elderly persons age 65 or older had substantially lower victimization rates of violent crime compared to younger people age 12 to 17 (Table 12.1; Morgan and Truman, 2020).

About 42 percent of those 65 or older reported incidents of violent crime to the police compared to and compared to 24 percent of those who were ages 12 to 17 (Table 12.2; Morgan and Truman, 2020).

Table 12.1 Total Violent Victimizations per 1,000 People by Age 2018–2019

Age	2018	2019
	Per 1,000 People	Per 1,000 People
12–17	34.2	35.2
18–24	35.9	37.2
25–34	31.8	25.0
35–49	25.2	19.5
50-64	18.3	18.9
65 and over	6.5	6.0

Source: Rachel E. Morgan and Jennifer Truman. (2020). *Criminal Victimization 2019.* September, US Department of Justice, Bureau of Justice Statistics. Available at: https://www.bjs.gov/content/pub/pdf/cv19.pdf

Table 12.2 Victimization Reporting Rates in the United States by Age 2019

Age	Percentage
12–17	24.0%
18–24	37.9%
25–34	46.4%
35–49	44.4%
50–64	47.1%
65 or older	41.9%

Source: Rachel, E. Morgan and Jennifer Truman. (2020). *Criminal Victimization 2019.* September, US Department of Justice, Bureau of Justice Statistics. Available at: https://www.bjs.gov/content/pub/pdf/cv19.pdf

An emerging threat to older Americans is identity theft. Persons aged 65 or older suffer higher incidents of identity theft than other groups, but this could be due to the fact that the elderly generally have more assets and resources (making them more attractive to identity thieves) than younger groups. In addition, the elderly are made more vulnerable to identity theft due to social isolation (discussed later) and discomfort or lack of familiarity with using the internet safely and protecting their digital data.

Elder Abuse

A particularly severe form of victimization is **elder abuse**. Because there is little consensus around what constitutes elder abuse, as well as a lack of a uniform reporting system, it is difficult to ascertain how many older Americans are abused, neglected, or exploited each year. According to the National Center on Elder Abuse, for every case of elder abuse, neglect, exploitation, or self-neglect reported to authorities, an estimated five more go unreported (National Center on Elder Abuse, 2016).

Types of abuse vary. One type involves financial exploitation. This is usually the result of some sort of confidence game or fraud committed against the elderly. According to one study, the overall reporting of financial exploitation is about 1 in 25 cases, which translates into about 5 million financial abuse victims each year (Wasik, 2000).

Elder abuse Older people are vulnerable to financial and physical abuse.

Another type of elderly victimization is physical abuse. A study of nursing homes found that among seven types of abuse, physical abuse was the most common type reported (National Center on Elder Abuse. 2016).

The National Center on Elder Abuse found that older women were far more likely than men to suffer from physical abuse or neglect. Almost two-thirds (65.7 percent) of elder abuse victims were women. This same study also found that 43 percent of abuse victims were age 80 or older (National Center on Elder Abuse, 2016).

The abusers in this study were primarily females (52.7 percent), and three-fourths of offenders were under age 60. About half of the perpetrators of **elderly abuse** were members of the victim's family—a third of the perpetrators were adult children and another 21 percent were other family members. Spouses or intimate partners accounted for only 11 percent of the total number of offenders. According to the study, caregiver neglect accounted for about 20 percent of all neglect cases (National Center on Elder Abuse, 2016; Lachs and Ramirez, 2014).

Elderly Offenders

The subject of **elderly offenders** has not received as much research attention as elderly victims. For the general public, the image of the elderly offender is shaped by stereotypes and misinformation. Because people think of the elderly as infirm, they may conclude that elderly offenders commit relatively "harmless" non-violent crimes, such as shoplifting. Further complicating the picture of elderly offenders is the fact that the agencies that collect data on crime vary considerably in their **operationalization** of age, or how they define it for the purpose of analysis.

For example, in their analysis of crime statistics, the FBI uses "65 and over" as the upper-most category in arrest data, but includes 55-59 and 60-64 age groups as well. Other agencies in the criminal justice system, such as the Federal Bureau of Prisons, use 45 as their cutoff point, while some state systems use 60. Some states use the degree of disability in their definition rather than chronological age. An added problem is that the elderly population tends to overlap with two other special needs categories: the chronically ill and the terminally ill (Shimmkus, 2007). This variability makes it difficult to compare information about elderly criminals from one study to the next.

According to the Uniform Crime Reports, which classifies arrests by age, there are three general categories to use in assessing elderly criminals: 55-59, 50-64, and 65 and older. Given the problems of operationalizing the term "elderly," for the purpose of this chapter, we will use these three categories.

Some researchers argue that crime rates among the elderly are actually much higher than what is officially recorded or even known about. These experts also note that the police are more likely to use discretion with the elderly, are less likely to arrest the elderly, and are more likely to just give the elderly warnings (Berger, 2018).

Although the elderly are significantly less likely to be arrested than younger people, elderly offenders are more likely to be arrested for alcohol and drug-related matters, such as intoxication and driving under the influence. Other types of criminal behaviors that the elderly are more likely to be arrested for involve larceny: theft, shoplifting, fraud, crimes against persons, white-collar crimes, and drug violations. Although the elderly are less likely than younger people to violently assault or physically harm other people, some data does indicate that overall rates of violence have gone up. Even though older offenders are less likely to be violent, some research has shown that rates of sexual offending have risen among the elderly, although overall rates are still relatively low (Berger, 2018).

Even if elderly offenders are less likely to commit violent crimes, the problems associated with elderly offenders are especially urgent in the field of corrections. A "get tough" approach to crime in the 1980s resulted in an unprecedented level of incarceration of offenders with very long sentences. Over time, these inmates have developed health problems beyond the scope of the correctional system's ability to deal with them. From 1995 to 2003 there was a 126 percent increase in the number of federal prisoners aged 65 and older, and by 2004 the prison population in America for inmates 55 and older grew from 44,200 to 69,900 (Berger, 2018).

HEALTH CARE AND AGING

The devastating effects of Covid-19 on the elderly demonstrated just how fragile the US social safety net is when it comes to that population. But there are chronic social, political, and medical problems that the elderly must contend with, and that US policymakers and other stakeholders have struggled to address—much less resolve. Problems such as a decline or loss of hearing and vision, along with arthritis, heart disease and diabetes are common among the elderly, according to the National Center for Health Statistics. The inevitability of aging also brings with it the need for assistance in day-to-day activities. Gerontologists estimate that, as the population continues to get older, the number of people who will need long-term care will increase over the next few decades as that group in the oldest age category increases. By 2060, 24 million older adults will need long-term care (Center for Disease Control and Prevention, 2017).

It is important to consider the disparate impacts of aging on the health of different populations. While the gender gaps in reported health have narrowed in recent years, with about as many elderly men reporting their health status as similar to elderly women, race plays a role. Older African Americans, for instance, are more likely to describe themselves as being in fair or poor health compared to elderly Asians or Whites, according to the National Center for Health Statistics (National Center for Health Statistics, 2017).

Chronic health issues of particular concern include expensive and personally devastating degenerative diseases like Alzheimer's and dementia; compassionate care for the dying; and a lack of safe, reliable, and affordable long-term care as life expectancies increase.

Long-Term Care

Traditionally, people were able to age in place, supported by close family and community. However, the current perception that most elderly people live in nursing homes is inaccurate. Data suggests that only about four percent of people age 65 and older live in long-term care facilities. One reason is that nursing home care is very expensive—upward of $75,000 per year, far beyond what most people can afford. Another factor is that most people do not need the intensive level of care that a nursing home provides until they are much older. (Genworth.com, n.d.).

Today only about one percent of people between the ages of sixty-five and seventy-four live in long-term facilities such as a nursing home. However, that percentage increases significantly among people eighty-five and over. As life expectancy rates increase, along with higher rates of chronic illness and higher rates of being unmarried (because women live longer than men), women make up about 75 percent of nursing home residents (National Center for Assisted Living, 2016).

It is more likely that an elderly person who needs care lives in an **assisted living facilities**. The main difference between an assisted living facility and a nursing home is the level of care needed for the resident. People in nursing homes require around the clock care and supervision, typically by skilled medical providers and may need a variety of treatments such as physical therapy, speech therapy, or respiratory care. Those living in assisted living typically have their own apartments and independence and generally only need custodial care (some type of supervision since it isn't safe to leave them alone) or have mobility issues that requires someone to assist them moving from one part of the apartment to another.

This is a booming industry, with more than 30,000 facilities currently operating in the United States. Assisted living comes in many forms, such as apartments for seniors with optional services such as housekeeping, food, and entertainment. Others provide more elaborate medical care, depending on the client's needs. Still others offer a transitional facility, which houses different types of units that allows the elderly person to remain with one organization as their needs change (National Center for Assisted Living, 2016). But assisted living is expensive too—with average costs approximately $40,000 per year, depending on the services offered.

The most likely living situation for the elderly in America is that they **age in place**. That is, they continue to live in the home in which they have lived for many years and may own outright. Here again it is important to consider the variables of race and class. Elderly White people, for example, are more likely than Black or Latino/a people to own their homes. Moreover, married couples are more likely to own a home than a single person. The distribution on the latter shows that among women over 65, White women and Black women were more likely than women of other races to live alone. Asian and Latino/a women were more likely to live with family members other than a spouse (US Census Bureau, 2017).

So where do the elderly end up living? Most rely on relatives to provide care, including cooking, cleaning, bathing, shopping, managing medications and ensuring their overall safety and well-being. Such intensive work, particularly by a spouse, can be stressful and expensive. Often these family members spend their own money to provide groceries, medications and other expenses not covered by insurance. Because the need for this type of care is likely to increase in the coming years as the costs of institutional long-term care become unsustainable, questions about relief for family members caring for elderly relatives will center on support from the government in the form of tax credits, respite care, paid family leave and other services. Currently, the federal Family Medical Leave Act allows for 12 weeks of leave from employment to care for a sick or disabled relative, but this is unpaid leave, an unrealistic option for most families to afford (US Department of Labor, n.d.).

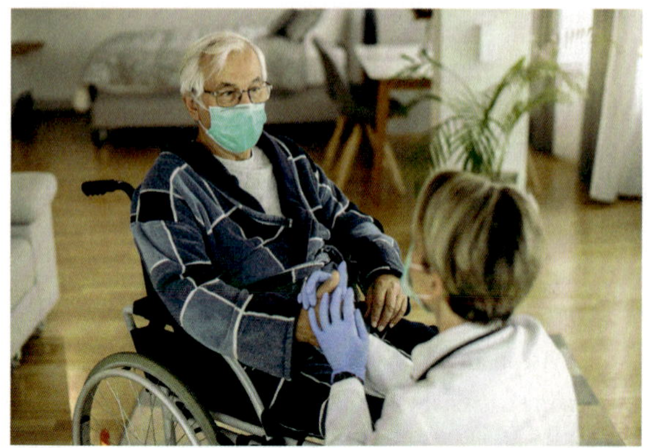

Assisted living An expensive option for many older people, assisted living provides support with day-to-day tasks as well as medical supervision while allowing for considerable independence.

Dementia

One of the most challenging health crises associated with aging is **dementia**, a progressive neurological disease that is always fatal. Symptoms of dementia include the loss of language (both speaking and understanding); an inability to identify objects or people, even close family members; and an inability to perform certain motor functions and to think and carry out complex tasks (Alzheimer's Association, n.d.).

One of the most common forms of dementia is Alzheimer's disease, which affects nearly 6 million people. It is always fatal, and is the seventh leading cause of death in the United States for people in general and fifth among people age 65 and over. The Alzheimer's Association estimates that over ten million baby boomers are expected to develop the disease, with a cost to the country at about $214 billion for long-term care and hospice. By 2050, that cost is expected to rise to over a trillion dollars (Alzheimer's Association, n.d.).

Death and Dying

With advances in health care and an overall increase in life expectancy, death in contemporary culture is perceived as something that happens primarily to the elderly. Even the terrible toll of the Covid-19 pandemic fell disproportionately on the elderly. Interestingly, most of the research on death shows that many people do not fear death itself as much as they are afraid of the possibility of pain and suffering, and the consequences of their death for loved ones. Most people would likely choose to have a painless death over a prolonged illness that places a burden on them and their families. Religion also factors into people's perceptions of death and the process of dying.

You may be familiar with the work of psychiatrist Elisabeth Kübler-Ross, who proposed a five-stage process of acknowledging death and grief. This **stage-based approach** begins with denial, then anger, followed by bargaining and negotiation, and ultimately acceptance. This theory was developed in the 1960s and has become so well-known it is used for a variety of life events, but particularly as it relates to death (Kilcrease, 2008).

Since the development of this stage-based approach, other models have been proposed for how people deal with death. Each model focuses on what happens to the dying person in terms of the length of time it takes to die as well as how they manage their expectations about a given stage. While some models contend that people attempt to normalize their lives until the illness or disease prevents them from performing their regular activities, others describe a period of disruption and depression, followed by a recalibration of their routines that adjusts to the declining stages of health (Kilcrease, 2008).

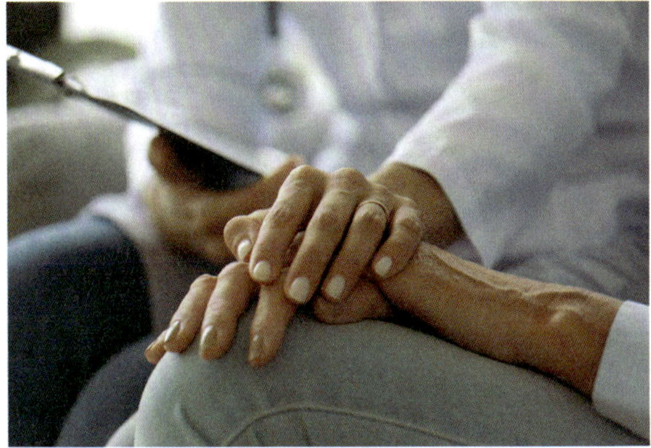

Hospice care Terminally ill seniors may choose hospice care at the end of their life. Hospice care provides for compassionate, often home-based medical support.

Because of advances in medicine and technology, many people can delay death and give themselves time to get their affairs in order. Living wills and advance directives are examples of ways that people can conveys their wishes when they are no longer able to communicate them to family members, such as whether heroic measures are to be used to keep them alive, while programs like hospice provide care for the terminally ill person which allows them to remain in a familiar environment and retain some control over the dying process ("Living Wills and Advance Directions for Medical Diseases,n.d.)

FAMILY RELATIONS AND AGING

Social dimensions to aging, such as the social isolation from family members and the loss of spouses and partners, present additional problems. These cultural and psychological effects are significant because even those who do not encounter the financial hardships of aging are likely to experience some of these issues at this stage in life.

Widowhood

Almost fifty years ago, two psychiatrists, Thomas Holmes and Richard Rahe, explored how and in what way stressful events influence or affects illness. In their study of the medical records of over 5,000 patients, Holmes and Rahe discovered 43 life events that they thought impacted one's health. The result was an index called the **Holmes and Rahe Stress Scale,** which assigns a particular value to a given stressful event. The scores assigned for each life event range from 11 to 100. Because life events do not occur in a vacuum, the Holmes and Rahe Scale calculates that a score of 300 or more puts the person at risk of illness; a score of 150-299 puts them at moderate risk; and a score of less than 150 means the person has only a slight risk of illness. Why is this important? At the top of the list for adults, with a score of 100, is the death of a spouse, followed by divorce and death of a close family member (Holmes and Rahe, 1967).

While widowhood can happen at any time during a marriage, it typically occurs as people get older. According to the US Census Bureau, there are over 14 million people classified as widowed in the United States. Given that women generally live longer than men, it makes sense that 75 percent of widows are women. Widowhood, meaning the death of a spouse, becomes a social problem due to the loss of financial stability, the emotional and psychological toll it takes on the surviving spouse, along with the loneliness that occurs once the person adapts to the loss (US Census Bureau, 2017; fivestarliving.com).

Social isolation As their social circle diminishes and after the loss of a spouse, social isolation can present a serious mental health challenge for many elderly people, especially women.

Social Isolation

In addition to widowhood, many elderly people become isolated from family members, friends, and their community. Older parents may not wish to be a burden to their children, or may feel that their opinions no longer matter. In either case, the elderly can easily feel isolated from family members. Living alone increases with age. Among those aged 75 and older, about half (44 percent) of women lived alone. Living alone can be a voluntary decision, as in the case of people who live alone because of divorce, widowhood, or because they are single (US Census Bureau, 2017). There is a relationship between one's social network and social class, with wealthier people tending to have a wider circle of friends and engage in a range of activities because they have the resources to do these things (US Census Bureau, 2017).

SOCIOLOGICAL THEORY AND AGING

Sociological theory provides insight into the changing roles for people as they age social inequalities based on age, and the perceptions of how members of society see older people and their value.

Functionalism and Aging

How do functionalists see the process of aging? Recall that functionalists want to maintain social equilibrium and ensure that people fulfill the roles necessary for society to thrive. This means there needs to be a process whereby people whose age makes them unable to perform those roles are replaced by people who can. In contemporary society, retirement serves as a reasonable and orderly mechanism that allows younger workers, who may have received the latest training and education on performing certain functions and roles, to take over while older workers have a means of surviving through programs like Social Security. This process accommodates older workers who want to distance themselves from previous roles or to take on new responsibilities (such as being a full-time grandparent). This process is referred to as **disengagement theory**, where people gradually disengage from previous positions in society. This orderly transition allows society to evolve (Deliema and Bengston, 2015).

However, there are limitations to this view of aging. For example, some people have great difficulty giving up their active roles in society, because they are still productive and fulfilled in those tasks. There is also the advantage gained from the mastery of a role by performing it for many years. Thus, while younger workers may bring innovative skills to a job, there is great value in the experience of older workers, whose experience in problem solving is important as well.

Some theorists argue that the policies and programs designed to address the elderly, such as Social Security and Medicare, are costly. Given the numbers of people using these programs compared to those contributing to it, functionalists would argue, they may be seen as dysfunctional for society. Finally, it is also important to recognize that the elderly may not be as financially secure even when they use programs like Social Security. As we discussed in the chapter on poverty, while Social Security protects millions of older Americans from poverty, this does not mean their quality of life is the same as it was when they were younger and working. Many elderly people take a part-time or full-time job to make ends meet, an especially difficult task if the reason they retired was due to a physical ailment that prevented them from working in that particular job or industry

Conflict Theory and Aging

From the conflict perspective, aging is not really a problem except as it relates to the loss of income, wealth and access to resources. In other words, getting older, particularly in a capitalistic society, generally means the person transitions into a lower social class. This is not necessarily a bad thing; after all, much of the retirement programs people participate in as working adults are designed so that their contributions are tax-free until they begin using them after retirement, when their income (and tax brackets) will be lower. Thus, part of the idea of getting older theoretically means there are fewer costs (mortgage is paid off, kids have graduated from college, etc.), which means a person can enjoy a leisurely life without needing to earn as much.

However, this perspective assumes that people are disciplined—and lucky—enough to have built up significant savings over the course of their working lives. It also overlooks, or at least underestimates, the higher medical costs of aging. For those did not save enough for retirement or for whom retirement programs were unavailable, the realities are quite different. They may have been forced to retire due to a physical injury or illness, and their fixed income forces them to continue working long after they expected to stop. Some politicians argue that the costs of supporting programs like Social Security and Medicare are unsustainable, and they are proposing cuts to the programs or modifying eligibility requirements. Along with the rising costs of health care in general, the out-of-pocket expenses for beneficiaries continue to increase. Add inflation to the mix, and the earning power of some retirees' limited incomes decreases each year. Because these individuals do not have access to or ownership of the means of production, retirement and aging present yet another type of struggle that prevents them from enjoying life in their golden years.

Feminist Theory and Aging

Feminist theory offers keen insight into how gender factors into the discussion of aging. For example, feminist theorists have demonstrated that aging for women carries a different set of challenges than it does for men. The primary reason for this **double marginality**, they say, stems from the beauty standards and appearance norms that require women to maintain a more youthful appearance as they age than for men. While older men are sometimes seen as having more power, influence, and experience, women who look older are seen as having less value other than as grandmothers or caregivers. This problem is magnified given how youthfulness is valued in American culture. For aging women, who are already struggling for equality in many areas of social life, aging exacerbates the problem (Sandberg, 2013).

Symbolic Interactionism and Aging

Wisdom and respect An elder of the Cherokee Nation talks with a member of the Warriors of AniKituhwa group and his young son at the annual Cherokee Southeast Tribes Festival in South Carolina.

A symbolic interactionist perspective to aging focuses on two main areas. The first relates to role theory and the social construction of appropriate societal roles for the elderly. As some interactionists have noted, in a modern industrialized society, there are limited roles for the elderly, thus making people's perceptions of their contributions to society harder to define. For some elderly people, the roles they play are defined by their relationships in the community or through their knowledge and understanding of the history of their race or ethnicity. They are perceived as community elders who provide context and a historical perspective for younger members of that community. In this way, some elderly members continue to define themselves in meaningful ways as they age.

A second way to understand aging from an interactionist perspective is to view aging not in terms of defining oneself in terms of a particular role, but as it relates to satisfaction levels derived as a result of the extent to which an aging person remains active. This is known as **activity theory**, where people who are more active tend to report higher levels of life satisfaction. This is predicated on the person being able to remain active, meaning they aren't suffering from an illness, disease, or disability that prevents them from being mobile and involved in a variety of activities. A social worker, sociologist, or policymaker who looks at the problem of aging through this perspective would focus on what types of activities provide the highest levels of life satisfaction, and how much activity is necessary for an elderly person to feel happy given their particular stage in life (Deliema and Bengston, 2015).

WHAT WORKS? EFFECTIVE SOLUTIONS TO THE PROBLEMS OF AGING

For many elderly people, the heavy dependence on Social Security as a primary source of income creates economic challenges and can lead to food insecurity. Many elderly people are also isolated from family and friends for various reasons, thereby creating psychological hardships. Both of these issues are social problems that can have a lasting impact on society as well as those individuals. One way to address both of these problems is the Meals on Wheels program, which delivers meals to isolated elderly who are also economically disadvantaged.

Meals on Wheels

While the Meals on Wheels program in the United States officially began in 1954 in Philadelphia, PA, the idea originated in England during World War II when the Women's Volunteer Service for Civil Defense delivered home-cooked meals to service personnel and civilians whose homes had been destroyed by bombs. Because the meals were often delivered in baby carriages, the name "meals-on-wheels" was applied.

In Philadelphia a community activist named Margaret Toy and a group of women delivered hot meals to the elderly and people in need during the winter. When Toy heard about the program in England, she modified the existing name of the group and called it Meals on Wheels. The program was largely organized by volunteers and supported by charitable institutions. Today, similar programs provide home-delivered foodstuffs and/or meals to those in need. In 2016, 2.4 million people were served by Meals on Wheels (meals on wheels.org).

The Older Americans Act (OAA) of 1965 provided rationale and funding for programs like Meals on Wheels. Nutrition services represent a major component of the OAA, which was particularly apparent during the 1970s. Home-delivered meals are intended for older adults who are considered homebound due to illness or disability and who cannot shop for groceries or prepare food for themselves. The home-delivered meals program is dependent upon volunteers to deliver meals, and the absence of a sufficient number of people willing to deliver meals means that less than five percent of eligible older Americans receive meals; and, on average, they receive less than three meals per week (Campbell, et. al, 2015).

As many elderly persons are alone and some are classified as shut-ins, the social interaction that occurs when volunteers visit their homes has a significant impact on their overall well-being. Evidence of this is seen in higher social isolation scores of people who are recipients of a Meals on Wheels program compared to those who do not (Campbell, et. al, 2015; Wright and Vance, 2014).

Physical Activity Programs for the Elderly

While the physical and emotional benefits of exercise are well known, just 40 percent of older adults are engaged in regular leisure-time physical activity (Office of Disease Prevention and Health Promotion, 2020). In recent years, researchers have begun to test evidence-based programs in physical activity, several of which have produced measurable positive outcomes for older participants.

According to a report by the Center for Disease Control and Prevention, exercise programs designed for the elderly have been shown to be effective in reducing the number of falls and injuries, along with improving flexibility, upper body strength, and slowing the onset of problems like osteoarthritis. Two such programs are Fit and Strong and A Matter of Balance (Belza and the PRC-HAN Physical Activity Conference Planning Workgroup, 2007).

Staying healthy together Women participate in a 1600-meter walk during the Detroit Recreation Department's Senior Olympics.

Fit and Strong is an evidence-based physical activity program that targets adults age 60 and above with osteoarthritis of their lower body. Research shows that osteoarthritis is the most common and disabling of all chronic conditions of older adults. Because the pain associated with the illness results in loss of muscle strength and an overall sedentary lifestyle, Fit and Strong provides flexibility exercises, aerobic conditioning, strength training, and an educational component on lifestyle change and arthritis disease management. (Belza and the PRC-HAN Physical Activity Conference Planning Workgroup, 2007).

A Matter of Balance is an evidence-based program that helps reduce the fear of falling among older adults and encourages them to increase their level of activity. Sessions involve low-to –moderate levels of exercise designed to increase flexibility, balance, strength and endurance. The program also teaches participants how to view falls and managing the fear of falling, along with goal setting for increased activity as well as changes to the environment that reduces the risk of falling (Belza and the PRC-HAN Physical Activity Conference Planning Workgroup, 2007).

Over the long-term, programs are designed to sustain the goals achieved by short-term intervention programs like Fit and Strong, by keeping people connected and focused on improving their overall health. One example is Active for Life, which offers insight for adults who are at risk for health problems because of their sedentary lifestyle. Through the use of pedometers and other tracking devices, coupled with counseling, older adults are encouraged to be more active. Research shows they are less likely to suffer from stress, depression, and higher levels of satisfaction about their appearance and body function (Belza and the PRC-HAN Physical Activity Conference Planning Workgroup, 2007).

SO WHAT CAN I DO?

After reading this chapter, you may be wondering what you can do to help the elderly population. You can't keep people from aging, you can't determine if they have saved enough for retirement, and you can't change social policies that impact the elderly, particularly when budget cuts are increasingly common.

However, there are a host of things you can do to help. For example, programs like depend on volunteers to prepare and deliver meals. You might also decide to volunteer at a local nursing home. Although Covid-19 restricted or suspended most volunteer opportunities in nursing homes, as the pandemic eases and vaccinations become widely available, volunteers will again be able to visit these facilities.

Another simple but effective strategy would be to look around your neighborhood and see if there are single elderly people living alone. You might arrange to routinely check on them, invite them to dinner, and help with yard work. They may have family members who care for them, but engaging with their neighbors helps keep them connected with and active participants in their communities.

CONCLUSION

Although the problems of crime, poverty, and access to health care affect all members of society, the elderly are especially challenged because of their vulnerability. Although it might be impossible to completely resolve these problems, they are most effectively addressed at the policy rather than the individual level. The disparate impact of the Covid-9 pandemic on elderly Americans made the extent of these problems tragically clear.

Thus, whether it be due to income, health care, social isolation, or the natural decline of one's body as a result of aging, the problems for the elderly have been and will continue to be, a significant concern for all of society, particularly as the population ages and the number of people who are considered elderly increases and requires societal programs to meet their needs.

YOU MAKE THE CALL: FIGHTING POVERTY AND LONELINESS

As the economic advisor to the President of the United States, you are asked to develop a series of programs to offset the costs that typically prevent millions of Americans from getting out of poverty. As a former sociology major, you decide that one of the critical needs of the poor relates to child care. As the costs of child care in this country average about $200 per week per child, this places an enormous burden upon working families. Given that the government is not in the child care business, the government cannot simply continue to subsidize child care for people nor can they realistically operate child care facilities.

To address this problem, you have decided to leverage existing resources and tackle two important issues: the cost of child care and keeping healthy retired individuals engaged in social activities. You create a child care supplemental program that uses volunteers, consisting of retired people who are interested in working with children, to assist low-income and working class families by meeting their child care needs for free.

You have leveraged many communities by finding locations in cities around the country that are willing to outfit buildings to serve as child care facilities and staff them with elderly volunteers. These individuals, many of whom are already grandparents, feel they are making a contribution to society and the local community, by donating their time to provide child care services to needy families. The research is fairly clear on the need for retirees to feel a sense of purpose and efforts to give back to others is an important way for retirees to feel valued. Workers in these facilities will be screened as any child care worker would be, meaning a background and security check will be conducted. Further, volunteers will receive the same type of training as any paid child care worker, so they will possess the same credentials as their private sector counterparts. All in all, this seems like a promising strategy to meet the needs of several populations.

Questions for you to consider:

1. How do you think for-profit child care facilities will react to this new program?
2. What are some of the problems you might expect to encounter when making use of senior citizens to care for children?
3. What about middle class and wealthy parents, who still have to pay for child care—is this fair to them and will they respond negatively to such a program?
4. Are there other issues to address with government-sponsored programs like this one? If so, what challenges might be presented as part of this plan?

SUMMARY

- Discuss the changing configuration of the elderly population in the United States.
    - The US population is getting older and with that trend come a series of challenges that the country will have to address.
    - Generational cohorts included in the definition of elderly are baby boomers and Generation X.
- Describe the economics of aging, including income, retirement issues, and job discrimination among the elderly.
    - The median income for an elderly person is approximately $25,000 per year and the bulk of that income, about $18,000, comes from Social Security.
    - For a large segment of the elderly population, Social Security is the primary source of income, even though the program was never intended to function in that capacity.
    - Because of low wages and the lack of adequate pensions in many industries, many elderly people do not have access to pensions or other sources of income in retirement.
- Analyze crime and the elderly, including victimization patterns among the elderly and crime as offenders.
    - While the elderly have high rates of fear regarding victimization, they have

some of the lowest victimization rates of any group.
    - Elderly offenders are becoming problematic for society, particularly as it relates to elderly inmates.
- Characterize the health care challenges facing the elderly in the United States.
    - The inevitability of aging also brings with it the need for assistance in day-to-day activities.
    - Gerontologists estimate that, as the population continues to get older, the number of people who will need long-term care will increase. For many people this will mean the use of nursing homes or assisted living facilities. However, such options are expensive and living at home or with relatives presents a host of challenges as well.
- Describe family relations and aging, including widowhood and social isolation, familial and health-related issues for the elderly.
    - Proposed changes to the Medicare system are a significant challenge for the elderly.
    - Illnesses such as dementia and Alzheimer's disease take a particular toll on the elderly and their families.
    - The elderly also wrestle with issues relating to social isolation and widowhood.
- Compare various sociological theories as it relates to aging and the elderly population.
    - Functionalists might study the ways in which people whose age makes them unable to perform important social roles are replaced by people who can.
    - From the conflict perspective, a key problem with aging in a capitalistic society is a transition into a lower social class.
    - Feminist theorists have demonstrated that aging for women implies a double marginality resulting in part from beauty standards that require women to maintain a youthful appearance as they age.
    - A symbolic interactionist perspective to aging focuses on two main areas. The first relates to role theory and the social construction of appropriate societal roles for the elderly. A second way to understand aging from an interactionist perspective is to view aging not in terms of defining oneself in terms of a particular role, but as it relates to satisfaction levels derived as a result of the extent to which an aging person remains active.
- Assess effective programs that assist the elderly and their empirical support, such as Meals on Wheels.
    - Programs shown to be effective in addressing the needs and concerns of the elderly include Meals on Wheels as well as programs offered to increase overall health and wellness.
- Discuss what individuals can do to address the challenges of an aging population.
    - Programs like Meals on Wheels depend on volunteers to prepare and deliver meals.
    - You might also decide to volunteer at a local nursing home. Although Covid-19 restricted or suspended most volunteer opportunities in nursing homes, as the pandemic eases and vaccinations become widely available, volunteers will again be able to visit these facilities.
    - Another simple but effective strategy would be to engage with elderly people living alone in your community.

KEY TERMS

Activity theory 361
Age in place 356
Ageism 349
Assisted living facilities 355
Dementia 356
Disengagement theory 359
Double marginality 360
Elderly abuse 353
Elderly offenders 353
Filial piety 342
Generation X (Gen Xers) 346
Holmes and Rahe Stress Scale 358
Operationalization 353
Stage based approach 357
The Age Discrimination in Employment Act (ADEA) 349
The Older Americans Act (OAA) of 1965 362

Discussion Questions

1. Why are American families so different in the way they perceive and care for elderly relatives? Is it an element of American culture that puts such an emphasis on youth and attractiveness or are there other factors at work?
2. What are some of the challenges that are created when so many elderly people rely on Social Security as a primary source of their income in retirement?
3. Should the government pay for health care for the elderly? What are your thoughts about the debate on Medicare and other entitlement programs? Critics of Medicare argue that the rising costs of health care are unsustainable and the program must be dramatically scaled back or eliminated altogether. However, proponents of Medicare argue that this is an entitlement program, where recipients paid into the program during their working lives based on the promise they would receive health care for the rest of their lives in return. Is there some middle ground or solution to this complex problem?
4. Many elderly people feel they still have something to offer society and can make a meaningful contribution even though they are no longer formally in the workforce. What suggestions might you offer about how to use this segment of the population? Can they be part of a solution to other problems facing society, such as child care, education, or other issues? If so, in what ways?

Learn more with this chapter's digital tools, including Data and Media Literacy Exercises, flashcards, and chapter self-assessments at **www.oup.com/he/mcnamara**.

13

Are You Feeling Okay? Health and Health Care

Chapter Outline

LEARNING OBJECTIVES

- Identify the reasons for the spiraling health care costs in the United States.
- Describe the inequalities in health care.
- Analyze how to address the spiraling costs of health care.
- Apply sociological theories to health care in the United States.
- Evaluate effective solutions to health care.
- Identify individual efforts to address the problems of health care in the United States.

A massive public health campaign In a scene repeated globally in 2021, people wait in line for a dose of COVID-19 vaccine.

The Covid-19 pandemic that began in 2020 placed extraordinary stress on health care around the globe. In the United States, health care was already one of the most pressing social problems. Public opinion polls indicate that health care has ranked in the top three categories for the first time since opinion polls began. Issues related to the pandemic and health care dominated the 2020 presidential election cycle, and they continue to reverberate with the enormous challenges of vaccinating an entire population.

Until the pandemic, it may have been difficult for the average healthy American to understand these issues. After all, healthy people don't access the health care system as often as sick people, so why would most Americans be concerned? But even the healthiest people probably have relatives who may need affordable health care, or work in jobs that don't carry health insurance. Healthy people also have children who need medical attention. As a result, issues related to access and cost make health care an urgent concern for everyone. Further, access and utilization of health care in this country is not evenly divided—the poor, minorities, women, and others often have significantly different experiences in getting the help they need and affording it.

Finally, it is important, much like the discussions we had regarding the economy and work, to objectively examine the ideas and solutions about improving the health care system in this country. For example, while many do not like the idea of a single payer system, as it is often equated with a form of socialism, it is important to consider all the possibilities when searching for solutions. In fact, some experts argue that we already have two types of single payer systems in this country: the Veterans Administration's system amounts to a single payer system and Medicare and Medicaid account for nearly half of the population's health care needs.

Thus, while we may not like the ideas suggested by some politicians who promote the benefits of a **single payer system**, in reality, we already have such a system in place. What is important is to examine whether the current model is sustainable (and no one really thinks it is) and if not, what are the most reasonable and thoughtful alternatives that ensures access to medical care.

A related issue to consider as you read this chapter is whether you think health care is a right or a privilege. After all the rhetoric and politics involving one model over another, at the heart of the matter, like housing and food, is whether you (along with the general public) think access to medical care is a guarantee as a citizen of this country.

SOCIOLOGICAL STORY TIME

- Despite the approval of Covid-19 vaccines, there appears to be a reluctance by many people to become vaccinated. In a January 2021 survey by the Kaiser Family Foundation, about 20 percent of US adults indicated they wouldn't get a vaccine, or would get one only if required. About 30 percent of respondents said they want to wait to get a vaccine to see how well it is working. The basis of the anti-vaccine movement stems from misinformation about vaccine side effects as well as conspiracy theories and mistrust of corporations and the federal government. Officials are concerned that antivaccine activists, including some state legislators, are impeding the ability to stem the spread of the virus (Pulliam, McKay, and Maher, 2021).
- According to TransUnion, a company the oversees the payment of patient bills, more than two-thirds of people with a hospital bill of $500 or less have not paid them over a two year period. The reason? Higher deductibles and out-of-pocket expenses for medical treatment (Lavito, 2017).
- Skepticism and a lack of trust about medicine among the general public is growing. In 1966, more than 75 percent of Americans had great confidence in doctors and medical leaders. Today, that number is 34 percent. Compared with people in other developed countries Americans are less likely to trust doctors and have lower levels of confidence in the health system (Khullar, 2018).
- In 2018, HealthCare Partners LLC, which is part of DaVita, Inc., a large dialysis company, was reported to have exaggerated how sick their patients were in an effort to inflate the amount they could bill Medicare and had been doing so for years. The company agreed to pay a $270 million fine (Schulte, 2018).

At a time when the news cycle is dominated by fears over the Covid-19 pandemic and the hopes and challenges of vaccinating an entire population, the ongoing issue of the rising costs of health care is all the more urgent. Health care reform continues to dominate election cycles, with politicians and policymakers labeling some strategies with emotion-laden terms like socialism. This chapter explores these issues as well as some of the proposals offered to remedy the problem. As we will see, like all the social problems we have discussed this far, the issues are complex and are intertwined with many other problems, such as poverty, race, the economy, jobs, and even crime.

The research points to three key factors that influence health care reform in this country: the explosive costs of health care, the specialization of medicine, and the aging of the American population (Alonzo-Zaldivar, 2016). There are also social factors to consider. People without health insurance, who tend to be poor, have a variety of medical issues and often use emergency rooms as their primary source of health care. This increases the overall costs of providing care and reduces the continuity of care for patients. Although the development of medications to treat patients for a variety of illnesses has addressed part of the issue, there have been dramatic increases in the cost of medications as well (Schumock et al., 2016).

Some experts contend that the current model is unsustainable and that the existing **fee for services model** will continue to increase costs to a point where very few will be able to pay unless the government is involved in health care (Nichols, 2017). Others point out that the single payer system, while popular in other countries, has not had a successful track record in the United States. As an example, critics of the single payer system point to the Veterans Administration (VA), where the problems with its infrastructure and ability to effectively treat patients is used as an illustration that the federal government is ill-equipped to handle such a large scale endeavor (Waldman, 2014).

THE COSTS OF HEALTH CARE IN THE UNITED STATES

In 2019, a report issued by the Department of Health and Human Services (DHHS) showed that health care spending is growing at a faster rate than the national economy. Growth is expected to average about 5.8 percent from 2015 to 2025. National expenditures for health care were $3.8 trillion in 2019, which is approximately $11,582 for every man, woman and child in the United States. These expenditures represented about 18 percent of the U.S. Gross Domestic Product in 2019. The rise in health care costs is expected to increase to 20 percent of the economy by 2025. The distribution of the $3.8 trillion in health care costs consists of hospitals, which comprise about a third of the costs, doctors and other providers account for another 20 percent, and prescription drugs bought through pharmacies comprise another 10 percent (Centers of Medicare and Medicaid Services, 2020).

These costs are extraordinary. Health care spending per capita in the United States is more than double that of other developed countries. Yet, the health outcomes from this additional spending show results that are no better than peer countries—and in some cases they are worse. Part of the reason for these poor results is incompetence, greed, and waste. The Institute of Medicine, for example, has estimated that about 30 percent of total health care spending goes to unnecessary, ineffective, overpriced, and wasteful services. This cost, more nearly $800 billion, is more than the entire budget for K-12 education in the United States (Peterson Foundation, 2017).

The DHHS report further showed that spending on prescription drugs also grew significantly. According to the Centers for Medicare and Medicaid Services, retail drug spending increased about 5.7 percent in 2019 to nearly $369 billion. These increases far exceeded any other rate of growth in health care and account for about 10 percent of the total health care spending (Centers of Medicare and Medicaid Services, 2020).

Efforts to curb the costs of prescription drugs have not had their intended effect. As an illustration, the dramatic costs in drugs such as epinephrine auto injectors, also known as the *EpiPen*, garnered considerable negative publicity when the manufacturer increased the cost from about $57 in 2007 to $615.58 in 2016. Since 2007, when Mylan Corporation took control of the drug, there has been a steady increase in the price. Mylan cites product improvements as the justification for the increased costs, but little in the way of actual improvements have been documented (Woodyard and Layton, 2016).

The Specialization of Medicine

A sizeable portion of the costs of health care involve physician fees. These fees are often the result of the need for patients to see a specialist. But overspecialization in medicine is a problem as well. As more medical students choose to specialize, the number of general and family practitioners, who see patients for a variety of illnesses and make recommendations to specialists, is reduced. There are many good reasons for specialization in medicine, particularly in developing a sense of expertise in a refined area, but managed care requires a referral from a primary care physician.

As information and technology improve the medical establishment's ability to diagnose and treat illnesses, the body of knowledge expands, making it quite challenging to stay abreast of all the changes. Specialization reduces some of that burden by allowing practitioners to refine their skill and knowledge base and to become better at treating patients than they would otherwise. Specialization also allows physicians to earn more by developing this level of expertise and reduce the administrative responsibilities as it relates to billing for insurance.

At the same time, however, with more specialties comes a shortage of **primary care physicians**, which creates a backlog of patients who need a referral to see a specialist. In 2010, the Association of American Medical College's Center for Workforce Studies predicted that there would be a shortage of nearly 45,000 primary care physicians and 62,000 non-primary care specialists by 2020, a prediction that has proven to be true (Woodyard and Layton, 2016).

Emergency rooms as primary care Many Americans lack access to a primary care physician, relying on emergency rooms for most medical care.

Such a dramatic shortage typically results people turning to hospital emergency rooms as the primary source of their medical care. This is the most expensive way to treat patients, thereby contributing to the escalating costs of health care, and it results in a lower continuity of care for the patient, since they see whichever provider is on duty, who may not have a comprehensive history of the patient's health. Thus, the end result of the specialization of medicine is a limited access to care, longer wait times to receive it, and the use of other alternatives to meet patient needs.

Longevity and the Aging of America

The 2018 DHHS report showed that Medicare and Medicaid are expected to grow more rapidly than private insurance as the population ages. In fact, by 2025, the government will account for 47 percent of all health care spending. Such a startling prediction indicates that we may end up with a single payer system simply as a result of the Baby Boom generation aging and the government paying the costs of their health care. However, the larger numbers of people being eligible for care does not tell the entire story. The DHHS estimates that about 5 percent of the population account for nearly half of the health care spending in a given year. This means that even with affordable health care for everyone, its use will remain significantly uneven. At the same time, half of the population has little or no health care costs, which accounts for about 3 percent of the spending (Centers for Medicare and Medicaid Services, 2020).

INEQUALITIES AND HEALTH CARE IN AMERICA

One of the most significant problems relating to the health care crisis in this country relates to unequal access for some members of the population. As we have seen in the discussions of crime, employment, substance abuse and its treatment, as well as with issues like access and utilization of health care, minorities are at a significant disadvantage when it comes to getting the medical help they need.

Table 11.1 Life Expectancy in Years by Race/Ethnicity

Category	Years
Whites	78.9
Blacks	74.6
Hispanic	82.8
Asian	86.5
Native American	76.9

Race, Ethnicity, Gender, and Social Class

One way to assess health status is **life expectancy**: on average how long a person is expected to live. White males can expect to live about four years longer than Black males, and even Native Americans, with all of the challenges they face, have a longer life expectancy than Blacks (Table 11.1; Kaiser Family Foundation, 2020.).

Another indicator of health status relates to **infant mortality rate**, which is the number of deaths in the first year of life for all live births. The rate for Blacks is twice as high as it is for Whites, according to the National Center on Health Statistics. The infant mortality rate for Blacks is 11.1 per 1,000 live births compared to 4.9 for Whites (National Centers on Health Statistics, 2018).

In addition, racial and ethnic minorities suffer more from almost every illness than do Whites and because minorities are less likely to be immunized in general, non-Whites suffer much higher rates of death from infectious diseases. Even in those cases where incomes are the same, the death rates remain higher for non-Whites. With the exception of Asian Americans, virtually every minority group rates their health as only fair or poor (National Centers on Health Statistics, 2018).

In fact, the most recent research on inequalities in health care in the United States shows that even with equivalent insurance, racial and ethnic minorities are likely to receive less care or care that is of lesser quality than Whites. People of color across all social class lines and low-income Whites receive less preventive care and lower quality management of chronic diseases. Under Medicaid, the poor often receive fewer services because of limitations placed on eligibility and the fee structure paid to doctors, who have little incentive to provide thorough treatment because they are paid a fixed amount per patient (Schpero et. al, 2017).

A 2018 report by the Center for Disease Control and Prevention (CDC) points out that there are many disparities in health based on race, ethnicity and class. For instance, African Americans and Hispanic/Latinos, compared to Whites, have higher rates of HIV, untreated hypertension, diabetes, and heart disease. The report also points out

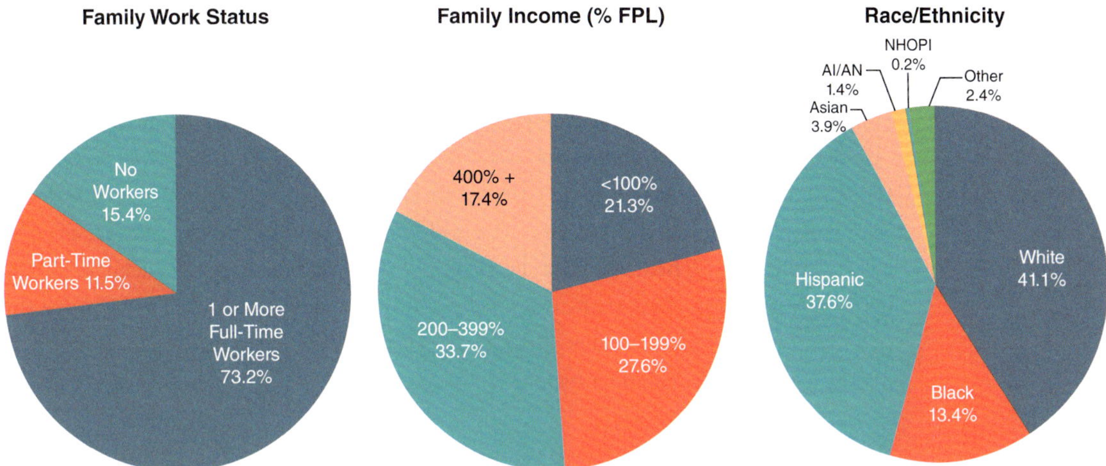

Figure 13.1 Characteristics of the Nonelderly Uninsured, 2019 Note: Includes nonelderly individuals ages 0 to 64. AIAN refers to American Indian/Alaska Native. NHOPI refers to Native Hawaiians and Other Pacific Islanders. Hispanic people may be of any race but are categorized as Hispanic; other groups are all non-Hispanic. The 2019 Census Bureau poverty threshold for a family of three was $20,578. SOURCE: KFF analysis of 2019 American Community Survey, 1-Year Estimates.

that Blacks and Hispanics generally report fewer average healthy days compared to Whites (National Center on Health Statistics, 2018).

There is also a lack of representation of people of color, Hispanics, and Native Americans, among medical providers. Although these three groups constitute about 25 percent of the population, they represent only 6 percent of practicing physicians in the United States. This trend appears to be continuing as enrollment in medical school by these three populations has only shown small increases, according to the American Medical Colleges (Association of American Medical Colleges, 2021).

In 2016, there were approximately 27.6 million Americans who did not have health insurance. This is true despite changes in health care policy, such as **Obamacare**, which mandates that people obtain health insurance. However, for many people, the costs associated with obtaining a health insurance policy (even with subsidies from the federal government) are out of reach (Henry J. Kaiser Foundation, 2017).

Most of the uninsured in this country are families with one or both parents employed full-time (Figure 13.1). Their employers simply do not provide health insurance, and the costs for the family to purchase private insurance is too high (Kaiser Foundation, 2020).

Also, about eight in ten people who are uninsured include families that made less than 400 percent of the federal poverty line (Kaiser Foundation, 2020). Why is this important? Low-income people and racial and ethnic minorities already tend to be in overall poorer health and need access to health care services (Henry J. Kaiser Foundation, 2017).

HOW TO ADDRESS THE SPIRALING COSTS OF HEALTH CARE

In addressing the challenges related to the problems relating to quality health care, one might think that health insurance would be the solution. But is it? As we have seen, those who have insurance fare far better than those who do not, so it is important for as many people to obtain it as possible. The problem is that an increasing number of companies are dropping health insurance as part of its employee benefits package, largely because of the costs. Has it always been this way? What are we doing to improve the situation for uninsured workers, given the unsustainable costs of caring for them in an overburdened public medical system?

The History of Health Insurance in America

During World War II, some companies began to offer health insurance as a "perk" or benefit to employees. Wage freezes were in effect and health insurance was an inexpensive way to provide an incentive to attract employees. This also allowed companies to compete for workers.

By the 1950s, health insurance was equated with what it meant to have a "good" job—one that offered a high salary and benefits like health insurance. While this feature was more of an accident than a thought-out strategy, no other developed country had such a feature of employment. Access to health care in many countries, then and now, is a right of citizenship.

What happened was that the costs of health care began to rise in the 1960s. As a result, companies began dropping coverage for workers. This trend continues today. According to one estimate, less than two-thirds of Americans have job-related health insurance. Among low-income workers, only about a third have health insurance through their employer (Kaiser Family Foundation, 2020).

While almost all workers were covered by some sort of plan by the 1950s, it wasn't until the 1960s that the remaining segment of the population that was not covered by health insurance, the poor and the elderly, were covered through Medicare and Medicaid.

From the outset, it appears that the medical community has generally opposed any legislation that curbed the autonomy and authority of physicians. In 1945, the American Medical Association argued that national health insurance would be a form of socialism and voiced its opposition. Over the next several decades the AMA continued to oppose governmental control over health care delivery and the potential loss of income for doctors, drug companies and hospitals. Insurance companies opposed it because of price controls, while labor unions and the elderly opposed the caps on their health benefits. It wasn't until 1994 that President Clinton was able to effect change in health care delivery with a plan that had two important features. It not only made health care reform a central issue for the general public, it also prompted a massive reorganization of American health care into a delivery system that resulted in what is now known as **managed care** (Cockerham, 2017).

Private Insurance

Private insurance companies, which emerged from the Great Depression, allow people to pay premiums in the form of insurance that in turn pays doctors and hospitals for each treatment a patient receives. This "third party" or fee for service approach has been arguably the best and most cost efficient method of delivering medical care. However, some contend that it is far too expensive a model. Why? The more services doctors provide, the more they charge in fees and the more money they make. Patients have no incentive to limit their visits because they have already paid the premiums and feel entitled to medical care. Such a system also excludes those who do not have health insurance. The costs and challenges in health care have only increased, as third party providers began paying for an increasingly larger portion of doctor and hospital bills for insured patients (Starr, 1983).

Health Maintenance Organizations (HMOs), which also emerged during the Great Depression, are a means of providing workers with health coverage at a reasonable rate by lowering costs. An HMO, for a fixed monthly fee, provides total health care for patients with an emphasis on prevention in an effort to avoid costly treatments in the future. In this model patients are required to be seen by providers are affiliated with their HMO. Critics of HMOs argue that since they are paid a fixed amount per patient, regardless of how much time they spend with that patient, the process contains few incentives for physicians to be thorough in their treatment of patients.

Another private approach to controlling health care costs is **managed care**, which emerged as corporations tried to control the escalating health care costs of their employees. In this system, **preferred provider organizations (PPOs)** "manage" or control the costs of health care by supervising and monitoring the work of health care providers, as well as limiting visits to specialists to a particular managed care network and requiring prior authorization for hospitalization. It has become, in effect, the most common form of health care delivery in this country (Cockerham, 2017). Thus, managed care brings a third party into the interaction between physicians and patients, someone who is paying more attention to the bottom line than questions of medical care. It is in fact the insurance company who sees to it that the care provided by the physician is reasonable and the least costly alternative. Managed care forced physicians to be accountable to those who had to pay the bill: insurance companies, the federal government, and employers. In the process, managed care became a business much like any other, where controlling costs and market sensitivity drove decision making. This model theoretically spelled the end of doctors making all of the decisions in terms of patient care and health care policy.

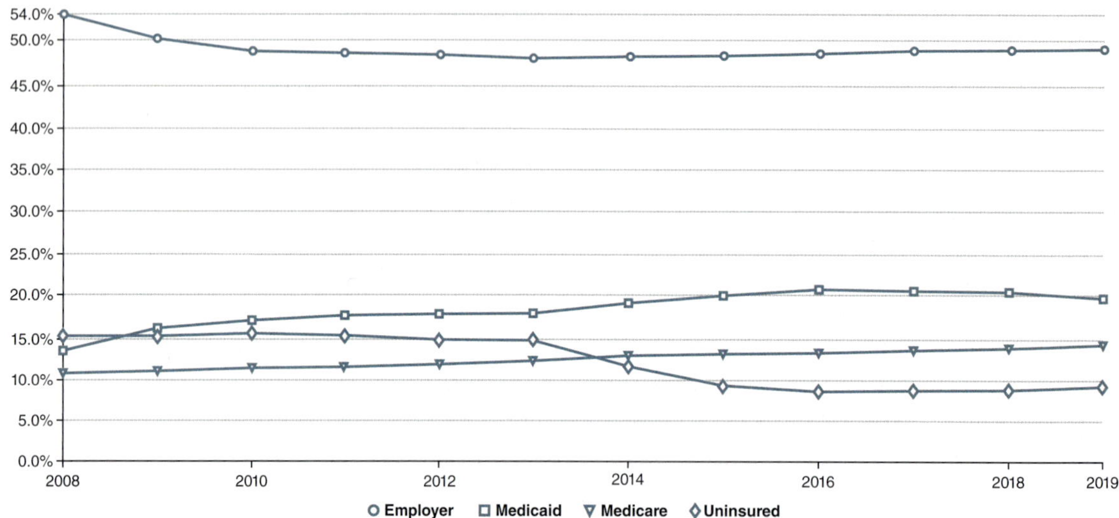

Figure 13.2 Health insurance coverage of the total US population, 2008–2019 KFF estimates based on the 2008–2019 American Community Survey, 1-Year Estimates.

So, has managed care controlled costs and made a positive impact on health care reform? The data suggests that initially costs were contained, but lately that trend has changed (Figure 13.2). Between 1993 and 1997, health care's portion of the Gross Domestic Product (GDP) was about 13.5 percent. Experts noted that until 2006, the percentage hovered around that mark, until 2007, when the costs jumped to 16.2 percent and steadily rose to 17.2 percent in 2013. As seen in the graph below, since 2013, the percentages have steadily climbed, with a projected 19.3 percent by 2023.

Some of the reasons for this increase may have been a result of dissatisfaction with managed care by consumers. Americans, by and large, are interested in choice and the freedom to select their preferred provider. As managed care evolved, with more insurance companies authorizing more referrals to specialists, costs to patients increased. Aside from the economic costs related to managed care are the social and cultural costs to medicine. As managed care changes the medical landscape, the role of physicians has changed as well. As a result of managed care and the changing way medicine is practiced, job satisfaction among physicians has become an issue, particularly with primary care physicians and general practitioners (Adams, 2012).

Public Insurance: Medicare and Medicaid

As early as the 1960s, evidence revealed private health insurance was limited in its success, particularly in meeting the needs of the poor and the elderly. Many experts realized that the AMA could not always be relied upon to put the public's interests regarding health care above its own.

The passage of the Medicare and Medicaid amendments of the Social Security Act of 1965 was a watershed event in the history of politics, as it represented the first time that Congress played a key role in health care policy. As we will see, this decision has played a pivotal role in how medicine has been understood since then (Adams, 2012).

Medicare provides medical and hospital insurance for people aged 65 or older regardless of their financial resources. It also includes people under the age of 65 who receive cash benefits from Social Security. There are specific deductibles and coinsurance payments for which the beneficiary is responsible, as well as overall limits to the program, but most of the cost is absorbed by the federal government. Hospital insurance is covered through Social Security deductions and does not require a monthly premium if the recipient paid Medicare taxes during their working lifetime (Cockerham, 2017).

Medicaid provides health care coverage for low-income persons or those who are disabled. It also covers a certain segment of senior citizens in nursing homes. Medicaid is funded by states, local government, and the federal government. Income and economic resources determine eligibility as well as a person's citizenship status. Medicaid provides medical, hospital and long-term care for people who are poor and disabled, blind, elderly, or pregnant. Whereas Medicare is largely funded by workers' payments into the system during their working lives, Medicaid is funded by the government. This leads many people to view Medicaid as a welfare program and Medicare as an entitlement program: the latter are those who have earned medical coverage through years of hard work and contributions to the system. Experts note that both programs are extremely expensive to manage and operate and contain no incentive to keep costs low. When the health care reform law was passed in 2010, both Medicaid and Medicare had grown faster than the economy and accounted for 25 percent of all federal spending—an estimated $760 billion per year (Cockerham, 2017).

The realities of health care costs have resulted in efforts by some states to create and implement their own health insurance plans for its citizens, especially the poor. However, the scope of this problem is so large and the costs so extraordinary, despite limited success in places like Massachusetts, Hawaii, and Vermont, most states are unable to resolve the issue. However, there is a growing body of evidence that people who have health insurance end up living longer and in better health than those who do not. It is this persistent finding that has led to so many efforts to reform health care in this country and it was also the impetus for the Affordable Care Act, also known as Obamacare (Cockerham, 2017).

The Affordable Care Act/Obamacare

President Barack Obama put health care reform at the top of the domestic agenda at a time when the country was experiencing a major recession. Despite this economic upheaval, along with the wars in Iraq and Afghanistan, Republicans strongly opposed health care reform. Concerns were raised about rising health care costs, the ability of

GLOBAL PERSPECTIVES

Health Care in Singapore

Given the challenges in the United States in providing affordable health care, how is it offered in other countries?

Singapore's two-tier system is heralded as one of the best in the world. In this model, two thirds of the spending comes from insurance while the remaining third is paid for through public spending. The government manages hospitals that provide low-cost or free care, and there are governmental regulations that control the cost of the entire health care system. Like other countries, people can purchase additional coverage if they so desire, but generally workers contribute 20 percent of their salary to a health care savings account called *Medisave* (in addition to a second, separate account for their retirement, and a third account for funding education, housing, and insurance), while employers pay an additional 16 percent into those accounts More than 90 percent of the population enrolls in Medishield, a catastrophic insurance program. Eldershield is another program that pays for nursing home care. Once an employee turns 40, a portion of their income is automatically deposited into the Eldershield account. In 2015, life expectancy was 83.1 years (Amadeo, 2018). Singapore also has created an effective government-funded contact tracing program for Covid19 called SafeEntry (Figure 3.4).

Contact tracing in Singapore The SafeEntry app, developed by the government of Singapore, helps to efficiently monitor the spread of COVID-19 and enforce quarantine measures. As a result of this and other public health initiatives, Singapore had one of the lowest COVID-19 fatality rates in the world.

Singapore is just one of several developed countries that offer free or reduced-cost health care while still offering individuals the option of purchasing additional coverage if they wish to do so. The quality of that coverage does not appear to affect life expectancy rates in an adverse way. Further, many of these countries provide comprehensive health care at far lower costs than what is offered in this country. The United States is the only developed country that does not offer full coverage to its citizens, and the costs of these programs continues to climb.

the government to operate and manage health care systems, along with concerns about the need for cuts in Medicare benefits.

The health care reform bill, officially called the **Patient Protection and Affordable Care Act**, also known as Obamacare, was passed in March 2010. Important elements of this legislation include:

1. The elimination of denying coverage to patients for preexisting conditions;
2. Minimum level of benefits, determined by the federal government, would be required of all health insurance plans;

3. State insurance exchanges were created so that a wide range of health insurance plans can be offered at competitive prices;
4. People who are not covered by health insurance through their employer can purchase coverage through state exchanges;
5. People under the age of 65 who already have health insurance can purchase plans from the exchanges and who earn up to four times the federal poverty line will receive government subsidies to help pay the cost;

Protesting "Obamacare" President Barack Obama was greeted by protesters in Minneapolis, MN on September 12, 2009. He was in the city to deliver a major speech on health care.

6. Low income people under the age of 65 earning below 133 percent of the poverty line will be covered by an expanded Medicaid program;
7. Small businesses can buy insurance for their employees through the exchanges and get tax credits.
8. Children can remain on their parents' health insurance plan until age 26;
9. People would generally be required to purchase health insurance or pay a penalty added to their federal income tax. Some groups are exempt from this rule, such as Native Americans, religious objectors, and people with hardships. Employers who have more than 50 employees but do not provide health insurance coverage also pay a penalty. Penalties for individuals can be less than $100 or more than $1,000, depending on their income, with penalties scheduled to increase in future years (Cockerham, 2017).

The cost for such a plan was estimated by the Congressional Budget Office to be approximately $1.1 trillion over the next decade. About half of these costs were to be covered by spending cuts and limits on Medicare payments and other savings while the other half was expected to come from higher Medicare taxes, fees and new taxes on drug manufacturers and others, along with penalties paid by businesses and uninsured individuals.

The ACA had several problems, beginning with the website for signing up, which was not operational. This made it difficult for some states to offer coverage until website had been fixed. Because individuals would be assessed a penalty if they did not sign up for health coverage, Obama was forced to waive the first year's penalties and extend the deadline for enrollment. When Obama did this without Congressional approval, Republicans in the House of Representatives filed a lawsuit charging the he had changed a federal law without Congress's approval (Schenecker, 2014).

Second, despite President Obama's promise that people would be allowed to keep the insurance coverage they already had, many individuals and families had their policies cancelled or were required to pay higher prices for new ones. The new plans included provisions that some people did not need or want—such as paying for prenatal care for women past childbearing age. The health plans also had very high deductibles: over half of the plans had deductibles of $3,000 or more (Schenecker, 2014).

In response, Obama allowed insurance companies to let people keep their old policies for another year, but some companies declined to do so because of the cost of issuing new policies with old benefits. Despite these challenges, as of 2020, about 9.6 million people enrolled in ACA health plans, a slight increase from 2019 (Norris, 2020; Reuter, 2020). On average, ACA insurance premiums decreased about 4 percent in 2020 from 2019. About 84 percent of people with ACA coverage received federal subsidies, in 2020, with the average amount $145 per month. In comparison, the average full price premium was approximately $545 per month (Norris, 2020).

Several legal challenges were raised to the ACA, including the mandate for individuals to obtain health insurance and for employers to provide it for their employees or pay a fine. Some states argued that it was unconstitutional to require people to purchase health insurance, similar to being forced to buy any commercial good or service as a condition of residency in the United States. Other issues focused on religious exemptions as well as forcing employers to purchase health insurance for their workers (Spakovsky, 2015).

The federal courts were inconsistent in their decisions on the constitutionality issue. In 2010, federal courts in both Virginia and Michigan found that the requirement to purchase health insurance was in fact constitutional, but another court in Virginia ruled that it was not. The argument in favor of the requirement asserted that the Commerce Clause of the Constitution allows Congress to oversee events and activities that impact interstate commerce. The federal government also argued that, because non-compliance with the law resulted in an income tax penalty, Congress was allowed to require health insurance based on its powers to tax citizens (Cockerham, 2017). The case was appealed to the U.S. Supreme Court and in *National Federation of Independent Small Businesses v. Sebelius* 576 U. S. ______ (2012), in a 5–4 vote, the Court agreed with the federal government. It also ruled that the expansion of Medicaid was legal but that Congress could not coerce states into participating by withholding existing Medicaid payments. The states were given the option of opting out of expanding their Medicaid programs (Liptak, 2012).

The Supreme Court also addressed the religious exemption and employer requirement issues. In *Little Sisters of the Poor v. Burwell*, 578 U. S. ______ (2016), Roman Catholic nuns had sought an injunction requiring them to provide contraceptive devices to their employees at a convent because it violated their religious beliefs. In a second case, *Hobby Lobby Stores v. Burwell* 568 U. S. ______ (2012), a family-owned business run on religious principles wanted an exception from having to pay for contraceptive devices as outlined in the ACA. The Supreme Court ruled in favor of the plaintiffs in these cases, granting the injunction by the Roman Catholic nuns and exempting Hobby Lobby from paying for contraceptive services of its employees.

Is universal health care socialism? Protesters in Phoenix, AZ in June 2013 believe that universal health care is equivalent to socialism, even though many US medical systems like Medicare and Medicaid are already very similar to socialized medicine.

The GOP Alternative to Obamacare

During the presidential election of 2016, Republican candidate Donald Trump promised that he would repeal the ACA and replace it with a better health plan. Instead, his term was marked by a chaotic approach to health care reform that culminated in the disastrous toll of Covid-19 on the American health care system and the American people.

On July 28, 2017, President Trump threatened to end government payments to health insurers if Congress did not pass a new health care bill. In a Twitter message, President Trump said, "if a new HealthCare Bill is not approved quickly, BAILOUTS for Insurance Companies and BAILOUTS for members of Congress will end very soon!" This Tweet occurred just after the Senate failed to repeal parts of the Affordable Care Act. Trump referenced the bailouts, which amount to approximately $8 billion in subsidies the federal government pays to insurers to lower the price of health coverage for some Americans (Kessler, 2017).

The ACA provides two types of subsidies to help low- and middle-income people pay for insurance on the exchanges. Premium subsidies defray the cost of premiums for people making less than four times the poverty level. For those who make even less, cost-sharing reductions help cover the costs of deductibles and other out-of-pocket expenses. (Zernike, 2017). House Republicans filed a lawsuit, *House v. Price*, that argued the ACA should not be able to offer cost sharing reductions as part of the law, since Congress never passed a law appropriating funds for that feature of the ACA (Zernike, 2017).

In 2016, a district court judge ruled that that the cost sharing payments were unconstitutional and ordered them stopped. The court delayed its injunction however to give the government time to appeal. Shortly after the appeal was filed by the Obama administration, Trump won the election. With the election of President Trump, the House asked the appeals court to put the case on hold because of the likely changes in health care policy that were forthcoming The appeals court agreed (Bagley, 2017). Since then, the Republican alternative to Obamacare, known as **the American Health Care Act**, has not been implemented. With the election of Joe Biden in 2020, along with Democratic control in both the House and the Senate, the viability of Obamacare seems secure for the foreseeable future.

Misinformation, Skepticism, and Denial

The politics associated with the ACA, coupled with the Covid-19 pandemic, have resulted in an extraordinary set of developments related to health care in the United States. Not only were many people impacted by the pandemic and required health care as a result of becoming infected with the coronavirus, there has been a continued misinformation provided about the causes of the virus along with proven treatments. Even the development of a vaccine has resulted in considerable skepticism, as conspiracy theories and misinformation have been presented by politicians, citizens, far-right advocates, and President Trump.

President Trump was heavily criticized for his failure to provide adequate leadership through the pandemic crisis as well as promoting misinformation. He first suggested (inaccurately) that the virus was under control and that it would simply disappear. Later, he promoted unproven and even dangerous treatments such as hydroxychloroquine (an experimental drug that has not been proven effective against Covid-19) and the use of disinfectant or ultraviolet light to kill the virus ("What do you have to lose?" he quipped; Newby, 2020).

Trump's unwillingness to follow his own team of experts, despite repeated warnings of its extraordinary impact on the country, contributed greatly to its spread throughout the United States (Clark, 2020; McCarthy, 2020). It has also altered people's understanding of the disease and effective measures to prevent its spread. This includes the misleading transformation by some activists of mask wearing and social distancing from a public health strategy to an issue of freedom and autonomy. Additionally, criticism of Trump's misinformation campaign, with his refusal to wear a mask or practice social distancing himself (despite contracting the disease) was met with dismissive comments that the scientific evidence was "fake news" (Pulliam, McKay and Maher, 2021).

The Trump administration focused on the creation and distribution of a vaccine, a program known as Operation Warp Speed. Once a vaccine was developed, the Trump administration promised 20 million doses by the end of 2020. Although two vaccines were developed, the Trump administration withheld millions of doses of the vaccines from the public. The Center for Disease Control estimated that by January 2021, only about 16.5 million doses had been administered (Lee, 2021).

Immediately upon taking office in January 2021, President Joseph Biden implemented a plan for 100 million vaccinations to be administered in his first 100 days in office. Biden released millions of doses of the first vaccine and plans to use the Defense Production Act if the second dose is not ready by the time the first wave is completed (Stolberg and Wu, 2021). The act allows the president to require private companies and industries to prioritize the needs of the federal government in the name of national defense (Siripurpu, 2021).

Biden also issued a federal mask mandate on all federal property within hours of taking office (Lee, 2021). However, much more work needs to be accomplished as there are still many more people vulnerable to Covid-19 than those who have been vaccinated. To date, over 450,000 people have died as a result of the disease (Lee, 2021), many of which could have been avoided had the federal government taken a more empirically based and science-driven approach to the threat and realities of the coronavirus and its treatment.

SOCIOLOGICAL THEORY AND HEALTH CARE IN THE UNITED STATES

From a sociological perspective, how can we better understand the nature of medicine and the health care crisis in this country? As we will see, the existing paradigms used to explain many of the social problems in this text offer keen insight into both the nature of the problem as well as offering a glimpse into possible solutions to them.

Functionalism and Health Care

To begin, functionalists would see something like illness as dysfunctional to society. Why? Because something like disease interferes with people's ability to perform the roles and functions necessary for society to operate smoothly and keeps society from growing in positive ways. The creation of a **sick role** is one that contains a limited level of responsibility to fulfill one's obligations as well as being seen as source of social consideration. Talcott Parsons, one of the most famous structural functionalists, offered the idea of the sick role to explain how people with illnesses are not held to the same behavioral standards nor are they required to meet certain social obligations if they are sick (Parsons, 1951).

Parsons argues that this sick role contains within it several expectations for those playing it. First, the sick person must not be responsible for their illness. That is, a person does not do anything to contribute to their illness. Second, people in the sick role are relieved of their responsibilities and obligations that are normally required of a healthy person. Third, in order to legitimate the sick role, the person must want to get better and want to be healthy. Finally, the person must seek out and adhere to the treatment plan of a medical provider (Parsons, 1951).

The sick role Talcott Parsons described the "sick role" from a functionalist perspective.

The sick role and its expectations suggest that it is generally dysfunctional for society. As such, it is a form of deviance that must be addressed in a meaningful way. The social control agents charged with limiting the sick role are physicians, who give the person the societal permission to be relieved of their normal roles and responsibilities (Parsons, 1951).

Conflict Theory and Health Care

The conflict approach sees health care as part of the larger capitalist economy. Under the current model, wealthy patients receive high-quality care and possess many choices in terms of treatment, while those who are poor or middle class either cannot afford quality care or have such high deductibles to their policies that health insurance essentially amounts to catastrophic insurance, not comprehensive health insurance.

Consistent with a conflict approach, physicians, hospitals and pharmaceutical companies possess a monopoly over health care in the United States. They set the fee structures and the delivery of services and products in the marketplace. In doing so, physicians can abuse the system by overcharging patients, billing for treatments they never provided, or offering unnecessary treatments. Similarly, hospitals can continue their efforts to gain a competitive advantage in the marketplace by purchasing new equipment and technologies and pass the costs along to consumers.

Drug companies set the prices and distribution of medication, particularly since they have no real competition in the market. Insurance companies also seek to profit by increasing premiums for coverage, maintaining high deductibles for policy holders, and limiting the costs of treatment. Conflict theorists argue that changes to the system are unlikely since the amount of money made by providers is so great that they would resist anything more than incremental improvements. Further, given the complexity of the system, with so many administrative layers built into the system, radical change would take years to implement and still contain numerous challenges.

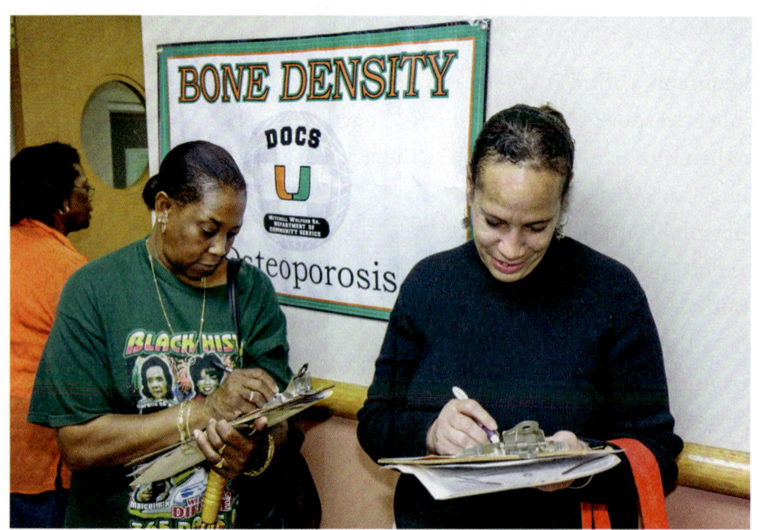

Building trust through information Outreach programs at community health centers, like this 2017 health fair in Miami, FL, encourage those who might distrust the medical establishment to empower themselves through accurate information.

Symbolic Interactionism and Health Care

From an interactionist approach, many of the problems relating to health and illness relate to the social construction of concepts like health, illness, and disease. Symbolic interactionists also examine the doctor-patient relationship. One of the most persistent problems in American health care and medicine today are complaints by patients that their physicians do not communicate with them, inform them adequately of options when considering treatment, and limit the amount of time they spend with patients. The latter is a function of reimbursement by insurance companies, because the only way doctors can make money is by seeing many patients during the day.

While patients have access to much more information about health and wellness than ever before, and while such information helps demystify the role of the physician as well as holding doctors accountable for patient care, there is an element of trust that drives much of the doctor-patient relationship. In the absence of meaningful and regular interaction, this trust either erodes or never develops in the first place. Such lack of trust, especially in an urgent public health crisis like a pandemic, has become a salient feature of how people view physicians and the field of medicine in general.

WHAT WORKS? EFFECTIVE SOLUTIONS TO PROBLEMS OF HEALTH CARE

The impact of Covid-19 on an already fragile and overburdened health care system made it clear that there are no simple solutions to the problems relating to the health care crisis in this country. The people of the United States will have to make difficult choices about the types of health care coverage they need and whether or not they can afford it. While many Americans are increasingly receptive to the idea of a universal type of coverage, there are many obstacles and opponents to making significant changes to the existing model.

On the positive side, with universal health care, health care costs overall would be lowered. Simply having one type of system for billing would greatly reduce administrative costs of filing claims and disputing fees. This means providers don't add staff to deal with the complexity of insurance company protocols and it forces hospitals to standardize their fees for services and focus on providing quality services at a low cost. Under the current model, hospitals leverage new technology and expensive services because they are more profitable, even if they are the types of services that most people don't need. This contributes to higher costs.

Preventive care also shows promise when it comes to reducing health care costs and increasing overall health in the population. In the past, many people used hospital emergency rooms as a source of primary care. This results in higher levels of health care inequality, because people with insurance received greater continuity of care. This emphasis on preventive care, which is not part of the current model, can be improved if the government regulated the system and imposed incentives for people to make healthier choices. Conversely, for those who want to engage in more risky behaviors, such as smoking or abusing alcohol, the government can impose additional taxes to compensate for the higher medical costs such behavior yields (Amadeo, 2018).

At the other end of the spectrum, universal health care requires healthy people to pay for the care provided to sick people. Chronic problems like diabetes and heart disease make up an enormous portion of health care costs (Lapointe, 2020; Centers for Medicare and Medicaid Services, 2020). As was mentioned, a small percentage of the population uses the vast majority of health care services in the United States—five percent of the population consumes 50 percent of the total health care costs in this country—often because of lifestyle decisions that lead to their illnesses. However, with free universal health care, there is no incentive for people to be careful about their health. Without a copay, people might simply overuse medical treatment (Lapointe, 2020).

Another disadvantage is that most universal health systems in other countries report long delays in elective procedures. Why? Because the government places greater emphasis on providing basic and emergency health care. Governments also tend to limit payments to reduce costs. This means physicians have less incentive to provide quality care and might spend less time with their patients to keep their costs low.

Universal systems are very expensive, which means higher taxes. It also means that governments may enact policies that limit services that have a low probability of success. This could mean denying coverage or medications for rare conditions. Under the current model in the United States, care for patients in the last six years of life makes up 25 percent of the Medicare budget.

What many experts have concluded is that we have what is known as **sick care** in this country, not health care. If you are sick—and you can afford it—the United States offers the best care in the world. But what the US health care system does not do is provide affordable health care that prevents people from needing medical care in the first place.

SO WHAT CAN I DO?

Given the complexity of this problem, you are probably wondering what you might be able to do about the challenges facing health care in this country. As a more macro-level issue (like most of the problems outlined in this book), the solutions might be beyond the level of the individual. However, there are some things you might be able to do in order to manage the impact health care has on your life.

One critical step is to take a greater level of responsibility for your own health. During 2020 you probably heeded the advice of public health professionals to wear masks, to wash your hands often, and to practice social distancing. These simple steps were not just to prevent yourself from getting sick with Covid-19, but to protect more vulnerable members of the population. Even after the pandemic subsides, you might consider maintaining a more preventive approach to your health rather than a reactive one, where you wait until you are sick to get treatment.

It also means you have to resist the cultural standard that is used to solve many problems in the United States: convenience. In this culture, we tend to want to take a pill to solve our inability to maintain an exercise regime or to be more disciplined in monitoring what we eat. Instead of making reasonable lifestyle changes, we opt for the easy solution. That convenience is not only expensive, it comes with it a host of consequences (think of side effects of medication) that cause other problems. This is not to say that being healthy is all about discipline; for some people with inherited medical issues and other challenges beyond their control, of course medicine and access to treatment is appropriate and necessary. But in other instances, we can and should take steps that might require a bit of sacrifice now for long-term health in the future.

Another thing that we can do in order to manage the health care crisis in this country is to reject the rhetoric about certain programs and practices. Many Americans believe that nationalized health care is bad because it is socialism, which seems to contradict American values of capitalism and a free market. In reality, we already have versions of nationalized health care. Is it perfect? No, but neither is the current system, which contains a host of intractable challenges including fraud, abuse, waste, and escalating costs.

Finally, as a taxpayer as well as a voter, it is important to make a reasonable assessment about what's the best way to proceed. Few experts think the current system of health care in this country is sustainable, and argue that eventually only the wealthy are going to be able to afford health care. But to reject a single payer system simply because of inaccurate and fear-mongering rhetoric about "socialism" demonstrates that we have been misled about some of its advantages. What you can do as an individual is to make sure you do not buy into the marketing and politically motivated narratives offered by people who want to maintain the status quo from which they benefit financially. Only then will we be able to make the difficult decisions about the future of health care in this country. While every option has its limitations, the focus should be on which ones give most people the best chance to get the care they need given the costs and other challenges of a particular model.

CONCLUSION

As the costs of health care continue to soar under the current model, it is important that you as a citizen and a consumer of health care understand the reasons for the dramatic and continued increases. The status quo also means that health care in the United States perpetuates inequality, as many people lack access to reliable and affordable health care. Unlike most developed countries, which see health care (like housing, food, and other basic necessities) as a right, many in the United States see it as a privilege. This inequality further burdens the health care system and the public in many ways. Even the healthiest among us are affected by those who are sick and who do not receive care.

It is also important to acknowledge that the United States already has a version of universal health care. Medicare and Medicaid are programs designed to help the elderly and poor populations by providing basic care for those who need it. Additionally, the US Department of Veterans Affairs provides universal coverage for military personnel. As the population continues to age, estimates are that nearly half of the US population will receive some form of universal health care. This means we are already on a pathway toward universal coverage, whether we like it or not.

Finally, dramatic changes to health care in the delivery of services are not likely to occur in the foreseeable future. There are trillions of dollars and millions of jobs dedicated to providing health care in its current form and restructuring or modifying the system will not happen quickly, efficiently, or without strong opposition from those who currently gain from the system in its current form. The Covid-19 pandemic has only increased the urgency of all of these issues.

YOU MAKE THE CALL: FINANCING MEDICAL CARE

As a physician and the owner of a family practice for 20 years, you make every effort to go above and beyond for your patients. In fact, you have had generations of family members see you as patients. In the past, for some patients, you have made concessions about their lapses in paying their bills for the services you provided. While it is a standard practice that all patients must pay their copay for each visit, once the insurance company reimburses you for your services, there is often an outstanding balance that must be paid by the patient. Under normal circumstances it is the practice's standard policy that a patient not be seen again unless they have made an arrangement with the office staff to pay their bills. You have been generally laid back about enforcing this policy; preferring to make sure people are taken care of than turning them away.

Now, however, as insurance companies reduce the reimbursement for services you provide, it is becoming obvious that in order to make ends meet, you must collect more from the patients in out-of-pocket expenses. This poses a dilemma for you: after all, your practice is located in a relatively low-income area, with many patients working in local factories or in the agricultural industry. While some have health insurance, you know that increased costs such as medical expenses make it difficult to make ends meet in other parts of their lives.

At the same time, however, you are running a business and last month you had trouble meeting payroll costs for your employees. It is right and appropriate that you are paid for the services you provide, and if the insurance company doesn't cover those costs, it is up to the patient to do so. Still, you are concerned that if you start enforcing the collection of fees from patients, they may choose to find another primary care provider. This could be devastating to your practice, which is already suffering because of higher overhead costs and lower reimbursement rates from insurance companies. You have recently learned that many other physicians are in a similar position and have accepted an offer from a local hospital to purchase their practices. In turn, these physicians then became hospital employees without any of the stressors of running a business. Recently, a representative of the hospital contacted you about selling your practice as well.

Questions for You to Consider

1. Do you follow the policy that patients agreed to when they started being seen by the practice and allow you to recoup some of the outstanding fees?
2. Do you 'write off" these balances, knowing that is lost revenue, because you do not want to antagonize patients, who might leave the practice? If they did, then all future revenue they would generate goes with them. So is it worth it in the short-term to lose money in favor of keeping the patients longer?
3. How do you continue to operate in the negative if you do not collect the fees? You already had difficulty meeting payroll last month because of low revenues, what happens if this

continues? You are already accepting new patients and trying to expand the practice through marketing strategies, but it is difficult to make up the lost revenue through increased volume—you are still faced with the problem of the costs of the practice compared to what comes in as revenue?

4. Do you accept the inevitable future of health care and take the paltry sum offered by the hospital? You have spent twenty years building this practice and the amount being presented is far less than its overall value. But do you take it and become an employee, without any of the headaches or difficult decisions?

SUMMARY

- Identify the reasons for the spiraling health care costs in the United States.
    - Much of the escalating costs stem from the specialization in medicine, the aging of the American population, and the rising costs of medications
- Describe the inequalities in health care.
    - This chapter also explored the inequalities relating to receiving health care in the United States, with its fee for service model virtually ensuring that some members of the population will receive lower quality care than others.
- Analyze how to address the spiraling costs of health care.
    - Universal care is expensive and requires higher taxes, along with challenges of how people use the system when there is no incentive to reduce costs and improve quality.
    - Obamacare. This law significantly reduced the number of people without health insurance by providing people with an affordable option if their employer did not offer health insurance as a benefit of employment.
    - The Trump administration promised to end Obamacare and replace it with a much more affordable, flexible and improved option. To date that has not occurred and Obamacare has continued.
- Apply sociological theories to health care in the United States.
    - Functionalists describe the sick role is one that contains a limited level of responsibility to fulfill one's obligations as well as being seen as source of social consideration.
    - Conflict theorists see health care as part of the larger capitalist system.
    - Consistent with a conflict approach, physicians, hospitals and pharmaceutical companies possess a monopoly over health care in the United States. They set the fee structures and the delivery of services and products in the marketplace.
    - Symbolic interactionists also examine the doctor-patient relationship.
    - The lack of communication between patients and physicians is a persistent problem and creates an absence of trust in the doctor/patient relationship.
- Evaluate effective solutions to health care.
    - Universal health care can reduce the costs of providing services by simplifying billing and administrative costs
    - Universal health care can provide incentives to people for making healthy

choices and an additional tax on those who engage in risky behaviors.
    - However, universal health care is expensive and will lead to higher taxes. It also results in delays in procedures and without incentives or copays, people can abuse the system.
    - Five percent of the population consume 50 percent of total health care costs in the United States. This is in part due to illnesses that result from risky behaviors, such as smoking, overeating, and neglecting preventative care.
- Identify individual efforts to address the problems of health care in the United States.
    - One critical step is to take a greater level of responsibility for your own health. During 2020 you probably heeded the advice of public health professionals to wear masks, to wash your hands often, and to practice social distancing.
    - Another important effort is for individuals to take greater responsibility for maintaining their overall health.
    - Reject the rhetoric about certain programs and practices. Many Americans believe that nationalized health care is bad because it is socialism, which seems to contradict American values of capitalism and a free market.
    - Vote to decide what is the best model and whether or not health care is a right or a privilege in this country.

KEY TERMS

American Health Care Act 383

Fee for services model 371

Health maintenance organizations (HMOs) 377

Infant mortality rate 374

Managed care 377

Medicaid 379

Medicare 379

Obamacare 375

Patient Protection and Affordable Care Act 380

Primary care physicians 373

Preferred provider organizations (PPOs) 377

Sick care 388

Sick role 385

Single payer system 370

Discussion Questions

1. Why do you think Americans are so opposed to the idea of universal health care, particularly given the costs involved in the current model?
2. What is the sick role and how is it used for secondary gains by people?
3. Why do you think doctors are either creating large practices or, more likely, closing their private practices and becoming employees of hospitals?
4. What would you say is the primary source of inequalities in the access and use of health care in the United States?

Learn more with this chapter's digital tools, including Data and Media Literacy Exercises, flashcards, and chapter self-assessments at **www.oup.com/he/mcnamara**.

14

What's that Smell? The Environmental Crisis

LEARNING OBJECTIVES

- Describe how technological advances and energy consumption contribute to environmental issues.
- Analyze the various types of environmental hazards, including air, land, and water pollution as well as solid and radioactive waste.
- Apply various sociological theories that help to explain environmental challenges.
- Analyze efforts to address environmental problems.
- Identify strategies that individuals can perform to limit the effects of environmental problems.

Chapter Outline

Dirty air Emissions from an oil refinery near Salt Lake City. Pollutants from such emissions contribute to global warming as well as health concerns.

Technology has changed how we function in society as well as how we interact with each other. Although technology makes our lives more convenient, its costs include a negative impact on the environment. In this chapter, we consider how technology both contributes to and can help solve social problems, particularly those related to the environment. We will also examine the intersections between environmental problems and topics discussed in previous chapters, such as poverty, work and the economy, as well as the prevailing themes of race and social class.

We also discuss the global consequences of American materialism. Although the convenience of living in a disposable society might offer a better quality of life for us, it has significant consequences for the environment and for people in other countries. The United States uses far more resources than virtually any other country, with consequences for the environment that impact nearly everyone with whom we share this planet.

SOCIOLOGICAL STORY TIME

- The devastating effects of Hurricane Florence on the town of New Bern, North Carolina resulted in thousands of people losing their homes and businesses and the cost to restore the town is estimated to be approximately $100 million (Bennett, 2018). Some blame the severity of the storm, and others like it, on global warming and climate control.
- According to Earth.org, one-third of all the food that is intended for human consumption, an estimated 1.3 billion tons valued at approximately a trillion dollars, is wasted or lost each year. This is enough food to feed an estimated

3 billion people. This is important given that there are an estimated 800 million people who suffer from severe malnutrition around the world (Earth.org. n.d.).

- In 2020, Australia witnessed one of the worst fires ever seen in the country, with nearly 18 million acres of land destroyed, which is an area larger than the countries of Belgium and Denmark combined. While some people offer natural causes for the fires, such as a severe drought, coupled with lightning strikes as well as people intentionally setting fires, most experts agree that climate change has increased the frequency and intensity of Australia's fire season (Yeung, 2020).
- In 2018, President Trump made an executive decision to allow an increase in ethanol in gasoline. Such a decision raised many questions about the impact of this change, which would essentially allow up to a 50 percent increase in the amount of ethanol contained in gasoline. The original idea to add ethanol to gasoline was to reduce environmental pollutants as well as America's dependency on foreign oil. However, the Environmental Protection Agency limited such amounts to ten percent or less during the Bush administration, because higher levels of ethanol in gasoline exceeded smog standards. Trump's decision was hailed as a victory for farmers, but critics point out it will contribute to damaging some vehicle engines and even increase the costs of food for consumers (Wald, 2018).

ENVIRONMENTAL ISSUES

How does technology influence problems in the environment? The impact of society on the environment is described by some experts as **environmental stress**. The development of technologies to improve our quality of life has resulted in the depletion of environmental resources as well as the addition of pollutants to the environment.

The United States and China are the largest energy consumers in the world and the largest contributors to the production of carbon dioxide and methane gases, both of which contribute to global warming (Table 14.1). While some countries saw modest decreases in their consumption in 2019, in most cases countries increased their use of energy since 2017.

Climate Change and Global Warming

Of all the problems facing the world today, few surpass the attention climate change is getting from the scientific community and environmental advocates. **Climate change** includes **global warming**, which is defined as the long-term warming of the planet but refers more to the broader changes that are taking place on Earth. These include rising

Table 14.1 World's Top Energy Consumers 2019 (Metric Tons of Energy Per Year-MTOE)

Country	MTOE
China	3,284
United States	2,213
India	913
Russia	779
Japan	421
South Korea	298
Germany	296
Canada	295
Brazil	288
Indonesia	269
Iran	258
France	241

Source: (Enerdata, 2020)

sea levels, acceleration of ice melting in Greenland, Antarctica and the Arctic, along with changes in growing seasons for plants and crops. These changes are due to increases in the temperature of the planet due primarily to the burning of fossil fuels, which emits pollutants into the atmosphere that trap heat. In addition, excessive breeding of methane-producing livestock like cattle emit gases into the atmosphere, while the destruction of forests that naturally absorb carbon dioxide limits the Earth's natural ability to address these problems (Australian Department of Environment and Energy, n.d.).

Livestock and global warming American reliance on beef and dairy makes the methane produced by cattle as they digest their food a contributing factor to global warming.

This type of overheating, even in small amounts, can have a disastrous effect not only on society, but on all life on Earth. Experts estimate that the global temperature is about 1.5 degrees centigrade above what it was in our preindustrial days. However, a rise in 2 degrees centigrade can cause severe storms; more acid rain, thus killing coral in the ocean and and disrupting the food chain; and melting of the polar ice caps. Melting the ice caps will result in dramatic increases in sea levels, which can wipe out islands and coastal regions and kill wildlife, further disrupting the food chain on land. The melting of the ice in Greenland and Antarctica also means there is less of it to deflect the sun's rays, thereby raising the earth's temperature even faster (National Aeronautic Space Agency, 2019).

California burning Climate change has contributed to worsening wildfire seasons around the globe. California has been especially hard-hit.

Climate change is also linked to the dramatic increase in wildfires. As mentioned in the Sociological Story Time example at the beginning of this chapter, wildfires in Australia had a significant impact across the country in 2020. Similarly, in California, wildfires across the state resulted in over four million acres of land being destroyed. Officials in California note that the 8,200 fires that occurred in 2020 was more than double the previous record. In offering an explanation for the dramatic increase in the number and intensity of the fires, officials note climate change as well as the buildup of dead and dried out vegetation across all 33 million acres of forestland in the state. The extended drought experienced by the state is also said to be the result of climate change, making the problem a chronic one in the future (Stelloh, 2020).

Addressing Climate Change and Climate Skeptics

One policy for addressing climate change was a regulatory system known as **cap and trade policy**. Under this policy, governments set a limit on overall emissions of pollutants and then let the market determine how industry would respond. However, by 2010, significant disagreements emerged about whether or not cap and trade could actually reduce pollution and slow global warming. In addition, some in government and industry dispute the existence of the greenhouse effect, and question the necessity of limiting the consumption of natural resources—especially the burning of fossil fuels. While some scientists also disagree about the existence of a greenhouse effect, the marked decreases of glaciers and the shift of vegetation patterns are not disputed (Experts Debate Global Impact of Greenhouse Gases, 2005).

There are opposing views on challenges to the environment. Scientists argue that we are facing an energy crisis and natural resource shortages that threaten human civilization. The United States is already experiencing a water shortage, which is so severe in places that states are suing each other over water rights. There are also water shortages around the globe as populations increase and industry expands to meet their needs. Thus, unless dramatic changes are made to conserve resources as well as find alternatives to fossil fuels (such as wind and solar power), we are facing a global calamity (Experts Debate Global Impact of Greenhouse Gases, 2005).

In contrast, other experts and scientists argue that such a position is inaccurate. They note that decreases in the price of energy, particularly coal and electricity, indicate a stable and even increasing supply of these forms of energy. Furthermore, advances in technology have historically solved many of the problems that impact the environment. Many optimistic scientists argue that technological advances in the future will address many of the environmental concerns we face today. This optimistic perspective also points out that concerns about the environmental crisis around the globe do not reflect the fact that life for many people is improving. One need only look at the increases in life expectancy around the world to indicate that the problems in the environment are not as drastic as environmentalists present. Experts from this perspective contend that when an environment deteriorates, life expectancy tends to decrease. Since that is not occurring, they conclude, concerns about the environment are unfounded (Experts Debate Global Impact of Greenhouse Gases, 2005).

In addition to cap and trade policies, another approach to address climate change is often referred to as **The Green New Deal**. This is a resolution by Congress that outlines a large-scale plan to resolve climate change. The proposal, which was introduced in Congress by Representative Alexandria Ocasio-Cortez of New York and Senator Edward Markey of Massachusetts, is designed to use the federal government as a tool to reduce the reliance on fossil fuels and reduce greenhouse gas emissions. The proposal also calls on the federal government to be a vehicle to guarantee high paying jobs in industries that promote and focus on clean energy (Friedman, 2019). How is this accomplished?

Green New Deal Advocates for climate justice protest ahead of the September 2020 presidential debates in Clevland, OH.

To address the climate change issue, the Green New Deal says the entire world needs to achieve net-zero emissions, where as much carbon is absorbed as released into the atmosphere, by 2050. Further, as a world leader and one of the largest users of the world's natural resources, the United States should take a leading role in achieving that goal. Specifically, the Green New Deal reduces carbon emissions by having 100 percent of the country's electricity from renewable and zero-emissions power, digitizing the nation's power grid, upgrading every building in the country to be more energy-efficient, and overhauling the nation's transportation system by investing in electric vehicles and high-speed rail systems (Friedman, 2019).

The second goal of the proposal involves social justice, where the federal government should not only recognize clean air, water and healthy food as basic human rights, but it should also be responsible for providing job training and new economic development so that companies and workers in the fossil fuel industries can effectively transition into the clean energy field (Friedman, 2019). Thus, the Green New Deal, named in part on President Roosevelt's famous New Deal legislation after the Great Depression of the 1930s (Chapter 4), has two goals: reducing climate change as well as trying to remedy societal problems like economic inequality and racial injustice.

Critics of the Green New Deal point out that such an ambitious effort is costly and will intrude on people's individual freedoms. For example, some members of Congress argued that the development of high speed rail systems and other efforts to reduce greenhouse effects could mean changes to the way Americans eat, travel, and live. The reduction of methane gases, for example, could be achieved with fewer livestock, particularly cows, which could reshape and restrict beef and dairy consumption (Friedman, 2019). While some reports in 2019 indicated that the Green New Deal would become a major issue in the 2020 Presidential elections, other issues surfaced that garnered more headlines (Freidman, 2019). This is not to say that climate change has gone away or become less important; indeed, with the election of President Biden and the shift of Congress to a Democratic majority, it is likely that climate change will be an important part of the new agenda for both branches of government.

High speed trains Mass transportation options, including zero-emissions high-speed trains, are one way address the problem of climate change. This is a Brightline train in Fort Lauderdale, FL.

Air Pollution

Photosynthesis is the process by which green plants combine water with carbon dioxide to produce oxygen. Under normal circumstances, this process removes pollutants from the atmosphere. The problem is that there is a limit to the capacity of the atmosphere to rid itself of contaminants, especially as the total biomass of the planet has declined due to deforestation (Nunez, 2019).

Forests still cover about 30 percent of the world's land area, but they are disappearing at an alarming rate. Between 1990 and 2016, the world lost 502,000 square miles of forest, an area larger than the country of South Africa. Since deforestation began, we have lost nearly half of the trees and a large portion of the Amazon rainforest has been destroyed. This is significant because trees absorb the carbon dioxide we exhale and the greenhouse gases we create in various industries (Nunez, 2019). According to one estimate, deforestation is responsible for about 10 percent of all global warming emissions (Union of Concerned Scientists, 2012).

According to the US Environmental Protection Agency, about 75 percent of the carbon monoxide in the air comes from the exhaust from motor vehicles. The rest comes from burning of oil and coal in airplanes and power plants, and the burning of trash. In addition, the chemical interactions that come from burning fossil fuels only exacerbates the danger of these pollutants when they reach the atmosphere (US Environmental Protection Agency, 2018).

The significance of deforestation is illustrated when one begins to consider how to reverse the effects of climate change. According to one report, tropical tree cover alone can provide a significant impact in slowing climate change over the next ten years (Nunez, 2019).

Smog and acid rain are two common terms used to describe the consequences of air pollution. **Smog** is a combination of nitrogen oxides, organic compounds (such as paint, cleaning products, and refrigerants), and sunlight. Together they create smog. This interaction causes ozone, which turns back into nitrogen dioxide, perpetuating the cycle. More of these organic compounds, like vehicle emissions, prevent the breakdown of the ozone, which then creates dense smog seen in places like Los Angeles and China. Some studies have found that smog can reduce the efficiency of photosynthesis by as much as 50 percent (Michelle, 2017).

Acid rain results when sulfur dioxide (SO_2) and nitrogen oxides (NO_X) are emitted into the atmosphere and transported by wind and air currents. The oxides react with water, oxygen and other chemicals to form sulfuric and nitric acids. These then mix with water and other materials before falling to the ground. Acid rain erodes buildings and vehicles and contaminates the water supply. Acid rains poison bodies of water and impact soil quality. Entire populations of fish in some ecosystems have died due to the acid quality of the water, while tracts of forests have been damaged or destroyed (US Environmental Protection Agency, n.d..; Michelle, 2017.).

Air pollution is especially severe in countries that have not taken steps to limit its effects through regulation of the burning of fossil fuels. In China, for example, the air quality has reached dangerous levels. Experts measure the air quality by using an index, called the **air quality indicator**, that ranges from zero to 300. Anything in the zero-to-50 range is considered good while anything above 300 is considered so dangerous it triggers a warning to the public to remain indoors. In Beijing, the air quality is routinely at the highest levels. In fact, because the air quality is so poor so often, people are frequently advised to stay indoors with the air conditioning set to its highest levels (Fleishman, 2018).

Smog in Los Angeles Downtown Los Angeles is seen through a haze of air pollution, or smog, in August 2019.

Air pollution in recent years has been exacerbated by extreme wildfire conditions brought about by climate change. During the summer of 2020, skies in much of the western United States turned orange due to wildfires and smoke particles in the atmosphere. Public health officials urged people to stay indoors and use both air conditioners and air purifiers to try to clean the air indoors (Vargas, 2020; Krishnakumar and Kanna, 2020).

The effects of air pollution are both physiological and economic. The health effects of long-term exposure to air pollution contributes to illness ranging from headaches to dizziness to asthma and cancer. Economically, air pollution results in lost productivity due to employees missing work, increased medical costs as people seek treatment for the effects of exposure to air pollution, and increased maintenance costs to buildings and cleaning costs, along with lost income for farmers and higher food prices as pollution destroys crops (US Environmental Protection Agency, 2018).

Water Pollution

The city of Flint, Michigan, was economically devastated by the downsizing of a General Motors factory (Chapter 5). This downsizing, which meant that many people lost their jobs, led to shortfalls in the city's budget. In an effort to reduce the deficit, the city built a new water pipeline to deliver water from Lake Huron, temporarily switching the city's water supply to the Flint River. By 2015, complaints from residents about the taste and smell of the water led the Environmental Protection Agency to test the water level for contaminants ("Flint Water Crisis—Fast Facts," 2018).

The EPA found high levels of lead in the water, and in addition discovered that the state was not adequately treating the water with an anti-corrosive additive meant to prevent lead from leaching from old water pipes into the water supply. There are serious health consequences related to lead consumption, especially to children, which is why federal law regulates the use of an additive to prevent it. More than a dozen lawsuits were filed, including several other class-action suits against the state and the city of Flint, claiming negligence on the part of those who were responsible for monitoring the water quality ("Flint Water Crisis—Fast Facts," 2018).

Poison in the water A member of the Michigan National Guard distributes bottled water and filters to residents of Flint, MI. The water supply in Flint is dangerously contaminated with lead.

The tragic situation in Flint is a good reminder of how fragile the water supply is for most people ("Flint Water Crisis—Fast Facts," 2018). Like the atmosphere, nature provides its own form of purification of water as it passes through the hydrologic cycle. As water vapor in the atmosphere falls as rain, snow, or dew, it is absorbed into the roots of plants and trees, or consumed by people or animals, or it may sink into underground reservoirs.

As with air pollution, humans have overloaded this natural purification process because we have contaminated much of it and rendered it unusable. This is a major social problem since there is only so much water available. Because of population growth and changing climate conditions, approximately 40 percent of the world's population suffers from serious water shortages. How do we use the water we have? Almost three-fourths of the water is used for crop irrigation, with industry as the second largest use. Less than ten percent of the water is used for household consumption (United Nations Environment, 2018).

Agriculture uses a tremendous amount of fresh water and contributes to the problem of water pollution. Rain and irrigation can cause the nitrates and phosphates in chemical fertilizers to leach into rivers and lakes, resulting in **algae blooms**, or huge amounts of algae that grow quickly and die. The decay of algae consumes oxygen, which can kill fish and animals. Moreover, as the algae decays, it settles to the bottom of the water along with other chemicals such as nitrogen and phosphorous (National Ocean Service, n.d.).

Toxic blooms Algae blooms are harmful to other plants, wildlife, and people. As the climate changes and pollutants increase in the water supply, algae blooms are more frequent.

Pesticides used in agriculture accumulate in the tissues of animals that are eaten by other animals. This is known as **biological magnification**—the concentration of a given substance increases as it moves up the food chain. As chemicals are consumed by smaller animals, who are then eaten by bigger ones, the intensity of the pesticide increases (Earth Eclipse, n.d.).

Industrial consumption of water has similarly dire environmental consequences, including **thermal pollution**. As factories and nuclear power plants release water and other substances into surrounding rivers and lakes, they can increase the temperature of the water by as much as 30 degrees. This can have a devastating effect on the cold-blooded animals which live in the water, as they are especially susceptible to temperature fluctuations. Temperature changes can also influence spawning and migratory patterns of animals, which can result in the extermination of some populations (O'Donnell, 2018).

The release (deliberate or accidental) of industrial chemicals into the water supply is another consequence of unchecked exploitation of natural resources. The oil spill is a particularly dramatic example. In March, 1989, the Exxon Valdez, which was carrying over 80 million gallons of oil aboard, collided with a reef in Prince William Sound, Alaska. More than 10 million gallons of oil spilled into the Sound. The Deepwater Horizon oil spill of 2010, which released over 200 million gallons of oil into the Gulf of Mexico, ranks as the worst oil spill in the United States (O'Donnell, 2018).

During the Gulf War in 1991, Kuwait experienced the largest oil spill in the world. Iraqi troops, retreating from their occupation of Kuwait, set fire to desert oil wells and opened the valves on oil rigs and pipelines. The goal was to impede US troops from attempting beach landings, but the spill resulted in upwards of 300 million gallons of crude oil being dumped into the Persian Gulf. This spill is one of the first times in military history where a natural resource and specifically pollution was used as a tactic of war (Catellani, 2018).

Land Pollution

Materialism and unchecked consumption are fundamental to American culture. As a consequence of this disposable lifestyle, America generates an enormous amount of **solid-waste pollution**. According to the US Environmental Protection Agency, in 2018 the United States generated about 292 million tons of municipal solid waste, which was an increase from the approximately 268 million tons in 2017 and 208 million in 1990. This roughly calculates into approximately 4.9 pounds of waste per person per day in the United States (Figure 14.1). This is comprised of various items such as paper (23 percent), food waste (21 percent), plastics (12 percent) and yard trimmings (12 percent). The remaining categories are things like rubber, leather, wood, textiles, metal, and glass (US Environmental Protection Agency 2018).

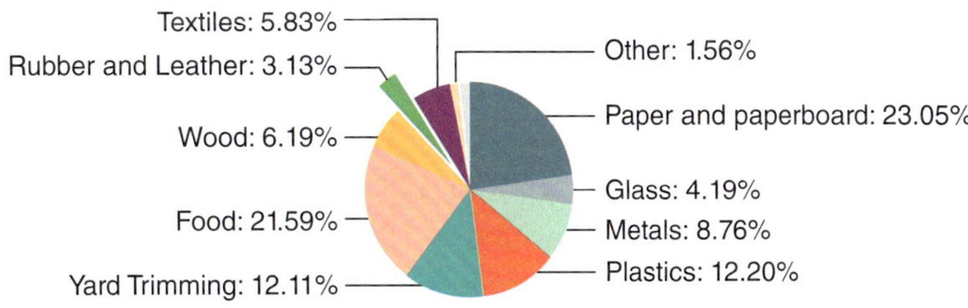

Figure 14.1 Municipal solid waste generated by material, 2018 (292.4 million tons). Source: EPA, 2018

Solid waste Municipal solid waste is collected in landfills like this one in Houston, TX.

You might be wondering about materials that are recycled or composted as a way to offset municipal solid waste. According to the EPA, the 292 million tons of waste collected, approximately 93.9 million tons (69 million tons were recycled, and 25 million tons were composted). Dividing this figure into the total amount of waste, the recycling and composting rate was approximately 32.1 percent. Such a figure shows that there remains far more waste than is reused (US Environmental Protection Agency, 2018).

Most people stop thinking about their trash and recycling once it's been picked up by a garbage hauler or sanitation engineer. However, recent evidence suggests that landfills are reaching capacity, resulting in concerns about **groundwater contamination**. Many communities work to prohibit the opening of new landfills in their area. While improvements in design and management of landfills have been made, property values near landfills are lower than in other areas and the quality of life of living near one is significantly different for those residents. As we will see, environmental racism contributes to the pattern of landfill location.

The problems of solid waste disposal don't end with landfills. Plastics and other synthetic items used in packaging don't break down organically. If they are incinerated rather than buried, the hydrocarbons and nitrogen oxides they release contribute to air pollution. About 12 percent of our solid waste in the United States consists of plastics and synthetic made items (US Environmental Protection Agency, 2018). Metals, which represent about 9 percent of the solid waste produced in the United States each year, are particularly difficult to dispose of safely in part because of their lead content (US Environmental Protection Agency, 2018). When these items are added to a landfill they can contaminate the soil and groundwater supply and pose a serious health hazard, including cancer.

Radioactive Waste

Nuclear power was at one time thought to be the solution to our energy problems. Worldwide, nuclear power generates about 10 percent of the world's electricity (International Atomic Energy Agency, 2020). In the United States, about 20 percent of the electricity produced here is done by nuclear power plants (Nuclear Energy Institute, 2020). Nuclear energy poses a problem because the dangerous fuel in the reactor's core must be replaced periodically. The spent fuel must be stored in stainless steel containers lined with concrete and must remain stable for 1,000 years, at which point the fuel becomes harmless. To date, the United States has over 90,000 metric tons of spent nuclear fuel and other nuclear wastes (Jacoby, 2020).

A particular challenge to the storage of spent nuclear fuel is the potential for catastrophic failure, either through human error or natural disaster. In the United States, nuclear waste is stored in about 80 sites across 35 states (Larson, 2020). This raises concerns about the transport of spent nuclear fuel (US Government Accountability Office, n.d.). The most noted example of a nuclear disaster occurred in 1979 at the Three Mile Island nuclear power plant in Pennsylvania. A mechanical or electrical failure in water pumps that helped cool the reactor core went unnoticed by employees. The nuclear fuel overheated and roughly half the reactor's core melted (Jacobs and Sedman, 2017).

Nuclear catastrophe The crippled nuclear reactor at Fukushima, Japan, after a catastrophic earthquake and tsunami on April 11, 2011.

Though investigators concluded that the radioactive water and gas did not escape the containment wall, the community was concerned about workers and nearby residents. In August 1993, fourteen years after the incident, the Nuclear Regulatory Commission announced that the cleaning of the 2.3 million gallons of contaminated water had been completed. Only a small amount of radiation people living in the area were exposed to radiation (Jacobs and Sedman, 2017).

The same cannot be said, however, for the 2011 catastrophe at a nuclear facility in Fukushima, Japan, after a massive earthquake and tsunami (Photo 14.100. The earthquake damaged three reactors, while the tsunami disabled the reactors' ability to be cooled. With no other option, Japanese authorities opened the floodgates to allow seawater to cool the reactor. However, the seawater then became contaminated as well. Initially, officials thought that they could release the seawater back into the ocean, but given the magnitude of the damage, such a strategy was not viable. Nearly a decade after the disaster, the damage is still being assessed (Motoko, 2017). In 2020, officials in Fukushima were considering releasing the contaminated water into the ocean. However, environmental groups and other advocates such as Greenpeace opposed this strategy, claiming the large amount of toxic water could have serious consequences for humans and wildlife. Japanese officials argue there is less risk and long-term storage of the contaminated water is not feasible (Woodyatt and Wakatsuki, 2020).

Environmental Racism

How do race, ethnicity and social class factor into social problems like pollution? Research suggests a pattern in the location of landfills, toxic waste facilities and areas that have been contaminated by pollutants. These sites are disproportionately located near low-income and minority neighborhoods. This pattern demonstrates **environmental racism,** since people living in low-income areas do not have the political or economic means to oppose and prevent this placement. Yet these are the populations most likely to suffer from the effects of these facilities. Data shows that low-income people, especially Blacks and Hispanics, have higher levels of illnesses because of contamination to water, land, and air by the toxic chemicals emitted from, leached out of, or dumped at these sites (Perlin Sexton, and Wong, 1999; Mikati et al., 2018; Newkirk, 2018).

For example, researchers at the National Center for Environmental Assessment found that people of color are much more likely to live near polluters and breathe polluted air. The study examined exposure to particulate matter, which includes automobile fumes, smog, soot, smoke, ash, and construction dust. Particulate matter is linked to serious health problems, and in some cases have been identified as known carcinogens by the International Agency for Research on Cancer. The EPA contends that particulate matter as a pollutant is linked to lung conditions, heart attacks, premature deaths, asthma, low birth weights in infants and high blood pressure (Mikati et al., 2018).

A 2012 and a 2016 study found that long-term exposure to particulate matter is also associated with race, in that people of color were exposed to higher levels of the pollutant and for longer periods of time than White people. The study found that people in poverty had about 1.3 times more exposure than people who are not impoverished. These findings join an ever-growing body of literature that has found that both polluters and pollution are often disproportionately located in communities of color (Bravo et al., 2016; Bell and Keita, 2012).

SOCIOLOGICAL THEORY AND ENVIRONMENTAL PROBLEMS

As sociologists developed an understanding of how people's attitudes, values, beliefs, and behaviors impact and influence the environment, an entirely new subfield of the discipline was created: **environmental sociology**. Environmental sociologists study people's perception of their place in society relative to the environment and the structures in society in response to environmental stressors.

Functionalism and the Environment

Recall the distinction in functionalism between manifest and latent functions. The former are those obvious contributions to society while the latter are the unintended consequences of certain practices, beliefs, and actions. Functionalists would point out that a latent function of technological innovation—which might otherwise be viewed positively as a sign of progress—is an exploitation of natural resources, resulting in higher levels of pollution. Functionalists might also point out optimistically that the problems of pollution and overuse have created new industries and opportunities for collective action inspired by the conservationist movement and the call to "go green."

At a global level, because the environmental problems are everyone's problems, such challenges forces countries to work together to find common solutions.

Conflict Theory and the Environment

From the perspective of conflict theorists, those who have the most economic, social, and political wealth will determine policy regarding how society responds to environmental crises. Given that profit means power, conflict theorists argue that the abuse of the environment can be considered a necessary evil required for the spread of capitalism. They might also suggest that inherent to capitalism is a belief that pollution and overuse of natural resources is minimized in importance, or not requiring conservation or regulation. Any challenges presented to the environment by industry are felt most by those who lack the power to resist. The discussion of environmental racism in this chapter is an example of how conflict theorists might frame the issue of what to do with solid waste and the pollution created by industry.

Symbolic Interactionism and the Environment

Symbolic interactionists tend to focus on micro-level approaches to understanding society and its issues. One way to understand the symbolic interactionist approach is the idea that perception is reality. That is, if people perceive a situation to be real, it is real to them, whether that situation is objectively true or not. As it relates to environmental problems such as pollution, if people believe that dramatic changes are necessary to our use of natural resources, they will work to promote behavioral changes as well as social policies that make conservation a priority. Conversely, if people believe that the problem of climate change is exaggerated and that the planet is not threatened by the overuse of resources, their understanding of how they use those resources will not make conservation a priority. Because the scientific community has not definitively determined the extent of the problem and the future outcome, a symbolic interactionist perspective helps us to understand why it is difficult to garner consensus.

WHAT WORKS? ADDRESSING ENVIRONMENTAL PROBLEMS

An optimistic view of the problem of climate change holds that technological innovation has already improved our ability to efficiently use natural resources, and that solutions for clean energy and remediating environmental pollution continue to be developed.

Most experts agree, however, that the greenhouse effect resulting from unchecked burning of fossil fuels as well as the destruction of biomass has resulted in a critical elevation of the earth's temperature. The consequences of such an increase include more frequent and extreme forms of weather, greater ice melting, and other disruptions to

Urban oasis Urban green spaces, like this garden created by volunteers in New York City, provide recreational spaces for residents while helping the environment.

the environment. One line of thinking about how to reduce the amount of carbon dioxide relates to nature's self-regulating system. Forests and soil store more than two and a half times as much carbon as the atmosphere. This, combined with other changes that reduce emissions, can be a significant part of the solution to the problem.

A growing forest, when sustainably managed, can reduce the amount of carbon dioxide in the atmosphere. Improved logging regulations can reduce deforestation. Changes in agricultural practices can also improve crop yields while reducing carbon content of the soils and discouraging the practice of slash-and-burn forest clearing. While reducing emissions is not enough to eliminate the problem, ecosystem restoration is a viable, achievable, and important short-term step. Such efforts yield economic benefits in the form of jobs and other opportunities while being more efficient (Adams, 2018).

Other solutions include the creation of what are called **urban green spaces**. According to the World Health Organization, creating urban green spaces, which is defined as the covering of all urban land with vegetation of any kind. This includes public and private spaces and provides a host of benefits to residents living in urban areas as well as mitigating some of the effects of climate change. The creation of urban green spaces not only has an impact on air and noise pollution, it also has an impact on weather, by protecting areas from flooding, heatwaves, and other challenges, it also promotes greater health and well-being among its residents by getting people outside and interacting with nature. There are a host of ways the creation of urban green spaces can be created but it starts with a recognition that urban areas will continue to grow more congested in the future and this has consequences for people and the environment as a whole (World Health Organization, 2017).

SO WHAT CAN I DO?

If only solving the problems of environmental degradation and pollution was as simple as driving less and carrying a reusable grocery bag! Such micro-level changes in behavior might have an impact if everyone participated. Simple strategies like recycling, reusing plastic materials when appropriate, conserving energy or finding ways to prevent excessive use are all reasonable, and if promoted widely, give people some semblance of improving the environment.

Part of the problem is that the general public is often unaware of the ways in which they contribute to pollution. In other cases, the information to which most people have access about complicated problems doesn't (or can't) provide simple, clear answers needed to make lifestyle changes. To the general public, it seems like experts argue either that the environment is doomed or that the problem is not nearly as dramatic as it is often portrayed. There is likely some truth to both sides of the debate, but what is the average person to make of all this information?

While it is certainly beyond the scope of the individual to change the way entire industries consume natural resources or create pollutants, we can certainly act intentionally and collectively to hold corporations accountable for their actions. You don't have to sacrifice all modern comforts and conveniences to take reasonable steps to help keep your community clean, or to improve its ability to recycle materials, or to be mindful of using public transportation instead of contributing to the carbon dioxide in the atmosphere every time you drive.

One specific way you might consider how to contribute to the problem is consider the challenge of plastic—specifically, plastic products that get dumped into the ocean. In 2018 a campaign was launched to eliminate the use of plastic straws in restaurants. Such an effort was heralded as a widely successful one, but alone it cannot solve the massive increase in the use of plastics. To be fair, eliminating plastics from society is neither feasible or a good thing—there are many advantages to using plastic in our everyday lives. However, there has been an explosion in the use of plastics across the globe and scientists conclude that half of all the plastic made occurred in the last fifteen years (Hancock, 2019).

A major problem relating to plastic is also its primary advantage—its durability. In fact, one of the great challenges for most people and organizations is figuring out what to do with plastic once its initial purpose is served. In fact, the majority of plastic waste that exists is largely a result of adequate recycling strategies. It doesn't matter if the plastic item we made is recyclable if there isn't a place to recycle it—and in the absence of a place to do that, most often the plastic ends up in landfills and the ocean. Current estimates suggest that of the most common type of plastic, known as polyethylene terephthalate (PET), such as a common soda bottle, only about 30 percent is recycled (Hancock, 2019).

There is evidence that the amount of plastics that are dumped into landfills and the ocean can be reduced by as much as 50 percent, provided there are mechanisms created to encourage reusing and recycling plastic products. At the individual level, you can contribute to reducing plastic in the following ways:

1. Carry a reusable shopping bag to the grocery store. You can also keep a water bottle or reusable coffee mug—or even bring your own utensils.
2. Instead of putting plastic furniture or dishes in the trash, consider donating them to a local charity.

3. Repurpose plastic items for some other task.
4. Recycle. Most estimates suggest that only about 9 percent of people in the United States recycle.
5. Volunteer to participate in a plastics clean-up effort. Some organizations solicit the help of boaters to participate in clean-ups of rivers and other areas.
6. Become active in improved efforts by local government regarding recycling efforts (Hancock, 2019).

CONCLUSION

There can be little doubt that the planet is being depleted of many of its natural resources—including perhaps two of the most essential ones to sustain life: air and water. This does not mean other types of pollution are not important, for our ability to grow food requires land and some of the damage we have done to the planet renders some of that land uninhabitable. Unless we make it a priority to begin conserving those resources and find alternative means to meet our energy needs, it is likely that we will soon be faced with serious consequences. There is also the need to consider the impact of race and social class on things like climate change and the depletion of environmental resources. As we have seen, while everyone is affected by climate change, issues relating to the location of landfills and other strategies disproportionately impact minorities and the poor. Policy decisions or programs designed to address this problem must consider these strategies in light of the disproportionate impact it has on some groups of people.

The good news is that we know some things actually do work. Efforts at the policy level need to be made to encourage conservation and promote sustainability. The problems discussed here are not unique to the United States, but as one of the biggest users of the world's resources, we have a responsibility to address the issues in meaningful ways.

YOU MAKE THE CALL: PROFIT OR PEOPLE?

You are the CEO of an oil company that is considering the use of fracking to access oil. Hydraulic fracturing, or fracking, is a technique designed to recover gas and oil from shale rock. Essentially, the process involves drilling down into the earth before a high-pressure water mixture is directed at the rock to release the gas or oil inside. The process can be carried out vertically or, more commonly, by drilling horizontally to the rock layer, which can create new pathways to release gas or used to extend existing channels (What is Fracking and Why is it Controversial?, 2018).

This process is risky in that the breakup of the shale and other hard rocks surrounding the oil pools increases the risk of earthquakes, sinkholes, and other challenges, not to mention the contamination of fresh water. The board of directors has directed you to implement fracking in several communities because the risks have not been proven to cause health problems or environmental damage.

Your company hired a consultant to assess these risks but you wonder if the results are really objective. The use of fracking will greatly enhance your company's ability to sustain itself in the future, not to mention providing an ample supply of oil for consumers. This means the United States will be less reliant on foreign oil and less vulnerable to price fluctuations. It also means significant bonuses for you and your executive team. However, community residents, environmentalists, and scientific experts express grave concerns about the costs of using this technique and the long-term consequences for the community.

Questions to Consider:

1. Do you move forward with the decision to increase production because at the end of the day you are responsible to your stockholders and the bottom line?
2. What are the potential costs involved if the community files a lawsuit that demonstrates the environmental, economic, and social costs to residents and the community at large? How does that weigh against the potential for profits?
3. What is the company's moral responsibility to the citizens of that community and society at large? If there are serious risks of injury as a result of this practice, is it ethical to continue? Does the company have an obligation to inform the community of the potential negative consequences?
4. What about your sense of morality and conscience? Do YOU have an obligation that extends beyond your career and job responsibilities to report dangerous practices that, while legal, create a host of concerns for residents and their children?

SUMMARY

- Describe how technological advances and energy consumption contribute to environmental issues.
  - While technological advances have many advantages, including the creation of many conveniences for people, they come at a cost.
  - The use of technology as it relates to the development of businesses and industry, sometimes called environmental stressors, result in the depletion of natural resources.
- Analyze the various types of environmental hazards, including air, land, and water pollution as well as solid and radioactive waste.
  - Problems of air, land, and water pollution present significant challenges to society and the planet, both now and in the future.
  - Nuclear power also presents opportunities but the disposal of radioactive waste and the costs of incidents where reactors fail have serious implications for society at large.

- Apply various sociological theories that help to explain environmental challenges.
    - Functionalists point out that a latent function of technological innovation—which might otherwise be viewed positively as a sign of progress—is an exploitation of natural resources, resulting in higher levels of pollution.
    - Functionalists might also point out optimistically that the problems of pollution and overuse have created new industries and opportunities for collective action inspired by the conservationist movement and the call to "go green."
    - At a global level, because the environmental problems are everyone's problems, such challenges forces countries to work together to find common solutions.
    - From the perspective of conflict theorists, those who have the most economic, social, and political wealth will determine policy regarding how society responds to environmental crises.
    - Given that profit means power, conflict theorists argue that the abuse of the environment can be considered a necessary evil required for the spread of capitalism.
    - Conflict theorists might also suggest that inherent to capitalism is a belief that pollution and overuse of natural resources is minimized in importance, or not requiring conservation or regulation.
    - The symbolic interactionist approach might promote behavioral changes as well as social policies that make conservation a priority.
    - Conversely, symbolic interactionists would also point out that if people believe that the climate is not threatened by the overuse of resources, their understanding of how they use those resources will not make conservation a priority.
- Analyze efforts to address environmental problems.
    - Creating a growing forest is one way to address issues relating to air pollution, but it will require us to prioritize how we are going to use the land we have.
    - Similarly, the creation of green urban spaces can also assist in addressing some of the issues many cities are confronting with regard to climate change and global warming.
- Identify strategies that individuals can perform to limit the effects of environmental problems.
    - The slowing of climate change and global warming is everyone's responsibility.
    - Steps individuals can take to alleviate climate change include recycling, community clean-up efforts, and lifestyle changes that make us less dependent upon fossil fuels as well as improving our overall health in the foods we eat.

KEY TERMS

Acid rain 400
Air quality indicator 400
Algae blooms 402
Biological magnification 402
Cap and trade policy 397
Climate change 395
Environmental racism 405
Environmental sociology 406
Environmental stress 395
Global warming 395
Green New Deal 398
Groundwater contamination 404
Nuclear waste 404
Oil spills 403
Smog 400
Solid waste pollution 403
Thermal pollution 403
Toxic waste 405
Urban green spaces 408

Discussion Questions

1. How does race and social class influence the discussion of environmental problems in the United States?
2. Given the extent of the US contribution to pollution, can it significantly impact the problem by conservation and other efforts? Why or why not?
3. Why haven't other forms of energy production, such as solar power, wind, and other strategies been more widespread in the United States?
4. Is nuclear power still a viable option for the United States or do you think the risks associated with it outweigh its potential advantages?

Learn more with this chapter's digital tools, including Data and Media Literacy Exercises, flashcards, and chapter self-assessments at **www.oup.com/he/mcnamara**.

15

Chapter Outline

Do We Need to Be Afraid? War and Terrorism

LEARNING OBJECTIVES

- Define war as a social problem and its impact on military personnel and civilians.
- Define terrorism and summarize its costs, types, and potential impact.
- Analyze sociological theories to explain and understand war and terrorism.
- Evaluate effective solutions to war and terrorism.
- Summarize what individuals can do to address the effects of war and terrorism.

The day everything changed The terrorist attacks of September 11, 2001 changed US policy towards terrorism and launched decades of war in the Middle East.

The social problems discussed in previous chapters have a disproportionate impact depending on unequal access to economic, social, and political power. When it comes to war and terrorism, however, everyone is at risk. To be sure, it is important to consider the ways in which US foreign policy decisions contribute to existing social problems at home. For example, some experts note that the costs of the war in Afghanistan and Iraq are resources that could be best used at home to address significant structural issues, such as higher education and the cost of affordable housing in the United States. And the ongoing cost of prolonged warfare on veterans and their families continues to mount.

When it comes to terrorism, the riot at the Capitol on January 6, 2021 made it shockingly clear that the threats are not just external but also permeate our own society. This finding is underscored by the fact that both the FBI and the Department of Homeland Security have identified domestic terrorism as a major threat to national security (US Department of Homeland Security, 2020; Sherman, 2020). While it is important to note different groups (foreign and domestic) and their respective ideologies, the fact that so many of them despise the United States and what it stands for should make us consider the roots of their hatred. Is it because we are enormous users and abusers of the world's scarce resources? Is it jealousy because we are one of the wealthiest countries on the planet, or is it due to the perception that the United States is arrogant, entitled, spoiled, and feels no real sense of responsibility for others around the globe? What role do domestic inequalities play in making some US citizens susceptible to false narratives about stolen elections or the threat of Covid-19 infection?

Finally, it is important to examine the role of technology in how warfare and terrorism is addressed. As we will see, the nature of warfare is changing as a result of drone technology, and other strategies of war are being developed that reduce the risk of human life. And information technology—especially social media—plays a significant role in the organization of domestic terrorism and the spread of false narratives and conspiracy theories that radicalize some people.

SOCIOLOGICAL STORY TIME

- In 2018, Russia blocked Ukraine's ships from entering a port that both used for shipping purposes. Russian border patrol planes also opened fire on Ukrainian ships that attempted to pass through the Kerch strait, a small area that links the Azov and Black seas. The tensions stem from the overthrow of a pro-Russian government in Ukraine in 2014, which resulted in Russia annexing Ukraine's Crimean Peninsula. It also set off an ongoing conflict between Pro-Russian rebels and Ukrainian troops. Fighting has claimed more than 10,000 casualties, and the blocking of shipsis the most recent in a long line of nearly daily skirmishes between the two countries (Ferris-Rotman and Stern, 2018).
- A 2016 report by the RAND Corporation found that deployments do not usually have long-term negative effects on spouses or children of soldiers. However, while service members were deployed, they were more likely to show symptoms of depression, and their spouses suffered elevated symptoms of depression, anxiety, and post-traumatic stress disorder (PTSD). In addition, although many couples returned to pre-deployment levels in terms of mental health and family status, when veterans experienced some form of trauma during deployment or suffered a physical injury, then higher levels of depression, anxiety, PTSD, and substance abuse were experienced among the service members and their spouses (Sutherland, 2016).
- In 2017, a report found that for the third consecutive year, the number of terrorist attacks across the globe had decreased. The Study of Terrorism and Responses to Terrorism (START) found that there were 10,900 terrorist attacks around the world last year, which killed a total of 26,400 people, including perpetrators. That was a drop from 2015 and 2016. Explanations for this downward trend may be due to law enforcement and counterintelligence efforts or it may be due to the fact that many of the Islamic States have lost territory through military action. Experts note that without a stable base, the number of attacks has declined (Taylor, 2018).
- The 2021 attack on the US Capitol shocked the nation, particularly when it was revealed that participants included military veterans and police officers. However, the presence and growth of involvement of veterans and law enforcement in domestic terrorist groups has been a long-standing concern for the intelligence community. Although the US Department of Homeland Security noted this trend in 2009, along with other reports, the attack on the

Capitol indicate that veterans are prime recruiting targets for domestic terrorist groups, largely because of their training and political views (US Department of Homeland Security, 2009; Lacour and Way, 2015).

In Chapter 2, we explored the reasons why crime is bad for society. Some sociologists argue that crime is a problem because of the harm it causes, while others offer insight into the societal costs associated with crime. In both cases, we noted that there are other events and circumstances that are either more harmful or costlier than crime, particularly street crime. We concluded from this discussion that the real reason crime is a social problem is due to the psychological harm it has on people—the fear of the possibility of being victimized or the chance that it could impact those we care about.

In examining the notion of war as a social problem, the costs and harms involved are far more significant and damaging than something like street crime. This does not, however, mean that victims of crime are not harmed or that those injuries should be minimized or ignored. What it does mean is that those harms and costs are much more visible and evident for victims of war. This includes the direct and indirect victims, including civilians and citizens, as well as the social, economic, and political impact war can have on a particular country.

WAR AS A SOCIAL PROBLEM

How do we define war? One definition is that **war** is an organized and armed conflict between nations or political factions. While most people think of war this way, as something that occurs between two or more countries in a specific location or area, sociologists often define war to be broader in scope. They argue that war includes those declared conflicts between countries but also incidents such as civil wars, covert operations and even some forms of terrorism. When considering war and the violence associated with it, sociologists examine the costs to combatants as well as collateral costs and harms, to civilians, families of military personnel, and others connected to the conflict.

Very few people in the United States see the effects of war, in part because at least since the twentieth century, wars have occurred outside of US soil. This makes the impact and relevance of war significantly lower, despite the fact that wars tend to have a lingering and persistent quality. In other words, when wars occur, they are rarely short-term events. As we have seen with the conflicts in Afghanistan and Iraq, wars endure for years and have a significant impact on the social, economic, and political landscape for the involved countries.

Costs

War is expensive, both in terms of its actual costs as well as in the costs to prevent it. During the period known as the **Cold War** (1947–1991), the United States and Russia were in a race for superiority over conventional and nuclear arms. The fear

Fallout shelter At the height of the Cold War, many Americans anticipated a nuclear attack by the Soviet Union. Some even built fallout shelters, like this one in Milwaukee, WI, at their homes.

of being vulnerable to an attack or, worse, the inability to deflect and respond to one, led to nearly unprecedented spending on the defense of the country. According to the Congressional Budget Office, during the Cold War, the US government spent nearly $11 trillion in defense spending and arms acquisition. In the end, when both sides realized they had more than enough missiles to wipe out the planet many times over, and détente was achieved as both countries were satisfied that the other would not initiate a first-strike against the other. Both countries also realized that the costs of a continued arms buildup were unsustainable (Higgs, 1988).

Today the global concerns about the nuclear capabilities of other less developed nations has continued to make defense spending a priority. According to the Congressional Budget Office, in 2020, the budget for 2020, passed in late 2019, was $738 billion, about 15 percent of all federal spending (Gould, 2019), with a projected budget for fiscal year 2021 to be $740 billion (Korb, 2020).

The costs of war go beyond the expense of producing weapons, missiles, and ancillary expenses. There are people costs as well. This includes not only the wages paid to military personnel, but the costs associated with compensation given to US veterans for injuries sustained in war-related activities. According to the US Department of Veterans Affairs, this was an estimated $87 billion in 2017 (Jowers, 2017). Because the compensation may be seen as both a harm and a cost, it makes sense to consider direct and indirect harms of war as well.

Harm

When people think about the harms involved in warfare, inevitably they think of the serious physical and emotional effect, including loss of life it has on participants and non-combatants alike. Over the sweep of history, the twentieth century was by far the most harmful in terms of loss of life. During World War I, for example, an estimated eight million soldiers and one million civilians died. The casualties during World War II were even higher, with nearly 17 million soldiers and 35 million civilians killed. Subsequent conflicts, such as the wars in Korea, Vietnam, the Gulf war, Iraq, and Afghanistan cost many more American and civilian lives. According to the US Department of Defense Casualty Report, between 2001 and 2014, there were a total of 2,395 deaths and 20,363 injured in and around Afghanistan as part of Operations Enduring Freedom and Freedom Sentinel. Between 2003 and 2010, as part of Operation Iraqi Freedom, there were 4,424 deaths and 31,957 wounded (Smith, 2018).

Commemorating their sacrifice The American Veterans Disabled for Life Memorial in Washington, DC, was dedicated in 2014. The memorial features glass panels etched with the personal testimonies of soldiers, as well as a reflecting pool and eternal flame.

Not all soldiers who fight in battles die, but many suffer physical and emotional injuries as a result of being in combat. More important, those injuries and their effects often last long after they have returned home. According to the Wounded Warrior Project, as a result of injuries, many soldiers are unable to hold a job or return to a normal life after serving in combat. According to the US Department of Veteran Affairs, in 2020, more than 6 million veterans are receiving some form of compensation due to disabilities sustained while serving in the military (National Center for Veterans Analysis and Statistics, 2020).

POST-TRAUMATIC STRESS DISORDER (PTSD)

While one does not have to be fighting on the front lines to experience emotional trauma, research suggests that the closer soldiers are to the action, the greater the likelihood they will experience **post-traumatic stress disorder (PTSD)**, which causes extreme stress reactions after experiencing a traumatic event. One of the consequences of the disorder is an excessive concern with danger.

PTSD support Iraq war veteran and military police office Sgt. 1st Class Jason Syriac with his PTSD companion dog, Rosco. Rosco has been trained to assist veterans with PTSD, and along with Syriac helps train rescue dogs as support animals for other injured veterans.

According to the US Department of Veterans Affairs, about 8 percent of the US population will experience PTSD at some point in their lives, and about 8 million adults have PTSD in any given year. Men are more likely to experience PTSD (60 percent) than women (40 percent). How they sustain PTSD also differs by gender, with men being more likely to experience it as a result of accidents, combat, disasters or witnessing death or injury. Women are more likely to experience PTSD as a result of sexual assault or child abuse. As it relates to veterans, the rates of PTSD are significantly higher than the general population. The National Center for PTSD estimates that about 30 percent of Vietnam veterans have experienced PTSD in their lifetime and about 15 percent are currently diagnosed. Similarly, about 12 percent of veterans of Iraq and Afghanistan have PTSD in a given year (US Department of Veterans Affairs, Center for PTSD, n.d.).

TRAUMATIC BRAIN INJURY

Another type of injury that has serious implications for soldiers and their families is **traumatic brain injury (TBI)**. This occurs from a sudden blow or jolt to the head. While a TBI is similar to a concussion, a direct blow to the head is not the only way one can sustain a TBI. A TBI is the result of the brain being shaken within the skull by a concussive force, causing bleeding between the brain and skull or bruises where the brain hits the skull. About 80 percent of all TBIs in civilians are mild, and most people who sustain them will return to normal within three months without specialized treatment (US Department of Veterans Affairs, n.d.).

As it relates to veterans and their experiences in combat, the wars in Iraq and Afghanistan have changed the nature of injuries for soldiers. **Improvised Explosive Devices (IEDs)** have resulted in a greater number of head injuries, particularly for soldiers on the ground, who often sustain these injuries near the blast site. According to the US Department of Veterans Affairs, the main causes of TBI among military service personnel are blasts, motor vehicle accidents (which can come as the result of IEDs going off on or near the roadside) and gunshot wounds. The Department of Defense estimate that nearly a quarter of all combat-related wounds are brain injuries, nearly double the rate of what occurred during the Vietnam War (US Department of Veterans Affairs, n.d.).

The data seems to indicate that veterans experience symptoms of TBI for longer periods of time than civilians. This may be because veterans often have more than one medical problem, such as chronic pain or PTSD, which may explain why veterans can experience symptoms for up to two years after sustaining the TBI. Dealing with multiple injuries may delay recovery from a TBI compared to a single injury (US Department of Veterans Affairs, n.d.).

The most common symptoms of TBI include feeling dizzy, trouble sleeping, memory loss, difficulty staying focused on a particular task or putting thoughts to words, as well as depression, anxiety, personality changes and impulse control problems. Many of the symptoms that relate to TBIs are also similar to those related to trauma. Many people who sustain a TBI also develop PTSD (US Department of Veterans Affairs, n.d.).

MILITARY SEXUAL TRAUMA

It should be pointed out that combat isn't the only way veterans can experience PTSD. Another example of a traumatic experience in the military relates to **military sexual trauma (MST)**. This is the term used to describe experiences of sexual assault or repeated sexual harassment of a veteran during his or her military service. According to Title 38 US Code 1720D, MST consists of "psychological trauma, which in the judgment of a VA mental health professional, resulted from a physical assault of a sexual nature, battery of a sexual nature, or sexual harassment which occurred while the Veteran was serving on active duty, active duty for training, or inactive duty training." (US Department of Veterans Affairs, n.d.).

This includes any sexual activity where a soldier is forced or pressured into sexual activities against their will or if they were unable to consent to sexual activities. It also includes offensive remarks about a person's body or sexual activities or unwelcome sexual advances. The important distinction in this definition is that it involves a service member who is on active duty at the time of the incident. It does not matter if the victim was on or off-duty or on or off base at the time of the incident—if the person was on active duty status or active duty training, the VA considers it an act of MST.

To determine the extent of MST, the VA uses a national screening program that asks every veteran seeking medical care whether they have experienced MST. The data suggests that about 25 percent of women and about one percent of men responded affirmatively to this question. Because this data is limited (in that it only includes those veterans who seek medical care from the VA), it cannot be used to determine the extent of sexual assault among all service members in the US military. It must be remembered that MST is not a diagnosis or a mental health condition, it is an experience that military personnel encounter. And although PTSD is commonly associated with MST, it is not the only disorder that can result from MST. Other challenges associated with MST include mood disorders, substance abuse, difficulty sleeping, and anxiety (US Department of Veterans Affairs, n.d.).

As is the case with sexual assault and rape in the general population, women are at far greater risk for victimization for this act than men, in part because there are many more men than women in the military. As policies relating to sexual orientation in the military have changed, with an increase in LGBTQ people enlisting in the military, it may be that an increase in the number of cases involving men will become more common.

FAMILIES AND CIVILIANS

Families of service members may also be impacted and harmed by warfare. Deployments place a significant stressor on families, particularly if the service member sustains an injury. According to the Substance Abuse and Mental Health Services Administration, a growing area of concern relates to the negative impact deployments have on children of US military personnel. The research suggests that children and youth experience multiple stressors before and during their parent's deployment and even after they return home. Evidence of this is seen in higher levels of academic, behavioral, and social difficulties for children of deployed personnel compared to non-military families (Lipari et al, 2016). If the service member comes home uninjured, there is a good likelihood that the family can return to its pre-deployment levels of stability. However, if the family member who was deployed sustains a physical or emotional injury, challenges remain for everyone in the household. About 20 percent of service members who return from a deployment have symptoms of posttraumatic stress disorder (PTSD) or major depression (Lipari, et al., 2016).

In addition to the service members injured or killed during war, non-combatant personnel can also be harmed. Part of the challenge of preventing women from serving in combat areas is that the modern nature of warfare has put anyone at risk of injury or death. Thus, how does the military determine the types of jobs women can perform if they are not allowed to be in a combat area and every location is a possible combat area? In addition to military support personnel being impacted by war, civilians and even private contractors are also at risk of being injured or killed as a result of sustained conflict.

REFUGEES AND WARFARE

Civilian non-combatants are also victims of warfare, especially those displaced as a result of conflict in their country. According to the United Nations High Commissioner for Refugees (UNHCR), the **forcibly displaced population** increased globally in 2017, when 68.5 million individuals were forcibly displaced worldwide as a result of persecution, conflict, or generalized violence. This was an increase of almost 3 million people from 2016 and a 50 percent increase since 2007. The UNHCR also reports that more than 60 percent of all refugees around the world come from five countries: Iraq, Syria, The Democratic Republic of the Congo (DRC), Nigeria and South Sudan. More than half (52 percent) of these refugees are children under the age of 18 (United Nations High Commissioner for Refugee, 2017).

Today one out of every 110 people in the world is displaced, compared with one in 157 a decade ago, with much of this increase having occurred over the last five years. While the Syrian conflict contributed significantly to this increase, there have been other major displacements throughout the world over the last five years, notably in and from Burundi, Central African Republic, the DRC, Iraq, Myanmar, South Sudan, Sudan, Ukraine, and Yemen. In 2017 an average of 44,400 people were newly displaced every day. At the same time, many others returned to their countries or areas of origin to try to rebuild their lives, including 4.2 million **internally displaced people (IDPs)** and at least 667,400 refugees. Syria continued to account for the largest forcibly displaced population globally. As of the end of 2017, there were 12.6 million forcibly displaced Syrians, comprising around 6.3 million refugees, 146,700 **asylum-seekers**, and 6.2 million IDPs. Colombia had the second-largest displaced population with

The misery of war The ongoing civil war in Syria has displaced millions of Syrians, forcing them into temporary camps like this one in Idlib Province, Syria.

7.9 million victims of conflict, the majority of whom were IDPs (United Nations High Commissioner for Refugees, 2017).

The Democratic Republic of the Congo (DRC) was the third-largest displacement situation with 5.1 million Congolese forcibly displaced, comprising 4.4 million IDPs, 620,800 refugees and 136,400 asylum-seekers. Some 4.8 million Afghans remained forcibly displaced, of whom 1.8 million were IDPs and 3.0 million were refugees or asylum seekers. Other large displaced populations at the end of 2017 included people from South Sudan (4.4 million), Iraq (3.3 million), Somalia (3.2 million), Sudan (2.7 million), Yemen (2.1 million), Nigeria (2.0 million), and Ukraine (2.0 million) (United Nations High Commissioner for Refugee, 2017).

The impact of wartime migration has social consequences as well. Not only is it likely that refugees will be disillusioned about the role of government or the type of government they wish to live under, they may also feel that their sense of belonging and levels of patriotism can be negatively affected. Indeed, it is unlikely that a group of people would likely remain loyal to a country or government that either persecutes them or forces them into a different way of life for reasons that might be controversial or even illegal. Moreover, the rule of law as a guiding principle, regardless of which form of government the people decide to use (which can be the source of serious disagreement and discouragement over the lack of progress), is also affected by the challenges each form of government presents.

Technology and Warfare

What role does technology play in warfare? Some might argue that it potentially escalates the likelihood of conflict, as different countries become better able to acquire sophisticated weapons of war. Other experts note that advanced technology could potentially reduce the harm and costs involved, given that greater precision of the destruction of targets can be achieved, which minimizes collateral damage and other loss of life. Thus, many experts point to the military's ability to be more precise in its use of bombs and missiles that minimizes collateral damage to both infrastructure as well as saving innocent lives.

Surveillance from afar Unmanned arial vehicles, or drones, have dramatically changed the way wars are fought. Here, US soldiers stand next to a drone used for surveillance.

However, critics point out that while technology has advanced the ability of the military to inflict greater and more precise forms of damage against an enemy, the continuing problem of civilian casualties and "friendly fire" incidents that suggest human error that cannot be eliminated through the use of technological innovation.

UNMANNED ARIAL VEHICLES AND CHANGING WARFARE LANDSCAPE

While drone technology is beneficial to society, proving useful in agriculture, energy conservation, and to humanitarian and disaster relief, drones are also an important asset to the US military. Although drones have been used by the military for over a decade, smaller, portable drones are now being used by ground forces on a regular basis.

Drones, or unmanned aerial vehicles (UAVs), are miniature planes that can be remotely controlled for short and long range military and civilian purposes. Drones are usually equipped with surveillance equipment or military armament such as missiles and can be used to either collect intelligence or inflict considerable physical and psychological damage against enemy combatants. According to a 2018 report the Pentagon now has some 7,000 aerial drones; the CIA has about 30 Predator and Reaper drones, which are operated by Air Force pilots from military bases; and the Department of Homeland Security has about 10 unarmed drones. The cost per flight hour varies by type of drone. Predator and Reaper drones cost about $2,500 to $3,500 per flight hour; larger armed systems such as the military's Global Hawk costs approximately $30,000 per flight hour (CBInsights, 2018). In addition to the use of new aerial technologies, militaries continue to use unmanned ground vehicles, or UGVs, to lead tactical initiatives (CBInsights, 2018).

While drone technology will inevitably change the nature of warfare, particularly as other countries begin acquiring drones and related technology, some argue that this will desensitize people to the harm and costs of war since it will increasingly be conducted from a video screen far away from the battlefield. Some research suggests that drone pilots are experiencing a similar form of psychological stress similar to PTSD, but without physically being on the front lines. In addition, many drone pilots experience high levels of anxiety, depression, and stress reactions similar to direct combat soldiers. Many drone pilots are overworked—often logging three to six times the number of flight hours as traditional pilots in the Air Force. While the Air Force is already experiencing a shortage of pilots, this higher workload has resulted in an increasing number of drone pilots seeking work in the private sector (Friends Committee on National Legislation, n.d.).

TERRORISM

There are different approaches to defining and understanding terrorism. One school of thought proposes that the use of violence for political purposes defines terrorism. Under this rubric, one researcher, Louise Richardson of Oxford University, defines terrorism as "violence—or equally important, the threat of violence—used and directed in pursuit of, or in service of, a political aim." Thus, if there is no political purpose for the actions, the behavior constitutes a criminal act; if there is no violence, those acts are not terrorist in nature (Ward, 2018).

There are two important questions stemming from the difficulty in defining terrorism: do forms of extremism constitute terrorism? And should groups that incite hatred be held responsible for attacks and identified as terrorists even if they don't directly participate in the violence? [The latter question was particularly relevant in January and February of 2021, as the second impeachment trial of Donald Trump was based largely on this issue.]

Coordinated violent attacks such as those committed by members of Al-Qaeda at the direction of the leadership of those groups are clearly terrorist acts committed by terrorist groups. But what about violent attacks are typically committed by individuals who are not a part of ideological groups? Are they terrorists or simply violent criminals (Ward, 2018)?

In 2015, in Charleston, South Carolina, Dylann Roof murdered nine African-Americans who were participating in a Bible study inside their church. Roof was said to have been influenced by information he found on a White supremacist group called the Council of Conservative Citizens. Some believe that Roof should have been charged with terrorism since he was a homegrown violent extremist even though he was not part of a terrorist cell or network. Instead, Roof was convicted of a federal hate crime (Ward, 2018).

It is also important to consider whether other groups in addition to the extreme far-right ones, should be considered in the definition of terrorism. As was mentioned in the Sociological Story Time example, the attack on the US Capitol was not conducted only by terrorists, but also by citizens who allegedly had no motive or goal to kill innocent people or to overthrow the government. Instead, as some of them argue, they were simply following the orders of their president, who told them to go and protest the results of the presidential election as Congress sought to certify the results.

Thus, the challenges found in defining terrorism, even when violence and a political objective are integral parts of the definition, is difficult, especially when the offenders are not actively involved in violent attacks or are not members of a given organization. Regardless of the

Incitement to violence On January 6, 2021, rioters stormed the US Capitol building at the encouragement of then-President Donald Trump, who falsely claimed that the 2020 presidential election was fraudulent.

definition used, and although terrorist groups sometimes attack government officials, government buildings, or military personnel or installations, a common theme is that terrorists are likely to target civilians or locations as a way to send symbolic messages to the people and the existing government of their vulnerability (Ward, 2018).

Costs of Terrorism

According to an annual report from the Costs of War project at Brown University's Watson Institute of International and Public Affairs, the total cost of the war on terror was $6.4 trillion in 2019 (Crawford, 2019).The report also factors in war-related spending by the Department of State, past and obligated spending for war veterans' care, interest on the debt incurred to pay for the wars, and the prevention of and response to terrorism by the Department of Homeland Security.

Nearly two decades later, America is conducting counterterror operations in 76 countries and US troops are fighting and dying everywhere from Afghanistan to Niger. In addition, according to the Costs of War project, about 801,000 people have been killed in the post-9/11 wars in Iraq, Afghanistan, and Pakistan (Crawford, 2019).

Types of Terrorism

There are many parallels between terrorist attacks and the nature of war. Both are threats to the stability and safety of groups of people and even entire countries. Both create significant levels of fear, destruction of property and the loss of life. As was mentioned, one definition of terrorism is that there is a political dimension to the activity; the same is true in warfare, where most conflicts are a result of different political ideologies. Within the phenomenon of terrorism itself, there are a few key distinctions.

Political terrorism uses intimidation, coercion, and violent acts to bring change or even overthrow an existing government. There are essentially three types of political terrorism: revolutionary terrorism, repressive terrorism, and state-sponsored terrorism.

The most common type of terrorism is **revolutionary terrorism**. This involves the use of violence against civilians by enemies of a particular government. The idea is that if there are enough seemingly random acts of terrorism conducted by dissident groups, it will disrupt the public's faith and confidence in the existing government's ability to keep them safe.

In contrast, **repressive terrorism** is the type of terrorism perpetrated by a government against its own citizens in an effort to preserve the existing political structure. One example of this type of terrorism is occurring in China, where over 1 million Muslim minorities in the Xinjian Uighur Autonomous Region have been detained in internment camps and forced to submit to reeducation and political indoctrination by the Chinese government (Greitans, Lee, and Yazici, 2020).

State-sponsored terrorism occurs when a government provides support, in the form of funding, training, weapons, and equipment, to terrorist groups so they can engage in terrorist activity in other countries. For the past twenty or more years, the United States has considered countries such as Iran, Iraq, Syria, Libya, North Korea and Sudan examples of state sponsored terrorist countries. In 2010, India demanded that Pakistan not allow territory under its control to be used for terrorism directed against India. Similarly, the United States accused Pakistan of harboring Osama bin Laden for several years prior to his capture and death (Haltiwanger, 2018).

The attacks on the US Capitol would fall into the category of revolutionary terrorism, since it was conducted by citizens who were protesting the election of Joe Biden as President and attempting to overthrow the existing government. By claiming that the government had rigged the election and that Democrats participated in a fraudulent election, insurgents, many of whom were right-wing extremists, were attempting to disrupt the activities of Congress and subvert the democratic process. Some rioters claimed a goal of executing Speaker of the House Rep. Nancy Pelosi as well as Vice President Mike Pence for his alleged "betrayal" of President Trump. The attack was clearly an attempt to install a leader who was not legitimately elected by the citizens (Crowley, 2021).

In addition to traditional terrorist activity, state-sponsored terrorism has been linked to cyberattacks, particularly against the United States. These are efforts by hackers, often in other countries, to infiltrate and disrupt economic and military structures against the United States.

For example, in March 2018, the city of Atlanta was crippled by a ransomware attack that lasted two weeks and cost nearly $3 million. In many US cities, cyberattacks have occurred even after government officials implemented greater security measures. The FBI reports that more than 4,000 ransomware attacks occur daily, while other research sources state that 230,000 new malware samples are produced every day. As a result, global security expenditure reached $86.4 billion in 2017, and approached $100 billion in 2018, as traditional security measures such as firewalls and anti-virus software prove to be inadequate (Erez, 2018).

The early viruses and worms that targeted networks have evolved into something altogether more powerful and problematic. These new attacks, or **advanced persistent threats (APTs)**, tend to be slow moving and remain embedded in the system undetected for long periods of time. An APT is a network attack by a third party that gains unauthorized access and remains undetected for a lengthy period. Hackers launch APTs at networks to access sensitive data and systems (Erez, 2018).

While APTs present problems for networks and existing systems, the problem is complicated by the lack of effective mechanisms to control them. In addition, there is a growing shortage of qualified computer personnel to keep up with various forms of cyberattacks. One estimate suggests that at the end of 2018, while about six million cyber security analysts are needed in the industry, only four to five million qualified people will be available to fill these positions (Erez, 2018).

While the challenges of cyberattacks are serious for corporations, an even more serious threat is when a country or nation-state attempts to hack another country's military, financial, or utilities and transportation networks, which can virtually disrupt an entire nation's operation. This becomes a form of cyberterrorism.

A major problem with this form of hacking is that it is nearly impossible to trace and track the activities and hold those individuals responsible for them. It is also a much easier, less costly, and more efficient way for terrorist groups to achieve their goals. One example of this trend is seen in the interference of hackers on social media in an effort to disrupt the 2016 and 2020 elections. In the 2016 election, there is evidence that Russian hackers created fake social media accounts to spread fake political news to over 126 million Americans. We also learned that fake political news tends to lean conservative in its views and that people 65 and older were seven times more likely to share fake news compared to younger people (Wright, 2020). As a two researchers pointed out in their 2016 study of the election, concerns about fake news and its impact on people's thinking has become an important element in shaping election outcomes. As Allcott and Gentzkow (2017) found, more people are using social media as their primary source of news and while the frequency of fake news stories about the election continues to grow, more people are believing the information they see and hear in those stories, with just over half of those who recalled seeing a fake news story believing it.

Part of the reason for this is that people are much more likely to believe stories that favor their preferred candidate, especially if they only use social media that supports their opinions (Allcott and Gentzkow, 2017). This makes the circulation of fake news stories a powerful and effective form of cyber attacking. More importantly, people may not even be aware that they are being influenced in a particular direction. This is perhaps one of the reasons so many people adamantly believed the 2020 election was "stolen" from President Trump, who claims he won the election in a landslide, despite any objective evidence. It also justified the attack on the US Capitol, since many Trump supporters believed that the election was invalid and that they had to "stop the steal," a campaign to invalidate the election results (Wright, 2020).

Fear and Public Opinion about Terrorism in the United States

As we explored in Chapter 2, fear of victimization in the United States remains high despite the fact that the crime rate has remained low for several years. In the same way, while the public was understandably concerned about terrorism after the 9/11 attacks, fear levels have remained high despite a decrease in the number of incidents.

In 2018, researchers from the Cato Institute observed that much of the counterterrorism efforts in the United States are a result of this fear, with little hope of reducing fear regardless of how much money is spent or how many programs and agencies are created to address the problem. More pointedly, the researchers pointed out that not only will allaying the public's fear be difficult to achieve, but that even if the coordinated efforts by agencies and the military managed to eradicate terrorist threats in the United States, it will be difficult to convince the public that they really are safe (Mueller and Stewart, 2018).

Empirically, there is little reason to fear terrorism. The probability that an American will be killed by a terrorist in the United States during the last half-century stands at about one in 4 million per year. For the period since 2001, the odds are far lower—something like one in 50 million per year. By comparison, an American's chance of being killed in an automobile crash is about one in 8,200 a year, while the chance of becoming a victim of homicide is about one in 22,000. Since 9/11, the number of Americans killed by Islamist terrorists is six per year. However, probabilities are estimates and while one might be able to convince themselves they are more at risk at home or driving a car than any other activity, as with the discussions of crime, the fear that is generated often overwhelms people beyond their ability to rationally consider the risks (Mueller and Stewart, 2018).

The recent events at the US Capitol in 2021 has likely raised the average American's fear about domestic terrorism and the threat some of these radical groups present. A 2020 report from the Center for Strategic and International Studies indicates that while white supremacists and other like-minded extremists were responsible for more than two-thirds of terrorist plots and attacks in the United States in 2020, the number of actual incidents and deaths related to them remains small (Jones, Doxsee, and Harrington, 2020). The report notes that the many demonstrations and protests that took place in 2020, provided a nearly ideal venue for some of these groups to attack protestors and increase the exposure and notoriety of their efforts (Figure 15.1). In addition to far-right extremists, there has also been an increase in the number of anarchist and antifascist or far-left groups in 2020, who also engaged in terrorist incidents. Separating the two is a difficult task, as both engage in nearly identical activities, although the targets may differ, with far-right extremists attacking African Americans, Jews, and immigrants (Jones, Doxsee, and Harrington, 2020).

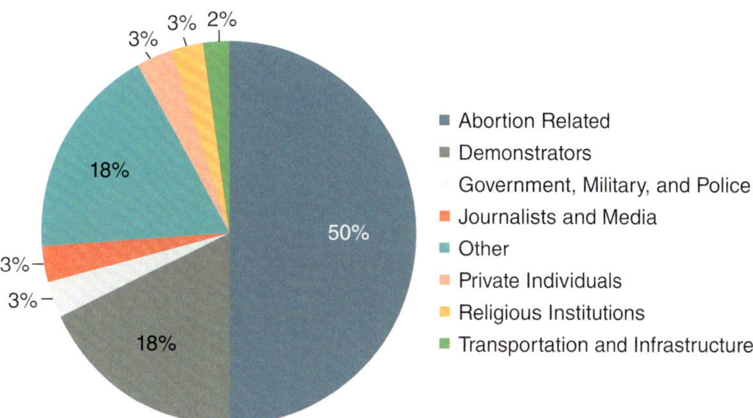

Figure 15.1 Targets of domestic far-right terrorist attacks and plots, January to August 2020 Source: Data compiled by CSIS Transnational Threats Project.

Still, it is important not to overstate the threat these groups present; the number of fatalities from these domestic groups, such as Proud Boys, Oath Keepers, Boogaloo Bois, Three Percenters, and QAnon, and the like, remains small as are the number of people injured or killed as a result

GLOBAL PERSPECTIVES

Incidences of Terror Around the Globe

The Institute for Economics and Peace created the Global Terrorism 2020 Index, which offers insight into the countries most affected by terrorism and most likely to sustain a future attack on a scale from zero to 10. In 2020, Afghanistan was one of 77 countries that experienced at least one death from terrorism last year, Total fatalities for 2020, however, fell for the second year in a row (Table 15.1).

The report showed that there are countries that are not at risk for a terrorist attack. Thirty countries were given a score of "0," representing no impact from terrorism and a low likelihood of future attacks, and another 42 countries had a score of less than 1.0 (Institute for Economics and Peace, 2020).

Table 15.1 Countries most affected by terrorism

Country	Score
Afghanistan	9.59
Iraq	8.68
Nigeria	8.71
Syria	7.78
Somalia	7.64
Yemen	7.58
Pakistan	7.54
India	7.35
Democratic	
Republic of Congo	7.17
Philippines	7.09

of these attacks. However, experts note that the continued political polarization, the Covid-19 pandemic, and concerns about immigration and racial injustice provide opportunities for these groups to engage in further and more widespread violence. It is also possible that the loose organization of the groups, and their lack of impact, may result in the groups deciding to develop a more organized structure to be more effective (Jones, Doxsee, and Harrington, 2020).

SOCIOLOGICAL THEORY ON WAR AND TERRORISM

Sociological theory offers important insight into understanding the issues surrounding war and terrorism and how these topics impact society, social life, and individual relationships.

Functionalism, War, and Terrorism

Functionalism offers useful insights into the nature of war and of terrorism. As it relates to war, functionalists would point out that war can have a physical and economic benefit to a society. Border wars occur as nations argue over territory and the encroachment of one country over another. The winning side in a war is then able to potentially expand its region. Recent examples in Russia point out that despite the independence of countries like Ukraine, Russia has continued its attempt to reclaim that territory as its own.

Another advantage of war according to the functionalist perspective is economic. War enhances a nation's economy through the use of its resources, such as land, oil, and crops. The requirements of warfare can also stimulate the economy of a country. For example, World War II was largely responsible for the end of the Great Depression in the United States as the war effort put millions of unemployed people back to work. More recently, the United States government has authorized the sale of military equipment and supplies to other countries fighting wars for billions of dollars. In 2020 alone, this amounted to approximately $175 billion (Mitchell, 2020). Not only does such activity generate profit for the corporations that own and manufacture the equipment, expansion results in job stability and increased employment in many states.

A third function of war is more political. While wars are often fought over disputes of territory, more often than not it is also about clashing ideologies, usually political or religious. For example, the involvement in wars by the United States are almost always over defending democracy and a democratic form of government. Similarly, the Taliban, ISIS, al Qaeda and other terrorist groups believe in a radical form of religious extremism that is the source of their violent acts, even against innocent civilians.

Functionalists also believe that war can be a source of significant social change, similar to Durkheim's observation about the unifying role of religion in society. This sense of solidarity, or **nationalism**, unites disparate groups in the face of serious adversity. Social change can also be practical and pragmatic, as the logistics of war necessitate changes in the operation of society. For example, during World War II, while many men were away fighting the war overseas, women took their places in the manufacturing sector, which contributed to the war effort. The country underwent an evolution of the roles of women that became part of the women's movement.

This is not to say that functionalists think war is a good thing for society. The harm and costs to society in human lives as well as damage to the infrastructure of society, along with the psychological effects of war, clearly outweigh any ancillary benefits.

Conflict Theory, War, and Terrorism

A discussion of war and terrorism seems to naturally lend itself to the conflict perspective. With its emphasis on economic, social and political power, war is a natural consequence of some disputes. Marx and other traditional conflict theorists might argue that all wars have an economic basis. That is, war and terrorism are more likely to result from potential economic gain or loss than from political or ideological disputes. Also, larger and more powerful countries may exercise their economic influence over others to achieve some type of gain, while smaller and less powerful groups may resort to terrorism to exert some level of power.

While there is inevitably a political dimension to all wars and even many terrorist activities, where traditional Marxists and contemporary conflict theorists merge is in the economic element of warfare. While Marxists might argue that the elite attempt to gain more ownership and control of private property as the primary motive for war and terrorism, others argue that profit may be the main reason for the decreased level of conflict around the world. That is, war is not necessarily in everyone's best economic interests, particularly international conflicts.

Symbolic Interactionism, War, and Terrorism

The symbolic interactionist approach offers insight into how and why certain groups believe, and act in particular ways in response to social problems. As it relates to war and terrorism, symbolic interactionists would likely examine the process by which people are transformed from citizen to soldier. How are individuals resocialized to adopt the attitudes, values, and beliefs that distinguish the non-combatant civilian from the warrior? As it relates to domestic terrorist groups, either far-right or far-left wing, how do these groups identify combat veterans as recruits and what messaging do they use to convince them to become members?

Symbols of protest—or of hate? A participant in a 2021 gun rights protest in Richmond, VA, flies the Gadsden Flag and the Betsy Ross flag. Along with the Confederate flag, these are symbols used by many far-right-wing activists and hate groups in the United States.

Whether it is the process of transitioning from citizen to soldier or in the case of veterans becoming involved in extremist groups, citizen to insurgent, the process involves an unquestioning obedience to the mission or cause. In combat situations, there isn't time for debates and discussions—and quick and decisive actions are needed. In addition, the resocialization process used in the military and by terrorist groups attempt to dehumanize the target or "enemy" so that killing becomes not only justified but righteous, even when those targets are American citizens. Similarly, civilian casualties are framed in such a way as they are seen as an inevitable consequence of war. In the case of the attack on the US Capitol, extremist groups see the execution of government leaders or those who have opposing views as a cost of war, even in those instances where innocent civilians do not pose a threat to their safety. Symbolic interactionists would also be interested in not only how former soldiers who became insurgents cope with these moral and ethical challenges, but also how they can return to everyday existence as American citizens once the armed conflict or attack ends.

Another way symbolic interactionists see war and terrorism is in the use of symbols to define an ideology, an act or response to a threat and how it shapes people's attitudes, values, beliefs and behaviors about particular groups. For instance, far-right extremist groups who participated in or supported the attack on the US Capitol often display Confederate and American flags, Christian crosses, and other patriotic memorabilia to justify their actions and ideology. Framing the behavior of a particular group in light of its patriotism or Christian righteousness is a powerful motivator for people to rationalize and justify what would otherwise be considered criminal and treasonous behavior (Stanton, 2021).

WHAT WORKS? EFFECTIVE SOLUTIONS TO THE PROBLEMS OF WAR AND TERRORISM

The number of terrorist attacks has decreased in recent years. One explanation for this trend relates to improved intelligence gathering and the ability of law enforcement to thwart potential attacks before they occur. In offering insight into what can be done to address the issues related to warfare and terrorism, there are a variety of approaches that have had some success.

The creation of the **United Nations (UN)** was an attempt to find a way for countries to have a neutral third party to intervene in border disputes and other conflicts between nations. What began as an organization designed to promote international peace as the **League of Nations** in 1919, after World War I, the onset of World War II showed that the mission of the League had failed. At the conclusion of the second world war, in 1945, the UN replaced the League of Nations (Shendruk, 2017).

While the United States is a primary supporter of the UN, with the contribution of about $10 billion per year, or about 20 percent of the UN annual budget, the 193 member organization has found mediating disputes to be of limited value. While there have been some notable successes on the part of the UN as a mediator in global conflict, such as the war between Israel and Arabs, the Greek civil war, the conflict in Bosnia and the Korean war, the UN has had less success in addressing conflicts involving larger nations. The research also shows that when the UN does intervene with peacekeeping troops, they are often forced to leave because of the severity of the conflict and nature of the violence between factions within a given country. Furthermore, there are significant challenges involved in UN peacekeepers maintaining a meaningful level of neutrality and managing "boots on the ground" diplomacy (Shendruk, 2017).

Another example of an effective approach to terrorism occurred in Minnesota. Between 2007 and 2008, a group of about 20 Somali-American adolescent boys and young men living in the Minneapolis–St. Paul area left their homes and flew to Somalia to join terrorist training camps. These young men, including academically talented high school and college students, ultimately were involved in suicide bombs and other activities. While it is tempting to conclude that these young men were mentally ill or emotionally unstable, experts have noted that involvement in violent extremism is more a result of a series of "push" and "pull" factors that led them to engaging in such radical behavior. These include exposure to war in their home country, forced migration to the United States, broken families due to being refugees, and the effects of racial and religious discrimination. These factors, coupled with Somali culture and savvy recruiters who influenced these young men about the importance of the use of violence and fulfilling their respective destinies, led to their involvement in terrorism (Weine and Osman, 2012).

These homegrown recruitment efforts were the starting point for the creation of the Building Community Resilience program, funded by the Obama administration. The program is based on the model Diminishing Opportunities for Violent Extremism (DOVE). This model was designed to assist community leaders and families to prevent extremism in the Somali-American community in Minneapolis-St. Paul area of Minnesota. The program helps to insulate young Somali men from the risk factors mentioned earlier, as well as offering concrete ways to create what are known as protective factors that give potential victims an opportunity to resist these influences. Much of the effort involves keeping Somali-American youth involved in constructive community-related activities while

Communities against extremism The Somali community in Minneapolis, MN, is working to address concerns about extremism while protecting their civil rights. In 2015, Council on American-Islamic Relations-Minnesota Executive Director Jaylani Hussein (with microphone) called for greater transparency in US government programs meant to counter extremist tendencies among Somali-American youth.

calling attention to the rhetoric offered by recruiters who attempt to convince them that violent extremism is an acceptable behavioral pathway (Weine and Osman, 2012).

This is an ambitious goal since it asks Somali youth, who struggle to understand what it means to be both an American and a Somali, to trust the federal government and law enforcement while suffering the effects of educational and employment inequalities and experiencing a backlash of prejudice and discrimination while living in the United States. One of the project's two main prongs is the development of "community-led intervention teams"—groups of Somali leaders and educators enlisted to identify and intervene with young people believed at risk for radicalization (Weine and Osman, 2012).

Another explanation for the decline in the number of terrorist attacks relates to the ability of the United States to disrupt the internal structure of many terrorist groups. As pointed out in the 2020 report by the Center for Strategic and International Studies, much of the violence we are seeing from domestic right-wing terrorist groups remains a small percentage of all attacks in part because these groups are small, have only a small number of followers and supporters, and remain organizationally loose and lacking in coordination (Jones, Doxsee and Harrington, 2020).

As a result of military attacks, assassinations, or other efforts to dismantle the leadership of these organizations, the planning and execution of these attacks on a larger scale has decreased. On the other hand, critics of such an approach argue that despite the death of Osama Bin Laden, the number of terrorist groups and scale of activity has remained. This raises questions about the overall importance and value of senior leaders in terrorist organizations and the ability of any country to reduce the level of activity against the United States.

Finally, there are hints that counterterrorism efforts may positively impact other aspects of social life, including reductions in crime. Unfortunately, while billions of dollars have been spent on efforts to prevent terrorist attacks in the United States, what seems to be missing are data that shows which programs work and which ones do not. A review of the literature by the Center for Evidence Based Crime Policy at George Mason University in Washington, DC found only a few studies that demonstrate how counterterrorism efforts, such as intelligence-led policing, can result in crime reductions.

For example, one study found that when police officers were assigned to protect synagogues following a terrorist attack in Buenos Aires, rates of auto theft showed significant decreases. In the United States, other research found that crime was lower in Washington, DC on those days when terrorist alerts were high. Intelligence-led policing offers a framework by which the intelligence gathering and sharing that are in important part of counterterrorism efforts can be applied to crime prevention, but it is clear that there is much more to be done to understand how and in what ways the prevention of terrorism can be evaluated empirically (Center for Evidence-Based Crime Policy, n.d.).

SO WHAT CAN I DO?

One might think that individuals can do very little to address the nature of war or terrorism, even in their own community. This makes sense in some ways since, like the other problems discussed in this textbook, warfare and terrorist activities are far beyond the scope of any individual's effort to thwart or minimize their effects. However, it is essential that the average person increase their understanding not only of the existence of these groups, particularly the far-right and far-left extremist groups at home, but also to educate themselves about social media platforms and the ways in which citizens appear to accept and share fake news perpetuates the problem and the threat.

The Center for Strategic and International Studies (2020) found that many domestic terrorist groups use social media platforms like Facebook, Instagram, Reddit and Twitter to spread propaganda and promote violence against minorities. Other platforms like Gab and Discord, while less mainstream, are also becoming popular with those who espouse conspiracy theories and other forms of misinformation. It is important to remain objective and focused on the facts, not the fiction, as it relates to the ideologies of these groups and to discern actual facts from rhetoric in the narratives that are presented. It is also important to debunk these false narratives, because the failure to address them is a form of acceptance. As more people start to believe the repeated false claims, the problems magnify.

CONCLUSION

A critical component of developing a sociological imagination is understanding how, for most people, perception is reality. That is, if people perceive something to be real, despite evidence to the contrary, it is a version of reality to them. Sociologist W.I. Thomas has noted that "if men define situations as real, they are real in their consequences" (Scott and Marshall, 2015). Such insight clearly applies to a societal understanding of warfare and terrorism. The fear of another attack like the 9/11 tragedy has remained a part of the public's consciousness. And yet while terrorism threats from the likes of Al Qaeda have decreased, we have perhaps not been aware of the growing new threat of domestic far-right terrorism.

Another important message of this chapter relates to the role of technology. In both warfare and in the battle against terrorism, technology is changing our understanding of conflict and war—in some ways by being more precise in attacking targets and minimizing collateral damage, but in other ways technology desensitizes us to the violence that makes up a critical component of war and terror. While technology may allow us to reduce the loss of life, such as using drones instead of troops, there may be other costs associated with technology that are not as easily understood.

YOU MAKE THE CALL

You are the CEO of a major social media platform. During the course of a presidential election campaign, you learn that the President of the United States has consistently provided false information about the election and the presence of a "deep state" conspiracy to remove him from office. Other supporters have also continually spread inaccurate claims. On one hand, you believe in the idea of free speech and do not want to censor people's views and opinions, since that is antithetical to a democratic society, but you are also concerned that people will believe the lies being told and that could change how they vote—which is also a threat to democracy. If you censor the President and his followers you will be accused of supporting his opponent and if you don't, your failure to act amounts to participating in a fraudulent election. The FBI and the Department of Homeland Security have informed you that Russian hackers created thousands of fake social media accounts and consistently fed the American people false information about the last election, making the current President's claims even more dangerous.

Questions to Consider:

1) Do you allow the President and his supporters to continue spreading what you know to be lies to the American people, arguing that it not your responsibility to convince citizens what to think?
2) Do you create a policy that verifies the information before allowing it to be published on your platform? Is such a policy enforceable given the amount of information that is presented—can you realistically fact-check all the information?
3) Should you suspend the accounts of those people who have provided "fake news" or misrepresented the facts about a particular issue if you can verify its accuracy because you have a responsibility to provide accurate information to people?
4) Knowing that the data indicates many people believe and share fake news, and social media has become a main mechanism in the advancing the ideology of extremist groups and helps in their recruitment of new members, should you filter information even though you are likely engaging in a form of censorship? In other words, is the greater good served by protecting the country and its members even though it means they have fewer freedoms?

SUMMARY

- Define war as a social problem and its impact on military personnel and civilians.
    - This chapter began with a discussion of the nature of warfare, including the costs and harms associated with it.
    - Beyond the immediate casualties and injuries sustained by war, such as PTSD, traumatic brain injury, or military sexual trauma, there are indirect costs and harms, particularly

to soldiers' families and refugees displaced as a result of conflict.

- Define terrorism and summarize its costs, types, and potential impact.
    - Terrorism has been a visible part of the US landscape since the attacks on September 11, 2001.
    - While there are many different types of terrorism and terrorist groups, fundamental to the process the use of violence and the attempts to disrupt the relationships and interactions between groups of people.
    - Cyberterrorism is increasingly becoming a part of the social landscape and many businesses as well as governmental agencies are taking steps to prevent attacks to their databases.
- Analyze sociological theories to explain and understand war and terrorism
    - Functionalism offers useful insights into the nature of war and of terrorism. As it relates to war, functionalists would point out that war can have a physical and economic benefit to a society.
    - Functionalists also believe that war can be a source of significant social change, similar to Durkheim's observation about the unifying role of religion in society. This sense of solidarity, or nationalism, unites disparate groups in the face of serious adversity.
    - Marx and other traditional conflict theorists might argue war and terrorism are more likely to result from potential economic gain or loss than from political or ideological disputes.
    - As it relates to war and terrorism, symbolic interactionists would likely examine the process by which people are transformed from citizen to soldier. How are individuals resocialized to adopt the attitudes, values, and beliefs that distinguish the non-combatant civilian from the warrior? Or, in the case of domestic terrorism, from citizen to insurgent?
    - Another way symbolic interactionists see war and terrorism is in the use of symbols to define an ideology, an act, or response to a threat and how it shapes people's attitudes, values, beliefs and behaviors about particular groups.
- Evaluate effective solutions to war and terrorism.
    - The creation of the United Nations (UN) was an attempt to find a way for countries to have a neutral third party to intervene in border disputes and other conflicts between nations.
    - The Building Community Resilience program, funded by the Obama administration. The program is based on the model Diminishing Opportunities for Violent Extremism (DOVE). This model was designed to assist community leaders and families to prevent extremism in the Somali-American community in Minneapolis-St. Paul area of Minnesota.
    - The Center for Evidence Based Crime Policy at George Mason University in Washington, DC found that there are only a few studies that demonstrate how counterterrorism efforts, such as intelligence-led policing, can result in crime reductions.

Summarize what individuals can do to address the effects of war and terrorism.

- Much of what can be done to address terrorism and the influence of extremist groups centers on making sure individuals can separate fact from fiction regarding the ideological arguments presented by terrorist groups. It also involves being willing to speak out against the false narratives and fake news that is becoming an increasing part of social media platforms and accepted by citizens.

KEY TERMS

Advanced Persistent Threats 427

Asylum-seekers 422

Cold War 417

Forcibly Displaced Population 422

Improvised Explosive Devices 420

Internally Displaced People (IDP) 422

League of Nations 433

Military sexual trauma (MST) 420

Nationalism 431

Political terrorism 426

Post-traumatic stress syndrome (PTSD) 419

Repressive terrorism 426

Revolutionary terrorism 426

State-sponsored terrorism 426

Traumatic brain injury (TBI) 420

United Nations 433

Unmanned Arial Vehicles (UAVs) 424

War 417

Discussion Questions

1) How has technology reshaped the nature of war? Will the use of drones and unmanned ground vehicles desensitize warfare and make it more likely to continue?
2) What are the long-term effects of having an increasingly larger segment of the population suffering from disorders such as PTSD, TBI, or MST?
3) How do we explain the downward trend of terrorist attacks—is it really due to better intelligence gathering and law enforcement efforts or have assassinations and other efforts really crippled many terrorist groups?
4) Do you think that the attacks on the US Capitol should be considered an act of domestic terrorism or is it simply a demonstration or protest that got out of hand?

Learn more with this chapter's digital tools, including Data and Media Literacy Exercises, flashcards, and chapter self-assessments at **www.oup.com/he/mcnamara**.

Glossary

#MeToo movement A social movement that began in the 1990s to address the problems of sexual harassment.

12-step model Treatment model that has been used for alcohol and drug abuse that involves following a series of steps toward recovery that include accepting one's inability to cope with addiction and relying on the support of sponsors and others to remain sober.

Absolute poverty Poverty that includes lacking of basic essentials such as food, housing, and clothing.

Acid rain Pollution that results when sulfur dioxide (SO_2) and nitrogen oxides (NO_X) are emitted into the atmosphere and transported by wind and air currents. The oxides react with water, oxygen, and other chemicals to form sulfuric and nitric acids. These then mix with water and other materials before falling to the ground.

Active Persistent Threats Computer viruses that tend to be slow moving and remain embedded in the system undetected for long periods.

Activity theory A psychological theory that suggests people who are more active tend to report higher levels of life satisfaction.

Affirmative action A program that provides preferential treatment for equally qualified minorities in education, employment, and other opportunities.

Age in place A trend wherein elderly people continue to live in the home in which they have lived for many years and may own outright.

Ageism A form of discrimination that focuses on the age of the person. Ageism is often experienced by elderly workers.

Air quality indicator Measuring tool that determines the safety of the air quality in a given area that ranges from zero to 300. Anything in the zero-to-50 range is considered good while anything above 300 triggers a warning to the public to remain indoors.

Alcohol counseling Form of treatment for alcohol abuse that involves group or individual therapy as part of the recovery from heavy drinking.

Alcohol use disorder Term used to describe someone who is suffering from alcohol abuse.

Alcohol user density Relates to the number of locations where alcoholic beverages are available, including bars and restaurants, which serve alcohol on the premises, and convenience and grocery stores.

Alcoholics Anonymous (AA) Organization that helps those suffering from alcoholism and drug abuse, which follows the 12-step model of treatment.

Algae blooms Huge amounts of algae that, when they die, result in the depletion of oxygen in the water that can kill fish and other wildlife in the water.

Alienation Concept from Marx's theory that workers feel disconnected from the work they do as a result of the exploitation they experience under capitalism.

Alt-labor movement A labor movement that is designed to bring the discussion of wages and labor issues to the public domain

Altruistic suicide A type of suicide wherein the individual over-identifies with a group rather than as an individual. As a result, such individuals are willing to sacrifice their own lives for the sake of the group.

Anomie Normlessness. A condition in which rules or norms no longer apply to a society or group of people.

Apartheid System of racial segregation in South Africa from 1948 to 1994. Non-white people were prevented from voting and lived in separate communities.

Assisted living facilities Institutional living arrangements with various options for people as they age.

Asylum-seekers Individuals and families who seek relocation to a particular country as a result of humanitarian crises in their native land.

Baby boomers A cohort of the population, born between 1946 and 1964, that represents about 28 percent of the overall US population

Bilingual/bicultural education A program designed to integrate students whose first language is not English.

Biological magnification The concentration of a given substance increases as it moves up the food chain.

Blended families Family with children created as a result of the previous divorce of one or both partners.

Blood alcohol concentration Formula that determines whether a person who has consumed alcohol is considered legally intoxicated and impaired.

Boomerang effect A phenomenon that occurs during research experiments in which the opposite effect of the independent variable occurs.

Bourgeoisie The ruling class in Marx's theory. This group owns the means of production and uses their economic, social, and political power to further their interests.

Broken windows theory A criminal justice theory that suggests an effective way to reduce crime and disorder is by addressing low-level problems in a community before they become more problematic.

Bullying and intimidation Harassing and intimidation others, either physically or psychologically.

Cap and trade policy A policy in which governments set a limit on overall emissions of pollutants and then let the market determine how industry would respond.

Capitalism A form of market economy involving the private ownership of the means of production.

Charter schools Schools that use taxpayer funds to create smaller and more specialized schools.

Child abuse Actions or behaviors that cause physical harm to a child.

Claims making The process by which people who feel a particular problem is dangerous to society and attempt to get the public to agree with them on the issues.

Class action suit Lawsuit brought to court on behalf of several people who have experienced a similar problem or issue.

Class consciousness A concept from Marx that all workers recognize their contribution to the production of wealth and capitalism in general.

Climate change Broad changes that are taking place on Earth. These include rising sea levels; acceleration of ice melting in Greenland, Antarctica, and the Arctic; along with changes in growing seasons for plants and crops.

Cohabitation A situation in which two adults live together without being formally married.

Cold War The period of tensions between the United States and Russia from 1947 to 1991 over the buildup of nuclear arms.

Collective conscience A concept coined by Durkheim to describe a group or society's acceptance and obedience to a set of values and rules that govern their way of life or morality.

Color-blind racism Mindset that essentially dismisses race in the discussion of social inequality.

Command economy An economy in which most of the system is controlled by the government or a central power. The government is involved in all aspects of economic development, including the distribution of resources and ownership of railroads, utilities, and airlines.

Communist society A Marxist ideal of a classless society.

Comparable worth Argument that similar jobs should be paid similar wages and that the wages paid should reflect the value placed on those tasks rather than the gender or race of the workers performing them.

Conditional Permanent Resident status (CPR) A way for immigrants to gain legal standing in the United States. To earn CPR, they must have entered the United States under the age of 18, have been living in the United States for four years, have not been convicted of a felony, have graduated high school, have obtained a GED, or are currently enrolled or admitted to an institution of higher education.

Conformity A form of adaptation to strain, in which people continue to accept the cultural goals and the institutional means to obtain them.

Critical race theory Argues that racism has become institutionalized in American society, especially in the legal system. This explains the disproportionate involvement of Blacks in the criminal justice system and the unfair treatment minorities generally receive when they become involved with the system.

Cultural capital Concept that suggests people develop an understanding of how social institutions function and use their social networks to gain an advantage over others.

Culture of poverty Explanation for the persistence of poverty that links the problem to a set of attitudes, values, and beliefs that encourage a form of fatalism and belief that people's situations will not improve.

Cybercrime Any type of crime that is committed through the use of a computer. This form of criminal behavior includes fraud, theft, computer hacking, bullying, terrorism, and a host of other criminal activities.

Cycle of violence A pattern of violence against a spouse that results in repeated offenses.

D.A.R.E. Drug abuse education program that was designed to teach youth about the negative effects of drug use.

Dark figure of crime The amount of crime that is not known or measured.

Deep poverty Term used to describe those people whose income is one half of the poverty line.

Deferred Action for Childhood Arrivals (DACA) Program created in 2012 to address those individuals who were brought into the United States illegally. This is a renewable, two-year deportation deferral and work permit to undocumented immigrants who had arrived in the United States as children and had no criminal records.

Deferred Action for Parents of Americans (DAPA) Program created in 2014 by the Obama administration to extend DACA benefits to undocumented parents of US citizens and permanent residents. This program was declared unconstitutional and eliminated.

Deferred gratification Concept that supports the idea of waiting for a reward of some type in favor of a larger one later.

Deindustrialization A concept in which countries that once made products to sell in a global market left these industries because of an inability to maximize profits.

Dementia A progressive neurological disease that is always fatal.

Democratic socialism Economic model combining elements of capitalism and socialism. In such a model, the government owns and manages key industries, but most property remains in the hands of private citizens.

Deportation Process by which immigrants are sent back to their home country for violating US laws.

Development, Relief, and Education for Alien Minors (DREAM) Act Law that attempts to outline a pathway to citizenship for undocumented youth who came into the United States. Despite support in Congress from various senators and congressmen, none of the versions of the legislation has become law.

Differential association A theory of crime that suggests people learn to commit crime by associating with those who find it acceptable.

Discrimination The behavioral component of mistreating those who are members of a particular group.

Disengagement theory A theory of aging that suggests people gradually disengage from previous positions in society. This orderly transition allows society to evolve.

Divorce The termination of a marriage.

Domestic partnerships Legal standing for people (often LGBTQ) who have either chosen not to marry or cannot legally marry, but still want the rights and privileges of a married couple.

Domestic violence Considered the most common violent crime in the United States, in which a spouse inflicts some type of physical injury against the other spouse.

Don't ask, don't tell Clinton-era policy that allowed soldiers to remain in good standing in the military if they did not reveal their sexual identity.

Double marginality A concept that suggests women have two stigmas associated with their status as they get older.

Dramaturgy The study of society and social interaction based on the premise that people are acting out roles and scripts as they go about their daily lives.

Dual enrollment programs High school students are enrolled in a local college while still attending high school, earning credit for both curricula.

Dual use The use both traditional cigarettes and e-cigarettes.

Early college high schools A program where high school students earn college credit by taking college courses in their respective high school.

E-cigarettes Electronic version of a cigarette. It involves a device and a cartridge that contains a substance with nicotine.

Economic determinism A Marxist concept that suggests a person's social and political place in society is determined by where they are in the economic structure.

Educational attainment The number of years of schooling completed.

Elderly abuse A type of physical, psychological, or medical abuse of a person over a certain age.

Elderly offenders People who commit a crime after a certain age. Traditionally the age is over 65, but there are a variety of definitions that use other age categories.

English-first movement Social movement that asserts that English should be the official language of the United States.

Environmental racism— The tendency to locate landfills and other potentially harmful storage sites in neighborhoods with high percentages of the poor and minorities.

Environmental sociology A subfield within sociology that focuses on environmental challenges, as well as inequalities in the use of strategies to address them.

Environmental stress The depletion of environmental resources and the addition of pollutants to the environment stemming from the development of technologies to improve our quality of life.

Ethnicity Shared culture, such as language, ancestry, practices, and beliefs.

Ethnography A form of qualitative research that focuses on spending a considerable amount of time with the people being studied and writing about their way of life.

Executive orders Changes in social policy that are enacted by the presidents of the United States based on their authority.

Expressive tasks Tasks that focus on nurturing, well-being, and group cohesion, traditionally performed by women.

Extreme poverty The most dire forms of poverty, in which people suffering from it attempt to exist on sometimes less than two dollars per day.

Failure to Thrive (FTT) A condition in which a child fails to grow at normal levels.

False consciousness A concept from Marx's theory of how workers accept exploitation by bourgeoisie and the unfair way employees are treated.

Family violence A broad term, which includes domestic violence, in which violence is committed against family members within the family unit.

Fatalism A perspective that suggests that little can be done to alter one's current economic or social position, thereby justifying doing little to actually improve it.

Federal Fair Housing Act of 1968 Federal law that provides protection against discrimination against members of minority groups in their attempt to secure housing.

Fee for services model The current health care model in the United States, whereby physicians charge patients a fee for their services.

Feminism A belief or doctrine that advocates equality in the social, economic, and political treatment of women in society.

Feminist movements Continuous efforts and campaigns promoting the belief that males and females should be politically, socially, and economically equal.

Feminist theory Originally an offshoot of Marxist doctrine, the theory argues that the unequal status of women in society is reflected in the justice system.

Feminization of poverty The tendency of poverty to fall disproportionately on women.

Fetal Alcohol Syndrome (FAS) A medical condition that occurs when a mother drinks alcohol during pregnancy. The effects can lead to birth defects, as well as a host of cognitive issues for the child.

Fight for $15 Labor movement that attempts to secure a $15 per hour minimum wage for workers.

Filial piety A term used to describe the virtue and primary duty of care for one's parents and elderly relatives.

Forcibly displaced population People who must relocate from their country as a result of war, conflict, or threat to their safety.

Foster care A type of care in which volunteers take in youth whose family situation is unsafe and provide them with the structure and support they need.

Free market economy An economy in which people act in their own self-interests. The allocation of resources, the types of goods that are produced, and who gets to buy them (and in what quantity) are determined by the market, not the government.

Free trade Trade between countries without tariffs on imported goods and services, or subsidies on exported ones.

Gender A social category that constructs roles and defines behaviors for men and women.

Gender-based violence Any act of violence that results in or is likely to result in physical, sexual, or psychological harm and suffering to women.

Generalizability A term used in scientific research that describes the findings of a particular study that can be applied to the entire population of people.

Generation X (Gen Xers) A cohort of the population, estimated to be about 41 million, born between 1968 and 1979.

Gig economy Economy that places an emphasis on part-time work without any stability or benefits—workers often provide goods and services to customers outside traditional industries.

Global warming The long-term warming of the planet.

Globalization The interconnectedness between all countries and their economies.

Grandparent-led families Families in which a child's grandparents assume caregiver roles and responsibilities.

Green New Deal— A resolution by Congress that outlines a large-scale plan to resolve climate change. The name is derived from President Roosevelt's New Deal plan during the Great Depression.

Groundwater contamination Contamination of water supplies as a result of the excessive use of fertilizers and other chemicals.

Head of household Role in which the person, typically a male, determines the rules and structure of managing the household.

Head Start Program to address some of the factors that affect early-childhood learning.

Health Maintenance Organizations (HMO) For a fixed monthly fee, an HMO provides total health care for patients with an emphasis on prevention in an effort to avoid costly treatments in the future.

Holmes and Rahe Stress Scale A stress scale that uses 43 major life events and assigns a particular value to a given stressful event.

Home school Students do not attend school but are taught by parents or others at home.

Homosexual advance theory Theory that suggests courts may allow a non-violent homosexual advance to constitute sufficient provocation to mitigate a murder charge to manslaughter.

Horatio Alger myths Concept based on Horatio Alger stories that focus on rags-to-riches explanations of success. What makes these myths is the tendency to use such extraordinary stories as a benchmark against which to compare others, rather than recognize them as the exceptions they are.

Hot spots policing A policing strategy that targets specific high-crime areas by concentrated levels of patrol.

Human trafficking The kidnapping and illegal transporting of people for the purposes of making them indentured servants or slaves.

Immigrant apprehension Catching individuals who are trying to cross the border illegally or detaining individuals by immigration officials inside the United States.

Immigration detention Refers to incarcerating individuals for violating immigration laws or those who are apprehended at the border who are destined for deportation.

Impression management A concept that suggests people attempt to convey a favorable impression to others. This is accomplished through the control of information and techniques to "save face" when interactions go astray.

Improvised explosive devices A bomb created from available parts, such as cell phones and accumulated projectiles.

Infant mortality rate The number of deaths in the first year of life for all live births.

Innovation As part of the strain theory, this form of adaptation involves accepting the goals of society but creating new means to achieve them.

Institutional discrimination Discriminatory behavior that is built into the structure of society. The impact of this is that people working within that system think everyone is treated equally.

Instrumental tasks Tasks requiring physical strength that were traditionally taken on by men in their role as breadwinners.

Internalization of label A consequence of being labeled involves accepting the stigma assigned by society.

Internally Displaced People (IDP) Refugees who were initially forced to relocate within their country of origin but were able to return to their homes once the conflict subsided.

Invisible hand A concept developed by economist Adam Smith that suggests the capitalist market, with profit and competition working against one another, will solve societal problems without government intervention.

Iron Cage of Rationality A concept coined by Max Weber whereby people become trapped by the conveniences and advantages of rationalization in all aspects of their lives.

Jury bias Tendency to discount the credibility or accuracy of a witness if their sexual identity as a non-heterosexual becomes known.

Labeling theory A theory that suggests crime is a product of a process in which people tag or label others as criminal.

Laissez-faire A form of government that plays a limited or no role in the economy. Found in free market systems.

Latent functions From a functionalist perspective, the unintended functions of education.

League of Nations The early version of the United Nations that began after World War I to promote international peace.

Legal Permanent Resident status (LPR) Also known as obtaining a green card. After maintaining LPR status for five years, a person can apply to become a US citizen

Legalization of marijuana Attempts to legalize or decriminalize the possession and use of marijuana for recreational purposes.

Legitimating the ex-status A way to cope with the labeling effects of crime, whereby offenders attempt to cope with negative labels by engaging in conforming behavior.

LGBTQ Acronym used to describe lesbian, gay, bisexual, transgender, and queer people.

LGBTQIA— Acronym used to describe lesbian, gay, bisexual, transgender, queer, intersex, and asexual people.

Liberal feminism Advocacy for equal opportunities for women and the freedoms that allow women to make decisions about their lives. Liberal feminists do not believe that the political system is inherently biased or that discrimination against women is institutionalized or systematic.

Life chances Opportunities provided by family, friends, and others to improve one's social standing or position.

Life expectancies A prediction of how long a person will live.

Living wage Wage based on the amount of income needed to live above the federal poverty level.

Macrosociology An area within sociology that explains society, social life, and social interaction by examining large-scale social institutions.

Managed care An attempt to regulate the costs of health care by placing an intermediary between the physician and patient. This made health care sensitive to costs and efficiencies like any other business.

Manifest functions From a functionalist perspective, the intended functions of education (e.g., reading, writing, math).

Mariel Boatlift A group of approximately 125,000 Cubans who fled Cuba for the United States, including many poor Cubans as well as some of whom Castro had released from hospitals and prison. Regrettably, many of these people were not criminals but were labeled "antisocial" by Cuban officials.

Marxist feminism Approach that contends that the control of private property in the early days of capitalism set in motion a series of events whereby men controlled the social institutions of society.

Mass incarceration of America Phrase used to describe the disproportionality of Blacks who were incarcerated as a result of the War on Drugs.

Mass murder The killing of more than one victim, either all at once or over time.

Means of production A Marxist idea that consists of everything a capitalist needs to produce wealth except labor. This includes the land, equipment, factories, and raw materials.

Mechanical solidarity A concept from Durkheim that explains the connectedness people have to one another based on the commonality of the tasks they perform.

Medicaid A federal program that provides health care to people who are disabled or have low-income.

Medicare A federal program that provides health care to people over the age of 65.

Meritocracy The idea that where a person goes in society is based on their efforts, or merit, and not on connections, family ties, or other factors not tied to the individual's actions.

Micro-aggressions Small acts of exclusion and marginalization committed by a dominant group toward a minority.

Microsociology An area of study within sociology that explains society, social life, and social interaction by examining details of everyday life and people's relationships with one another.

Military sexual trauma (MST) The experiences of sexual assault or repeated sexual harassment of a veteran during their military service.

Minority groups A group denied access to social, economic, and political power and resources that are given to the dominant groups in society.

Mixed economy A combination of different types of economic systems in which the government generally stays out of market involvement but controls critical areas such as defense, transportation, or some similar industry.

Moral entrepreneurs This concept is used to describe how social problems are constructed. They consist of influential people in society who are able to convince people that the challenges they identify as problematic for society are worthy of the public's consideration.

Mortgage-backed securities An investment package that consisted of low-interest mortgages with variable rates.

Multiple partner fertility (MPF) Mothers having children by different fathers.

Nationalism A sense of solidarity that unites disparate groups in the face of serious adversity.

Naturalization The process of becoming a US citizen.

Neglect Occurs when parents or guardians do not provide the kind of care needed, even though they have the ability to do so.

New Deal Federal programs created by President Roosevelt that were designed to address many of the problems relating to poverty in the United States.

No Child Left Behind Act of 2001 A federal law designed to hold schools accountable and to standardize the learning that takes place in all public schools.

North American Free Trade Agreement (NAFTA) Trade agreement between the United States and Mexico and Canada that led to the outsourcing of US jobs.

Nuclear family Family unit composed of parents and their children.

Nuclear waste The byproduct of nuclear power plants that is highly dangerous and must be disposed of in carefully designed caskets.

Obamacare A health care program that mandates health insurance for citizens in the United States.

Oil spills Accidental spills of oil into waterways as a result of damage to oil tankers or cargo ships.

Operationalization Process by which terms such as "elderly" are defined for research purposes.

Opioid addiction The physical and psychological dependency of opioid-based drugs.

Opioid epidemic An event that has occurred in the United States in which people become addicted to opioid drugs, largely as a result of abuse of prescription pain medication.

Opioid Fraud and Abuse Detection Unit Specialized unit in the US Department of Justice charged with the detection of abuse and fraud related to the manufacture and distribution of opioid drugs.

Organic solidarity A concept from Durkheim that explains the connectedness people have to one another based on their interdependence of the tasks they perform in society.

Overstayers Individuals who remain in the United States illegally after their visas expire.

Oxycontin A prescription painkiller.

Pain reliever use disorder Term used to describe someone who has become addicted to opioid drugs largely as a result of becoming dependent upon painkiller medication.

Panacea phenomenon A tendency for the public, policymakers, politicians., and others to seek a single cure-all solution to a problem such as crime.

Parental rights All of the legal rights and obligations that are associated with being a parent of a child.

Patient Protection and Affordable Care Act Legislation that created what is known as Obamacare.

Patriarchal society Male domination of every aspect of economic, social, and political life.

Patriarchy A male-dominated society that tends to discredit or devalue the contributions of women.

Personal attribution An explanation of poverty that links or attributes the cause to the talents and efforts of the individuals involved and not on structural factors beyond their control.

Personal troubles A concept developed by C. Wright Mills that defines social problems. Individuals with particular problems are not the focus of social problems, since they do not affect a large number of people. This is in contrast to public issues, where broader problems are identified based on the number of people impacted by them.

Phenomenological feminism Approach that focuses on how women and girls are treated by the system. Phenomenological feminists examine the discriminatory treatment of female delinquents by the juvenile justice system.

Plea bargain A strategy used by prosecutors and defense attorneys in which the defendant pleads guilty in exchange for a lesser punishment.

Political terrorism Intimidation, coercion, and violent acts to bring change or even overthrow an existing government.

Postmodernism A theory that argues there are no absolute truths and that there are many versions of reality, all of which are equally valid. Postmodernism rejects the notion of science and facts, since this is but one version of how to understand the universe.

Post-traumatic stress syndrome (PTSD) A disorder that causes extreme stress reactions after experiencing a traumatic event.

Praxis A Marxist term that refers to concrete or practical action. It is not enough, says Marx, to simply understand the problems in society—one must also attempt to change and improve society through meaningful activity.

Preferred provider organizations (PPOs) Organizations that manage or control the costs of health care by supervising and monitoring the work of health care providers, as well as limiting visits to specialists to a particular managed care network and requiring prior authorization for hospitalization.

Prejudice A negative attitude toward a group of people.

Prejudiced discriminator One who has negative attitudes against groups is said to engage in negative forms of discrimination.

Prejudiced non-discriminator One who has negative attitudes against others but does not discriminate is identified as a closet bigot.

Present orientation A mindset held by some people to live for the moment instead of saving or planning for the future. It is the opposite of deferred gratification.

Primary care physicians General practitioners who provide general medical care to patients and make referrals to specialists when needed.

Primary deviance The first step in the labeling process. The person is not seen as criminal and their act is not seen as part of their identity.

Private military contractors Former soldiers with combat experience who hire themselves out to other countries for their expertise.

Proficient English speakers Those immigrants who either speak English very well or only speak English at home.

Proletariat A Marxist concept describing people who must sell their labor to the Bourgeoise under capitalism because they have no other means of survival.

Public issues— a concept developed by C. Wright Mills that defines social problems. Public issues are broader problems that involve a large number of people and are not focused on individual cases.

Queer Historically used to disparage homosexual men, this term today is used affirmatively to describe a wide range of sexual identities.

Queer theory A branch of critical theory that rejects the idea of a binary heterosexual/homosexual identity categorization. Instead, queerness reflects a more nuanced and detailed approach to sexuality.

Race Physical differences that groups and cultures consider socially significant.

Race to the Top A federally funded program allowing schools to opt out of the No Child Left Behind requirements but still create measures of accountability for students, teachers, administrators, and schools.

Racial profiling A police practice that targets minorities for scrutiny, stops, or arrests.

Racial steering A practice by which real estate agents attempt to convince minority home buyers to live in neighborhoods with more minorities.

Racism Behavior based on the belief that humans have distinctive characteristics that determine their abilities.

Radical feminism Approach that views the control of society by males to be the source of all social inequality.

Rationalization A Weberian concept that removes all subjective aspects of people in their relationships with others. It also consists of identifying standardized criteria to evaluate people, and other aspects of society.

Rebellionism A form of adaptation to strain, which the person either accepts or rejects societal goals and the means to achieve them based on an attempt to change the entire system.

Red-light districts Urban districts considered sex markets for prostitution and sex workers.

Redlining The practice that essentially justified racial discrimination and prevented many Blacks from being eligible to purchase homes.

Refugees People across the globe who are fleeing conflict, poverty. and persecution within their home countries.

Relative definition of poverty A definition of poverty that takes into account the variation in how poverty is defined. Instead of absolute standards, this definition explains poverty relative to some other group or groups.

Remarriage The notion that someone gets married again after divorce or the end of a previous marriage.

Repressive terrorism Terrorism perpetrated by a government against its own citizens in an effort to preserve the existing political structure.

Retreatism A form of adaptation in which the person rejects cultural goals and the societal means of achieving them.

Retrospective interpretation A part of the labeling process in which people in society reinterpret the behavior and attitudes of a person based on their label.

Reverse discrimination A perspective that opposes affirmative action in the mistaken belief that it unfairly discriminates against Whites.

Revolutionary terrorism The use of violence against civilians by enemies of a particular government.

Ritualism A form of adaptation where a person continues to accept the means of obtaining societal goals but does not accept the goals.

Same-sex marriages A marriage between two people of the same gender.

Sanctuary cities Cities that have resisted working with federal immigration officials to enforce current zero tolerance policies related to immigration.

School vouchers A program in which parents can apply tax dollars that would have supported their child's public education to the child's tuition at a private or charter school instead.

Second shift The tendency for women to deal with the demands of a career, as well as management of household and family.

Secondary deviance A more systematic form of crime and deviance that occurs as a result of the offender being labeled.

Second-hand smoke exposure The effects of being exposed to the negative effects of cigarette, cigar, or pipe smoking. Some estimates suggest that the illnesses generated from being exposed to second-hand smoke are as dangerous as actually smoking.

Secure Communities Program A program in which state and local police provide fingerprints of suspects to federal immigration authorities and transfer individuals who were assumed to be illegal immigrants to federal authorities.

Self-report studies A type of research that asks offenders about their experiences with criminal behavior.

Separatism The idea that the United States should remain separate from other countries in order to protect the United States and its way of life.

Service economy A consequence of deindustrialization, this type of economy provides services instead of products.

Sex The biological difference between males and females.

Sexism Prejudice or discrimination based on sex or gender that gives rise to or perpetuates inequality.

Sexual abuse A type of abuse in which a child is sexually harmed.

Sexual harassment A form of gender discrimination that violates Title VII of the Civil Rights Act of 1964. It involves all unwelcome sexual attention that affects an employee's job and work environment.

Sexual orientation Sexual attraction toward people of the same gender, the opposite sex, or both.

Sexual victimization Victimization in which the victim is sexually abused by an offender against their will.

Sick care The tendency for a society to offer care to people in the event they become ill, but little in the way of preventive care.

Sick role A role given to a person with an illness or disease that reduces their societal expectations.

Single payer system A free health care system that provides medical coverage for everyone and is managed by the government.

Single payer system A system where the government operates the health care system.

Single-parent family Family in which one parent does not live with their children.

Smog A combination of nitrogen oxides, organic compounds (such as paint, cleaning products, and refrigerants), and sunlight.

Social construction of race Observation that the particular physical characteristics a society uses to distinguish one racial group from another are relatively meaningless.

Social constructionist view of social problems A perspective that asserts the creation of social problems is the result of policymakers, politicians, and others who deem a particular condition as worthy of being considered a problem for society.

Social inequality The idea that some people are not given the same opportunities to succeed in life based on factors beyond their individual effort, such as their race, gender, minority status, etc.

Social mobility The upward or downward movement of people in terms of their social standing or social class.

Social reality of crime A theory of crime that suggests the way any behavior is defined and understood by the public is a result of the influence of the wealthy and powerful, who control the media.

Social reproduction The process and consequences of passing social class from one generation to the next.

Social stratification The segmenting of people into different groups based on some set of criteria.

Socialism A command economy in which the means of production are owned by all citizens (the government).

Socialist feminism Approach that argues that it makes no sense to think of only one of these variables at a time. Looking at the larger picture, socialist feminists suggest that crime results from the lack of access to political power for women.

Socioeconomic status (SES) Index comprised of income, education level, and occupational prestige.

Sociological imagination A concept in sociology that looks for larger explanations of people's behavior. These larger explanations may involve the influence of race, social class, religion, economics, or politics in creating a context to understand a person's life and their behavior.

Solid waste pollution Pollution consisting of trash, plastic and other solid materials.

Stage based approach A coping mechanism which involves a five-stage process of acknowledging death and grief. It begins with denial, then anger, followed by bargaining and negotiation and ultimately acceptance.

State-sponsored terrorism When a government provides support, in the form of funding, training, weapons, and equipment, to terrorist groups so they can engage in terrorist activity in other countries.

Status degradation ceremony A step in the labeling process where the offender is made to accept the label.

Stay-at-home parent A parent who forgoes career opportunities to remain home with his or her children.

Stonewall Uprising Police raid of a gay bar in New York City in 1969 that resulted in three days of protests and the start of the "gay power" movement.

Strain theory A theory of crime that suggests the cause of crime is based on a strain between society's goals and people's ability to achieve them.

Structural factors Factors that explain poverty based on links to the way society is structured and functions.

Synthetic marijuana Artificial form of marijuana that has been chemically created instead of using its plant-based origins.

Systemic attribution An explanation of poverty that suggests the problem is primarily related to elements in the social structure or the way society operates.

Systemic racism Denial of African Americans to access to opportunities and advantages through the structural features of many social institutions.

Temporary Assistance for Needy Families (TANF) Federal welfare program that provides small cash amounts for recipients for incidental expenses.

The Age Discrimination in Employment Act (ADEA) A law that makes it illegal for employers to discriminate against employees who were 40 years of age or older.

The American Health Care Act— Legislation that is seen as the Republican party's alternative to Obamacare.

The Fostering Communities to Success and Increasing Adoptions Act of 2008 Legislation that allows foster children to remain with their foster families until they reach age 21.

The Older Americans Act (OAA) of 1965 Legislation that provided services and funding for programs like Meals on Wheels.

The panacea phenomenon A theory that suggests people in society attempt to find simple solutions to complex problems like crime.

Theory of social reproduction Developed by Pierre Bourdieau, who asserts that children acquire habits, ideas, and expectations from their parents, leading to the development of cultural capital.

Thermal pollution The increase in water temperature as a result of water from industrial plants being dumped into waterways.

Toxic waste— Any waste that is harmful to humans or the environment.

Trade deficit The difference between the cost of a country's goods and services that are exported and the cost associated with the goods and services they receive from other countries.

Traditional economy Also known as a preindustrial economy; one in which involves the growing and bartering of agricultural products.

Traditional family values A perspective which contends families should consist of a father and mother, with the father working and the mother remaining home to raise the children and maintain the household.

Traumatic brain injury (TBI) An injury that results from the brain being shaken within the skull by a concussive force, causing bleeding between the brain and skull or bruises where the brain hits the skull.

Tribal schools/tribal colleges Educational institutions designed to meet the cultural needs of American Indian/Alaskan native students.

Troubled Asset Relief Program (TARP) Program authorized by Congress in response to the financial crisis in 2008 that allowed the federal government to bail out failing banks and the automobile industry.

US Equal Employment Opportunity Commission Federal agency that ensures companies and individuals do not discriminate against minorities in the workplace.

Underground economy Any economic activity that results in unreported income.

Uniform Crime Reports A tool that measures crime based on incidents that are reported to the police.

United Nations Organization that serves as a neutral third party to intervene in border disputes and other conflicts between nations.

Universal Basic Income a Strategy that suggests providing people with a certain amount of money, regardless of whether or not they work, as a substitute for welfare benefits.

Universal income Concept that suggests providing people with a small but fixed amount of money to cover living costs in place of traditional welfare benefits.

Universalism A concept found in social democracies where all members of society receive free or heavily subsidized services.

Unmanned Arial Vehicles (UAVs) Also known as drones, these are smaller aircraft that do not require a human to pilot them inside the aircraft.

Unprejudiced discriminator One who may discriminate against certain groups but the reasons for doing so may not relate to negative attitudes against them.

Unprejudiced non-discriminator One who holds no negative attitudes against other groups nor do they discriminate against them.

Urban green spaces Parks and gardens created in otherwise unused sections of urban areas to limit the effects of pollution.

Vaping The process of using an e-cigarette, either with the nicotine-filled cartridge or marijuana.

Victimization surveys A tool that measures crime based on reports from victims of crime.

Victimless crimes Crimes that occur whereby there is no clearly defined victim or offender. Often used to describe crimes such as prostitution.

Wage gap The difference between what women and men earn.

War An organized and armed conflict between nations or political factions.

War on Poverty Programs that were created by the Johnson administration to address the many factors relating to poverty, such as housing, food, health care, and child care.

Weed and Seed A program sponsored by the US Department of Justice that attempts to improve the quality of life in communities by eliminating the criminal element and promoting economic and social development by residents.

Welfare Programs designed to assist the poor. This includes initiatives like food stamps, Medicaid, Section 8 housing, and other efforts.

Welfare reform A 1993 law that redefined how welfare operated in the United States. Instead of the federal government operating a host of programs across the country, block grants were given to states to customize their programs for its particular recipients.

White collar crime Crime that are committed by people as part of their normal business activity.

White fragility A state of denial which for some White people leads to outrage when their privilege is called out.

White privilege The set of benefits granted to those who resemble the people—almost always White—who dominate powerful positions in US institutions.

Working poor Individuals who are working but make too much to qualify for assistance. However, their income is not sufficient to improve their overall quality of life.

References

Chapter 1

Abramson, Alana. (2018). "President Trump Signs Executive Order to Keep Families Together." *Time*, June 20th. Available at: http://time.com/5317367/trump-executive-order-immigration/

Babbie, Earl. (2015). *The Practice of Social Research*. 13th ed. Los Angeles, CA: Wadsworth.

Berger, Peter. (1963). *Invitation to Sociology*. New York: Anchor Books.

Bergo, Harvard. (2014). *The Secret of Japan's Mysteriously Low Crime Rate. Nation Master,* Available at: http://www.nationmaster.com/blog/?p=74

Blumer, Herbert. (1986). *Symbolic Interactionism: Perspective and Method*. Berkeley, CA: University of California Press.

Coser, L. (1999). *Masters of Sociological Thought*. Belmont, CA: Sage.

Davis, Alyssa. (2018). *"In U.S., Concern About Crime Climbs to 15-Year High."*

Gallup. April 6th. Available at: https://news.gallup.com/poll/190475/americans-concern-crime-climbs-year-high.aspx Gallup polls

Daynes, Sarah, and Terry Williams. (2018). *On Ethnography*. New York: Polity.

Delgado, Richard. (2017). *Critical Race Theory: An Introduction*. 3rd ed. New York: New York University Press.

Durkheim, Emile. (1893:1960. *The Division of Labor in Society*. Glencoe, IL: The Free Press.

Durkheim, Emile.. (1897:1965). *Suicide*. Glencoe, IL: The Free Press.

Fox, James A., Levin, Jack, and Fridel, Emma. (2019). *Extreme Killing*, 4th edition. Belmont, CA: Sage.

Gallup. (2019). "Most Important Problem." Available at: https://news.gallup.com/poll/1675/most-important-problem.aspx

Gans, H. (1964). "The Positive Functions of Poverty." *American Journal of Sociology*, 78(2):275–289.

Geertz, Clifford. (1973). *The Interpretation of Cultures*. New York: Basic Books.

Goffman, Erving. (1969). *The Presentation of Self in Everyday Life*. New York: Anchor Books.

"Harvey Weinstein Expected to Surrender in Sexual Misconduct Case in Manhattan." (2018). *NBC Nightly News,* May 24th, Available at: https://www.nbcnews.com/nightly-news/video/harvey-weinstein-expected-to-surrender-in-sexual-misconduct-case-in-manhattan-1241361987763

Held, David. (1980). *Introduction to Critical Theory: Horkheimer to Habermas*. Berkeley, CA: University of California Press.

Hobsbawm, Eric. (1999). *Industry and Empire: The Birth of the Industrial Revolution*. London: The New Press.

Hollinger, Robert. (1994). *Postmodernism and the Social Sciences: A Thematic Approach*. Belmont, CA: Sage.

hooks, bell. (2014). *Feminist Theory: From Margin to Center.*3rd edition. New York: Routledge.

Kenney, Dennis. (1985). *Crime, Fear, and the New York City Subways: The Role of Citizen Action*. Westport, CT: Praeger.

Lunden, Walter A. (1958). "Pioneers in Criminology XVI: Emile Durkheim (1858–1917)" *Journal of Criminal Law and Criminology*, 49(1). Available at: https://scholarlycommons.law.northwestern.edu/cgi/viewcontent.cgi?article=4674&context=jclc

Mehl-Madrona, Lewis. (2010). *Healing the Mind through the Power of Story*. New York: Inner Traditions/Bear Company.

Mills, C. W. (1959). *The Sociological Imagination*. New York: Oxford University Press.

Ritzer, George, and Jeffery Stepinsky. (2017). *Sociological Theory*, 10th ed. Belmont, CA: Sage.

Rubington, Earl, and Martin Weinberg. (2010). *The Study of Social Problems: Seven Perspectives* (7th ed.). New York, NY: Oxford University Press.

Sternheimer, Karen. (2018) "Higher Education and Goal Displacement." *Everyday Sociology*. New York: W.W. Norton and Company. Available at: http://www.everydaysociologyblog.com/karen_sternheimer/

Sullivan, Nikki. (2003). *A Critical Introduction to Queer Theory*. New York: New York University Press.

Tooze, Adam. (2020). "Is the Coronavirus Crash Worse than the 2008 Financial Crisis?" *Foreign Policy*, March 18, Available at: https://foreignpolicy.com/2020/03/18/coronavirus-economic-crash-2008-financial-crisis-worse/

U.S. Department of Justice, Federal Bureau of Investigation. (2019). *Crime in the United States 2018*. Available at: https://ucr.fbi.gov/crime-in-the-u.s/2018/crime-in-the-u.s.-2018/topic-pages/rape

U.S. Department of Justice, Office of Juvenile Justice and Delinquency Prevention. (2018). *Juvenile Arrests*. Available at: https://www.ojjdp.gov/ojstatbb/crime/qa05101.asp?qaDate=2018&text=yes

Van Maanen, John. (2011). *Tales of the Field: On Writing Ethnography*. Chicago, IL: University of Chicago Press.

Weber, Max. (1921:2019). *Economy and Society*. Boston, MA: Harvard University Press.

Weber, Max. (1905:2003). *The Protestant Ethic and the Spirit of Capitalism*. New York: Dovers..

Yan, Holy, Christina Maxouris, and Steven Almasy. (2020). "US Coronavirus Cases Soar Past 8,700 as Officials Try to Head off Overwhelming Effects." *CNN*, March 19th. Available at: https://www.cnn.com/2020/03/18/health/us-coronavirus-case-updates-wednesday/index.html

Chapter 2

Alexander, Michelle. (2012). *The New Jim Crow: Mass Incarceration in the Age of Colorblindness*. New York: The New Press.

Baum, K., Catalano, S., Rand, M., and Rose, K. (2009). "Stalking Victimization in the United States." *National Crime Victimization Survey*. http://www.victimsofcrime.org/docs/src/baum-k-catalano-srand-m-rose-k-2009.pdf?sfvrsn=0.

Becker, Howard. (1966). *The Outsiders*. Chicago: University of Chicago Press.

Bekiempis, Victoria. (2020). "Everything to Know About the Harvey Weinstein Trial." *Vulture*, January 6th. Available at: https://www.vulture.com/article/harvey-weinstein-case-update.html

Bergo, Harvard. (2014). The Secret of Japan's Mysteriously Low Crime Rate. *Nation Master*, Available at: http://www.nationmaster.com/blog/?p=74

Bousso, Rob. (2018). "BP Deepwater Horizon Costs Ballon to $65 Billion." *Reuters*. January 16th. Available at: https://www.reuters.com/article/us-bp-deepwaterhorizon/bp-deepwater-horizon-costs-balloon-to-65-billion-idUSKBN1F50NL

Braga, Anthony A., and Brenda J. Bond. 2008. "Policing Crime and Disorder Hot Spots: A Randomized Controlled Trial." *Criminology 46*(3):577–607

Braga, Anthony, Brendon Welsh, and Corey Schnell, (2015). "*Broken Windows Theory*." Center for Evidence-Based Crime Policy. Available at: https://cebcp.org/evidence-based-policing/what-works-in-policing/research-evidence-review/broken-windows-policing/

Cima, Rosie. (2016). DARE: The Anti-Drug Program that Never Actually Worked. *Priceonomics*. Available at: https://priceonomics.com/dare-the-anti-drug-program-that-never-actually/

U.S. Department of Justice, Federal Bureau of Investigation. (2019). Crime in the United States 2018. Available at: https://ucr.fbi.gov/crime-in-the-u.s/2018/crime-in-the-u.s.-2018/tables/expanded-homicide-data-table-6.xls

Clear, Todd R; Resig, Michael, D.; Petrosino, Carolyn, and Cole, George F. (2018). *American Corrections*. 3rd Edition. Cincinnati, OH: Wadsworth.

Cowley, Stacy. (2018). "Wells Fargo Agrees to Settle With Shareholders for $480 Million." *New York Times*, May 4th. Available at: https://www.nytimes.com/2018/05/04/business/wells-fargo-shareholder-suit-phony-accounts.html

Davis, Alyssa. (2018). "In U.S., Concern About Crime Climbs to 15-Year High." *Gallup*. April 6th. Available at: https://news.gallup.com/poll/190475/americans-concern-crime-climbs-year-high.aspx Gallup polls

Dawson, M. (2006). "Intimacy and violence: Exploring the role of victim-defendant relationship in criminal law." *The Journal of Criminal Law & Criminology* 96(4), 1417–1450.

Dickson, Mike. (2018). "John Gotti: The Teflon Don and Gambino Boss." *American Mafia History*, October 19th. Available at: https://americanmafiahistory.com/john-gotti-the-teflon-don/

Finckenauer, James. (1982) *Scared Straight and the Panacea Phenomenon*. Englewood, NJ: Prentice-Hall.

Fox, James A., Levin, Jack, and Fridel, Emma. (2019). *Extreme Killing*, 4th edition. Belmont, CA: Sage.

Garfinkel, Harold. (1956). "Conditions of a Successful Status Degradation Ceremony." *American Journal of Sociology*, *61*(5): 420–424.

Gavin, Patricia and Finckenauer, James. (1999). *Scared Straight Revisited*. Belmont, CA: Waveland Press.

Hanna, Jason, Karimi, Faith, Grinberg, Emanuella. (2018). "Gunman Confessed to Florida High School Shooting Police Say." *CNN*, February 15th, available at: https://www.cnn.com/2018/02/15/us/florida-high-school-shooting/index.html

Holler, Madeline. (2019). "17 Staggering Sexual Assault Statistics Everyone Should Read." *MSN*, April 8th. Available at: https://www.msn.com/en-us/health/medical/17-staggering-sexual-assault-statistics-everyone-should-read/ar-BBVK6WB https://news.gallup.com/poll/1603/crime.aspx

Innocence Project. (2018). *Report: Guilty Plea on the Rise, Criminal Trials on the Decline*. Available at: https://www.innocenceproject.org/guilty-pleas-on-the-rise-criminal-trials-on-the-decline/

Kann, Drew. (2019). "5 facts behind America's high incarceration rate." *CNN*, April 21st. Available at: https://www.cnn.com/2018/06/28/us/mass-incarceration-five-key-facts/index.html

Katz, Jack. 1989. *Seductions of Crime*. New York: Basic Books.

Kyodo. (2018). "Japan's Crime Rate Hits Record Low as Theft Rates Plummet." *Japan Times*, January 18th. Available at: https://www.japantimes.co.jp/news/2018/01/18/national/crime-legal/japans-crime-rate-hits-record-low-number-thefts-plummets/#.Xh9aGUZKjIU

Latzman, N., Viljoen, J., Scalora, M., and Ullman, D. (2011). "Sexual offending in adolescence: A comparison of sibling offenders and non-sibling offenders across domains of risk and treatment need." *Journal of Child Sexual Abuse 20*(3), 245–263. See also Darkness to Light. *Child Sexual Abuse Statistics*. Available at: https://www.d2l.org/wp-content/uploads/2017/01/all_statistics_20150619.pdf

Lemert, Edwin. (1951). *Social Pathology*. Thousand Oaks, CA: Sage.

Lopez, German. (2018). "Japan Has Exceptionally Low Crime Rates. But there's a Dark Side to its Justice System." *The Vox*, Dec. 13th, Available at: https://www.vox.com/world/2015/12/13/9989250/japan-crime-conviction-rate See also https://www.cbsnews.com/news/gun-death-rate-rises-for-second-year-in-a-row/

Mahdavi, Pardis. (2018). How #MeToo Becamae a Global Movement." *Foreign Affairs*, March 6th. Available at: https://www.foreignaffairs.com/articles/2018-03-06/how-metoo-became-global-movement

McKollop, Matt and Boucher, Alex. (2018). "*Aging Prison Populations Drive up Costs*." Pew Charitable Trusts, February 20th. Available at: https://www.pewtrusts.org/en/research-and-analysis/articles/2018/02/20/aging-prison-populations-drive-up-costs

McNamara, Robert and Burns, Ronald. (2020). *Multiculturalism, Crime, and Criminal Justice*, 2nd Edition. New York: Oxford University Press.

McNeil, David. (2018). "Japan's Crime Problem? Too Many Police, Not Enough Criminals." *Irish Times*, April 8th. Available at: https://www.irishtimes.com/news/world/asia-pacific/japan-s-crime-problem-too-many-police-not-enough-criminals-1.3451997

McKollop, Matt and Boucher, Alex. (2018). "*Aging Prison Populations Drive up Costs*." Pew Charitable Trusts, February 20th. Available at: https://www.pewtrusts.org/en/research-and-analysis/articles/2018/02/20/aging-prison-populations-drive-up-costs

Merton, Robert (1938). "Social Structure and Anomie". *American Sociological Review*. **3** (5): 672–682.

Morgan, Rachel, and Kenna, Grace. (2017). *Criminal Victimization, 2016*. Washington, DC: U.S. Department of Justice, Office of Justice Programs, Bureau of Justice Statistics. Available at: https://www.bjs.gov/content/pub/pdf/cv16.pdf

Murphy, Heather. (2019). "El Paso Shooting Suspect Indicted on Capital Murder Charges." *New York Times*, September 12th. Available at: https://www.nytimes.com/2019/09/12/us/el-paso-suspect-capital-murder.html

National Institute of Justice. (2011). *Program Profile: Hot Spots Policing: Lowell, MA*. Available at: https://www.crimesolutions.gov/ProgramDetails.aspx?ID=208

Quinney, Richard. (1970). *The Social Realities of Crime*. Boston, MA: Little, Brown.

Ramsland, Katerhine. (2005). *Inside the Minds of Mass Murderers: Why They Kill*. Westport, CT: Praeger.

Roman, Caterina Gouvis, Meagan Cahill, Mark Coggeshall, Erica Lagerson, and Shannon Courtney. 2005. *The Weed and Seed Initiative and Crime Displacement in South Florida: An Examination of Spatial Displacement Associated with Crime Control Initiatives and the Redevelopment of Public Housing*. Washington, DC: Urban Institute Justice Policy Center. http://www.jrsa.org/ws-eval/studies_other/displacement-final-report.pdf

Schur, Edwin. (1971). *Labeling Deviant Behavior*. New York: Harper and Row.

Schweinhart, Lawrence, J., Helen Verdain Barnes, and David P. Weikart. 1993. "Significant Benefits: The High/Scope Perry Preschool Study Through Age 27." In *Monographs of the High/Scope Educational Research Foundation, No. 10*. Ypsilanti, Mich.: High/Scope Press.

Segal, Ida. (2017). "Bookkeeping Pastor Robs Plumbing Company of $700,000, Prosecutors." *New York Live*, May 28th, available at: https://www.nbcnewyork.com/news/local/Bookkeeping-Pastor-Robs-Plumbing-Company-of-700000-Prosecutors-417326033.html

Sentencing Project (2018). *Criminal Justice Facts*. Available at: https://www.sentencingproject.org/criminal-justice-facts/

Simpson, Sally, S. (1989). "Feminist Theory, Crime, and Justice." *Criminology*, *27*(4): 605-632.

Singh Brar, Harmandeep and Kumar, Gulshan. (2018). "Cybercrimes: A Proposed Taxonomy and Challenges." *Journal of Computer Networks and Communication*, April 12th. Available at: https://new.hindawi.com/journals/jcnc/2018/1798659/

Smith, Matt. (2015). "NCJJ Report Shows Juvenile Crime Keeps Falling, But Reasons, Elusive." *Juvenile Justice Information Exchange*, February, 26th. Available at: https://jjie.org/2015/02/26/ncjj-report-shows-juvenile-crime-keeps-falling-but-reasons-elusive/

Sutherland, Donald. (1939). *Principles of Criminology*. Chicago: University of Chicago Press.

Sutherland, Edwin. (1949). *White Collar Crime*. New York: Harden Press.

Tierney, Joseph P., Jean Baldwin Grossman, and Nancy L. Resch. 2000. *Making a Difference: An Impact Study of Big Brothers/Big Sisters*. Philadelphia, PA: Public/Private Ventures. http://ppv.issuelab.org/resource/making_a_difference_an_impact_study_of_big_brothersbig_sisters_re_issue_of_1995_study

Tragardh, Karin; Nilsson, Thomas; Granth, Svan; and Sturup, Joakim. (2016) "A Time Trend Study of Swedish Male and Female Homicide Offenders from 1990 to 2010." *International Journal of Forensic Mental Health*, *15*(2): 125–135.

Tuttle, Brad. (2016). "More Cars Being Stolen Because Owners are Basically Asking for it." *Money*, November 1st. Available at: http://time.com/money/4553620/cars-stolen-keys-ignition-fob-unlocked/

U.S. Department of Justice, Bureau of Justice Statistics. 2016. *Burglary Victimization*. Available at: https://www.bjs.gov/content/pub/ascii/vdhb.txt

U.S. Department of Justice, Executive Office of Weed and Seed. (2010). Available at: https://ojjdp.ojp.gov/sites/g/files/xyckuh176/files/pubs/gun_violence/sect08-e.html

U.S. Department of Justice, Federal Bureau of Investigation. (2019a). *Uniform Crime Reports: Crime in the United States 2018*. Available at: https://ucr.fbi.gov/crime-in-the-u.s/2018/crime-in-the-u.s.-2018/topic-pages/violent-crime

U.S. Department of Justice, Federal Bureau of Investigation. (2019b). *Uniform Crime Reports: Crime in the United States 2018*. Available at: https://ucr.fbi.gov/crime-in-the-u.s/2018/crime-in-the-u.s.-2018/topic-pages/rape

U.S. Department of Justice, Office of Juvenile Justice and Delinquency Prevention. (2018). *Juvenile Arrests*. Available at: https://www.ojjdp.gov/ojstatbb/crime/qa05101.asp?qaDate=2018&text=yes

United Nations Population Fund. (n.d.) Gender-based Violence. Available at: https://www.unfpa.org/gender-based-violence

The Sentencing Project. (n.d.) "Criminal Justice Facts." Available at: https://www.sentencingproject.org/criminal-justice-facts/

U.S. Department of Justice, Executive Office of Weed and Seed. Available at: https://ojjdp.ojp.gov/sites/g/files/xyckuh176/files/pubs/gun_violence/sect08-e.html

U.S. Department of State. (2018). *Human Trafficking Report*. Available at: https://www.state.gov/documents/organization/282799.pdf

Wilson, David B., Doris L. MacKenzie, and Faw Ngo Mitchell. (2008). Effects of Correctional Boot Camps on Offending. *Campbell Systematic Reviews 1*. http://www.campbellcollaboration.org/lib/download/3/

Wilson, James Q. and Kelling, George. (1982). "Broken Windows." *The Atlantic*, March. Available at: https://www.theatlantic.com/magazine/archive/1982/03/broken-windows/304465/

Wombell, James A. (2009). *Army Support During Hurricane Katrina Disaster*. U.S. Army Combined Arms Center, Combat Studies Institute. Available at: http://www.dtic.mil/dtic/tr/fulltext/u2/a494535.pdf

Chapter 3

Action on Smoking and Health. (2019). *"ASH Fact Sheet: Tobacco and the Developing World."* Available at: https://ash.org.uk/wp-content/uploads/2019/10/Tobacco-Developing-World.pdf

Addiction Center. (2018). *"The 12 Step Model."* Available at: https://www.addictioncenter.com/treatment/12-step-programs/

Alexander, Michelle. (2012). *The New Jim Crow: Mass Incarceration in the Age of Color Blindness*. New York: The New Press.

American Civil Liberties Union. (2013). *"The War on Marijuana in Black and White."* Available at: https://www.aclu.org/report/report-war-marijuana-black-and-white?redirect=criminal-law-reform/war-marijuana-black-and-white

American Civil Liberties Union. (2006). *"Cracks in the System: 20 Years of the Unjust Federal Crack Cocaine Law."* Available at: https://www.aclu.org/other/cracks-system-20-years-unjust-federal-crack-cocaine-law

Auriacombe, M., M. Fatseas, J. Dubernet, J. P. Daulouede, and J. Tignol. (2004). "French Field Experience with Buprenorphine." *American Journal of Addiction, 13*(1):17–28.

Burns, Ken. (n.d.) "The Roots of Prohibition." PBS. Available at https://www.pbs.org/kenburns/prohibition/roots-of-prohibition/

Centers for Disease Control. (2018). Fast Facts and Fact Sheets." Available at: https://www.cdc.gov/tobacco/data_statistics/fact_sheets/index.htm?s_cid=osh-stu-home-spotlight-001

Centers for Disease Control. (n.d.). *Smoking and Tobacco Use*. https://www.cdc.gov/tobacco/basic_

information/e-cigarettes/about-e-cigarettes.html

CNN. (2018). "Opioid Crisis: Fast Facts." https://www.cnn.com/2017/09/18/health/opioid-crisis-fast-facts/index.html

Cullen, James. (2018). "The History of Mass Incarceration." *Brennan Center for Justice*. Available at: https://www.brennancenter.org/our-work/analysis-opinion/history-mass-incarceration

DiBenedetto, David J., Valerie F. Weed, Kelly M. Wawrzyniak, Matthew Finklelman, Mathew Paolini, Janelle Paolini, Michael E. Schatman, David Herrera, and Ronald J. Kelich J. (2018). "The Association between Cannabis Use and Aberrant Behaviors During Chronic Opioid Therapy for Chronic Pain." *Pain Medicine 19* (10):1997–2008.

Deming, Jenny. (2018). "*Why Just Say No Won't Stop the Opioid Crisis*." *Skywood Recovery*. https://skywoodrecovery.com/why-just-say-no-wont-stop-the-opioid-crisis/

Depinto, Jennifer. (2019). "Support for Marijuana Legalization Hits New High, CBS News Poll Finds." *CBS News*, April 19. Available at: https://www.cbsnews.com/news/support-for-marijuana-legalization-hits-new-high-cbs-news-poll-finds/

Dodes, Lance. (2016). *The Sober Truth*. New York: Basic Books.

Drug Policy Alliance. (2018). "*From Prohibition to Progress: A Status Report on Marijuana Legalization*." Available at: http://www.drugpolicy.org/sites/default/files/dpa_marijuana_legalization_report_feb14_2018_0.pdf#page=27

Ebbs, Stephanie. (2018). "FDA Calls e-Cigarettes 'an Epidemic' among Minors, Cracks Down on Retailers." ABCNews, September 12. Available at: https://www.yahoo.com/gma/fda-calls-e-cigarettes-epidemic-among-minors-cracks-162706382—abc-news-topstories.html?soc_src=newsroom&soc_trk=com.apple.UIKit.activity.Mail&.tsrc=newsroom

Filby, Max. (2017). "Student Death Has Area Colleges Re-evaluating Binge Drinking." *Dayton Daily*, March 10. Available at: https://www.mydaytondailynews.com/news/student-death-has-area-colleges-evaluating-binge-drinking/ez6SrJDOCoR4aT1eTLmGQO/

Glandtz, Stanton. (2018). "CDC Should Employ Evidence-Based Strategies to Help People Quit Using Tobacco that Support Quit Attempts and Abstinence." *University of San Francisco: Center for Tobacco Control and Research Education*. Available at:https://tobacco.ucsf.edu/cdc-should-employ-evidence-based-strategies-help-people-quit-using-tobacco-support-quit-attempts-and-abstinence

Glassner, Gabriel. (2015). "*The Irrationality of Alcoholics Anonymous*." *The Atlantic*, March, available at: https://www.theatlantic.com/magazine/archive/2015/04/the-irrationality-of-alcoholics-anonymous/386255/

Grant Bridget, Chou Patricia, Tulshi, Sada. (2017). "Prevalence of 12-Month Alcohol Use, High-Risk Drinking, and DSM-IV Alcohol Use Disorder in the United States, 2001–2002 to 2012–2013: Results from the National Epidemiologic Survey on Alcohol and Related Conditions." *Journal of the American Medical Association, Psychiatry 74* (9):911–923.

Haffajee, Rebecca, and Michelle Mello. (2017). "Drug Companies' Liability for the Opioid Epidemic." *New England Journal of Medicine*. December 20. Available at: https://www.nejm.org/doi/full/10.1056/NEJMp1710756

Hansen, H., and J. Netherland. (2016). "Is the Prescription Opioid Epidemic a White Problem?" *American Journal of Public Health, 106* (12):2127–2129. https://www.cnn.com/2018/06/19/us/no-more-new-york-city-marijuana-arrests/index.html

Hendricks, LaVelle, and Angie Wilson. (2013). "The Impact of Crack Cocaine on Black America." *National Forum Journal on Counseling and Addiction, 2* (1). Available at: http://www.nationalforum.com/Electronic%20Journal%20Volumes/Hendricks,%20LaVelle%20The%20Impact%20of%20Crack%20Cocaine%20on%20Black%20America%20NFJCA%20V2%20N1%202013.pdf

Hsaio, Timothy. (2019). "7 Arguments for legalizing marijuana that no one should believe." *The Federalist*, March 7th. Available at: https://thefederalist.com/2019/03/07/7-arguments-legalizing-marijuana-no-one-believe/

Ingraham, Christopher. (2017). "One in Eight American Adults is an Alcoholic." *The Washington Post*, August 11th. Available at: https://www.washingtonpost.com/news/wonk/wp/2017/08/11/study-one-in-eight-american-adults-are-alcoholics/?utm_term=.aa3a6c7f0564

Insurance Information Institute. (2018). *"Facts and Statistics About Alcohol-Impaired Driving."* Available at: https://www.iii.org/fact-statistic/facts-statistics-alcohol-impaired-driving

Jernigan, David, H.; Sparks, Michael; Yang, Evelyn; Schwartz, Randy. (2013). "Using Public Health and Community Partnerships to Reduce Density of Alcohol Outlets." *Preventing Chronic Disease, 10*. Available at: https://www.cdc.gov/pcd/issues/2013/12_0090.htm

Johnson, B. 2018. "*The Drug Policy of Amsterdam and the Netherlands*." Available at: https://www.beejonson.com/single-post/2017/11/17/The-Drug-Policy-of-Amsterdam-and-the-Netherlands

Jones, Jeffrey. (2019). "U.S. Support for Legal Marijuana Steady in Past Year." *Gallup*, October 23. Available at: https://news.gallup.com/poll/267698/support-legal-marijuana-steady-past-year.aspx

Kurtzleben, Danielle. (2010). "Data Show Racial Disparity in Crack Sentencing." *U.S. News and World Report*, August 3. Available at: https://www.usnews.com/news/articles/2010/08/03/data-show-racial-disparity-in-crack-sentencing

Lopez, German. (2018). "The Spread of Marijuana Legalization, Explained." *The Vox*, August 20, available at: https://www.vox.com/cards/marijuana-legalization/-popular-opinion-changing-marijuana-legislation

Lopez, German. (2016) "The War on Drugs Explained." *The Vox*, May 8th. Available at: https://www.vox.com/2016/5/8/18089368/war-on-drugs-marijuana-cocaine-heroin-meth

Lopez, German. (2018). "We Really Do Have a Solution to the Opioid Epidemic—and One State Is Showing It Works." *The Vox*. May 10. Available at: https://www.vox.com/policy-and-politics/2018/5/10/17256572/opioid-epidemic-virginia-medicaid-expansion-arts

Mann, Brian. (2013). The Drug Laws That Changed How We Punish." *NPR*, February 14. Available at: https://www.npr.org/2013/02/14/171822608/the-drug-laws-that-changed-how-we-punish

Miech, Richard, Patrick Megan, Patrick O'Malley, and Lloyd Johnson. (2017). "What Are Kids Vaping? Results from a National Study." *Tobacco Control, 26* (4):386–391.

Minchon, Kathleen. (2018. Tobacco Litigation: History and Recent Developments. Nolo.com, available at: https://www.nolo.com/legal-encyclopedia/tobacco-litigation-history-and-development-32202.html

National Institute on Alcohol Abuse and Alcoholism. (2018). *Treatment for Alcohol Problems: Finding and Getting Help*. https://pubs.niaaa.nih.gov/publications/treatment/treatment.htm

National Institute on Drug Abuse. (2018). "*Cigarettes and Other Tobacco Products*." Available at: https://www.drugabuse.gov/publications/drugfacts/cigarettes-other-tobacco-products

National Survey on Drug Abuse and Health. (2015). *Results from the 2015 National Survey on Drug Use and Health: Detailed Tables*. Available at: https://www.samhsa.gov/data/sites/default/files/NSDUH-DetTabs-2015/NSDUH-DetTabs-2015/NSDUH-DetTabs-2015.htm#tab1-1a

National Transportation and Safety Board. (2018). *Alcohol Abuse and Cost*. Available at: https://www.nhtsa.gov/risky-driving/drunk-driving#alcohol-abuse-and-cost-5091

Project Know. (2018). "*Five Tragic Cases of Drug-fueled Child Abuse*." Available at: https://www.projectknow.com/5-tragic-cases-of-drug-fueled-child-abuse/

Ryan, Harriet, Lisa Girion, and Scott Glover. (2016). "You Want a Description of Hell? OxyContin's 12 Hour Problem." *Los Angeles Times*, May 5. Available at: http://www.latimes.com/projects/oxycontin-part1/

Sawyer, Wendy, and Peter Wagner. (2019). "*Mass Incarceration: The Whole Pie 2019*." *Prison Policy Initiative*. Available at: https://www.prisonpolicy.org/reports/pie2019.html

Thompson, Madeline. (2018). "*New York Police to Relax Policy on Smoking Pot in Public.*" *CNN*, June 19th. Available at: https://www.cnn.com/2018/06/19/us/no-more-new-york-city-marijuana-arrests/index.html

U.S. Department of Health and Human Services. (2014). "*The Health Consequences of Smoking—50 Years of Progress: A Report of the Surgeon General.*" Atlanta: U.S. Department of Health and Human Services, Centers for Disease Control and Prevention, National Center for Chronic Disease Prevention and Health Promotion, Office on Smoking and Health.

U.S. Department of Health and Human Services, Office of the Surgeon General. (2018). "*Facing Addiction in America: The Surgeon General's Spotlight on Opioids.*" Available at: https://addiction.surgeongeneral.gov/sites/default/files/OC_SpotlightOnOpioids.pdf

U.S. Department of Health and Human Services, Substance Abuse and Mental Health Services Administration. (2017). "HHS, SAMHSA to Maintain Funding Formula for $1B Opioid Grant Program." *Press Release.* October 30. Available at: https://www.samhsa.gov/newsroom/press-announcements/201710300530

U.S. Department of Justice. (2017). "Attorney General Sessions Announces Opioid Fraud and Abuse Detection Unit." *Press Release.* Available at: https://www.justice.gov/opa/pr/attorney-general-sessions-announces-opioid-fraud-and-abuse-detection-unit

U.S. Food and Drug Administration. (2020). "FDA Finalizes Enforcement Policy on Unauthorized Flavored Cartridge-Based e-Cigarettes that Appeal to Children, Including Fruit and Mint." January 2, available at: https://www.fda.gov/news-events/press-announcements/fda-finalizes-enforcement-policy-unauthorized-flavored-cartridge-based-e-cigarettes-appeal-children

U.S. National Transportation and Safety Board. (2018). *Alcohol Abuse and Cost.* Available at: https://www.nhtsa.gov/risky-driving/drunk-driving#alcohol-abuse-and-cost-5091

U.S. Sentencing Commission. (2015). "*Report to the Congress: Impact of the Fair Sentencing Act of 2010.*" Available at: https://www.ussc.gov/sites/default/files/pdf/news/congressional-testimony-and-reports/drug-topics/201507_RtC_Fair-Sentencing-Act.pdf#page=7

Willingham, A. J. (2017). "Study Finds 1 in 8 Americans Struggles with Alcohol Abuse." *CNN*, August 17. Available at: https://www.cnn.com/2017/08/10/health/drinking-alcoholism-study-trnd/index.html

Chapter 4

Adams, James Truslow. (2001). *Epic of America*. New York: Simon Publishing.

Arango, Tim. (2018). "In Los Angeles, Where the Rich and the Destitute Cross Paths." *New York Times*, July 2. Available at: https://www.nytimes.com/interactive/2018/07/02/us/homeless-los-angeles-homelessness.html?rref=collection%2Ftimestopic%2FHomeless%20Persons&action=click&contentCollection=timestopics®ion=stream&module=stream_unit&version=latest&contentPlacement=3&pgtype=collection

Axim, June, and Mark Stern. (2005). *Social Welfare: A History of the American Response to Need*. 6th ed. Boston: Allyn and Bacon.

Bauer, Lauren, Emily Moss, and Jay Shambaugh. (2019). Who Was Poor in 2018? *The Brookings Institution*, December 5. Available at : https://www.brookings.edu/blog/up-front/2019/12/05/who-was-poor-in-the-u-s-in-2018/

Bendix, Aria. (2020). "One of the World's Largest Basic-Income Trials, a 2-Year Program in Finland, Was a Major Flop. But Experts Say the Test Was Flawed." *Business Insider*, December 8. Available at: https://www.businessinsider.com/finland-basic-income-experiment-reasons-for-failure-2019-12

Braunstein, Adam. (2017). "The Poverty Rate in Finland: A Success Story." *The Borgen Project, August 15.* Available at: https://borgenproject.org/poverty-rate-in-finland/

Booker, Brakton. (2018). "Report: Rural Poverty in America an Emergency." *NPR*, May 31st. Available at: https://www.npr.org/2018/05/31/615578001/report-rural-poverty-in-america-is-an-emergency

Center for Budget Analysis and Policy Priorities. (2019). *"Chart Book: Economic Security and Health Insurance Programs Reduce Poverty and Provide Access to Needed Care."* December 11. Available at: https://www.cbpp.org/research/poverty-and-inequality/chart-book-economic-security-and-health-insurance-programs-reduce

Center for Budget Analysis and Policy Priorities. (2018). *"House Farm Bill, SNAP Cuts, Work Requirements, Hurt Children."* Available at: https://www.cbpp.org/sites/default/files/atoms/files/5-1-18fa-brief-children.pdf

Center for Budget Analysis and Policy Priorities. (2019). *"Where Do Our Federal Tax Dollars Go?"* Available at: https://www.cbpp.org/research/federal-budget/policy-basics-where-do-our-federal-tax-dollars-go

Handren, Nathaniel, Robert Mandura, and Jimmy Narang. (2017). "The Fading American Dream: Trends in Absolute Income Mobility Since 1940." *Science*, April 28, *356* (6336): 398–406.

Dickinson, Maggie. (2019). "The Ripple Effect of Taking SNAP Benefits from One Person." *The Atlantic*. December 10. Available at: https://www.theatlantic.com/family/archive/2019/12/trump-snap-food-stamps-cuts/603367/

Doob, Christopher. (2012). *Social Inequality and Social Stratification in U.S. Society*. Boston, MA: Pearson.

Edin, Kathryn, and Luke Shaefer. (2016). *$2 a Day: Living on Almost Nothing in America*. New York: Houghton Mifflin.

Egan, Timothy. (2018). "Down and Out in San Francisco on $117,000 a year." *New York Times*, July 6. Available at: https://www.nytimes.com/2018/07/06/opinion/san-francisco-housing-homelessness.html?rref=collection%2Ftimestopic%2FHomeless%20Persons&action=click&contentCollection=timestopics®ion=stream&module=stream_unit&version=latest&contentPlacement=2&pgtype=collection

Fisher, Gordon. (1997). *History of Poverty Thresholds*. U.S. Department of Health and Human Services. Available at: https://aspe.hhs.gov/history-poverty-thresholds

Gans, Herbert. (1995). *The War against the Poor: The Underclass and Antipoverty Policy*. New York: Basic Books.

Griswold, Allison. (2014). "Here's the Startling Degree to which Your Parents Determine Your Success." *Business Insider*. January 24. Available at: https://www.businessinsider.com/parents-determine-child-success-income-inequality-2014-1

Grusky, David B. (2018). *Inequality: Classic Readings in Race, Class and Gender*. London: Routledge.

Grusky, David B. (2014). *Social Stratification: Class, Race, and Gender in Sociological Perspective*, 4th ed. Boulder: Westview Press.

Halikias, Dimitrios, and Richard V. Reeves. (2016). "How Many People are Better Off Than Their Parents? Depends on How You Cut the Data." *Brookings Institution*. August 10th. Available at: https://www.brookings.edu/blog/social-mobility-memos/2016/08/10/how-many-people-are-better-off-than-their-parents-depends-on-how-you-cut-the-data/

Hamm, Trent. (2014). "A Dose of Financial Reality." *The Simple Dollar*, August 1. Available at: https://www.thesimpledollar.com/a-dose-of-financial-reality/

Hauhart, Robert C. (2015). "American Sociology's Investigations of the American Dream, Retrospect and Prospect." *The American Sociologist*, *46* (1): 65–98. March.

Herberg, Will. (1955). *Protestant, Catholic, Jew*. New York: Knopf, Doubleday.

Hochschild, Jennifer. (1996). *Facing Up to the American Dream: Race, Class, and the Soul of the Nation*. Princeton, NJ: Princeton University Press.

Jagannathan, Meera. (2020). "As Andrew Yang Drops Out, Here's What Other 2020 Democrats Say about Universal Basic Income." *Marketwatch*, February 13, 2020. Available at: https://www.marketwatch.com/story/heres-what-2020-democratic-candidates-for-president-have-said-about-universal-basic-income-2019-07-09

Kaiser Family Foundation. (2019). 2018 *Poverty Rates by Race/Ethnicity.* Available at: https://www.kff.org/other/state-indicator/poverty-rate-by-raceethnicity/?currentTimeframe=0&sortModel=%7B"colId":"Location","sort":"asc"%7D

Kornblum, William, Karen Seccombe, and Joseph Julian. (2017). *Social Problems.* 15th ed. Boston, MA: Pearson.

Lewis, Oscar. (1966). *La Vida: A Puerto Rican Family in the Culture of Poverty.* New York: Random House.

"Living on $2 a day: Exploring Extreme Poverty in America." (2018). *Nation,* Dec. 27, available at: https://www.pbs.org/newshour/nation/poverty

Lowery, Annie. (2017). Give People Money: How a Universal Basic Income Would End Poverty, Revolutionize Work, and Remake the World. New York: Crown.

McNamara, Robert H. (ed.) (2008). *Homelessness in America: Three Volumes.* Westport, CT: ABC:CLIO.

National Alliance to End Homelessness. (2018). *Homelessness in America.* Available at: https://endhomelessness.org/homelessness-in-america/who-experiences-homelessness/children-and-families/

National Center for Children in Poverty. (2018). *Child Poverty.* Available at: http://www.nccp.org/topics/childpoverty.html

Rank, Mark, Thomas A. Hirschl, and Kirk Foster. (2014). *Chasing the American Dream: Understanding What Shapes Our Fortunes.* New York: Oxford University Press.

Siddiqui, Sabena. (2018). "Homeless in America." *International Policy Digest,* Feb 13. Available at: https://intpolicydigest.org/2018/02/13/homeless-in-america/

Trattner, Walter. (1999). *From Poor Laws to Welfare State: A History of Social Welfare in America.* 6th ed. New York: The Free Press.

United Nations Development Programme. (2016). *Human Development for Everyone.* New York: UN.

University of California, Davis, Center for Poverty Research. (2016). "*What Are Poverty Thresholds Today.*" Available at: https://poverty.ucdavis.edu/faq/what-are-poverty-thresholds-today"

U.S. Department of Health and Human Services. (2019). *2019 Poverty Guidelines Computations Table.* Available at: https://aspe.hhs.gov/computations-2019-annual-update-hhs-poverty-guidelines-48-contiguous-states-and-district-columbia

U.S. Department of Housing and Urban Development. (2020). *Fair Market Rents.* Available at: https://www.huduser.gov/portal/datasets/fmr.html

Vesoulis, Abby. (2020). "Coronavirus May Disproportionately Hurt the Poor—And That's Bad for Everyone." *Time,* March 11. Available at: https://time.com/5800930/how-coronavirus-will-hurt-the-poor/

Weber, Max. (1922). *Economy and Society.* San Francisco, CA: University of California Press.

Wilson, William, J. (1987). *The Truly Disadvantaged.* Chicago, University of Chicago Press.

Yglesias, Matthew. (2016). "Rising Inequality Has Crushed the Dream of Upward Mobility." *Vox,* December 14. Available at: vox.com/new-money/2016/12/14/13936920/inequality-mobility-chetty

Chapter 5

Berman, S. (2006). *The primacy of politics: Social democracy and the making of Europe's twentieth century.* New York, NY: Cambridge University Press.

Chen, Michelle. (2018). "No, Seattle's $15 minimum wage is not hurting workers." *The Nation.* June 30th. Available at: https://www.thenation.com/article/no-seattles-15-minimum-wage-is-not-hurting-workers/

Collins, Michael. (2015). "The Pros and Cons of Globalization." *Forbes,* May 6th. Available at: https://www.forbes.com/sites/mikecollins/2015/05/06/the-pros-and-cons-of-globalization/#46fbd1a2ccce

Cox, Jeff. (2020). "January Adds a Much Stronger Than Expected 225,000 Jobs with a Boost from Warm Weather." *CNBC,* February 7th. Available at: https://www.cnbc.com/2020/02/07/us-non-farm-payrolls-january-2019.html

Crossman, Ashley. (2018). "Three Causes of Deindustrialization." *Thoughtco,* July 20th.

Available at: https://www.thoughtco.com/reasons-for-deindustrialization-3026240

Democratic Socialists of America. (n.d.) "*What is Democratic Socialism?* Available at: https://www.dsausa.org/about-us/what-is-democratic-socialism/

Depersio, Greg. (2019) "What are some examples of free market economies?" *Investopia.com*, Available at: https://www.investopedia.com/ask/answers/040915/what-are-some-examples-free-market-economies.asp

Economic Times. (2018)."*Definition of Invisible Hand.*" Available at: https://economictimes.indiatimes.com/definition/invisible-hand

Foran, Clare and Barrett, Ted. (2020). "Trump Signs Coronavirus Relief Legislation." *CNN*. March 19th. Available at: https://www.cnn.com/2020/03/18/politics/coronavirus-congress-relief-senate-house/index.html

Frazier, John. (2019). "How the Gig Economy is Reshaping Careers for the Next Generation." *Forbes*, February 15th. Available at: https://www.forbes.com/sites/johnfrazer1/2019/02/15/how-the-gig-economy-is-reshaping-careers-for-the-next-generation/#6e950a949ada

Gallup and Northeastern University. (2018). "*U.S, U.K. and Canadian Residents Call for a Unified Skills Strategy for the AI Age.*" Available at: https://www.northeastern.edu/gallup/#_ga=2.134320049.1985678662.1563135517-965286709.1561913491

Godstene, Claire. (2014). *The Struggle for America's Promise: Equal Opportunity at the Dawn of Corporate Capitalism*. Mississippi: University Press of Mississippi.

Greenhouse, Steven. (2019). *Beaten Down and Worked Up: The Past, Present and Future of American Labor*. New York: Alfred Knopf.

Grunwald, Michael. (2017). "*The Trade Deal We just Threw Overboard.*" *Politico*, March/April. Available at: https://www.politico.com/magazine/story/2017/03/trump-tpp-free-trade-deal-obama-renegotiate-nafta-214874

Hadden, Joey, Casado, Laura, and Sonnemaker, Tyler. (2020). "Oracle, Apple, Google, and Amazon are among the largest global companies who have restricted travel or asked their employees to work remotely as a precaution against the novel coronavirus—here's the list." *Business Insider*, March 12th. Available at: https://www.businessinsider.com/companies-asking-employees-to-work-from-home-due-to-coronavirus-2020

Johnson, Keith. (2018). "Trump's $12 Billion Bailout is no remedy for farmers caught in trade war." *Foreign Policy*, July 31st. Available at: https://foreignpolicy.com/2018/07/31/trumps-12-billion-bailout-no-i-remedy-for-farmers-caught-in-trade-war/

Johnston, Mark. (2019). "How Big is America's Underground Economy?" *Investopedia*, November 9th. Available at: https://www.investopedia.com/articles/markets/032916/how-big-underground-economy-america.asp

Kim, Tammy. (2020). "The Gig Economy is Coming for Your Job." *New York Times*, January 10th. Available at: https://www.nytimes.com/2020/01/10/opinion/sunday/gig-economy-unemployment-automation.html

Kopf, Dan. (2019). "Union Membership in the US Keeps on Falling, Like Almost Everywhere Else." *Quartz*, February 5th. Available at: https://qz.com/1542019/union-membership-in-the-us-keeps-on-falling-like-almost-everywhere-else/

Krupa, Charles. (2018). "What would a Socialist America look like?" *Politico*, September 3rd. Available at: https://www.politico.com/magazine/story/2018/09/03/what-would-a-socialist-america-look-like-219626

Levitz, Eric. (2018). "Study: Minimum Wage Hikes Are Paying Off." *New York Magazine*, September. Available at: http://nymag.com/daily/intelligencer/2018/09/study-minimum-wage-hikes-increase-pay-without-killing-jobs.html

Lipse, Mark. (2020). "What countries have a traditional economy?" *Quora*, available at: https://www.quora.com/What-countries-have-a-traditional-economy

Long, Heather and Bhattarai, Abha. (2020). "As layoffs skyrocket, US safety net is underprepared." *The Washington Post*, March 19th.

Available at: https://www.washingtonpost.com/business/2020/03/19/unemployment-insurance-today-coronavirus/

Miller, Michael J. (2019). "What do AI and automation changes mean for your job? *PC magazine*, December 19th. Available at: https://www.pcmag.com/news/what-do-ai-and-automation-changes-mean-for-your-job

Moser, Sarah. (2018). What is a mixed exonomcy and what countries have them? *Quora*. Available at: https://www.quora.com/What-is-a-mixed-economy-and-what-countries-have-them

Movahed, Masoud. (2016). "The Persistence of Manufacturing in Deindustrialized America." *Harvard Economics Review*. April 10th. Available at: http://harvardecon.org/?p=3258

Peterson Institute for International Economics. (n.d.). *What is Globalization?* Available at: https://www.piie.com/microsites/globalization/what-is-globalization

Press, Gil. (2019). "Is AI Going to be a Jobs Killer? New Reports about the Future of Work." *Forbes*, July 15th. Available at: https://www.forbes.com/sites/gilpress/2019/07/15/is-ai-going-to-be-a-jobs-killer-new-reports-about-the-future-of-work/#7871257eafb2

Segran, Elizabeth. (2017). "Sweatshop Protests Keep NikeSweating." *FastCompany*.Availableat;https://www.fastcompany.com/40444836/escalating-sweatshop-protests-keep-nike-sweating

Sherman, Erik. (2018). "Sure unemployment went down because the number of people left the workforce." *Forbes*, May 5th. Available at: https://www.forbes.com/sites/eriksherman/2018/05/05/sure-unemployment-went-down-because-the-number-of-people-working-did/#6ffd66e0408b

Taylor, Tess. (2019). "How Flextime and Telecommuting benefits transform the workplace." *Thebalancecareers.org*. September 17th. Available at: https://www.thebalancecareers.com/flextime-and-telecommuting-benefits-3876763

Torpey, Elka and Hogan, Andrew. (2016). *Working in a Gig Economy*. U.S. Bureau of Labor Statistics, available at: https://www.bls.gov/careeroutlook/2016/article/what-is-the-gig-economy.htm

U.S. Bureau of Economic Analysis. (2020). "*2019 Trade Gap is $616.8 billion*." Available at: https://www.bea.gov/news/blog/2020-02-05/2019-trade-gap-6168-billion

Wike, Richard and Stokes, Bruce. (2018). "In advanced and emerging countries alike, worries about job automation." *Pew Research Center*, September 13th. Available at: https://www.pewresearch.org/global/2018/09/13/in-advanced-and-emerging-economies-alike-worries-about-job-automation/

World Population Review. (2020). *Command Economy Countries*. Available at: http://worldpopulationreview.com/countries/command-economy-countries/

Chapter 6

American Sociological Association. (n.d.) "*Race and Ethnicity*."Available at: https://www.asanet.org/topics/race-and-ethnicity

Banks, Duren; Ruddle, Paul; and Kennedy, Erin. (2016). "Arrest Related Deaths Program Redesign Study: 2015-2016 Preliminary Findings." *Bureau of Justice Statistics*, Available at: https://www.bjs.gov/content/pub/pdf/ardprs1516pf.pdf

Bezrukova, Katerina, Chester S. Spell, Jamie L. Perry, and Karem A. Jehn. (2016). "A Meta-Analytical Integration of Over 40 Years of Research on Diversity Training Evaluation, " *Psychological Bulletin* (Volume *11*).

Brookfield, Stephen. (2019). *Teaching Race: How to Help Students Unmask and Challenge Racism*. New York: John Wiley and Sons, Inc.

Bureau of Labor Statistics. (2019). *Labor Force Characteristics by Race and Ethnicity, 2018*. Available at: https://www.bls.gov/opub/reports/race-and-ethnicity/2018/pdf/home.pdf

Carrega, Christina and Ghebremedhim, Sabina. (2020). "Timeline: Inside the Investigation of Breonna Taylor's Killing and its Aftermath." *ABC News*, June 20th. Available at: https://abcnews.go.com/US/timeline-inside-investigation-breonna-taylors-killing-aftermath/story?id=71217247

Carson, E. A. 2020. *Prisoners in 2018*. U.S. Department of Justice, Bureau of Justice Statistics, available at: https://www.bjs.gov/content/pub/pdf/p18.pdf

Centers for Disease Control and Prevention. (2017). *"Health in the United States, 2016. Chartbook on Long-Term Health Trends."* Available at: https://www.cdc.gov/nchs/data/hus/hus16.pdf

Clair, Michael and Denis, Jeffery S. (2015). *"Racism, Sociology of."* Boston, MA: Harvard University. Available at: https://projects.iq.harvard.edu/files/deib-explorer/files/sociology_of_racism.pdf

Colby, Sandra, L. and Ortman, Jennifer M. (2015) "Projections of the Size and Composition of the U.S. Population: 2014 to 2060." *U.S. Census Bureau.* Available at: https://www.census.gov/content/dam/Census/library/publications/2015/demo/p25-1143.pdf

Conley, D. (1999). *Being Black, Living in the Red: Race, Wealth and Social Policy in America.* Berkeley: University of California Press.

Covid Tracking Project, *The Atlantic* (2021). Available at: https://covidtracking.com/race

Davis, Elizabeth; Erika Harrell, and Grace Kena. (2018). *National Crime Victimization Survey, Police-Public Contact Survey, 2018.* Available at: https://www.bjs.gov/index.cfm?ty=dcdetail&iid=251

Delgado, Richard and Jean Stefanic. (2012). *Critical Race Theory: An Introduction.* 2nd ed. New York: New York University Press.

DiAngelo, Robin. (2018). *White Fragility: Why It's So Hard for White People to Talk About Racism.* Boston, MA: Beacon Press.

Dixson, Adrienne. (2017). "What's Going On?": A Critical Race Theory Perspective on Black Lives Matter and Activism in Education. *Urban Education.* 53(4):004208591774711. 10.1177/0042085917747115

Dobbin, F. and Kalev, A. (2016). "Why diversity programs fail." *Harvard Business Review,* available at: https://hbr.org/2016/07why-diversity-programs-fail

Duffin, Erin. (2020). "Educational Attainment in United States in 2018 by Ethnicity." *Statista.com,* February 11th. Available at: https://www.statista.com/statistics/184264/educational-attainment-by-enthnicity/

Elliott, Debbie. (2020). "Protests are Bringing Down Confederate Monuments in the South. *NPR,* June 8th, Available at: https://www.npr.org/sections/live-updates-protests-for-racial-justice/2020/06/08/872659015/protests-are-bringing-down-confederate-monuments-around-the-south

Feagin, Joe R. (2006). *Systematic Racism: A Theory of Oppression.* New York: Routledge.

Haney Lopez, Ian. (1995). "The Social Construction of Race," in Delgado, Richard (ed.). *Critical Race Theory: The Cutting Edge.* Philadelphia, PA: Temple University Press, pp.191–203.

Hochschild, Arlie R. (2016). *Strangers in Our Own Land.* New York: The New Press.

Jencks, Christopher. (1999). *Rethinking Social Policy.* Boston, MA: Harvard University Press.

Kelly, R. (2010). "Why we still need Affirmative Action." *Newsweek,* Feb. 17th. Available at: http://www.newsweek.com/why-we-still-need-affirmative-action-75297

Langton, L., and Durose, M. 2013. *Police Behavior during Traffic and Street Stops.* Washington, DC: Bureau of Justice Statistics, available at http://www.bjs.gov/content/pub/pdf/pbtss11.pdf

Laub, Zachery. (2019). "Hate Speech on Social Media: Global Comparisons." *Council on Foreign Relations,* June 7th. Available at: https://www.cfr.org/backgrounder/hate-speech-social-media-global-comparisons

Lowry, Rich. (2018). *"Harvard's Ongoing Anti-Asian-American Micro Aggression." National Review,* June, Available at: https://www.nationalreview.com/2018/06/harvard-admissions-policies-unfair-to-asian-americans/

Lucero, Marissa. (2020). "Meaning Behind Black Lives Matter Movement." *University of New Mexico,* June 26th. Available at: https://news.unm.edu/news/meaning-behind-the-movement-black-lives-matter

Martinez, Peter. (2020). "White Woman Faces Charges After Calling 911 on Black Man in Central Park." *CBS News,* July 6th. Available at: https://www.cbsnews.com/news/amy-cooper-faces-charge-for-calling-911-on-black-man-central-park-video/

Massey, D. S. and J. J. Fisher. (2004). "The Ecology of Racial Discrimination," *City and Community, 3,* 221–224.

Merton, Robert K. (1949). *"Discrimination and the American Creed,"* in Robert M. MacIver (ed.), *Discrimination and National Welfare,* pp. 99–126. New York: Harper and Brothers.

Mitchell, O. and MacKenzie, D. L. 2014. *The Relationship Between Race, Ethnicity, and Sentencing Outcomes: A Meta-Analysis of Sentencing Research.* Washington, DC:

Montenaro, Domenico. (2020). "Trump Downplays Police Violence, Deaths of Black Americans." *NPR,* July 14th. Available at: https://www.npr.org/sections/live-updates-protests-for-racial-justice/2020/07/14/891144579/trump-says-more-white-people-killed-by-police-violence-than-blacks

Ordway, Denise; Wihby, John; and Kille, Leighton. (2020). "Deaths in Police Custody in the U.S.: Research Review." June 7th, Journalist's Research. Available at: https://journalistsresource.org/studies/government/criminal-justice/deaths-police-custody-united-states/

Perry, Todd. (2017). "The World Value's Survey Map of Intolerance." *Good is,* Available at: https://www.good.is/articles/america-isnt-as-racist-as-you-think

Peter G. Peterson Foundation. (2019). *Income and Wealth in the United States: An Overviews of Recent Data.* Available at: https://www.pgpf.org/blog/2019/10/income-and-wealth-in-the-united-states-an-overview-of-data

Plaut, V. C., Garnett, F. G., Buffardi, L. E., and Sanchez-Burks, J. (2011). "What about me?" Perceptions of exclusion and Whites' reactions to multiculturalism. *Journal of Personality and Social Psychology, 101,* 337–353.

Richardson, Brenda. (2020). "Redlining's Legacy of Inequality: Low Homeownership Rates, Less Equity for Black Households." *Forbes,* June 11th. Available at:https://www.forbes.com/sites/brendarichardson/2020/06/11/redlinings-legacy-of-inequality-low-homeownership-rates-less-equity-for-black-households/#5a7f40162a7c

Robertson, Dwanna, L. (2015). "Invisibility in the Color-Blind Era: Examining Legitimized Racism against Indigenous Peoples." *American Indian Quarterly* 39(2): 113–153.

Schumer, Lizz. (2020). "What Black Lives Matter Means and Why It's Problematic to Say All Lives Matter." *Good Housekeeping,* July 4th. Available at: https://www.goodhousekeeping.com/life/a32745051/what-black-lives-matter-means/

Starkey, Brandon. (2017). "Why do so many white people deny the existence of white privilege?" *The Undefeated,* March 1st. Available at: https://theundefeated.com/features/why-do-so-many-white-people-deny-the-existence-of-white-privilege/

Steinhauer, Jason. (2015). "William Julius Wilson Discusses "The Declining Significance of Race" on Voice of America's Press Conference USA" *Library of Congress,* July 2nd. Available at: https://blogs.loc.gov/kluge/2015/07/william-julius-wilson-discusses-the-declining-significance-of-race-on-voice-of-americas-press-conference-usa/

Stokely, C. and Hamilton, C.V. (1967). *Black Power: The Politics of Liberation in America.* New York: Vintage Books.

U.S. Census Bureau. (2019). "*Quick Facts.*" Available at: https://www.census.gov/quickfacts/fact/table/US/PST045217

U.S. Department of Education, National Center for Education Statistics. (2017). *Fast Facts: High School Graduation Rates by Race.* Available at: https://nces.ed.gov/fastfacts/display.asp?id=805

U.S. Department of Justice, Federal Bureau of Investigation. 2018. *Crime in the United States.* https://ucr.fbi.gov/crime-in-the-u.s/2018/crime-in-the-u.s.-2018/tables/table-43

Williams, David R. and Salina Mohommed. (2018). "Racism and Health, Pathways and Scientific Evidence" *American Behavioral Scientist, 57*(8): 1152–1173.

Chapter 7

American Immigration Council. (2017). "*The Dream Act, DACA, and Other Policies Designed to Protect Dreamers. Fact Sheet.*" September 6th. Available at: https://americanimmigrationcouncil.org/research/dream-act-daca-and-other-policies-designed-protect-dreamers

Associated Press. (2020). *"Questions and Answers on the State of Trump's Border Wall."* August 20th. Available at: https://www.usatoday.com/story/news/politics/elections/2020/08/20/trumps-border-wall-questions-and-answers-its-status/3403811001/

BBC.com. (2020). *"Yemen Crisis: Why is there a War?* June 19th. Available at http://bbc.com/news/world-middle-east 29319423

Budiman, Abby. (2020). "Key Findings about U.S. Immigrants." *Pew Research Center,* August 20. Available at: https://www.pewresearch.org/fact-tank/2020/08/20/key-findings-about-u-s-immigrants/

Budiman, Abby, Christian,Tamir, Lauren Mora, and Luis Noe-Bustamante. (2020). "Facts on U.S. Immigrants, 2018." *Pew Research Center,* August 20th. Available at: https://www.pewresearch.org/hispanic/2020/08/20/facts-on-u-s-immigrants/

Clemens, Michael. (2017). "What the Mariel Boatlift of Cuban Refugees Can Teach Us about the Economics of Immigration: An Explainer and a Revelation." *Center for Global Development.* May 22nd. Available at: https://www.cgdev.org/blog/what-mariel-boatlift-cuban-refugees-can-teach-us-about-economics-immigration

Connor, Phillip. (2018). "Most displaced Syrians are in the Middle East, and about a million are in Europe." *Pew Research Center.* January 29th. Available at: http://www.pewresearch.org/fact-tank/2018/01/29/where-displaced-syrians-have-resettled/

East, Chloe. (2020). "Secure Communities: Broad Impacts of Increased Immigration Enforcement." *Econofact.org,* January 13th. Available at: https://econofact.org/secure-communities-broad-impacts-of-increased-immigration-enforcement

Felter, Claire and Renwick, Danielle. (2018). "The U.S. Immigration Debate." *Council on Foreign Affairs.* July 2nd. Available at: https://www.cfr.org/backgrounder/us-immigration-debate-0

History.com Editors. (n.d.). *"U.S. Immigration Before 1965."* Available at: https://www.history.com/topics/immigration/u-s-immigration-before-1965-video

Gramlich, John. (2020). "How Border Apprehensions, ICE Arrests, and Deportation Have Changed under Trump." *Pew Research Center,* March 2nd. Available at: https://www.pewresearch.org/fact-tank/2020/03/02/how-border-apprehensions-ice-arrests-and-deportations-have-changed-under-trump/

Immigration Direct. (2018). *"Protestors Want Greyhound to Refuse Border Patrol Checks."*October 22nd. Available at: https://www.us-immigration.com/us-immigration-news/us-immigration/protestors-want-greyhound-to-refuse-border-patrol-checks/

Jawetz, Tom. (2019). "Restoring the Rule of Law Through a Fair, Humane, and Workable Immigration System." *Center for American Progress.* July 22nd. Available at: https://www.americanprogress.org/issues/immigration/reports/2019/07/22/472378/restoring-rule-law-fair-humane-workable-immigration-system/

Kelemen, Michelle. (2019). "The U.S. and War in Yemen." *NPR,* August 29th. Available at: https://www.npr.org/2019/08/29/755323036/the-u-s-and-the-war-in-yemen

Lind, Dara. (2018). "The Migrant Caravan Explained." *Vox,* October 25th. Available at: https://www.vox.com/2018/10/24/18010340/caravan-trump-border-honduras-mexico

Lopez, Gustavo, Kristen Bialik, and Jynnah Radford. (2018). "Key Facts About U.S. Immigration." *Pew Research Center.* November 30th. Available at: http://www.pewresearch.org/fact-tank/2018/11/30/key-findings-about-u-s-immigrants/

Marshall, Serena. (2016). "Obama has Deported More People than Any Other President." *ABC News,* August 29th. Available at: https://abcnews.go.com/Politics/obamas-deportation-policy-numbers/story?id=41715661

McNamara, Robert H. (2020). *The Criminalization of Immigration: Truth, Lies, Tragedy and Consequences.* Westport, CT: Praeger.

National Immigration Forum. (2019). *"Polling Update: American Attitudes on Immigration Steady, but Showing More Partisan Divides."* April 17th. Available at: https://immigrationforum.

org/article/american-attitudes-on-immigration-steady-but-showing-more-partisan-divides/

Office of United Nations High Commissioner on Human Rights. 2018. Available at: https://www.ohchr.org/EN/pages/home.aspx

Sanchez, Gabriella and Romero, Mary. (2010). "Critical Race Theory in the U.S. Sociology of Immigration." *Sociology Compass*, 4(9):779–788.

Shear, Michael. (2020). "Naturalization ceremony at RNC at odds with Trump Stance on Immigration." *New York Times*, August 25th, Available at: https://www.nytimes.com/2020/08/25/us/politics/trump-convention-white-house.html

Sipress, Alan, Karklis, Laris, and Meko, Tim. (2018). "Five Reasons the Yemen Crisis Matters." *The Washington Post*, June 8th. Available at: https://www.washingtonpost.com/graphics/2018/world/why-yemen-matters/?noredirect=on&utm_term=.742c0bad410e

Stableford, Dylan. (2018). "Trump uses terror attack in France to push U.S. border wall." *Yahoo News*, December 12th. Available at: https://www.yahoo.com/news/trump-uses-terror-attack-france-push-u-s-border-wall-141205455.html

Thompson, Derek. (2018). "How Immigration Became so Controversial." *The Atlantic*, February 2nd. Available at: https://www.theatlantic.com/politics/archive/2018/02/why-immigration-divides/552125/

U.S. Immigration and Customs Enforcement. (2020). *Criminal Charges and Convictions: U.S. Immigration and Customs Enforcement Fiscal Year 2019: Enforcement and Removal Operations Report*. Available at: https://www.ice.gov/sites/default/files/documents/Document/2019/eroReportFY2019.pdf

White House.gov (2020). *"Proclamation Suspending Entry of Immigrants Who Present Risk to U.S. Labor Market During Economic Recovery Following COVID-19 Outbreak."* April 22nd. Available at: https://www.whitehouse.gov/presidential-actions/proclamation-suspending-entry-immigrants-present-risk-u-s-labor-market-economic-recovery-following-covid-19-outbreak/

Younis, Mohamed. (2020). "Americans Want More, Not Less, Immigration for First Time." *Gallup*, July 1st. Available at: https://news.gallup.com/poll/313106/americans-not-less-immigration-first-time.aspx

Zeitz, Joshua. (2017). "The real history of American immigration." *Politico Magazine*, August 6th. Available at: https://www.politico.com/magazine/story/2017/08/06/trump-history-of-american-immigration-215464

Chapter 8

American Psychological Association. (2008) *Are Zero Tolerance Policies Effective in the Schools? An Evidentiary Review and Recommendations.* Available at: https://www.apa.org/pubs/info/reports/zero-tolerance.pdf

Avelar, Robin, Johnson, LaSalle, Johnson, Ruth. (2018). *"Hidden Labels Hold Students Back" Education Weekly, Feb 5th. Available at:* https://www.edweek.org/ew/articles/2018/02/07/hidden-labels-hold-students-back.html

Balonon-Rosen, Peter. (2017). *"The Promise and Peril of School Vouchers."* NPR, May 12th, Available at: https://www.npr.org/sections/ed/2017/05/12/520111511/the-promise-and-peril-of-school-vouchers

Beckhusen, Julia. (2019). "About 13 million US workers have more than one job." *US Census Bureau.* June 18th. Available at: https://www.census.gov/library/stories/2019/06/about-thirteen-million-united-states-workers-have-more-than-one-job.html

Berger, Andrea; Turk-Bicakci, Lori; Garet, Michael; Knudson, Joel; and Hoshen Gur. (2014). "Early college continued success: Early college high school initiative impact study." *American Institutions for Research*, January 15. Available at: http://www.air.org/resource/early-college-continued-success-early-college-high-school-initiative-impact-study-2014

Capelli, Peter. (2015). *Will College Pay Off? A Guide to the Most Important Financial Decisions You'll Ever Make*. New York: Public Affairs.

Carey, Kevin. (2017). "Dismal Voucher Results Surprise Researchers as De Vos Era Begins." *New York Times*, Feb 23rd. Available at: https://www.nytimes.com/2017/02/23/upshot/

dismal-results-from-vouchers-surprise-researches-as-devos-era-begins.html

Carnevale, A., Cheah, B., and Hanson, A. R. (2015). "The Economic value of college majors." *Georgetown University Center on Education and the Workforce*. Available at: https://cew.georgetown.edu/cew-reports/valueofcollegemajors/

Carpentier, Megan. (2016). "No Child Left Behind has been unsuccessful, says bipartisan report." *The Guardian*, August 9th. Available at: https://www.theguardian.com/education/2016/aug/09/no-child-left-behind-bill-unsuccessful-report-us-schools

Cavanagh, Sean. (2017). "Data snapshot: who are the nation's homeschoolers?" *Edweek*, November 20th. Available at: https://marketbrief.edweek.org/marketplace-k-12/data-snapshot-nations-homeschoolers/

Chuck, Elizabeth. (2015). "Just Over Half of All College Students Actually Graduate, Report Finds." *NBC News*, November 18th, Available at: https://www.nbcnews.com/feature/freshman-year/just-over-half-all-college-students-actually-graduate-report-finds-n465606

Clarron, Rebecca. (2017). "How America is Failing Native American Students." *The Nation*, July 24th. Available at: https://www.thenation.com/article/left-behind/

CNN. (2019). *"10 years. 180 school shootings. 356 victims."* July, Available at: https://www.cnn.com/interactive/2019/07/us/ten-years-of-school-shootings-trnd/#storystart

CollegeBoard. (2018). *Trends in Higher Education*. Available at: https://trends.collegeboard.org/college-pricing/figures-tables/average-published-undergraduate-charges-sector-2017-18

College and Career Academy Support Network. (2018). *Career Academies/SLC*. Available at: https://casn.berkeley.edu/services-and-workshops/career-academies-slcs/

Cottom, Tressie McMillan. (2017). *Lower Ed: The Troubling Rise of For-Profit Colleges in the New Economy*. New York: The New Press.

"Fact Sheet: White House Unveils America's College Promise Proposal: Tuition-Free Community College for Responsible Students." *The White House*, January 9th. Available at: https://obamawhitehouse.archives.gov/the-press-office/2015/01/09/fact-sheet-white-house-unveils-america-s-college-promise-proposal-tuition

Federal Safetynet.com. (2019). *Head Start and Child Care*. Available at: http://www.federalsafetynet.com/head-start-and-child-care.html

Gertzmann, Evan. (2019). "Why the Asian American Students Lost Their Case Against Harvard (But Should Have Won)." *Forbes*, October 1st. Available at: https://www.forbes.com/sites/evangerstmann/2019/10/01/why-the-asian-american-students-lost-their-case-against-harvard-but-should-have-won/#32a6721a63c1

Greer, Colin. (1972). *The Great School Legend*. New York: Basic Books.

Harris, Elizabeth. (2020). "It was just too much: how remote learning is breaking parents." *New York Times*, June 12th. Available at: https://www.nytimes.com/2020/04/27/nyregion/coronavirus-homeschooling-parents.html

Headstart. (2017). *Access to Head Start Funding*. Available at: https://www.nhsa.org/facts

H.R.987 - Gun-Free Schools Act of 1993 https://www.cbsnews.com/video/teach-us-all-documentary-explores-education-inequality/

Isenberg, Eric; Max, Jeffrey; Gleason, Phillip; Johnson, Matthew; Deutsch, Jonah; Hansen, Michael; and Lauren Angelo. (2016). *Do Low-Income Students Have Equal Access to Effective Teachers? Evidence from 26 Districts*. Washington, DC: National Center for Education Evaluation and Regional Assistance. Available at: https://ies.ed.gov/ncee/pubs/20174008/pdf/20174007.pdf

Kaur, Harmeet. (2018). "FYI: English FYI: English isn't the official language of the United States." *CNN*, June 15th, available at: https://www.cnn.com/2018/05/20/us/english-us-official-language-trnd/index.html

Klein, Alison. (2015). "No Child Left Behind: Overview." *Education Week*. April 10th. Available at: https://www.edweek.org/ew/section/multimedia/no-child-left-behind-overview-definition-summary.html

Kozol, Jonathan. (1999). *Savage Inequalities*. New York: Crown.

Locke, John. (1728). *Some Thoughts on Education*. 9th Edition. Dublin, Ireland: S. Powell.

Loveless, Tom. (2017). *How Well Are American Students Learning? The Brookings Institute*. Available at: https://www.brookings.edu/wp-content/uploads/2017/03/2017-brown-center-report-on-american-education.pdf

Loveless, Tom. (2016) Tracking and Advanced Placement. *The Brookings Institute*, March 24th. Available at: https://www.brookings.edu/research/tracking-and-advanced-placement/

Lu, Mei-Yu. (1998). "English-Only Movement: Its Consequences on the Education of Language Minority Children." *Eric Digest*, April. Available at https://www.ericdigests.org/1999-4/english.htm

McFarland, Joel; Cui, Jiasham; Holmes, Juliet; and Wang, Xialoi. (2020). *Trends in High School Dropout and Completion Rates 2019. National Center for Education Statistics*. Available at: https://nces.ed.gov/pubs2020/2020117.pdf

Musu-Gillette, Lauren; Cristobal de Bray; Joel McFarland; William Husser; William Sonnenberg; Sidney Wilkinson-Flicker. (2018). *Status and Trends in the Education of Racial and Ethnic Groups 2017*. Washington, DC: U.S. Department of Education, National Center for Education Statistics. Available at: https://nces.ed.gov/pubs2017/2017051.pdf

National Center for Education Statistics. (2020). Fast Facts. Available at: https://nces.ed.gov/fastfacts/display.asp?id=805

U.S. Department of Education, National Center for Education Statistics. (2020). *The Condition of Education 2020 (NCES 2020-144)*, Undergraduate Retention and Graduation Rates.

National Center for Education Statistics. (2019). *Status and Trends in The Education of Racial and Ethnic Groups*. Available at: https://nces.ed.gov/programs/raceindicators/indicator_red.asp

National Center on Education Statistics. (2020). *The Condition of Education: English Learners in Public Schools*. Available at: https://nces.ed.gov/programs/coe/indicator_cgf.asp

National Center for Education Statistics. (2017). *Trends in International Math and Science Study*.

Northwest Evaluation Association. (2014). "*Bureau of Indian Education Report on Student Achievement and Growth 2009–2010 to 2012–2013*." http://www.bie.edu/cs/groups/webteam/documents/document/idcl-028067.pdf

Pew Research Center. (2014). *The Rising Cost of Not Going to College*. Available at: http://www.pewsocialtrends.org/2014/02/11/the-rising-cost-of-not-going-to-college/

Pulliam, John D. (2002). *The History of Education in America*. Upper Saddle River, NJ: Prentice-Hall.

Redford, J., Battle, D., and Bielick, S. (2016). *Homeschooling in the United States 2012*. Washington, DC: U.S. Department of Education, National Center for Education Statistics.

Sparks, Sara D. (2013). "Poor children are not a majority in 17 states' public schools." *Education Week*, October. Available at: http://www.edweek.org/ew/articles/2013/10/23/09poverty.h33.html

Strauss, Valerie. (2015). "No Child Left Behind's test-based policies failed. Will Congress keep them anyway?" *The Washington Post*, Feb.13th. Available at: https://www.washingtonpost.com/news/answer-sheet/wp/2015/02/13/no-child-left-behinds-test-based-policies-failed-will-congress-keep-them-anyway/?utm_term=.828730c4367e

Strauss, Valerie. (2018). "The Bottom Line on Opting Out of High Stakes Testing." *The Washington Post*, June 8th. Available at: https://www.washingtonpost.com/news/answer-sheet/wp/2018/06/08/the-bottom-line-on-opting-out-of-high-stakes-standardized-tests/?noredirect=on&utm_term=.efc7c3d8d886

Taylor, Astra and Hannah Appel. (2014). "Subprime Students: How For-Profit Universities Make a Killing by Exploiting College Dreams." *Mother Jones*, September 23rd, available at: https://www.motherjones/com/politics/2014/09/for-profit-university-subprime-student-poor-minority

Totenberg, Nina. (2007). "Supreme Court Squashes School Desegregation." *NPR*, June 29th. Available at: https://www.npr.org/templates/story/story.php?storyId=11598422

U.S. Department of Labor, Bureau of Labor Statistics. (2018). *Household Unemployment Rates*. Available at: https://www.bls.gov/news.release/pdf/empsit.pdf

Vogel, Emily A. (2020). "59% of U.S. parents with lower incomes say their child may face digital obstacles in school work." *Pew Research Center*, September 20th. Available at; https://www.pewresearch.org/fact-tank/2020/09/10/59-of-u-s-parents-with-lower-incomes-say-their-child-may-face-digital-obstacles-in-schoolwork/

Vogel, Emily A; Perrin, Andrew; Rainie, Lee; Anderson, Monica. (2020). "53% of Americans say the internet has been essential during COVID-19." *Pew Research Center*, April 30th. Available at: https://www.pewresearch.org/internet/2020/04/30/53-of-americans-say-the-internet-has-been-essential-during-the-covid-19-outbreak/

Wang, Ke; Chen, Yongjiu; Zhang, Jizhi; and Oudekerk, Barbara A. (2020). *Indicators of Crime and School Safety 2019*. National Center for Education Statistics. Available at: https://nces.ed.gov/pubs2020/2020063.pdf

Wang, Ke, Rathbun, Amy, and Musu, Lauren. (2019). *School Choice in the United States: 2019. National Center for Education Statistics*. Available at: https://nces.ed.gov/pubs2019/2019106.pdf

Wong, Alia, and Ross, Terrence. (2015). "When Teachers Cheat." *The Atlantic*, April 2nd . Available at: https://www.theatlantic.com/education/archive/2015/04/when-teachers-cheat/389384/

Chapter 9

Adler, Freda. (1975). *Sisters in Crime*. New Brunswick, NJ: Rutgers University Press.

Ahern, Meg. (2019). "Six graphs in GPE's results in gender equality and girls education." *Global Partnership for Education*, June 26th. Available at: https://www.globalpartnership.org/blog/6-graphs-gpes-results-gender-equality-and-girls-education

Savran, D. 1998. *Taking It like a Man: White Masculinity, Masochism, and Contemporary American Culture*. Princeton, NJ: Princeton University Press.

Berger, Ronald J. (1996). "Explaining female delinquency: does gender make a difference?" in Berger, Ronald J. (ed.) *1996, Sociology of Juvenile Delinquency*, 2nd edition, pp. 282–291 Washington DC: National Institute of Justice.

Case, Menoukha Robin and Craig, Allison V. (2019). *Introduction to Feminist Thought and Action*. New York: Routledge.

Center for American Women and Politics. (2020). *Women in the U.S. Congress, 2019*. Available at: https://cawp.rutgers.edu/women-us-congress-2019

Constitutional Rights Foundation. (2014)."*Women in the Military*." Available at: http://www.crf-usa.org/images/pdf/gates/Womin-in-Military.pdf

Coon, D., and Mitterer, J. O. 2008. *Psychology: Modules for Active Learning*, 11th ed. Belmont, CA: Cengage.

Dawsey, Josh and Sonmez, Felicia. (2018). " Trump mocks Kavanaugh accuser Christine Blasey Ford." *The Washington Post*, October 2nd. Available at: https://www.washingtonpost.com/politics/trump-mocks-kavanaugh-accuser-christine-blasey-ford/2018/10/02/25f6f8aa-c662-11e8-9b1c-a90f1daae309_story.html?utm_term=.2db314e28cf8

Evans, Megan L.; Lindauer, Margaret; Farrell, Maureen E. (2020). "A pandemic within a pandemic: intimate partner violence during COVID-19." *The New England Journal of Medicine*, September 16th. Available at: https://www.nejm.org/doi/full/10.1056/NEJMp2024046

Gilligan, C. 1990. *Making Connections: The Relational Worlds of Adolescent Girls at Emma Willard School*. Cambridge, MA: Harvard University Press.

Graves, Lucia. (2020). "Women's domestic burdens just got heavier with the coronavirus." *The Guardian*, March 16th, Available at: https://www.theguardian.com/us-news/2020/mar/16/womens-coronavirus-domestic-burden

Greenfiled, L., and Brunberg, J. J. 2002. *Girl Culture*. San Francisco: Chronicle Books; Maine, M., and

Kelly, J. 2005. *The Body Myth*. New York: John Wiley.

Halpern, D., and LaMay, M. 2000. "The Smarter Sex: A Critical Review of Sex Differences in Intelligence." *Educational Psychology Review, 12*: 229–246.

Hochschild, Arlie and Machung, Ann. (2012). *The Second Shift: Working Families and the Revolution at Home*. New York: Penguin.

Jackson, T. and Hong, C. 2007. "Sociocultural Predictors of Physical Appearance Concerns among Adolescent Girls and Young Women from China." *Sex Roles, 58*(5-6): 402–411.

Lippa, R. A. 2005. *Gender, Nature and Nurture*. New York: Routledge. See also Freeman, N. H. 2007. "Preschoolers Perceptions of Gender Appropriate Toys and Their Parents' Beliefs about Genderized Behaviors, Miscommunication: Mixed Messages or Hidden Truths?" *Early Childhood Education Journal, 34*(5): 357–366.

Morgan, Rachel, and Jennifer Truman,. (2020). *Criminal Victimization 2019*. Washington DC: Bureau of Justice Statistics. Available at: https://www.bjs.gov/content/pub/pdf/cv19.pdf

Progressive Women's Leadership. (2019). *The Four Waves of Feminism and Why They Matter for All Women*. Available at: https://www.progressivewomensleadership.com/four-waves-feminism-matter-women/

Savran, D. 1998. *Taking It like a Man: White Masculinity, Masochism, and Contemporary American Culture*. Princeton, NJ: Princeton University Press.

Task and Purpose. (2017). *Timeline A History of Women in the U.S. Military*. Available at: https://taskandpurpose.com/timeline-history-women-us-military/

"There's a Reason Men Take Up So Much Space When They Sit." (2017). *Vice.com*, June 24th. Available at: https://www.vice.com/en_au/article/xwz37q/theres-a-reason-men-take-up-so-much-space-when-they-sit

The Sentencing Project. (2019). *Incarcerated Women and Girls*. Available at: https://www.sentencingproject.org/publications/incarcerated-women-and-girls/

Ward, L. M., and Aubrey, J. S. (2017). "Watching gender: How stereotypes in movies and on TV impact kids' development." *San Francisco*, CA: Common Sense

Whitmire, Richard. (2011). *Why Boys Fail*. New York: Amacon books.

Wolf, N.1990. *The Beauty Myth: How Images of Beauty Are Used Against Women*. New York: Morrow.

Chapter 10

Bronski, Michael. (2012). *A Queer History of the United States*. Boston, MA: Beacon Press.

Brooks, Adrian. (2015). *Right Side of History: 100 Years of LGBTQI Activism*. New York: Start Publishing LLC.

Brunelli, H. C. (2004). "The Double Bind: Unequal Treatment for Homosexuals Within the American Legal Framework." *Boston College Third World Law Journal*.

Center for Disease Control. (2020). "YRBS Data Survey and Trends." Available at: https://www.cdc.gov/healthyyouth/data/yrbs/yrbs_data_summary_and_trends.htm

DeVogue, Ariane. (2017). "LGBT employees protected from workplace discrimination, appeals court rules." *CNN*, April 4th. Available at: https://www.cnn.com/2017/04/04/politics/lgbt-employees-appeals-court/index.html

"Each Year, Immigration Equality fields inquiries from over 1,000 LGBT or HIV-positive foreign nationals and their loved ones about their options under U.S. Immigration law." Available at *Immigration Equality* at http://immigrationequlaity.org/about/

Faderman, Lillian. (2016). *The Gay Revolution: The Story of the Struggle*. New York: Simon and Schuster.

Ganna, Andrea; Verweij, Karin J. H.; Nivard, Michel G.; Maier, Robert; Wedow, Robbin. (2019). "Large Scale GWAS Reveals Insights into the Genetic Architecture of Same Sex Sexual Behavior." *Science*, vol. 365, issue 6456, eaat 7693, August 30th. Available at: https://science.sciencemag.org/content/365/6456/eaat7693

Ghose, Tia. (2015). "*Being Gay Not a Choice: Science Contradicts Ben Carson.*" Live Science, March

6th. Available at: https://www.livescience.com/50058-being-gay-not-a-choice.html

Goffman, Erving. (1963). *Stigma: Notes on the Management of a Spoiled Identity*. New York: Simon and Schuster.

Greenblatt, A. (2013). "In Some Cities, Gays Face Greater Risk of Becoming Homeless" *National Public Radio*, August 7, available at http://wwwnpr.org2013/08/06/209510271/in-some-cities-gays-face-greater-risk-of-becoming-homeless

Hanssens, Catherine; Moodie-Mills, Aisha C.: Ritchie, Andrea J.; Spade, Dean; and Urvashi Vaid. (2014). *A Roadmap for Change: Federal Policy Recommendations for Addressing the Criminalization of LBGT People and People Living with HIV*. Columbia University. Available at: https://web.law.columbia.edu/sites/default/files/microsites/gender-sexuality/files/roadmap_for_change_full_report.pdf

Harrell, W. (2013). "Prisons: The Next Frontier for LGBTI Rights," *The Life of the Law*, available at http://www.lifeofthelaw.org/prisons-the-next-frontier-for-lgbti-rights/

Human Right Campaign. (2012). *HRC Issue Brief: Housing and Homelessness*, available at http://www.hc.org/files/assets/reources/housingand-homeless_document.pdf

James, S. E.; Herman, J. L.; Ranklin, S.; Kensley, M.; Mottet, G.; and Anafi, M. (2017). *Executive Summary of the Report of the 2015 Transgender Survey*. Washington, DC: National Center for Transgender Equality. Available at: https://transequality.org/sites/default/files/docs/usts/USTS-Executive-Summary-Dec17.pdf

Kinsey, Alfred. (1948). *Sexual Behavior in the Human Male*. New York: Rockafeller Foundation.

Kinsey, A; Pomery, W.; Martin, C.; and Gebhard, P. (1953). *Sexual Behavior in the Human Female*. Philadelphia, PA: Saunders.

Levy, Diane K.; Wissoker, Douglas A; Aranda, Claudia; Howell, Brent; Pitingolo Rob; Sewell, Sarale H. (2017). "A Paired-Testing Pilot Study of Housing Discrimination against Same-Sex Couples and Transgender Individuals." *The Urban Institute*. Available at: https://www.urban.org/research/publication/paired-testing-pilot-study-housing-discrimination-against-same-sex-couples-and-transgender-individuals

Marcus, Eric. (2002). *Making Gay History: the Half Century Fight for Lesbians and Gay Equal Rights*. New York: HarperCollins.

Masci, David; Brown, Anna, and Jocelyn Kiley. (2019). "5 Facts about Same Sex Marriage." *Pew Research Center*, June 24th. Available at: https://www.pewresearch.org/fact-tank/2019/06/24/same-sex-marriage/

McCann, Hannah and Monaghan, Whitney. (2019). *Queer Theory Now*. London: Macmillan Education.

Minson, R. (1992). "Homophobia in Manslaughter: The Homosexual Advance As Insufficient Provocation." *California Law Review 80*, 133.

Morris, Bonnie. (2017). "*History of Lesbian, Gay, Bisexual and Transgender Social Movements*." American Psychological Association. Available at: https://www.apa.org/pi/lgbt/resources/history

Mustanski, Brian; Burkett, Michelle; Greene, George J.; Rossini, Margaret; Bostwick, Wendy; and Everett, Bethany. (2014). "The Association Between Sexual Orientation Identity and Behavior Across Race/Ethnicity, Sex, and Age in a Probability Sample of High School Students." *American Journal of Public Health*, February, *104*(2):237–244.

National Coalition of Anti-Violence Programs. (2012). *Lesbian, Gay, Bisexual and Transgender Hate Violence*. Available at http://www.avp.org/storage/documents2012_mr_ncavp_hvreport.pdf

National Prison Rape Elimination Commission. (2011). *National Prison Rape Elimination Commission Report*. Available at http://static.nicic.gov/usershared/2013-03-29_nprec_finalreport.pdf

Pew Research Center. (2019). "Majority of Public Favors Same-Sex Marriage, but Divisions Persist." May 19th. Available at: https://www.pewresearch.org/politics/2019/05/14/majority-of-public-favors-same-sex-marriage-but-divisions-persist/

Piantato, G. (2016). "How has queer theory influenced the ways we think about gender?" working paper in public health, Azienda Ospedaliera Nazionale "SS. Antonio e Biagio e Cesare Arrigo"

Rupp, Leila and Freeman, Susan K. (eds.) (2017). *Understanding and Teaching U.S. Lesbian, Gay, Bisexual and Transgender History*. 2nd edition. Madison, WI: University of Wisconsin Press.

Topper, Alexandra. (2015). "*A Proposed Suicide Prevention Intervention for LGBTQ Youth*." Master's Thesis, University of Pittsburgh.

U.S. Equal Employment Opportunity Commission. (2020). *What You Should Know: The EEOC and Protections for LGBT Workers*. Available at: https://www.eeoc.gov/laws/guidance/what-you-should-know-eeoc-and-protections-lgbt-workers

Welfare Warriors Research Collaborative. (2010). *A Fabulous Attitude: Low Income LGBTGNC People Surviving and Thriving With Love, Shelter and Knowledge*. New York: Queers for Economic Justice. Available at Http://d38a8pro7vhmx.cloudfront.net/q4ej/pages/22/attachments/original/1375201785/compressed_afabulousattitudefinalreport.pdf?1375201785

Wyman, Peter A.; Brown, Hendricks, C.; LoMurray, Mark; Schmeelk-Cone, Karen; Petrova, Mariya; Yu, Qin; Walsh, Erin. (2011). "An Outcome Evaluation of the Sources of Strength Suicide Prevention Program Delivered by Adolescent Peer Leaders in High Schools." *American Journal of Public Health, 100*: 1653–1661. Available at: https://ajph.aphapublications.org/doi/full/10.2105/AJPH.2009.190025

Zhou, Wen; Yan, Xiaoying; Chen, Kepu; Cai, Peng; He, Sheng; Jiang, Yi. (2014). "Chemosensory Communication of Gender Through Two Human Steroids in a Sexually Dimorphic Manner." *Current Biology, 24*(10):1091–1095. Available at: https://www.cell.com/current-biology/fulltext/S0960-9822(14)00327-3

Chapter 11

Allen, Samuel H. and Mendez, Shawn N. (2018). "Hegemonic Heteronormativity: Toward a New Era of Queer Family Theory." *Journal of Family Theory and Review, 10* (1): 70–86.

Anderson, J. (2014). "The Impact of Family Structure and Health of Children: Effects of Divorce." *Linacre Q 81*(4): 378–387.

Association of American Medical Colleges. (2017) "*More Women Than Men Enrolled in U.S. Medical Schools in 2017*." Available at: https://news.aamc.org/press-releases/article/applicant-enrollment-2017/

Baker, Billy. (2017). "The Biggest Threat Facing Middle Age Men Isn't Smoking or Obesity, It's Loneliness." *The Boston Globe*. March 9th. Available at: https://www.bostonglobe.com/magazine/2017/03/09/the-biggest-threat-facing-middle-age-men-isn-smoking-obesity-loneliness/k6saC9FnnHQCUbf5mJ8okL/story.html

Banfield, E. 1970. *The Unheavenly City Revisited*. Chicago: University of Chicago Press.

Bianchi, S. M.; Robinson, J. P.; and Milkie, M. A. 2006. *Changing Rhythms of the American Family Life*.New York: Russell Sage Foundation

Brand, JE; Moore, R; Siang, X; Xia, Y. (2019). "Parental divorce is not uniformly disruptive to children's educational attainment." *Proceedings of the National Academy of Sciences, 116*(15):7266–7271.

Childwelfare.gov (2019). Fact Sheet. Available at: https://www.childwelfare.gov/pubPDFs/about.pdf

Christnacht, Cheridan and Sullivan, Briana. (2020). "The Choices Mothers Make." *U.S. Census Bureau*, May 8th. Available at: https://www.census.gov/library/stories/2020/05/the-choices-working-mothers-make.html

Cohen, Patricia and Hsu, Tiffany. (2020). "Pandemic Could Scar a Generation of Working Mothers." *New York Times*, June 3rd. Available at: https://www.nytimes.com/2020/06/03/business/economy/coronavirus-working-women.html

DeVogue, Ariane. (2018). "Supreme Court rules for Colorado baker in same-sex wedding cake case." *CNN*, June 4th. Available at: https://www.cnn.com/2018/06/04/politics/masterpiece-colorado-gay-marriage-cake-supreme-court/index.html

Duffin, Erin. (2019). "*Number of Single Person Households in U.S. 1960-2019*." Statistica.

com, November 22nd. Available at: https://www.statista.com/statistics/242022/number-of-single-person-households-in-the-us/

Eberstadt, M. 2001. "Home Alone America: The Consequences of Children Raising Themselves." *Policy Review107.* Available at http://www.hoover.org/publications/policyreview/3476711.html.

Horowitz, Juliana. (2019). "Despite Challenges at Home and Work, most Working Moms and Dads Say Being Employed is What's Best for Them." *Pew Research Center, September 19th.* Available at: https://www.pewresearch.org/fact-tank/2019/09/12/despite-challenges-at-home-and-work-most-working-moms-and-dads-say-being-employed-is-whats-best-for-them/

Horowitz, Juliana, Graf, Nikki, and Livingston, Gretchen. (2019). " *The Landscape of Marriage and Cohabitation in the U.S.*" Pew Research Center, November 6th. Available at: https://www.pewsocialtrends.org/2019/11/06/the-landscape-of-marriage-and-cohabitation-in-the-u-s/

Jaschik, Scott. (2016). "Law School Gender Gaps." *Inside Higher Education*, November 30th. Available at: https://www.insidehighered.com/quicktakes/2016/11/30/law-school-gender-gaps

Khimm, Suzy. (2015). "The New Nuclear Family." *The New Republic*, July 23rd. Available at: https://newrepublic.com/article/122349/new-nuclear-family

LaRossa R., Reitzes D.C. (2009) Symbolic Interactionism and Family Studies. In: Boss P., Doherty W.J., LaRossa R., Schumm W.R., Steinmetz S.K. (eds) *Sourcebook of Family Theories and Methods.* Springer, Boston, MA

Livingston, Gretchen. (2018). "Stay-at-home moms and dads account for about one-in-five U.S. parents." *Pew Research Center.* September 24th. Available at: http://www.pewresearch.org/fact-tank/2018/09/24/stay-at-home-moms-and-dads-account-for-about-one-in-five-u-s-parents/

Livingston, Gretchen and Thomas, Deja. (2019). "Why is the teen birth rate falling?" *Pew Research Center*, August 2nd. Available at: https://www.pewresearch.org/fact-tank/2019/08/02/why-is-the-teen-birth-rate-falling/

McNamee, S. J. and Miller, R. K. 2004. "The Meritocracy Myth." *Sociation Today* 2(1) available at http://www.ncsociology.org/sociationtoday/v21/merit.htm

Monte, Lindsey M. (2017). *Multiple Partner Fertility in the United States: A Demographic Portrait.* Available at: https://www.census.gov/content/dam/Census/library/publications/2017/demo/SEHSD-WP2017-45.pdf

Morgan, Rachel E and Kena, Grace. (2017). *Criminal Victimization, 2016.* Available at: https://www.bjs.gov/index.cfm?ty=pbdetail&iid=6166

National Conference of State Legislators. (2017). *Extending Foster Care Beyond 18.* Available at: http://www.ncsl.org/research/human-services/extending-foster-care-to-18.aspx

O'Hara, Mary Emily. (2018). "Domestic Violence: Nearly Three U.S. Women Killed Every Day by Intimate Partners." *NBC News*, April 11th. Available at: Domestic Violence: Nearly Three U.S. https://www.nbcnews.com/news/us-news/domestic-violence-nearly-three-u-s-women-killed-every-day-n745166

Orford, J. 2008. *Community Psychology: Challenges Controversies and Emerging Consensus.* New York: Wiley

Parsons, Talcott and Bales, Robert F. (1955). *Family: Socialization and Interaction.* New York: The Free Press.

Payne, Krista. (2017). "Change in the U.S. Remarriage Rate, 2008 and 2016." *National Center on Family and Marriage Research.* Available at: https://www.bgsu.edu/ncfmr/resources/data/family-profiles/payne-change-remarriage-rate-fp-18-16.html

Popenoe, D. and Whitehead, B. (2006). *The State of Our Unions, 2006, The National Marriage Project.* New Brunswick, NJ: Rutgers University.

Redden, G. 2008. *Violence in the Family.* National Association of Children of Alcoholics. http://www.nacoa.org/famviol.htm

Rosenberg, Rachel, and Abbott, Samuel. (2019). "Supporting Older Youth Beyond Age 18: Examining Data and Trends in Extended Foster Care." *Child Trends*, June 3rd. Available at: https://www.

childtrends.org/publications/supporting-older-youth-beyond-age-18-examining-data-and-trends-in-extended-foster-care

Schondelmyer, Emily. (2017). "Fewer Married Households and More Living Alone." *U.S. Census Bureau*, August 9th. Available at: https://www.census.gov/library/stories/2017/08/more-adults-living-without-children.html

Scutti, Susan. (2017). "US teen birth rate drops to all-time low." *CNN*, June 30th. Available at: https://www.cnn.com/2017/06/30/health/teen-birth-rate-prenatal-care-2016/index.html

Sham'ah Md-Yunus. (2017). "Development of Well-being in Children Raised by Grandparents." *Child Research Net*. October 20th. Available at: https://www.childresearch.net/papers/rights/

Stein, Perry and Lindsey Bever. (2018) "The opioid crisis is straining the nation's foster-care systems." *The Washington Post*, July 1st. Available at: https://www.washingtonpost.com/national/the-opioid-crisis-is-straining-the-nations-foster-care-systems/2017/06/30/97759fb2-52a1-11e7-91eb-9611861a988f_story.html?utm_term=.b83b68ba5da1

Stepler, Renee. (2017). "Number of U.S. adults cohabiting with a partner continues to rise, especially among those 50 and older." *Pew Research Center*, April 6th. Available at: http://www.pewresearch.org/fact-tank/2017/04/06/number-of-u-s-adults-cohabiting-with-a-partner-continues-to-rise-especially-among-those-50-and-older/

U.S. Census Bureau. (2018). *Subject Definitions.* Available at: https://www.census.gov/programs-surveys/cps/technical-documentation/subject-definitions.html

U.S. Census Bureau. (2016). *The Majority of Children Live With Two Parents, Census Bureau Reports.* Available at: https://www.census.gov/newsroom/press-releases/2016/cb16-192.html

U.S. Department of Health and Human Services. *Study of National Incidence and Prevalence of Child Abuse and Neglect.*

U.S. Department of Health and Human Services, Administration for Children and Families. (2020). *"Child Abuse, Neglect Data Released"* Available at: https://www.acf.hhs.gov/media/press/2020/child-abuse-neglect-data-released

U.S. Department of Health & Human Services, Administration for Children and Families, Administration on Children, Youth and Families, Children's Bureau. (2017). *Child Maltreatment 2015.* Available from http://www.acf.hhs.gov/programs/cb/research-data-technology/statistics-research/child-maltreatment.

US Department of Health and Human Services, Administration for Children and Families, Children's Bureau. (2017). *Child Maltreatment 2016.* Available at: https://www.acf.hhs.gov/cb/resource/child-maltreatment-2016

U.S. Department of Health and Human Services, Administration for Children and Families, Children's Bureau. (2020). *Child Maltreatment 2018.* Available at: https://www.acf.hhs.gov/sites/default/files/cb/cm2018.pdf#page=31

U.S. Department of Health and Human Services, Center for Disease Control. http://www.cdc.gov/ncbddd/FAS/fasask.htm

U.S Department of Health and Human Services, Center for Disease Control and Prevention (2019). *Child Abuse and Neglect Prevention.* Available at: https://www.cdc.gov/violenceprevention/childabuseandneglect/index.html

U.S Department of Health and Human Services, Center for Disease Control and Prevention (2019). *Child Abuse and Neglect Prevention.* Available at: https://www.cdc.gov/violenceprevention/childabuseandneglect/index.html

U.S. Department of Health and Human Services, Strengthening Families Program. Available at: https://strengtheningfamiliesprogram.org/

U.S. Department of Justice, Office of Juvenile Justice Delinquency Prevention. 2001. *The Nurturing Parenting Programs.* Washington, DC http://www.ncjrs.gov/pdffiles1/ojjdp/172848.pdf

U.S. Department of Justice, Office of Juvenile Justice and Delinquency Prevention. 2000. *Safe From the Start: Taking Action on Children Exposed to Violence*, Washington, DC. Available at http://www.ncjrs.gov/pdffiles1/ojjdp/182789.pdf

Wallace, H. 2005. *Family Violence: Legal, Medical and Social Perspectives*, 4th ed. Boston: Allyn and Bacon.

Wang, Wendy. (2018). "The Majority of U.S. Children Still Live in 2 Parent Families." *Institute for Family Studies*, October 4th. Available at: https://ifstudies.org/blog/the-majority-of-us-children-still-live-in-two-parent-families

Zimbardo, P. G. and Boyd, J. 2008. *The Time Paradox*. New York: Simon and Schuster.

Chapter 12

Adler, F.; G.O.W. Mueller, and W.S. Laufer. 1995. *Criminology*. New York: McGraw-Hill.

Administration on Aging. (2020). "2019 Profile of Older Americans." *The Administration for Community Living, US Department of Health and Human Services*. May, Available at: https://acl.gov/sites/default/files/Aging%20and%20Disability%20in%20America/2019ProfileOlderAmericans508.pdf

Alzheimer's Association. *Facts and Figures*. Available at: https://www.alz.org/alzheimers-dementia/facts-figures

Backman, Maurie. (2017). "Here's How Much the Average 50-Something American Has Saved for Retirement." *The Motley Fool*, October 22nd. Available at: https://www.fool.com/retirement/2017/10/22/heres-how-much-the-average-50-something-american-h.aspx

Belza B. and the PRC-HAN Physical Activity Conference Planning Workgroup (2007). *Moving Ahead: Strategies and Tools to Plan, Conduct, and Maintain Effective Community-Based Physical Activity Programs for Older Adults*. Centers for Disease Control and Prevention: Atlanta, Georgia. Available at: https://www.cdc.gov/aging/pdf/community-based_physical_activity_programs_for_older_adults.pdf

Berger, Raquota. (2018). "Criminal Behavior Among the Elderly: A Look into What People Think About this Emerging Topic." *Advances in Aging Research*, 7, 1–16. Available at: https://file.scirp.org/pdf/AAR_2018013014004382.pdf

Belza B. and the PRC-HAN Physical Activity Conference Planning Workgroup (2007). *Moving Ahead: Strategies and Tools to Plan, Conduct, and Maintain Effective Community-Based Physical Activity Programs for Older Adults*. Centers for Disease Control and Prevention: Atlanta, Georgia. Available at: https://www.cdc.gov/aging/pdf/community-based_physical_activity_programs_for_older_adults.pdf

Bloom, Esther. (2017). "Here's How Much the Average American Spends on Health Care." CNBC, June 23rd. Available at: https://www.cnbc.com/2017/06/23/heres-how-much-the-average-american-spends-on-health-care.html

Campbell, Anthony, D.; Godfryd, Alice; Buys, David R.; Locher, Julie L. (2015). "Does Participating in Home Delivered Meals Improve Outcomes for Older Adults?" *Journal of Nutritional Gerontology, 34*(2): 124–167. Available at: https://www.ncbi.nlm.nih.gov/pmc/articles/PMC4480596/

Center for Disease Control and Prevention. (2017). *Long-Term Care Facilities*. Available at: https://www.cdc.gov/longtermcare

Center on Budget and Policy Priorities. (2020). "Policy Basics: Top Ten Facts About Social Security." August 13th. Available at: https://www.cbpp.org/research/social-security/policy-basics-top-ten-facts-about-social-security

Cubanski, Juliette; Koma, Wyatt; Damico, Anthony; and Neuman, Tricia. (2019). "How Much do Medicare Beneficiaries Spend Out of Pocket on Health Care?" *Kaiser Family Foundation*, November 4th. Available at: https://www.kff.org/medicare/issue-brief/how-much-do-medicare-beneficiaries-spend-out-of-pocket-on-health-care/

Deliema, Marguarite and Bengtson, Vern. L. (2015). "Activity Theory, Disengagement Theory, and Successful Aging," in *Encyclopedia of Geropsychology*, Nancy Pachana (ed.) Available at: https://link.springer.com/referenceworkentry

Genworth.com. (n.d.). *Compare Long Term Care Costs Across the United States*. Available at: https://www.genworth.com/aging-and-you/finances/cost-of-care.html

Holmes T.H. Rahe R.H. (1967). "The Social Readjustment Rating Scale." *Journal of Psychosomatic Research, 11* (2): 213–218.

Kilcrease, Worth. (2008). "Stages of Grief: Time for a New Model." *Psychology Today,* April 20th. Available at: https://www.psychologytoday.com/us/blog/the-journey-ahead/200804/stages-grief-time-new-model

Konish, Lorie. (2020). "Social Security Cost of Living Adjustment will be 1.3% in 2021." CNBC, October 13th. Available at: https://www.cnbc.com/2020/10/13/social-security-cost-of-living-adjustment-will-be-1point3percent-in-2021.html

Kraus, Markus. (2017). "Comparing Gen X and Gen Y on their Preferred Emotional Leadership Style." *Journal of Applied Leadership and Management,* 5:62–75.

Lachs, M.; Teresi, J. A.; Ramirez, M. 2014. *Documentation of Resident to Resident Elder Mistreatment in Residential Care Facilities. Final Report to the National Institute of Justice,* grant number 2009_IJ-XC-0001.

Leonhardt, Megan. (2019). "Americans Now Spend Twice as Much on Health Care as they did in the 1980s." *CNBC,* October 9th. Available at: https://www.cnbc.com/2019/10/09/americans-spend-twice-as-much-on-health-care-today-as-in-the-1980s.html

Livingston, J. 1992. *Crime and Criminology.* Clifton Hills, NJ: Prentice-Hall.

"Living Wills and Advance Directions for Medical Decisions." *The Mayo Clinic.* Available at: https://www.mayoclinic.org/healthy-lifestyle/consumer-health/in-depth/living-wills/art-20046303

Meals on Wheels.org. (2020.) "Fact Sheet and Sources and Methods." Available at: https://www.mealsonwheelsamerica.org/docs/default-source/fact-sheets/2020/2020-national/mowa_2020factsheet_issue_sourcesmethods.pdf?sfvrsn=71a8b53b_2

Medina, Lauren; Sabo, Shannon; and Vespas, Jonathan. (2020). "Giving Longer, Historical and Projected Life Expectancy in the United States, 1960–2060." *US Census Bureau,* February, Available at: https://www.census.gov/content/dam/Census/library/publications/2020/demo/p25-1145.pdf

Morgan, Rachel, E. and Truman, Jennifer. (2020). *Criminal Victimization 2019.* September, US Department of Justice, Bureau of Justice Statistics. Available at: https://www.bjs.gov/content/pub/pdf/cv19.pdf

National Center for Assisted Living. (2016). *Fact Sheet.* Available at: https://www.ahcancal.org/ncal/facts/Pages/Communities.aspx

National Center on Elder Abuse. 2016. *Fact Sheet. Available at:* https://www.cdc.gov/violenceprevention/pdf/em-factsheet-a.pdf

National Center for Health Statistics. (2017). *Fact Sheet.* Available at: https://www.cdc.gov/nchs/data/factsheets/factsheet_overview.htm

Office of Disease Prevention and Health Promotion at https://www.healthypeople.gov/2020/topics-objectives/topic/older-adults

Sandberg, Linn (2013). "Affirmative Old Age: the Ageing body and Feminist theories on Difference." *International Journal of Aging and Later Life,* (8), *1,* 11–40.

Seigel, L.J. 2005. *Criminology.* New York: West Publishing.

Shimmkus, J. 2007. *The Graying of America's Prisons: Corrections Copes with Care for the Aged. National Commission on Correctional Healthcare.* Washington, DC.

Snelling, Sherri. (2020). "3 Reasons There Will be a Wave of Nursing Home Closures." *Marketwatch.com,* November 17th. Available at: https://www.marketwatch.com/story/3-reasons-there-will-be-a-wave-of-nursing-home-closures-11605221403

Sykes, G.M. and Cullen, F.T. 2005. *Criminology.* New York: Harcourt Brace and Jovanovich.

U.S. Department of Labor. *Need Time? The Employee Guide to the Family Leave Act.* Available at: https://www.dol.gov/whd/fmla/employeeguide.pdf

US Senate, Special Committee on Aging. (2017). *America's Aging Workforce: Opportunities and Challenges.* Available at: https://www.aging.senate.gov/imo/media/doc/Aging%20Workforce%20Report%20FINAL.pdf

Wasik, J. 2000. "The Fleecing of America's Elderly." *Consumer's Digest*, March/April.

Wright, Lauri Y. and Vance, Lauren M. (2014). "The Impact of Participation in Meals on Wheels on Nutritional Risk, Dietary Intake, Food Security, Loneliness, and Well-being." *Meals on Wheels.org*. Available at: https://mowtampa.org/wp-content/uploads/2014/09/Abstract.pdf

Zemke, R., Raines, C. and Filipczak, B. 2000. *Generations at Work: Managing the Clash of Veterans, Boomers and Xers and Nexters in your Workplace.* New York: American Management Association.

Chapter 13

Adams, S. (2012). "Why do so Many Doctors Regret Their Job Choice?" *Forbes*, April 27th. Available at: https://www.forbes.com/sites/susadams/2012/04/27/why-do-so-many-doctors-regret-their-job-choice/#10521d8c371fa

Alonzo-Zaldivar, R. 2016. "$10,345 per person: US health care spending reaches new peak." *Associated Press*, July 13th, available at: http://www.pbs.com/newshour/rundown/new-peak-us-heaht-care-spending-10345-per-person/

Amadeao, Kimberly. (2018). "Universal Health Care in Different Countries, Pros and Cons of Each." *The Balance*, September 15th. Available at: https://www.thebalance.com/universal-health-care-4156211

Association of American Medical Colleges. (2021). *Physician Specialty Report*. January 26th. Available at: https://www.aamc.org/data-reports

Bagley, N. (2017). "Trump's Ominous Threat to Withhold Payment From Health Insurers, Explained." *Vox*, April 27th. Available at: https://www.vox.com/the-big-idea/2017/3/29/15107836/lawsuit-aca-payments-reimbursement-unconstitutional

Bryan, B. (2017a). "Three States Proved That One Move From Trump Could Send Healthcare Costs Skyrocketing for Millions of Americans." *Business Insider*, August, 1st. Available at:http://www.msn.com/en-us/news/us/3-states-proved-that-one-move-from-trump-could-send-healthcare-costs-skyrocketing-for-millions-of-americans/arAApgu74?li=BBmkt5R&ocid=spartandhp

Centers for Medicare and Medicaid Services. (2020). *NHE Fact Sheet*. Available at: https://www.cms.gov/Research-Statistics-Data-and-Systems/Statistics-Trends-and-Reports/NationalHealthExpendData/NHE-Fact-Sheet

"CBO: 20% Premium Rise Without Obamacare Insurance Subsidies." *Newsline*. August 15th. Available at: https://newsline.com/cbo-20-premium-rise-without-obamacare-insurance-subsidies/

Clark, Dartunorro. (2020). "Trump suggests 'injection' of disinfectant to beat coronavirus and 'clean' the lungs." *NBC News*, April 23rd, available at: https://www.nbcnews.com/politics/donald-trump/trump-suggests-injection-disinfectant-beat-coronavirus-clean-lungs-n1191216

Cockerham, John. (2017). *Medical Sociology*. 15th edition. New York: Elseiver.

Henry J. Kaiser Foundation. (2017). *Key Facts About the Uninsured Population*. Available at: https://www.kff.org/uninsured/fact-sheet/key-facts-about-the-uninsured-population/

Kaiser Family Foundation. (2020). "Health Insurance Coverage of the Total Population 2008-2019." Available at: https://www.kff.org/other/state-indicator/total-population/?activeTab=graph¤tTimeframe=0&startTimeframe=11&selectedDistributions=employer—medicaid—medicare—uninsured&selectedRows=%7B%22wrapups%22:%7B%22united-states%22:%7B%7D%7D%7D&sortModel=%7B%22colId%22:%22Location%22,%22sort%22:%22asc%22%7D

Khullar, Dhruv. (2018). "Do You Trust the Medical Profession?" *New York Times*, January 23rd. Available at: https://www.nytimes.com/2018/01/23/upshot/do-you-trust-the-medical profession.html

Lapointe, Jacqueline. (2020). "1% of people account for 22% of total healthcare spending." *Revcycle Intelligence*, February 26th, Available at: https://revcycleintelligence.com/news/1-of-people-account-for-22-of-total-healthcare-spending

LaVito, Angelica. (2017) "Two in three patients can't pay off their hospital bills." *CNBC*, June 26th. Available at: https://www.cnbc.com/2017/06/26/two-in-three-patients-cant-pay-off-their-hospital-bills.html

Lee, MJ. (2021). "Biden inheriting non-existent coronavirus vaccine distribution plan and must start from scratch, sources say." *CNN*, January 21st. Available at: https://www.cnn.com/2021/01/21/politics/biden-covid-vaccination-trump/index.html

Liptak, J. (2012). "Supreme Court Upholds Health Care Law 5-4 in Victory for Obama." *New York Times*, June 28th. Available at http://www.nytimes.com/2012/6/29/US/Supreme-Court-lets-health-care-law-largely-stand.html

National Center on Health Statistics. (2018). *NCHS Data on Racial and Ethnic Disparities Fact Sheet*. Available at: https://www.cdc.gov/nchs/data/factsheets/factsheet_disparities.pdf

Newby, Robert. (2020). "Column: Injection of disinfectant: what do you have to lose?" *The Morning Sun*, May 5th, available at: https://www.themorningsun.com/opinion/column-an-injection-of-disinfectant-what-do-you-have-to-lose/article_3a8de932-8e3d-11ea-b55a-2f753fd087ad.html

Nichols, J. 2017. "Single Payer is a Rational Health Care System." *The Nation*, September13th. Available at: https://www.thenation.com/article/single-payer-is-a-rational-health-care-system-an-exclusive-interview-with-bernie-sanders-on-his-medicare-for-all-plan/https://www.thenation.com/article/single-payer-is-a-rational-health-care-system-an-exclusive-interview-with-bernie-sanders-on-his-medicare-for-all-plan/

Norris, Louise. (2020). "Will You Receive an Obamacare Premium Subsidy?" *Healthinsurance.org*, May 23rd. Available at: https://www.healthinsurance.org/obamacare/will-you-receive-an-obamacare-premium-subsidy/

Parsons, Talcott. (1951). *The Social System*. Glencoe, IL: The Free Press.

Peterson Foundation. (2017). "*Infographic: U.S. Healthcare Spending.*" Available at http://www.pgpf.org/infographic/infographic-us-healthcare-spending

Punke, H. 2013. "Survey: 42% of Physicians are Dissatisfied." *Jackson Healthcare*. Available at http://www.beckershospitalreview.com/hospital-physician-relationships/survey-42-of-physicians-are-dissatisfied.html

"Republicans Question Legality of Obamacare Payments to Insurance Companies." *Washington Free Beacon*, June 11th, (2014). available at: http://freebeacon.com/issues/-question-legality-of-obamacare-payments-to-insurance-companies/

Schencker, L. (2014). "Republicans file their suit against the Affordable Care Act." *Modern Healthcare*, November 21st. Available at: http://www.modernhealthcare.com/article/20141121/NEWS/311219970

Schpero, Willaim, L.; Morden, Nancy, E.; Sequist, Thomas, D.; Rosenthal, Meridith, B. (2017). "For selected services, Blacks and Hispanics more likely to receive low value crare than whites." *Journal of Health Affairs*, *36*(6), available at: https://www.healthaffairs.org/doi/abs/10.1377/hlthaff.2016.1416.

Schulte, Fred. (2018). "Feds Settle Huge Whistleblower Suit Over Medicare Advantage Fraud." *Kaiser Health News*, October 1st. Available at: https://khn.org/news/feds-settle-huge-whistleblower-suit-over-medicare-advantage-fraud/

Schumock, G. t.; Li, E.C.; Wiest, M.D.; Suda, K.J.; Stubbings, J.; Matusiak, L.; Hunkler, R.; Vemereuleun, L. C. (2017). "National Trends in Prescription Drug Expenditures and Projections for 2017." *American Journal of Health System Pharmacy*, August, 74(15) 1158–1173. Available at: https://doi.org/10.2146/ajhp170164

Stolberg, Cheryl Gay and Wu, Katherine J. (2021). "Biden Plans Coronavirus Vaccination Blitz After Inauguration." *New York Times*, January 8th. Available at: https://www.nytimes.com/2021/01/08/us/politics/biden-coronavirus-vaccinations.html

Spakovsky, H. (2015). "Several States Launch New Lawsuit Against Obamacare: here's Why it Will Likely Go to the Supreme Court." *The Daily Signal*, October 21st. Available at: http://www.dailysignal.com/2015/10/21/several-states-launch-new-lawsuit-againsts-obamacare-heres-why-it-will-go-to-the-supreme-court/

Starr, Paul. (1983). *The Social Transformation of Medicine*. Glencoe, Il: The Free Press.

Waldman, D. (2014). "Single Payer is Root Cause of VA Deaths." *American Thinker,* June 4th. Available at: http://www.americanthinker.com/articles/2014/06/single_payer_is_root_cause_of_va_deaths.html

Woodyard, C. and Layton, M. J. 2016. "Massive Price Increase on EpiPens Raise Alarm." *USA Today,* August 22nd. Available at: https://www.usatoday.com/story/money/business/2016/08/22/two-senators-urge-scrutiny-epipen-price-boost/89129620/

Zernike, K. (2017). "The Hidden Subsidy that Helps Pay for Health Insurance." *New York Times,* July 7th. Available at: https://www.nytimes.com/2017/07/07/health/health-insurance-tax-deduction.html

Chapter 14

Adams, Justin. (2018). "There is a forgotten solution to climate change that we must invest in – nature." *World Economic Forum,* August 30th. Available at: https://www.weforum.org/agenda/2018/08/investing-in-a-forgotten-solution-to-climate-change-nature/

Australian Department of Environment and Energy. *"Greenhouse Effect."* Available at: http://www.environment.gov.au/climate-change/climate-science-data/climate-science/greenhouse-effect

Bell, Michelle and Keita, Ebisu. (2012). "Environmental Inequality in Exposure to Airborne Particulate Matter Components in the United States." *Environmental Health Perspectives, 120*(12): 1699–1704.

Bennett, Abbie. (2018). "New Bern is counting up the damage from Hurricane Florence. It's at $100 million so far." *News Observer,* September 23rd. Available at: https://www.newsobserver.com/news/local/article218889660.html

Bravo, Mercedes; Anthopolos, Rebecca; Bell, Michelle; Miranda, Marie Lynn. (2016). "Racial Isolation and Exposure to Airborne Particulate Matter and Ozone in Understudied US Populations: Environmental Justice Applications of Down Scaled Numerical Model Output." *Environmental International,* 92-93 July/August: 247–255.

Catellani, Michael. (2018). "The Gulf War Oil Spill: A Man Made Disaster." *Environment and Society,* Available at: http://www.environmentandsociety.org/tools/keywords/gulf-war-oil-spill-man-made-disaster

Earth Eclipse. *"What is BioMagnification?"* Available at: https://www.eartheclipse.com/ecosystem/causes-effects-process-of-biomagnification.html

Earth.org. (n.d.). *"20 Facts about Food Waste."* Available at: https://earth.org/facts-about-food-waste/

Enerdata. (2020). *Global Energy Statistical Yearbook, 2020, Total Energy Consumption*. Available at: https://yearbook.enerdata.net/total-energy/world-consumption-statistics.html

"Experts Debate Global Impact of Greenhouse Gases." (2005). *The Guardian,* February 1st. Available at: https://www.theguardian.com/environment/2005/feb/01/research.climatechange

Fleishman, Glenn. (2018). "Seattle's Air Quality Was Five Times Worse than Beijing's This Week. Here's Why it's The Future." *Fortune*. August 21st. Available at: http://fortune.com/2018/08/21/seattle-air-quality-beijing-five-times-worse-fires-natural-gas/

"Flint Water Crisis—Fast Facts." (2018). *CNN,* April 8th. Available at: https://www.cnn.com/2016/03/04/us/flint-water-crisis-fast-facts/index.html

Friedman, Lisa. (2019). "What is the Green New Deal? A Climate Proposal Explained." *New York Times,* February 21st. Available at: https://www.nytimes.com/2019/02/21/climate/green-new-deal-questions-answers.html

Hancock, Lorin. (2019). "Plastics in the Ocean." *World Wildlife Magazine,* Fall. Available at: https://www.worldwildlife.org/magazine/issues/fall-2019/articles/plastic-in-the-ocean

International Atomic Energy Agency. (2020). "Preliminary Nuclear Power: Facts and Figures for 2019." Available at: https://www.iaea.org/newscenter/news/preliminary-nuclear-power-facts-and-figures-for-2019

Jacobs Julia and Seidman, Bianca. (2017). "A brief history of the Three Mile Island nuclear plant known for 1979 reactor accident." *ABC News*, May 31st. Available at: https://abcnews.go.com/US/history-mile-island-nuclear-plant-1979-reactor-accident/story?id=47731028

Jacoby, Mitch. (2020). "As nuclear waste piles up, scientists seek the best long-term storage solutions." *Chemical and Engineering News*, March 30th. Available at: https://cen.acs.org/environment/pollution/nuclear-waste-pilesscientists-seek-best/98/i12

Krishnakumar, Priya and Kanna, Swetha. (2020). The WorstFireSeasonEver."*LA Times*,September15th. Available at: https://www.latimes.com/projects/california-fires-damage-climate-change-analysis/

Larson, Lance N. (2020). "Nuclear Waste Sites in the United States." *Congressional Research Service*, April 13th. Available at: https://fas.org/sgp/crs/nuke/IF11201.pdf

Michelle, Meg. (2017). "Types of Air Pollution: Smog and Acid Rain." *Sciencing*, April 25th. Available at: https://sciencing.com/types-air-pollution-smog-acid-rain-23483.html

Mikati, Ihab; Benson, Adam F.; Luben, Thomas J.; Sacks, Jason, D.; Richmond-Bryant, Jennifer. (2018). "Disparities in Distribution of Particulate Matter Emission Sources by Race and Poverty Status." *American Journal of Public Health, 108*:480–485.

Motoko, Rich. (2017). "Struggling With Japan's Nuclear Waste, Six Years After Disaster." *New York Times*, March 11th. Available at: https://www.nytimes.com/2017/03/11/world/asia/struggling-with-japans-nuclear-waste-six-years-after-disaster.html

National Aeronautic Space Agency. (2019). *"Climate Change: How Do We Know?"* Available at: https://climate.nasa.gov/evidence/

National Ocean Service. *"Harmful Algae Blooms."* Available at: https://oceanservice.noaa.gov/hazards/hab/

Newkirk, Vann. (2018). "Trump's EPA Concludes Environmental Racism Is Real." *The Atlantic*, February 28th. Available at: https://www.theatlantic.com/politics/archive/2018/02/the-trump-administration-finds-that-environmental-racism-is-real/554315/

Nuclear Energy Institute. (2020). *"US Nuclear Generating Statistics."* Available at; https://www.nei.org/resources/statistics/us-nuclear-generating-statistics

Nunez, Christina. (2019). "Deforestation Explained." *National Geographic*, February 7th. Available at: https://www.nationalgeographic.com/environment/global-warming/deforestation/#close

O'Donnel, Josy. (2018). "What You Need to Know About Thermal Pollution and its Causes." *Conservation Institute*, April 27th. Available at: https://www.conservationinstitute.org/thermal-pollution/

Perlin, Susan, A.; Sexton, Ken; and Wong, David S. (1999). "An Examination of Race and Poverty for Populations Living Near Industrial Sources of Air Pollution." *Journal of Exposure Analysis and Environmental Epidemiology, 9*:29–48.

Stelloh, Tim. (2020). "California Exceeds 4 Million Acres Burned by Wildfires in 2020." *NBC News*, October 4th. Available at: https://www.nbcnews.com/news/us-news/california-exceeds-4-million-acres-burned-wildfires-2020-n1242078

Union of Concerned Scientists. (2012). *"Tropical Deforestation and Global Warming."* December 9th. Available at: https://www.ucsusa.org/resources/tropical-deforestation-and-global-warming

United Nations Environment. (2018). *"Mainstreaming Fresh Water Ecosystem."* Available at: https://www.unenvironment.org/explore-topics/water/what-we-do/mainstreaming-freshwater-ecosystem-health

United States Government Accountability Office. (n.d.). *"Disposal of High-Level Nuclear Waste."* Available at: https://www.gao.gov/key_issues/disposal_of_highlevel_nuclear_waste/issue_summary

US Environmental Protection Agency. (2018). *"Advancing Sustainable Materials Management: 2015 Fact Sheet."* Available at: https://www.epa.gov/sites/production/files/2018-07/documents/

2015_smm_msw_factsheet_07242018_fnl_508_002.pdf

US Environmental Protection Agency. (2018). *"Air Pollution: Current and Future Challenges."* Available at: https://www.epa.gov/clean-air-act-overview/air-pollution-current-and-future-challenges

US Environmental Protection Agency. (2018). *National Overview: Facts and Figures on Materials Waste, and Recycling."* Available at: https://www.epa.gov/facts-and-figures-about-materials-waste-and-recycling/national-overview-facts-and-figures-materials

US Environmental Protection Agency. (n.d.). *"What is Acid Rain?"* Available at: https://www.epa.gov/acidrain/what-acid-rain

Vargas, Monica. (2020). "Public Health Officials Urge Californians to Stay Indoors When Possible due to Unhealthy Air Quality in Wildfire Areas." *California Offices of Emergency Services*, August 20th, available at: http://www.oesnews.com/public-health-officials-urge-californians-to-stay-indoors-when-possible-due-to-unhealthy-air-quality-in-wildfire-areas/

Wald, Ellen. (2018). "Trump's New Ethanol Rule Explained (And What It Means For Gasoline)." *Forbes*. October 9th. Available at: https://www.forbes.com/sites/ellenrwald/2018/10/09/trumps-new-ethanol-rule-wont-change-your-gasoline/#1c3911087d96

"What is Fracking and why is it controversial?" (2018). *BBC*, October 15th. Available at: https://www.bbc.com/news/uk-14432401

World Health Organization. (2017). *Urban Green Spaces: A Brief for Action*. Available at: https://www.euro.who.int/__data/assets/pdf_file/0010/342289/Urban-Green-Spaces_EN_WHO_web3.pdf%3Fua=1#:~:-text=Consider%20various%20types%20of%20urban,on%20%E2%80%93%20to%20satisfy%20different%20needs.&text=Make%20use%20of%20biodiversity%2C%20using%20different%20plants%20to%20create%20diverse%20settings.&text=Use%20signing%20within%20parks%20or%20for%20greenways%20and%20trails.

Woodyatt, Amy, and Wakatsuki, Yoko. (2020). "Fukushima water release could change human DNA Greepeace warns." *CNN*, October 24th. Available at: https://www.cnn.com/2020/10/24/asia/japan-fukushima-waste-ocean-intl-scli/index.html

Yeung, Jessie. (2020). "Australia's deadly wildfires are showing no sign of stopping. Here's what you need to know." *CNN*, January 13th. Available at: https://www.cnn.com/2020/01/01/australia/australia-fires-explainer-intl-hnk-scli/index.html

Chapter 15

Allcott, Hunt, and Matthew Gentzkow. 2017. "Social Media and Fake News in the 2016 Election." *Journal of Economic Perspectives, 31* (2): 211–236.

CBInsights. (2018). *"33 Ways Drones Will Impact Society: From Fighting War to Forecasting Weather, UAVs Change Everything."* May 9th. Available at: https://www.cbinsights.com/research/drone-impact-society-uav/

Center for Evidence-Based Crime Policy. (n.d.). *Counterterrorism Strategies*. Available at: https://cebcp.org/evidence-based-policing/what-works-in-policing/research-evidence-review/counterterrorism-strategies

Crawford, Neta C. (2019). US Budgetary Costs and Obligations of Post 9/11 Wars Through Fiscal Year 2020, $6.4 trillion." *Watson Institute on International and Public Affairs, Brown University*, November 13th. Available at: https://watson.brown.edu/costsofwar/files/cow/imce/papers/2019/US%20Budgetary%20Costs%20of%20Wars%20November%202019.pdf

Crowley, James. (2021). "Protestors Following President's Orders Hurt Argument that Trump Didn't Incite Violence." *Newsweek*, January 16th. Available at: https://www.newsweek.com/protesters-following-presidents-orders-hurt-argument-that-trump-didnt-incite-violence-1562134

Erez, Noam. (2018). "Cyber attacks are shutting down countries, cities and companies. Here's how to stop them." *World Economic Forum*, June 22nd. Available at:https://www.weforum.org/

agenda/2018/06/how-organizations-should-prepare-for-cyber-attacks-noam-erez/

Ferris-Rotman, Amie and Stern, David. (2018). "Black Sea standoff intensifies tensions between Russia, Ukraine." *Washington Post*, November 25th. Available at: https://www.washingtonpost.com/world/russia-closes-water-route-in-fresh-confrontation-with-ukraine/2018/11/25/a57adc3e-f0c1-11e8-99c2cfca6fcf610c_story.html?utm_term=.682485914c4a

Friends Committee on National Legislation. (n.d.). *Understanding Drones*. Available at: https://www.fcnl.org/updates/understanding-drones-43

Gould, Joe. (2019). "Pentagon Finally Gets Its 2020 Budget." *Defense* News.com, December 19th. Available at: https://www.defensenews.com/congress/2019/12/19/pentagon-finally-gets-its-2020-budget-from-congress/

Greitans, Sheena; Lee, Myunghee, and Yazici, Emir. (2020). "Understanding China's 'preventive repression' in Xinjiang." *Brookings Institute*, March 4th. Available at: https://www.brookings.edu/blog/order-from-chaos/2020/03/04/understanding-chinas-preventive-repression-in-xinjiang/

Haltiwanger, John. (2018). "America's 'war on terror' has cost the US nearly $6 trillion and killed roughly half a million people, and there's no end in sight." *Business Insider*, November 14th. Available at: https://www.businessinsider.com/the-war-on-terror-has-cost-the-us-nearly-6-trillion-2018-11

Higgs, Robert. (1988). US Military Spending in the Cold War Era: Opportunity Costs, Foreign Crises, and Domestic Constraints. *The Cato Institute*. November 30th. Available at: https://www.cato.org/publications/policy-analysis/us-military-spending-cold-war-era-opportunity-costs-foreign-crises-domestic-constraints

Jones, Seth; Doxsee, Catrina; and Harrington, Nicholas. (2020). "The War Comes Home: The Evolution of Domestic Terrorism in the US." *Center for Strategic and International Studies*, October 22nd. Available at: https://www.csis.org/analysis/war-comes-home-evolution-domestic-terrorism-united-states

Jowers, Karen. (2017). VA chief: Time to rethink disability system; current setup 'not sustainable' *Military Times*, June 23rd. Available at:https://www.militarytimes.com/veterans/2017/06/23/va-chief-time-to-rethink-disability-system-current-setup-not-sustainable/

Korb, Lawrence. (2020). "Pentagon Fiscal Year 2021 Budget More than Meets US National Security Needs." *American Progress*.org, May 6th. Available at: https://www.americanprogress.org/issues/security/reports/2020/05/06/484620/pentagons-fiscal-year-2021-budget-meets-u-s-national-security-needs/

Lacour, Greg and Way, Emma. (2015). "Veterans and Domestic Terrorism." *Charlotte Magazine*, August 5th. Available at: https://www.charlottemagazine.com/veterans-and-domestic-terrorism/

Lipari, Rachel; Forsyth, Barbara; Bose, Jonaki; Kroutil, Larry, A.; and Lane, Marian. (2016). "Spouses and Children of US Military Personnel: Substance Abuse and Mental Health Profile from the 2015 National Survey on Drug Use and Health." *Substance Abuse and Mental Health Services Administration*. Available at: https://www.samhsa.gov/data/sites/default/files/NSDUH-MilitaryFamily-2015/NSDUH-MilitaryFamily-2015.htm

Mueller, John and Stewart, Mark. (2018). "Public Opinion and Counterterrorism Policy." *The Cato Institute*, February 20th. Available at: https://www.cato.org/publications/white-paper/public-opinion-counterterrorism-policy

Mitchell, Ellen. (2020). "US Approved $175 Billion in Weapons Sales to Other Countries in 2020." *The Hill*, December 4th. Available at: https://thehill.com/policy/defense/528826-us-approved-175b-in-weapons-sales-to-other-countries-in-2020

National Center for Veterans Analysis and Statistics. (2020). *"VA Utilization Profile, 2017."* Available at: https://www.va.gov/vetdata/docs/Quickfacts/VA_Utilization_Profile_2017.pdf

Scott, John, and Marshall, Gordon. (2015). *A Dictionary of Sociology*. New York: Oxford University Press.

Shendruk, Amanda. (2017). "Funding the United Nations: What Impact Do US Contributions Have on UN Agencies and Programs?" *National Council on Foreign Relations*, September 21st. Available at: https://www.cfr.org/article/funding-united-nations-what-impact-do-us-contributions-have-un-agencies-and-programs

Sherman, Amy. (2020). "Fact Check: Did the FBI Director Warn About White Supremacist Violence?" *Austin American-Statesman*, October 9th. Available at: https://www.statesman.com/story/news/politics/elections/2020/10/09/fact-check-did-fbi-director-warn-about-white-supremacist-violence/114251512/

Smith, Stew. (2018). "*The Costs of War Since September 11, 2001.*" The Balance Careers, November 1st. Available at: https://www.thebalancecareers.com/the-cost-of-war-3356924

Stanton, Zach. (2021). "It's Time to Talk About Violent Christian Extremism." *Politico*, February 4th. Available at: https://www.politico.com/news/magazine/2021/02/04/qanon-christian-extremism-nationalism-violence-466034

Stein, Jeff. (2018). "US military budget inches closer to $1 trillion mark, as concerns over federal deficit grow." *The Washington Post*, June 19th. Available at: https://www.washingtonpost.com/news/wonk/wp/2018/06/19/u-s-military-budget-inches-closer-to-1-trillion-mark-as-concerns-over-federal-deficit-grow/?utm_term=.f9ceb9588f40

Sutherland, Ann. (2016). "How Deployments Affect Military Families." *Institute of Family Studies*, April 21st, Available at: https://ifstudies.org/blog/how-deployment-affects-military-families

Taylor, Adam. (2018). "Terrorist attacks are quietly declining around the world." *Washington Post*, August 15th. Available at: https://www.washingtonpost.com/world/2018/08/15/terrorist-attacks-are-quietly-declining-around-world/?utm_term=.1f6fdb7240a8

Institute for Economics and Peace. Global Terrorism Index (2020). *Measuring the Impact of Terrorism*, November. Available from: http://visionofhumanity.org/reports

United Nations High Commissioner for Refugees. (2017). *Global Trends: Forced Displacement in 2017.* Available at: https://www.unhcr.org/en-us/statistics/unhcrstats/5b27be547/unhcr-global-trends-2017.html

US Department of Homeland Security. (2020). *Homeland Threat Assessment 2020.* Available at: https://www.dhs.gov/sites/default/files/publications/2020_10_06_homeland-threat-assessment.pdf

US Department of Homeland Security. (2009). *Right-wing Extremism: Current Economic and Political Climate Fueling Resurgence in Radicalization and Recruitment.* Available at: https://fas.org/irp/eprint/rightwing.pdf

US Department of Veterans Affairs. (n.d.). *Traumatic brain injury: A guide for patients.* Available at: http://www.mentalhealth.va.gov/docs/tbi.pdf.

US Department of Veterans Affairs. (n.d.) *Military Sexual Trauma.* Available at: https://www.ptsd.va.gov/understand/types/sexual_trauma_military.asp

US Department of Veterans Affairs, National Center for PTSD. (n.d.). *How Common is PTSD?* Available at: https://www.ptsd.va.gov/understand/common/common_veterans.asp

Ward, Antonia. (2018). "How do you define terrorism?" *The National Interest*, May 31st. Available at: https://nationalinterest.org/feature/how-do-you-define-terrorism-26058?nopaging=1

Weine, Stevan, and Osman Ahmed. (2012). *Building Resilience to Violent Extremism Among Somali-Americans in Minneapolis-St. Paul*, Final Report to Human Factors/Behavioral Sciences Division, Science and Technology Directorate, U.S. Department of Homeland Security. College Park, MD: START.

Wright, Chrysalis. (2020). "Political Fake News and the 2020 Election." *Psychology Today*, November 8th. Available at: https://www.psychologytoday.com/us/blog/everyday-media/202011/political-fake-news-and-the-2020-election

Credits

PHOTOS

Chapter 1

[Photo 1.1] giuseppelombardo; [Photo 1.2] Steve Skjold/Alamy Stock Photo; [Photo 1.4] Hananeko_ Studio; [Photo 1.5] INTERFOTO/Alamy Stock Photo; [Photo 1.6] Richard Ellis/Alamy Stock Photo; [Photo 1.7] Kevin RC Wilson/Alamy Stock Photo; [Photo 1.8] Jim Lambert; [Photo 1.9] Jeffrey Isaac Greenberg 1+/Alamy Stock Photo

Chapter 2

[Photo 2.1] Darko Cacic; [Photo 2.3] Distinctive Shots; [Photo 2.4] Patrik Urban/Alamy Stock Photo; [Photo 2.5] ohrim; [Photo 2.6] Mikael Karlsson/ Alamy Stock Photo; [Photo 2.7] mark reinstein/ Alamy Stock Photo; [Photo 2.8] Simone Hogan

Chapter 3

[Photo 3.1] AGENZIA SINTESI/Alamy Stock Photo; [Photo 3.3] Chicken Strip; [Photo 3.4] Finn-b; [Photo 3.5] Steve Skjold/Alamy Stock Photo; [Photo 3.8] Lukassek; [Photo 3.9] Pictorial Press Ltd/Alamy Stock Photo

Chapter 4

[Photo 4.1] LOU Collection/Alamy Stock Photo; [Photo 4.2] ClassicStock/Alamy Stock Photo; [Photo 4.3] RossHelen editorial/Alamy Stock Photo; [Photo 4.4] Jim West/Alamy Stock Photo; [Photo 4.6] Jim West/Alamy Stock Photo; [Photo 4.9] Boaz Rottem/Alamy Stock Photo; [Photo 4.10] Vic Hinterlang

Chapter 5

[Photo 5.1] Gukzilla; [Photo 5.2] LifeInCaption; [Photo 5.3] UPI/Alamy Stock Photo; [Photo 5.4] Kapi Ng; [Photo 5.5] Jason Raff; [Photo 5.6] AB Forces News Collection/Alamy Stock Photo; [Photo 5.7] Judith Bicking/Alamy Stock Photo; [Photo 5.8] Maskot/Alamy Stock Photo; [Photo 5.10] James Schwabel/Alamy Stock Photo; [Photo 5.12] Cultura Creative RF/Alamy Stock Photo; [Photo 5.13] Robert K. Chin/Alamy Stock Photo

Chapter 6

[Photo 6.1] David Brickner; [Photo 6.2] Stuart Monk; [Photo 6.3] Tom Wurl; [Photo 6.4] Kim Kelley-Wagner/ Shutterstock; [Photo 6.5] Alexander Oganezov; [Photo 6.12] MediaPunch Inc/Alamy Stock Photo

Chapter 7

[Photo 7.1] Joebeth Terriquez/EPA-EFE/Shutter-stock; [Photo 7.2] Glasshouse Images/Shutterstock; [Photo 7.5] Moises Castillo/AP/Shutterstock; [Photo 7.9] YAHYA ARHAB/EPA-EFE/Shutterstock; [Photo 7.10] Steve Helber/AP/Shutterstock; [Photo 7.11] nik wheeler/Alamy Stock Photo; [Photo 7.12] Wilfredo Lee/AP/Shutterstock; [Photo 7.13] Brynn Anderson/AP/Shutterstock

Chapter 8

[Photo 8.1] Al Seib/Shutterstock; [Photo 8.2] Charlie Riedel/AP/Shutterstock; [Photo 8.4] Jim West/Alamy Stock Photo; [Photo 8.5] Bob Daemmrich/Alamy Stock Photo; [Photo 8.6] Marcio Jose Sanchez/AP/ Shutterstock; [Photo 8.13] Marjorie Kamys Cotera/ Bob Daemmrich Photography/Alamy Stock Photo

Chapter 9

[Photo 9.1] Andrew Harnik/AP Photo/Shutterstock; [Photo 9.2] Alena A; [Photo 9.3] Yulia Reznikov; [Photo 9.4] Shawshots/Alamy Stock Photo; [Photo 9.5] Sundry Photography; [Photo 9.6] Broadimage/Shutterstock; [Photo 9.7] Tyler Olson; [Photo 9.9] J Scott Applewhite/AP/Shutterstock; [Photo 9.11] Chirag Wakaskar/Shutterstock; [Photo 9.12] Marc Bruxelle

Chapter 10

[Photo 10.1] bakdc; [Photo 10.2] PT Hamilton; [Photo 10.3] Frances Roberts/Alamy Stock Photo; [Photo 10.5] Yakoniva/Alamy Stock Photo; [Photo 10.7] Bob Daemmrich/Alamy Stock Photo; [Photo 10.8] Richard Levine/Alamy Stock Photo

Chapter 11

[Photo 11.1] AJR_photo; [Photo 11.5] fizkes; [Photo 11.8] David Pereiras; [Photo 11.10] Monkey Business Images

Chapter 12

[Photo 12.1] Richard Levine/Alamy Stock Photo; [Photo 12.6] YAKOBCHUK VIACHESLAV; [Photo 12.10] Jim West/Alamy Stock Photo; [Photo 12.12] Richard Levine/Alamy Stock Photo; [Photo 12.13] CGN089; [Photo 12.14] Drazen Zigic; [Photo 12.15] fizkes; [Photo 12.16] FrameAngel; [Photo 12.17] Luc Novovitch/Alamy Stock Photo; [Photo 12.18] Jim West/Alamy Stock Photo

Chapter 13

[Photo 13.1] Jim Ruymen/UPI/Shutterstock; [Photo 13.2] Chaikom; [Photo 13.6] kandl stock; [Photo 13.7] miker; [Photo 13.8] Norma Jean Gargasz/Alamy Stock Photo; [Photo 13.9] Photoroyalty; [Photo 13.10] Jeffrey Isaac Greenberg 16+/Alamy Stock Photo

Chapter 14

[Photo 14.1] Rick Bowmer/AP/Shutterstock; [Photo 14.2] Terry Chea/AP/Shutterstock; [Photo 14.3] Myung J Chun/Los Angeles Times/Shutterstock; [Photo 14.4] Amy Harris/Shutterstock; [Photo 14.5] Wilfredo Lee/AP/Shutterstock; [Photo 14.6] ETIENNE LAURENT/EPA-EFE/Shutterstock; [Photo 14.7] Paul Sancya/AP/Shutterstock; [Photo 14.8] Cristobal Herrera/EPA-EFE/Shutterstock; [Photo 14.10] AP/Shutterstock; [Photo 14.11] Quirky China/Shutterstock; [Photo 14.12] Diane Bondareff/AP/Shutterstock

Chapter 15

[Photo 15.1] Charles Sykes/Shutterstock; [Photo 15.2] Anonymous/AP/Shutterstock; [Photo 15.3] David Goldman/AP/Shutterstock; [Photo 15.4] PJF Military Collection/Alamy Stock Photo; [Photo 15.5] Ghaith Alsayed/AP/Shutterstock; [Photo 15.6] PHILIPP GUELLAND/EPA-EFE/Shutterstock; [Photo 15.7] Sipa USA/Alamy Stock Photo; [Photo 15.9] Richard Ellis/Alamy Stock Photo; [Photo 15.10] Jim Mone/AP/Shutterstock

FIGURES

Chapter 6

[Figure 6.2] Hum Historical/Alamy Stock Photo; [Figure 6.3] US Department of Education, Office of Elementary and Secondary Education; [Figure 6.5] Carson, E. A. 202. Prisoners in 2018. U.S. Department of Justice, Bureau of Justice Statistics, available at: https://www.bjs.gov/content/pub/pdf/p18.pdf

Chapter 8

[Figure 8.5] National Center for Education Statistics; [Figure 8.6] National Center for Education Statistics

Index

Tables, figures, and boxes are indicated by an italic *t*, *f*, and *b* following the page number.